# The Habit of Being

# FLANNERY O'CONNOR

# THE HABIT OF BEING

LETTERS EDITED AND

WITH AN INTRODUCTION

BY *Sally Fitzgerald*

VINTAGE BOOKS

*A Division of Random House • New York*

*Library of Congress Cataloging in Publication Data*

*O'Connor, Flannery / The habit of being*

*Reprint of the 1979 ed. published by Farrar, Straus & Giroux, New York*

*Includes index*

*1. O'Connor, Flannery—Correspondence*

*2. Novelists, American—20th century—Correspondence*

*I. Fitzgerald, Sally / II. Title*

*PS3565.C57Z48 1980 /813'.5'4 [B] / 79-23319*

*ISBN 0-394-74259-1*

*To Regina Cline O'Connor*

*in gratitude for letting readers*

*come to know her daughter better*

# Contents

# Introduction

Among the papers in the Flannery O'Connor Memorial Room of the library of her college, Georgia College, in Milledgeville, I came across a tiny, scrappy notebook, about three inches by four, kept by Flannery when she was twelve. It was scrappy in both senses of the word. On the first page a warning to snoopers—"I know some folks that don't mind thier own bisnis"—called me to order and reminded me that it would be well to walk gingerly through her correspondence, bearing in mind what she herself would have objected to as a breach of privacy, particularly the privacy of her friends. No great loss, for there was something here of much greater interest. Reading through her letters, I felt her living presence in them. Their tone, their content, and even the number and range of those she corresponded with, revealed the vivid life in her, and much of the quality of a personality often badly guessed at.

Katherine Anne Porter wrote to Flannery's friends, the Gossetts, after they had taken her to lunch with Flannery and her mother at the farm, "I am always astonished at Flannery's pictures which show nothing of her grace. She was very slender with beautiful, smooth feet and ankles; she had a fine, clear, rosy skin and beautiful eyes. I could wish I had some record of her as she appeared to me . . ."

Most of her friends wish the same thing, both literally and figuratively. But she was not photogenic in maturity, or at least the camera was often as unjust as what was written about her. I have come to think that the true likeness of Flannery O'Connor will be painted by herself, a self-portrait in words, to be found in her letters. Read in sequence—from the beginning in 1948, when she wrote asking Elizabeth McKee to become her literary agent, through to the last note of 1964 on her bedside table, waiting to be posted—her letters sketch the lineaments, add the chiaroscuro of depth and space and the color of life itself. There she stands, to me, a phoenix risen from her own words: calm, slow, funny, courteous, both modest and very sure of herself, intense, sharply penetrating, devout but never pietistic, downright, occasionally fierce, and honest in a way that restores honor to the word. Perhaps because I remember her as smiling and laughing often when she was a part of our family in the Connecticut woods, her self-portrait wears, for me at least, a smile I recall very clearly. The mindless camera records on Flannery's face the ravages of ill health; her letters wipe them all away, not in a cosmetic sense, but by means of something that lay within and imparted the fine clarity and youthfulness Katherine Anne Porter perceived. And her offhand way of speaking of her physical ordeal, when she did, tells more about her gallantry than any encomium could make real.

Letters were always important to her. When she lived with us, she took a daily walk to the mailbox, half a mile away at the bottom of our ridge. One thing it always contained was a letter from Regina O'Connor, who wrote to her, and to whom she wrote, every single day. This daily exchange of news and talk between them ought to be mentioned, just to keep the record straight, since none of those letters will appear in the collection. Flannery shared news items from Milledgeville with us, and we came to feel that we knew all her kin well, long before we met them. Her strong family feeling was manifest even then.

On the subject of Mrs. O'Connor herself, I can report a remark that Flannery made to me the last time I talked to her. She told me that she had fully come to terms with her confinement, and with the physical danger in which she lived; that she had, in fact, only one great fear—that her mother would die before she did. "I don't know," she said, "what I would do without her." The letters themselves are full of Mrs. O'Connor: she is quoted, referred to, relished and admired, joked with and about, altogether clearly loved.

What else, though, do the letters tell us of the storyteller herself? The overriding impression is of a *joie de vivre*, rooted in her talent and the possibilities of her work, which she correctly saw as compensating her fully for any deprivations she had to accept, and as offering her a scope for living that most of us never dream of encompassing. From this sensibility grew a wonderful appreciation of the world's details: the vagaries of human personality; the rich flow of the language she heard around her; the beauty of Andalusia, the family farm outside Milledgeville where the O'Connors went to live after Flannery fell ill, and of the birds, homely or regal, with which she peopled it; the hospitality she and her mother offered to friends and strangers alike; good food, always a pleasure to her; talk, books, and letters. These letters reveal her to have been anything but reclusive by inclination: to have been, on the contrary, notably gregarious. She enjoyed company and sought it, sending warm invitations to her old and new friends to come to Andalusia. Once her inviolable three-hour morning stint of writing was done, she looked for, and throve on, companionship. When people couldn't come, she wrote to them, and looked forward to hearing from them in return. She participated in the lives of her friends, interested herself in their work, their children, their health, and their adventures. Anything but dour, she never ceased to be amused, even in extremis. In a letter after her return from the hospital and surgery, in 1964, she wrote: "One of my nurses was a dead ringer for Mrs. Turpin. Her Claud was named Otis. She told all the time about what a good nurse she was. Her favorite grammatical construction was 'it were.' She said she treated everybody alike whether it were a person with money or a black nigger. She told me all about the low life in Wilkinson County. I seldom know in any given circumstances whether the Lord is giving me a reward or a punishment. She didn't know she was funny and it was agony to laugh and I reckon she increased my pain about 100% ."

The world of the absurd delighted her. She regaled us with Hadacol advertisements; birth announcements of infants with names that had to be read to be believed; such news items as the attendance of Roy Rogers' horse at a church service in California, or the award of first prize in an amateur contest to a crimped and beribboned seven-year-old singing "A Good Man Is Hard to Find"; and the wonderful mugs of a gospel quartet promised as a Coming Attraction somewhere. All these things filled her with glee, and gleefully she passed them on. She could write fine country talk, of course, and often did, to amuse her friends and herself. The next letter, however, might set forth in strong clear style a literary or theological insight that shed light in every direction. She was capable, at twenty-three, of flooring a patronizing publisher with one courteous but steely letter when he proposed to "work with her" to "change the direction" of her first book. He later complained in a note to her former teacher, Paul Engle, that she suffered from "hardening of the arteries of cooperative sense," adding, "It seems most unbecoming in one so young." But she escaped and went on to a publisher and to editors who were better able to recognize the originality of her gift and who encouraged her to develop in her own way.

However inordinate her self-confidence seemed, she never failed to send her manuscript drafts to those of her friends who she felt understood what she was trying to do, and whose literary judgment she respected. There is continual discussion of work-in-progress throughout the letters over the years, and she was always open to suggestion or instruction, and almost always acted upon any advice that helped her to improve a particular piece of writing. She had the true humility that is based on a just assessment of one's own worth. She certainly knew hers, and at the same time knew that it could always be increased by a willingness to learn. One thing she had little interest in learning, however, was how to spell. In the ragged little journal mentioned above, she complained, "Teacher said I dident know how to spell what of it?" Well, what of it? Possibly because her ear was so fine, it was enough for her to get things down more or less as they sounded. In any event, she was what she described as "a very innocent speller." Except for obvious misslicks on the typewriter, I have retained her own versions of what words ought to look like; to have corrected them would have destroyed some of the savor of her letters.

One commentator has remarked unkindly that "any crank could write to her and get an answer." I expect it is true that she answered any letter someone had taken the trouble to write to her. She mentions several cranky, furious, funny, or simply foolish letters that found their way to her. But on the whole, her correspondence was an enrichment of her life, to say nothing of the lives of her correspondents, and was by no means conducted with fools or cranks. One of her most valued friendships began with an exchange of letters with a reader whose comments interested her and whom she encouraged to continue to write to her. They met only later, became close friends, and their correspondence flourished for nine years. Another equally cherished comradeship began in the same way and endured until her death seven years later. Almost all her close friendships were sustained through the post. I have tried, with each of Flannery's correspondents, to use enough of the letters to give a sense of the continuity, or lack of it, in their correspondence, and so to give a sense of continuity to her life. Isolated "statements" to be found in her letters are too much just that. No sense of her existence, and of some aspects of her personality, can be gained from these alone; nor can any sense be gained from them of the various people who were most important to her, or of the kind of importance they had in her life. One needs to follow her in a correspondence for these things to emerge.

There is much discussion of books in Flannery's letters, not just her own but all kinds of books. Understandably, reading was one of the great pleasures and interests in her life. She exchanged books with friends, and commentaries in turn. She liked to discuss ideas, and she liked to discuss theology, and she made a striking apologist for Catholicism, which was, to say the least, an arguable system of belief and thought to many, even most, of the people she wrote to. This faith was her intellectual and spiritual taproot, and it deepened and spread outward in her with the years. Her real love for Christianity and for the Church as its guardian is inescapable in her letters, and so is her impatience with fatuity and obtuseness among Catholics. On the latter subject she is not so much astringent as withering. In her letters to an intelligent Jesuit friend, she would demolish the Catholic press and some Catholic education with a blast and, at the same time, ask a dispensation to read two authors listed on the late, unlamented Index of proscribed works. She maintained throughout her life that the Church in no way impaired her true freedom, either in the practice of her art or in her personal life. She gladly honored the prerogatives claimed by the Church, holding that what the Church gave her far outweighed any demands it made in return. To the novelist John Hawkes, Flannery wrote, "There are some of us who have to pay for our faith every step of the way and who have to work out dramatically what it would be like without it and if being without it would ultimately be possible or not." There is in her letters not a hint of deviation from her orthodox position, even in her mind. She says in so many words to one correspondent that she has simply never doubted, or for a moment wanted to leave the fold.

She did, however, at one point want to leave the South. Like so many gifted young people, she was sure, at twenty-one, that she could never properly "work" in her own native region. As it turned out, after two years of study in Iowa and less than a year as guest of one of the foundation estates offering hospitality to promising artists, she fetched up in our country house in Connecticut where, if she wasn't in the South, she was living with another emigré Southerner, and there was plenty of spoonbread and mutual understanding to feed on. She wasn't far from home, after all, least of all in her thoughts, in the ensuing two years.

When she came home to Georgia for good, it was of course under the hard constraint of disseminated lupus erythematosus, a dangerous disease of metabolical origin—incurable but controllable by steroid drugs—which exhausts the energies of its victims and necessitates an extremely careful and restricted life. But her return was for good, in more ways than one. She herself acknowledged this, describing it in one of her letters as not the end of all work she had thought it would be but only the beginning. Once she had accepted her destiny, she began to embrace it, and it is clear from her correspondence that she cherished her life there and knew that she had been brought back exactly where she belonged and where her best work would be done.

Here her mature growth began. When she learned how matters really stood, and when her health had been more or less stabilized and meticulous treatment worked out to control her illness, she set about building a life with her mother, under Regina O'Connor's care, at Andalusia. Her living and working habits were established so as to ensure that her diminished strength could go almost entirely into her writing. She wrote us that she was able to work at her fiction no more than two or three hours a day. If she had a long struggle accepting loneliness, and the reality of a permanently curtailed life, or if she felt resentment or self-pity (and how could she have failed to suffer these, and much more, to some degree?), she gave no sign of such feeling to any of us. There is no whining. A characteristic description of how she stood is contained in a 1953 letter to Robert Lowell and his wife: "I am making out fine in spite of any conflicting stories . . . I have enough energy to write with and as that is all I have any business doing anyhow, I can with one eye squinted take it all as a blessing. What you have to measure out, you come to observe more closely, or so I tell myself."

But her life was becoming pleasurable, too. She had doted on chickens from early childhood, and now the long love affair with her flock of peafowl, and attendant Muscovy ducks, Chinese geese, and one-eyed swans began, and she wrote constantly of these; of the reading she was doing; of Mrs. O'Connor's farming adventures; of her numerous visitors and friends; of the progress of her novel, and the relief she felt when she occasionally put it aside for the comparative ease of writing a story. She began to travel on occasion, as well, to give readings or talks, and she enjoyed these trips until they became too difficult and costly to her strength; and she learned to love getting home to Andalusia. She went to Europe, though not very willingly, and was even gladder to get home.

With time, her correspondence enlarged greatly, widening her contact with the world beyond Milledgeville. She was as generous with her correspondents as she and her mother were in their hospitality. She received many manuscripts and, though spared the wear and tear of classrooms, counseled and taught these "students" with gentleness and patience, offering them any kind of help and encouragement she was able to give. As the years passed, we cannot fail to see in her letters the increase in her own being, commensurate with and integrally related to her growth in stature as a writer.

When Flannery went home, expecting to return to us, she left behind a book, *Art and Scholasticism*, by Jacques Maritain. I had mislaid it, and bought another copy to send her when I forwarded her things. She told me to keep her copy when I found it, and I have it still, underlined here and there by her. It was from this book that she first learned the conception of the "habit of art," habit in this instance being defined in the Scholastic mode, not as mere mechanical routine, but as an attitude or quality of mind, as essential to the real artist as talent. Maritain writes:

Operative habit resides chiefly in the mind or the will . . . Habits are interior growths of spontaneous life . . . and only the living (that is to say, minds which alone are perfectly alive) can acquire them, because they alone are capable of raising the level of their being by their own activity: they possess, in such an enrichment of their faculties, secondary motives to action, which they bring into play when they want . . . The object [the good of the work] in relation to which (the habit) perfects the subject is itself unchangeable—and it is upon this object that the quality developed in the subject *catches*. Such a habit is a virtue, that is to say a quality which, triumphing over the original indetermination of the intellective faculty, at once sharpening and hardening the point of its activity, raises it in respect of a definite object to a maximum of perfection, and so of operative efficiency. Art is a virtue of the practical intellect.

Flannery consciously sought to attain to the habit of art, and did, by customary exercise and use, acquire it in the making of her novels and stories. Less deliberately perhaps, and only in the course of living in accordance with her formative beliefs, as she consciously and profoundly wished to do, she acquired as well, I think, a second distinguished habit, which I have called "the habit of being": an excellence not only of action but of interior disposition and activity that increasingly reflected the object, the being, which specified it, and was itself reflected in what she did and said.

It is to this second habit that her letters attest, even as they shed a great deal of new light on the novels and stories she gave us in the practice of the first. This is not to say that the selection of letters is an exercise in hagiography. Although she was far from being as self-centered as either her genius or her invalidism might have made her, she was not without vanity, and her tongue could take on a quite unsaintly edge. And there was an area of sensibility in her that seems to have remained imperfectly developed, as her letters suggest, although I believe that she touched it in what she often described as probably the best thing she would ever write, "The Artificial Nigger"—a story that she said contains more than she herself understood. That she *did* understand somewhat, however, is plainly suggested in a letter she wrote to Ben Griffith: "What I had in mind to suggest with the artificial nigger was the redemptive quality of the Negro's suffering for us all." I had understood this to be her intention when I first read it, and to my mind this story contains the germ of a final enlargement of understanding for Flannery O'Connor. There is important evidence of a developing sense of this mystery in *The Violent Bear It Away*. Buford Munson, the old country black, monumental astride his mule, looks down at the renegade Tarwater, moments before— almost as though in conjunction with—the boy's compelling epiphany, and reproves him in these significant words: "It's owing to me he's resting there. I buried him while you were laid out drunk. It's owing to me his corn has been plowed. It's owing to me the sign of his Saviour is over his head." And there are other flashes, integral to the particular story she is telling, winks of light in her own prophetic vision, which, if she had lived long enough to see it whole and to give it concrete form, might have perfected that vision and completed the extraordinary work in which she was to embody it.

Moreover, I have found myself thinking that her own being would have been likewise raised and perfected, completed, by a greater personal empathy with the blacks who were so important a part of the tissue of the South, and of the humanity with whose redemption she was so truly and deeply concerned. Her will was never in danger on the score of racism; she describes herself as bridling at a contemptuous jape from a bus driver addressed to a group of blacks waiting to board, and says that from that moment on she was an integrationist. But large social issues as such were not the subject of her writing, and she never thought in those terms. She wrote: "The uneducated Southern Negro is not the clown he is made out to be. He's a man of very elaborate manners and great formality which he uses superbly for his own protection and to insure his own privacy." There is a great deal of respect in this characterization but, sentimental about no one else, she was equally unsentimental about blacks as individuals. Frequently she was impatient with them, and said so. She disliked the stridency of the militant movement and some of its spokesmen, although she recognized the need for, and approved of, Martin Luther King's crusade. The blacks on the O'Connor farm were as primitive as some of the whites she wrote about, and they perhaps served as trees obscuring her view of the social forest. Certainly they sometimes vexed her sorely. In any case, she evidently felt unable to "get inside their heads," in her own phrase. This may have been humility. In her letters, she uses the prevailing locution of the South as easily, and as unmaliciously, as it often occurs there, among blacks and whites alike. It was simply natural to her in her time and place. And if she did not live to envision fully and dramatize their role in the divine comedy, it was perhaps because it was her well-met responsibility to her gift to give dignity and meaning to the lives of individuals who have far fewer champions, and enjoy considerably less sympathy, and are far lonelier than they. In the last year of her life, Flannery wrote to Sr. Mariella Gable, "I've been writing eighteen years and I've reached the point where I can't do again what I know I can do well, and the larger things I need to do now, I doubt my capacity for doing." You write, she repeatedly said, what you can. And you become, we can further infer, what you can. Her accomplishments in both making and being are too impressive to support cant from any side.

This is enough, or more than enough, to hear about her letters before proceeding to read them. The sharp little journal calls me again to order: "I've got a lot of *faults* but I *hope* I won't ever hang on the line like Mrs. S."

*Sally Fitzgerald*

*Cambridge, Massachusetts*
*March 1978*

# Editor's Note

I should like to express my gratitude to all those who so generously made their letters from Flannery O'Connor available to me for this selection. I am indebted to Gerald Becham, curator of the O'Connor papers in the Georgia College Library in Milledgeville, for his unfailing courtesy and helpfulness. I am indebted, as well, to Professor Mary Barbara Tate and Dr. Sarah Gordon, also of Georgia College, and to Mary Ann Tate, who all three braved some steamy August days to scan the galley proofs with me. I am grateful to Marian Schlesinger, Betsy Walsh, Frances McFadden, and Eileen Simpson, who read the introduction in draft and offered useful comments. Robert Giroux was invariably patient and supportive in the face of all the difficulties and delays that ensued in the course of preparing this book. Professor Charles Haar, showing remarkable tolerance of the absent mind at the secretarial desk, gave me every encouragement. Robert Fitzgerald, Flannery's literary executor, read the entire manuscript and made some needed corrections. Thanks are owing to Fr. John Boles, of St. Paul's Church in Cambridge, for the indispensable cell he so kindly lent in the last year of my labors. And, finally, I want to thank my children for all they did to keep me afloat on my sea of papers.

Except for the first and last letters, no salutations or closing words are reproduced, in order to avoid pointless repetition and save space. The name of a correspondent is given only with the first of a series of letters; the absence of a name indicates another exchange with the same person. Similarly, Flannery's address is given only with the first of a series or when her location changes, which (except for the first few years) is rare. After July 1952, almost every letter Flannery wrote came from Milledgeville. Even accounts of her trip abroad in April 1958 were mostly written after she reached home.

Brackets indicate editorial interpolations, usually factual, to clarify obscurities. Dots indicate editor's deletions. Footnotes have been kept to a minimum. Flannery's sometimes bizarre spelling and punctuation have in general been respected. In the few instances of alteration, her meaning would not have been (as she always wished it to be) perfectly clear.

*S.F.*

# PART I

---

## UP NORTH AND

## GETTING HOME

## 1948 – 1952

Most of the readers of these letters are probably familiar with the simpler facts of Flannery O'Connor's life: that she was born in Savannah, Georgia, on March 25, 1925, the only child of Edward Francis O'Connor and Regina Cline O'Connor; that she moved to Milledgeville, Georgia, her mother's birthplace, when she was twelve years old, after her father had fallen gravely ill. He died when Flannery was fifteen. Thereafter she lived in Milledgeville with her mother, in the fine old home of the Cline family, and attended Peabody High School and Georgia State College for Women (now Georgia College) in the same town. By the time she received her A.B. degree in 1945, she knew very well what she could and wanted to do.

When Flannery left Milledgeville to "go north," it was to the School for Writers, conducted by Paul Engle at the State University of Iowa. Her promise had been recognized in college, and she received a scholarship for her Master's studies. This seems to have been an interesting and fruitful time for her: she read a great deal and she learned a lot about writing. Her first publication, in Accent magazine, of her story "The Geranium," occurred in 1946 while she was still a student. In 1947 she won the Rinehart-Iowa Fiction Award for a first novel, with part of Wise Blood.

On the strength of this, she was recommended for a place at Yaddo, in Saratoga Springs, New York, a philanthropic foundation offering artists periods of hospitality and freedom, enabling them to concentrate on their work. For a few months she enjoyed working there, but in the spring of 1949, together with all the other guests, she left Yaddo, which was undergoing a turmoil described on page 11. After a few disagreeable weeks in New York City, she went back to Milledgeville, returned to New York for the summer, then came with her half-finished novel *in September of the same year to join the Robert Fitzgerald family in a hidden house on a wooded hilltop in Ridgefield, Connecticut. There she lived and wrote until, in 1951, illness redirected her life.*

*None of the letters she wrote while she was in Iowa has been made available for this selection. Most of them were probably to her mother, who feels that they are purely personal and contain nothing of literary interest. Her close college friend, the late Betty Boyd Love, wrote us, soon after Flannery's death, that they had corresponded monthly in the first few years after they graduated, when Flannery went her way and Betty Boyd set off for the University of North Carolina to take her own master's degree in mathematics. Inevitably, some of these letters were lost, and unfortunately none at all from Iowa turned up in the search.*

*So it must be that Flannery's correspondence during her years in the North begins with the letter she wrote, in 1948, at the outset of her professional life, on a professional matter of great importance. As it turned out, it was a lucky letter, for it marked the beginning of an association and a friendship that continued throughout her life and, on the part of her correspondent, until the present day.*

## To Elizabeth McKee

Yaddo
Saratoga Springs, New York
June 19, 1948

Dear Miss McKee,

I am looking for an agent. Paul Moor [another writer at Yaddo] suggested I write to you. I am at present working on a novel [*Wise Blood*] for which I received the Rinehart-Iowa Fiction Award ($750) last year. This award gives Rinehart an option but nothing else. I have been on the novel a year and a half and will probably be two more years finishing it. The first chapter appeared as a short story, "The Train," in the Spring 1948 issue of the *Sewanee Review*. The fourth chapter ["The Peeler"] will be printed in a new quarterly to appear in the fall, *American Letters*. I have another chapter ["The Heart of the Park"] which I have sent to *Partisan Review* and which I expect to be returned. A short story of mine ["The Turkey"] will be in *Mademoiselle* sometime in the fall.

The novel, except for isolated chapters, is in no condition to be sent to you at this point. My main concern right now is to get the first draft of it done; however as soon as *Partisan Review* returns the chapter I sent them, I would like to send it to you, and probably also a short story ["The Crop"] which I expect to get back from a quarterly in a few days.

I am writing you in my vague and slack season and mainly because I am being impressed just now with the money I am not making by having stories in such places as *American Letters*. I am a very slow worker and it is possible that I won't write another story until I finish this novel and that no other chapters of the novel will prove salable. I have never had an agent so I have no idea what your disposition might be toward my type of writer. Please consider this letter an introduction to me and let me know if you would like to look at what I can get together when I get it together. I expect to be in New York a day or two in early August, and if you are interested, I would like to talk to you then.

Yours sincerely,

(Miss) Flannery O'Connor

July 4, 1948

It was good to get your letter and I am glad you look kindly on handling my work.

My chapter has been a month at the *Partisan Review*. I understand things are regularly lost around there but I will hope to get it back before the novel is finished. The story I had out at a quarterly came back and I find it much too bad to send to you.

I want you to put through the details of my contract with Rinehart if they take up their option. John Selby [editor-in-chief of Rinehart] has written me that they want to see the first draft before considering a contract. I am a slow six months before the end of a first draft, and after that, I will be at least a year cleaning up. I think I will need an advance for that year.

Paul tells me that you will be in Europe when I go through New York. I am very sorry that I won't have the chance to talk to you.

July 21, 1948

I enclose a few things you might like to see.

What you say about the novel, Rinehart, advances, etc. sounds very good to me, but I must tell you how I work. I don't have my novel outlined and I have to write to discover what I am doing. Like the old lady, I don't know so well what I think until I see what I say; then I have to say it over again. I am working on the twelfth chapter now. I long ago quit numbering the pages but I suppose I am past the 50,000 word mark. Of the twelve chapters only a few won't have to be re-written; and I can't exhibit such formless stuff. It would discourage me to look at it right now and anyway I yearn to go about my business to the end. At this point I think the novel will run about 100,000 words. The chapters I enclose should give you some idea. They are the best chapters in it.

If I find I am able to come to New York before the 31st I will write you. If I don't come before then, I will probably skip New York this time altogether, although I would like to meet John Selby and George Davis [fiction editor of *Mademoiselle*]. There is a possibility that I may come back to Yaddo in the fall and/or winter.

The enclosed story "The Crop" is for sale to the unparticular.

July 21, 1948

Thank you for returning the chapter. I agree that compression at both ends would help "The Crop" but unless you think there is a possibility of its being taken anywhere, I don't care to fool with it now.

I'll be interested to hear if the *Partisan* has lost the "Heart of the Park" and of the outcome of the lunch with Selby. I don't want an advance from Rinehart until I finish the first draft and they see what they are getting—six or eight months hence. I cannot really believe they will want the finished thing.

[P.S.] My address after August 1 will be, Box 246, Milledge-ville, Georgia.

Milledgeville<br>September 3, 1948

I plan to stop in New York September 14th and 15th on my way back to Yaddo, and I shall hope to see you. You suggested once that you make appointments with John Selby and George Davis for me. I would like to have you do this if you would. I get in the afternoon of the 13th and will be free anytime the next two days.

I sent John Selby a copy of Chapter Nine which the *Partisan Review* decided to take.

[P.S.] In case you should want to call me, you would find me at the Woodstock Hotel.

Yaddo
September 18, 1948

Dear Elizabeth [first use]:

I was glad to get your letter and am anxious to hear if Mr. [Philip] Rahv or Mr. [Robert Penn] Warren or Mrs. Porter [Arabel Porter, editor of *New World Writing*] will recommend me [for a Guggenheim Fellowship]. I haven't been able to face the blanks yet but I suppose there is no need to until I know by whom I am going to be recommended.

You will probably hear from me asking you to make hotel reservations for me in November sometime. There will be only three of us here this winter (Clifford Wright, Robert Lowell, and myself) so I shall probably be more than ready to take off for a few days by that time.

I'll send you a copy of "The Crop" as soon as I can type one up.

I am altogether pleased that you are my agent.

September 30, 1948

I am sending you two copies of "The Geranium" and one of "The Train" which if you think advisable you can show to Mr. Rahv or anybody. I don't know that this is enough or good enough to influence him one way or the other, but it is all I have . . .

The novel is coming very well, which is why you haven't got the copy of "The Crop." *American Letters* may be out. The editor doesn't know my address now so I won't get a copy. It would be a good thing for Mr. Rahv to see, if it is out. Thank you for your trouble.

November 14, 1948

Robert Lowell has said he will recommend me for the Guggenheim, so if it is not too late to add a name, I would appreciate your calling Mr. Moe's secretary [Henry Allen Moe, president of the John Simon Guggenheim Foundation] and having it put on. Lowell's address is Yaddo.

December 15, 1948

Enclosed is the letter from George Davis. After re-reading as much of the story ["The Crop"] as I could stand, I am more than ready to agree with his criticism. Please send the manuscript back to me. I should not write stories in the middle of a novel.

I appreciate his reading it and writing the Guggenheim letter.

Paul Engle sent me a copy of his report and I have seen Robert Lowell's, so there should be three anyway with Mr. Moe.

Perhaps I shall get down in January and perhaps before that send you the chapters I am working on of the novel. I have decided, however, that no good comes of sending anything (that story) off in a hurry so you may expect it when you see it.

*Alfred Kazin, who was at Yaddo with Flannery, was at that time a consultant to Harcourt, Brace and Company; he recommended her work to Robert Giroux, editor-in-chief of the publishing house, as did Robert Lowell. In February 1949, when Flannery accompanied Lowell on a visit to Giroux at the publishing offices, then located at 383 Madison Avenue, she met her future editor and publisher for the first time.*

January 20, 1949

Here are the first nine chapters of novel, which please show John Selby and let us be on with financial thoughts. They are, of course, not finished but they are finished enough for the present. If Rinehart doesn't want the book, what about Harcourt, Brace? Alfred Kazin, who is up here now and works for them, said they were interested.

I am going to send the sixth chapter to the *Kenyon Review* and if they don't want it to the *Sewanee*.

January 28, 1949

My visit here [Yaddo] is sure only through April. I have asked to stay through July and to come back again next October but I have my doubts about either of these requests being granted. I won't know until the end of March whether I can stay longer than April, but considering the improbability of it and the improbability of my getting a Guggenheim this year, an advance on the book is more than necessary.

I would like to come down to New York but not until I have to. How long is it supposed to take the Brothers Rinehart to decide if they want to risk their money on me? . . .

James Ross, a writer who is here, is looking for an agent. He wrote a very fine book called, *They Don't Dance Much*. It didn't sell much. If you are interested in him, I daresay he would be glad to hear from you. Right now he wants to sell some stories he is reworking.

February 3, 1949

I am very much pleased about what you have done with the manuscript. Until I hear from Selby, there is not much I can say, but $1,500 for an advance from Harcourt sounds altogether good to me, and I don't see Rinehart giving me that much. I want mainly to be where they will take the book as I write it. I gather it is also well to be where they will try to sell some copies of it, but if Harcourt would give me $1,500 I presume they would try to get that much out of it anyway.

When I hear from Selby I will write you again and probably ask you to make a hotel reservation for me so I can come down and talk to you and to Amussen [Theodore Amussen, an editor at Harcourt who had previously worked at Rinehart] before I make up my mind.

*The long-awaited letter from Mr. Selby to Flannery opened with the remark that she seemed a "straight shooter," an approach that did not go down very well with her, as she wrote Elizabeth McKee.*

February 17, 1949

I received Selby's letter today. Please tell me what is under this Sears Roebuck Straight Shooter approach. I presume Selby says either that Rinehart will not take the novel as it will be if left to my fiendish care (it will be essentially as it is), or that Rinehart would like to rescue it at this point and train it into a conventional novel.

The criticism is vague and really tells me nothing except that they don't like it. I feel the objections they raise are connected with its virtues, and the thought of working with them specifically to correct these lacks they mention is repulsive to me. The letter is addressed to a slightly dim-witted Camp Fire Girl, and I cannot look with composure on getting a lifetime of others like them. I have not yet answered it and won't until I hear further from you, but if I were certain that Harcourt would take the novel, I would write Selby immediately that I prefer to be elsewhere.

Would it be possible for you to get the manuscript back now and show it to Harcourt, or does Rinehart hang onto it until we break relations? Please advise me what the next step is to be, or take it yourself. I'll probably come down week after next if you think it advisable. I am anxious to have this settled and off my mind so that I can get to work . . .

I received your letter of the 17th today and I have decided to come down next Wednesday since you say that will be quicker. I have my doubts about the efficacy of personal conversation with Selby as my experience with him is that he says as little as possible as vaguely as possible. With this in mind, I am writing him a letter, stating what my position about the book is, so that he can collect himself and have something specific to say. I enclose a copy of same.

Would you make an appointment with him or Raney [William Raney, an editor at Rinehart] or whomever for Thursday the 24th? I would also like to see Amussen on this visit, if that would not be rushing things. I will be down the 24th, 25th, and part of the 26th. I am going to stay in Elizabeth Hardwick's apartment so it won't be necessary to make a hotel reservation for me . . . I'll be there probably around five Wednesday afternoon.

## To John Selby

February 18, 1949

Thank you for your letter of the 16th. I plan to come down [from Yaddo] next week and I have asked Elizabeth McKee to make an appointment with you for me on Thursday. I think, however, that before I talk to you my position on the novel and on your criticism in the letter should be made plain.

I can only hope that in the finished novel the direction will be clearer, but I can tell you that I would not like at all to work with you as do other writers on your list. I feel that whatever virtues the novel may have are very much connected with the limitations you mention. I am not writing a conventional novel, and I think that the quality of the novel I write will derive precisely from the peculiarity or aloneness, if you will, of the experience I write from. I do not think there is any lack of objectivity in the writing, however, if this is what your criticism implies; and also I do not feel that rewriting has obscured the direction. I feel it has given whatever direction is now present.

In short, I am amenable to criticism but only within the sphere of what I am trying to do; I will not be persuaded to do otherwise. The finished book, though I hope less angular, will be just as odd if not odder than the nine chapters you have now. The question is: is Rinehart interested in publishing this kind of novel?

I'll hope to see you Thursday and hear further what you think.

## To Elizabeth McKee

February 24, 1949

I am sorry you will have to break the Tuesday appointment with Selby. I get in Tuesday night and will call you Wednesday morning. Anytime after that will do for the appointment.

We have been very upset at Yaddo lately and all the guests are leaving in a group Tuesday—the revolution. I'll probably have to be in New York a month or so and I'll be looking for a place to stay. Do you know of anything? Temporarily I'll be staying at something called Tatum House but I want to get out of there as soon as possible. All this is very disrupting to the book and has changed my plans entirely as I definitely won't be coming back to Yaddo unless certain measures go into effect here.

I hope you are finished with the grip and feel well again.

*The "upset" at Yaddo centered on a well-known journalist, Agnes Smedley, who by all accounts made no attempt to disguise the fact that she was a Communist Party member in good standing. She had lived at Yaddo for five years, while most guests were invited for a few precious months. She left Yaddo in 1948. Miss Smedley had not only lived there for years but had published almost nothing during her stay, although the function of Yaddo was to free guests to do their work. Partly because of her long sojourn, the F.B.I. had for some time had Yaddo under surveillance. When a newspaper stated (inaccurately, as it turned out) that Agnes Smedley's name had appeared in an army report, the investigation became an open one. There were four writers-in-residence that winter: Robert Lowell, Edward Maisel, Elizabeth Hardwick, and Flannery O'Connor. When Maisel and Elizabeth Hardwick were questioned, they of course told the other two. Hindsight now seemed to clarify much that had bothered them only as a vaguely unpleasant atmosphere of hostility and evasiveness. Concerned about the possible misuse of a benevolent institution, meant to be devoted to the arts, the four decided to inform the board of directors of the Yaddo Corporation privately of the presumed misconduct of the directress in the form of collusion with Agnes Smedley. The directors they reached did not disregard their charges as incredible, and a formal meeting of the entire board was quietly convened.*

*The four plaintiffs chose Robert Lowell—a powerful personality at any time—as their spokesman at the hearing. Possibly they needed good legal counsel, or at least clearer knowledge of the rules of evidence. The evidence they had was largely circumstantial, and some of it was sub-*

jective. What they had to say was neither conclusive nor implausible enough to permit an immediate decision, and it was agreed that another meeting would be held three weeks later and a final decision made.

It was further agreed that nothing would be said publicly, and the four writers honored this agreement. But in the interim one of the board members leaked the stenographic transcript to some of his literary friends in New York, who at once circulated to eighty or ninety others a hasty and inaccurate letter describing the events at Yaddo as a public inquisition carried out in an atmosphere of hatred, panic, and fanaticism. They enclosed a petition, in the nature of a shriek, describing the charges as "preposterous . . . a cynical assault . . . smear technique," to be signed and returned to the Yaddo board. This was hardly fair. The four had made their charges in good faith, in private, and in open confrontation with their adversary, who was unlikely to be hurt if those charges could not be thoroughly substantiated. The kind of injurious attack launched, chiefly against Lowell, by people he had thought were his friends, was a profound shock to him, and to the others. The board, buffeted by forty-odd signed petitions, and threatened by wide publicity, abandoned its inquest, appointed a new admissions committee, and retired. The directress retained her place. This was all very instructive to Flannery. Nothing in it reflects discredit on her motives or her intelligence. Someone less young than she, less naïve, might have been wary of the jungle of political and literary infighting, but she behaved honestly throughout and in accord with her convictions.

The episode left a deep impression on her, especially the unexpected and violent attack from the organized left, which I think did more to convince her of the possible justice of their charges than anything that had happened until then. In any case, she quite detachedly judged that concerted assault to be an evil, and this surprised her possibly less than it did her friends. She lost no respect from anyone at Yaddo as a result of the episode. On the contrary, she was later cordially invited to return. The idea amused her.

It was when she came down to New York from Saratoga Springs in the company of Elizabeth Hardwick and Lowell, in the time between the two hearings, that my husband and I first met her, alert and coolly sensible as always. As events developed, she silently watched and listened, seeing and understanding clearly what was occurring at every stage. Toward the end of March she returned to Milledgeville for a few weeks, and then came back to New York for the summer, before moving to Connecticut.

## To Paul Engle

I am in the process of moving. I left Yaddo March 1 and have since been in transit and am now getting ready to go back to New York City where I have a room and where I hope to keep on working on the novel as long as my money holds out, which is not due to be long. Therefore, being in a swivit, I am writing you in brief what I take the situation with Rinehart to be but when I get to New York in ten days I will write you further and send back the letter Rinehart sent you. Thank you for sending it to me.

When I was in New York in September, my agent and I asked Selby how much of the novel they wanted to see before we asked for a contract and an advance. The answer was—about six chapters. So in February I sent them nine chapters (108 pages and all I've done) and my agent asked for an advance and for their editorial opinion.

Their editorial opinion was a long time in coming because obviously they didn't think much of the 108 pages and didn't know what to say. When it did come, it was *very* vague and I thought totally missed the point of what kind of a novel I am writing. My impression was that they want a conventional novel. However, rather than trust my own judgment entirely I showed the letter to Lowell who had already read the 108 pages. He too thought that the faults Rinehart had mentioned were not the faults of the novel (some of which he had previously pointed out to me). I tell you this to let you know I am not, as Selby implied to me, working in a vacuum.

In answer to the editorial opinion, I wrote Selby that I would have to work on the novel without direction from Rinehart, that I was amenable to criticism but only within the sphere of what I was trying to do.

In New York a few weeks later, I learned indirectly that nobody at Rinehart liked the 108 pages but Raney (and whether he likes it or not I couldn't really say), that the ladies there particularly had thought it unpleasant (which pleased me). I told Selby that I was willing enough to listen to Rinehart criticism but that if it didn't suit me, I would disregard it. That is the impasse.

Any summary I might try to write for the rest of the novel would be worthless and I don't choose to waste my time at it. I don't write that way. I can't write much more without money and they won't give me any money because they can't see what the finished book will be. That is Part Two of the impasse.

To develope at all as a writer I have to develope in my own way. The 108 pages are very angular and awkward but a great deal of that can be corrected when I have finished the rest of it— and only then. I will not be hurried or directed by Rinehart. I think they are interested in the conventional and I have had no indication that they are very bright. I feel the heart of the matter is they don't care to lose $750 (or as they put it, Seven Hundred and Fifty Dollars).

If they don't feel I am worth giving more money to and leaving alone, then they should let me go. Other publishers, who have read the two printed chapters, are interested. Selby and I came to the conclusion that I was "prematurely arrogant." I supplied him with the phrase.

Now I am sure that no one will understand my need to work this novel out in my own way better than you; although you may feel that I should work faster. Believe me, I work ALL the time, but I cannot work fast. No one can convince me I shouldn't re-write as much as I do. I only hope that in a few years I won't have to so much.

I didn't get any Guggenheim.

If you see Robie [Macauley, author] tell him to write me.


*Betty Boyd, then in California, was about to take a job among the computers of Los Alamos, New Mexico.*

## To Betty Boyd

> [postmarked 8/17/49]
> 255 W. 108 NYC
> After Sept 1:
> Care of Fitzgerald, RD 4,
> Ridgefield, Conn.

I am wondering about you and Los Alamos?

Me & novel are going to move to the rural parts of Connecti-cut. I have some friends named Fitzgerald who have bought a house on top of a ridge, miles from anything you could name. An exaggeration . . . I have no particular desire to leave New York except that I will save a good deal of money this way & my publishing connections still being in a snarl, that is a great considera-tion. I am on a tightrope somewhere between Rinehart and Harcourt, Brace. There should be some kind of insurance to take care of such cases.

I learned by the Alumna Junnal that [a former teacher] is not ten blocks from me, filling her noddle full of Lord knows what at the Columbia trough. Fancy the mental champaine (sp?) that will be brought back, brimming & bristling, to be dispensed in Parks basement. Also fancy it mingling there with the vinegar, pop, & the hogwash.

Isn't Los Alamos in California? I would be obliged for your impressions of California if you go there. It puzzles me about like the thinking machine.

*The contract mentioned in this letter is one that Robert Giroux had sent from Harcourt, Brace and Company for* Wise Blood. *Rinehart had failed to pick up the option, and no legal impediment to contracting with another publisher remained. Mavis McIntosh, partner of Elizabeth McKee at McIntosh & McKee, had written to Mr. Selby at Flannery's direction, out of respect for whatever moral obligation to Rinehart might yet exist. When Selby did not respond, the HB contract was forwarded to Flannery. Later, the wording of the "release" by Selby deeply offended Flannery and created further trouble.*

## To Mavis McIntosh

> 70 Acre Road
> Ridgefield, Conn.
> October 6, '49

Thank you for your letter and the contract received today. I doubt if my novel will come to 90,000 words but since this contract is only to be looked at, I presume that is no consideration at present.

Thank you for so much to and fro business. I'll be anxious to hear from you again.

[P.S.] My typewriter is being analyzed.

## To Betty Boyd

> 10/17/49

Well, I can't equal you in the matter of clippings, but I enclose a token as I thought you might like to look at An Honest Smiling Face and read some Real Art.* I am obliged for the

---

* A laundry ad in the Ridgefield weekly paper, featuring a smiling picture of the laundryman and a poem he had chosen to quote.

accounts. They fit in fine with what I can imagine and with a novel I read by Nathanael West called *The Day of the Locust* (which you would like); I also thought of the character in *Sanctuary* who "had the depthless quality of stamped tin." I can't believe New York where the culture fog is thicker is much better, but then I am of the school that wants rotgut labelled whether it's in a rosewater bottle or not and that believes fornication is the same thing in New York as in Los Angeles (sp?). A wonderful novel has just been written by a man named Nigel Dennis called *A Sea Change*. You should get your hands on that one . . .

My publishing snarl is still snarled. I have a provisional contract with Harcourt, Brace in my desk drawer but can't sign it because I am still unreleased by Rinehart; however all I really want to be about is getting this book finished. I am living in the country with some people named Fitzgerald, and writing about four hours every morning which I find is the maximum. Mr. Fitzgerald is a poet (*A Wreath for the Sea*) and has just translated the *Oedipus* with Dudley Fitts. I think it is a very fine translation. He teaches Aristotle and St. Thomas at Sarah Lawrence College and has a lot of books which I am getting to read. There are no other people around here but them and their two children so I presume I am at the farthest remove from the spirit of Los Angeles . . .

*Flannery, troubled about the contretemps with Rinehart, explains her position.*

## To Elizabeth McKee

October 26, 1949

Thank you for your letter and the copy of Selby's "Statement of release." I find it, like most of Selby's documents, in the highest degree unclear. They want it definitely understood that in the event of trouble with Harcourt they see the novel before any other publisher. This is no release. However, I suppose the best thing to do is sign the Harcourt agreement and hope there will be no further trouble; but I want it definitely understood that it is *not* definitely understood that in the event of trouble with Harcourt, Rinehart see the manuscript again. I suppose it would be impossible to get anything better out of Selby and I am certainly much obliged to you and Mavis for all your effort in my behalf. If there was ever any doubt in my mind about the possibility of working with Selby, it has been done away with by his letter.

I will be in town in a few weeks and would like to talk with you or Mavis. I am anxious to know with what amount of difficulty the Harcourt agreement was obtained and also about Mavis' talk with Selby, although I realize that his conversation is no more enlightening than his prose. I'll try to write you for an appointment.

It seems to me I should at least be getting proofs on that chapter ["The Heart of the Park"] the *Partisan* has. You can do what you please about asking for payment; my understanding is that they pay on publication. I would like to know mainly when they plan to use it.

I would like to have some of that *Flair* [magazine] money but I don't have any chapters that would do for anybody now; please remember me to George Davis when you see him.

The novel is going well, almost fast.

*The release written by John Selby described Flannery as "stiff-necked, uncooperative and unethical." The last word especially made her feel that her personal honesty was being impugned, and she wanted no doubt in anyone's mind on that score.*

## To Mavis McIntosh

October 31, 1949

I have been pondering Selby's statement of release for some days now. I think it is insulting and shows very clearly that I could not work with him. However, since they still feel that they have an option and that I am being dishonest, it seems to me that I should present them with more of the manuscript one more time.

Now since if I sign the contract with Harcourt, I won't get any money until next fall anyway, and that providing they take the book, it seems to me that it would be better all around to try to arrange something like this with Rinehart: that next March, I show them what I have done up to that date. This will be considerably more than what they saw last year at the same time and the direction of the book will be more apparent. If they are not able by that time to know if they want it, then they will never know. Now it seems that if I do this, they should agree IN WRITING to release me without condition or any such malicious statement as accompanied the present release if they don't want the book. It should also be made clear that I will not work with them or sign any contract which includes an option on the next book or any such thing as that. I feel certain that they will not want the book if they see it in the spring or at any time later, for that matter.

This would simply be an attempt on my part to be fair with them and to give them a chance to be fair with me. As you said, they owe me something. The announcement of the contest was so worded that I am held to a "moral" obligation and they are not. Further, I understood last spring that they would make up their minds on six chapters. Selby told Elizabeth and me that at lunch. It wasn't in writing and apparently dealings with them should be.

Perhaps after all your trouble this seems unnecessarily scrupulous to you or anyway, a late-in-the-day scrupulosity. It may well be, but the fact remains that the statement of release was not much of a release; if Harcourt doesn't take the book, we are back where we started from. If Rinehart will make this agreement with me, in writing, we might get the thing settled by summer and I would be free to work with an open mind; which I am certainly not now.

I am going to try to be in town Thursday and Friday of this week. I will call you and hope to see you, but I am writing this beforehand so that you will know what is on my mind. I wrote Elizabeth that I thought it would be best to go ahead and sign the contract with Harcourt, but this letter is the fruit of more thought.

Thank you for bothering with such unrewarding people.


*To Betty Boyd*

[postmarked 11/5/49]

Congratulations on Los Alamos. Was Los Alamos a place before the bomb? My notions of the southwest are very vague but I should think you would have definite sensations about living in a place completely Post Bomb. Anyway, how can you give up the old culture? I mean Wheels & Dr. T. B. Chew.* I was particularly impressed with Dr. Chew as I thought he had an elevated face; I mean elevated beyond most elevated faces. If you see another of his recommendations of himself with the picture, I wish you would send it to me as I passed that on to a friend with dispepsia (sp?). It is possible that I should subscribe to a Los Angeles paper.

I have been released with a nasty note from Rinehart & now have the contract with H. B. . . . .

---

* A Chinese herb doctor who advertised in the Los Angeles paper.

I had a long letter from Miss Helen Green [former teacher] a few weeks ago. I have always thought she was the smartest woman at that college, & during my last spell home last March, I talked to her a good bit on the subject of my Yaddo deal and the general rottenness of S. Science and soforth. I still think she's the brighest thing they have around. Unfortunately, I could make out only a few words in the entire letter. On the envelope she had scribled, "Saw your poem in Seydell's Quarterly, Fall 48." Of course I have never heard of any such quarterly & have not written anything but prose since I got out of stir. But several awful ghosts come to mind. Do you remember the poems we sent to an anthology and had accepted—called *America Sings*, printed by offset somewhere in California? I have only a vague reccolection of what the poems were about but they were bad enough. This may be where Seydell's Q. reprints from. I plan to investigate & if I find you in it, will send you a copy.

I don't read *Orphan Annie*. Am I missing something significant?

I have just got back from 2 days in NYC. There is one advantage in it because although you see several people you wish you didn't know, you see thousands you're glad you don't know.

*Betty Boyd had just announced her engagement to James Love.*

[postmarked 11/17/49]

In honor of my nuptial blessing I am writing on white paper, 16 pound bond, suitable (and left over from) 2nd and 3rd copies of theses. The following are violets:
[a row of three disheveled flowers]
or at least I would have you think of them as such.

Marriages are always a shock to me.

Will you live in Los Angeles & take a Los Angeles paper?

I would like to send you a teasespoon. What kind would you like me to send? . . .

I am leaving a large space at the bottom to make this look more nuptial.

An abundance of peace.

*Flannery went home to Milledgeville for Christmas with her mother, and for an operation to correct a floating kidney. This was the first health problem of the many that were to afflict her. She made light of it to us, and at that time there was no other indication of a fragile physique.*

## To Elizabeth and Robert Lowell

Milledgeville
[undated; early 1950]

I won't see you again as I have to go to the hospital Friday and have a kidney hung on a rib. I will be there a month and at home a month. This was none of my plan . . .

Please write me a card while I am in the hospital. I won't be able to do anything there but dislike the nurses.

## To Elizabeth McKee

February 13, 1950

Thank you for your note. I am out of the hospital and don't expect to be ill again any time soon after such a radical cure. I hope to be back in Connecticut by March 20th . . .

I'm anxious to be on with the book but don't have any strength yet.

Ridgefield
April 27, 1950

Thank you for your letter, received after my manuscript was sealed. I expect to get down in May sometime and would like then to have lunch with you. I had a note from Bob Giroux the other day, asking how the book was coming. This seems to be a question that extends itself over the years.

## To Robie Macauley

[undated; 1950]

I wrote Dilly [Mrs. John Thompson] to find out where you and Ann were this year and she said at Iowa. I congratulate you on your endurance. I had a letter from Paul Engle and he intimated that everything out there was filthy rich and florishing and said they would be in *Life* in December. This must be the end. There must be going to be a picture of Engle surrounded by foreign students and looking like the Dean of American Letters, and one of P.G. surrounded by natives and trying to look as if he were in

Paris, and one of M. surrounded by bottles and looking as if he didn't know he wasn't in Paris. What about you? I hope you manage to escape.

Me and Enoch are living in the woods in Connecticut with the Robert Fitzgeralds. Enoch didn't care so much for New York. He said there wasn't no privetcy there. Every time he went to sit in the bushes there was already somebody sitting there ahead of him. He was very nervous before we left and somebody at the *Partisan Review* told him to go to an analyst. He went and the analyst said what was wrong with him was his daddy's fault and Enoch was so mad that anybody should defame his daddy that he pushed the analyst out the window. You can see why we would never last in New York. Enoch is going to be in the *Partisan Review* again in December or January but he don't like it at all and is mad with me because I didn't get him in *Click,* which has pictures.

This summer I chanced on a copy of *Furioso* and I liked that story of yours in it very much and was glad they didn't waste their $250. I haven't seen the other stories as I have largely given up reading polite magazines since I have given up trying to be a gracious lady . . . I am going back to raising mandrils . . .

The Brothers Rinehart and I have parted company to our mutual satisfaction and I have a contract with Harcourt, Brace, but I am largely worried about wingless chickens. I feel this is the time for me to fulfill myself by stepping in and saving the chicken but I don't know exactly how since I am not bold. I only know I believe in the *complete* chicken. You think about the complete *chicken* for a while.

The best to you and Anne.


## To Elizabeth McKee

September 22, 1950

Thank you for your note. I am still here and still at it. The last time I saw Bob Giroux, he said we would push the date of the agreement up to the first of the year but that there was nothing magic in that date. There is nothing magic in my speed or progress at this time, but I don't know anything for it. I plan to last until the first of the year and then see what I've got . . .


*When, in December 1950, I had put Flannery on the train for Georgia she was smiling perhaps a little wanly but wearing her beret at a jaunty*

*angle. She looked much as usual, except that I remember a kind of
stiffness in her gait as she left me on the platform to get aboard. By
the time she arrived she looked, her uncle later said, "like a shriveled
old woman."*

*A few nights later her mother called to tell us that Flannery was
dying of lupus. The doctor had minced no words. We were stunned.
We communicated regularly with Mrs. O'Connor while she went through
this terrible time and the days of uncertainty that followed, during
Dr. Arthur J. Merrill's tremendous effort to save Flannery's life.*

*As she emerged from the crisis, debilitated by high fevers and the
treatment alike, she began to communicate again herself—chiefly on
the subject of her novel, which had never been much out of her mind,
even when the lupus attack was most severe.*

*For the next year and a half, living at Andalusia, the beautiful farm
that was to become her permanent home, she stayed close to the house,
regaining her strength and her youthful looks, and enduring the trying
strictures necessary to control what she believed to be rheumatoid
arthritis. One of these was a totally salt-free diet: not even milk was
permitted, as being too naturally salty. She required daily medication,
ACTH by inoculation, and she learned to manage this for herself. It
was all an ordeal, but she believed that it was to be temporary, and her
greatest concern was for Wise Blood, which she rewrote, correcting and
polishing it, while she was still in the hospital. While she occupied herself with preparations for its publication, she began to write some
stories.*

*In this letter written while she was still in the hospital, she gives
little hint of what she was going through.*

## To Betty Boyd Love

Baldwin Memorial Horspital as usuel
12/23/50

Thanks yr. card. I am languishing on my bed of semi affliction, this time with AWTHRITUS of, to give it all it has, *the* acute
rheumatoid arthritis, what leaves you always willing to sit down,
lie down, lie flatter, etc. But I am taking cortisone so I will have
to get up again. These days you caint even have you a good psychosomatic ailment to get yourself a rest. I will be in Milledgeville Ga.
a birdsanctuary for a few months, waiting to see how much of an
invalid I am going to get to be. At Christmas the horsepital is full
of old rain crows & tree frogs only—& accident victims—& me,
but I don't believe in time no more much so it's all one to me.
And hope you are the same & and have some chuldrun by now. I
always want to hear.

I have been reading *Murder in the Cathedral* & the nurses thus conclude I am a mystery fan. It's a marvelous play if you don't know it, better if you do.

Write me a letter of sympathy.

## To Elizabeth McKee

[undated; probably January 1951]
Emory University Hosp.
Atlanta, Georgia

Thank you for your letter that I received after Christmas. I am in Atlanta right now at the Emory University Hospital, much improved and expect to go home next week.

During the cortisone period I managed to finish the first draft of the novel and send it to Mr. Fitzgerald in Conn. He is satisfied that it is good and so am I. I think I have found somebody here in Atlanta to make me some copies. Anyway I am trying to get you a copy and one to Harcourt.

When I get home I plan to add an extra chapter and make some changes on a few others.

It will all just take some time.

## To Robert Giroux

Milledgeville
March 10, 1951

Thank you for your letter. Enclosed is the manuscript of the book [*Wise Blood*] and I hope you'll like it and decide to publish it. I'm still open to suggestion about improving it and will welcome any you have; however, I'm anxious to be done with it and if it could be out in the fall that would suit me fine.

Miss McKee or Miss McIntosh will probably see you about it. Miss McKee has the notion that some more of the chapters will be salable, but I don't.

I am up and around again now but won't be well enough to go back to Connecticut for some time.

Thank you for Dr. Stern's book [*A Pillar of Fire*, by Karl Stern]. I've wanted to read it.

## To Elizabeth McKee

March 10, 1951

I enclose a letter from Giroux. I sent the manuscript to him directly today as I had only one copy of it corrected. I plan to mail you a corrected copy Monday. I wrote him that you or Miss McIntosh would see him.

So far as I am concerned this is the last draft of the book, unless there is something really glaring in it that may be pointed out to me. I don't think any of the chapters are salable, as is, but you can see what you think.

If Harcourt doesn't want it, what about Scribner's?

I am full of ACTH and much better.

## To Betty Boyd Love

4/24/51

I got your letter a long time ago when I was at Emory Hospital. I stayed there a month, giving generous samples of my blood to this, that and the other technician, all hours of the day and night, but now I am at home again and not receiving any more awful cards that say to a dear sick friend, in verse what's worse. Now I shoot myself with ACTH oncet daily and look very well and do nothing that I can get out of doing. I trust you are as well.

The other day one of my cousins wrote me that she was leaving her secretarial job in Atlanta and that somebody . . . who knew me, was taking it. My cousin thought this a remarkable coincidence, illustrating how remarkable coincidences can be. Now ain't it? I expect to have a letter from [the acquaintance] shortly, probably asking me if I like men or some such . . .

I have finished my opus nauseous and expect it to be out one of these days. The name will be *Wise Blood*.

Let me hear how you do.

*Acceptance of her unusual manuscript was not immediate. Six weeks after sending it, she wrote to her agent.*

## To Elizabeth McKee

April 24, 1951

Would you check on my manuscript at Harcourt, Brace? I sent it on the 12th of March but have had no acknowledgement of their receipt of it. They ought to know by now if they want it or not, and I am anxious to get it off my mind. If they don't want it, please get the manuscript back and send it somewhere else.

*At last word came from Elizabeth McKee's office that Harcourt had accepted her novel, and Flannery wrote to the agency.*

## To Mavis McIntosh

June 8, 1951

I am mighty pleased that Harcourt took the book and hope we'll get on with it now. I haven't heard from Bob Giroux but I suppose I will in whatever he considers the fullness of time.

Thank you for all your trouble in this.

## To Mavis McIntosh

September 1, 1951

Bob Giroux and Mrs. Tate [Caroline Gordon*] made some suggestions for improving my book and I have been working on these and have by now about come up with another draft of it, of which I will have one copy—readable but with a good many inked-in corrections—I hope in a few weeks.

I'm not familiar with the necessities or the niceties of sending a final draft to the publisher. Is it alright for me to send this copy? Or is their deadline for the spring already up anyhow? If so, there's no need for me to hurry myself. I have been in and out of the hospital this summer and am too decrepit to type a hundred and fifty pages under a month.

Will you need a copy? I hate to think of that other draft batting around at British publishing houses when this improved version exists. There is not much chance of its being bought there, however, I would think.

Giroux sent me the other ms. back and I have been inserting the additions and corrections, etc., into it and that is the copy I'll have in a few weeks. He said they would like to have it as soon as possible; but that is nothing definite.

I'd be much obliged for what information you can give me. Regards to Elizabeth.

* *Caroline Gordon, Mrs. Allen Tate, herself a distinguished novelist, became a generous mentor to Flannery, giving her invaluable criticism from the beginning to the end of her writing life.*

## To Sally and Robert Fitzgerald

9/20/51

I reckon you all are underway with the academic yer (*year*) '51–'52 and No. 5. I hope this one will be a girl & have a fierce Old Testament name and cut off a lot of heads. You had better stay down and take care of yourself. Your children sound big enough to do all the work. By beating them moderately and moderately often you should be able to get them in the habit of doing domestic chores.

Me & Maw are still at the farm and are like to be, I perceive, through the winter. She is nuts about it out here, surrounded by the lowing herd and other details, and considers it beneficial to my health. The same has improved. I am down to two moderate shots a day from four large ones when we first got to the farm. The large doses of ACTH send you off in a rocket and are scarcely less disagreeable than the disease so I am happy to be shut of them.

I am working on the end of the book while a lady around here types the first part of it. I think it's a lot better but I may be mistaken and will have to be told.

I got as far in Cal's [Robert Lowell] book as the quotation in the front from Dr. Williams. The local librarian brought me George Santayana's *Dominations & Powers*, what I have been reading for the style, not being able to take in the thought; and one of my English-teacher friends was so good as to leave with me *twenty old Saturday Reviews*—only a loan—they like to save them. The face of Malcolm Cowley shines out in every issue.

I have twenty-one brown ducks with blue wing bars. They walk everywhere they go in single-file.

Let us hear how you do; and steel yourselfs to read the changed parts of that manuscript again . . .

[P.S.] . . . I am reading Dr. Johnson's *Life of Dryden*. Dryden "embraced Popery" but Dr. Johnson is very lenient with him about it and says the measure of his sincerity was, he taught it (Popery) to his children . . .

*Flannery had been much amused when I told her that I had an aunt whom we called Aunt Car, because she was the only one of my father's three maiden sisters who could drive. She proposed to call one of her characters Mrs. Wally Car Hitchcock.*

Tuesday (mid-September, 1951)

Enclosed is Opus Nauseous No. 1. I had to read it over after it came from the typist's and that was like spending the day eating a horse blanket. It seems mighty sorry to me but better than it was before. My mother said she wanted to read it again so she went off with it and I found her a half hour later on page 9 and sound asleep. I sent it on to Giroux and said if he thought it was alright to go on with it but I doubt if the poor man puts himself to reading it again. Do you think Mrs. [Caroline Gordon] Tate would? All the changes are efforts after what she suggested in that letter and I am much obliged to her. If you think she wouldn't mind, would you send this copy on to her after you read it as I don't have another copy or her address? I would like to thank her for reading it the first time so if you would send me her address I would be obliged for that too. I am also obliged, while I am at this, for your reading it again. My vocabulary don't touch such a service.

Note that I changed the Car to Bee. If you are possessed of an Aunt Bee, let know and I change it to Flea. If you have an Aunt Flea . . .

I hope you got the pickle recipe. Regina had never made any such but got the recipe out of a very dirty old cookbook so it should be alright.

Regina says I should invite you to visit us on this farm. I tell her you have 5 or 6 children and couldn't hardly do such a thing but she says I should anyway, that it would be the *nice thing to do*.

I have read about that book *Catcher in the Rye* and will be glad to see it when it comes.

I have just discovered that my mother's dairyman calls all the cows *he*: he ain't give but two gallons, he ain't come in yet,— also he changes the name endings: if it's Maxine, he calls it Maxima. I reckon he doesn't like to feel surrounded by females or something.


[undated; mid-September 1951]

I certainly enjoyed *Catcher in the Rye*. Read it up the same day it came. Regina said I was going to RUIN MY EYES reading all that in one afternoon. I reckon that man owes a lot to Ring Lardner. Anyway he is very good. Regina said would she like to read it and I said, well it was very fine. She said yes but would *she* like to read it, so I said she would have to try it and see. She hasn't tried it yet. She likes books with Frank Buck and a lot of wild animals.

Thank you for sending the ms. to Caroline. She sent it back to me with some nine pages of comments and she certainly increased my education thereby. So I am doing some more things to it and then I mean to send it off for the LAST time . . .

You ought to hear all the hollering down here about the Separation of Church & State. They are having conventions all over the place and making resolutions and having the time of their lives. You'd think the Pope was about to annex the Sovereign State of Georgia.

What ever happened to Jacques Maritain? Is he still at Princeton or did Frank the Spell man [Cardinal Francis Spellman] get him a job in some Catholic institution?

Regina is glad you liked the cake and will send you the recipe when she finds it. I think she just throws stuff in. She likes em dry and Sister [Miss Mary Cline] likes em wet. That was Sister's recipe.

I am glad you have come to favor chickens. You won't favor them so much when you have to clean up their apartment but the eggs are certainly worth it. I have got me five geese. We also have turkeys. They all have the sorehead and the cure for that is liquid black shoe polish—so we have about fifteen turkeys running around in blackface. They look like domesticated vultures.


## To Robert Giroux

October 16, 1951

I am sending my revised manuscript under separate cover today. I've tried to clear up the foggier places and to make the changes suggested by Mrs. Tate. It looks better to me but I have no one here to read it who could tell me. If it seems all right to you, or to her, please go on with it; if not, I'd like to work on it again.

P.S. I've sent a copy to the Fitzgeralds who have agreed to undergo another session with it. They may have some suggestions.


## To Betty Boyd Love

10/18/51

I have been afraid that Margaret Ellen [the Loves' first child] would be up working on a calculating machine before I got around to congratulating you on her. I don't know what the proper word on children is but I am glad you've got one and hope you'll soon have a whole bunch of them. My advice to all parents is beat your children moderately and moderately often; and anything that Wm. Heard Kilpatrick & Jhn. Dewey say do, don't do . . .

I spent the summer in and out of Emory hospital but am hoping I can avoid it for the winter. I have got my last draft off to the publisher and now am raising ducks like a respectable citizen. I have twenty-one. However, if the Lord is willing, I am shortly going to eat all twenty-one of them and start another novel.

Mail is very eventful to me. Let me hear how you do.


## To Robert Giroux

November 23, 1951

I have had a long letter from Caroline about some things that need to be done yet to that novel. I suppose it is not set up and if not, I would like to do some more to the three or four places she has mentioned. Would you let me know? I apologize for all this shilly-shallying. And keep on doing it.


December 3, 1951

I am enclosing the changes and I will be much obliged to you if you can get them substituted at the printers. I think they make a lot of difference. I had a good many more for the first chapter but I presume it is too late for that. Caroline thought that some places went too fast for anybody to get them; also that I needed some preparation for the title. About how much can I mess around on the proofs without costing myself a lot of money? Fifteen percent of the cost of composition doesn't mean anything to me. What I want to know is: how many paragraphs (approximately) could I insert?

The biographical statement: Born, Savannah, Georgia, March 1925. Attended Georgia State College for Women, A.B. degree; State University of Iowa, M.F.A. degree. Published stories in *Accent, the Sewanee Review, Partisan Review, Mademoiselle,* and *Tomorrow.* No prizes except the Rinehart money which shouldn't be mentioned. (Doubtless Miss McIntosh didn't show you their letter of release. It said I was "stiff-necked, uncooperative, and unethical.") I have lived in Connecticut and am at present living in Milledgeville, Georgia, raising ducks and game birds, and writing. (This is the way all those things sound to me. If you need any more, I will have to make it up.)

I'll have to have the picture taken and will send it to you but I doubt if they give it to me by the 10th.

Please send me the proofs here.

Thank you for all this trouble I am putting you to about the changes.


## To Sally and Robert Fitzgerald

[Christmas 1951]

A very noisy Christmas to you all and assorted blessings for the new year. My mamma is getting ready for what she hopes will be one of her blessings: a refugee family to arrive here Christmas night. She has to fix up and furnish a house for them, don't know how many there will be or what nationality or occupation or nothing. She and Mrs. P., the dairyman's wife, have been making curtains for the windows out of flowered chicken-feed sacks. Regina was complaining that the green sacks wouldn't look so good in the same room where the pink ones were and Mrs. P. (who has no teeth on one side of her mouth) says in a very superior voice, "Do you think they'll know what colors even is?" Usually the families that have been got around here for dairy work have turned out to be . . . shoemakers and have headed for Chicago just as soon as they could save the money. For which they can't be blamed. However, we are waiting to see how this comes out.

What I forgot to say the last time I wrote was don't send me any two weeks rent that you may think you owe me. If the Lord is with me this next year I aim to visit you, at which time I will be glad to eat it out. I am only a little stiff in the heels so far this winter and am taking a new kind of ACTH, put up in glue, and I am on a pretty low maintenance dose. I only hope I can keep it that way.

My momma sends hers for the season.


## To Robert Giroux

January 23, 1952

The corrected galleys and the manuscript are enclosed. I hope the corrections and insertions are plain and not too numerous. They were all suggested by Caroline.

The shrub Enoch sits under in galleys in 20 and 21 is "abelia," not lobelia. The buzzard in galley 53 will have to stand on the roof if he can't stand on a television aerial in 1946; any other kind wouldn't support him. I don't think there is any other change that there can be any questions about.

I liked the sample page very much. When is this book supposed to come out?

## To Sally and Robert Fitzgerald

Thursday [undated; early 1952]

I certainly am enjoying [Philip Hughes's] *The Reformation in England.* I feel like I was at it. I showed it to the college Librarian so she would get it for them. Sometimes the students check out a good book by mistake; not often, according to her. They are very careful. She says they all go in for sociology and case studies. Case studies are the big thing.

My mama's refugees haven't come yet; she don't know why. She is very anxious to get them here and have the difficulties begin. She says I ought to be able to teach them English (educ!) and I say well I ain't able to and she says well *she* could if she wanted to and I say how and she says CAT: C—A—T. and you draw a picture of one. I don't doubt but what she could do it.

The Macauleys have asked me to come to Greensboro in March for an Arts Forum thing that Catherin Ann Porter is to be the phenomenon at. I may try this to see how my travelling legs are . . .

I had to go have my picture taken for the purposes of Harcourt, Brace. They were all bad. (The pictures.) The one I sent looked as if I had just bitten my grandmother and that this was one of my few pleasures, but all the rest were worse.

We liked your Christmas card very much and recognized yer assorted children.

*The enclosure sent with the following letter was a telegram regarding the acceptance of "Enoch and the Gorilla," one of the chapters in* Wise Blood, *by a new paperback periodical,* New World Writing, *an anthology of the best new young American writers. Flannery was unaware of the "second serial" provision in her contract, and the telegram from Victor Weybright and Arabel Porter of* New World Writing *mystified her. Giroux had also just completed an agreement with New American Library for a paperback reprint edition of* Wise Blood, *which he was about to reveal to her together with the anthology news. Mrs. Semmes was Flannery's much loved "Cousin Katie" in Savannah, then in her eighties, who retained a lively interest in Flannery and her writing. Mrs. Semmes was the widow of a nephew of the Civil War figure Admiral Raphael Semmes of the Confederate Navy.*

## To Robert Giroux

February 6, 1952

The enclosed came for me yesterday but I don't know what it's about. Could you enlighten me?

From February 16 to 22 I will be in Savannah and if those page proofs are to get here during that time, I could get them back to you quicker if you would send them to me there: care of Mrs. Raphael T. Semmes . . .

*Proofs of* Wise Blood *were sent on February 20, and returned within four days, with the following note to her publisher.*

February 24, 1952

The galley proofs and marked page proofs are enclosed. I have made insignificant changes on pages 20, 26, and 185, which you can dispense with if they would cost the printer any unhappiness or me any money.

I was glad to hear about the [paperback] reprint.

*On March 12, 1952, in response to a telegraphed query, Flannery also instructed Giroux to dedicate her novel to "Regina," her mother.*

## To Elizabeth McKee

March 14, 1952

Thank you for your letter and check. I am glad you and Mavis went into high dudgeon and got me some advance money [from the New American Library paperback agreement]. It is very nice of them to accomodate me in this way; however I don't want to be accomodated now with money that I will eventually have to accomodate them by paying back. Please let me know if and when the contract is signed.

## To Sally and Robert Fitzgerald

[undated; April 1952]

I thank you for the information about the Ford book. I don't have anything good enough right now to send to high-class places and it's also necessary for me to convert everything I can into ACTH, so I'll spare old Blackmur the pleasure of using my return envelope. Do they use reprints? I could ask Giroux to send them a book. One [serial] reprint has been bought for something called *New World Writing*—the part about Enoch and the gorilla. Then my agent wrote me that the New Am. Lib. had bought [paperback rights of] the whole thing for $4,000, and that I would get $2,000. Then she writes that that ain't actually the case yet but is going to be. I never believe nothing until I got the money. However, they advanced me $500 against the guarantee of $4,000, but I still suspicion the whole thing, as my mama's dairyman's wife says.

Have you seen the book? They haven't sent me any copy but they sent one to the lady here who is going to sell it and she kindly showed it to me. The book itself is very pretty but the jacket is lousy with me blown up on the back of it, looking like a refugee from deep thought. It has Caroline's imprimatur on it so that ought to help. My current literary assignment (from Regina) is to write an introduction for Cousin Katie [Mrs. Semmes] "so she won't be shocked," to be *pasted* on the inside of her book. This piece has to be in the tone of the *Sacred Heart Messenger* and carry the burden of contemporary critical thought. I keep putting it off.

Regina is getting very literary. "Who is this Kafka?" she says. "People ask me." A German Jew, I says, I think. He wrote a book about a man that turns into a roach. "Well, I can't tell people *that*," she says. "Who is this Evalin Wow?"

I am having a terrible time getting out of parties . . . I have to be very stealthy, all eyes and ears. You will see me very early in June.

Did that book I sent you come? If not I'll write them as I ordered it from a place in Chicago.

I have eleven enfant geese.

[P.S.] They just sent me a copy. I will ast them to send you one.

*In response to a request for suggestions of writers or critics to whom advance copies of her book might be sent, and for a list of those to whom she wished to send personal copies, Flannery wrote her publisher.*

## To Robert Giroux

April 16, 1952

Thank you for sending me the copy of the book. I think it is a very pretty book and I like the details all except meeting myself in that thunderclap fashion on the back of the jacket. I found that very grim indeed.

I think a good word might be squeezed out of the following list: John Palmer of *Sewanee Review*, Philip Rahv, Kerker Quinn of *Accent*, Frederick Morgan of *Hudson Review*, Paul Engle, Andrew Lytle, Robie Macauley, John Wade of *Georgia Review*, R. P. Blackmur, Francis Fergusson, Robert Penn Warren.

I am sure that the above people ought to be sent books whether they like them or not.

As for the ones with the cards in them that I get the 40% off of, please one to each of the following: Mr. and Mrs. Allen Tate, Mr. and Mrs. Robert Fitzgerald, Mr. and Mrs. John Thompson, Miss Margaret Sutton, Mr. and Mrs. J. D. Way, Miss Lydia Bancroft.

I will be very much obliged. My nine copies have to go to a set of relatives who are waiting anxiously to condemn the book until they get a free copy.

*Giroux sent Flannery some of the comments that had come in on her novel, and she wrote to him.*

April 30, 1952

Thanks so much for the comments which I'll always be anxious to get, good or bad. Robie Macauley is a good friend of mine but I don't know Mr. [Jerre] Mangione. [Evelyn] Waugh was very nice to comment at all. Is that the sort of thing you can use? Caroline wrote me yesterday that she could not review the book. [Someone] told her she was ineligible because her comment had been used on the jacket. As for reviewing I don't know whether it is worse to be ignored or to fall into the hands of L., but this is no concern of mine . . .

I forgot to ask you to send a copy of *Wise Blood* to Cal and Elizabeth Lowell.

Many thanks as usual.

## To Robie Macauley

Harcourt, Brace will be very glad to hear from you as I think they try to get all the favorable comments they can and stick them in ads—not that I've seen nair ad for that book. You will be interested to know about Enoch's daddy. I had him inside that ape suit at first . . . and thought it was terribly funny but Caroline said No and she was right. It was a little too logical. Old man Emery has to keep away from Enoch because Enoch makes him break out. He broke out in the ape suit—hives. He is after Enoch and hopes someday to kill him. He keeps Baby Ruth candy bars full of arsenic in his pocket all the time so he can offer Enoch one if he meets him . . .

Thanks so much for your letter. I am very glad to hear you have a novel that will be out in November. I hope you won't have as much trouble about keeping people from having parties for you as I am having. Around here if you publish the number of whiskers on the local pigs, everybody has to give you a tea. If you don't send me a copy of your book, I will go to the extreme of buying one.

## To Robert Lowell

May 2 [1952]

I was powerful glad to hear from you and I am pleased that you liked the gorilla. I hope you'll like the whole thing. I asked Bob Giroux to send you one.

I've been in Georgia with the buzzards for the last year and a half on acct. of arthritis but I am going to Conn. in June to see the Fitzgeralds. They have about a million children, all with terrific names and all beautiful. I'm living with my mother in the country. She raises cows and I raise ducks and pheasants. The pheasant cock has horns and looks like some of those devilish people and dogs in Rousseau's paintings. I have been taking painting myself, painting mostly chickens and guineas and pheasants. My mother thinks they're great stuff. She prefers me painting to me writing. She hasn't learned to love Mrs. Watts. Harcourt sent my book to Evelyn Waugh and his comment was: "If this is really the unaided work of a young lady, it is a remarkable product." My mother was vastly insulted. She put the emphasis on *if* and *lady*. Does he suppose you're not a lady? she says. WHO is he?

I'm all with Elizabeth on the sightseeing and will take mine sitting down or not at all. I like food with mine instead of politics, though.

If you ever see Omar [Pound] give him my regards. I met a doctor recently who had been at St. Elizabeth's and knew Mr. and Mrs. [Ezra] Pound, and liked them very much. He said a lot of people came out to see Pound and one who came insistently had sprouted a beard and a French collar.

The best to you both.

## To Betty Boyd Love

[postmarked 5/23/52]

Cocktails were not served but I lived through it anyway and remember signing a book for you sometime during it. It was very funny to see relics like Miss N. toting home a copy and to imagine it going on inside particular minds, etc. I got a good review from *Newsweek*—May 19—and from the NY *Tribune* and NY *Times* but I ain't seen any cash yet.

Who should appear for it—and to spend the night with my aunt Mary [Cline]—but Miss B. She said she felt she should be in New York and I said I felt that way too with the voice she had developed —American Stage or something. She is still violently interested in finding herself a husband and still asks personal questions without any preparation and at the most inconvenient times. I do wish somebody would marry the child and shut her up. I am touched by her but you know what a long way a little goes.

I also saw Lucynell Cunningham Smith who is my idea of a very nice person indeed.

I guess with an enfant stalking your problems you have your hands full. Do you all ever aim to visit Georgia?

## To Robert Giroux

May 24, 1952

I have had a request for a complimentary copy of *Wise Blood* from Captain W. of the Salvation Army . . . for their reading room and would be much obliged if you would send them a copy that I get the 40% off of. I'm always pleased to oblige the Salvation Army. According to some of the reviews you have sent me, I ought to be in it.

Thank you for sending me the clippings, and [Mary McCarthy's] *The Groves of Academe.*

I am steeling myself for even more dreadful reviews.

*That summer Flannery was well enough to come to Ridgefield to visit us. R.F. was teaching at the Indiana School of Letters, but our household was sufficiently crowded even so, containing besides Flannery and myself, four small children (all under four years old), Mary Loretta, a twelve-year-old black child I had invited for a vacation through the Fresh Air Fund, and Maria Ivancic, a Yugoslav displaced person we had brought over to help me with the children. Maria was instantly allergic to our guest (she had never seen a black before) and began to behave very badly, afflicting us all with scowls, mutterings, and tantrums of varying intensity, in Slovenian. After a few days of this, I was threatened with a miscarriage; and Flannery came down with a virus, which of course alarmed us all. Happily, her visit was almost over and was not much shortened by her immediate return to Georgia.*

*Flannery left her things in Ridgefield during all this time, in the expectation of coming back to us one day. When, in the summer of 1952, she learned the true nature of her illness, she took stock characteristically and began to plan her life in the light of reality. Only then did she send for her suitcases and books, order a pair of peafowl, and begin getting home in earnest.*

## To Robert Giroux

Milledgeville
July 19, 1952

I would be much obliged if you would send me six copies of *Wise Blood* and charge them to my account. I'd also be obliged if you would send a review copy to [a Ridgefield neighbor]. He is a friend of the Harcourts(?) and asked that it be sent. I wouldn't know what for.

Caroline suggested that one be sent to Herbert Read in England, who has just bought her book for publication there.

I had a nice stay in Connecticut but had to come home in a hurry on account of fever, leaving the Fitzgeralds (Sally) sick also. Robert was still in Indiana.

## To Sally Fitzgerald

I hope your situation has improved and that [a friend] didn't show up with his girl friends for lunch Tues. I thought I should have called him but I didn't think about it until I was on the plane.

I got Loretta on the train and sat her down by a stern-looking man and I sat across from her. As soon as the busboy came through I bought her some candy and she licked and sucked all the way in and didn't bother me at all. Her mother was at the gate to meet us. She was a very nice-looking pleasant woman and said that she had been very worried that Loretta might have mis-behaved. I assured her this wasn't the case. A noble lie, I thought. Then me and the momma turned her over to a welfare woman and I gave her the note. Loretta reminded me about the dollar every five minutes or so, so she got that.

My plane was 20 minutes early getting into Atlanta and Regina had arranged an appointment with Dr. Merrill. He said he thought I had got a virus infection up there and that usually about three days after you had one of those, it reacted on your own disease and set it off. I am to increase my dose and rest. He also had a letter there ready to be mailed to me, which I will send you and ask that you send it back, as I think it's a nice letter. He told Regina that he had told me and she said that was alright.

As soon as she saw me my mamma said, "Oh you've gotten fat," but when I weighed I weighed a half pound less than when I started to see you five weeks ago so I certainly must not have got any salt. You were mighty nice to cut it out of your food however. You know how much I enjoyed the vacation and how sorry I was to go. Let me hear how you do. Regards to Maria and Mr. L. and yer 4 children.

## To Robert Fitzgerald

I hated to leave Sally there with only Maria when she was sick, but as I seemed to be getting sick myself, I thought I had better. Also I was able to take M. Loretta back to New York with me and leave her in the lap of the welfare woman. I felt that when she was gone, Sally would be better. Loretta would perhaps have been controllable if there had been a Federal Marshal in the house, though I have my doubts. She had to stay in the room with Sally and she was full of wise sass and argument and there was no rest for Sally with her there.

I went over to E.H.'s* Sunday afternoon and told her that Sally was there and not supposed to get out of bed. She immediately came over. She drives and she speaks Italian and I think she likes to take charge. Also [her husband] was going away Monday so she wouldn't have much to do but mind Sally's business. She took all the telephone numbers and was very nice. Nicer by far than her daughter, who didn't even come up. Mr. L. said he would stay up there Monday and Tuesday nights. His son didn't want him staying any longer lest he overdo himself. In my opinion the old man likes it better at the Fitzgeralds . . .

I tried to call you Sunday night but the operator never could get you. S. was debating if she should call her mother but she couldn't make up her mind about it. I was afraid myself that her mother might not add to the quiet, and I thought quiet was what was needed most, but Mr. L. was prepared to call her if Sally decided she wanted her to come. I also suggested calling Eileen [Mrs. John] Berryman but S. was afraid that would upset Maria who had already been upset by Loretta . . . She was allergic to Loretta on first sight.

I saw my doctor as soon as I got to Atlanta. He said I had had a virus infection and it had reacted on my complaint (I now know that it is lupus and am very glad to so know) and he increased my dose but doesn't think I will have any trouble. It was a great boon to me to be able to spend a month in Connecticut and the Lord knows I appreciate your hospitality. I only wish I could have done more for Sally before I left. Please keep me informed on how she does. I think with food and rest she will be all right.

[P.S.] Mr. Isaac Rosenfeld unburdened himself on the subject of *Wise Blood* in the *New Republic*. He found it completely bogus, at length.

## To Sally and Robert Fitzgerald

Sunday [Summer 1952]

Greetings from my bed of affliction to yourn. I have been on it two weeks with the fevers & etceteras and am like to be two

* *Our next-door neighbor, a strong-minded Lucy Stoner of whom we were all somewhat in awe.*

more but I seem to be avoiding Emory at least which is a gret place to avoid.

You and Robt. would do me a great favor if you would read the enclosed document & return it to me with comment soon after. The man that wrote it teaches philosophy here—an exLutheran preacher who was an editor of *Theatre Arts* magazine for some years. He has sent this opus to the *Kenyon Review* and I am supposed to send him my reactions to it. Mine are as follows: that I am not clear on how he uses such terms as contemplation & meditation interchangeably, or whether he is making prayer & poetry the same thing or what. Then the last part about the impiety & lack of love in the book & all that. (It seems to me the form of love in it is penance, as good a form as any other under Mr. Motes circumstances.) But anyhow this guy is one of these learned gents & I don't aim to stick my neck out too far arguing with him. I am sure Robt. will know at a glance whether it's any good but do read it all and let me have it back. Great favor. This man is writing a book on Ethics now that will probably eventually get to that crafty crusty old reviewer, S. M. Fitzgerald.

I owe you $2.85 which I'll send when I get up & begin to prowl. Miss Washington's ticket was $1.15 & she got her sterling behavior buck added on . . .

I've never read Simone Weil but a good bit about her & and you sound right to me on the subject.

Regards to Maria & yr 4 children.

*I sent Flannery my own medical report, and suggested that J. F. Powers might like to review* Wise Blood.

## To Sally Fitzgerald

[undated; Summer 1952]

. . . I think that is a wonderful idea to ask Powers to review the book . . . Will you send me Caroline's address in Princeton so I can write her and thank her for the invitation. I am still having fever though I have doubled my dose, however the heat here is terrific. I have gotten a kind of Guggenheim. The ACTH has been reduced from 19.50 to 7.50 . . .

Regina says Dr. Merrill diagnosed it as lupus before he even saw me. Over the phone.

## To Sally and Robert Fitzgerald

Thursday [Summer 1952]

I was distressed to hear you had been so up & down. Please forget about the suitcases until it's convenient to send them. I am all for transfusions. We have found that you have to have two. The first pint don't do much but the 2nd sets you up. Maybe another one or two would help you.

You would relish the [present farm help]. My mama says she has never read *Tobacco Road* but she thinks it's moved in. I don't know how long they will be with us but I am enjoying it while it lasts, and I aim to give my gret reading audiance a shot of some of the details sometime. Every time Regina brings in some new information, our educ. is broadened considerably.

Please keep me posted on how you do.

[P.S.] Got your card and am much obliged. Also the enclosed from [the former teacher] which I think shows him in a better light. I didn't know Chaucer was at heart a pagan myself or what a recompense theology is. I am just hoping I don't have to *talk* any of this claptrap with him.

I hope S. is picking up.

Tuesday [Summer 1952]

I hope the vacation was a great success. It's hard to imagine Maria on the beach. Did you happen to see the Ways [Elizabeth Fenwick Way and her husband]?

I've had two blood transfusions and on the strength of that was able to get the enclosed off to [the former teacher] but with my tongue hanging on the keys most of the time. I have no notion that he will think anything but that I have misunderstood his piece. [He] is the one that one day in a class says, "The Medieval Church was politheistic." I rise and say, "The Medieval Church was not politheistic." [He] fixes me very coldly. "I am speaking," says he, "as an anthropologist." . . .

I would be much obliged if you would send on those two suitcases of stuff, dropping me a card on the day you do it so we can be on the lookout for it as they don't deliver out here. There are things in it that the new [farm help] crowd out here can use to begin school on. They don't have nothing and are shiftless into the bargain, and as my mother notes from their garbage—they threw it out on the highway—use Bailey's Supreme Coffee which costs 80¢ a pound while she uses the A&P brand at 49¢.

I'd also be obliged if you'd send me the copy of *Art and Scholasticism* of mine that I meant to bring and forgot. I want to read it before I have to encounter [the aforementioned teacher]. I'd enjoy that *Epitaph to a Small Winner*, I'm sure . . .

I finally enclose the check for the change in Loretta's ticket.

Thursday [Summer 1952]

The suitcases came and also the *Art and Scholasticism* and I am highly obliged but sorry you had to buy the book as there was one in my room. You keep that.

I hope you are better. I am much better myself—up and working on a story ["A Late Encounter with the Enemy"] which promises to be not so bad. Those transfusions were mighty good but I am also on an increased dose—nair drop of salt.

If Powers does review my book in the *Hudson Review* and you see it, would you send me a copy? It wouldn't be possible to get a copy around here as nobody ever heard tell of it.

Much politicking around here. The lady across the street went down and got herself an Eisenhower button the other day and that afternoon he said he would put a qualified Negro in the cabinet if he could find one. She returned the button before that evening sun went down. Maw is for Eisenhower but Stevenson is good enough for me though I hope he has quit applying the words of Christ to himself. That father-remove-this-cup etc. was too much for me . . .

## To Elizabeth McKee

July 16, 1952

I am now back in Georgia.

A man named Martin Greenberg from the *American Mercury* wrote and asked if I had any stories. I referred him to you. He wrote again and said he had called you and you were going to send him the stories. This is fine if you can get any money out of them . . . Please keep me informed on what happens to these two stories.

I had lunch with Caroline Tate one day while I was in New York and she suggested sending a copy of *Wise Blood* to Herbert Read in England, who had just bought her book for publication over there. Perhaps your representative in England has already sent it there. I would like to know about that.

I hope you are surviving the heat in New York. One day there was enough for me.

*Flannery's story, "A Late Encounter with the Enemy," was accepted at* Harper's Bazaar *by Alice Morris, the fiction editor.*

August 30, 1952

The changes improve the story and I'm much obliged to Miss Morris for making them. Do you know when they plan to use it? [It appeared one year later, in September 1953.]

*I sent back her Bible, along with other effects. She now bought her first pair of peafowl.*

## To Sally and Robert Fitzgerald

Tuesday [late Summer 1952]

Thanks for sending the Bible—just in time for *Bible Week!* All the local churches are going in big for Bible Week . . .

We are anxious to hear that you are better. I am better, up, and working and have just ordered myself a pair of peafowl and four peachicks from Florida—at a price far exceeding my means but I am learning from the [farm help].

Let me hear when you can.

## To Betty Boyd Love

[postmarked 9/20/52]<br>Bird Sanctuary

It was real good to get the picture and letter a while back. The stalking enfant looks as if she could handle an earthquake and so do you. I felt a split second's shake once but never anything like a minute. I imagine a minute of it would feel like an hour. I hope you are shet of them for a while.

I remember now I signed a book for Lucynell to send you. She is one of the nicest people I know. Her husband's brother married B.A. in the spring, what give the local ladies a chance to use their hats at about 60 functions, some of which she came over to and I saw her at, which was the only part of them I enjoyed except the ice cream.

I'm afraid my judgment on B. was overharsh. I only learned recently (from a cousin who worked in the office with her and had to see her employment record) that she was subject to epilepsy. This is a great affliction and I think anyone deserves a lot of credit who has it and don't go around telling everybody like Brother M.

( 43 )

I wonder if poor F. still thinks she's living with Walt Whitman? If it was he she thought he was.

Thanks for writing me about my book this spring. I wanted to answer the letter but I was on the way to Connecticut. I stayed up there five weeks, got sick, flew home, spent the next six in bed, and now am up again, slow. The book was not agin free-will certainly, which all the characters had plenty of and exercised I felt with deadly determination. The thought is all Catholic, perhaps overbearingly so. Do you like the novel *Dead Souls*? I like Tolstoy too but Gogol is necessary along with the light.

All the tra-la-la is about to begin at the instution of higher larning across the road, folderol and poopppoopado, M.G., the Humorist . . . The Psychologist . . . , the retired, the superannuated, the almost dead, the not-quite dead a year or more, the spirit of Progress, advancement, and progressive education in pursuit of happiness and holding the joint open as long as possible without funds. Hey nonny nonny and ha hah ha . . .

## To Elizabeth McKee

October 15, 1952

The enclosed is a corrected version of what you now have as "The World Is Almost Rotten" ["The Life You Save May Be Your Own"]. I like the new title better. If *Discovery* doesn't want it please get it back and send it to the *Sewanee Review* and then the rest of the quarterlies if you haven't already. I'd like to know where all it goes and what is said about it.

Isn't this about the time for me to get a royalty statement? Will I have to pay them any money back at this time, and when are they going to give me the rest of that money from the reprint sale? Do I have to wait two years on it? I am mighty anxious to see that royalty statement.

Could you ask for me when *Harper's Bazaar* plans to use the story they bought?

I am writing on something that may turn out to be a short novel or something of the kind.* I may be sending you some parts of it eventually.

Regards to Mavis.

* *This was probably "You Can't Be Any Poorer Than Dead," or what was later published under that title, and it became the first chapter of* The Violent Bear It Away.

## To Robie Macauley

I've read your book with great delight and I wish I had some reasons to tell you why I think it's so fine. However, I merely enjoys, I does not analyze. Doubtless as soon as it comes out officially all the jokers will turn up and tell the folks exactly what you haven't said and exactly how you haven't said it. I particularly liked Gorden and the parties—I've seen the winner and the jockey. It's a book that's alive all the way through and that is as close as I can come to saying anything intelligent about it.

Also I was very pleased to get a free copy. I'm developing a Scrooge-like character and collecting things (anything) against the coming Republican depression. I'm in a new business too. I've bought a hen and rooster peafowl from Eustis, Florida and four peachickens. You get $65 dollars for a pair of three-year-old peafowl, so you see where I'll be in a couple of years. The man I bought them from in Eustis assures me that the demand always exceeds the supply.

I had a letter from Paul Engle this summer about my book. He didn't like the title or think the end was clear but otherwise he thought it was fine etc. etc. and he would permit himself "only one note of harshness," to wit: from the jacket nobody would have known I had ever been at Iowas WHEREAS my book had really been "shaped" there and this was a "simple honorable fact that I should have thought of myself." I was sick at the time so I didn't answer it, but I got around to it recently and told him that in the information I had sent Harcourt I had of course put in that I had been to Iowa and studied under him but that I hadn't had anything to do with the jacket and didn't know how it would look until I saw it, but I told him I'd fix it up on the drugstore reprint that has been sold to the New American Library. I told him that would really be a jacket, with Mrs. Watts on the front cover, wearing the least common denominator, and I would certainly see that everything about Iowa etc. etc. was on that one. He's in New York now on a Ford Fellowship; he said he intended to get out a book of poetry and a book of prose during the year.

Where are the Lowells these days? There were some wonderful letters in the last issue of the *Commonweal* that Santayana had written Cyril Clemens, in which he mentioned his interest in Cal and told about some visits from him. When your book is out, you'll probably get a fancy scroll from Clemens saying you have been elected an Honorary Member of the Mark Twain Society (along with Winston Churchill, Lord Smuts, TSEliot, Dorothy Canfield Fisher & Several of The Living & The Dead) and that contributions are gratefully accepted. He is apparently in on this with an old bird [who is] a cousin of Caroline's, who is filthy rich and, she says, pure goat. Before I was talking to her about it, I sent them two dollars in memory of Mark Twain and "to Unite the Whole World in Bonds of Cultured Peace . . ."

[P.S.] I am going to write the lady that sent the book how much I liked it.

## To Sally Fitzgerald

The Sabbath [undated; 1952]

I have just read the review [of *Ushant*] by Conrad Aiken in the *Commonweal* and I think you have nailed the lid on his box. He makes me sick just to read about and I don't see how you got through his book. Also the S.M. is very impressive. I would suspect it stood for something like Smernkchs Maupasuntanti if I wasn't so up on the literary WORLD. I never have read Aiken or Henry Miller or that dope that wrote the *Jurgen* things, but from what I have read about them they all sound like steps on the same ladder —with old Aiken the high rung. There is a very funny piece on Henry Miller in the second *New World Writing*.

I thank you extremely for sending the coat and camera, and enclose the postage for same. Parent has taken passionate dislike of coat and waits for colder weather when I won't have to wear it. She is composing you a fruit cake but I don't know if it will be composed in time for Thanksgiving or not. I don't know when Thanksgiving is. Anyway it'll be along.

I had a note from John Crowe Ransom, saying there was such a thing as a *Kenyon Review* Fellowship in Fiction that they got from Rockerfeller money and would I like to apply, that Robt. Fitzgrld & Peter Taylor had mentioned me to him. I applied before the envelope was opened good but I reckon there are a lot of others as would like to come off with it too. Anyway, I thank Robt. for the mentioning. [Ransom] said he had read my book and had been impressed, so that is a help. I am wondering did he also see [the former teacher's] piece. [He] has been violently writing letters to the *Atlanta Constitution* about the election—he always calls Stalin Uncle Joe in the letters; they sound mad and sporty too, with just a dash of art and a dash of philosophy. I am going to try to force a loan of *Art and Scholasticism* on him when I see him.

I hear tell the Lowells are in Rome. I thought those were good pieces on Santayana in the *Commonweal*.


Tuesday [November 1952]

I would certly be obliged for some word on this ["The Life You Save May Be Your Own"]. I have been working on it two months & it's cold as a fish to me. I don't know the front from the back & I don't want to send it around if it's not good & I can, some way, make it better.

I got to have another transfusion but I am doing all right & work every day. The [farm family] have moved out but I learned a lot while they were here. I am sending you a copy of Robie Macauley's novel, as Random House sent me one & he sent me another. I think it's a good book. My mamma & I are on the way to the polls to cancel out each other's vote.

Many thanks for this great service you render me.


Thursday [undated; Fall 1952]

I am much obliged for both letters and think I have fixed up the story ["The Life You Save May Be Your Own"] much better now on acct. of same. I had to send some stuff to the *Kenyon Review* in applying for that fellowship so I sent that one and the first chapter of what proposes itself to be a novel [*The Violent Bear It Away*]—the one with the hero named Tarwater.

We hope the cake got there in time for Thanksgiving. There was also one enclosed for Maria to take to her room and eat with her secret beer. I never got to send her that screwdriver I was going to on acct. of being sick and whatnot.

We are real glad there will be a fifth small devil in June. I recomment turnip green potliquor with cornbread broke up in it, and hope you will continue to be well.

I agree with you about the Macauley book. I thought it was very funny but as the guy in the *Commonweal* said "no theological dimension," a fact of which Bro. Macauley is unfortunately proud I am afraid . . .

My parent is out chasing two visiting mules off the premises. She runs the car after them for about thirty feet. Then they stop, turn around and stand there looking at the car. Then she gets out and says SHOO and throws up her arms. Then they run about twenty feet. Then she gets in the car and looks as if she is going to run smack over them. They stand and look at the car, she gets out again and says SHOO and throws up her hands. It goes on that way all down to the entrance of the place. She will chase them out and then I suspect they will follow the car back, and be where they were when she arrives . . .

Mrs. P. [the farm wife] was telling about how her new preacher sings his sermons. He puts a chair out on the platform and then calls up various Biblical characters to testify. "Paul," he says, "will you come up and testify?" They imagine the Apostle Paul getting up and taking a seat in the chair I suppose. Then the preacher sings "Rock of Ages." Then he says, "Peter, will you come up and testify?" and sings something for Peter to testify. [She] thinks it's wonderful. "Evy eye is on him," she says. "Not a breath stirs."


## To Elizabeth McKee

November 26, 1952

I enclose another story ["The River"] which I suggest you send to the *Hudson Review* unless you think strongly otherwise. What has happened to Mr. Shiftlet [of "The Life You Save"] and where is my royalty statement that they were supposed to send in October? They are mighty slow folks . . .

I have started on a novel and may send you a chapter after I think about it for a while.

Do you know when *Harper's Bazaar* intends to use that story ["A Late Encounter with the Enemy"]?


December 20, 1952

I hate to bother you so near Christmas but my business this time is urgent. I applied last month for a Kenyon Fellowship ($2,000 furnished them by the Rockerfeller Foundation) and in applying sent, along with a chapter of the novel I am working on, a copy of "The Life You Save" and one of "The River," mentioning that these were unpublished stories. Mr. Ransom writes me that he will take either of them for the *Kenyon* if one is available. I would like him to have "The Life You Save," so I hope you have not sent it on to the *Sewanee*. If it is still at *New World Writing*, can you get it away from them *now*? They have had it long enough certainly.

If I am not able to send him "The Life You Save," I'll have to send him "The River." I would much prefer to see the former in the *Kenyon Review* since you think you might be able to get some money for the other.

He has copies of both stories so when you find out about it, write me and I'll write him. I don't want to mention money to him so I won't ask that the check be sent to your office but if one comes to me (they used to pay) I'll send you the ten percent.

Incidentally, I received the Fellowship. They are giving three, one to a poet, one to a novelist, and one to a critic. The $2,000 will come in mighty handy. They haven't announced their choices yet so please don't mention me in connection with it.

A merry Christmas to you all and I'll hope to hear from you shortly.

[P.S.] Please thank Mavis for the royalty statement. I'm glad it was no worse.


## To Sally and Robert Fitzgerald

12/20/52

Merry Christmas to you all from Grimrack. I got the Kenyon Fellowship, thanks being no doubt to your saying to him this summer that I was an existing writer. My mamma is getting a big bang out of notifying all the kin who didn't like the book that the Rockerfeller Foundation, etc. etc.—this very casual like on the back of Christmas cards. Money talks, she says, and the name of Rockerfeller don't hurt a bit. It don't, except that all they'll think is that the Foundation is going to pot. I reckon most of this money will go to blood and ACTH and books, with a few sideline researches into the ways of the vulgar. I would like to go to California for about two minutes to further these researches, though at times I feel that a feeling for the vulgar is my natural talent and don't need any particular encouragement. Did you see the picture of Roy Rogers's horse attending a church service in Pasadena? I forgot whether his name was Tex or Trigger but he was dressed fit to kill and looked like he was having a good time. He doubled the usual attendance.

I think [my friend] is going to think he was solely responsible for my getting the Fellowship. They finally came out and the first thing he said was he was reading *Ushant.* So I pull out SM Fitzgerald's review and set him to reading it and he said it was right. He didn't seem to think much of Aiken though he liked some of the puns and named a few which made me cringe. I told him SM was the wife of Robt and he says oh the translator and knows all about that because he uses the first two; he hadn't seen the *Edipus* but I think now he will order it for the library . . .

Mrs. P. [farm wife] met Mrs. O. [former farm wife] wandering around downtown yesterday. They didn't take to each other atall but Mrs. P. never loses an opportunity to get any information about anything whatsoever so she stopped her and asked if Mr. O. was working *yet*. Well, says [his wife] (whine), dairy work is so reglar, we decided he better just had get him a job where he could work when he wanted to. Mrs. P. has not got over this yet. She never will. She manages to repeat it every day in [Mrs. O.'s] tone of voice. . . .

Would you mind sending me the address of the place where I write to subscribe to *The Month*? I am going to let old Rockerfeller furnish me with that journal for a while. Incidentally I see where Miss Gertrude Himmelfarb has come forth with her treatise on Acton. I am going to read Acton and leaver lay.

[P.S.] Mr. Ransom said he would take either "The River" or "The Life You Save May Be Your Own" for the *Kenyon Review* (the one with Mr. Shiftlet—your title) . . .


Monday [December 30, 1952]

I had a card from the *Kenyon Review* saying you were giving me that learned journal for the year. This is certainly a treat and also I am very glad I didn't have to write them myself and say to send me a subscription like now that I was using their dough I would give them this bone. Now I will get to see Mr. Shiftlet in there. I see Mr. Shiftlet and somebody like Ivor Winters, blank wall to blank, between two unintelligible poems.

A letter from Caroline and another from some people in Iowa City said the Lowells were going to take Paul Engle's place out there again in February . . .

My mamma got her hand caught in the electric mixer but both survived and I have had the shingles, a disease, the doctor says, that "confers no distinction." Mrs. P.'s boy has had a bad foot brought on by the *sugar diabetes* he had when he was ten, and her niece Starene, age 6, says the boys nearly drive her crazy. She has told her teacher this but has got no relief yet.

I thought you would enjoy the name of the horse in the enclosed piece. ["MacArthur." The clipping concerned a "saddle pastor" about to go on an evangelizing tour of Florida on horseback.]

# PART II

---

# DAY IN AND

# DAY OUT

# 1953 – 1958

*The letters in this section were written during the years after Flannery had come to terms with the way of life circumstances now dictated. Her acceptance was more graceful than merely stoic. She has written that "vocation implies limitation," and it can only be supposed that she regarded the circumscription of her life as a necessary aspect of her vocation as a writer and as an individual. She knew that her literary gift made special demands on her, and I think that she saw the restrictions on her life in the same light.*

*From Teilhard de Chardin she eventually learned a phrase for something she already knew about: "passive diminishment"—the serene acceptance of whatever affliction or loss cannot be changed by any means—and she must have reasoned that the eventual effect of such diminishment, accompanied by a perfecting of the will, is to bring increase, which is not to say that acceptance made matters easy. So now she set about making the most she could of both her gift and her circumstances, from day to day.*

*There were consolations. She loved Andalusia; she was interested in the farm, and in her mother's Laocoön struggles with it. And she was by no means a complete misfit in Milledgeville. As Betty Boyd Love, her close friend at college, has written: "I don't believe for a minute that the conventionality of her private life represented any repression of instinct on her part. It was a life in which she felt comfortable, and I see no inconsistency between her private life and her private vision." Inevitably, she practiced her vocation in solitude. She scorned the notion of the loneliness of the artist, but she knew that what she was making she had to make alone. Once something had been made, however, she usually invited several people into the process, asking for and respecting criticism and suggestions.*

*Flannery was a likable young woman, and she had many friends. These were important to her, and letters far too numerous to include here show her willing involvement in the lives of her friends, and the welcome she gave them into her own. She wrote to her closest correspondent that she needed people. Her letters suggest that many of those with whom she came in contact came to realize that they needed her as well.*

## To Sally and Robert Fitzgerald

Milledgeville
1/25/53

My first issue of *Kenyon Review* came yestiddy and I felt very learned sitting down reading it. There was a chapter of a novel by Randall Jarrell [*Pictures from an Institution*] in it. I suppose you would say it was good Randall Jarrell but it wasn't good fiction. It was of the School of Mary [McCarthy]. The *Kenyon Review* sent me a thoouusand bucks the other day, no note, no nothing; just the dough. My kinfolks think I am a commercial writer now and really they are proud of me. My uncle Louis [Cline] is always bringing me a message from somebody at [his company] who has read *Wise Blood*. The last was: ask her why she don't write about some nice people. Louis says, I told them you wrote what *paid*. There was another message from "the brains of [his] company." He said, yeah it was a good book well written and all that but tell her the next time to write about some rich folks, I'm mighty tired of reading about poor folks . . .

My mamma has been dickering (negotiating) with [a new farm family] to take the [former farm help's] place. Old man P. looked like he might have had an ancestor back a couple of centuries ago who was at least a decayed gentleman (he wouldn't wear overalls; only khaki) but these . . . look like they've been joined up with the human race for only a couple of months now. Mrs. W. says she went to school for one day and didn't loin nothin and ain't went back. She has four children and I thought she was one of them. The oldest girl is 14 with a mouth full of snuff. The first time I saw her she had long yellow hair and the next time it was short in an all-over good-for-life permanent and Regina says— they were standing outside the car and we were in—"I see you have a new permanent." "Got it Sad-day," she says and then another pair of hands and eyes pulls up on the window of the car and says, "I'm gonter git me mine next Sad-day." Mamma has one too. I was all set for [them] but he traded with the sawmill man instead of Regina. I hope he gets tired of it and quits though.

The Notre Dame business sounds very good to me. I had some friends who were there and were crazy about it. I visited them but I didn't get to see the university. If sometime next summer proves convenient for you to have me visit you, I would like to come if I am well; but I imagine you will have a crowded schedule, as your prospective children don't always travel by the doctor's clock. If my presence would be convenient at any particular time, I would be pleased to try to manage to have it on hand. My mamma is none too favorable toward any kind of travel for me, or at least nothing longer than two weeks she says, because you know who has to do the nursing when you get sick; and I do. However, I think I will go to New York anyways sometime next summer if it ain't but to spend the week. I am doing fairly well these days, though I am practically bald-headed on top and have a watermelon face. I think that this is going to be permanent. There is another lady in town now with lupus. She went to the hospital a couple of weeks ago and couldn't open her hands but now she is full of ACTH and up cooking her dinner. Now that I know I have the stuff I can take care of myself a lot better. I stay strictly out of the sun and strictly do not take any exercise. No great hardship.

2/1/53

The Maple Oats really send me. I mean they are a heap of improvement over saltless oatmeal, horse biscuit, stewed Kleenex, and the other delicacies that I have been eating. They send Regina too but I think it is because they smell like what the cows here eat. We are going to get Louis to see if he can get them in Atlanta for us. I also like the O'Faoláin book but I like all he writes that I have seen.

The enclosed is a poem. I tell you this. The Poetry Society of Georgia (a social outfit) is offering 50 bucks for one and I thought I would bite but I would like to know first if it works, as they say. Beinst as your occupation is properly poetry, please let me know. This is my first and last. I think it is a filthy habit for a fiction writer to get into. The novel seems to be doing very well. I have a nice gangster of 14 in it named Rufus Florida Johnson. Much more in my line.

My mamma and I have interesting literary discussions like the following which took place over some Modern Library books that I had just ordered:

SHE: *"Mobby Dick. I've always heard about that."*
ME: *"Mow-by Dick."*
SHE: *"Mow-by Dick. The Idiot.* You would get something called *Idiot.* What's it about?"
ME: "An idiot."

I am sending you a subscription to something called the *Shenandoah* that is put out at Washington and Lee University. I told them to begin it with the autumn issue that has a review in it of my book by a man named Brainard Cheney. It also has a review of *The Old Man and the Sea* by Wm. Faulkner, the review I mean, that is nice. He says that Hemingway discovered God the Creator in this one. What part I like in that was where the fish's eye was like a saint in a procession; it sounded to me like he was discovering something new maybe for him.


### The Peacock Roosts

The clown-faced peacock
Dragging sixty suns
Barely looks west where
The single one
Goes down in fire.

Bluer than moon-side sky
The trigger head
Circles and backs.
The folded forest squats and flies
The ancient design is raised.

Gripped oak cannot be moved.
This bird looks down
And settles, ready.
Now the leaves can start the wind
That combs these suns

Hung all night in the gold-green silk wood
Or blown straight back until
The single one
Mounting the grey light
Will see the flying forest
Leave the tree and run.

## To Elizabeth and Robert Lowell

17 March 1953

I'm glad you liked the story. That is my contribution to Mother's Day throughout the land. I felt I ought to do something like Senator Pappy O'Daniels. He conducted the Light Crust Dough Boys over the radio every Mother's Day and recited an original poem. One went: "I had a mother. I had to have. I lover whether she's good or bad. I lover whether she's live or dead. Whether she's an angel or a old dope head." You poets express yourselves so well in so little space.

I suppose Iowa City is very restful after Europe, it being naturally blank. I always liked it in spite of those sooty tubercular-looking houses. When I was there there was a zoo with two indifferent bears in it and a sign over them that said: "These lions donated by the Iowa City Elks Club." But they had a good collection of game bantams that I used to go and admire, and I admired that electric railroad car that ran to Cedar Rapids.

I am making out fine in spite of any conflicting stories. I have a disease called lupus and I take a medicine called ACTH and I manage well enough to live with both. Lupus is one of those things in the rheumatic department; it comes and goes, when it comes I retire and when it goes, I venture forth. My father had it some twelve or fifteen years ago but at that time there was nothing for it but the undertaker; now it can be controlled with the ACTH. I have enough energy to write with and as that is all I have any business doing anyhow, I can with one eye squinted take it all as a blessing. What you have to measure out, you come to observe closer, or so I tell myself.

Last summer I went to Connecticut to visit the Fitzgeralds and smuggled three live ducks over Eastern Airlines for their children, but I have been inactive criminally since then. My mother and I live on a large place and I have bought me some peafowl and sit on the back steps a good deal studying them. I am going to be the World Authority on Peafowl, and I hope to be offered a chair some day at the Chicken College.

## To Sally and Robert Fitzgerald

5/7/53

I am much obliged for the word on the story and for the poem [by R.F.]. I liked the poem. I have to smell them out beinst I have no critical equipment to go by but there are some that hit you at once and that is one of them. I hope HB is going to do the *Sophia* book [a project Robert was considering at the time] . . .

I never heard of *Conversations at Newburgh* (sp?), but there was a man by here the other day who was a textbook salesman from Harcourt, Brace who told me that was one of D[orothy] Day's farms. This man was from Denmark, not a Catholic but had some Russian aunt who was a Catholic and somebody or other with a magazine called *Nightwatch* or *Watchguard* or somesuch. Anyway he had studied philosophy at Fordham and taught German there and knew Fr. Lynch and was much interested in Dorothy Day, only he couldn't see he said why she fed endless lines of endless bums for whom there was no hope, she'd never see any results from that, said he. The only conclusion we came to about this was that Charity was not understandable. Strange people turn up. The Cheneys said that when they went to St. Simons they would stop by to see me so I am hoping they will.

I hope you have selected a resounding name for #5 and will let us know when same gets here. I have thought of several but won't discompose you with them.

Somebody was telling me that Malcolm Cowley had delivered himself of an essay in the last *Harper's Magazine* on the state of the novel. He didn't find them now as good as in the '30s when folks were protesting. I didn't rush out to buy one.

I hope if I am eating salt in August I can get to see you before you start off in the airplane. I don't make no plans.

6/7/53

I am wondering if you are sitting in the city waiting on #5 and write to enquire. We hope all goes well and recomment you daily to the Lord.

The Cheneys stopped by yesterday on their way to South Ga. and we liked them very much. They wanted to know what *Conversations at Newburgh* were but I couldn't enlighten them. Is it some more philosophers and bums and priests conversing at a retreat at one of those farms or what? They had a Japanese Fulbright student with them whose gold teeth fascinated Regina. Mrs. C. is a liberry science teacher at Peabody but she is very nice inspite of that. In fact you would never know it. Also appeared, at the same time but not connected, a Ph.D. student from Princeton who had heard your lectures there and liked them. His real admiration seemed to be Francis Fergusson. He apparently taught at Princeton (assistant, I guess) but had spent the last year at Oxford on a Fulbright. Named Lane. He thought yr. friend

[R. P.] Blackmur "threw up a dust of words," and that the [Allen] Tates were faddists—first the old South & now HMC [Holy Mother Church]. I demurred, on the part about the Tates.

I sold "A Good Man Is Hard to Find" to the *Partisan Review Reader,* another of those 50¢ jobs.

I am reading M. Gabriel Marcel that the jacket says is a Christian Existentialist. I certainly like it but oncet the book is shut I have no idea what it's all about. Since I can't take the continental tour on Mr. Rockefeller, I am buying books.

[P.S.] I liked old S. M. Fitzgerald—the freelance critic's— review in the *Commonweal.*

## To Robert Giroux

June 14, 1953

I was surprised that the pocket edition [of *Wise Blood*] should be out so soon and that the cover was no worse than it was. I had expected Mrs. Watts to be on it and was hoping the new Georgia Literature Commission would take it off the drugstore racks. We have a fine new literature commission in this state, composed of a preacher, a picture-show manager, and some other worthy who I keep thinking must or should be the warden at the state penitentiary.

The review you enclosed was of considerable interest to me and I appreciate your sending it. I have 50 or 60 pages on the [new] novel but I still expect to be a long time at it. It's a theme that requires prayer and fasting to make it get anywhere. I manage to pray but am a very sloppy faster.

## To Sally and Robert Fitzgerald

[undated; Summer 1953]

I did like the Shakespeare poem and thank you for sending it. My mamma asked me the other day if I knew Shakespeare was an Irishman. I said no I didn't. She said well it's right there in the Savannah paper; and sure enough some gent from the University of Chicago had made a speech somewhere saying Shakespeare was an Irishman. I said well it's just him that says it, you better not go around saying it and she said listen SHE didn't care whether he was an Irishman or a Chinaman. She is getting ready to build herself a pond for the cows to lie down in and cool off in the summertime. The government says it has to go down two feet straight to keep from breeding mosquitoes but she don't want it that way for fear the cows will break their legs getting in.

The Tates sent me the piece in the *New Republic* about orthodoxy & the standard of literature. I wrote Caroline that I liked the piece but that my line about the Cardinal was: if we must have trash this [*The Foundling*] is the kind of trash we ought to have. Of course this was the wrong thing to say to them, and I got a letter back saying Allen said we shouldn't have trash in the first place and the Cardinal was the last person who ought to write it in the second. Caroline also said you had written Allen a letter of reprimand about the piece. Well I thought the piece was all right but that it shouldn't have been in the *New Republic* of all places. I also shudder to think what would happen if Francis Cardinal acquainted himself with the masters of the novel in the 19th century. Caroline said Allen wasn't allowed to contribute to *Thought.* That piece would have been all right expanded in a Catholic publication. She said it was originally a talk to a Newman Club around there somewhere.

Today I had a letter from Cal who said he was thirty-six years old and feeling very elderstatesmanish and peaceful to be in Iowa City again. He had just been to Kenyon to visit Peter Taylor . . .

I sold the story about the child that got baptized ["The River"] to the *Sewanee Review*.

I am taking painting again but none of my paintings go over very big in this house although mamma puts them up and is loth to take them down again. Sister [Miss Mary Cline] used to teach painting classes in her youth and she says she doesn't like this modern art because it's not "smoothed down." My mamma says it's *not* modern art (insulted), it's very true to nature and there's no use spending five hours on a painting you can do in two. This refers to the fact that I have been painting with a palette knife because I don't like to wash the brushes.


Friday [undated; 1953]

I enclose you two items, one out of the peacock and the other out of me ["A Good Man Is Hard to Find"]. I would be much obliged to know what you think of the story before I send it to market. Thow it away when you get through with it.

I had a letter from Brainard Cheney and he said that both he and his wife had come into the Church the Saturday before.

When do you aim to set off for Siena? We had a visitor the

other day, an old man, who said he wouldn't go to Europe if they gave it to him. Said a feller went over there and set down on some steps he seen in front of a church. Another feller come along and held out his hand. First one said, What for now? Feller holding out his hand said, Step rent.

I painted me a self-portrait with a pheasant cock that is really a cutter but Regina keeps saying, I think you would look so much better if you had on a tie. The Easter rabbit brought her a man with a bulldozer so she has just finished her pond. She says she's not going to have but four feet of water in it because if anybody drowns she wants to be able to go in and get them out without draining it. Practical.

I liked Powers' story ["The Devil Was the Joker"] very much and am obliged as I don't take the *New Yorker*. Wasn't that funny what Edith Sitwell said about her visit to Hollywood?

## To Sally Fitzgerald

Friday [undated; Summer 1953]

Greetings to you and Barnaby but I am sure this child is not to be called Barnaby Only. If you all have run out of resounding names I offer the following: Barnaby Borromeo Counter-Reformation Fitzgerald. St. Charles Borromeo belonged to the 16th cen. too and really did some cleaning up. Acton couldn't stand him. I should think you could work him in somewhere. I was privately hoping it would be a girl and you would name her Essence and call her Essie but you can be thinking about that for the future.

I am sending you a copy of the 25¢ edition of *Wise Blood* that you may consider the cover. I think it's very funny.

We went to Atlanta yesterday to visit the scientist and he says I am doing better than anybody else that has what I got and he's very pleased with his work. Therefore, sometime this summer I would like to come to see you. My mamma says a week is all I can stay, that my trouble is overdoing everything etc. etc. So would you let me know what time would be most agreeable to you if it is still convenient at all, and if it isn't don't hesitate to say so.

Mrs. P. is having [her church] ladies to her house tomorrow and she has to give the lesson. The lesson is how in this town in Florida there was a rowdy crowd on the street every night. Loud talking. So the young people decides they would get behind it. So they come out. The old people encourage them. The first night they come out everybody is surprised how things change. Some, after these young people have talk on the street corner, only stand there and do not say a word. It just goes to show you what the young people can do when the old people encourage them. She says she ain't studied it very good yet but she is going to work it up by the time the ladies meet. They have a book with all these lessons in it and I suppose have a lesson each meeting.

Doubleday must have decided there's money in Homer [*The Odyssey* was to be translated by Robert Fitzgerald]. My word.

## To Sally and Robert Fitzgerald

[undated; August 1953]

The only plane I could get comes in at the Newark Airport and it strikes me that this may be inconvenient for you to get to. If so, I can maneuver as I said but the hour anyhow is 4:20 p.m. EDT, Flight 514, Tues. August 11. and if I don't see you and the fraction, I will take myself a bus to the railroad station.

Last weekend I flew to Nashville to see the Cheneys and Ashley Brown (a friend of theirs & correspondent of mine) and had a most agreeable time. I asked the steward on the airplane what he did with the dirty dishes. When we get to Chicago, he says, we push them down a slot. I would like to work out some such arrangement.

Maw is expecting a [farm] family Monday. They are hired sight unseen. She and Mrs. P. are busy plumbing. Mr. P. can't plumb—it makes him nervous. He is taking a correspondence course in Catholicism. He is not going to be a Catholic or anything —he just likes to get things free in the mail.

*Her visit that year was pleasant and uneventful, and she stayed almost three weeks, stopping off for a conference with Robert Giroux in New York on September 2, on her way back to Milledgeville. She was not strong, but her condition seemed stabilized, and she was not yet having the bone trouble that impended.*

*A letter or two to us is missing from this time, but in late September she wrote to me:*

Tues. [undated; September]

I am sending you one of these blouses, only they don't make them anymore with the round collars the lady says. This ain't exactly what you want but anyways I want to give it to you as I wanted to send you something for the house after my visit but beinst you won't be in the house, I will send thisyer instead. Which reminds me that if I can send you anything to Italy particularly in the hardware line to let me know. I had a letter from Caroline from Paris & from Ashley [Brown] in Dublin & feel like the world is moving off and leaving me in the United States alone. When do you take off etc. etc.?

[P.S.] Did you read about Fr. Divine's meeting with the Prophet Jones?

## To Robie Macauley

13 October 53

I have just recently been reading your story in the *Partisan* 35¢ thing and feel called upon to tell you how much I like it and what your stories remind me of. Of course I offer all my critical opinions on long sticks that can be jerked back at once because I really seldom know what I'm talking about but I'm willing to defend this one like a fox terrier. Conrad. They remind me of Conrad's (I mean like in the *Secret Agent* or *Under Western Eyes,* etc.) and I have read just about everything he wrote by now. I don't have one perception about the novels, but I keep reading them hoping they'll affect my writing without my being bothered knowing how. Anyway I have thought this about several of your stories that I have seen and I asked that woman that sent me your book why they didn't publish your stories and she said she wouldn't be surprised or some such politeness. I never pay any attention to what they say.

I have recently been to Connecticut to visit the Fitzgeralds and stopped on the way back to have an accounting with Harcourt, Brace and a lovely time I had. You see, he says, 208 [copies] returned before the first statement but only 200 before the second, now that is a difference of *eight,* you see that is much better, etc. etc.

Some time during the summer a young man named Lane appeared who had been to a party where you and Anne were. He seemed to have a very vague idea about that, but he was investigating one of our local killings and visiting everybody in town who could speak understandable English . . . I have never seen him since and wouldn't know about him but my opinion is that the Southern Young Man of Parts is busy building himself up to be

Quentin. I think they all want to go to Harvard or Princeton so they can sit in a window and say I hate it I hate it but I have to go back. Or maybe they only learn to say it after they get up there.

Also this summer I went to Nashville to see the Cheneys who had stopped by previously to see me on their way to St. Simons. They had Ashley at the same time. I heard a lot of Tennessee politics and more literary talk, most of it over my head, than since I left Iowa. Ashley managed to board his dog, Tiejens, with a family named Ford when he went to Europe. The last I heard from him he had stumbled over Swift's birthplace in Dublin.

*We left for Italy in mid-October, and wrote Flannery a description of our new ménage, which sounds a good deal spiffier than it turned out to be: we were freezing to death among our new lackeys.*

## To Sally and Robert Fitzgerald

11/11/53

If you have a cook, a gardener, and a nurse I suppose we will never see you again. My mother was not impressed by the 16½ hours [flight time]. In fact there was no comment at all from her. She wants to send you a fruit cake; however it actually takes her about two months to bring one into being. It's like building a nest. First she thinks about it, then she begins to gather the material, then she begins to put it together. Right now she has hinted that I may pick out the nuts. I ain't sure my health permits this. Anyway, sometime or other it will arrive.

Caroline sent me your address on the back of a letter of hers a few days ago but didn't say if she had seen you. I have been sending poor Caroline stories by the dozen it seems to me. I have written three in a row, all in the interest of excusing myself from writing on the novel. But now I have seven good stories and two lousy ones for my collection.

I had a letter from the Cheneys and they were very pleased to have seen you, and thought everything very attractive, particularly the children.

Mamma has a new silage cutter and Mrs. W. has a new set of teeth. Otherwise nothing that I know of has happened in the United States since you left.

I hope you are keeping the whip hand on all your help and learning to act like a tyrant. Regina says she has broken Shot [a farm hand at Andalusia] of the habit of borrowing money from Louis [Cline]. However, Shot is doing well by his insurance these days. He is always cutting his hand and having to go to the doctor. Regina has a policy which takes care of all his accidents, but he has one too and never fails to collect on it at the same time. He made four dollars on his last cut. She says [they] are smart as tacks when it comes to looking out for No. 1.

## To Elizabeth and Robert Lowell

1 January 53 [1954]

I am real glad to hear you have a hale automobile. My mother says every nigger she knows has a better-looking car than she does. I can't drive myself. I am waiting until it's all automatic, and you sit there and it goes.

I didn't mean I was fat when I said I was disgustingly healthy. I'm not fat yet but I don't have any room to grow. I just meant I don't look very intelligent. I was in Nashville a couple of weeks ago visiting the Cheneys and met a man who looked at me a while and said, "That was a profound book. You don't look like you wrote it." I mustered up my squintiest expression and snarled, "Well I did," but at the same time I had to recognize he was right.

The Fitzgeralds are in Fiesole, put all those children in an airplane and went . . . I went to see them this summer . . . I suggested [a name for the new one] but they weren't up to it.

I'm writing a novel but it's so bad at present that I'm writing a lot of stories so as not to have to look at it. I did have one in *Harper's Bazaar* about a Confederate General who was a hundred and four years old, but nobody sees things in those magazines except the ladies that go to the beauty parlors. I'm getting up a collection of stories that I'm going to call *A Good Man Is Hard to Find*. I send them all to Caroline and she writes me wherein they do not meet the mark . . .

## To Sally and Robert Fitzgerald

Jan. 4 [1954]

We are distressed that that cake hasn't arrived as we sent it before Thanksgiving, complete with all the govermint stickers and stamps and other paraphernalia. Doubtless some official along the way ate it. I was going to ask you how you fared for peanut butter and if you needed it was going to send you some, but I won't if things don't get there any better than that. I hate to think of your suffering for want of peanut butter though and I doubt if they have advanced to the state of culture where they have it over there. If you ever do get the cake it should be good and stale.

I got word the other day that I had been reappointed a Kenyon Fellow so that means the Rockerfellers will see to my blood and ACTH for another year and I will have to keep on praying for the repose of John D.'s soul, Also I sold a story to *Kenyon* and another to *Harper's Bazaar*. I don't know if I ought to buy AT&T or go in for colored rental property. I am wondering if I own colored houses with outdoor privies that drain into the water supply if my burden of social guilt will be so great it offsets the little income? Maybe I'll write a book called *Prudence and Low Finance . . .*

Today I got a letter from *Jimmie Crum* of Los Angeles, California who has just read *Wise Blood* and wants to know what happened to the guy in the ape suit. He would also like an autographed picture of me for his office. He has a rare stamp and coin shop and is a notary public and has had an article accepted in a technical magazine; I feel that since I have now reached the lunatic fringe there is no place left for me to go. I am also corresponding with the Secretary of the Chefs' National Magazine, *The Culinary Review*. This lady has written me five letters and sent me a sonnet since September. I had a note from Cal who says next year they are going to live in the house in Duxbury and that Elizabeth has at last learned to cook.

I would certainly like to think of coming come spring but I doubt if it will get out of the stage of thought. Where would I be coming should I come and what airline should I write for information? I wouldn't even know how to get a passport.

I am glad to hear the *Odyssey* is ahead of schedule and that we'll see you again . . .


*Elizabeth Fenwick [Way] was at Yaddo when Flannery first went there in 1948, and the two women, very different temperamentally, became good friends. She found a place for Flannery to live in New York, near her own, before Flannery came to us, the summer after she left Yaddo in 1949. When she was living with us, Flannery spoke of Elizabeth, whom she always referred to as "Miss Fenwick," often and fondly. In 1958, when I saw her in Europe, she told me that Elizabeth, too, had been diagnosed as having lupus, and Flannery fretted anxiously that she didn't seem to realize how serious it was, or even to believe that she had it. Flannery pursued the subject in her letters, scolding her friend for her placidity, suggesting doctors she might see, including her own, and urging her to take every precaution. If Elizabeth Fenwick did have the disease, it was of a milder kind than Flannery's, and she is alive today and in reasonably good health. The two never saw each other again after their Ridgefield meeting in 1958, when E.F. came to spend an afternoon during Flannery's summer visit with us. Only a few of Flannery's letters to her have survived. These she sent me, however, and this is the earliest.*

## To Elizabeth Fenwick

2/12/54

I am at a loss where to send this as the Birches doesn't sound like a winter residence. I forget now that people do have to live in the North in the wintertime—it seems a pity. I am becoming mighty unreconstructed. I have been wondering about you since about a month ago when I saw Bob Giroux in Atlanta. He was on tour seeing various people, and I went up and had lunch with him and consulted about the story collection; anyway when I asked about you, he said they had decided not to use your book. He seemed distressed about it himself. I gathered that he had liked the one called "People from Detroit" better than this last one. However all this has set me to inquire about you & hope that you are in a state of well-being, and perhaps back at Stonington—which sounds to me more appropriate for a Yankee winter than the Birches. No offense to the Birches but I HAVE BEEN TO STONINGTON. I hope the novel proves to be retrievable. I enjoy retrieving mine better than I do writing them. Perhaps you finished it under a strain. Try rearranging it backwards and see what you see. I thought this stunt up from my art classes, where we always turn the picture upside down, on its two sides, to see what lines need to be added. A lot of excess stuff will drop off this way.

I have developed a decided limp but I am told it has nothing to do with the lupus but is rheumatism in the hip, and I trust them to be telling me this straight as otherwise they would increase my dose of ACTH. However it galls me to have supported the lupus for four years and then to be crippled with rheumatism (a vulgar disease at best) of the hip. I am not able enough to walk straight but not crippled enough to walk with a cane so that I give the appearance of merely being a little drunk all the time. No spots or butterfly wings.*

My peachicken has turned out to be a cock which means that in three years if he survives dogs, foxes, weasels, mink, and internal worms, he will have a tail-spread of four feet. He has one

---

* *The acute phase of lupus is characterized by a rash, over the bridge of the nose and cheeks, in the shape of a butterfly.*

trick: he runs up to anyone holding a cigaret and snatches it away and eats it. He has eaten two hot cigarets so far.

*Ben Griffith, a writer, was then teaching at Bessie Tift Women's College (now Tift College) in Forsyth, Georgia, and is now Dean of the Graduate School at West Georgia College.*

## To Ben Griffith

13 February 54

Thank you so very much for your kind letter. I am much more like Enoch than like the gorilla and I always answer any letter I get, at once and at length. This may be because I don't get many.

I don't know how to cure the source-itis except to tell you that I can discover a good many possible sources myself for *Wise Blood* but I am often embarrassed to find that I read the sources after I had written the book. I have been exposed to Wordsworth's "Intimation" ode but that is all I can say about it. I have one of those food-chopper brains that nothing comes out of the way it went in. The Oedipus business comes nearer home. Of course Haze Motes is not an Oedipus figure but there are the obvious resemblances. At the time I was writing the last of the book, I was living in Connecticut with the Robert Fitzgeralds. Robert Fitzgerald translated the Theban cycle with Dudley Fitts, and their translation of the *Oedipus Rex* had just come out and I was much taken with it. Do you know that translation? I am not an authority on such things but I think it must be the best, and it is certainly very beautiful. Anyway, all I can say is, I did a lot of thinking about Oedipus.

My background and my inclinations are both Catholic and I think this is very apparent in the book. Something is usually said about Kafka in connection with *Wise Blood* but I have never succeeded in making my way through *The Castle* or *The Trial* and wouldn't pretend to know anything about Kafka. I think reading a little of him perhaps makes you a bolder writer. My reading is botchy. I have what passes for an education in this day and time, but I am not deceived by it. I read Henry James, thinking this may affect my writing for the better without my knowing how. A touching faith, and I have others.

Right now I am working on another novel and a collection of short stories. I was five years writing WB and will perhaps be that many on the one I am working on now. The effort to maintain a tone is a considerable strain, particularly as I never know exactly what tone I am maintaining.

Since you show an interest in the book I presume you are a foreigner, as nobody in Georgia shows much interest. Southern people don't know anything about the literature of the South unless they have gone to Northern colleges or to some of the conscious places like Vanderbilt or Sewanee or W&L. At least this is my theory.

I have heard of Bessie Tift but never saw one they put out. What is it—adulterated Methodist or militant genteel? We have a girls' college here too but the lacy atmosphere is fortunately destroyed by a reformatory, an insane asylum, and a military school.

3 March 54

I am amused by the "tare" in his throat. I had to look it up in the dictionary. The truth is, it was my error; not the printer's. I meant it in the sense of "split" in his voice. I have always been a very innocent speller. I never sense that I am spelling something incorrectly and so don't look up the words. The simpler the word, the more liable I am to come up with a rare spelling. If anybody else asks me about this, I am certainly going to say I meant it in the sense of first principle, a seed of evil, and thus pass myself off for a scholar. "Tear in his throat" must be a colloquial expression as it comes very naturally to me (whereas someone else might think it mannered). However, the omniscient narrator is not properly supposed to use colloquial expressions. I send a good many of my things to Caroline Gordon (Tate) for her criticism and she is always writing me that I mustn't say such things, that the om. nar. never speaks like anyone but Dr. Johnson. Of course, it is a great strain for me to speak like Dr. Johnson. Most of the images I make up when the need arises but I suppose some of them are to be found in the local idiom.

Vaguely I remember passing Java's Oasis but I am not able to get there to make their acquaintance as I don't drive and no one else I know would be interested in such a place. It sounds very interesting to me, however.

Let me assure you that no one but a Catholic could have written *Wise Blood* even though it is a book about a kind of Protestant saint. It reduces Protestantism to the twin ultimate absurdities of The Church Without Christ or The Holy Church of Christ Without Christ, which no pious Protestant would do. And of course no unbeliever or agnostic could have written it because it is entirely Redemption-centered in thought. Not too many people are willing to see this, and perhaps it is hard to see because H. Motes is such an admirable nihilist. His nihilism leads him back to the fact of his Redemption, however, which is what he would have liked so much to get away from.

When you start describing the significance of a symbol like the tunnel which recurs in the book, you immediately begin to limit it and a symbol should go on deepening. Everything should have a wider significance—but I am a novelist not a critic and I can excuse myself from *explication de textes* on that ground. The real reason of course is laziness.

I don't know anything about the Peabody sisters so your children's biography will be just the thing for me. I do seem to have in mind that one of them married Hawthorne and my opinion of Hawthorne is that he was a very great writer indeed.

I think H. M. McLuhan's piece in the *Southern Vanguard* is one good one. It possibly takes a Canadian to throw a sharper light on things here. I notice I have marked in my copy the sentence "Formality becomes a condition of survival." That apparently struck me when I first read it and it strikes me now, out of context, as true. The formality that is left in the South now is quite dead and done for of course.

*To Sally and Robert Fitzgerald*

3/5/54

I am sending you off the mixes and whatnot tomorrow and I hope you get them before the worm does. I found it all but the Maltex. The Southern Child lives in such a rich environment that he don't need Maltex and it is not to be found in this community. I substituted an angel-food cake mix that Mama dotes on. All you do is spit on it or something and you got an angel-food cake.

I will send you a copy of the story that is coming out in *Harper's Bazaar* in April ["A Temple of the Holy Ghost"]. The others are in the same state that the novel ms. was in. I don't know what happens to the copies but there is one I don't even have a copy of myself, though it will be in the spring *Kenyon* and they have it. This getting up the collection is a great nuisance and I have to drive myself to it.

One of my Atlanta cousins informed me that she had written a book review on *Wise Blood* for her class (9th grade). Why? said

I. Because, said she, I had to write one on some book the Sister wouldn't read. I asked her what she said about it. She said she said her cousin wrote this book and then she said everything that was on the jacket.

Is Cal at Iowa or Cincinnati? I got a note at Christmas from him at Iowa. Regards to the Oddisey & yr. children.

## To Robert Giroux

March 29, 1954

I have forgotten about the manuscript for the collection of short stories but the last story ["The Displaced Person"] has just been sold to the *Sewanee Review* and I don't think they will be able to print it before next spring; so I don't see any need to startle myself into activity about making up the manuscript. I have eleven stories anyway . . .

I'd be much obliged if you'd send me Peter Taylor's book [*The Widows of Thornton*] when it comes out.

## To Sally and Robert Fitzgerald

26 April 54

. . . Big doings around here. Mrs. P.'s youngest, age 17, is going to get married on the 4th of July. We get all the gruesome details, twenty-four hours a day. They are going to Nashville Tennysee on their wedding trip. Well, that's lovely, Regina says, what are they going to Nashville for? The music, Mrs. P. says, Grand Ole Opry . . .

Cal Lowell [writes that he is not] "rejoining the flock." He thought he "could do more good outside, at least for myself." And some other claptrap about Henry Adams being a Catholic anarchist and he was the same, only agnostic too. I wrote him that his not being in the Church was a grief to me and I knew no more to say about it. I said I severely doubted he would do any good to anybody else outside but that it was probably true he would do good to himself inasmuch as he would be the only one in a position to. I said the Sacraments gave grace—and let it go at that. I got a post-card back saying thank you, that we did speak the same language but he wasn't as young as he used to be and not so quick on his feet anymore. Well, maybe he plans to get on them eventually. He had just been to see that Randall Jarrell.

The enclosed is a snapshot of my self-portrait. Maw says it shows exactly how awful it is but it don't really show how good it is because the colors are nice in the original.

## To Robert Giroux

3 September 54

I find that the *Sewanee Review* is going to use my story in the next issue instead of waiting until spring so I am wondering whether, [if] I get this collection [*A Good Man Is Hard to Find*] in to you in October, you could publish it in the spring. Of course I am anxious to get it out of the house and I have the manuscript practically ready. I enclose a list of the stories. One or two of them might be left out, according to what you think.

I liked Peter Taylor's collection so much and thank you for sending it to me.

*Wise Blood* finally found a publisher in England—something called Neville Spearman, Ltd, which for all I know may be the British equivalent of Gory Stories. Anyway, they plan to put it out in the spring.

I'll be anxious to hear from you about this collection.

15 November 54

I sent the manuscript for the story collection to Mavis today and asked her to get it to you by December 1.

I have included only the long version of "The Displaced Person" but if you don't like it, we can substitute the short one, which I can send you. Also I include the story that was in *Mademoiselle* [as "The Capture"]—with the title changed to "An Afternoon in the Woods" and the whole thing much rewritten. Then I have rearranged the table of contents, putting the long story last. That's all I've done, I think.

Mr. [John Crowe] Ransom took "The Artificial Nigger," but I have rewritten it since and the amended version is in the ms.

Caroline says to ask you to send her the proofs as soon as you have them as she has asked the *Times* to let her review it. I hope she will . . .

Sally [Fitzgerald] is coming back to the states at the end of the month to see her father who is dying in Houston. We are hoping she will stop over in Milledgeville.

The next time you come to Atlanta, I hope you will stop with us in Milledgeville. It is just as central as the Biltmore.

*However eager she was to "get it out of the house," the habit of perfectionism was strong.*

30 November 1954

I have conferred with Caroline about the story called, "The Artificial Nigger," and am consequently rewriting it. When should I send the new version to you in order to get it in the collection instead of the old one? The corrections are not such as could be made on the proofs. I am sorry about this shilly-shallying, but the story will be much better in consequence of it.

*When Giroux told her when she would have to have the revised version in, if the publication date was to be met, she sent her new schedule.*

6 December 54

In as much as this is the 6th I won't be getting the revised story to you on the 5th; however, I will absolutely have it to you by the 20th of December. And also a new first page for the story called "The Displaced Person."

*Giroux was reassuring as to the possibility of meeting the schedule if the revisions arrived by the twentieth. He sent the bad news, however, that the book now exceeded its prescribed length, and that one of the stories would have to be deleted. He suggested deleting either "A Stroke of Good Fortune" or "An Afternoon in the Woods."*

11 December 54

Why not cut out both "An Afternoon in the Woods" and "A Stroke of Good Fortune." Nine stories ought to be enough when one of them is as long as "The Displaced Person."

However, if it must be one or the other, I think I would prefer leaving in "A Stroke of Good Fortune" because it seems more tied in with the others thematically. I may be wrong; I'm not wildly fond of either and I leave it up to you. I would really like both left out.

The revised story and two first pages for "The Displaced Person" will be mailed Monday so you should get them by the 15th.

## To Sally Fitzgerald

26 Dec 54

We are sorry you missed us but it sounds like a ghastly trip and I think you did well to get home. Regina and I are having a mass said for your father and will continue to pray for him . . .

I have finally got off the ms. for my collection and it is scheduled to appear in May. Without yr kind permission I have taken the liberty of dedicating (grand verb) it to you and Robert. This is because you all are my adopted kin and if I dedicated it to any of my blood kin they would think they had to go into hiding. Nine stories about original sin, with my compliments.

I have been invited to go to Greensboro to the Women's College in March to be on an arts panel. That is where Brother Randall Jarrell holds forth. I accepted but I am not looking forward to it. Can you fancy me hung in conversation with the likes of him?

When I had lunch with Giroux in Atlanta he told me about Cal's escapade in Cincinnati. It seems [Cal] convinced everybody it was Elizabeth who was going crazy . . . Toward the end he gave a lecture at the university that was almost pure gibberish. I guess nobody noticed, thinking it was the new criticism . . .

I just got a check for $200 for the 2nd prize in the O. Henry book this year. My ex-mentor Paul Engle does the selecting. Jean Stafford got the first one.

I am walking with a cane these days which gives me a great air of distinction. The scientist tells me this has nothing to do with the lupus but is rheumatism. I would not believe it except that the dose of ACTH has not been increased. Besides which I now feel it makes very little difference what you call it. As the niggers say, I have the misery.

I am reading everything I can of Romano Guardini's [Italian priest and theologian]. Have you become acquainted with his work? A book called *The Lord* of his is very fine.

## To Elizabeth McKee

13 January 1955

The carbon of "An Exile in the East" is enclosed, but I don't know if you realize or not that this is a rewritten version of "The Geranium" originally printed in *Accent*. *Accent* didn't pay me for it and it is rather much changed, but I enclose both stories so [the editor] can see what she's doing. I don't want to go to the penitentiary for selling a story twice (but if I do I would like to get a good price for the story).

## To Robert Giroux

22 January 55

Nothing has been said about a picture for the jacket of this collection *but if you have to have one,* I would be much obliged if you could use the enclosed so that I won't have to have a new picture made. This is a self-portrait with a pheasant cock, that I painted in 1953; however, I think it will do justice to the subject for some time to come.

26 February 55

I have just written a story called "Good Country People" that Allen and Caroline both say is the best thing I have written and should be in this collection. I told them I thought it was too late, but anyhow I am writing now to ask if it is. It is really a story that would set the whole collection on its feet. It is 27 pages and if you can eliminate the one called "A Stroke of Good Fortune," and the other called "An Afternoon in the Woods," this one would fit the available space nicely. Also I remember you said it would be good to have one that had never been published before. I could send it to you at once *on being wired.* Please let me know.

*Giroux wired Flannery that every effort would be made to include the story. After he had read it, he wrote suggesting that an appearance by the mother and Mrs. Freeman at the end might improve it. Flannery recognized the value of the suggestion and added the sentences that are now a part of the story.*

7 March 55

I like the suggestion about the ending of "Good Country People" and enclose a dozen or so lines that can be added on to *the present end.* I enclose them in case you can get them put on before I get the proofs. I am mighty wary of making changes on proofs . . .

## To Sally and Robert Fitzgerald

1 April 55

We are wondering if #6 is here yet or due to arrive momentarily. Let us hear and if you need any names, I'll be glad to cable you a rich collection. I have just got back from Greensboro where I said nothing intelligent the whole time, but enjoyed myself. Mr. Randall Jarrell, wife and stepdaughters I met and et dinner with. I must say I was shocked at what a very kind man he is—that is the last impression I expected to have of him. I also met Peter Taylor, who is more like folks. Mrs. Jarrell is writing a novel. You get the impression the two stepdaughters may be at it too and maybe the dog. Mr. Jarrell has a beard and looks like Mephistopheles (sp?) only fatter. Mrs. Jarrell is very friendly & sunkist.

The Easter rabbit is bringing my mother a three-quarter ton truck.

I trust Giroux will be sending you a copy of the book soon. I wrote a very hot story at the last minute called "Good Country People": so now there are ten.

While I was in NC I heard somebody recite a barroom ballad. I don't remember anything but the end but beinst you all are poets I will give it to you as it is mighty deathless:

> "They stacked the stiffs outside the door.
> They made, I reckon, a cord or more."

I call that real poetry.

I have put the cane up and am walking on my own very well. Let us hear. Regards to children.

---

*On March 31, 1955, Robert Giroux resigned from Harcourt, Brace & Company to join Farrar, Straus and Company. This was dismaying to Flannery, but she was fortunate to have Catharine Carver as her new editor and Giroux assured her she was in the best of hands. Denver Lindley became the new editor-in-chief at HB. Informed of the turn of events by her agent, and before she had heard from Giroux directly, Flannery wrote to Catharine Carver.*

## To Catharine Carver

April 2, 1955

I had not heard that Bob Giroux had left Harcourt but since he has gone, I am very glad that you will be my editor. He told me once that you did all the work anyhow, which was what I might have suspected. I appreciate your interest in my writing and I will rely on you to tell me when what I do needs more doing. The last time I was at the Harcourt office, I stayed around longer than I was expected, hoping you would come in, but I had to leave before you returned from lunch. I don't expect to get to New York this year or next. If you make any of these trips that editors seem to make, I hope you will include Milledgeville. Meanwhile, perhaps I'll see Mr. Lindley . . .

I'll be very glad to get the reviews, though they don't always elate me. And I'll be particularly glad to see any that come in on the British edition as I can't fancy what the British will make of *Wise Blood*. You probably noticed in the Neville Spearman catalogue that they said I was *finishing* my second novel—and they would publish it in the fall. I am not finishing it or anywhere near finishing it, and it is fortunate they don't say which fall.

Many thanks for all your kindnesses to me.


## To Elizabeth McKee

5 April 55

After thinking it over, I suppose *New World Writing* is as good a place for this as any, since they seem to favor novels-in-progress, but if you think more money could be got from *Harper's Bazaar* I am all for more money. Anyhow I want it published as a chapter and not as a short story ["You Can't Be Any Poorer Than Dead"]. And the title is just for the chapter and not for the whole novel.

Did I tell you that I recently was a guest at a Penwoman's breakfast in Atlanta and had to sit for two hours next to my old friend, Long John Selby? . . . We both overflowed with politeness.

I am sorry Giroux is elsewhere but I will like Miss Carver fine. I reckon Mr. Lindley will come to see me if he is expert in penetrating the Georgia wilderness. The only way to get here is by bus or buzzard. At least I don't live in the Okefenokee Swamp.


## To Alice Morris

28 April 55

The society editor of the Macon paper has never sent me the picture although she said she would do so . . . If she does get around to sending it to me, I'll send it on to you, although I dislike it heartily. As a matter of fact, she has two of them but I have only seen the one she used. The other might be better. Some turkeys came and got in it and she didn't care for that.

I am very glad you like "Good Country People" and that it will appear in *Harper's Bazaar*. A lady in Macon told me that she read me under the dryer. I was gratified.

## To Ben Griffith

4 May 1955

I have gotten one other letter about "The Artificial Nigger" and in that one I was asked if Mr. Head didn't represent Peter and Nelson the Christ-Child. I had to say that Mr. Head's behavior certainly resembled Peter's a little but that I found it harder to gin up Nelson's character so he could suitably represent the Christ-Child. What I had in mind to suggest with the artificial nigger was the redemptive quality of the Negro's suffering for us all. You may be right that Nelson's reaction to the colored woman is too pronounced, but I meant for her in an almost physical way to suggest the mystery of existence to him—he not only has never seen a nigger but he didn't know any women and I felt that such a black mountain of maternity would give him the required shock to start those black forms moving up from his unconscious. I wrote that story a good many times, having a lot of trouble with the end. I frequently send my stories to Mrs. Tate and she is always telling me that the endings are too flat and that at the end I must gain some altitude and get a larger view. Well the end of "The Artificial Nigger" was a very definite attempt to do that and in those last two paragraphs I have practically gone from the Garden of Eden to the Gates of Paradise. I am not sure it is successful but I mean to keep trying with other things.

I am writing Harcourt, Brace to send you an advance copy of *A Good Man Is Hard to Find*, which is my collection of short stories (ten) due to be published June 6. There is one very long story in it, 60 pages, that I would like you to see, and another called "Good Country People" that pleases me no end. You will observe that I admire my own work as much if not more than anybody else does. I have read "The Artificial Nigger" several times since it was printed, enjoying it each time as if I had had nothing to do with it. I feel that this is not quite delicate of me but it may be balanced by the fact that I write a great deal that is not fit to read which I properly destroy.

The people on our place always say, "we gone to see it," or "we gone and done it," when the action is past—never "went" when "went" would be correct. I had Nelson say "I'm glad I've went once," because I couldn't resist the "went once."

I am at home every afternoon but Monday and would be most happy to have you come over. We live 4 miles from Milledgeville on the road to Eatonton in a two-story white farm house. The place is called Andalusia. Any time in the afternoon would be fine but if you drop me a card when you plan to come, I will make it a point to be here.

Occasionally I see the *Georgia Review* but not often; however, it would be very agreeable to me to see something written about my work for local consumption by somebody who knows something. Recently I talked in Macon (nobody had ever heard tell of me, of course) and it was announced in the paper the next day that I was a "writer of the realistic school." I presume the lady came to this conclusion from looking at the cover of the drugstore edition of *Wise Blood.* In a few weeks I am going to talk to some more ladies in Macon and I am going to clear up that detail. I am interested in making up a good case for distortion, as I am coming to believe it is the only way to make people see.

## To Catharine Carver

8 May 55

My books came yesterday and this is only to tell you that I like it fine. It is nice not to have to look at myself on the back of the jacket and I am glad the Waugh quotation was used in full. My agent sent me a copy of a review out of the Virginia Kirkus Bulletin that said I was no short-story writer but seemed to leave a little hope that I might be able to write a novel or something. Which was rather consoling. That first chapter has been sold to the *New World Writing* thing under the title "Whom the Plague Beckons." Miss Porter wondered if I couldn't think of a more provocative title but so far I haven't been able to. [The title was later changed to "You Can't Be Any Poorer Than Dead"].

Please tell Mr. Lindley I hope he will make it next time. I fear I left him the impression that he would need a map, compass, guide, and mule to get here.

## To Sally and Robert Fitzgerald

8 May 1955

We were certainly glad to get our notice about CMT's [Caterina Fitzgerald] arrival and then the letter. I reckon my mother is now convinced that a child can be born in Europe. I think she thought forin children could but not regular children—and then to have its blood changed too! My my. Well, as she says, showing that she can add correctly, this makes six, three boys and three girls. She approves of this one's being a girl.

I have been discovered by the Club ladies of middle Georgia. Last month the Macon Writers Club had a breakfast IN MY HONOR and allowed me to address them for 25 minutes. I tell you it was a great success. One old lady told me that it was a very important day, "April 23, the birthdays of William Shakespear, Harry Stillwell Edwards, and Shirley Temple." I have been wasting my time all these years writing—my talent lies in a kind of intellectual vaudeville. I leave them not knowing exactly what I have said but feeling that they have been inspired. On the 20th I am to address the Book Review Group of the Macon Women's Club on Southern Letters and the fact that I have never read any Southern Letters ain't holding me back none. My mother thinks this is very fine and likely to *broaden* me; she finds me very narrow in my outlook.

Harcourt is supposed to send you a copy of the book but I reckon it will take some time to get there. Old Giroux took himself off and is now Vice President of Farrar, Straus as I reckon you have been informed. There is a Catharine Carver there who is also fiction editor of *Partisan Review,* a friend of the Lowells, and she is taking care of me in so far as I have to be taken care of. Your friend Denver Lindley is in charge and was recently in the South and inquired could he come to see me. So I gave him explicit instructions how to get here, making it seem as if I lived in the middle of the Okefenokee Swamp, and he didn't come. I don't think I would have known exactly what to do with him if he had. Some Very Peculiar Types have beat a path to my door these last few years and it is always interesting to see my mother hostessing-it-up on these occasions.

Today is The Great Commercial Feast but we were spared a sermon on mothers and merely asked to give generously to the special collection.


## To Robie Macauley

18 May 55

I certainly am glad you like the stories because now I feel it's not bad that I like them so much. The truth is I like them better than anybody and I read them over and over and laugh and laugh, then get embarrassed when I remember I was the one wrote them. Unlike *Wise Blood,* they were all relatively painless to me; but now I have to quit enjoying life and get on with the second novel. The first chapter of it is going to be published in the fall in the *New World Writing* thing and is to be called "You Can't Be Any Poorer Than Dead"—which is the way I feel every time I get to work on it.

Nobody has given me any gold even in a medal, but you are right about the television. I am going to New York on the 30th to be, if you please, interviewed by Mr. Harvey Breit (on the 31st) on a program he is starting up over NBC-TV [*Galley-Proof*]. They are also going to dramatize the opening scene from "The Life You Save" etc. Do you reckon this is going to corrupt me? I already feel like a combination of Msgr. Sheen and Gorgeous George [a wrestler]. Everybody who has read *Wise Blood* thinks I'm a hillbilly nihilist, whereas I would like to create the impression over the television that I'm a hillbilly Thomist, but I will probably not be able to think of anything to say to Mr. Harvey Breit but "Huh?" and "Ah dunno." When I come back I'll probably have to spend three months day and night in the chicken pen to counteract these evil influences.

Although I am a prominent Georgia Author I have never went to Washington but I have went over it and shall this time at an altitude of 14,000 feet compliments Eastern Airlines.

Greensboro was moderately ghastly, the more so than it would have been if you and Anne had come down. The panel was the worst as I never can think of anything to say about a story and the conferences were high comedy. I had one with a bearded intellectual delinquent from Kenyon who wouldn't be convinced he hadn't written a story, and the rest with girls writing about life in the dormitory.

A couple of weeks ago Ashley came down of a Sunday afternoon with [a friend] and they took in the architecture and had supper with me. Ashley was telling me that you are an admirer of Dr. Frank Crane [a newspaper columnist], my favorite Protestant theologian (salvation by the compliment club). I was glad to hear this because I think the doctor ought to be more widely appreciated. He is really a combination minister and masseur, don't you think? He appears in the Atlanta *Constitution* on the same page as the funnies. I like to hear him tell Alma A. that she can keep her husband by losing 75 pounds and just the other day he told a girl who was terrified of toads how not to let this ruin her life—know the truth & the truth shall make you free. However, his best column was where he told about getting the letter from the convict who had joined the compliment club. I hope you saw that one.

Please thank Mr. W. P. Southard for liking my stories. I am always glad to know I have a reader of quality because I have so many who aren't. I get some letters from people I might have created myself . . . [like] one from a young man in California who was starting a magazine to be called *Hearse*—"a vehicle to convey stories and poems to the great cemetery of the American intellect." Then I got a message from two theological students at Alexandria who said they had read *Wise Blood* and that I was their pin-up girl—the grimmest distinction to date. I got a real ugly letter from a Boston lady about that story called "A Temple of the Holy Ghost." She said she was a Catholic and so she couldn't understand how anybody could even HAVE such thoughts. I wrote her a letter that could have been signed by the bishop and now she is my fast friend and recently wrote me that her husband had run for attorney general but hadn't been elected. I wish somebody real intelligent would write me sometime but I seem to attract the lunatic fringe mainly.

I will be real glad when this television thing is over with. I keep having a mental picture of my glacial glare being sent out over the nation onto millions of children who are waiting impatiently for *The Batman* to come on.

Best to you and Anne and write me again before my next book comes out because that may be in 1984.

## To Catharine Carver

24 May 55

Thanks so much for the information and the copies of the letters, all very agreeable. Also I'd like to see the play. Last week I "lectured" in Macon and a club lady asked me if Tennessee Williams was from Tennessee. I didn't know.

I am going to start being a nuisance at once and ask you to change my hotel reservation. I went to the doctor yesterday and he told me not to walk any more than I could help it in New York and as the Woodstock is three or four long blocks west, I am wondering if you could change the reservation to that hotel over Grand Central or the one behind it. I forgot the names of either. All this winter I walked with a cane but have been able to discard it this spring and the doctor says if I do too much walking I will undo my progress. It is a great temptation to strike out from the Woodstock and walk so I will be much obliged if you will make the change and let me know where you make the new reservation . . .

I am sure the only people who look at TV at 1:30 p.m. are children who are not financially able to buy *A Good Man Is Hard to Find*.

*Ben Griffith had in the meantime visited Andalusia, bringing a story of his for Flannery's criticism. She wrote him after his departure.*

## To Ben Griffith

6/8/55

Thanks so much for the review and the Plunkett [radio husband and wife evangelists] Rainbow prayers and the story. Too bad we both can't write like Plunkett—tears would roll down everybody's cheeks. The review I naturally liked very much . . . You brought out a lot of points I wanted to see brought out.

As soon as I read your story I thought of two other stories that I felt you should read before you start rewriting this one. One of these is "The Lament" by Chekhov, the other "War" by Luigi Pirandello. Both of these stories are in a book called *Understanding Fiction* by Cleanth Brooks and R. P. Warren, which you may know but should if you don't. It is a book that has been of invaluable help to me and I think would be to you.

Your story, like these other two, is essentially the presenting of a pathetic situation, and when you present a pathetic situation, you have to let it speak entirely for itself. I mean you have to present it and leave it alone. You have to let the things in the story do the talking. I mean that, as author, you can't force it and I think you tend to force it in your story, every now and then. The first thing is to see the people at every minute. You get into the old man's mind before you let us know exactly what he looks like. You have got to learn to paint with words. Have the old man there first so that the reader can't escape him. This is something that it has taken me a long time to learn. Ford Madox Ford said you couldn't have somebody sell a newspaper in a story unless you said what he looked like. You have to learn to do this unobtrusively of course. The old man thinks of the daughter-in-law and son talking and recalls their conversation—well he should see them, the reader should see them, should feel from seeing them what their conversation is going to be almost before he hears it.

Let the old man go through his motions without any comment from you as author and let the things he sees make the pathetic effects. Do you know Joyce's story "The Dead"? See how he makes the snow work in that story. Chekhov makes everything work—the air, the light, the cold, the dirt, etc. Show these things and you don't have to say them. I think what the colored man says in your story is very good. But you don't have to say the colored man is about 45—instead paint him there so the reader will know he's a fat middle-aged insolent Negro and as hurt by the old man as the old man will shortly be by him.

The deaf and dumb child should be seen better—it does no good just to tell us she is seraphically beautiful. She has to move around and make some kind of show of herself so we'll know she's there all the time.

Also in a story like this you don't want to rely on local effects, such as calling the paper he picks up the *Macon Telegraph*. This is not the kind of story that gets its effects from local things, but from universal feeling of grief that old age and unwantedness call up. I think it could be made into a very fine story if you have the time to work on it. I am a great hand at rewriting myself. It takes a long time to make a thing like this work. Looks simple but is not.

If you do rewrite it, I hope you will let me see it again. This is just the repressed schoolteacher in me cropping out.

Please do bring your wife and children over any time you get ready. Merrill, Lynch, Pierce, Fenner and Bean [ducks] are slated for the deep freeze in August but Clair Booth Loose Goose is going to live a natural life until she dies a natural death. My mother is head of the horse department, so I will have to ask her about an Oveta. I hope you enjoy North Carolina.

[P.S.] The television was mildly ghastly and I am very glad to be back with the chickens who don't know I have just published a book.

*Flannery didn't want to be too subject to another unexpected editorial change at Harcourt. With this in mind she asked that a provisional voidance clause be written into her contract.*

## To Elizabeth McKee

9 June 55

I have just been told that the clause I signed on the Harcourt contract should have read "void unless . . ." and I don't believe it did. Of course I have signed it now so I suppose it is too late, but would you check on this and let me know. I only signed one copy.

I enclose my excellent self-portrait so you can see what a marvelous painter I am . . .

## To Sally and Robert Fitzgerald

10 June 55

Gladjer got the book. You are right about "A Stroke of Good Fortune." It don't appeal to me either and I really didn't want it there but Giroux thought it ought to be. It is, in its way, Catholic, being about the rejection of life at the source, but too much of a farce to bear the weight . . .

I have just got back from a week in New York at the expense of Harcourt, Brace, being, if you please, on a television program with Harvey Breit. They dramatized "The Life You Save" up to the point where the old woman says she'll give $17.50 if Mr. Shiftlet will marry the idiot daughter. Harvey Breit narrated the story and they had three live actors and then he interviewed me. It was all mildly ghastly as you may well imagine. I had interviews with this one and that one, ate with this one and that one . . . and generally managed to conduct myself as if this were all very well but I had business at home. This book is getting much more attention than *Wise Blood* and may even sell a few copies.

The atmosphere at Harcourt, Brace, at least in regard to meself, has changed to one of eager enthusiasm. I had tea with Giroux and he told me all about it. He looks better than when I saw him in the fall. He advised me to have a clause in my contract saying that my editor had to be a certain Miss Carver whom I like or the contract would be void so this has been done. If she leaves I can escape the textbook people if they prove to be too much. I liked Denver Lindley fine and am satisfied at Harcourt, Brace as long as he and Miss Carver are there.

I spent the weekend in Conn. with Caroline [Gordon Tate] and Sue Jenkins [friend of Mrs. Tate]. They had a party at which the chief guests were dear old Malcolm Cowley and dear old Van Wyke Brooks. Dear old Van Wyke insisted that I read a story at which horror-stricken looks appeared on the faces of both Caroline and Sue. "Read the shortest one!" they both screamed. I read "A Good Man Is Hard to Find" and Mr. Brooks later remarked to Miss Jenkins that it was a shame someone with so much talent should look upon life as a horror story. Malcolm was very polite and asked me if I had a wooden leg.

Congratulations on the Shelley Memorial Award which certainly sounds elegant. I am going to apply for a Guggenheim, hoping that now that my need is not so great they may see fit to reward me . . .

I have never read *The Golden Bowl* but I guess that condition will have to be corrected.


## To Alice Morris

10 June 1955

Thank you so much for sending me the Dead Sea scrolls piece (which I want to keep a little longer) and the Hartford remarks (which I return at once). I recognize Brother Hartford all too easily: my kinfolks and neighbors have been saying these same things for years. The other is fascinating and I want to read it again before I return it.

I also enclose my correspondence with Mrs. N. of Boston whose letter is probably not unlike those you received. I'd like it back as I guess there will be other Mrs. N.'s that I'll have to write to in the future. I don't deserve any credit for turning the other cheek as my tongue is always in it . . .

If I could be of any assistance in providing an answer to any complaints you might get about "Good Country People," I'll be glad to; but perhaps the complaints this time will be from pious atheists and not from irate Catholics.


## To Catharine Carver

16 June 55

Thanks for the contract [for the new novel] and for seeing about the pictures. I thought the pictures were very good considering the subject.

Maybe all these fierce reviews are doing some good. Anyway I hope you don't get stuck on another printing.

You would be amused at some of the mail I am getting—one from a "real west Virginia mountineer to his writer-friend . . . I have a serious heart and blood vessel condition, don't want a penny or pity but sure do like how you form words—sinsationally, wow, ha ha." Another from young man who says he has written a novel that is a combination of *The Yearling, Random Harvest,* and *Gone with the Wind* and that with all I know about it, he thinks he and I could write one together as good as *Gone with the Wind.* He then adds that he is 35 years old, weighs 160 pounds, is six feet tall, considered "handsome, intellegent and great ambition and broke my leg in four places in Miami Florida on April 20 so have plenty time to write." The latest came from a Mr. Semple of Cincinnati who has not read anything of mine but doesn't really see how I can say a good man is hard to find. He is an industrial engineer, likes to play bridge, is the active type, 31 years old, single etc. etc. I wrote Mr. Semple that I didn't think I'd like him a bit but he would be crazy about me as I had seven gold teeth and weighed 250 pounds. Yesterday I got a picture postcard from the West Virginia mountaineer. It showed a baby bear sitting on a boulder with the caption, "I just can't bear to leave the West Virginia mountains!"

Lon and Brainard [Cheney] are one and the same but I always forget he's Brainard. He writes speeches for the Governor of Tenn. and I reckon he thinks in terms of nuclear fission and the Cold War.

Please thank Denver for me for the Prescott review.

*The following letter was written to her former editor just as the book of stories was published.*

## To Robert Giroux

16 June 55

My copy of the [Harcourt] contract came today and I see the clause reads as follows:

> It is understood Catharine Carver will act as editor for this book. If, for any reason, she is unable to do so, the author shall have the option, upon repayment of the advance, of cancelling this contract.

There is no "void unless . . ." but it is not as bad as I had remembered it. The time limit she put on it is five years, during which time Mr. Ivanovitch [Jovanovich] may decide to sell text-books exclusively or Miss Carver may take the veil or I may join Uncle Roy and his Red Creek Wranglers.

They sent me the Orville Prescott review [of *A Good Man Is Hard to Find*] and said it was as near as he ever came to ecstasy and that on that day they sold 300 copies. They are going to have another printing but I am still not worried that they will sell too many copies.

Thanks again for all your advice and if you don't think this clause is right, please let me know.

## To Catharine Carver

27 June 55

Will you please send a copy of *A Good Man,* charged to me, to Carol Johnson . . .

By the way, have you read this girl's poetry? It comes out every so often in the *Sewanee* and I believe some in the *Hudson.* Anyway, it is something else. I finally had to write her and tell her how much I liked it. I thought—all these idiots write me, why can't I write her? So I did and asked her if she would read the stories if I had them sent to her and she seemed very pleased.

I have been hoping that my erstwhile British publisher had gone bankrupt but I had a note from him today saying *Wise Blood* would come out next month; I don't guess I can expect him to go bankrupt before then.

[P.S.] Did you see the nice little notice in the *New Yorker?* I can see now why those things are anonymous.


## To Elizabeth McKee

29 June 55

Thanks for the word on the contract. It's all right with me as it is if you say so.

Thanks also for the copy of the Gollancz letter. I had a note from Neville Armstrong, very cheerful, unfortunately, saying *Wise Blood* would come out in the middle of next month; so I reckon his shoestring is still holding him up. It's holding me up too.

Would you look in my contract with him and see if I am tied up with him for the book of short stories? I know he has an option on the novel and something was put in about the short stories but I have forgotten what.

Also you have a copy of a story called "An Exile in the East" that they didn't put in the collection. Please send this back to me and in my spare time I may give it a shot of ACTH and send it back in some better shape. I gather it is too much still like it was in *Accent* to be published anywhere else.

I'm glad you like the self-portrait. The colors are real nice too. I'm sorry you can't see the colors . . .

I didn't like Tennessee Williams' play. I thought I could do that good myself. However, on reflection I guess it is wise to doubt that.

## To Ben Griffith

Thanks for lending my books around to the scholars. I relish the idea of being read by scholars. I have been getting some very funny fan mail—a lot of it from gentlemen who have got no farther than the title—"Do you really think a good man is hard to find? I am 31 years old, single, work like a dog . . ." etc. etc. etc. . . . One from a West Virginia mountaineer whose favorite word is "literature" which he spells "litatur."

I agreed about the similarity of other characters to Haze Motes (Motes, not Moates); in fact, Mrs. Tate wrote me that she thought the Bible salesman was a super Haze Motes, one with all his evil potentialities realized. Of course, I think of Haze Motes as a kind of saint. His overwhelming virtue is integrity. I also liked what you said about some of the stories being about children who meet theological truths beyond their understanding.

My editor wrote me that the book was selling better than anything on their list except Thomas Merton—which doesn't say much for their list, I guess. However, they have ordered a second printing. The review in *Time* was terrible, nearly gave me apoplexy. The one in the *Atlanta Journal* was so stupid it was painful. It was written I understand by the lady who writes about gardening. They shouldn't have taken her away from the petunias.

I have never read Krafft-Ebing or *Memoirs of Hecate County*. A little self-knowledge goes a long way . . .

I passed Plunkett on to a friend in Nashville. Plunkett is really real modern when you come down to it—"pray and your food will taste better" is just another version of "Grace before meals is an aid to digestion" which is what religion is coming to in some parts.

*Now Flannery received a letter from a young woman, unknown to her, whose comments so interested her that she asked her to write again. It was the beginning of a nine-year friendship and correspondence. Flannery was obviously hungry for conversation on matters of primary interest to her, and she found with her new correspondent exactly the kind of exchange she needed. We are fortunate that they met late, and not very frequently, so that all she had to say to this almost uniquely important friend did not go up in talk but had to be written down. In setting down what she was thinking, Flannery was of course forced to clarify it for herself first of all, and this enhances the value of these letters. The recipient, who wishes to remain completely anonymous, will be referred to throughout as "A." She has given me copies of all the letters she had; the following was the first.*

## To "A."

20 July 55

I am very pleased to have your letter. Perhaps it is even more startling to me to find someone who recognizes my work for what I try to make it than it is for you to find a God-conscious writer near at hand. The distance is 87 miles but I feel the spiritual distance is shorter.

I write the way I do because (not though) I am a Catholic. This is a fact and nothing covers it like the bald statement. However, I am a Catholic peculiarly possessed of the modern consciousness, that thing Jung describes as unhistorical, solitary, and guilty. To possess this *within* the Church is to bear a burden, the necessary burden for the conscious Catholic. It's to feel the contemporary situation at the ultimate level. I think that the Church is the only thing that is going to make the terrible world we are coming to endurable; the only thing that makes the Church endurable is that it is somehow the body of Christ and that on this we are fed. It seems to be a fact that you have to suffer as much from the Church as for it but if you believe in the divinity of Christ, you have to cherish the world at the same time that you struggle to endure it. This may explain the lack of bitterness in the stories.

The notice in the *New Yorker* was not only moronic, it was unsigned. It was a case in which it is easy to see that the moral sense has been bred out of certain sections of the population, like the wings have been bred off certain chickens to produce more white meat on them. This is a generation of wingless chickens, which I suppose is what Nietzsche meant when he said God was dead.

I am mighty tired of reading reviews that call *A Good Man* brutal and sarcastic. The stories are hard but they are hard because there is nothing harder or less sentimental than Christian realism. I believe that there are many rough beasts now slouching toward Bethlehem to be born and that I have reported the progress of a few of them, and when I see these stories described as horror stories I am always amused because the reviewer always has hold of the wrong horror.

You were very kind to write me and the measure of my appreciation must be to ask you to write me again. I would like to know who this is who understands my stories.

( 90 )

## To Catharine Carver

. . . I am real glad you are still selling copies of the book. I have just got back from a weekend in Nashville and met the people who run the local bookstore there and they informed me they were selling a lot of copies of it. My mail continues to arrive but by this time it is getting me down—another one from a mental institution. I am beginning to think every mental institution should offer a writing course . . .

I have hatched thirteen peachickens this year in the incubator. Next year I hope to have them all over the place, hope to be stepping on them.

I hope you beat the heat. It is never as hot in Georgia as in New York City as I found out by spending one August on 108th St.


28 July 55

Thank you for my mother for the pictures. For myself I think they're horrible but she is overjoyed. I am glad you are not going to use either of those. They are not suitable for anyone but a parent . . .

I have been asked to talk on The Significance of the Short Story (UGH) at a wholesale gathering of the AAUW in Lansing, Michigan—next April. It will take me from now until next April to find out what the significance of the short story is. Have you any idea? I think I will just tell them that this is no concern of the short-story writer.

Did you all publish Karl Stern's book, *The Third Revolution?* If you did, the next time Harcourt, Brace elects to send me a book, I wish they would send me that.

The total of peachickens is 16 today.


## To "A."

2 August 55

Thank you for writing me again. I feel I should apologize for answering so promptly because I may seem to force on you a correspondence that you don't have time for or that will become a burden. I myself am afflicted with time, as I do not work out on account of an energy-depriving ailment and my work in, being creative, can go on only a few hours a day. I live on a farm and don't see many people. My avocation is raising peacocks, something that requires everything of the peacock and nothing of me, so time is always at hand.

I believe too that there is only one Reality and that that is the end of it, but the term, "Christian Realism," has become necessary for me, perhaps in a purely academic way, because I find myself in a world where everybody has his compartment, puts you in yours, shuts the door and departs. One of the awful things about writing when you are a Christian is that for you the ultimate reality is the Incarnation, the present reality is the Incarnation, and nobody believes in the Incarnation; that is, nobody in your audience. My audience are the people who think God is dead. At least these are the people I am conscious of writing for.

As for Jesus' being a realist: if He was not God, He was no realist, only a liar, and the crucifixtion an act of justice.

Dogma can in no way limit a limitless God. The person outside the Church attaches a different meaning to it than the person in. For me a dogma is only a gateway to contemplation and is an instrument of freedom and not of restriction. It preserves mystery for the human mind. Henry James said the young woman of the future would know nothing of mystery or manners. He had no business to limit it to one sex.

You are right that I won't ever be able entirely to understand my own work or even my own motivations. It is first of all a gift, but the direction it has taken has been because of the Church in me or the effect of the Church's teaching, not because of a personal perception or love of God. For you to think this would be possible because of your ignorance of me; for me to think it would be sinful in a high degree. I am not a mystic and I do not lead a holy life. Not that I can claim any interesting or pleasurable sins (my sense of the devil is strong) but I know all about the garden variety, pride, gluttony, envy and sloth, and what is more to the point, my virtues are as timid as my vices. I think sin occasionally brings one closer to God, but not habitual sin and not this petty kind that blocks every small good. A working knowledge of the devil can be very well had from resisting him.

However, the individual in the Church is, no matter how worthless himself, a part of the Body of Christ and a participator in the Redemption. There is no blueprint that the Church gives for understanding this. It is a matter of faith and the Church can force no one to believe it. When I ask myself how I know I believe, I have no satisfactory answer at all, no assurance at all, no feeling at all. I can only say with Peter, Lord I believe, help my unbelief. And all I can say about my love of God, is, Lord help me in my lack of it. I distrust pious phrases, particularly when they issue from my mouth. I try militantly never to be affected by the pious language of the faithful but it is always coming out when you least expect it. In contrast to the pious language of the faithful, the liturgy is beautifully flat.

I am wondering if you have read Simone Weil. I never have and doubt if I would understand her if I did; but from what I have read about her, I think she must have been a very great person. She and Edith Stein are the two 20th-century women who interest me most.

Whether you are a Christian or not, we both worship the God Who Is. St. Thomas on his death bed said of the *Summa*, "It's all straw,"—this was in the vision of that God.


9 August 55

I have thought of Simone Weil in connection with you almost from the first and I got out this piece I enclose and reread it and the impression was not lessened. In the face of anyone's experience, someone like myself who has had almost no experience, must be humble. I will never have the experience of the convert, or of the one who fails to be converted, or even in all probability of the formidable sinner; but your effort not to be seduced by the Church moves me greatly. God permits it for some reason though it is the devil's greatest work of hallucination. Fr. [Jean] de Menasce told somebody not to come into the Church until he felt it would be an enlargement of his freedom. This is what you are doing and you are right, but do not make your feeling of the voluptuous seductive powers of the Church into a hard shell to protect yourself from her. I suppose it is like marriage, that when you get into it, you find it is the beginning, not the end, of the struggle to make love work.

I think most people come to the Church by means the Church does not allow, else there would be no need their getting to her at all. However, this is true inside as well, as the operation of the Church is entirely set up for the sinner; which creates much misunderstanding among the smug.

I suppose I read Aristotle in college but not to know I was doing it; the same with Plato. I don't have the kind of mind that can carry such beyond the actual reading, i.e., total non-retention has kept my education from being a burden to me. So I couldn't make any judgment on the *Summa*, except to say this: I read it for about twenty minutes every night before I go to bed. If my mother were to come in during this process and say, "Turn off that light. It's late," I with lifted finger and broad bland beatific expression, would reply, "On the contrary, I answer that the light, being eternal and limitless, cannot be turned off. Shut your eyes," or some such thing. In any case, I feel I can personally guarantee that St. Thomas loved God because for the life of me I cannot help loving St. Thomas. His brothers didn't want him to waste himself being a Dominican and so locked him up in a tower and introduced a prostitute into his apartment; her he ran out with a red-hot poker. It would be fashionable today to be in sympathy with the woman, but I am in sympathy with St. Thomas.

I don't know B.R. well, but he came out here one evening and had dessert with us. I have a friend who is very fond of him and so I hear a lot about him and his troubles, of which he seems to be so well supplied that it's a miracle he's still alive. My impression was that he was a very fine and a very proud man. When he was sick about a year ago, I sent him a copy of St. Bernard's letters and in thanking me, he said he was an agnostic. You are right that he's an anachronism, I guess, strangely cut-off anyway. I wrote to my friend who is so fond of him that perhaps he might be sent something to read that would at least set him thinking in a wider direction, but I am afraid this filled the poor girl with apprehension, she thinking I would probably produce Cardinal Newman or somebody. I had had in mind Gabriel Marcel whose Gifford Lectures I had just read. This girl is a staunch and excellent Presbyterian with a polite horror of anything Romish.

I am highly pleased you noticed the shirts, though it hadn't occurred to me that they suggested the lack of hairshirts. I am chiefly exercised by the hero rampant on the shirt and the always somewhat-less occupying it. This is funny to me. The only embossed one I ever had had a fierce-looking bulldog on it with the word GEORGIA over him. I wore it all the time, it being my policy at that point in life to create an unfavorable impression. My urge for such has to be repressed, as my mother does not approve of making a spectacle of oneself when over thirty.

I have some long and tall thoughts on the subject of God's working through nature, but I will not inflict them on you now. I find I have a habit of announcing the obvious in pompous and dogmatic periods. I like to forget that I'm only a storyteller. Right now I am trying to write a lecture that I have been invited to deliver next spring in Lansing, Mich. to a wholesale gathering of the AAUW. I am trying to write this thing on the justification of distortion in fiction, call it something like "The Freak in Modern Fiction." Anyway, I have it borne in on me that my business is to write and not talk about it. I have ten months to write the lecture in and it is going to take every bit of it. I don't read much modern fiction. I have never read Nelson Algren that you mention. I feel lumpish.

## To Catharine Carver

10 August 55

. . . Today I got a letter from a man who said he had spent his childhood among characters such as I had portrayed. Poor man. He said since he had seen them in print they burdened his conscience less.

I would be much obliged if you would send me and charge to me five copies of *A Good Man*. My mother again. She wants to send them to sick friends.

## To "A."

21 August 55

I am really much obliged to you for sending me this book of Algren's to read, as it is something I ought to be familiar with. I have read almost 200 pages so far. I don't think he is a good writer. This may be a hasty judgment and I suspect the book as a whole has an impact, but I have the impression page by page of a talent wasted by sentimentalism and a certain over-indulgence in the writing. In any fiction where the omniscient narrator uses the same language as the characters, there is a loss of tension and a lowering of tone. This is something that it has taken me a long time to learn myself; Mrs. Tate is my mentor in matters of this kind and she has drummed it into me on every occasion so I am very conscious of it.

It may be that a writer can sentimentalize certain segments of the population and get away with it, but he cannot sentimentalize the poor and get away with it. I don't have much to compare Nelson Algren with in this country as I have never read J. T. Farrell or Steinbeck or any of the people who deal with the afflicted (economically afflicted, that is). I have read Céline though (*Journey to the End of the Night*) and there is no comparison. Nelson Algren doesn't look like a serious writer beside Céline. It may be that no American can write about the poor the way a European can.

It may also be that poverty in this country is not a matter of physical want anyway, except in certain particular areas. In any case, when you write about the poor, you have to be writing about yourself first, everybody else second, and the actual poor third. The particular appeal of the poor for the fiction writer is existential not economic, but a great deal of the writing about them since and during the '30s seems to consist in numbering their lice (not that I think Algren particularly guilty of that). I have been reading an essay of Wyndham Lewis's (Percy, not D. B.) on George Orwell. It seems Orwell felt he had to force himself to get used to the poor physically; he was repulsed by the way the lower classes smelled. Lewis says that the Orwells had only one servant whereas he, Lewis, came up in a family with a cook, two chambermaids and a nurse, and "being exposed to four stinkers instead of one," felt no necessity of making a special effort to get used to their odor.

All of which is a little beside the point of Algren. I think my particular objection is as a writer—that this is sloppy writing. I write that way myself all the time, and tear it up. I hope.

### To Sally and Robert Fitzgerald

August 25 [1955]

I take it you all have survived the summer, which I am thankful for it is almost over. Midseason the W.'s [farm help] up and left us—which puts me in the Minor Prophet's League. They finally, we presume, got so jealous of the G.'s [new help] that they couldn't stand it any more. Now my mamma has only the G.'s and two negroes but she is going strong.

I am taking the newest wonder drug, Meticorten, so for the first time in four years don't have to give myself shots or conserve on salt. I feel very fine about that.

The collection they tell me is in the third printing. Most of the reviews still regard me as the Sour Sage of Sugar Creek but I am minding my own bidnis down on the farm and in my spare time I multiply various numbers by .35 and entertain myself thataway.*

---

* At twelve, Flannery had made the following entry in her journal, and put to herself the following question: "I do not see much use of A's B's & D's in Ari. I can add and sub. and mul. and know the tables up to twelve. What good'll it do me?" As it turned out, she could figure out her royalties.

*To "A."*

I wish St. Thomas were handy to consult about the fascist business. Of course this word doesn't really exist uncapitalized, so in making it that way you have the advantage of using a word with a private meaning and a public odor; which you must not do. But if it does mean a doubt of the efficacy of love and if this is to be observed in my fiction, then it has to be explained or partly explained by what happens to conviction (I believe love to be efficacious in the loooong run) when it is translated into fiction designed for a public with a predisposition to believe the opposite. This along with the limitations of the writer could account for the negative appearance. But find another word than fascist, for me and St. Thomas too. And totalitarian won't do either. Both St. Thomas and St. John of the Cross, dissimilar as they were, were entirely united by the same belief. The more I read St. Thomas the more flexible he appears to me. Incidentally, St. John would have been able to sit down with the prostitute and said, "Daughter, let us consider this," but St. Thomas doubtless knew his own nature and knew that he had to get rid of her with a poker or she would overcome him. I am not only for St. Thomas here but am in accord with his use of the poker. I call this being tolerantly realistic, not being a fascist.

Another reason for the negative appearance: if you live today you breathe in nihilism. In or out of the Church, it's the gas you breathe. If I hadn't had the Church to fight it with or to tell me the necessity of fighting it, I would be the stinkingest logical positivist you ever saw right now. With such a current to write against, the result almost has to be negative. It does well just to be.

Then another thing, what one has as a born Catholic is something given and accepted before it is experienced. I am only slowly coming to experience things that I have all along accepted. I suppose the fullest writing comes from what has been accepted and experienced both and that I have just not got that far yet all the time. Conviction without experience makes for harshness.

The magazine that had the piece on Simone Weil is called *The Third Hour* and is put out spasmodically (when she can get the money) by a Russian lady named Helene Iswolsky who teaches at Fordham. I used to go with her nephew so I heard considerable about it and ordered some back issues. The old lady is a Catholic of the Eastern Rite persuasion and sort of a one-man Catholic ecumenical movement. The enclosed of Edith Stein came out of there too. I've never read anything E. Stein wrote. None of it that

I know of has been translated. There is a new biography by Hilda Graef but I have not seen it. My interest in both of them comes only from what they have done, which overshadows anything they may have written. But I would very much like you to lend me the books of Simone Weil's when you get through with them . . .

Mrs. Tate is Caroline Gordon Tate, the wife of Allen Tate. She writes fiction as good as anybody, though I have not read much of it myself. They, with John Crowe Ransom and R. P. Warren, were prominent in the '20s in that group at Vanderbilt that called itself the Fugitives. The Fugitives are now here there and yonder. Anyway Mrs. Tate has taught me a lot about writing.

Which brings me to the embarrassing subject of what I have not read and been influenced by. I hope nobody ever asks me in public. If so I intend to look dark and mutter, "Henry James Henry James"—which will be the veriest lie, but no matter. I have not been influenced by the best people. The only good things I read when I was a child were the Greek and Roman myths which I got out of a set of child's encyclopedia called *The Book of Knowledge*. The rest of what I read was Slop with a capital S. The Slop period was followed by the Edgar Allan Poe period which lasted for years and consisted chiefly in a volume called *The Humerous Tales of E.A.Poe*. These were mighty humerous—one about a young man who was too vain to wear his glasses and consequently married his grandmother by accident; another about a fine figure of a man who in his room removed wooden arms, wooden legs, hair piece, artificial teeth, voice box, etc. etc.; another about the inmates of a lunatic asylum who take over the establishment and run it to suit themselves. This is an influence I would rather not think about. I went to a progressive high school where one did not read if one did not wish to; I did not wish to (except the *Humerous Tales* etc.). In college I read works of social-science, so-called. The only thing that kept me from being a social-scientist was the grace of God and the fact that I couldn't remember the stuff but a few days after reading it.

I didn't really start to read until I went to Graduate School and then I began to read and write at the same time. When I went to Iowa I had never heard of Faulkner, Kafka, Joyce, much less read them. Then I began to read everything at once, so much so that I didn't have time I suppose to be influenced by any one writer. I read all the Catholic novelists, Mauriac, Bernanos, Bloy, Greene, Waugh; I read all the nuts like Djuna Barnes and Dorothy Richardson and Va. Woolf (unfair to the dear lady of course); I read the best Southern writers like Faulkner and the Tates, K. A. Porter, Eudora Welty and Peter Taylor; read the Russians, not

Tolstoy so much but Dostoevsky, Turgenev, Chekhov and Gogol. I became a great admirer of Conrad and have read almost all his fiction. I have totally skipped such people as Dreiser, Anderson (except for a few stories) and Thomas Wolfe. I have learned something from Hawthorne, Flaubert, Balzac and something from Kafka, though I have never been able to finish one of his novels. I've read almost all of Henry James—from a sense of High Duty and because when I read James I feel something is happening to me, in slow motion but happening nevertheless. I admire Dr. Johnson's *Lives of the Poets*. But always the largest thing that looms up is *The Humerous Tales of Edgar Allan Poe*. I am sure he wrote them all while drunk too.

I have more to say about the figure of Christ as merely human but this has gone on long enough and I will save it. Have you read Romano Guardini? . . . In my opinion there is nothing like [his book, *The Lord*] anywhere, certainly not in this country. I can lend it to you if you would like to see it.

6 September 55

I looked in my Webster's and see it is 1948, so you are five years ahead of me in your vocabulary and I'll have to concede you the word. But I can't concede that I'm a fascist. The thought is probably more repugnant to me than to you, as I see it as an offense against the body of Christ. I am wondering why you convict me of believing in the use of force? It must be because you connect the Church with a belief in the use of force; but the Church is a mystical body which cannot, does not, believe in the use of force (in the sense of forcing conscience, denying the rights of conscience, etc.). I know all her hair-raising history, of course, but principle must be separated from policy. Policy and politics generally go contrary to principle. I in principle do not believe in the use of force, but I might well find myself using it, in which case I would have to convict myself of sin. I believe and the Church teaches that God is as present in the idiot boy as in the genius.

Of course I do not connect the Church exclusively with the Patriarchal Ideal. The death of such would not be the death of the Church, which is only now a seed and a Divine one. The things that you think she will be added to, will be added to her. In the end we visualize the same thing but I see it as happening through Christ and His Church.

But I can never agree with you that the Incarnation, or any truth, has to satisfy emotionally to be right (and I would not agree that for the natural man the Incarnation does not satisfy emotionally). It does not satisfy emotionally for the person brought up under many forms of false intellectual discipline such as 19th-century mechanism, for instance. Leaving the Incarnation aside, the very notion of God's existence is not emotionally satisfactory anymore for great numbers of people, which does not mean that God ceases to exist. M. Sartre finds God emotionally unsatisfactory in the extreme, as do most of my friends of less stature than he. The truth does not change according to our ability to stomach it emotionally. A higher paradox confounds emotion as well as reason and there are long periods in the lives of all of us, and of the saints, when the truth as revealed by faith is hideous, emotionally disturbing, downright repulsive. Witness the dark night of the soul in individual saints. Right now the whole world seems to be going through a dark night of the soul.

There is a question whether faith can or is supposed to be emotionally satisfying. I must say that the thought of everyone lolling about in an emotionally satisfying faith is repugnant to me. I believe that we are ultimately directed Godward but that this journey is often impeded by emotion. I don't think you are a jellyfish. But I suspect you of being a Romantic. Which is not such an opprobrious thing as being a fascist. I do hope you will reconsider and relieve me of the burden of being a fascist. The only force I believe in is prayer, and it is a force I apply with more doggedness than attention.

To see Christ as God and man is probably no more difficult today than it has always been, even if today there seem to be more reasons to doubt. For you it may be a matter of not being able to accept what you call a suspension of the laws of the flesh and the physical, but for my part I think that when I know what the laws of the flesh and the physical really are, then I will know what God is. We know them as we see them, not as God sees them. For me it is the virgin birth, the Incarnation, the resurrection which are the true laws of the flesh and the physical. Death, decay, destruction are the suspension of these laws. I am always astonished at the emphasis the Church puts on the body. It is not the soul she says that will rise but the body, glorified. I have always thought that purity was the most mysterious of the virtues, but it occurs to me that it would never have entered the human consciousness to conceive of purity if we were not to look forward to a resurrection of the body, which will be flesh and spirit united in peace, in the way they were in Christ. The resurrection of Christ seems the high point in the law of nature . . .

You are right about "A Stroke of Good Fortune." In fact I didn't want it in the collection but was prevailed upon by my editor. It is much too farcical to support anything. Actually it was intended as a part of *Wise Blood* but I had the good sense to take it out of there. I suppose "The Artificial Nigger" is my favorite. I have often had the experience of finding myself not as adequate to the situation as I thought I would be, but there turned out to be a great deal more to that story than just that. And there is nothing that screams out the tragedy of the South like what my uncle calls "nigger statuary." And then there's Peter's denial. They all got together in that one.

You are also right about this negativity being in large degree personal. My disposition is a combination of Nelson's and Hulga's. Or perhaps I only flatter myself.


## To Robie Macauley

11 September 55

Thanks so much for sending *AGMIHTF* to the people connected with *Encounter*. I know what *Encounter* is but I have never seen it as it don't penetrate to the backwoods—nor nothing much else either. My agent says she is offering the book to French publishers but no French publishers are offering to buy it. The latest report from Harcourt is that it has now sold 4,000 copies, which doesn't get me ready for retirement just yet, but is certainly better than anybody expected. I wish I could write one in a year. I have been at this for ages and I am just like a squirrel on a treadmill; I remain in chapter 2.

I am real glad you are getting up a collection of stories as I think those stories of yours set in Germany and Japan are hard to beat. I wonder at how you can pick up the feeling of foreign places like that as I cannot put down any idiom but my own. I presume there are some advantages to not being a Southerner.

Which reminds me that I am going to your country for a visit next spring—to Lansing, to talk, if you please, to a convention of the AAUW. Fancy me in this role. The lady called me up and asked me if I would talk on "The Significance of the Short Story." I don't have the foggiest notion what the significance of the short story is but I accepted at once as I like to make trips by plane, etc., and I figured I had ten months to find out . . . I think I'll tell them something very grand, such as that the short story restores the contemplative mentality, but I don't know exactly how I'll work it up. Maybe I'll write Dr. Crane and ask him what is the significance of the short story. He tackles *any* subject.

I am sorry the enclosed columns don't have his picture on

them but some days the sun doesn't come out. Anyway, these will answer your questions about education and if you weren't entirely successful as a teacher, well dear boy here's why and you had better face it. I would advise you to read it twice and send off for the booklet, "Test for a Good Teacher." Lately the doctor has been concerning himself with what to tell your child when he asks where he came from. I won't even repeat his advice as it is much too naturalistic for me. He says they'll ask the first question and then it'll be several years before they ask the second. I don't doubt it a bit. I always thought he was just a doctor of divinity but he is talking now about "we medics," so I presume he is both.

Best to you and Anne. If Doctor Crane comes up with anything that could make life more worth living, I'll send it special delivery.

## To "A."

15 September 55

I didn't mean to suggest that science is unreliable, but only that we can't judge God by the limits of our knowledge of natural things. This is a fundamental difference in your belief and mine: I see God as all perfect, all complete, all powerful. God is Love and I would not believe Love efficacious if I believed there were negative stages or imperfections in it.

Also I don't think as you seem to suppose that to be a true Christian you believe that mutual interdependence is a conceit. This is far from Catholic doctrine; in fact it strikes me as highly Protestant, a sort of justification by faith. God became not only a man, but Man. This is the mystery of the Redemption and our salvation is worked out on earth according as we love one another, see Christ in one another, etc., by works. This is one reason I am chary of using the word, love, loosely. I prefer to use it in its practical forms, such as prayer, almsgiving, visiting the sick and burying the dead and so forth.

I don't think LaCroix is reconciled to atheists as "useful lost." He makes no judgment about the "lost," but leaves that to the providence of God. I read recently somewhere about a priest up for canonization. It was reported in the findings about him that he had said of a man on the scaffold who had been blasphemous up to the last that this man would surely go to hell; on the basis of this remark he was denied canonization.

I guess by emotion you mean something like our deepest

psychological needs. I have recently been reading some depth psychologists, mainly Jung, Neumann, and a Dominican, Victor White (*God and the Unconscious*). All this throws light momentarily on some of the dark places in my brain but only momentarily. I have also read a book which is fairly elementary I suppose but certainly profound in spots, by Karl Stern, called *The Third Revolution*. His remarks on the subject of guilt are very interesting and parallel yours to some extent—an interesting contrast of the Greek idea of guilt (the Furies) and the Christian.

About the fascist business: don't consider calling me that out of order as I would rather know what you are thinking than not, and it is proper to let me defend myself against such if it can occur to you. Your writing me forces me to clarify what I think on various subjects or at least to think on various subjects and is all to my good and to my pleasure.

About the vacuum my writing seems to create as to (I suppose) a love of people—I won't say the poor, because I don't like to distinguish them. Everybody, as far as I am concerned, is The Poor. Anyway, it occurs to me to put forward that fiction writing is not an exercise in charity, except of course as one is expected to give the devil his due—something I have at least been scrupulous about. I suppose it is true, however, that one's personal affection for people or lack of it carries over and colors the work. Henry James (actually) could write better about vulgar people than any writer I can think of, and this I take it was because there was very little vulgarity in him and he must have hated it thoroughly. James said the morality of a work of fiction depended on the *felt life* that was in it; and St. Thomas said that art didn't require rectitude of the appetite. When you start thinking of a phrase like *felt life*, you can get beyond your depth in a minute. But St. Thomas's remark is plain enough: you don't have to be good to write well. Much to be thankful for . . .

When I call myself a Catholic with a modern consciousness I don't mean what might be implied in the phrase "modern Catholic," which doesn't make sense. If you're a Catholic you believe what the Church teaches and the climate makes no difference. What I mean is that I am conscious in a general way of the world's present historical position, which according to Jung is unhistorical. I am afraid I got this concept from his book, *Modern Man in Search of a Soul*—and am applying it in a different way.

*Andrew Lytle is a novelist and critic, and was a longtime editor of* The Sewanee Review. *He taught Flannery at Iowa.*

## To Andrew Lytle

15 September 55

This is to ask you if I may use your name as a reference on the application for a Guggenheim fellowship that I am making this fall. I am still working on my novel and as I haven't been made rich or even self-supporting yet by the collection of stories, I am going to apply for this fellowship.

I want to thank you for the letter you sent Harcourt, Brace last spring. What you said in it is what I see in the stories myself but what nobody who reviews them cares to see. To my way of thinking, the only thing that keeps me from being a regional writer is being a Catholic and the only thing that keeps me from being a Catholic writer (in the narrow sense) is being a Southerner; but the religious element is largely ignored and I was glad to have it pointed out. They have incorporated part of your letter in some of their ads.

The first chapter of my novel is going to appear this fall in *New World Writing* and I asked Mrs. [Arabel] Porter to send you a copy of it. It goes mighty slow.

## To "A."

24 September 55

I am learning to walk on crutches and I feel like a large stiff anthropoid ape who has no cause to be thinking of St. Thomas or Aristotle; however, you are making me more of a Thomist than I ever was before and an Aristotelian where I never was before. I am one, of course, who believes that man is created in the image and likeness of God. I believe that all creation is good but that what has free choice is more completely God's image than what does not have it; also I define humility differently from you. Msgr. Guardini can explain that. I think it is good to have these differences defined. I really don't think *folly* is a wise word to use in connection with these orthodox beliefs or that you should call Aristotle "foolish and self-idolizing." At least, not until you have coped with all the intricacies of his thought. These things may look tortuous to you because they take in more psychological and metaphysical realities than you are accounting for. Of course, I couldn't say about that, but in any case I don't think it's good critical language. However, my crutches are my complete obsession right now. I have never used such before and I am to be on them for a year or two. They change the whole tempo of everything. I no longer am going to cross the room without making a major decision to do it.

I hope I have not left you with the impression that I tote any flags for Céline. All I can say for him is that from what I have read (*Journey to the End of the Night*) I find him superior as a writer to N. Algren. I can't take Algren seriously in spite of his good intentions whereas I can take the other seriously in spite of his bad ones. He is, I think, a REAL Fascist. I believe he was even tried as a collaborator of the Germans, though I may be wrong here. Mauriac recently made the statement that *Bonjour Tristesse* was written by the devil, so I read it. Well it was a very stupid remark for Mauriac to make because the devil writes better than Mademoiselle Saigon [Sagan]. Your comments on how much of oneself one reveals in the work are a little too sweeping for me. Now I understand that something of oneself gets through and often something that one is not conscious of. Also to have sympathy for any character, you have to put a good deal of yourself in him. But to say that any complete denudation of the writer occurs in the successful work is, according to me, a romantic exaggeration. A great part of the art of it is precisely in seeing that this does not happen. Maritain says that to produce a work of art requires the "constant attention of the purified mind," and the business of the purified mind in this case is to see that those elements of the personality that don't bear on the subject at hand are excluded. Stories don't lie when left to themselves. Everything has to be subordinated to a whole which is not you. Any story I reveal myself completely in will be a bad story.

I am reading the Weil books now, having finished the *Letters to a Priest* and got onto the other one and I am very much obliged to you and will keep these books until you want them. I am struck by the coincidence (?) of title of *Waiting for God*, and *Waiting for Godot*—have you read that play, by an Irishman naméd Beckett? The life of this remarkable woman still intrigues me while much of what she writes, naturally, is ridiculous to me. Her life is almost a perfect blending of the Comic and the Terrible, which two things may be opposite sides of the same coin. In my own experience, everything funny I have written is more terrible than it is funny, or only funny because it is terrible, or only terrible because it is funny. Well Simone Weil's life is the most comical life I have ever read about and the most truly tragic and terrible. If I were to live long enough and develop as an artist to the proper extent, I would like to write a comic novel about a woman—and what is more comic and terrible than the angular intellectual proud woman approaching God inch by inch with ground teeth?

I must be off on my two aluminum legs.

30 September 55

I can't imagine either who would think the Lord would need defending on the score of romanticizing sin. It seems more or less like a crutch Guardini is using to get to the next thought on; or possibly he has come across some such notion in the German youth he instructs. Such is possible. Somewhere lately I read about some child who asked his mother why he should take Jesus' word for anything and she replied, "Because He was a gentleman." This was announced with much approval by the columnist. I wish I could remember where I saw it. I should have cut it out. It might have been Billy Graham or Dr. Crane but I wouldn't accuse them as I'm not sure. Do you read Dr. Crane? I never miss him. He is an odd mixture of fundamentalism (against the grape), psychology, business administration and Dale Carnegie. The originator of The Compliment Club. He appears in the *Atlanta Constitution* on the same page as the comic strips.

By saying Simone Weil's life was both comic and terrible, I am not trying to reduce it, but mean to be paying her the highest tribute I can, short of calling her a saint, which I don't believe she was. Possibly I have a higher opinion of the comic and terrible than you do. To my way of thinking it includes her great courage and to call her anything less would be to see her as merely ordinary. She was certainly not ordinary. Of course, I can only say, as you point out, this is what I see, not, this is what she is—which only God knows. But I didn't mean that my heroine would be a hypothetical Miss Weil. My heroine already is, and is Hulga. Miss Weil's existence only parallels what I have in mind, and it strikes me especially hard because I had it in mind before I knew as much as I do now about Simone Weil. Hulga in this case would be a projection of myself into this kind of tragic-comic action—presumably only a projection, because if I could not stop short of it myself, I could not write it. Stop short or go beyond it, I should say. You have to be able to dominate the existence that you characterize. That is why I write about people who are more or less primitive. I couldn't dominate a Miss Weil because she is more intelligent and better than I am but I can project a Hulga. However, writing this wouldn't be a thing I would see as a duty. I write what I can and accept what I write after I have given it all I can. This is loose language and doesn't say what I am after saying exactly, but you might piece it out.

I have forgotten Guardini's definition of Romanticism. There are so many definitions of it that I suppose it is a meaningless word to use unless you throw in another definition of your own. I think it was only suggested to me to think you Romantic by ideas you express that would perhaps more properly be seen as pantheistic or something of that sort. As to jellyfish, I read in a filler the other day that there were jellyfish so diaphanous that you could be next to them in the water and you wouldn't know they were there. This does not seem to fit you and it is all I know about jellyfish. If you are going to read 1500 pages of St. Thomas and 650 pages of Aristotle, you will at least be an ossified jellyfish when you get through —if such is possible. I am currently reading Etienne Gilson's *History of Christian Philosophy in the Middle Ages* and I am surprised to come across various answers to Simone Weil's questions to Fr. Perrin. St. Justin Martyr anticipated her in the 2nd century on the question of the Logos enlightening every man who comes into the world. This is really one of her central questions and St. Justin answered it in what I am sure would have been her own way. Gilson is a vigorous writer, more so than Maritain; the other thing I have read of his is *The Unity of Philosophical Experience*, which I am an admirer of.

My being on the crutches is not an accident or the energy-depriving ailment either but something that has been coming on in the top of the leg bone, a softening of it on acct. of a failure of circulation to the hip. They say if I keep the weight off it entirely for a year or two, it may harden up again; otherwise in my old age I will be charging people from my wheelchair or have to have a steel plate put on it. Anyway, it is not as great an inconvenience for me as it would be for somebody else, as I am not the sporty type. I don't run around or play games. My greatest exertion and pleasure these last years has been throwing the garbage to the chickens and I can still do this, though I am in danger of going with it.

You are very good to offer to get me books from the Atlanta library and if there is something I especially need and can't get here, I will not hesitate to ask you. The enclosed article is about a woman I have never heard of before [Elizabeth Sewell]. I wrote the place in New York where I buy books and asked them if they could get her books for me but that was a month ago and they haven't even answered the letter. I don't think there is the remotest chance any of them would be in the Atlanta library but if you would ask the next time you have time there, I would be very glad to know. I am going to write to Fordham and try to get the back issues of *Thought* that have the Graham Greene thing and *The Death of the Imagination*. She sounds interesting to me. I think she contends that in spite of Greene's Catholic convictions, he writes from the standpoint of "neo-Romantic decadence." This much I got from a review of my own stories, a review by a priest who said that while my convictions might be Catholic, my sensibility appeared to be Lutheran. This after I announce to you in grand terms that I write the way I do because I am a Catholic. Anyhow, I do not agree with the reverend Father but no matter. I just read another review from a Kansas City paper that ended with the sentence: "These stories are technically excellent; spiritually empty."

My friend in Atlanta who is so fond of B.R. wrote me that she was sending me his book. What she wants is an opinion and it will have to be a pleasant one for the sake of her feelings, so I am glad to hear that it is not so bad. I would like to be able to write him too and say I like it, so I hope I will. Few poets have any business to write novels.

[P.S.] I have an interesting article on St. Thomas and Freud—if you think you could stand it.


## To Sally and Robert Fitzgerald

30 September 55

This would be a fine time for me to come to Italy if it were not for the fact that I have just been put on crutches. It requires some decision for me at this point to cross the room, much less the ocean. This has nothing to do with the lupus, which is fine and all but controlled with the Meticorten. This is something NEW. Or at least it has been coming on and has only just got here. A softening of the top of the leg bone due to a failure of the circulation to the hip.* They say if I take the weight off the hip for a year or two, I may be able to save it, otherwise a wheelchair or an operation where they put in a steel cap or something. So I am swinging around on two aluminum legs . . . I am real awkward and there is always a crash going on behind me, but I am learning. I hope by next spring I will be able to make it to Michigan but I am not

---

*I got this <u>straight</u>, having seen the X rays and spoken with the scientist <u>before</u> the parental conference with him.

so enthusiastic about the thought of that anymore. You had better set your praying children on the subject of my leg bone. I will be much obliged. Crutches make a big difference in the tempo you live at. Mine always was slow, but now!

*Wise Blood* came out in England this summer and I have seen three reviews, all respectful but not very perceptive.

Mama sends hers. Regards to children.


## To "A."

12 October 55

About the Weil books—you finish them first as I haven't even got through *Waiting for God*. It certainly don't remind me of *Waiting for Godot* but I think the second title may have been used on acct. of the first.

I do like the articles back though I don't have any file. I live in a rat's nest of old papers, clippings, torn manuscripts, ancient quarterlies, etc. etc. etc. I can tell more or less by instinct or smell at what level in the impedimenta some article is. I tunnel about in this mess like a mole making his way underground.*

The item with the book chapter should have arrived long since but I am afraid I didn't wrap it up very good; if it never comes let me know. I'll start off those [Elizabeth] Sewell books in good time since it takes so long and will send them as you say. I'll also send Nelson—Algren, not Head. I have almost finished *The Structure of Poetry*, which is interesting in part though anything the least mathematicalish sends me running for cover; but don't send the book on Valéry as there is enough Valéry in this one. As for the novel, it's not Mrs. Woolfesh but it is impossible. They will probably send me the other two books from New York sooner or later as they move in a very lackadaisical fashion. This place is the Cross Currents Bookstore and I buy books there because they give me a 20% discount, which is quite a lot, and you don't have to pay the tax. What I should have done is to have ordered the books from England. English books are much cheaper even with the postage. I get lists from Peter Russell, an English 2nd hand place and I will pass them on to you if you would be interested. I am like the little boy who just liked to *feel* candy; I like to read booklists.

I had not heard that a textbook of Dr. Crane's is being used

---

* *The twelve-year-old Flannery had also taken her stand on this point, with another entry in her journal: "I do not see why a person wants a room if they can't keep all my litter in it."*

at the U. of Ga. It is later than I think. His current obsession is a *scientific* dating bureau, but go to the source for information on this. You will not regret it.

I'll read the article on Freud and St. T. over and assure myself that it won't give you apoplexy before I send it. Of course, it's a comfort to me that Guess Who comes out on top but it would give you less satisfaction. As to Sigmund, I am against him tooth and toenail but I am crafty: never deny, seldom confirm, always distinguish. Within his limitations I am ready to admit certain uses for him.

I, crutches and all, am going to Nashville this weekend where I hope to hear Russell Kirk lecture at Vanderbilt. He wrote a book called *The Conservative Mind,* which I admire, and one called *Academic Freedom* that I haven't read.

It occurs to me to ask you if I may stop calling you Miss A. and if you will stop calling me Miss O'Connor. It makes me give myself airs hearing myself called Miss. I have a mental picture of you as a lady 7 ft. tall, weighing 95 lbs. Miss A. fits this image better than [your first name] but I think I can still make the shift without disabusing myself of the vision. You can let me know after you meditate on it.

20 October 55

I go from bad to worse in your imagination—first a fascist and now Cupid. I can defend myself on the first score but the Lord only knows what line I'm to take against this other. I'd rather be the Minotaur or the Gorgon or that three-headed dog at the river Styx, or ANYBODY. Just reconsider. The enclosed should help you. I don't want it back. I am the one on the left; the one on the right is the Muse. This is a copy of a self-portrait I painted three years ago. Nobody admires my painting much but me. Of course this is not exactly the way I look but it's the way I feel. It's better looked at from a distance.

I have adjusted my image of you to five three, one thirty. This was less trouble than I thought as I also am five three and in the neighborhood of one thirty. It is a neighborhood I would like to get out of as I have to pick it up on my two wrists now. Anyway, I now distinguish you with thick hornrimmed spectacles, a Roman nose, and ash-blonde hair.

The reason your packages go quicker than mine is that they look more respectable; consequently I got me some Scotch tape and some of those stickers and the two books I returned today do not look like that Mentor package, as if mailed by one of the great unwashed. I used the same paper you used. Now if you send me another book, just reverse this paper and use your old sticker already licked and addressed and when I return it I will reverse it again and use mine. I envision this going on for several years, same paper, same stickers, at a saving to us both of 15 or 20¢ over the annual period. Frugality is next to cleanliness which is next to Godliness. The next time you are at the library will you see if they have Percy Wyndham Lewis' novel, *Tarr*? I can't get it here and W/L is much worth my study.

I have put Nelson Algren on the respected shelf of Books Given, Not Paid For, where it looks excellent. Many thanks.

What translation of the Theban cycle are you reading? *A Good Man* is dedicated to Robert Fitzgerald (and his wife) who translated the plays with Dudley Fitts. I think their translation is the best going from the standpoint of poetry. I have it in a paperback Harcourt book that I'll send you if you don't have it. I lived with the Fitzgeralds for several years in Connecticut.

I am glad you read the stories aloud as I like to do it myself and I think most of them gain in the reading. I do it every time I go to Nashville or anytime anybody asks me, which is not often. Usually it works very well; however, the funnier the story, the straighter the face it should be read with and I am the kind who laughs heartily at my own jokes. This weekend I read the first story in the book and disgraced myself in this fashion.

There is a story in the Mentor thing called "We're All Guests," by George Clay. I don't know him but he has written me some letters about my stuff, the first one being about "Good Country People" which he thought very successful. I asked him to read the rest and recently he has written me about that. He said *WB* bored and exasperated him because H. Motes was not human enough to sustain his interest and he thought "A Good Man," "A Temple of the Holy Ghost" and "A Circle in the Fire" were substantially marred by the "religious reference that didn't fit in." About *WB* I think he is in a sense correct but of course he doesn't know what he's talking about about the others. However, his interesting comment was that the best of my work sounded like the Old Testament would sound if it were being written today—in as much (partly) as the character's relation is directly with God rather than with other people. He points out, correctly, that it is hard to sustain the reader's interest in a character like that unless he is very human. I am trying to make this new novel more human, less farcical. A great strain for me.

I didn't hear Russell Kirk lecture as that turned out to be on Mon. instead of Sat. as I had thought; however, he and I were visiting the same people for the weekend so I saw a plenty of him. He is about 37, looks like Humpty Dumpty (intact) with constant cigar and (outside) porkpie hat. He is non-conversational and so am I, and the times we were left alone together our attempts to make talk were like the efforts of two midgits to cut down a California redwood. However, at one point we burst forth into the following spurt of successful uncharitable conversation:

ME: I read old William Heard Kilpatrick died recently. John Dewey's dead too, isn't he?

KIRK: Yes, thank God. Gone to his reward. Ha ha.

ME: I hope there're children crawling all over him.

KIRK: Yes, I hope he's with the unbaptized enfants.

ME: No, they would be too innocent.

KIRK: Yes. Ha ha. With the baptized enfants.

ME: Yes.

Curtain

He is starting a bi-monthly magazine to be called *The Conservative Review* which will be out in two weeks. It should be very good.

The business of the broken sleep is interesting but the business of sleep generally is interesting. I once did without it almost all the time for several weeks. I had high fever and was taking cortisone in big doses, which prevents your sleeping. I was starving to go to sleep. Since then I have come to think of sleep as metaphorically connected with the mother of God. Hopkins said she was the air we breathe, but I have come to realize her most in the gift of going to sleep. Life without her would be equivalent to me to life without sleep and as she contained Christ for a time, she seems to contain our life in sleep for a time so that we are able to wake up in peace.

On the purely spiritual side, I refer you to *Atl. Const.* Tues. Oct 18, pp 18, Dr. Crane: who recommends that pastors get their congregations to contribute tangible gifts to the Church like water coolers, kitchen stoves, typewriters, folding steel chairs, because Jesus stated (sic): "Where your treasure is, there will your heart be also."

Hi yo silver.

## To Robert Giroux

21 October 55

I applied for a Guggenheim this year and put your name down as a reference like you said I could but I thought I had better let you know lest it come as a shock to you when they ask if I am worthy.

*Wise Blood* finally came out in England and has gotten good reviews. It is printed in offset and looks as if it will come apart in the hand, but has such a jacket as would stop the blindest Englishman in the thickest fog. I think Neville Spearman will do the stories next and not wait on the novel as I have given him to understand it will be a long wait . . .


## To "A."

30 October 55

I think Mlle. Weil was a far piece from the Church too but considering where she started from, the distance she came toward it seems remarkable. And jackass is your word. She was obviously no pantheist. I accept that a saint is a soul in heaven but then I am a strong believer in Purgatory. I already have a berth there reserved for myself. Have you ever read St. Catherine of Genoa's *Treatese* (not the way to spell *Treatiss, eze, aeze*????) on Purgatory? I got interested in St. Catherine of Genoa when I saw her picture—a most beautiful woman. I have the T. with her picture in it if you'd like to see it.

The enclosed is more of my articles. These two are re the question of false mysticism. There's only one answer to that, which I'll refrain from forcing on you. It can be found in St. Teresa, St. John of the Cross, St. Catherine of Siena or whomever you will. Should I say it, it would smack of the too apt. I have recently been reading one of Mr. [Frank] Sheed's collection called *Born Catholics* (which the too apt makes me think of). This was forced on me by the nun from whom I took piano lessons (I despise the piano and all its works and pomps but this is a way of supporting the good Sisters who teach the bad children). Anyway I found it more interesting than I had thought as there are many and diverse degrees of experience in it (some very dull) and I think more should be written about conversion within the Church. It is a more difficult subject than conversion without.

I am only too glad to swap all my images of you for the ginger beer bottle with the head of Socrates. Being dammed by a faint prettiness turned a mite sour, I wish I looked like that but as I don't I'm at least glad I can write somebody who does. I first sent *Harper's Bazaar* my self portrait and can you imagine, they said: This is not exactly what we want, a little stiff, couldn't you send us a snapshot? I also sent it to Harcourt, Brace to use on the jacket of my book. They said: This is a little odd, we don't think it would increase the sale of the stories, etc.

I take it you are propelled by great energy if you stay up reading until 1. All my mental lights are out by 9.

A study should be made of Dr. Crane's face. (The lower-class form, "puss," might be more adequate here.) He lately reported that C-students who make a practice of delivering *sincere* compliments will be found, over a ten-year period, to earn more money in their professions than A-students who preserve a close-mouthed and sour demeanor. Blessed are the smilers; their teeth shall show.

*John Lynch was a young writer and teacher at Notre Dame who had reviewed Flannery's* A Good Man Is Hard to Find.

## To John Lynch

6 November 55

I am extremely obliged to you for sending me the copy of the review and very much surprised and pleased that a Catholic magazine would want it and would get somebody intelligent to do it. The silence of the Catholic critic is so often preferable to his attention. I always look in the Catholic magazines my mother reads, to see if my book has been reviewed, and when I find it hasn't, I say an act of thanksgiving. This should not be the case but it is, and for me, the ironical part of my silent reception by Catholics is the fact that I write the way I do because and only because I am a Catholic. I feel that if I were not a Catholic, I would have no reason to write, no reason to see, no reason ever to feel horrified or even to enjoy anything. I am a born Catholic, went to Catholic schools in my early years, and have never left or wanted to leave the Church. I have never had the sense that being a Catholic is a limit to the freedom of the writer, but just the reverse. Mrs. Tate told me that after she became a Catholic, she felt she could use her eyes and accept what she saw for the first time, she didn't have to make a new universe for each book but could take the one she found. I feel myself that being a Catholic has saved me a couple of thousand years in learning to write. I don't want to bother you but I would like to know if this has been your experience, since you write fiction. I have never talked to another Catholic writer of fiction, except converts, and the experience there is different. They have been formed by other things, I have been formed by the Church, and perhaps you have also.

I am wondering too if you teach writing at Notre Dame and if they go about it there any differently from what they do at Stanford or Iowa—if they go on about "reflecting Christian values," etc. I am not very sure that I think the business of the Catholic writer is to reflect anything but what he sees the most of; but the subject of what is and what isn't a Catholic novel is one I give a wide berth to. Ultimately, you write what you *can*, what God gives you.

I have not read any of your fiction but I am familiar with your name from, I presume, the *Commonweal*, which I read. However, I'll get the 1947 O. Henry and read your story in there. My first story was published along about that time (*Accent*, 1946) but was not very good.

Thank you again for the review and your special kindness in sending it to me.

## To "A."

10 November 55
. . . I have looked at the Messenier [Meissonier]. It's nothing I would like to form a hasty judgment about. I think that if I saw it framed and in a place proper to it, after considerable time I might grow to have some feeling for it; but I don't know enough about art to appreciate the purely formal qualities. I think I approve of distortion but not of abstraction. There is at least enough I can recognize in this that I would be willing to stand around and let it have its way with me. Actually I know nothing about it. I am in the unenviable state where the plastic arts are concerned of knowing what is bad but not knowing what is good. What do you think of it? I am always prepared for a violent opinion from you. It must have struck you forcibly one way or the other.

About Clay—I don't agree with you that he has no talent. I just think that is all he has. He can create a believable character and set him about his business with some grace; but there it ends. "We're All Guests" wasn't related to anything larger than itself. He has written me that he believes that the highest thing the writer can do is to explain the reasonable man to himself. He then explained that the reasonable man was a legal concept (he studied law a year)—juries try to decide if the reasonable man would act thus and so, etc. He went on to admit that H. Motes might ultimately be found to be more reasonable than the legal reasonable man, but nevertheless . . . his reasonable man is the legal one.

Mine is certainly something else—God's reasonable man, the prototype of whom must be Abraham, willing to sacrifice his son and thereby show that he is in the image of God Who sacrifices His Son. All H. Motes had to sacrifice was his sight but then (you are right) he was a mystic and he did it. The failure of the novel seems to be that he is not believable enough as a human being to make his blinding himself believable for the reasons that he did it. For the things that I want them to do, my characters apparently will have to seem twice as human as humans. Well, it's a problem not solved by the will; if I am able to do anything about it, it will simply be something given. I never understand how writers can succumb to vanity—what you work the hardest on is usually the worst. Tell me what you mean by a limitation of categories. What's categories? This is too abstract to do me any good. Do you mean feeling or experience or some social range or what? There is an interesting review of the stories in the fall *Kenyon Review* that if you ever see, I would like to know what you think of.

About Dante—the Church leaves the judgment of art and artists up to the individual. Of course if the work is a danger to faith or morals it may be put on the Index but this is not a judgment of its artistic value or of the character of the artist, e.g., Gide may have produced works of art and may now be resting in peace but his works are on the Index as a warning to the Catholic that they are dangerous. For my money Dante is about as great as you can get.

About yclept Pseudo-Dionysius—he was Somebody who wrote between 475 and 525 and ascribed his works to Dionysius the Areopagite who was a friend of St. Paul's. He addressed certain letters on mysticism to Timothy, St. Paul's fellow-worker. He was probably, according to Evelyn Underhill (from the back of whose book this learning comes) a Syrian monk and he wrote treatises on the Angelic Hierarchies and on the Names of God which were very influential for medieval mysticism. You would enjoy this book, *Mysticism,* by Evelyn Underhill, a paperbound Meridian book. I read it last spring is how come I know all this. It's a mine of information. I would like to read Baron von Hügel's book, *The Mystical Element in Religion.* Do you reckon the Atlanta PL would have that?

I have decided I must be a pretty pathetic sight with these crutches. I was in Atlanta the other day in Davison's. An old lady got on the elevator behind me and as soon as I turned around she fixed me with a moist gleaming eye and said in a loud voice, "Bless you, darling!" I felt exactly like the Misfit and I gave her a weakly lethal look, whereupon greatly encouraged, she grabbed my arm and whispered (very loud) in my ear. "Remember what they said to John at the gate, darling!" It was not my floor but I got off and I suppose the old lady was astounded at how quick I could get away on crutches. I have a one-legged friend and I asked her what they said to John at the gate. She said she reckoned they said, "The lame shall enter first." This may be because the lame will be able to knock everybody else aside with their crutches.

25 November 55

You are in many ways an uncanny girl and very right about the lacking category, which reminds me that Chekhov said "he-and-she is the machine that makes fiction work," or something near that. Of course I think it is too exclusive a view. You are right that this is the category lacking but wrong that I don't associate it with the virtuous emotions. I associate it a good deal beyond the simply virtuous emotions; I identify it plainly with the sacred. My inability to handle it so far in fiction may be purely personal, as my upbringing has smacked a little of Jansenism even if my convictions do not. But there is also the fact that it being for me the center of life and most holy, I should keep my hands off it until I feel that what I can do with it will be right, which is to say, given. Purity strikes me as the most mysterious of the virtues and the more I think about it the less I know about it. "A Temple of the Holy Ghost" all revolves around what is purity. The enclosed is a correspondence I had on the subject with a Boston lady, whose wrath I managed to turn away. I doubt if the same would work with my California friend. As to Brother E., he probably don't admit that this kind of virtue exists so he couldn't be expected to make much out of that story. I never have anything balanced in my mind when I set out; if I did I'd resign this profession from boredom and operate a hatchery.

I suppose what you work hardest on is what you know least, but listen, I never had a moment's thought over Enoch but I struggled over Haze. Everything Enoch said and did was as plain to me as my hand. I was five years writing that book, and up to the last I was sure it was a failure and didn't work. When it was finished I came down with my energy-depriving ailment and began to take cortisone in large doses and cortisone makes you think night and day until I suppose the mind dies of exhaustion if you are not rescued. I was, but during this time I was more or less living my life and H. Mote's too and as my disease affected the joints, I conceived the notion that I would eventually become paralyzed and was going blind and that in the book I had spelled out my own course, or that in the illness I had spelled out the book. Well, God rescues us from ourselves if we want Him to.

The displaced person did accomplish a kind of redemption in that he destroyed the place, which was evil, and set Mrs. McIntyre on the road to a new kind of suffering, not Purgatory as St. Catherine would conceive it (realization) but Purgatory at least as a beginning of suffering. None of this was adequately shown and to make the story complete it would have had to be—so I did fail myself. Understatement was not enough. However, there is certainly no reason why the effects of redemption must be plain to us and I think they usually are not. This is where we share Christ's agony when he was about to die and cried out, "My God, why have You forsaken Me?" I needed some instrument to get this across that I didn't have. As to the peacock, he was there because peacocks might be found properly on such a place but you can't have a peacock anywhere without having a map of the universe. The priest sees the peacock as standing for the Transfiguration, for which it is certainly a most beautiful symbol. It also stands in medieval symbology for the Church—the eyes are the eyes of the Church. All this would be lost to Mr. E. and I suppose all priests are addled to him because they are priests—those who aren't addled will be sinister. Anyway, he was not addled and nothing survived but him and the peacock and Mrs. McIntyre suffering. Isn't her position, entirely helpless to herself, very like that of the souls in Purgatory? I missed making this clear but how are you going to make such things clear to people who don't believe in God, much less in Purgatory?

The scholar known to you as Benjamin is one Ben C. Griffith who until last year taught at Bessie Tift . . . He now teaches at Mercer but anyhow two years ago, finding *Wise Blood* in the drugstore, he read and favored it and wrote me a very intelligent letter about it and after that kept up with my stories. Last spring he came over to see me as he proposed to write a piece for the *Ga. Review* about my stuff. I think the *Ga. Review* gave to understand they weren't terribly interested in a piece about my stuff. They took one from him on James Jones, his other critical interest! I have not read James Jones so I'm not judging myself by the company I keep. But Mr. Griffith is a nice man anyway, with a slight stutter. I have never met anybody with a stutter who was not nice. He remarked that in these stories there was usually a strong kind of sex potential that was always turned aside and that this gave the stories some of their tension—as for instance in "A Circle in the Fire" where there is a strong possibility that the child in the woods with the boys may be attacked—but the attack takes another form. I really hadn't thought of it until he pointed it out but I believe it is a very perceptive comment.

I am sending you along the issue of *Thought* with the Sewell piece on Graham Greene in it. I admire her but all through the piece, my sympathy goes out to Mr. Greene, or his carcus, which has to suffer this lady-like vulture dining off him. What I feel I suppose is that she is right without much effort but that he is the one sweating to bring something to birth. A much better piece is the one following by Fr. Lynch, one of the most learned priests in this country I think. I haven't read Greene lately enough to know what I think of him. I don't know whether pity is the beginning of love or the corruption of it, or whether it is harder to love something perfect or something feeble.

I read *Kristin Lavransdatter* long years ago and remember being much gripped with that love and that writing, although in those days I wasn't thinking of it as writing. Do you think she could have done it without returning to the 13th century?

I'll pass up the biographies of the Baron von Hügel. I intend to order off after his *Letters to a Niece* which has recently been put out by Regnery. The other books came—don't feel you have to hurry with these things. A man wrote me yesterday, never heard of him, and said he had enjoyed *Wise Blood* more than any book to come out of the South since Newman's *HBV*. Well I racked my brain as to who Newman was and I finally remembered Frances Newman, an Atlanta woman, who wrote in the '20s. I had read one story of hers but she did write a novel called *The Hard Boiled Virgin* I find, which now I must read. I am going to see if they have it in the GSCW library—the title may keep it out of there, but if they don't have it, I will ask you to get it for me at the Atlanta Public Library.

## To Catharine Carver

2 December 55

Thanks for the manuscript which I had forgotten existed and also for sending the book to the hospital gratis. They sent me a thank-you note which you properly deserve but which I won't inflict on you.

Elizabeth writes me she has sold [the French rights of] *Wise Blood* to Gallimard.

I have just got through talking to one of our honorable regional (with a vengence) bodies . . . After my talk, one lady shook
my hand and said, "That was such a nice dispensation you gave
us, honey." Another said, "What's wrong with your leg, sugar?"
I'll be real glad when I get too old for them to *sugar* me.

## To Elizabeth McKee

5 December 55

I have just heard from Catharine Carver that she is leaving
Harcourt, Brace. Now what?

This seems to be my time either to leave or to stay. If I stay
with them, I want the contract made over to read that I will stay
only so long as Denver Lindley is my editor. If he goes, then so far
as I am concerned there won't be anybody there that I want to
work with.

If I leave what do I do? Just give them back their $500 or
what?

Will you please talk to Giroux about it because I wouldn't
leave Harcourt, Brace unless he was willing to take me on.

This is all considerably upsetting, and I will be glad to hear
from you about it soon . . .

## To "A."

8 December 55

. . . Charity is hard to come by and I value you more for your
charity than your perception. Nevertheless, you are mighty perceptive. But on the matter of the possible attack on the child in
"A Circle in the Fire," I think you are off because you assume I
think that would be an act of passion, that the boys, if they
attacked her, would do it because there was an attraction. No.
There couldn't be any attraction or any dependence. They would
do it because they would be sharp enough to know that it would
be their best revenge on Mrs. Cope; they would do it to humiliate
the child and the mother, not to enjoy themselves. And children,
particularly in numbers, are quite capable of using themselves in
this way, of committing the most monstrous crimes out of the urge
to destroy and humiliate. They might well have done this if they
had seen the child behind the tree. I didn't let them see the child
behind the tree. I couldn't have gone through that myself.

It has always seemed necessary to me to throw the weight of

circumstance against the character I favor. The friends of God suffer, etc. The priest is right, therefore he can carry the burden of a certain social stupidity. This may be something I learned from Graham Greene . . . or it may just be instinct. Anyhow, it seems to me proper.

I have read two of the [Shirley] Grau stories—one about a small colored boy who steals a coat off a dead man and the other about the colored convict who goes home and his children throw bottles at him. They didn't seem to me to have any moral focus, which made them tedious, but I daresay there is considerable talent there and that she is too young yet to make any judgment about. The ugly truth is that of young people writing fiction now, besides myself, I don't like any of it but Peter Taylor's (*A Long Fourth*), some of J. F. Powers' (*Prince of Darkness* and one that will be out soon called *The Presence of Grace*), some, mostly early, of Eudora Welty's. Mr. Truman Capote makes me plumb sick, as does Mr. Tenn. Williams. Of foreigners living I like Frank O'Connor. I keep waiting for some club lady to ask me if I am kin to Frank O'Connor. At which I hope to reply, "I am his mother." So far no opportunity.

Your friend was generous in the report about my talk, but the truth is these clubs seldom have anybody to talk to them who thinks they are worth being serious with. Everybody tells them how to write and sell, which is what they think they want to know, but they are always grateful to hear something else, or so they always appear to be to me. I always come away with a lot of faces without names and a lot of names without faces and it is very frustrating . . .

About the woman who is the Realist: this is a complicated subject but the only light I have to throw on it is that poetry is always dependent on realism, that you have to be a realist or you can't be a poet. Mrs. Hopewell is a realist but not a poet, whereas Hulga has tried to be a poet without being a realist. Where the poet and the realist are truly combined you have St. Catherine of Genoa maybe. I do not think of the realist anyhow as the ogre . . .

What I was thinking about Undset was that she did write a couple of novels set in the 20th century that were not so successful as the others. I take this on what I have vaguely read. I haven't read the novels so I don't really know.

## To Robert Giroux

9 December 55

Thank you so much for sending the very generous recommendation to the Guggenheim Foundation. I'll be hoping it does some good.

You have probably heard or will hear shortly that Catharine Carver is leaving Harcourt, Brace as of the 15th of December. She wrote me about it last week and said she didn't know what she would do next. Of course I don't know what to do at this point. I have written Elizabeth McKee and she says to wait until she returns from England the middle of next month, that the clause in my contract about Catharine being my editor doesn't say I have to do anything right away. I have not heard from Harcourt, Brace.

I like Denver Lindley but he is the only one there now that I know anything about; I mean anything about good . . .

## To Sally and Robert Fitzgerald

12 December 55

The manuscript [a year's work on *The Odyssey*] came Saturday and I sat myself down and read it all then and thar and besides being proud to read it I am proud to own it. If I am ever faced with the Little Sisters of the Poor, I intend to sell it to the Library of Congress for a large sum and go instead to Sarasota, Florida and live the high life. I think it's a knockout though I naturally don't know why. Throughout the seven books only one word irritated me and I will give you the benefit of my semantic considerations on this point: Tulemacusses' *nervy* speech to the suitors. This may be merely rural Georgia usage but in my neck of the woods, *nervy* has other connotations besides "requiring nerve." It means in Georgia that it requires nerve because it ain't justified, whereas in the case of Tulemacus, the speech required nerve but was justified. But I don't know what it means in the dictionary. In any case I am real pleased to have it and also the stamps, which I cut off. Those Italian stamps are beautiful, particularly after you've spent your life looking at George Washington's pan on the 3¢ envelopes.

Have you all seen the Cheneys? I certainly wish I could have come with them, but my battling around on crutches is going to be limited to the continental United States. I've been asked to go to the University of Washington for a week as a visiting writer but I will have to wait on that too . . .

*Wise Blood* has been sold to Gallimard. The French think Erskine Caldwell is the nuts so maybe they'll like me, provided the translation is bad enough.

My mamma is roaring as usual and sends you her best for Christmas. I have sixteen peachickens so my sense of well-being is at its height. Let us hear from you and all the best of the season to you and all regards to children . . .

## To Denver Lindley

16 December 55

I was much distressed to hear from Catharine that she has left and I think the loss is Harcourt, Brace's.

I'll be very glad indeed to accept you for my editor; the only question in my mind, after having two such respected ones depart from under within the year, is how long you will be my editor. My sense of the stability of editorial positions at Harcourt, Brace is not being increased with time.

With this in mind, I wrote Elizabeth McKee and asked her what to do and she has written me that the terms of the contract don't call for any immediate action on my part, and that I should wait until she returns from England around the middle of January at which time she will see about it. In any case, I'll want your name substituted for Catharine Carver's in the clause I had put in the present contract, for it is only your presence there that inclines me to stay. For the time being, I presume the decision can ride.

I'm glad Miss Lillian Smith [a Georgia writer] liked the speech. It was no more than plain language from truthful James but nobody in these parts is accustomed to that so it at least takes them by surprise. You didn't miss anything.

## To "A."

16 December 55

The subject of the moral basis of fiction is one of the most complicated and I don't doubt that I contradict myself on it, for I have no foolproof aesthetic theory. However, I think we are talking about different things or mean different things here by moral basis. I continue to think that art doesn't require rectitude of the appetite but this is not to say that it does not have (fiction anyway) a moral basis. I identify this with James' *felt life* and not with any particular moral system and I believe that the fiction writer's moral sense must coincide with his dramatic sense. I don't like Nelson Algren because his moral sense sticks out, is not one with his dramatic sense. With the Grau stories, I can't discover that life is felt at a moral depth at all. As I remember Céline, I felt that he did feel life at a moral depth—or rather that his work made me feel life at a moral depth; what he feels I can't care about. Focus is a bad word anyway.

When I said that the devil was a better writer than Mlle. Saigon [Sagan], I meant to indicate that the devil's moral sense coincides at all points with his dramatic sense.

As I understand it, the Church teaches that our resurrected bodies will be intact as to personality, that is, intact with all the contradictions beautiful to you, except the contradiction of sin; sin is the contradiction, the interference, of a greater good by a lesser good. I look for all variety in that unity but not for a choice: for when all you see will be God, all you will want will be God.

About it's being cowardly to accept only the nun's embrace: remember that when the nun hugged the child, the crucifix on her belt was mashed into the side of the child's face, so that one accepted embrace was marked with the ultimate all-inclusive symbol of love, and that when the child saw the sun again, it was a red ball, like an elevated Host drenched in blood and it left a line like a red clay road in the sky. Now here the martyrdom that she had thought about in a childish way (which turned into a happy sleeping with the lions) is shown in the final way that it has to be for us all—an acceptance of the Crucifixtion, Christ's and our own. As near as I get to saying what purity is in this story ["A Temple of the Holy Ghost"] is saying that it is an acceptance of what God wills for us, an acceptance of our individual circumstances. Now to accept renunciation, when those are your circumstances, is not cowardly but of course I am reading you short here too. I understand that you don't mean that renunciation is cowardly. What you do mean, I don't in so many words know. Understand though, that, like the child, I believe the Host is actually the body and blood of Christ, not a symbol. If the story grows for you it is because of the mystery of the Eucharist in it.

I was once, five or six years ago, taken by some friends to have dinner with Mary McCarthy and her husband, Mr. Broadwater. (She just wrote that book, *A Charmed Life*.) She departed the Church at the age of 15 and is a Big Intellectual. We went at eight and at one, I hadn't opened my mouth once, there being nothing for me in such company to say. The people who took me were Robert Lowell and his now wife, Elizabeth Hardwick. Having me there was like having a dog present who had been trained to say a few words but overcome with inadequacy had forgotten them. Well, toward morning the conversation turned on the Eucharist, which I, being the Catholic, was obviously supposed to defend. Mrs. Broadwater said when she was a child and received the Host, she thought of it as the Holy Ghost, He being the "most portable" person of the Trinity; now she thought of it as a symbol and implied that it was a pretty good one. I then said, in a very shaky voice, "Well, if it's a symbol, to hell with it." That was all the defense I was capable of but I realize now that this is all I will ever be able to say about it, outside of a story, except that it is the center of existence for me; all the rest of life is expendable.

Why didn't the lady say I identified myself with St. Thomas? I was recommending to these innocents self-knowledge as the way to overcome regionalism—to know oneself is to know one's region, it is also to know the world, and it is also, paradoxically, a form of exile from that world, to know oneself is above all to know what one lacks, etc. etc. etc. I then went on to say that St. Catherine of Siena had called self-knowledge a "cell," and that she, an unlettered woman, had remained in it literally for three years and had emerged to change the politics of Italy. The first product of self-knowledge was humility, I said, and added that this was not a virtue conspicuous in the Southern character. Well, betwixt us two, I do not identify myself with St. Catherine. What's furthermore, I never quoted St. Augustine. Anyway, I'm real pleased to have impressed with my attire. Nothing shocks like conventionality and this will remind me when attending the fire sales where I buy my clothes not to get anything the Duchesser Windsor wouldn't eat with the Duke in.

Tuesday I attended another one of these things [a literary gathering]. There are always one or two that I would like to see again although I never can remember the names or am not given them. I reported on the characteristics of the short story and afterwards they asked questions, such as, "What do you think of the frame-within-a-frame short story?" They know all the "frames." Most of them live in a world God never made. There is one of them who attends all these things who reminds you of Stone Mountain on the move. She's a large grey mass, near-sighted, pious, and talks about "messages" all the time. I haven't got her name yet but she is going to pursue me in dreams I feel.

If the fact that I am a "celebrity" makes you feel silly, what dear girl do you think it makes me feel? It's a comic distinction shared with Roy Rogers's horse and Miss Watermelon of 1955. In a great many ways it makes things difficult, for the only friends you can have are old friends or new ones who are willing to ignore it. I am very thankful that you are willing to ignore it.

1 January 56

The enclosed says where my thought heads on the subject of all things working toward becoming a woman—a phrase I am made suspicious of naturally, when you go on to mention the artistic sterility "that woman is." I guess you mean "can be." Also what I call a moral basis is a good deal more than a masculine drive—it is, in part, the accurate naming of the things of God (in fiction and poetry, that is). Remember that I am not a pantheist and do not think of the creation as God, but as made and sustained by God.

I don't assume that renunciation goes with submission, or even that renunciation is good in itself. Always you renounce a lesser good for a greater; the opposite is what sin is. And along this line, I think the phrase "naive purity" is a contradiction in terms. I don't think purity is mere innocence; I don't think babies and idiots possess it. I take it to be something that comes either with experience or with Grace so that it can never be naive. On the matter of purity we can never judge ourselves, much less anybody else. Anyone who thinks he's pure is surely not.

I sent you the other Sewell piece and the one on St. Thomas & Freud. This latter has the answer in it to what you call my struggle to submit, which is not struggle to submit but a struggle to accept and with passion. I mean, possibly, with joy. Picture me with my ground teeth stalking joy—fully armed too as it's a highly dangerous quest. The other day I ran up on a wonderful quotation: "The dragon is at the side of the road watching those who pass. Take care lest he devour you! You are going to the Father of souls, but it is necessary to pass by the dragon." That is Cyril of Jerusalem instructing catechumens.

There is a new Sewell thing in the latest *Thought* on Chesterton but I haven't read it. Would you be interested in reading Guardini's monograph on the Grand Inquisitor section of *The Brothers Karamazov*? The librarian never came through with the HBV [*Hard Boiled Virgin*]; she must have disapproved of it too strongly. I'd like to see it if the time on it isn't up but if so I can do without it all right. I am interested in seeing something called

*The Bridge*, edited by John M. Oesterreicher. This hasn't been out long so they may not have it. It has a piece in it on Simone Weil that was criticized in the *Commonweal* recently and one on the Finaly case and one on the growth of human conscience by Raïssa Maritain that I would like to see.

My novel is at an impasse. In fact it has been at one for as long as I can remember. Before Christmas I couldn't stand it any longer so I began a short story. It's like escaping from the penitentiary. It may well be that I'll have another book of stories before I have a novel. I work from such a basis of poverty that everything I do is a miracle to me. However, don't think I write for purgation. I write because I write well.

As for the crutches, I am used to them and I might as well be as I think I will be on them for considerable time. He didn't look for any improvement under a year and then he said, what's a year or two or three off your life? Truly not much, as I was inactive anyway. I get around about as much as I ever did.

I got two beautiful things for Christmas. Robert Fitzgerald sent me a manuscript copy of the first seven books of the *Odyssey* which he is translating (for an Anchor book) and somebody sent me a poinsetta (sp) without any name on it. I never got anything before without any name on it and I was much touched with it. . . .

My current problem is: are Northern ladies more intelligent than Southern ladies? I have to write this talk for the AAUW in Michigan and I see it is going to drive me nuts. The subject is supposed to be "Some Aspects of Modern Fiction." It revolts me to think of it.

## To Elizabeth McKee

8 January 56

After thinking it over, I have decided that any change now would be unnecessary and upsetting to me, so if you would just see about having my Harcourt contract fixed so that Denver Lindley's name is substituted for Catharine Carver's, I will be much obliged.

I hope you had a good trip. My best for the new year.

12 January 56

Enclosed is the contract. Much ado I guess about nothing, as in all probability I will have a book of stories ready before I finish this novel. You will be getting a story from me I think in the next month or so.

I think Neville Spearman ought to pay me that other 60 before I sign any contract for the stories?

I am fine and get about on crutches now as if I had been born on them.


## To "A."

The two Weils and the *HBV* and the magazines all received and with thanks. I haven't started these two Weil ones but I have read fifty or so pages in the *HBV*—dear Lord, it's all reported; the most undramatic fifty pages I have been exposed to since *Marius the Epicurean*. She must have been a very intelligent miserable woman—but no fiction writer. After a while the eye merely glides over all that cleverness, there's nothing to stop it (the eye not the cleverness).

I enclose the Guardini and another section of a report from Iowa that I just got. It will make you even gladder that you didn't get a degree. I can see [two participants in the writer's workshop] chained together by mutual hate on one of the less important circles of the inferno, eternally arguing if church steeples are phallic symbols. My days there were not like this boy's I must say. I did pretty much nothing, which seems to be a better thing to do than he's doing.

I suppose when I say that the moral basis of Poetry is the accurate naming of the things of God, I mean about the same thing that Conrad meant when he said that his aim as an artist was to render the highest possible justice to the visible universe. For me the visible universe is a reflection of the invisible universe. Somewhere St. Augustine says that the things of the world poured forth from God in a double way: intellectually into the minds of the angels and physically into the world of things. (I am sure that an angelic world is no part of your belief but of course it is very much a part of mine.) Since you believe that the world itself is God, that all is God, this can hardly meet with your sympathy. No more than [Father Walter] Ong. About him, let me say that his position would be the same if Freud had never been alive and that it is certainly no part of his concern whether one sex is superior to another. He's off on an entirely different track, and whether the male or female is the superior sex ain't going to ruffle his orthodoxy any; or mine. You may be right that a man is an incomplete woman. It don't change anybody's external destination however, or the observable facts of the sex's uses (a nice phrase). Anyway, we can be thankful we aren't between the crossfire of [the pair in Iowa] . . . She [one of the contestants] fascinates me, though.

The Church it should be said is no less a Gospel reader than the separated brethren. Beginning in the 16th century it was less emphasized for obvious reasons—anyhow an acquaintance with the liturgy is enough to show it without the commentaries of the Church Fathers. While Christ sometimes seemed impatient of his mother, he performed his first miracle at her request, and on the cross he gave her to John and John to her.

To get back to the accurate naming of the things of God, I am wondering if what worries you about that, what may seem THE contradiction for me to say such a thing is the fact that I write about good men being hard to find. The only way I can explain that is by repeating that I think evil is the defective use of good. Perhaps you do too . . .

I am very happy right now writing a story ["Greenleaf"] in which I plan for the heroine, aged 63, to be gored by a bull. I am not convinced yet that this is purgation or whether I identify myself with her or the bull. In any case, it is going to take some doing to do it and it may be the risk that is making me happy.


*To Denver Lindley*

15 January 56

I have read Caroline's novel [*The Malefactors*] with all my usual admiration for everything she writes. I look at it from the underside, thinking how difficult all this was to do because I know nothing harder than making good people believable. It would be impertinent for me to comment on the book, simply because I have too much to learn from it . . .

It would be good to be translated by Maurice Coindreau but I suppose that is up to Gallimard. I have just read an unpleasant book called *The American Novel in France*, which says that the translations are usually terrible and that the French think Erskine Caldwell is a great writer. Apparently they (the publishers) get any translator who cares to call himself one . . .

*The recipient of this letter, Rev. James McCown, S.J., became a devoted friend of Flannery's. His unexpected appearance in her life is described in her letters to the Fitzgeralds (January 22, 1956) and to "A." (February 11).*

## To Father J. H. McCown

16 January 56

Thank you for the books sent in the mail and the ones [your friend] brought. I'm returning the Michelfelder novel and several of the magazines that I have enjoyed very much, and I also enclose in that package a pocket-book copy of *Wise Blood* which I forget whether you said you had seen or not. If you have time to read sometime, I'd like to know what you think of it.

The Michelfelder book is amazing and I am very glad to have read it. It interests me particularly because it deals with loss of faith which was the underlying subject of my novel, though I didn't use a Catholic background. A Catholic has to have strong nerves to write about Catholics.

I have read almost everything that Bloy, Bernanos, and Mauriac have written. The Catholic fiction writer has very little high-powered "Catholic" fiction to influence him except that written by these three, and Greene. But at some point reading them reaches the place of diminishing returns and you get more benefit reading someone like Hemingway, where there is apparently a hunger for a Catholic completeness in life, or Joyce who can't get rid of it no matter what he does. It may be a matter of recognizing the Holy Ghost in fiction by the way He chooses to conceal himself.

I hadn't read the Eric Gill autobiography and am enjoying it . . .

## To "A."

17 January 56

I'm never prepared for anything. I felt sure you were 7 ft. tall and ash blonde and you turn out to be dark and shaped like a ginger beer bottle and I have been equally positive that you were a Pantheist in good standing with whatever they're in good standing with and now you allow you're as orthodox as I am if not more. More, I suppose, as baptism is something you choose and I had it thrust upon me. To my credit it can be said anyway that I never considered you unbaptized. There are the three kinds, of water, blood, and desire, and with the last I thought you as baptized as I am. So that may be the reason I have nothing to say about this when I ought to say something. All voluntary baptisms are a miracle to me and stop my mouth as much as if I had just seen Lazarus walk out of the tomb. I suppose it's because I know that it had to be given me before the age of reason, or I wouldn't have used any reason to find it.

In any case I can't climb down off the high powered defense reflex whateveritis. The fleas come with the dog as Mr. McG. [Ralph McGill, Atlanta newspaper editor] says. If you were Pius XII, my communications would still sound as if they came from a besieged defender of the faith. I know well enough that it is not a defense of the faith, which don't need it, but a defense of myself who does. The Church becomes a part of your ego and gets messed in with your own impurity. It's a situation I can't handle myself so I wait for purgatory to do it for me. Anyway, I know it exists.

I frequently disagree with priests who get themselves printed in various places but generally it's not with the contents but the tone. My mind is usually at ease, but my sensibilities seldom so. Smugness is the Great Catholic Sin. I find it in myself and don't dislike it any less. One reason Guardini is a relief to read is that he has nothing of it. With a few exceptions the American clergy, when it takes to the pen, brings this particular sin with it in full force. One reason I favor *Cross Currents* is the frequency of articles without the American-clerical tone. *Thought* seldom has it either . . .

It's a very pompous phrase—the accurate naming of the things of God—I'll grant you. Suitable for a Thomist with that ox-like look. But then I said it was a basis. What I suppose I mean is an aim. Anyway, I don't mean it's an accomplishment. It's only trying to see straight and it's the least you can set yourself to do, the least you can ask for. You ask God to let you see straight and write straight. I read somewhere that the more you asked God, the more impossible what you asked, the greater glory you were giving Him. This is something I don't fail to practice, although not with the right motives.

I don't want to be any angel but my relations with them have improved over a period of time. They weren't always even speakable. I went to the Sisters to school for the first 6 years or so . . . at their hands I developed something the Freudians have not named—anti-angel aggression, call it. From 8 to 12 years it was my habit to seclude myself in a locked room every so often and with a fierce (and evil) face, whirl around in a circle with my fists knotted, socking the angel. This was the guardian angel with which the Sisters assured us we were all equipped. He never left you. My dislike of him was poisonous. I'm sure I even kicked at him and landed on the floor. You couldn't hurt an angel but I would have been happy to know I had dirtied his feathers—I conceived of him in feathers. Anyway, the Lord removed this fixation from me by His Merciful Kindness and I have not been troubled by it since. In fact I forgot that angels existed until a couple of years ago the *Catholic Worker* sent me a card on which was printed a prayer to St. Raphael. It was some time before it dawned on me Raphael was an archangel, the guide of Tobias. The prayer had some imagery in it that I took over and put in "The Displaced Person"—the business about Mrs. Shortley looking on the frontiers of her true country. The prayer asks St. Raphael to guide us to the province of joy so that we may not be ignorant of the concerns of our true country. All this led me to find out eventually what angels were, or anyway what they were not. And what they are not is a big comfort to me . . .

I have just sold *Wise Blood* to a French publisher, Gallimard. I can't feature H. Motes in French, and my own French is too sorry to be able to tell if the translation will be any good or not. Which may be a blessing . . . The bull, yes. He is the pleasantest character in this story.


## To Sally and Robert Fitzgerald

22 January 56

Enclosed is the Pound piece [R.F.'s "Gloom and Gold in Ezra Pound"]. It ought to be printed in THIS country as nothing is about Pound but such as you read by Hynes, only usually much worse. This ought to be in the *Commonweal* but they probably wouldn't print it. I don't want those pieces back. Incidentally, you like not to have seen this one again or me seen it at all as it came unsealed and the gent at the postoffice said he didn't know if it was all there or not. Anyway, I'm very glad it came because I wanted to see something unmessy written on that situation. All my erstwhile boy friends visit Pound at St. Elizabeth's and think he is made and finished—he calls them all funny names and they think its wonderful, touched by the holy hand, etc.

The business of "living in music" reminds me of a piece I am reading called "Theology and the Imagination," by yr friend, Fr. Wm. Lynch of *Thought*. It's about the manichean (sp?) vs. the anagogical or Christian imagination. Have you seen it? I have at length subscribed to *Thought* and find it very valuable.

Yours very truly is being accepted these days by the Cathlicks as being a Cathlick writer! I just got asked to talk at a Cathlick Litry Gild Book Fair in Providence, R.I. and would have done it too if it hadn't been in Providence but I can't get to Providence on crutches. Also I have been reviewed favorably in something called *Books on Trial*. *America* has not come across but the other day a white Packard drove up to our humble yard and out jumped an unknown Jesuit; he turnt out to be from a nearby metropolis and had come to express his devotion to *A Good Man Is Hard to Find*. I told him about the Sister at Minneapolis that writes such good poetry (the one Caroline knows) and he said: "Boy, I bet she's crucified". . .

The translator for Gallimard that is going to do *WB* is Maurice Coindreau, a friend of Caroline's, and I hear he's a good translator.

I have just read Caroline's novel and it's all very fine. She certainly had a hard job to do making those *CW* [*Catholic Worker*] people at all believable. The one who is Dorothy Day is a little *bodiless* and I can't decide if this was intentional or not. She keeps emphasizing that this is a large woman but the effect is different . . .

I thought you would like to see some real spiritual faces is why I enclose the Sunshine Boys. Regards to children.


## To "A."

30 January 56

I sent you off the Dialogues [of St. Catherine of Siena] last week to have something the Atl. PL didn't. That is just like a library—four biographies and not her own work which is available. I am repelled and attracted by her too. I read one biography, the one by that Dane, Jörgensen, I think. Anyway he was repelled by her at first. He came to write the biography of her after he had written one of St. Francis of Assisi and the change of personality was too drastic. She was apparently what she believed so entirely that it colored even the comical things—such as the incident of her eating the lettuce leaf after one of her long fasts and then vomiting it up with the remark, "Here comes this miserable sinner up for justice." There's no hurry for this back. I don't intend to read it again any time soon and it can't be read in a hurry—a little goes a long way.

Incidentally, I have another of Guardini's books that you may not have seen—*The Church and Modern Man*—that I'll send you if you want to see it. Him discussing such things as dogma and free will. I have a good many books that you might be interested in but I haven't put them forth because I thought they were "too Catholic" and I did not want you to think I was trying to stuff the Church down your throat. This is a peculiar thing—I have the one-fold one-Shepherd instinct as strong as any, to see somebody I know out of the Church is a grief to me, it's to want him in with great urgency. At the same time, the Church can't be put forward by anybody but God and one is apt to do great damage by trying; consequently Catholics may seem very remiss, almost lethargic, about coming forward with the Faith. (Maybe you ain't observed this reticence in me.) I try to be subtle and succeed about as well as the gents in Washington Square, nevertheless, now that you approach this of your own accord, it's all right for me to appear on the surface with such books as I wouldn't have appeared with on it before.

I doubt if your interests get less intellectual as you become more deeply involved in the Church, but what will happen is that the intellect will take its place in a larger context and will cease to be tyrannical, if it has been—and when there is nothing over the intellect it usually is tyrannical. Anyway, the mind serves best when it's anchored in the word of God. There is no danger then of becoming an intellectual without integrity . . .

My packages get neater beinst they are your packages inside out.


## To Father J. H. McCown

6 February 56

. . . I wrote Fr. Gardiner but after seeing the review of the Michelfelder book, I am afraid I expressed myself badly and that he will think I am an advocate of Michelfelder's position that you only don't have to be "in collusion with sin" in order to write a moral book. Even Milton is now thought of by some high-toned critics as being on the devil's side, so I don't know how the likes of Michelfelder and myself could safely say we weren't, even with the best intentions and the correct doctrine.

However, it does seem to me that you don't have to rely on the virtue of prudence to prevent pornography in your writing, but that you must first anyway rely on the virtue of art. Pornography and sentimentality and anything else in excess are all sins against form, and I think they ought to be approached as sins against art rather than as sins against morality. At least this is practical in these times when most writers are pagans and if you are going to talk in terms they can understand. The pious style is a great stumbling block to Catholics who want to talk to the modern world . . .

I have just read a very funny book by a priest named Fr. Robo—on St. Theresa Lisieux. It's called *Two Portraits of St. Theresa.* He has managed (by some not entirely crooked means) to get hold of a photograph of her that the Carmelites have not "touched up" which shows her to be a round-faced, determined, rather comical-looking girl. He does away with all the roses, little flowers, and other icing. The book has greatly increased my devotion to her.

My mother and I enjoyed your visit and hope you'll continue to come to see us when you're in this direction.

## To Sally and Robert Fitzgerald

2/6/56·

. . . These Jesuits work fast. Ten days after I had the visit from the one in Macon, I receive a communication from Harold C. Gardiner, S.J. asking me to contribute to *America.* Fancy me contributing to *America.*

Caroline's book was to be dedicated to Dorothy Day, but Miss Day on inspecting the page proofs declared she would burn every copy she could get her hands on if she had her way. So the dedication has been withdrawn at the request of both author and dedicatee and now, with that tree off the road, Miss D. begins to like the book better.

Blessings and cheers.

*Mrs. Rumsey Haynes, head of the Lansing, Michigan, chapter of the AAUW, had invited Flannery to speak there.*

## To Mrs. Rumsey Haynes

9 February 56

Thank you for both of your kind letters. I have always wanted to be able to keep this appointment in Lansing, but it seemed too much to ask you to meet me in Detroit at 10:30 p.m. which is the only schedule I could make going up. I'd also have to be taken back to Detroit to get a plane that leaves there at 12:35 p.m.—so that this would mean two trips to Detroit for you.

Of course if you are willing to go to all this trouble, I'll be most happy to come. I don't think my merits as a speaker can make up for the inconvenience to you, but I'd like to come anyway. But if this is too much for you, feel free to say so.

You are lovely to ask me to spend the week, and I would like to stay a day or two extra to get my breath before boarding more planes. I think the meeting is on Tuesday and that I should fly up on Monday and return Thursday or Friday.

As for the talk—I don't mind either talking or reading my own work; but it is easier to talk if you know what your audience is interested in. I don't talk about other writers' work because I don't know enough, and I am reluctant to talk about my own because I know too much, but somewhere in between there is room for some remarks on the nature of fiction. Or it may be that you would rather hear something about what the "regional" writer, so-called, has to cope with (being a Southern writer has its disadvantages). I have made a good many talks in the past year but all in the South, which is like talking to a large gathering of your aunts and cousins—I know exactly what they don't know— but talking to Northern ladies is a different thing. I can't imagine that there's anything they don't know. Maybe you could enlighten me a little on this.

I feel it is an imposition to ask you to meet me in Detroit at a disagreeable hour and then to have to take me back too, so again, if it is too much, just say so. Crutches have changed the tempo of my existence and I can no longer get anywhere without inconveniencing someone else.


## To "A."

11 February 56

What you say about there being two [sexes] now brings it home to me. I've always believed there were two but generally acted as if there were only one. I guess meditation and contemplation and all the ways of prayer boil down to keeping it firmly in sight that there are two. I've never spent much time over the bride-bridegroom analogy. For me, perhaps because it began for me in the beginning, it's been more father and child. The things you have said about my being surprised to be over twelve, etc., have struck me as being quite comically accurate. When I was twelve I made up my mind absolutely that I would not get any older. I don't remember how I meant to stop it. There was something about "teen" attached to anything that was repulsive to me. I certainly didn't approve of what I saw of people that age. I was a very ancient twelve; my views at that age would have done credit to a Civil War veteran. I am much younger now than I was at twelve or anyway, less burdened. The weight of centuries lies on children, I'm sure of it.

According to a recent communication from S., Mrs. R.'s thought for the week is: "Nobody would have paid any attention to Jesus if he hadn't been a martyr but had died at the age of eighty of athlete's foot." I told S. that [her] trouble was she was orthodox and didn't know it. S., incidentally, is a youth I have never seen. He wrote me last summer and sent a story he had written and asked me to recommend him at Iowa. The story was not good but it showed some talent so I did. He had a long history of being in institutions but now he takes one of those new drugs. Last summer he would write me twice a week letters of from 30 to 50 type-written pages—full of violence and all kinds of foolishness. He's highly anti-Catholic. I finally wrote him that I couldn't read the things and not ever to write me a letter over two pages—which is a terrible cramping of his spirit .·. . He has written a story which he is convinced is shocking and he's terribly pleased with himself.

I have put the bull aside for further thought on it. It's finished but I'm not sure it works yet. Meanwhile I occupy myself with busy-work—a talk to the Council of Teachers of English in March and this ordeal in Michigan and a book review for the *Bulletin*. This latter being my first emergence into the Catholic Press. The other week a white Cadillac drove up into the yard and out jumped an unknown priest. He turned out to be [a Jesuit], come over to tell me that he had read and liked my stories. This almost knocked me out, as no priest has ever said turkey-dog to me about liking anything I wrote. In he came and we had a lively discussion. Ten days later I had a letter from the literary editor of *America* asking me to contribute to their columns—this was the result of the other visit. The one from Macon called again a few days ago, this time in a black and white Cadillac. I asked him where he got his Cadillacs and he said they belonged to a [man] he is bringing into the Church. I sent him off with the Sewell article on Greene and with a 25¢ edition of *Wise Blood* for [the man who], as he said, was much impressed that I had a book out in a drugstore edition and said that was really where you made the money. [This man] said a book had to have a good many trashy spots for him to be able to appreciate it. I am waiting for his comment on *Wise Blood*.

[P.S.] On the subject of my guile I will preserve the ominous silence. The ominous silence is preserved best when I can't think of anything to say.

## To John Lynch

19 February 56

I was glad to hear from you and to know more about what they do—or don't do as appears to be the case—about writing at Notre Dame. I had thought they did more with it as a friend of mine, Robert Fitzgerald, went out there one summer to teach poetry for a week or two at some special writing thing. He is a poet, translator, journalist, what-have-you, and has six children. Supporting six children in Connecticut got to be something else so he put them all on a plane for Italy and now they live in Genova. He's translating the *Odyssey* for an Anchor book. He and a Fr. Gardiner of *America* were there for this summer thing. I gather that Fr. Gardiner was supposed to see that art did not intrude savagely upon doctrine; according to Robert he performed this function with some tact and an absence of unction.

I have just had the doubtful honor of reviewing *All Manner of Men* for the diocesan paper, yclept the *Bulletin*. Of course, "The Knife" was one of the few good stories in it. If you have seen the collection you know how few there were. As for fiction, the motto of the Catholic press should be: We guarantee to corrupt nothing but your taste. I also read "The Burden" in the Martha Foley collection. I thought it a better story than "The Knife" because it seemed to me more complete. But I have no critical sense. I write entirely by smell as it were and criticize the same. I did have the feeling that your stories were stories written by a poet. I think it must be easier on the nerves to publish poetry because it's not generally misunderstood as it is not generally read. Anyone who can read the telephone book thinks he can read a story or a novel.

I hope the Atlantic Press takes your stories; however, there's no money in it and little consolation except that it looks good when you have to fill out a form. Somebody will take them eventually. And a year later you will get a few letters from your friends saying they saw your book for 33¢ on a remainder table. At least this is what is always happening to me. Robert Giroux at Farrar, Straus is one of the best editors, if you start looking around for another. He was my editor at Harcourt, Brace but left them last year.

The *Ave Maria* I have never seen but can only too well imagine. Of course this vapid Catholicism can't influence you except to want to be shut of it. The Catholic influence has to come at a deeper level. I was brought up in the novena-rosary tradition too, but you have to save yourself from it someway or dry up. I was struck in *All Manner of Men* with how limited the range of experience was—all those baby stories and nun stories and young girl stories—a nice vapid-Catholic distrust of finding God in action of any range and depth. This is not the kind of Catholicism that has saved me so many years in learning to write, but then this is not Catholicism at all . . .

I once had the feeling I would dig my mother's grave with my writing too, but I later discovered this was vanity on my part. They are hardier than we think. I also had an 83-year-old cousin who was fond of me and I was convinced that my novel was going to give her a stroke and that I was going to be pursued through life by the Furies. After she had read it, I waited for a letter announcing her decline but all I got was a curt note saying, "I do not like your book." She is now 88 . . .

I do think you do better to have a large family than any number of books and I don't know if working for the *Ave Maria* is worse than teaching. I have never taught but I can imagine its being a terrible drain on your creative powers. I don't suppose there is much danger of any of your creative energy going into the *Ave Maria*. I heard about a lady who said to Wallace Stevens once, "Oh but Mr. Stevens, you can always fall back on the insurance business!" . . .

## To Father J. H. McCown

20 February 56

. . . It's a shame to send you a book I don't want to keep myself but, as my mother points out, plenty of people like what I don't. In any case this is a collection of stories taken from the Catholic press; they are therefore guaranteed to corrupt nothing but your taste. I enclose my review.

I have heard of [your friend] but never read anything of hers. I take it she is, or was, a Macon lady. I never mind writing any-body. In fact it is about my only way of visiting with people as I don't get around much and people seldom come to see us in the country. I hope you will come and bring Fr. Edwards. I am almost always here in the morning unless we go to Atlanta for the day.

Next Monday we are going to Savannah for the day but that is the only trip scheduled for a while.

I enclose a letter which I think will interest you and which I'd like back. It is from the man who reviewed my book in *Today* [John Lynch]. I had thought he taught at Notre Dame and I wrote and asked him what they did there in the way of teaching writing. A sad answer . . .

I had a nice letter from Fr. Gardiner, giving me five or six names of reviewers who would be interested in Caroline Gordon's book. He said my ideas for a critical piece were very interesting and he hoped I would come up with one before too long. However, there is a good deal more that I must come up with right now.

My mother went cow-buying a couple of years ago and asked an old man for directions how to get to a certain man's house. He told her to go thus and so and that she couldn't miss it because it was the only house in town with an artificial nigger. I was so intrigued with that that I made up my mind to use it. It's not only a wonderful phrase but it's a terrible symbol of what the South has done to itself. I think it's one of the best stories I've written, and this because there is a good deal more in it than I understand myself . . .

## To "A."

25 February 56

What I reviewed for the *Bulletin* was something called *All Manner of Men*—25 short stories taken from the Catholic press. It is Lent and we are advised to practice mortification. This can be fitted nicely into Catholic Press week, a point I should press in a pious article maybe. Anyway, I shall send you a copy of this worthy review when it appears, for if you have survived an illustrated catechism, the *Bulletin* should be as nothing to you. The *Bulletin*'s book page contains such information as: "Reviewed by M.R., age 13." A protection to the unwary reader. I resisted the impulse to put under mine, age 30 . . .

S. hadn't read my works when he sent me his but when he did read *Wise Blood*, he sent me a detailed criticism running to I don't know how many pages, the gist of which was that this kind of work was not to his liking. He thought one or two things acceptable about it but for the most part it was not the sort of thing he favored. He wished to argue each point so I told him I never discussed my work. I think Iowa has been a big help to him, to judge by the tone of the letters.

You are probably right about its being the parents—or their world—that creates the weight. The Church makes a difference but it can't kill the age. I think my elders absorbed the physical goods of the age without absorbing its meaning. I don't think mine have ever been in a world they couldn't cope with because none of them that I know of have left the 19th century. It's very complicated though. I was too self-righteous myself to resolve to be an enormity in my own right. I only resolved to be an enormity to them, but right now, right then. I never allowed myself to picture me as an adult.

When Tarwater goes to the city, he goes of course to the uncle who is, in principle and practice, the Atheist of Protestant descent. And I am having great trouble with him because I have not yet created a human being out of him but only an Atheist of Protestant descent; perhaps because he wasn't somebody I grew up with, I am having such a hard time. I know plenty of them but I found them all after I was grown. Well back to it I go.

The story with the bull also has the sun in a very prominent place in it, but I think the reason I use such is just because it is obvious. I am not one of the subtle sensitive writers like Eudora Welty. I see only what is outside and what sticks out a mile, such things as the sun that nobody has to uncover or be bright to see. When I first started to write, I was much worried over not being subtle but it don't worry me any more.

The yammer in Michigan is going to last 30 minutes only, by the clock so help me, that is if I live through writing it. My outlook is going to be increasingly dark until April 24. Never am I going to commit myself like this again. Expect nothing but incoherency from me until May . . .


*To Father J. H. McCown*

4 March 56

The enclosed letter is from one of my correspondents whom I've never seen. I helped him to get into the University of Iowa and now he favors me with letters describing his friends. He has been telling me for some time about this [lady] whose chief characteristic is that she can't stand Jesus. Thinks he was a lunatic. She is the psychoanalytical school . . . So now I get this further information about her background. It should doubtless be posted on the bulletin board at the Sisters of Mercy Mother House. What I want to know is if I am right in contradicting the Sister who told [the lady] that anybody who hadn't heard of Jesus would be dammed? So far as I understand it the Church does not teach any such thing, but then I know this is a matter with complications and I don't want to tell him what I am not absolutely sure about . . .

I don't know anybody in Augusta. I visited there once when I was four—at the convent where my cousin was Mother Superior and celebrating her something-or-other jubilee. They had ice cream for dessert in the shape of calla lilies. That was the only time I was ever tempted to join an order—I thought they ate that way every day. We hope you will get over on the 19th.

*A student sent her a letter full of questions.*

## To Shirley Abbott

7 March 56

I'll try to answer these questions as I find them in your letter.

I'm working on a novel now, the first chapter of which was published in *New World Writing* #8. The name of the chapter (not the whole novel) is "You Can't Be Any Poorer Than Dead." I couldn't tell you anything about this novel as I am not very good at talking about what I haven't completed. I hope there'll be surprises in store for me in it . . . As an undergraduate I didn't even know what fiction was but in graduate school I began to find out by reading and writing it. I think this is about the only way to find out . . .

*Mrs. Eileen Hall edited the book page of* The Bulletin, *the diocesan paper for which Flannery wrote many book reviews over a period of years.*

## To Eileen Hall

10 March 56

I'm enclosing a copy of an essay that has answered some of my questions and may answer some of yours, but I'd be much obliged if you'd send it back when you're through with it, because I don't have but this one copy.

About scandalizing the "little ones." When I first began to write I was much worried about this thing of scandalizing people, as I fancied that what I wrote was highly inflammatory. I was wrong—it wouldn't even have kept anybody awake, but anyway, thinking this was my problem, I talked to a priest about it. The first thing he said to me was, "You don't have to write for fifteen-year-old girls." Of course, the mind of a fifteen-year-old girl lurks in many a head that is seventy-five and people are every day being scandalized not only by what is scandalous of its nature but by what is not. If a novelist wrote a book about Abraham passing his wife Sarah off as his sister—which he did—and allowing her to be taken over by those who wanted her for their lustful purposes—which he did to save his skin—how many Catholics would not be scandalized at the behavior of Abraham? The fact is that in order not to be scandalized, one has to have a whole view of things, which not many of us have.

This is a problem that has concerned Mauriac very much and he wrote a book about it called, *God and Mammon*. His conclusion was that all the novelist could do was "purify the source"—his mind. A young man had written Mauriac a letter saying that as a result of reading one of his novels, he had almost committed suicide. It almost paralyzed Mauriac. At the same time, he was not responsible for the lack of maturity in the boy's mind and there were doubtless other souls who were profiting from his books. When you write a novel, if you have been honest about it and if your conscience is clear, then it seems to me that you have to leave the rest in God's hands. When the book leaves your hands, it belongs to God. He may use it to save a few souls or to try a few others, but I think that for the writer to worry about this is to take over God's business.

I'm not one to pit myself against St. Paul but when he said, "Let it not so much as be named among you," I presume he was talking about society and what goes on there and not about art. Art is not anything that goes on "among" people, not the art of the novel anyway. It is something that one experiences alone and for the purpose of realizing in a fresh way, through the senses, the mystery of existence. Part of the mystery of existence is sin. When we think about the Crucifixtion, we miss the point of it if we don't think about sin.

About bad taste, I don't know, because taste is a relative matter. There are some who will find almost everything in bad taste, from spitting in the street to Christ's association with Mary Magdalen. Fiction is supposed to represent life, and the fiction writer has to use as many aspects of life as are necessary to make his total picture convincing. The fiction writer doesn't state, he shows, renders. It's the nature of fiction and it can't be helped. If you're writing about the vulgar, you have to prove they're vulgar by showing them at it. The two worst sins of bad taste in fiction are pornography and sentimentality. One is too much sex and the other too much sentiment. You have to have enough of either to prove your point but no more. Of course there are some fiction writers who feel they have to retire to the bathroom or the bed with every character every time he takes himself to either place. Unless such a trip is used to further the story, I feel it is in bad taste. In the second chapter of my novel, I have such a scene but I felt it was vital to the meaning. I don't think you have to worry much about bad taste with a competent writer, because he uses everything for a reason. The reader may not always see the reason. But it's when sex or scurrility are used for their own sakes that they are in bad taste.

What offends my taste in fiction is when right is held up as wrong, or wrong as right. Fiction is the concrete expression of mystery—mystery that is lived. Catholics believe that all creation is good and that evil is the wrong use of good and that without Grace we use it wrong most of the time. It's almost impossible to write about supernatural Grace in fiction. We almost have to approach it negatively. As to natural Grace, we have to take that the way it comes—through nature. In any case, it operates surrounded by evil.

I haven't so much been asked these questions as I have asked them of myself. People don't often even have the courtesy to ask them—they merely tell you where you have failed. I don't take the questions lightly and my answers are certainly not complete, but they're the best I can do to date.

Don't feel you have to review the Gordon book if you think it would cause the *Bulletin* embarrassment or trouble. I will certainly understand. Most of your readers wouldn't like *The Malefactors* if it were favorably reviewed by Pius XII.

Have you read *Art and Scholasticism* by Jacques Maritain? This *God and Mammon* is published by Sheed & Ward. Maybe that should be reviewed in the *Bulletin!* About twenty years late, but better late than never.


*To "A."*

10 March 56

Well I am overawed to have *The Bridge* [edited by Fr. John Oesterreicher]—but this is no library book. Does that mean I can keep it so long as I please and if inspired by the Holy Ghost write in the margins? You couldn't have had a chance to look at it yourself as it appears to be formidable. I am plagued by my ignorance of the Old Testament and this is going to throw light on some more dark places. I am more than obliged to you—for many things . . .

That they harbor an ex-dancer among the Sisters at the cancer home is just another indication of the Grace that must move through that place. I have more admiration for them than any other order I know. You know it was founded by Hawthorne's daughter? My evil imagination tells me that this was God's way of rewarding Hawthorne for hating the Transcendentalists. One of my Nashville friends was telling me that Hawthorne couldn't stand Emerson or any of that crowd. When one of them came in the front door, Hawthorne went out the back. He met one of them one morning and snarled, "Good Morning Mr. G., how is your Oversoul this morning?"

The old lady that novenas don't send sounds very pleasant. Having grown up with them, I think of novenas the same way I think of the hideous Catholic churches you all too frequently find yourself in, that is, after a time I cease to see them even though I'm in them. The virtue of novenas is that they keep you at it for nine consecutive days and the human attention being what it is, this is a long time. I hate to say most of these prayers written by saints-in-an-emotional-state. You feel you are wearing somebody else's finery and I can never describe my heart as "burning" to the Lord (who knows better) without snickering.

I have just been disgusted to read the review of Caroline Gordon's book in *Time*. They could not be expected to like such a book but what seems particularly low in the review is that it implies there is not even any honesty of intention in the writing. I read the book in page proofs. I don't think it is entirely successful as she is trying to do something impossible, but I think it is a good deal better than most of what they will recommend during the year. I am a *Time* subscriber but I think it is a stupid magazine . . . This is the lady who has taught me so much about writing . . .

It is hard to make your adversaries real people unless you recognize yourself in them—in which case, if you don't watch out, they cease to be adversaries. I don't know if that was Dostoevsky's trouble or not. As for me you are mighty right I could do with some learning about souls not my own—only I wouldn't be knowing where I'm to get that from.

This pride in the tin leg* comes from an old scar. I was, in

* In a previous letter Flannery noted her astonishment that William Sessions had once danced professionally in ballet. She said that she herself had a "tin leg." This echoes an entry in her youthful journal: "Do not see why children twelve years old have to take dancein."

my early days, forced to take dancing to throw me into the company of other children and to make me graceful. Nothing I hated worse than the company of other children and I vowed I'd see them all in hell before I would make the first graceful move. The lessons went on for a number of years but I won. In a certain sense.

The enclosed ["Greenleaf"] is for you. I sent it to Mr. Ransom last week and got word today that they will use it probably in the summer issue. If you don't like it, don't fail to say so. I have a heart of pure steel.


## To Elizabeth McKee

15 March 56

I don't have any strong feelings on the matter of the young man who is interested in the stories for a film; however, I wouldn't want to tie up but a story or two at the time. I had two letters from one Jerry Wald last fall, Columbia, I believe, expressing a vague interest in my sometime writing something for a film; I don't have any interest in that.

Some friends of mine in Nashville have a plan afoot for the establishment of a Provincial Theatre. I might eventually be interested in adapting some of my things for that—myself. Therefore, I wouldn't want everything tied up.

I finished the story ["Greenleaf"] I was working on, and after some deliberation, sent it to Mr. Ransom. It is a good story and I am sure *Harper's Bazaar* would have taken it and paid twice as much as *Kenyon* but Mr. Ransom has been very good to me and I would like as long as he's there (they say he's soon going to retire) to send him a story every year. I don't want this to be unfair to you however, and if you think it proper, I'll be most glad to send you the commission. But since he's a friend I like to send them to him myself. Just let me know how you feel about it and I'll do whatever you say . . .

My mother and I were amused (startled) to read in Mr. F. W. Dupee's letter in *Perspectives* that I lived in an unlikely sounding place called Milledgeville where my mother raised hogs and I raised peacocks. My mother can't stand pigs and has never allowed one on the place—but now she is raising them it seems in French, German and Italian.

## To Shirley Abbott

Thanks so much for the copy of the feature. You write very well indeed and proceed with a great deal more sophistication than I could have mustered when I was your age.

I'd say in general that there is less fire and more pattern than you've accounted for but I certainly think it's a most creditable job. There are only two things that I would question. One I only question. The other I must contradict.

The one question: "Her message is immoralistic, in the Gidean sense." I don't know what the Gidean sense is. Gide is one of the few writers who really nauseates me so I am naturally not an authority on him. But my "message" (if you want to call it that) is a highly moral one. Now whether it's "moralistic" or not I don't know. In any case, I believe that the writer's moral sense must coincide with his dramatic sense and this means that moral judgment has to be implicit in the act of vision. Let me make no bones about it: I write from the standpoint of Christian orthodoxy. Nothing is more repulsive to me than the idea of myself setting up a little universe of my own choosing and propounding a little immoralistic message. I write with a solid belief in *all* the Christian dogmas. I find that this in no way limits my freedom as a writer and that it increases rather than decreases my vision. It is popular to believe that in order to see clearly one must believe nothing. This may work well enough if you are observing cells under a microscope. It will not work if you are writing fiction. For the fiction writer, to believe nothing is to see nothing. I don't write to bring anybody a message, as you know yourself that this is not the purpose of the novelist; but the message I find in the life I see is a moral message.

The one I have to contradict follows from the above. ". . . she merely states that it is probably impossible to know how to be one (a good man)." Not at all. It is possible to know how to be one. God became man partly in order to teach us, but it is impossible to be one without the help of grace. Naturally, every story is a unique statement—experience is the better word—and no abstract meaning can be drained off from it, but if you are going to say, "she merely states" at all, you need something that is theologically more accurate.

The truth in any such matter as this is always a great deal more stodgy-sounding than what we would like to believe. Many of my ardent admirers would be roundly shocked and disturbed if they realized that everything I believe is thoroughly moral, thoroughly Catholic, and that it is these beliefs that give my work its chief characteristics.

I like very much what you've done with the Agrarian business. I haven't seen it mentioned before in connection with my work and I think it should be.

## To Denver Lindley

18 March 56

We hope by now you have safely returned yourself to New York and also that you'll come to see us again. My mother enjoyed your visit very much and so did I. I hope you didn't have to look at too many local monuments.

You are real nice to want to buy one of my pictures and I would be glad to furnish you with a dozen for the price of three Octagon soap coupons but my mother has always declared that my pictures are not to leave her walls. I am sure if they did leave her walls they would be followed by some abominations, as our attic is full of paintings of dewdrops and sweetpeas done by my great aunts in their youth. The only way I keep these in the attic is by providing something else. Anyhow, I am glad you liked my pictures, as I feel you know something about it . . .

## To "A."

24 March 56

So the fender is not the thing that goes across the front? It was my conviction that the fender went across the front and the bumper went across the back. This still seems eminently logical to me but I am willing to take your word for it because a similar embarrassment happened to me before. In the *Kenyon Review* Mr. Shiftlet started his car by stepping on the clutch. I was afterwards told that this was against the nature of the automobile and I changed it before it got in the book. I will attend to this other on the page proofs and also change faught to fought. Mrs. Tate had to tell me once that there was no such thing as bob-wire. It is barbed wire. Isn't that silly? My mother says, "You talk just like a nigger and someday you are going to be away from home and do it and people are going to wonder WHERE YOU CAME FROM."

I thought Mrs. Greenleaf was a sympathetic character. She and the sun and the bull were connected and sympathetic. At one point Mrs. May sees the bull as the sun's shadow cast at an oblique angle moving among the cows, and of course he's a Greenleaf bull! What personal problems are worked out in stories must be unconscious. My preoccupations are technical. My preoccupation is how I am going to get this bull's horns into this woman's ribs. Of course why his horns belong in her ribs is something more fundamental but I can't say I give it much thought. Perhaps you are able to see things in these stories that I can't see because if I did see I would be too frightened to write them. I have always insisted that there is a fine grain of stupidity required in the fiction writer.

Well you should read my latest interpreter for a real chill— this is a young lady from Texas State College for Women who is entering a *Mademoiselle* contest with a feature story on my work. She is twenty-one and SUCH SOPHISTICATION—of a sort. She sent me a copy of the feature, not for my approval as she had already sent it to *Mademoiselle;* possibly for my edification. It is called "Flannery O'Connor: The Pattern in the Fire," and contains such statements as "Her message is immoralistic, in the Gidean sense." . . . I had to tell her I had no idea what the Gidean sense was so maybe that will make her feel better. Now they latch onto Gide when they are twenty-one.

The Tates were great friends of Hart Crane. Last summer I spent a weekend with Caroline in Connecticut near the place where they and Crane lived one winter. There was a lot of his stuff piled up in a corner, a pair of snowshoes and some other things. Allen has written a piece about him that is in *The Man of Letters in the Modern World*—a Meridian book worth reading—that I think is very fine. You are right about her not being timid. She lays about her right and left and has considerable erudition to back herself up with. She says my trouble is I don't have a classical education, I don't know what Sophocles' "middle diction" is. (I do now, as she has told me.) Nobody my age, says she, has an education—which is true. She is currently at the University of Kansas teaching a course in contemporary writers. She says she is going to *make* them see the difference in *Wise Blood* and the works of Truman Capote if she has to use the word "religion." According to her, the two words not allowed to be used at the U. of K. are "whiskey" and "religion." She takes great pains and is very generous with her criticism. Is highly energetic and violently enthusiastic. When I am around her, I feel like her illiterate grandmother.

I am making progress with *The Bridge*. The piece on Simone Weil is very good I think. When you get ready for it let me know and also *The Malefactors*.

I want to do something celebrative when you come into the Church, which desire brings me sharply up against the idiocy of all human gestures. You can imagine me holding some kind of figurative candle and croaking the proper responses. But what I will do is go to Communion for you and your intention Easter morning, and since we will then share the same actual food, you will know that your being where you are increases me and the other way around. I have a sentence in mind to end some story that I am going to write. The character all through it will have been hungry and, at the end, he is so hungry that "he could have eaten all the loaves and fishes, after they were multiplied."

7 April 56

After this revelation about the turtles, it's doubtful if there will ever again appear in my works anybody weighing over 92 pounds. Hereafter you better had screen your zoological information before you transmit it to me or you are liable to paralyze great areas of my creative imagination. Now I don't love these fat women and I do love Mrs. May, Mrs. Cope, Mrs. Hopewell & Bailey's mother; but old lady Greenleaf was virtuous, you'll have to admit. She prayed for the whole world . . .

I enclose only the book page of the *Bulletin*. The rest of it was devoted to descriptions of the various St. Patrick's Day parades—the kind of literature I approve of burning. The last thing Mrs. Hall sent me to review was Msgr. Guardini's book on the Rosary. I asked her please to quit putting that "author of *A Good Man Is Hard to Find*" business after my name. Holy Mother!

Enclosure from Mr. Wilyum Sessions. Such formality makes me feel very respectable. I sent him the article and a note expressing equal admiration of his *Bulletin* review.

Last week I had a letter from an unknown lady who said she had to tell me this story: a friend of hers, the widow of a Methodist minister, has a son who is working his way through college selling Bibles and contraceptives from door to door. He has found Indiana a fertile field and plans to return there next summer. The lady said she was too shocked to inquire if the same customers bought both items. I suspect they do and that the young man is studying for the ministry . . .

I've read *Swann's Way* but not other Proust. I feel this is very uncultured of me but I don't see the day when I am going to rectify it. I feel I ought to do something about this lack of a classical education so I am currently reading Cicero. I aim to read Cicero, Caesar, Tacitus and any other of them boys that I can think of. Then I will at least have a classical veneer.

Noise of expected presence in Lansing Michigan has produced

a letter to the local curate from the local curate in Lansing, inquiring if I am a practicing Catholic. On being informed that I am that, they have inquired would I speak to the Newman Club at Michigan State or let them give a tea for me. The moral of this is either (1) they have not been able to ascertain from my works what kind of a Catholic I am; or (2) they have not read my works. In any case, for this laxness on their part I am going to let them give a tea for me.

I went to Atlanta Wednesday to get another X-ray as I have been on the crutches six months now. I'm informed that it's crutches for me from now on out. Putting a cap on it won't be possible because the bone is diseased. So, so much for that. I will henceforth be a structure with flying buttresses . . .


## To J. F. Powers

19 April 56

This is a review [of *The Presence of Grace*] from the backwoods and it is very backwoodsy of me to send it to you but I would like you to know that I admire your stories better than any others I know of even in spite of the cat who, if my prayers have been attended to, has already been run down.

My best wishes to you and your family.


## To Denver Lindley

19 April 56

Thanks so much for the advice. I've written them to drop the matter of publication [of *Wise Blood*] in any Russian-occupied country. They would probably use The Misfit to represent the Typical American Business Man . . .


## To "A."

21 April 56

St. Catherine in hand. I have never got beyond page 87 in that book myself. I located the spot with difficulty. It's very interesting. All my books are spotted with Ovaltine which has put me and Little Orphan Annie to sleep these many years. I sent you *The Malefactors* and when you get through with it, keep it or leave it in a basket on somebody's doorstep. One copy is sufficient for me.

I put in the sentence about Jung because, according to C., this is the first Jungian novel—as distinguished from Freudian. I think Jung is probably just as dangerous as Freud. I see Scury T. has latched onto Freud this week. Last week I guess you observed they latched onto yer friend Walter Ong, S.J. This time I will have to be the one to disagree with Walter, S.J. This may be a better age for the Faith, but this is certainly not an age of Faith.

I agree with you that nothing in this present collection of [J. F.] Powers equals the best in the first. However, who am I to be saying that in public? These are the only reviews I have ever written and I make the discovery that they are not the place for that kind of absolute honesty. In the first place you can be so absolutely honest and so absolutely wrong at the same time that I think it is better to be a combination of cautious and polite. I prefer the good manners of an idiot to his honesty and while I am not an idiot in these matters, I have found myself mighty far wrong mighty often. Well, Mauriac says *only* fiction does not lie and I believe him.

You ask about Cal Lowell. I feel almost too much about him to be able to get to the heart of it. He is a kind of grief to me. I first knew him at Yaddo. We were both there one fall and winter. At that time he had left his first wife, Jean Stafford, and the Church. To make a long story short, I watched him that winter come back into the Church. I had nothing to do with it but of course it was a great joy to me. I was only 23 and didn't have much sense. He was terribly excited about it and got more and more excited and in about two weeks had a complete mental breakdown. That second conversion went with it, of course. He had shock treatments and all that, and when he came out, he was well for a time, married again a very nice girl named Elizabeth Hardwick, and since then has been off and on, in and out, of institutions. Now he is doing very well on one of these drugs—but the Church is out of it, though I don't believe he has been able to convince himself that he doesn't believe. What I pray is that one day it will be easy for him to come back into the Church. He is one of the people I love and there is a part of me that won't be at peace until he is at peace in the Church. Pray for him because the Lord knows he is in a hard position. The last thing he wrote was called *The Mills of the Kavanaughs*. Right now he is writing an autobiography. This is part of some kind of analytical therapy.

I have no letter-writing duties . . . Anyway, be it understood that my writing to you is a free act, unconnected with character, duty or compulsion. I am afraid that if I tell you your writing to me is a kindness, you will lay this to some more of my guile or feel obliged to write me when you don't feel like it. Don't do that, but do be assured that these letters from you are something in my life. I have the sense that they are too much concerned with me and my works but I don't know how to avoid that, as the works do interest me.

I think the lady [mentioned in letter of 7 April 56] thought the story merely funny. She went on to say that she didn't allow quite so much freedom to her college-age sons. What's funny about it is that it represents so well an illogical position, represents it in the concrete. I have a friend, a man in his fifties, who claims he quit going to [his] Sunday school because he attended one Mother's Day and listened to a discussion in favor of birth control. Now he's a follower of Robert Graves and the white goddess or something so it's frequently a matter of out-of-the-frying-pan.

Monday I departs for Lansing, Friday, d.v., I returns. After that I will shut up about it. I am to stay with one Mrs. Rumsey Haynes. She says her spouse will help me up and down the stairs; but I am just going to tell Rumsey to stand by at the bottom as there is nothing more dangerous to the safety of those on crutches than a gentleman's assistance. She allows there are many interesting young writers and intellectuals there that I will enjoy meeting. Anything I can't stand it's a young writer or intellectual. Well, I brought this on myself. May the Lord have mercy on my soul.


## To Elizabeth Fenwick Way

[April 1956]

This letter from Dr. Merrill sounds very good to me. You could make an afternoon appointment with him, leave New York about 7:15, get to Atlanta at 12:30 flying, spend the night at the Cox Carlton Hotel (a place a few blocks from his office) and let me come up the next day and retrieve you for a visit to Milledgeville . . . Should you want to make a reservation at the Cox Carlton the address is Peachtree Street, Atlanta. It's about four blocks from his office, a small hotel but okay and not exorbitant. Dr. Merrill's office is an old house—nothing fancy or new. They have their offices downstairs and a lab and X-ray machine and so forth upstairs.

I suppose you can always take it for granted that an emotional situation makes these things worse but there is nothing for those but time, and the one you have now may not be as bad as the one you run into next—besides which all this works both ways—when you feel better, having the right medicine in you, the emotional situation will be less of a strain. Everybody now talks about it's all-in-the-mind. When I was in the hospital even the nurse's aides that didn't have sense enough to do anything but empty the ice-water were full of that chatter.

Well, anything I can do, let me know.

## To Mrs. Rumsey Haynes

29 April 56

You must really know how much I enjoyed being in Lansing and staying with you, so I won't bore you with another recital of all my pleasures there. I enjoyed everything, but the best part of it for me has been my getting to know you and Rumsey and that is a pleasure that won't end with my visit to Lansing. My mother was delighted with the box of candy and the cookies you made and plans to write you herself. She took the occasion of my absence to clean up my room and I find that it will take me at least two months to reestablish the customary disorder. This is a danger I incur everytime I go anywhere . . .

While I was gone, the peachickens ate all the strawberries out of my mother's strawberry patch, so she is taking a dark view of peachickens right now and I have to reestablish relations between her and them—as next year I plan to have twice as many birds as this year.

Please remember me to all the lovely people I met and thank you and Rumsey many times again.

## To "A."

5 May 56

I'll be real pleased to be your sponsor for Confirmation—that is, if I read that right and am not just inviting myself. Once I was godmother for a child in California by proxy and I had to send a statement saying I was willing. I don't know if that's necessary for sponsors but if it is, drop me a card and I will send it on. I never have been anybody's sponsor before. What's it mean? I am supposed to come and ask you what the fruits of the Holy Ghost are once a year or something? Anyway, I am highly pleased to be asked and to do it and as for your horrible history, that has nothing to do with it. I'm interested in the history because it's you but not for this or any other occasion.

We have got crossed up on our book intentions all around as

when I got your instructions I had already [sent] *The Malefactors* to Mrs. Rumsey Haynes who had expressed an interest. They were really very nice people and I enjoyed them. Rumsey collects postcards and gave me a bunch of them to send out . . . You always like these people better than you had expected to and perhaps the dreary part is that you will never see them again.

As for the Catholic function—one is always paid for one's sins. They decided against both the tea and the talk to the Newman Club and instead, decreed that I should be invited to a huge convention luncheon of the Nat. Asso. of Cat. Women. If ever there has been devised something suitable for the remission of temporal punishment due to sin, this is it. It lasted three hours, included a talk by a priest and one by a bishop, the introduction of sixteen guests (I was the sixteenth like Gen. Tennessee Flintrock Sash), pledges, resolutions, welcomes, responses, and dedications. There were about five hundred attending. I sat at a table with 8 ladies I had never seen before and an ancient deaf priest named Fr. Murphy—next to him. Said he to me:

> And wharre are you from?
> Milledgeville, Georgia, Father.
> Eh?
> Milledgeville, Georgia.
> I didn't get that.
> MILLEDGEVILLE GEORGIA
> What city is that near?
> M A C O N (great volume)
> Mi-kun? I never heard of that.
> Where are you from, Father?
> (Pause—waiting to get the ladies' attention.) Purrrgatory.
> (Laughter)

During the priest's and bishop's addresses he took out his breviary and read it under the table. I wished I had had one.

Mr. Billy [William Sessions] has been invited down here to visit Dr. Rosa Lee Walston, the head of the English Department and twice I have had notes from him saying he would be around at such and such a time, but every note contradicted the last one, and now it is that he may come next Thursday when their president is getting some kind of award. So it may well be I will get to see Billy in person but I doubt it . . .

I think, or anyway, hope, that I have heard the last of S. The two letters I sent you were sane. The last couple I have had have not been. They have been full of abuse, obscenity, real hate. The first one I didn't answer. Then there was another one waiting on me when I got back from Michigan so I wrote him that since there was nothing I could do for him, I saw no reason to keep up the correspondence. The letters were filthy but terribly pathetic as well. There's nothing you can do for such people but pray for them. The boy is homosexual and apparently scizophrenic (sp?) to boot and he tried to make you feel personally responsible for both conditions in him.

Would you be interested in reading Baron von Hügel's letters to his niece? I've just reviewed it for the *Bulletin* and according to me it is absolutely finer than anything I've seen in a long long time. You can read one letter a night without straining yourself much. I'll send it if you'd be interested. No hurry to return any of these books . . .

Oh. My TSCW prodigy has been chosen as one of the twenty guest editors for the month of June at *Mademoiselle*. She wrote me a very nice and intelligent letter, explaining what she meant about Gide. I still don't exactly understand what but I'm pleased she is going to get this reward, since she wants it. I once visited the *Mlle.* offices—full of girls in peasant skirts and horn-rimmed spectacles and ballet shoes.

[P.S.] Oh. Jean Stafford. She's the one you think. The first book was *Boston Adventure,* then *The Mountain Lion,* and then something called *The Catherine Wheel.* Also a lot of stories . . . She must be a very nice person who has had a hard time, from all I can hear. I never met her.

## To Ben Griffith

7 May 56

I'd love to have you and Mr. [Thomas] Gossett come over Friday and bring Alfred Kazin. I met him a good many years ago and he is very pleasant but I don't know him well.

That weren't no peacock in that self-portrait. That was a pheasant. However, some people have referred to it as a turkey so you can be forgiven . . .

[P.S.] Thanks for the invitation to come to the lecture but I won't be able to make that. I call myself working in the mornings.

## To Father J. H. McCown

9 May 56

. . . After taking as much as I could stand of [a book he had sent], I decided that since I might get a chance to meet [the author], it would be better not to have read her books—as I wouldn't possibly be able to say I like them, it's better to be able to say I haven't read them. I agree with her children.

I think a person who didn't know anything about fiction could read it and enjoy it. It's all done with dialogue and the dialogue could have been tape-recorded from Macon to Atlanta. She has an awfully good ear but absolutely no discrimination in using it. [Her book] is just propaganda and its being propaganda for the side of the angels only makes it worse. The novel is an art form and when you use it for anything other than art, you pervert it. I didn't make this up. I got it from St. Thomas (via Maritain) who allows that art is wholly concerned with the good of that which is made; it has no utilitarian end. If you do manage to use it successfully for social, religious, or other purposes, it is because you make it art first . . .

## To "A."

19 May 56

No, what I mean by the technical achievement [of *The Malefactors*] doesn't have anything to do with a theory of the evolution of a conversion (horrible thought) as I reckon every conversion is unique and nothing to have theories about. What I mean has strictly to do with point of view in the telling. She [Caroline Gordon] is a disciple of James, and James started this business of telling a story through what he called a central intelligence—like he did with Strether in *The Ambassadors* and like she does with Claiborn. Start writing a novel and you will soon discover this to be a problem. She follows a kind of modified use of the central intelligence and the omniscient narrator, but she never gets in anybody else's mind but Claiborn's, and that's quite something to do. It gives the thing a dramatic unity that's hard to get otherwise. Point of view runs me nuts. If you violate the point of view, you destroy the sense of reality and louse yourself up generally. She and Allen Tate have a textbook called *The House of Fiction* in which she explains all this. It's more complicated than I make it out to be. Anyway you can't just sit down and write a novel. You have to know who's seeing what and all that kind of stuff. Of course, she didn't HAVE to do it that way, but seeing she did, she had to be consistent with it and she was.

I agree with you about the bulls. Nothing wrong with artificial insemination as long as it's animals and bringing those Hookers or Shakers or whatever they were and their disapproval to bear just confused the moral point, if any. But I suspect that she just wasn't able to resist doing that inseminator, as she had him down. About the old nun. Again this is a matter of point of view. The author, the omniscient narrator, don't tell you that Claiborn is to learn something about Buggs Butts from the sister. It's Claiborn that thinks that's what he's going to do—all that comes through Claiborn—the author knows better.

Don't know where she got those blue eyes from. You are way out of my reach when you say these two books show a sexual need of hers for somebody she really doesn't like. That hadn't occurred to me . . . I think it's a more profound feeling with her than what you make out from the books. Fiction doesn't lie, but it can't tell the whole truth. What would you make out about me just from reading "Good Country People"? Plenty, but not the whole story. Anyway, you have to look at a novel or a story as a novel or a story; as saying something about life colored by the writer, not about the writer colored by life. She distorts herself to make a better story so you can't judge her by the story. But anyway, I suspect it's a purgatorial more than a hellish love—and what I mean is, she don't deserve to do it halfway . . . He is a very brilliant man but he has told me he's mighty hard to live with when he's not writing, and if she unconsciously maybe is thinking of God as a means to aid [his] works, well, that is perhaps something that God puts up with in us because we are only children—like there is perfect and imperfect contrition and imperfect will do.

There was a review of it in the *Commonweal* by a Fr. Simons (the same boy who said I had a Lutheran sensibility) which did you see? Do you take *Commonweal*? I take it and I used to send it to a girl in a T.B. sanitarium every week when I finished it but she got well, then I sent it to a patient at the local state sanitarium but he escaped so now they are just piling up, so if you don't take it and would like to see it, I'll send it to you. My room is getting worse and worse. Everything collects on the floor. I can't put the books in the bookcase very well because I can't tote them and there ain't any more room in the bookcases anyway, so there are books all over the bureau and books all over the floor and a large collection under the chair. Every now and then my mother declares that she can stand the sight of it no longer and she and the colored woman assault it and this is an operation that makes me feel I am being sawed in two without ether. I forget what issue that review was in. I sent it to Robt. Fitzgerald. He wrote a letter to *Time* castigating them for the review they wrote of it but they declined to print it. Robt. reviewed for *Time* for fifteen years . . .

I sent that review of mine to Powers and got the enclosed note from him which I think is nice. Waugh reviewed his book in *Commonweal* and didn't like the cat either, but I am surprised at the number of reviewers that admired the cat.

The two colored people in "The Displaced Person" are on this place now. The old man is 84 but vertical or more or less so. He doesn't see too good and the other day he fertilized some of my mother's bulbs with worm medicine for the calves. I can only see them from the outside. I wouldn't have the courage of Miss Shirley Ann Grau to go inside their heads.

[P.S.] Back to *The Malefactors*. I ain't exhausted that subject. I didn't think Catherine was a good character, I mean well done. I thought she had a kind of bodiless quality. She wasn't one-third as real as the inseminator, but of course she would be about a hundred times as hard to make real. I had a letter from Sally Fitzgerald (Robt's wife) about the book. She found a lot to object to and made this point: ". . . it seemed to me too bad that she had invented for Catherine Pollard a history suggesting that she had begun her work after being rejected by a husband to whom she had offered to return. What with two ladies in the book flying to religion and religious works at the loss of their husbands, the Faith is unintentionally made to seem too much like chiefly a refuge for the losers in the battle between the sexes. I am always dismayed when people regard faith as chiefly compensatory . . ." I hadn't thought of that, though perhaps she is right. On the other hand, some kind of loss is usually necessary to turn the mind toward faith. If you're satisfied with what you've got, you're hardly going to look for anything better. Well, I am only thinking out loud. And I have forgot as usual what side I am supposed to be arguing on.

Oh. I am sending you a rather garish-looking book called *A Short Breviary* which I meant to get to you when you came into the Church but which has just come. I have a 1949 edition of it but this is a later one, supposed to be improved but I don't think it is. Anyway, don't think I am suggesting that you read the office every day. It's just a good thing to know about, I say Prime in the morning and sometimes I say Compline at night but usually I don't.

But anyway I like parts of my prayers to stay the same and part to change. So many prayer books are so awful, but if you stick with the liturgy, you are safe.

## To Father J. H. McCown

20 May 56

It was good to see you turn up with that crowd from Macon. It reminded me slightly of one of those early books of Waugh's that has Fr. Rothschild, S.J. in it. He is always appearing in unlikely company, usually in disguise, and if I remember correctly, usually on a motorcycle. He was the last of the Rothschilds, become a Jesuit—certainly one of Waugh's best strokes . . .

## To "A."

1 June 56

. . . What carries over (into the novel) [*The Malefactors*] of the writer's soul is bound, according to me, to be the most natural elements of it, so that what all you see there may well be there, but just isn't all, can't be the whole story. Nobody not engaged in it realizes what energy it takes to write a novel; what comes easiest is what is most natural and what is most natural is what is least affected by the will. For instance, I wrote GCP ["Good Country People"] in about four days, the shortest I have ever written anything in, just sat down and wrote it; but I was two or three months writing "The Artificial Nigger"—which is a story in which there is an apparent action of grace. As stories both of those are equally successful (I insist) but the amount of creative energy put out was entirely different; and this is not to say that more energy expended on GCP would have made it a better story. Anyway, what this adds up to is to say that what her [Caroline Gordon's] books say to you about their relationship may be what is most fundamental to it, but is not what you can judge it by, is not what God judges it by, is not what it is, finally.

Apparently about four or five years before he actually came into the Church, A.T. had taken instructions and was ready to be baptized but when the priest was questioning him just before this was to come off, he asked him something and A. gave him a flip answer—not disrespectful to the priest but, I gather, disrespectful to the Church. Whereupon, said the priest, "You are not ready," and would not receive him. This was probably the finest thing that ever happened to him. I can fancy it rid him of a great deal of spiritual pride and that he is a better Catholic now for it. I admire him in spite of the fact that charity has probably a hard time taking root in him. I think it has taken root.

Mrs. Fitzgerald is 5 feet 2 inches tall and weighs at most 92 pounds except when she is pregnant which is most of the time. They have been married nine years and expect their seventh child next week. She says she is gliding around as usual "like Moby Dick." Her face is extremely angular; in fact, horse-like, though attractive, and she does have the pulled-back hair and the bun. Robert was brought up a Catholic but left the Church when he was about eighteen to become an intellectual. Subsequently married outside it. That marriage didn't work and was annulled and by that time he had worked his way back to the Church. The present Mrs. F. is a convert. They are very intense Catholics and their religion colors everything they do. When I lived with them, they said the Benedictine grace before meals in Latin every day while the dinner got cold. I am more for expressing my appreciation by eating heartily while it's still warm.

I am "reviewing" Russell [Kirk's] latest for *The Bulletin*, if you please. It's a collection of his essays called *Beyond the Dreams of Avarice*. You want to see it? Old Russell lays about him. I also have *The Conservative Mind* if you want that—or any of those books I review for *The Bulletin*, if you want them, holler. It don't bother me to wrap up packages. I have a large ugly brown desk, one of those that the typewriter sits in a depression in the middle of and on either side are drawers. In front I have a stained mahogany orange crate with the bottom knocked out and a cartridge shell box that I have sat up there to lend height and hold papers and whatnot and all my paraphernalia is somewhere around this vital center and a little rooting produces it. Besides which, I always seize on busy-work.

I'm glad you like the breviary. The Fitzgeralds put me onto that five or six years ago and it has meant a lot to me.

I'd be interested in the Bedoyere but I have just had a scare about mailing books. I have a friend in Nashville who is a fiend about Wyndham Lewis. He lent me his *Demon of Progress* and when I got through with it I dutifully mailed it back but it never arrived. Fortunately it was his own and not a library book but if any I sent you back didn't get there, you would have some explaining to do and I wouldn't want to put you in that fix. I got him another *Demon of Progress* but a lot of library books are out of print and couldn't be replaced even.

It was Mrs. Tate sent me off on the Greeks and Romans but

the old man gimme another shove. I have bought me the Modern Library Tacitus. Everybody in Tacitus dies either by poisoning or suicide . . .

Would you spend the weekend with us sometime this summer? The bus trip is direct and air conditioned and I have an uncle who goes back to Atlanta in his car every Sunday after supper with two or three riders. There's nobody here but me and my mother and the upstairs is empty. There is nothing to do here but sit and walk and collect redbug bites but there are a lot of things I would like to show you—the peacock for one thing before his tail gets ratty. I have five peahen eggs in the incubator and in three weeks, I ought to have some peachickens. Anyway, consider it and if you will we can find a time convenient to you.


## To Elizabeth Fenwick Way

8 June 56

The book came yesterday and I have just finished it and have been much impressed throughout. I see now why Catharine Carver liked it so much. I have liked each of your books better than the last and this seems much the sharpest to me, I mean as to characterization. It is just right and never overdone and everything in it is necessary and works. I never know though why I like anything. It's either dead or alive to me and this is alive. When does it come out officially? I intend to write to Margaret Marshall (I hope that's her name) and congratulate them on publishing it, though I guess the credit for their taking it goes to Catharine.

Also it's the best-looking jacket I've seen in a long time—real respectable as to color and the nice portrait on the back. My books they always make orange with blood-red letters or purple with pimento spots.

Why don't you come NOW to see Dr. Merrill? Make them give you an advance on the next one or something. I went to him last week and he said they were using a new treatment for lupus. You might ask your boy up there about it. They take something from somebody with lupus and shoot it into you. He said I was doing all right with what I was doing with, but if it proves to be spectacular, he may try it on me later. It might be just the thing for you since it isn't, I gather, a drug.

My mother has now started on your book, having affirmed her approval of it from the jacket. "Refined," she said, "very refined."

Let us know if you can't come on now. I can guarantee it will be hot enough for you.

*This was written after her new friend's first visit to Milledgeville.*

## To "A."

28 June 56

You always make of me what I would like to be but if I took your notion of me for present reality, I'd be in the devil's hands right now; however, I only take your idea of what I am as an indication of what I should become, and the Lord has never instructed me in such a pleasant way before.

I had the impression that all the time you were here you were poised for flight—a lark with a jet engine—and that if I had turned my back, you would have been gone. The next time I'll know better and will use the commanding tone since I am capable of it, at least through the mail. In person I lack command.

Nobody attains reality for my mother until he eats. Therefore she is not quite convinced that you exist on a plane with the rest of us, but when you come again, you can correct that by staying long enough to take in some of your meals. She is wondering if you eat on the 7th day, in the middle of it, that is. I approve of the iron will but it should be used only on what resists with an equal force. To meander further, you don't look anything like I expected you to as I always take people at their word and I was prepared for white hair, horn-rimmed spectacles, nose of eagle and shape of ginger-beer bottle. Seek the truth and pursue it: you ain't even passably ugly.

You are wrong that it was long ago I gave up thinking anything could be worked out on the surface. I have found it out, like everybody else, the hard way and only in the last years as a result of I think two things, sickness and success. One of them alone wouldn't have done it for me but the combination was guaranteed. I have never been anywhere but sick. In a sense sickness is a place, more instructive than a long trip to Europe, and it's always a place where there's no company, where nobody can follow. Sickness before death is a very appropriate thing and I think those who don't have it miss one of God's mercies. Success is almost as isolating and nothing points out vanity as well. But the surface hereabouts has always been very flat. I come from a family where the only emotion respectable to show is irritation. In some this tendency produces hives, in others literature, in me both.

According to [a friend] the only way you can help a person on crutches is going down the steps to hold on to her belt in the back. Then if she falls, you got her. But she says if anybody takes your arm or your crutch, he'll throw you every time. After which she describes all the occasions on which she has been thrown and the resulting fractures. For my part I am always glad to have the door held open but that's all that's necessary. I don't want any of those apple-eyed old boys helping me on any busses. Did you have to sit with any of those boys? The delegation from Cornelia? To get back to the crutches, the truth about them is that they worry the on-looker more than the user . . .

Oh, I meant to ask you. Do you read the *National Geographic* or do you smell it? I smell it. A cousin gave me a subscription when I was a child as she noted I always made for it at her house, but it wasn't a literary or even a geographical interest. It has a distinct unforgettable transcendent apotheotic (?) and very grave odor. Like no other mere magazine. If *Time* smelled like the *Nat'l. Geo.* there would be some excuse for its being printed.

*After William Sessions, Georgia writer, came to Andalusia to meet Flannery, they became friends, and his devotion to her and to her mother grew with the years. At this time, he was about to enter the Church.*

## To William Sessions

8 July 56

. . . I went to Communion for your intentions on Friday the 8th (June) and have been praying for you since. Coming into the Church must have its terrors but born Catholics are always a little envious of them. When I made my First Communion I was six and it seemed as natural to me and about as startling as brushing my teeth. Having been a Protestant, you may have the feeling that you must feel you believe; perhaps feeling belief is not always an illusion but I imagine it is most of the time; but I can understand the feeling of pain on going to Communion and it seems a more reliable feeling than joy.

Do you know the Hopkins-Bridges correspondence? Bridges wrote Hopkins at one point and asked him how he could possibly learn to believe, expecting, I suppose, a metaphysical answer. Hopkins only said, "Give alms."

I remember the name Phillip Burnham frequently being in the *Commonweal* some years ago—maybe he was editor. All editors of Catholic magazines seem to retire to Catholic book stores. Write me about him, and about what you are doing, when you have time.

## To "A."

13 July 56

I am considerably at a loss as to how I can thank you enough for these books [a life of Baron von Hügel and the *Essays and Addresses* of von Hügel]. I had started on the biography but when the essays came, I dropped that for them. I didn't know the essays existed where they could be got hold of and I can think of nothing that I am gladder to be reading. This is more than you should be doing for me, though, and I will accept them only if I can share them with you. I take it you have read the biography but have you read the essays? They are better than the letters to Gwendolyn. The old man I think is the most congenial spirit I have found in English Catholic letters, with more to say, to me anyway, than Newman. I would never have seen these essays if you hadn't sent them, as I lack the facilities (and the initiative) to get out and find out where what I need is. I have had considerable time to read this last week as Monday I managed to drop one of the doors to the chicken brooder on my good foot and smash the toe, thereby making myself more or less stationary, so I have marked up the first three essays thoroughly. They require to be read many times and you have given me something for a lifetime and not any passing pleasure . . .

I bought myself a chess set a few years ago because I like to feel the pieces but I can't play. I suppose you have to be mathematically minded to enjoy it and I can't even make change without agony. If I am going to play a game I don't want to have to THINK. I can't play bridge or canasta or any of those things, though I can, or could when I was a child, play poker. There it's given and all a matter of luck more or less. I'd like to learn how to play chess but I could never play with anybody who cared about it more than just pushing those pieces around. A sensualist I am. This is in the same category as smelling the *Natl. Geo.* . . .

Naw, I don't want to read *Dying We Live*, or not right now anyway. I am too busy reading the Baron's essays, after which I will finish the biography, after which I may go back and read the Baron's essays again. I have just reviewed a most interesting one for the

*Bulletin* about [Ernest] Fénelon and Madame Guyon by the same fellow that wrote the Baron's biography. Would you be interested in it or in this book of [Paul] Horgan's? Also have you read St. Theresa of Avila's *Interior Castle*? I have it.

When you were here I was much affected to hear you say that your aunt spoke of my father in tones not usually applied to members of the Legion. I always sensed myself that the Legion was something other for him, not a rowdy organization, but something it would have been surprised to find itself. He died when I was fifteen and I really only knew him by a kind of instinct. Last year I read over some of the speeches he made and I was touched to see a kind of patriotism that most people would just laugh at now, something childlike, that was a good deal too good and innocent for the Legion. But the Legion was the only thing provided by the country to absorb it. And your saying what you did made me feel that it was not entirely lost and I was very grateful.

## To William Sessions

22 July 56

I am about midway into the [Jean] Guitton book. At first I was irritated by the "freethinker's journal" business and wondered why he didn't just write it straight. In the meantime, I have been reading the life of Baron von Hügel and Baron von Hügel's *Essays and Addresses*, and I begin to see why such a form may have been necessary for Guitton. Anyway, I like the book very much. My trouble is wanting to read everything at once. I find Baron von Hügel very congenial and the biography [by Michael de la Bedoyere] fascinating. I am getting all this Modernist business more or less straight for the first time.

What you say about Hopkins' answer to Bridges strikes me as right. It didn't for that matter serve Bridges. I find myself lately applied to by all sorts of people—through the mail usually—that I don't seem to be able to help, and I am always left wondering how much of it is laziness on my part. You have to learn to have patience to go behind the formula and in some way that will be applicable to the person in question. This is apparently what Baron von Hügel always tried to do.

I wish the lady in the bookshop could see Maritain's letter to Caroline about *The Malefactors*. I lent it to somebody in Nashville who hasn't returned it to me or I would send it to you to show her. He didn't think she had been unkind or superficial to [Dorothy Day] or [Peter Maurin] and the Lord knows that was far from her intention. I don't know anybody who has a greater respect for Dorothy Day. In any case, it's as a novel that the thing has to stand or fall . . . Caroline is going to write an introduction to the French edition of my short stories or maybe it's my novel, I don't know which. She is also currently writing a book called *How to Read a Novel* and an article for *Books on Trial* called "How I Write a Novel" . . .

*For the first time, Flannery identifies her chronic lupus to her new friend.*

## To "A."

28 July 56

As soon as I lay hands on that Jesuit I will get the [Elizabeth] Sewell piece. I'm sure he must be the one who has it. What do you call her little Sewell for? I bet that old girl wears a number-nine boot and could blow us both down with one exhale.

We just yesterday got our telephone out here. The lineman that put it in wanted to see the peacock so I took him out there and he looked for a while, not saying anything. Overcome, thinks I. Finally he turns away. "How do you like him?" I say. "Longlegged rascal, ain't he?" he says. "I bet he could outrun a Greyhound bus."

. . . This week I have finished the biography of the Baron. When I came to the essay on Troelch I realized I would do better to finish the biography so I would know better what I was reading, which proved to be the case. That is a very splendid biography, very painstaking and complete and it puts another dimension on the essays. As to the *Mystical Element,* I much appreciate your trying to get it and finding out it is out of print. I am determined to read it anyhow and I am thinking that when the college gets going in the fall I will induce the librarian to see where she can locate it and get it on an interlibrary loan. She got me one of Lewis's books that way—it proved to be at two libraries in the state —Agnes Scott and Atlanta U. I should have gone to Atlanta U. Don't think I could have stood Agnes Scott. A friend of mine that Agnes Scott turned out came to see us the other day and was telling me that she was reading her children Uncle Remus but that she took out all the bad grammar as she went along.

The book on Fénelon has a good cops and robbers background I'll have to admit. It also explains Madame Guyon handily I think. I'll let you consider it a while longer but it's here if you want it . . .

I suppose my father toted around some of my early produc-

tions.* I drew—mostly chickens, beginning at the tail, the same
chicken over and over, beginning at the tail. Also occasional verse.
My father wanted to write but had not the time or money or training
or any of the opportunities I have had. I am never likely to romanticize him because I carry around most of his faults as well as his
tastes. I even have about his same constitution: I have the same
disease. This is something called lupus. At the time he had it there
was nothing for it but the undertaker. When he died my mother
asked the doctor if it might be inheritable but the doctor said no,
in fact he had never heard of its occurring twice in the same family.
Ten years later I came up with it but by that time it could be controlled, though not cured. Anyway, whatever I do in the way of
writing makes me extra happy in the thought that it is a fulfillment
of what he wanted to do himself.

The *Commonweal* protest was not adequate but it was at least
a protest of some sort and the only one I've seen. I'm much obliged
to that and *America,* which I read where and only where you had
marked . . . I observe your Militant Feminist reaction to the Rev.
Whatshisname—only one thing: don't say the Church drags around
this dead weight, just the Rev. So&So drags it around, or many
Rev. So&Sos. The Church would as soon canonize a woman as a
man and I suppose has done more than any other force in history
to free women . . .

11 August 56

Well you are mighty right about the low rate of pious exchange. I told Mrs. H. I would pray for her but I doubt if I have
thought about it twice . . . But remember the prayer in the Mass
for the 11th Sun. after Pentecost, asking "to take away from us
those things which our conscience feareth and to add that which
our prayer presumeth not to ask." No more can be said in the way
of asking for anything.

Reading yr review of the German martyrs makes me think I
ought to read the book but I am about to embark on Vol 2 of the
Baron's essays. Vol 1 is much marked up; when you want it let
me know. I am currently engaged in writing a talk on the problems
of the Catholic fiction writer which I am to give to the ladies of the
Macon Parish Council and the which I will send you when I get
through with it as you have thought of some I ain't from the read-

* A relative of this correspondent had known Edward O'Connor during his
lifetime, and told her that he had usually had with him a piece of writing or
a drawing of Flannery's and liked to show his daughter's work to his friends.

ing side. Anyway, I have found several things out of the Baron that I quote in this . . .

You may be right about Msgr. Guardini not wearing well but I haven't read *The Lord* but once and that some time ago. The book on the Rosary is a watered-down version of the former. In the fall there is going to be a new one called *The End of the Modern World*, which Mrs. H. was to get for me. I have been meaning to read *The Lord* again and will do it with what you say in mind. However, my evaluations of these people all have a background . . . to go against which makes them seem highly superior. If Msgr. Guardini is the Msgr. Sheen of Europe then that only says how far Europe is ahead of us on that score . . . Furthermore, almost any spiritual writer *ought* to wear thin for you. It's like reading criticism of poetry all the time and not reading the poetry. Spiritual writers have a limited purpose and can be very dangerous, I suppose.

But about his moving in too close—I never noticed it but I'm not very sensitive to such things, but it may be that if he moves in close it is as a reaction against the modern tendency to think you can't move in at all. I think more and more of what writers with Christian concerns write against. I don't mean in a polemical way, I mean maybe the climate they write in. It affects fiction writers as well as people like him. But I must have said this before. I forget by now whatall of my mental mumblings I have laid in your lap. When I first started writing to you I was careful to try to say what I had to say in a clear way as I was conscious of the fact that I might be the only person inside the Church who would get a chance to talk to you. But now if I relapse into my natural vagueness, it is because I find that you sometimes appear to know better what I am trying to say than I do; and also it is you now who is in a position to help me. And do.

I suppose what I mean about my father is that he would have written *well* if he could have. He wrote all the time, one thing or another, mostly speeches and local political stuff. Needing people badly and not getting them may turn you in a creative direction, provided you have the other requirements. He needed the people I guess and got them. Or rather wanted them and got them. I wanted them and didn't. We are all rather blessed in our deprivations if we let ourselves be, I suppose. Which is why Mrs. Fitzg. is wrong about C.'s book . . .

Me I'm all for the telephone. A great invention. A great mother-saver. She sits in the back hall now and talks to the vet, the seed man, the feed man, the tractor & implement man . . . instead of running herself ragged going to town four times a day in the burning-down heat. I have spoke over it oncet myself. Yesterday in the midst of the heat of composition it rang and on the other end was a female voice . . . who, she said, had heard that I had published books well she had written this song and wondered did you have to send money when you got a book published not that a book was a song or anything but she thought maybe I would know since I had had a book published though it is harder to get a song published than a book she knew because there was this fellow on "Name This Tune" that had written a song and he said he had sent it to two or three song-publishing companies and they wouldn't pay any attention it was hillbilly so he sang it over "Name This Tune" and it was real catchy and caught on and now he can get any song publisher he wants well she hadn't written a hillbilly song because she didn't like hillbilly hers was just a real sweet song but she had written to this man in California and he said send a hundred dollars and sign this long contract and he would get the song across well her husband said well that's just the way you get jipped and you better find out from somebody that knows so she was just calling me up to see would I know. Well I didn't know but I listened for twenty minutes and enjoyed every second of it . . .

24 August 56

. . . About GCP ["Good Country People"] let me say that you are not reading the story itself. Where do you get the idea that Hulga's need to worship "comes to flower" in GCP? Or that she had never had any faith at any time? or never loved anybody before? None of these things are said in the story. She is full of contempt for the Bible salesman until she finds he is full of contempt for her. Nothing "comes to flower" here except her realization in the end that she ain't so smart. It's not said that she has never had any faith but it is implied that her fine education has got rid of it for her, that purity has been overridden by pride of intellect through her fine education. Further it's not said that she's never loved anybody, only that she's never been kissed by anybody—a very different thing. And of course I have thrown you off myself by informing you that Hulga is like me. So is Nelson, so is Haze, so is Enoch, but you cannot read a story from what you get out of a letter. Nor I repeat, can you, in spite of anything Sister Sewell may say, read the author by the story. You may but you shouldn't— See T. S. Eliot.

That my stories scream to you that I have never consented to be in love with anybody is merely to prove that they are screaming an historical inaccuracy. I have God help me consented to this frequently. Now that Hulga is repugnant to you only makes her more believable. I had a letter from a man who said Allen Tate was wrong about the story that Hulga was not a "maimed soul," she was just like us all. He ended the letter by saying he was in love with Hulga and he hoped some day she would learn to love him. Quaint. But I stick neither with you nor with that gent here but with Mr. Allen Tate. A maimed soul is a maimed soul.

I have also led you astray by talking of technique as if it were something that could be separated from the rest of the story. Technique can't operate at all, of course, except on believable material. But there was less conscious technical control in GCP than in any story I've ever written. Technique works best when it is unconscious, and it was unconscious there.

What Fr. Simons was talking about saying "Lutheran sensibility" he explained this way: Luther said a man was like a horse, ridden either by Christ or the devil. My characters are ridden either, said he, by Christ or the devil and therefore lack any self-determination, hence Lutheran sensibility. ?????????

What you say about your experience last August and since all rings true to me though I have never experienced anything like that myself. When you are born in it I suppose that is gift enough without asking for anything else. In any case you now have the Church and don't need anything else. And that about Edith Stein rings true too. I have been reading about eternity in a book of Jean Guitton's called *The Virgin Mary*—one that [a friend] left here—and have had considerable light thrown on the subject for me. He says that eternity begins in time and that we must stop thinking of it as something that follows time. It's all very instructive and I recommend it.

Sunday I am to entertain a man who wants to make a movie out of "The River." He has never made a movie before but is convinced "The River" is the dish for him—"a kind of documentary," he said over the telephone. It is sort of disconcerting to think of somebody getting hold of your story and doing something else to it and I doubt if I will be able to see my way through him. But we shall see. How to document the sacrament of Baptism???????

## To Father J. H. McCown

28 August 56

Thanks for reading the piece. I'll put in some more examples and doctor up those places that are confusing. I just have the usual

Catholic desire not to be a heretic. There is a letter to the editor in the current *Jubilee* from a Brooklyn lady who takes them to task for praising *The Quiet American,* which, says she, she would not have "resting on her bookshelf." Why don't Catholic magazines review *wholesome* books, she wants to know. Maybe I should change my whole approach and discuss "What is a wholesome book?" Answer: one that is whole.

You are the one who should write the pamphlet. They would take it from a priest where they wouldn't from a novelist.

## To John Lynch

2 September 56

Thank you so much for sending me the stories. The longer one is certainly powerful and the power seems to me to be in the prose itself, which I took to be the case in the story of yours I read that was in the Martha Foley collection. All of which makes me wonder if you aim sooner or later to write a novel. I am not one to advise anybody to do it since my own is driving me nuts, but some are more suited to the ordeal than others. Me I prefer something where the agony is over quicker.

I had never seen *Four Quarters* before but after I read your story and that symposium in it, I forthwith wrote for two extra copies of that issue and a subscription. I had a letter back from one Brother Edw. Patrick who described his troubles after they had printed parts of a letter from Philip Wylie and gotten roundly condemned for their liberalism by a Catholic paper "on the Coast." The voice of one who will never get clearance from the Catholic Press. I congratulate you on yours. The Voice of St. Jude reminds me that I have an aunt all of whose financial affairs he conducts . . .

My current project is writing a talk I am to give to the Macon Parish Catholic Women's Council on the dizzying subject—"What Is a Wholesome Novel?" I intend to tell them that the reason they find nothing but obscenity in modern fiction is because that is all they know how to recognize.

## To "A."

8 September 56

My objection to the Luce thesis about writers goes farther than I was able to say in that paper. I believe they are wrong in general as well as in particular. I don't believe that you can ask an artist to be affirmative, any more than you can ask him to be negative. The human condition includes both states in truth and "art," according to Msgr. Guardini, "fastens on one aspect of the world, works through its essence, to some essential thing in it, and presents it in the unreal arena of the performance." I mortally and strongly defend the right of the artist to select a negative aspect of the world to portray and as the world gets more materialistic there will be more such to select from. Of course you are only enabled to see what is black by having light to see it by—but that is no part of the Luce contention. Furthermore, the light you see by may be altogether outside of the work itself. The question is not is this negative or positive, but is it believable. The Luces say the negativeness of our novels is not believable because statistics tell us that we are rich and strong and democratic. In which case Dr. Kinsey and Dr. Gallup are sufficient for the day thereof. I don't believe that in all this you can be so cavalier about particulars. When the particulars are wrong, the general is usually wrong too. If you are too cavalier about particulars you will find yourself a Manichean without knowing how it happened.

Sent you a piece out of the *Catholic Worker* that I thought was about Edith Stein until I read it but maybe in the next issue he will get back to the subject of her. If she is ever canonized, she will be one saint that I don't think they can sweeten up on holy cards and write a lot of "pious pap" about. Do you see the *Catholic Worker?* It irritates me considerably because I don't go for the pacifist-anarchist business, but every now and then you will find something fine in it—it is where I first came across the name of Miss Sewell. It also has the distinction of costing 25¢ a year—the ideal subscription rate.

The enclosed was sent me recently by a friend of mine [John Lynch] who lives in South Bend and used to be the editor of something called *Ave Maria*, which he claimed was the worst magazine in the Catholic Press. He was recently fired from there to the satisfaction of all concerned I think and now writes for an aircraft corporation. Anyway, this is interesting for the symposium. I immediately wrote off for a subscription.

When I saw *The Mechanical Bride* before it had fairly arrived, I said to myself—hate at first sight, no doubt. Then later I wondered how you could tell it wasn't your kind of thing on such a quick perusal. Then when I saw you had decided it was comic, I began to understand. No mam, it isn't comic or meant to be and it isn't sociology or written by a sociologist. To be understood, it has to be read completely and slowly, as [Herbert Marshall] Mc-

Luhan has a packed style. I will admit that occasionally he says something crudely funny—as when he calls the hero of the ad "Big Barnsmell"—this seems just right to me I must admit but it's not why I appreciate the book. Also you can omit the little captions by the pictures. The meat is in the text and has to be read carefully. McLuhan teaches English at some Canadian Catholic college or used to, the last I heard. A friend of mine was telling me that there is a fictional portrait of him in Wyndham Lewis' novel, *Self-Condemned.* Apparently McLuhan was very kind to Lewis when Lewis was in Canada during the war. I first came across McLuhan in an article on Southern writers in the *Southern Vanguard* and was taken by it. I see he occasionally has an article in *Thought* but I will be looking around for something shorter of his that may make a better impression on you.

The fellow who wants to make the movie arrived. He's never made a movie before but he envisions "The River" as just the thing for a low-cost movie made by him. My agent is opposed to the whole idea but I rather liked the man. He stuttered. But we shall see. Anyway, I have just sold the television rights to "The Life You Save May Be Your Own" to what I understand is called the General Electric Playhouse. All I know about television is hearsay but somebody told me that this was a production conducted by Ronald Regan (?). I don't know if this means RR will be Mr. Shiftlet or not. A staggering thought. Mr. Shiftlet and the idiot daughter will no doubt go off in a Chrysler and live happily ever after. Anyway, on account of this, I am buying my mother a new refrigerator. While they make hash out of my story, she and me will make ice in the new refrigerator.


## To Elizabeth Fenwick Way

13 September 56

I have been wondering how you and the lupus epizooticus were. Me and mine are as usual. I am going to make a trip to Arthur J. [Dr. Merrill] before long and catch up on all the new discoveries. My poor cousin really has trouble but hers is arthritis— she can't use her hands at all and is about bent double. After seeing her, the lupus looks pretty good to me and I don't mind the crutches a bit.

I had a note from Margaret Marshall and she said she liked your book and then I had a note from Denver Lindley saying he liked it too. I saw the review in the *NY Times Book Section* by accident but it only repeated the story and it does look like the *Times* would print better reviews than that.

My finances have taken a turn for the better as I have just sold the television rights to "The Life You Save" to something called Revue Productions. Harcourt gets 10% and the agent 10% but that leaves me with a tidy sum still. I'm thinking you ought to get your agent to look into selling some of yours this way. It is certainly a painless way to make money. You never have to see the thing or do anything but sign the check. Anyway, I have bought us a new refrigerator—the kind that spits the ice cubes at you, the trays shoot out and hit you in the stomach, and if you step on a certain button, the whole thing glides from the wall and knocks you down . . .

Should you still be of a mind to come see Dr. Merrill, please plan to come here before or after and pay us a visit. Anyhow, let me hear how you do.

## To Mrs. Rumsey Haynes

13 September 56

Last week was my week to hear from Michigan—a letter from D.H., a letter from Yereth [Knowles] (still Michigan to me) and a box of tulip bulbs from you for my mother. She is delighted with them and has Henry (the 86-year-old yardman) preparing a place to set them out now.

I was interested in your comment on the story—that Scofield and Wesley were my first upper-class young men. I hadn't thought of it but I guess you're right. It usually takes somebody else to point out to you what you're doing. I have just finished another story called "A View of the Woods," which I like, at present. I've sent it to *Harper's Bazaar* but I don't know if they'll take it—it may be a little grim for the dryer set. On the other hand that's a pretty grim set and *Harper's Bazaar* has published my other ones . . .

I suppose the sense of unreality you get in some of the stories has something to do with style or stylization; also with the fact that in art you are impressing an idea on matter and this gives a sense that you do not have in real life. You use reality to make a different kind of reality . . .

Remember me to Rumsey and to the AAUW and thanks again for the bulbs. My mother is going to write you herself but she is currently building a water tank (22,000 gallons) and has welders, carpenters, engineers and other creatures about, and I don't know when she'll be through with it.

It's always a treat to hear from you.

## To "A."

22 September 56

That wagon you describe sounds like the perfect example of clerical taste. I have never seen one of the travelling chapels but I heard about one called Our Lady of the Mountains that travelled around North Georgia. It was painted that morning-glory blue that the clergy so admires. Possibly the Lord just thinks all of this is funny. It is funny if you can stand it.

If you are going to pass on the Luces and the *Bulletin,* I will pass on being Miss Delayed Development, though not without me inner groan. Anyway, I ain't going to worry about stomping over your ego: it's just the patter of little feet, though it may be the little feet of the baby rhinoceros at the zoo. Once or twice people have written me that I have been barbarous or rude about one thing or another and all the time it will be something that I have been wondering if I have made even a slight impression about.

On the subject of the feminist business, I just never think, that is never think of qualities which are specifically feminine or masculine. I suppose I divide people into two classes: the Irksome and the Non-Irksome without regard to sex. Yes and there are the Medium Irksome and the Rare Irksome.

You may well be right about L. I've never met him. He reviewed my stories for *Today* . . . and sent me a copy and there begunst a correspondence . . . all his stories are about the War or some facet thereof. And my notion is that The War is all he'll ever have to write about and that The War is over. However, the story you read is not the best of his. The others have a certain power in the prose which the one in *FQ* lacked entirely. He writes poems too and sent me one but I didn't know if it was any good or not . . . Also [his circumstances] are a handicap to being a writer in this day and age. There is a great deal that has to either be given up or be taken away from you if you are going to succeed in writing a body of work. There seem to be other conditions in life that demand celibacy besides the priesthood.

I guess you are right too about the greatest potential showing up in monstrous forms first. Only there are a lot of monstrous forms floating around that are not due to great potential.

The agent has a cold eye but very accurate and I reckon she is right; anyway, that's what I got her for. I don't want to write a movie, I want to write what I'm writing. I seem to myself right now to be working all the time in the realm of the impossible with this novel, but no matter, it's better than writing a movie . . .

6 October 56

Well I have now acted on yr three suggestions with much profit to the story ["A View of the Woods"]. The business about traveling too close to the embankment is meant to show the old man's concern for her safety at all times but seeing it doesn't give that impression, I have extended it with a sentence to the effect that Mr. Fortune was always careful to see that she avoided dangers. "He would not let her sit in snakey places or put her hand in bushes that might hide hornets." Broadening it out like that relieves the suggestion that she may fall over the embankment. About removing "the bodies" you are ABSOLUTELY AND PROFOUNDLY correct and I find furthermore that when "them" is substituted the rest of the paragraph almost falls into place. The one sentence can't be "that the sky had left in their eyes" because eyes has already been used once in the sentence but I think that this will do maybe: "For almost a minute he stood still and then, his knees buckling, he squatted down by their sides and stared into their eyes, into the pale blue pools of rainwater, that the sky had filled." I ain't sure about this yet but it may be an improvement. Anyway, my complete thanks. There is every reason why I should let you see what I write before it's printed . . .

Yesterday Regina, N. and I went to a cattle auction down near Dublin. R. is an old hand at cattle auctions but it was my first. N. and I looked like a white edition of the Gold Dust Twins, being both on crutches, and got some very thorough looks from the assembled. The cows went cheap and Regina bought ten. She's usually the only lady present at these things and gets treated in highstyle by the auctioneer, this time a gent in a white broad-rimmed hat, which may be traditional for cow auctioneers. His tie had the likeness of a Hereford bull embroidered on it. One of the very sorriest-looking cows I have ever seen came in the ring and they tried to start her off at fifty dollars but nobody would bid. Somebody finally said $35 and eventually by persuading them that they could get more than that out of her by beefing her, the auctioneer got it up to $41. So she went for $41 and then they tried to get her out of the ring. She would get to the gate every time and refuse to go through. Finally a loud voice was heard to drawl from the bench, "She ain't satisfied with what she brought." They finally got her out. I intend to attend them all after this. N. entertained us on the way to and back with tales of the barnyard, the most graphic being about a pig that had screwworms in his head. At the dinner table one day she told us that the ONLY thing to do for a dog that was constipated was to give him an enema. I thought my mother's expression very odd for the next several minutes. If you will come and spend the weekend with us, I will produce N. for a meal.

I suppose gambling is not a virtue but it almost seems like one in a society where there is such an exaggerated respect for the dollar. Part of Purgatory must be the realization of how little it would have to take to make a vice into a virtue. But I reckon the Lord excuses us for bad training. One thing I like in the Tate essay on [Hart] Crane was the statement that God did not despise circumstances. This would apply to the fact that though the act may not have been good, good did come out of [it] . . . The Communion of Saints has something to do with the fact that the burdens we bear because of someone else, we can also bear for someone else.

Letter just interrupted when Parent came in with your note and the cookies. She was much amused by note, but Shot will not get them. We both et heartily but she was as much pleased with having a tin box as with the contents. She always has something to put in a tin box.

Your interpretation of the story is good enough for me, though far be it from me to have worked it out in any abstract way. I don't know why the bull and Mrs. May have to die, or why Mr. Fortune and Mary Fortune: I just feel in my bones that that is the way it has to be. If I had the abstraction first I don't suppose I would write the story . . .


## To William Sessions

11 October 56

. . . I have just seen the Signet (35¢) edition of my stories. The cover features a leacherous-looking gent grabbing for a discheveled (sp?) looking lady in a pile of straw, pitchfork to the side, suitcase full of whisky behind. I suggested to them that they put wooden legs all over the cover but I guess they figure they know what they're doing.

Never heard of an athlete's heart but I sympathize with anyone who has to take exercise of any kind.

The tank is up but it leaks and the project is still being nursed by Mr. Clavin. I feel we won't see the end of it any time soon.

*To "A."*

The recording is supposed to be played November 23 (Friday) 7:30 p.m. station WGKA (FM). It is very bad. [The recorder] played some of it over for me but I couldn't stand much of it. I sound like a very old woman with a clothespin on her nose and her teeth in a dish beside her. Flat ain't the word. Dead is better. The voice is a great deal better in the dialogue as I actually sound like a real hillbilly girl.

I am entranced with the report of H. C. Gardiner, S.J. If he had known you and your perceptive apparatus were concealed in that innocent-looking audience, he would have been afraid to utter a word. The trouble is, I suppose, that he is delivering a *sermon* on literature. But you can't even begin to talk about anything of interest with an audience like that . . . I have just read in the *Bulletin* that I said "*Americans* make the mistake of thinking that the writer is writing excusively for them." When what I plainly said was *Catholics* make that mistake. I never mentioned Americans in the whole damm speech. They didn't want to hear what I said and when they had heard it they didn't want to believe it and so they changed it. I also told them that the average Catholic reader was a Militant Moron but they didn't quote that naturally. I wonder why he couldn't admit that Madame de Beauvoir could lead people to the Church? I daresay she has led a many a one. All of which has nothing to do with the Index or its purpose. Of course, it is really harder for a priest to answer those questions than a lay person. No matter what he says in the way of his own opinion, people are going to take it for the Church speaking so that there is such a responsibility laid on him to begin with that he can hardly get off the ground.

Next installment I will describe giving of handsome scroll [to Flannery by the Georgia Writers' Association] but if you will come down I will also show it to you. It not only extolls my merits as a writer but spells my name in two interesting ways.

What you say about *Self-Condemned* and the last paragraph seems very true. His mother said early in the book, "Don't be a fool, son," and in spite of his sympathy with René [Wyndham] Lewis was with her all the way; but he's a rationalist through and through I guess . . . I'm more interested in the way Lewis writes than what he has to say. Sometimes as you say it's very tedious but when he moves, he moves. Have you seen the collection of stories, *Rotting Hill?* I liked it.

There was great excitement here yesterday. A Holstein cow elected to leap into the water trough—which is concrete, about five feet deep and three feet wide and four feet high. She was found apparently several hours after she came to this decision. She was on her side more or less with one or two feet sticking out and she was swollen tight in there. The wrecker was called and a rope somehow got under her and she was hauled out. My mother tells this story better than I.

You are right of course about not understanding the ordinary emotions any better than the extraordinary ones. But the writer doesn't have to understand, only produce. And what makes him produce is not having the experience but contemplating the experience, and contemplating it don't mean understanding it so much as understanding that he doesn't understand it. Where conservatism comes into this I haven't decided. I certainly have no idea how I have written about some of the things I have, as they are things I am not conscious of having thought about one way or the other. Experiences must have some parallel relationship. This must have some connection with the anagogical way of seeing. The enclosed is what I am going to say at Wesleyan in December and I touch on this here and there. I manage to be dogmatic about it, in fact. I am sending you this speech without even reading it over I am so sick of it. I don't seem to get out of one before I am into another. Now it is Emory. They are having some courses in their winter quarter—a different writer every week . . . in other words a zoo, featuring a different animal every week. I wrote the man that as far as I was concerned this was entertainment and not education. However, the people at Emory have been rather nice to me and if I use old stuff, it shouldn't be much of a pain.

I have other things to say but they can wait and you will have had enough of this incoherence.


## To William Sessions

23 November 56

I certainly think without any doubt or equivocation that you should send these stories out and that you should keep on writing them. I like the texture of both of them very much; the prose is relaxed and yet controlled and there is no feeling of strain.

It seems to me that the one called "A Summer at Madame's" is the less ambitious and probably the more successful technically of the two. It holds together as one piece very well I think and I think that visually it is beautifully realized. I am not sure that I so much "get the point" as that I see the summer at Madame's. This is not everything you could accomplish but it is a good deal to accomplish and I would send the story out as it is.

Now the other is a good deal more interesting to me, more ambitious and therefore I am more hesitant about giving you any advice about it. Each individual scene seems fine; I have the feeling that the whole thing could have a little more dramatic unity. I was not certain what the uncle saw at the funeral parlor that changed his expression. Later the boy comes to some realization about it in his room but it is a little choppy, it falls into such distinct pieces. I hesitate to suggest you change it unless you have some definite feeling about this too. The trouble with being a writer and taking on the activity of critic is that you tend to think everybody else's work should be like your own. You tend to a kind of diffusion which is pretty foreign to my way of writing a story, but after all you have to work out the unity of your way of doing things. In one or two places the story seems a little awkward in the wording —as where you call the uncle "the man" two or three times as if we hadn't been introduced to him. Check it for things like that.

But I would send these stories out and I would send them out together so they can see that you ain't no flash in the pan and that you can write two stories. The world is full of people who can write only one story . . .

Cheers, and I hope the goose didn't give you indigestion.


*To Elizabeth Fenwick Way*

24 November 56

Ever since I got your letter saying you had written a book in six weeks I have been thinking well the lupus is good for her. Why don't it do something for me? But now as you tell me it was just an old corny nervous breakdown, I guess I'll have to change my theory. Anyway, make HBCo send me a copy as soon as it's out as I am anxious to read it. Me, I'm fine. My nose is to the novel but I seem to produce nothing but lectures, letters, and short stories. One ["Greenleaf"] in the *Kenyon* this summer and Catharine Carver took one for *PR* ["A View of the Woods"]. The standard price for a lecture (by one of my lack of steam) at a college seems to be $50, but as I now have 25 peachickens to support, I cannot scorn it. Scratchfeed is going up. I intend to write the President a letter about it and send a copy to Ezra Taft Benson.

Even if you can't claim the lupus as an excuse, I wish you would come down and see me. I am not liable to reach the city again though I consider myself very good on crutches—not anyway until I am rich enough to ride everywhere in taxis and have a personal robot to tote the bags. Whereas you on your two feet could come to see me handily . . .

Cheers and if you ever find out what spheroid means, lemme know.

## To "A."

29 November 56

Sunday morning I read the thing in the paper that said what the play was about, and I decided that just couldn't be mine and that if it was, I better not see it. I'm sure it couldn't have been from what you say, because my contract specifically stated that I was to get story credit. If I don't I can sue them for a million bucks and buy my mama a jeep with nylon cushions.

Nobody with any connections at Doubleday or any connection with the O. Henry has notified me about the O. Henry prize but according to [a friend] at Davidson's I am going to get it . . . Don't tell me that bird announced it over that program when I read? It would be mighty funny if it weren't true and people thought I had spread the word. Well I didn't. But if I am going to get it, fine and dandy, as I think it is $300 untaxable dollars . . . The enclosed from Powers on the subject of "Greenleaf." I'll look up the letters from C.J. and send them to you if I can produce them out of my purgatorial filing system. Actually, I haven't much idea what those sonnets mean. I guess you'd have to sit down and read them every day for a month—but the point is, you probably could sit down and read them every day for a month—so I conclude they're real poetry . . .

I was honestly able to say that I thought [B.] should keep on writing his stories and that he should send these two out—which is what he allowed he wanted to know. I think, as a matter of fact, that he has a natural gift for presenting a scene without strain. Anybody who talks as much as he does and as much about trivia could hardly help having a facility for fiction, a lot of which depends on the ability to mimic the social scene. He didn't tell me anything about what he meant them to mean so I wasn't troubled with thinking that dancing one had any deep level—everything in it is quite well *seen*. If he deludes himself into thinking it is full of symbols, all well and good, but it certainly never occurred to me. I liked the one about the funeral better as there was potentially more to it and all the separate scenes were quite good. I wasn't sure it hung together so well but I am afraid to give advice on such things as I am seldom sure. Anyway, I think [he] can achieve a certain gracefulness in writing stories . . .

I suppose I am not very severe criticizing other people's manuscripts for several reasons, but first being that I don't concern myself overly with meaning. This may be odd as I certainly believe a story has to have meaning, but the meaning in a story can't be paraphrased and if it's there it's there, almost more as a physical than an intellectual fact. The person who teaches writing is not much more than a midwife. After you help deliver the enfant, it is ungracious to say, Madame, your child has two heads and will never grow up. The procedure I follow is, after its here, to announce only if its alive or dead. Another reason I would be less severe than probably either you or B. is that I remember my own early stories—if anybody had told me actually how bad they were, I wouldn't have written any more. Also, what is on the other side of the story is flesh and blood and you temper the wind to the lamb. B. informed me that he had read a story of yours and that there were some wonderful things in it or something like that. At which Outraged Vanity screamed: how does he get to read it and I don't? All he has been doing is jumping from his left foot to his right whilst I have spent these last eleven years in the mines. Well, I am glad he told you I would like to see the story and you need not be afraid of any compliments on it from me. He hasn't sent it yet but just from reading your letters I have several prejudices about how you might be expected to write. I have always thought that you should write but have never said so. I doubt very much though if you should write anything as concentrated and circumscribed as short stories, particularly if you tend to the grotesque. However, I will continue in my pedagogical vein after I have seen the culprit.

At the Ga. Wr. Thing I asked [a participant writer] if he had any good students at Emory. No, he said in a severe voice, teaching writing is a fraudulent occupation. I thought, yes and brother you would have been better off if you had been exposed to a little more of it.

I hadn't seen the picture but I was glad you sent it as it will stop my ugly tongue. I sent you *The Blue River* and a Mauriac that I got out of one of those sales in the newspaper. Those sales are always very funny—amongst the *Flower Arrangements Made Easy* and *Sex in the South Sea Islands* there is always one lonesome Christian tucked away.

Incidentally, it is never possible to put anything over on a goose. That goose you saw is probably still happily causing his eaters indigestion. I convinced my parent to cook a goose for Thanksgiving, though she is opposed in principle to geese, on or off the table. This one had summered in the deepfreeze and I thought we ought to be eating him. I finally persuaded her against her better judgement. She looked in the cook book to see how she should do it and the first thing she read was: wash goose in soap and water. This did not increase her enthusiasm. When she began to cook it, she kept coming into my room with a drawn face and saying: Do you smell that thing? She poured the water off once and began again. When she served it, it didn't look much but it tasted all right. We are still eating it and it don't improve with age. Tonight N. is coming and says she will finish it.

I will have to try to do something to that lecture to make it clear that what I am talking about is experience for its own sake when I say that the writer stands off from experience, but as I say, I am entirely sick of it at this point and I doubt if the little girls will pay much attention to it anyhow. When B.L. talked over there, she didn't talk about writing but about Women—"we must be better sweethearts wives & mothers," etc. etc. and when she talked to the Ga. Writers I gather that she talked about "The Struggles and Loneliness of the Writer" and according to [one hearer] it was superb and brought tears to the eye. I always want to throw up when I hear people talk about "The Loneliness of the Artist." I'd rather hear we must be better sweethearts wives & mothers. But I guess I'll have to stick to the appointed topic myself—though I really should get me some alternates ("The Polish Crested Bantam in America").

More in due time on the subject of the grotesque in stories.

*Post Scriptum:* I wish you could come but I respect your reasons. Perhaps what I should have said is that you are more than your history. I don't believe the fundamental nature changes, but that it's put to a different use when a conversion occurs and of course it requires vigilance to put it to the proper use . . .

Look in your last *Commonweal* and see a poem by a girl named Carol Johnson. She is the only writer I ever initiated a correspondence with. Caroline [Gordon] put me onto her poems, which have appeared from time to time in the *Sewanee Review*. She was not a Catholic but was a student at St. Catherine's College in Minnesota, run by the Sisters of St. Joseph of Corondele, and according to C. she was the only girl they ever graduated and told never to come back. She was "difficult." I don't know how. Anyway, the year after she graduated from there, back she came, a Catholic and wanting to join the order. She had been a great reader of Rimbaud and announced that she had followed Rimbaud as far as he went and had found herself, much against her will, at the Church. She therefore entered, with I presume, love and a profound distaste. When I first wrote her about a year ago, she was Sister M. I wrote her that I had read her poems and thought they were real poetry, though I didn't know anything about poetry and I sent her a copy of *A Good Man*. I liked her letters very much. They didn't sound like any Sister of St. Joseph I had ever heard from before. We only exchanged a letter or two and then I didn't hear from her again, but last week I did and she is out of the convent—"having followed my vocation where it seemed to lead and out again"—but still a Catholic and doing graduate work and teaching at Marquette. Anyway, I think hers is the poetry to watch.

## To J. F. Powers

9 December 56

I guess I'll have to resurrect Mrs. May as Mrs. Somebody-else and start over. There are some of us that just have to get the agony over with in a hurry. Anyway, I'm afraid you have hit upon my initial embarrassment: after thirty pages death is the great temptation. Right now I am writing myself ragged on a novel [*The Violent Bear It Away*] that died a natural death after the first chapter when it ceased to be a short story.

I gather you are teaching at the University of Michigan. Last year I visited in East Lansing and wandered over the plant there. If you are up and coming you can get a degree there in Hotel Management. I met some of the English faculty and they were a very disgruntled crew. They said their library was brand new and specialized in the second volumes of trilogies . . .

## To Sally and Robert Fitzgerald

10 December 56

We were real glad to hear from you and get the picture of the large and sturdy brood. They look like a formidable crew and I hope you have gained a few pounds. I think you should each weigh about a hundred and eighty so your mere presence will scare hell out of them and you never have to resort to violence of word or deed. This is my theoretical contribution to child care and development.

I enclose a little morality play ["A View of the Woods"] of mine for your Christmas cheer but as it is not very cheerful, I'd advise you to leave off reading it until after the season. It's sold to the *Partisan Review* but any criticism would be appreciated because I can still make corrections before they get around to using it. I'm looking forward to getting my year's batch of Telemacus . . .

I have just learned via one of those gossip columns that the story I sold for a TV play is going to be put on in the spring and that a *tap-dancer* by the name of Gene Kelly is going to make his tellyvision debut in it. The punishment always fits the crime. They must be going to make a musical out of it. This is the story about Mr. Shiftlet who marries the old woman's idiot daughter.

I am fine but still on the crutches, of course. However, after the last X-rays the scientist has definitely decided that it is not lupus of the bone but just a roughening of the bone, about which nothing can be done except to continue on the crutches. Which don't bother me none.


## To "A."

12/11/56

This Chicago magazine is being lent me by Ben Griffith, the man who admires the respective works of me and James Jones, but I can't resist sending it to you as I'm sure he won't mind. G. wrote an article on Jones in the *Georgia Review*. I didn't see it but I think it was called "A Backwoods Robin Hood," or something like that, though *backwoods* don't sound right. Should you ever run across it in your researches, do gimme a report. This article on the Handy Institute is by the same boy Ashley read, though not the same article, probably a condensation. Anyway it's hard to see why Mrs. Handy and her boys shouldn't stay dead and buried after what he's done to them here.

Also enclosed are the four letters I've had from C.J. I can't see an escape from *that* [religious] order for *her* as a defeat. I bet she was like a hyena in a cage full of doves there. Either she would have gone plumb slap nuts or she would have just dried up and blown away. But doubtless she learned something there that will do her in good stead for whatever she has to face outside. Of the books she mentions, the only one I have is the *New Tower of Babel* if you'd be interested.

It remains to be seen whether we see me in *America* or not. It seems that Fr. McCown sent a copy of my talk to the Macon girls to H. C. Gardiner, SJ. I had sent it to Fr. McCown before I gave it to make sure it was theologically correct, as I wanted to be on firm ground . . . After considerable time Harold C. writes me that he would like to condense it (himself) for *America*. Well, I can see where it would have to be condensed, but I can't see me letting Harold C. condense it. If my name is going to be attached to it, I am the one that is going to do the condensing. The which, in politer terms, I wrote him; and have not heard again. So we shall see. I showed Fr. McCown the letter I wrote him and asked if he thought it might hurt Fr. G.'s feelings, if they were delicate. He said no, you ought to just tell him to keep his dirty red pencil off your manuscript. That was about three weeks ago and no reply.

Your letter about *The Forest of the South* [by Caroline Gordon] immediately put my sins before me: I had never read *The Forest of the South*. Only [her] "Old Red" in an anthology. So I called the college librarian and asked her if she had it and she did and I went and got it, and so I am now up with you enough to be able to say that I have read "Summer Dust." The first thing that hit me in the face was the child's quoting the Bible verse—"He who calls his brother a fool is subject to hell's fire." Mary Fortune quoted the exact verse in "A View of the Woods." Now I am in a quandary as to whether I should change that in "A View of the Woods." What do you think? I find it effective there and I hate the thought of having to take it out. Caroline has read the story and didn't mention it. She probably never dreams that "Old Red" is all of her stories I had read. Some prediction of hell for the old man is essential to my story. This has never come up before. What do you think?

But to get on to "Summer Dust"—it's a good example I guess of what you would call an impressionistic short story. You read it and then you have to sit back and let your mind blend it together —like those pictures that you have to get so far away from before they come together. She is a great student of Flaubert and is great on getting things there so concretely that they can't possibly escape —note how that horse goes through that gate, the sun on the neck and then on the girl's leg and then she turns and watches it slide off his rump. That is real masterly doing, and nobody does it any better than Caroline. You walk through her stories like you are walking in a complete real world. And watch how the meaning comes from the things themselves and not from her imposing anything. Right when you finish reading that story, you don't think you've read anything, but the more you think about it the more it grows.

I haven't read enough to know much what she does with her

men but I would think from "Old Red" that she makes a contrast between the kind of man her father was, the Aleck Maury [of her novel, *Aleck Maury, Sportsman*], and the kind of man who has to come to the surface when he's spoken to. She is saying the Aleck M. kind is the more complete certainly, and I don't doubt but what she's right . . .

According to Lon [Brainard] Cheney, the best of Caroline's novels is *None Shall Look Back*. I haven't read it, but he says the unnamed adversary is Death in it and it is all understatement, which is Caroline's specialty.

Last spring a quarterly by the name of *Critique* published an entire issue on Caroline. I had a copy and lent it to [a friend] and he made three trips here expressly to return it, forgetting it on each one. So I wrote him last week to put it in an envelope and mail it to you. There are some things in it you may enjoy . . . I am in no hurry for it whatsoever if he does send it to you. Never lend a book to a man as you will have to set a stick of dynamite under him before you get it back. I'll probably get a frantic letter saying he has misplaced it.

I am very handy with my advice and then when anybody appears to be following it, I get frantic. Anyway, the thought of your writing something—anything—as a kind of exercise has got me down. It may just be the word exercise. Experiment but for heaven sakes don't go writing exercises. You will never be interested in anything that is just an exercise and there is no reason you should. Don't do anything that you are not interested in and that don't have a promise of being whole. This doesn't mean you have to have a plot in mind. You would probably do just as well to get that plot business out of your head and start simply with a character or anything that you can make come alive. When you have a character he will create his own situation and his situation will suggest some kind of resolution as you get into it. Wouldn't it be better for you to discover a meaning in what you write than to impose one? Nothing you write will lack meaning because the meaning is in you. Once you have done a first draft then read it and see what it says and then see how you can bring out better what it says. If I don't shut up I will get to sounding like Lowney Handy.

The man who lives with the family of bears reminds me of Cal Lowell who has an imaginary friend named Arms, a policeman, kind of half man and half bear. Arms of the law, he calls him, and Arms says all the outrageous things that Cal is too polite to say. That man sounds very nice.

I am writing my agent to make haste and sell all my stories

for musical comedies. There ought to be enough tap dancers around to take care of them, and there's always Elvis Presley. Momenti mori.

## To William Sessions

27 December 56

I have been highly enjoying the beautiful book [*Three Mystics*] about St. Theresa and St. John and El Greco and so for that matter has my mother. And we christened the water pitcher last Sunday and she proclaimed it was just suited to her needs and was highly gratified that the spout didn't drip. So we are both most grateful. Me I am glad that at least half the holidays are over and I hope we soon get rid of the fruit cake and turkey. We had our Christmas dinner on Sunday and for Christmas I demanded and got meatballs and turnip greens.

I also finished reading [Fr. George] Tavard's book and I think it ought to be in every Catholic hand and paw . . . Also I wrote Arabel Porter so I hope your seccetery got off the ms.

## To "A."

28 December 56

The Lord knows I never expected to own the *Notebooks* of Simone Weil. This is almost something to live up to; anyway, reading them is one way to try to understand the age. I intend to find that *Time* with her picture (some weeks ago) and cut out the picture and stick it in the front. That face gives a kind of reality to the notes. I am more than a little obliged to you. These are books that I can't begin to exhaust, and Simone Weil is a mystery that should keep us all humble, and I need it more than most. Also she's the example of the religious consciousness without a religion which maybe sooner or later I will be able to write about.

You were good to read AVOTW ["A View of the Woods"] again and if you are like me you are now thoroughly sick of it; however, it ain't over until it is finished and I am always long in finishing anything. The first point is whether Pitts is or can be a Christ symbol. I had that role cut out for the woods. Pitts is a pathetic figure by virtue of the fact that he beats his child to ease his feelings about Mr. Fortune. He is a Christian and a sinner, pathetic by virtue of his sins. And I don't feel that a Christ figure can be pathetic by virtue of his sins. Pitts and Mary Fortune realize the value of the woods, and the woods, if anything, are the Christ symbol. They walk across the water, they are bathed in a red light, and they in the end escape the old man's vision and march off over the hills. The name of the story is a view of the woods and the woods alone are pure enough to be a Christ symbol if anything is. Part of the tension of the story is created by Mary Fortune and the old man being images of each other but opposite in the end. One is saved and the other is dammed and there is no way out of it, it must be pointed out and underlined. Their fates are different. One has to die first because one kills the other, but you have read it wrong if you think they die in different places. The old man dies by her side; he only thinks he runs to the edge of the lake, that is his vision. I changed the verb to the conditional which makes that clearer now. He runs in imagination. I have thought that since the old last paragraph* was only an appendage anyhow, that it might be added to the new ending, but I don't really think it does anything for it. You can see what you think. I also changed the sentence that was confusing. And spelled them words right. I don't see how you can tell about the words. Dain looks just as good to me as deign. In fact better.

I ought to defend Powers. I don't take him as meaning it was a mistake to kill Mrs. May for a short story, but only that I should have left her alive so that I could write a novel about her. Powers' instincts are too good on what to do with short stories for him to mean anything else; besides, he was only giving half a mind to it and being pleasant. And I ought to defend myself against the charge of producing in this second ending something "slick." I only worry in these things about serving my own artistic conscience, not a mythical set of admirers who expect a certain thing. God and posterity are only served with well-made articles.

* *The paragraph that was eventually deleted from "A View of the Woods" suggests a somewhat different conclusion as to the ultimate fate of the two warriors. Flannery notes here that she meant to convey that the old man was damned. This is a rather extreme verdict, given his unawareness of the nature of what he was doing all along, and the killing of the child was clearly accidental. The paragraph she omitted seems to suggest that although both were* doomed, *having destroyed each other, in the end both had their eyes opened and filled with rain, even possibly with tears. This is the ending she discarded:*

"Pitts, by accident, found them that evening. He was walking home through the woods about sunset. The rain had stopped but the polished trees were hung with clear drops of water that turned red where the sun touched them; the air was saturated with dampness. He came on them suddenly and shied backward, his foot not a yard from where they lay. For almost a minute he stood still and then, his knees buckling, he squatted down by their sides and stared into their eyes, into the pale blue pools of rainwater that the sky had filled."

Apropos of the Christ image business, the fall issue of *Cross Currents* has an essay on *The Idiot* as a Christ symbol by Msgr. Guardini. I ordered you a subscription to it and told them to make it retro what you call it to the fall issue. Yesterday I get an extra copy of the fall issue, I don't know if they just made a mistake or not. Anyway, if you don't get a fall issue of it before long, let me know. They are a very slipshod organization and it takes months for them to do anything and then like as not they do it backwards.

In my novel I have a child—the schoolteacher's boy—whom I aim to have a kind of Christ image, though a better way to think of it is probably just as a kind of redemptive figure. None of this may work however; but I have made some progress these last three months or think I have . . .

Harold C. Gardiner SJ has not seen fit to answer my communication of November 22 . . . I have never heard from O. Henry.

. . . A letter from my agent today announces that "The Life You Save" will be presented February 1 on the Schlitz Playhouse at 9:30 New York time. My eager beaver friend in NY keeps sending me clippings of gossip columns, one announcing that Kelly will star in Flannery O'Connor's "backwoods love story." Another saying Kelly says "It's a kind of hillbilly thing in which I play a guy who *befriends* a deaf-mute girl in the hills of Kentucky. It gives me a great chance to do some straight acting, something I really have no opportunity to do in movies." See? He ain't had the opportunity before. There'll be no singing & dancing, Kelly says. I think it's chanel 5 and people tell me you can't get it very good here, so I hope you will absolutely be in front of your set this time at the correct hour, as I must have some representative there to give Kelly a good leer every now and then for me. I don't know who his leading lady will be, but doubtless my NY friend will be providing that information before long. She thinks this is all hilariously funny and keeps writing me, "Has dignity no value for you?" etc. It will probably be appropriate to smoke a corncob pipe while watching this. All my kinfolks are going to think that it is a great improvement over the original story.


29 December [56]

Correction: O. Henry sent me the money this morning. Now we will see what "Greenleaf" is subjected to by the people who review the book.

I am glad you are working on the long thing. I like that length myself but it is never wise to decide beforehand what length a thing will be. It will be as long as it takes to do it . . .

I will keep in the Bible quotation in AVOTW. All I needed was the strong voice of encouragement. I sometimes suffer from literary scruples.

I have two books that I think would help you in your writing—not immediately perhaps but in the long run—but I won't send them unless you want me to. One is a book by Percy Lubbock called, *The Craft of Fiction*. This sounds like a how-to-do-it book but it is not; it's a very profound study of point of view. Lubbock is a Jamesian. The other is a textbook I used at Iowa. It is pure textbook and very uninviting and part of the value of it for me was that I had it in conjunction with Paul Engle who was able to breathe some life into it; but even without him, it might help you some—called *Understanding Fiction*, Brooks and Warren.

Well, a happy new year and more thanks than I can tell you for the many things you have done for me, for Baron von Hügel and Simone Weil, but even more for your own letters.

## To Sally and Robert Fitzgerald

I January 56 [57]

The sweater, the like of which I have never seen before [it was full-length] arrived yesterday and I assure you that no day from now until the hot weather will see me outside of it. It's the answer to an uninsulated house and I have told my mother she needn't bother to chink up the cracks around the windows in here with newspaper this year. Do all the I-talians go about in these garments or is it a new invention? It couldn't be better for my needs and purposes and I do thank you no end . . .

That lay committee to advise Cardinal Spellman on how to keep his feet out of his mouth should certainly reorganize. He is at it again, this time over a movie called *Baby Doll*, a dirty little piece of trash by Tennessee Williams, which he is on good ground in condemning but not the way he did it. The rector of the Episcopal Cathedral (Pike) immediately answered him in a sermon, pointing out that *Baby Doll* was no more obscene than *The Ten Commandments* which the Cardinal had recommended highly.

I have got the O. Henry prize this year—$300—for the thing that was in the *Kenyon* this summer ["Greenleaf"]. I keep hearing that Mr. Ransom is going to retire and go back to Nashville but I don't believe it.

I was not satisfied with the ending of that story I sent you for Christmas ["A View of the Woods"] and have redone the last paragraph, which I enclose just for the record.

We haven't got the Hungarians [a proposal Mrs. O'Connor was entertaining]. She keeps dragging along with the [refugees]. She gave the old man a pair of glasses this Christmas that cost her $19 but as she said, he never said Thank you or Merry Christmas or kiss-my-foot. She also gave him a shirt and he came over with it on and, she said, stood there grinning at her. So after a while she says, "Well how do you like your shirt?" He pulls at the collar and says, "Leetle bit too beeg." "Well," she says, "you just grow into it." I think she sometimes feels for the Russians . . .

*In late December of 1956, Flannery found a vivid new friend, one who was to be immensely important to her. Maryat Lee, a playwright then living in New York but a Kentuckian by birth, whose brother had just been made president of the Georgia State College for Women in Milledgeville, was visiting her family there. It had been suggested to Miss Lee that the two should meet, although her own work and interest in the theater were so absorbing that she was not yet familiar with Flannery's writing. Coincidentally, on the last day of her visit, Flannery telephoned and invited her to come out to Andalusia. Expecting the worst in "lady writers" or "Graham Greene sensibilities," Maryat Lee went; they met, they talked, and their long friendship was born. Flannery liked her and she liked Flannery, and that evening, after she had read one of the stories Flannery had given her, the lady-writer image crumbled once and for all.*

*There are no other letters among Flannery's like those to Maryat Lee, none so playful and so often slambang. For one thing, Flannery obviously took some mischievous vicarious pleasure in the fluttering of the dovecotes that usually followed the visits of her rebellious and unconventional friend to formal Milledgeville. They settled early on into a running joust on two subjects, race and religion, that lasted throughout their friendship.*

*Maryat Lee writes: "Flannery permanently became devil's advocate with me in matters of race, as I was to do with her in matters of religion. Underneath the often ugly caricatures of herself . . . I could only believe that she shared with me the sense of frustration and betrayal and impotency over the dilemma of the white South." She did to a great extent, of course, but the solution in which she placed her hopes was not the activist and immediate one to which Maryat Lee was devoting her generous energies. Flannery's hope lay in a slower process, best described when she wrote, in answer to an interviewer's question: "[The Southerner's] social situation demands more of him than that elsewhere in the country. It requires considerable grace for two races to live together, particularly when the population is divided fifty-fifty between them and when they have a particular history. It can't be done without a code of manners based on mutual charity . . . [The] old manners are obsolete, but the new manners will have to be based on what was best in the old ones—in this real basis of charity and necessity . . . For the rest of the country, the race problem is solved when the Negro has his rights, but for the Southerner, whether he's white or colored, that's only the beginning. The South has to evolve a way of life in which the two races can live together with mutual forbearance. You don't form a committee to do this or pass a resolution; both races have to work it out the hard way. In parts of the South these new manners seldom make the papers."*

*Maryat Lee, for her part, threw herself into the black movement with all the fervor of her nature. At the same time, writing to Flannery, she caricatured institutional religion, to which Flannery was committed at her deepest levels, on the theory, she writes, "that scandalizing religious institutional people did more good than harm." So they went at it over the years, jeers flying, on these two subjects, casting each other in the roles of Rayber and Tarwater. Flannery addressed Maryat Lee under an endless array of names: Raybucket, Rayfoot, Raybog, Raybush, etc., and signed herself by as many variants of Tar and Water; and she awarded her combative friend "half interest" in Mary Grace, the surly Wellesley girl in "Revelation."*

*Behind all the mockery, however, lay the greatest mutual fondness. Maryat Lee was a joy to Flannery, and a devoted friend. The correspondence begins with this letter, which refers to Maryat Lee's drive back to the Atlanta airport in the automobile of her family's black gardener: a real deed of derring-do twenty years ago in Georgia. Flannery was merely ironic in her reaction, and admired the finesse of M.L.'s brother in the matter.*

## To Maryat Lee

9 January 57

A few days after you left, my mother and I saw E. [the Lees' gardener] rolling down the street. He looked as if he were in the state of euphoria that follows being psychodramatized, and I decided that you had had them at that all the way to Atlanta. I find it mighty hard to imagine any conversation that might have taken place in that car. When you left, my mother said to me, "Don't you tell a soul that she is going in E.'s car. Don't you even tell Sister. If that got out, it would ruin Dr. Lee." A few days ago, Dr. Lee called Sister to find out something and Sister asked him if you got there all right with E. "Oh," he said, "she went with friends." Sister later told us that you hadn't gone with E. after all, that you had gone with *friends* and that SHE thought that was much better. I think Dr. Lee will last a long time here; in fact as long as he cares to last.

It is often so funny that you forget it is also terrible. Once about ten years ago while Dr. Wells was president, there was an education meeting held here at which two Negro teachers or superintendents or something attended. The story goes that everything was as separate and equal as possible, even down to two Coca-Cola machines, white and colored; but that night a cross was burned on Dr. Wells' side lawn. And those times weren't as troubled as these. The people who burned the cross couldn't have gone past the fourth grade but, for the time, they were mighty interested in education.

Our "contact"—on the strength I guess of having done me one favor by seeing that I got introduced to you—forthwith sent me four more poems to criticize. The next time you come we will get you out here before you are ready to leave. Incidentally, neither my mother nor I was conscious of any rudeness. However, the parental presence never contributes to my articulateness, and I might have done better at answering some of your questions had I entertained you in the hen house. That's a place I would like to keep two cane-bottomed chairs in if there were any way to keep the chickens from sitting in my absence. My ambition is to have a private office out there complete with refrigerator. My mother's contention would be that my own room looks enough like a chicken pen that I ought to be satisfied.

I'm glad you liked the stories of mine you read and felt that they weren't a dead-end taken. Many's the dead-end I have taken, however, but the results of those trips are I hope in the trashcan. I suppose you come to know yourself as much by what you throw away as what you keep and at times it is appalling. I wonder if you can have thought the dead-end a likely possibility for me because of the orthodoxy, which I remember you said was a ceiling you had come through? I take it that what you have come through is some expression of orthodoxy. I have come through several of those myself, always with a deepened sense of mystery and always several degrees more orthodox.

Meanwhile, I'll be looking forward to reading the play and to hearing from you when you are inclined to write me and to seeing you out here again under more leisurely (sp?) circumstances.

*To "A."*

Enclosed for yr edification please find Harold C. Observe mention of "admirable work," observe general charitable tone, observe burden of Christmas rush. I have been working on the little article all week as it will run me nuts until it is finished. I can't have that hanging over me. Will send you same next week probably for your minute scrutinizing of for loophole & folly. Also possible unique spelling.

You have convinced me that the Christ symbol is Pitts if there at all. You are right. It's got to be human. But you have not convinced me that the first ending is better than the second or that M.F. and the old gent should die in the same breath . . .

Don't worry about my spending any time computing the little figures in the Simone notebooks. I just go on to the next page. There are remarkable things there and if I really own the complete Simone Weil I feel very rich. Sally Fitzgerald was once much interested in her and reviewed some of her books for the *Commonweal*—under the initials S. M. Fitzgerald, but that was when I was sick and I didn't see the reviews. Sally had it figured out what *kind* of a heretic she was but I forget.

When you were writing about Lowell's wife that B. admired I naturally presumed you were talking about Jean Stafford and your remarks seemed to fit her well enough. Then when I read the postscript I saw you meant Elizabeth, and I wondered what of Elizabeth's you had read first to give you that opinion, the one you had before you read *The Simple Truth*. I liked *The Simple Truth* and I think Elizabeth is a lot better writer than she gets credit for being. She is a long tall girl, one of eleven children, from Kentucky. She's a great friend of Mary McCarthy. I haven't heard about the baby. Maybe somebody will be writing me. I used to go up to Elizabeth's apartment to see her when I lived in New York and the elevator man always thought I was her sister. There was a slight resemblance.

N. called up the other day and told my mother that she had taken a job and was on the way out to tell ALL about it—first job she has ever had. My mother hung up and said, "I'm afraid she's selling those pots and pans and if she wants to have a demonstration out here, you know we'll have to let her." So I offered a strong silent prayer that N. was not selling pots and pans. Shortly N. hove up and yells, "You want to hear my speel? I repersent the Curtis Circulation Company. I am your local repersentative! Do you take any magazines? Are you interested in renewal? I have a special offer on the *Ladies' Home Journal!*" She has been at it a week and is having a wonderful time, going to all the houses in the country and not missing a thing and repeating it all as good as if she had memorized it. She is also hoping to be able to make some money as the commission they get is very good, 60% on some magazines and 40% on the rest. She visited a crazy woman in the country, an old man wanted to know if she believed in a literal hell and told her if there was a literal hell everybody in the Bible ought to be in it, a woman with her neck in a cast etc. etc. etc . . .

My mother is busy nursing a giant azalea that some unknown sent us for Christmas. She being from Savannah thinks there is nothing so fine as azaleas and she is determined that no draft shall touch this one until spring when she aims to put it out in some protected place. She has been wanting one of these bushes with the orange berries whatever they are and so she gave me one for Christmas and got Jack to plant it. They were planting it and she said, "Be careful with that now, I've given it to Miss Mary Flannery for Christmas." "This ole bush?" he said. "It's a very nice bush," she said. "She yo only chile," he said, "and you ain't going to give her nothing but this ole bush?" She gave my uncle Louis a pecan tree. Anyway, whoever sent her the azalea hit the nail on the head without knowing it.

I have sent you the two books. I see the Brooks & Warren is full of my juvenile notes. Keep these books as long as you please as I have no use or need of them.

[P.S.] When my head clears I will utter some remarks on the subject of mysticism and technique.


## To Elizabeth Bishop

13 January 57

You were very kind to write me and it means considerable to me to know that you have read and liked my stories. The stories are, by now, much better travelled than I am, as I have never been out of the United States and have been few places in it. Every now and then I get some perception of how they might be taken by someone out of the country and it is a revelation that enlarges my own view. I hadn't realized that life in Brazil might resemble life here in the South but I guess there are many similarities. We have a lot of students who come here from South America. A friend of mine who taught a special course designed for them and their problems with English told me he found them much disgruntled at having to read the short stories he assigned. "Why do we have to read stories like these?" one of them asked him. "Nobody gets married in them." Which is an attitude I am right familiar with from hearing my connections estimate my own work.

You were good to mention them to the editor of *Revista Contemporanea* and I would like to see some of them used. There is a French translation in the making but that is the only one. They have received a little critical attention in Italy; at least, Robert Fitzgerald, who is now living in Genova, sent me a translation of an essay on Miss Eudora Welty's stories and mine, done by Mario Praz, the *Romantic Agony* man. He described the story called "A Circle in the Fire" in such a way that I barely recognized it but otherwise he appeared to know what they were about and to approve. He had apparently once visited Savannah which he described as "a city of decayed 19th century elegance, Negro shacks, suffocating heat, lugubrious large trees draped with 'Spanish moss' and innumerable mosquitoes."

Once Cal Lowell showed me a picture of you (I am supposing the same Miss Bishop) sitting on a porch in Florida; he left me with the vague notion (how much owing to him and how much to my imagination I don't know) that you travelled up and down the coast, sort of with the seasons. If that is the case and you ever pass by here or near us, my mother and I would be so pleased to have you stop and visit us. She and I live in the country a few miles outside of Milledgeville. The place is a dairy farm and I am glad to say that most of the violences carried to their logical conclusions in the stories manage to be warded off in fact here—though most of them exist in potentiality . . . Off and on we find ourselves with some not-so-good country people but they are the type always on the move and we never have them for long.

Thank you again for writing me. I have a great respect for your own work though I am almost too ignorant ever to know why I like what I like. I used to live with the Fitzgeralds in Connecticut and I remember that Robert always spoke of you with great admiration.


*To "A."*

25 January 57

I have just read the story, once only so far, but I think it is just about perfect. I want to keep it until I have a chance to read it again. I think it is a little too long and I think one or two places could be toned down. The only other qualm I have is about the hero? being as you say not even quite genuinely human. He is what you call a moral moron or what the old psychologists used to call that, a person who apparently is incapable of feeling the difference between right and wrong and therefore is incapable of sin—like that one that put the bomb in his mamma's suitcase and blew up the plane. And if he is incapable of sin, then the old man is not really a buckgoat for sin. Occasionally, however, you show that he does have a perception of right, or perhaps you don't show it but could. But I think you can't just posit a moral moron and expect the reader to have any interest. If there is no possibility for change in a character, we have no interest in him. You wouldn't write a story about someone hopelessly insane. I think you could correct this by having the boy not quite so evil, by having him hesitate before each of his evil acts and decide on the evil for a reason which he figures out. Otherwise there is no use to write about him. You've got to show him killing the little bit of good in himself; and it seems to me you could do this fairly easy. Let him be a monster because he wants to be a monster, not just because he is a monster. He seems to me evil but not sinful. Sin is interesting but evil is not. Sin is the result of an individual's free choice, but evil is something else.

His language is wonderful and everything is dramatic and this is all about 350% better than that last one.

I think your use of the Mass is all right, though I don't think this apey boy would be able to repeat the Latin so well and I'm not sure that altar boys at low Mass wear red cassocks—not generally anyway.

Janelle is not quite right. I don't think she should make the pious speech about the scar or I think anyhow that it should be shorter and the scar too should probably not be so obvious. He is obviously interested in her ONLY because she goes to Church, but why she is interested in him beyond the natural pull of evil is hard to understand. I would just say tone her down a little. And don't put that she is going to baby sit for a *Catholic* family in San Francisco. The Mass scene is enough.

The tramp is fine and just as he ought to be. Jennie Mae could probably say less.

If possible we should have some indication as to why or what in his past life has made this boy such a monster. It would heighten his credibility. In fiction everything that has an explanation has to have it and the residue is Mystery with a capital M.

This story is quite worth your getting down to and rewriting with some of these things in view. And when you have rewritten it to your satisfaction, then you should send it out . . . to some of the quarterlies that are willing to print new people—*Accent, Epoch, New World Writing,* or some such place.

Two minor items: don't name any streets Oak and Main. Even if they are that kind of street, cease and desist.

The story is very well constructed. Amen. If you write it over, let me see it again. Amen 2.

Naw, the story in the Martha Foley collection was "The Artificial Nigger." Don't ask me how they figure what they'll use. Paul [Engle] wanted to use it the year before, but he can't use anything that has appeared in a book; apparently Sis Foley can. One year "A Circle in the Fire" was in both collections. Hers comes out before his. His is usually better than hers. I have them both if you want to read them. They have some really lousy stories in them I can tell you.

I have just finished reading Frank O'Connor's book on the novel, *The Mirror in the Roadway.* He expresses many of me prejudices perfectly but he does go off on wild explanations à la the life and oddities of various of the authors. I can't judge because I have usually not read what he's talking about

The Lowells have a girl, came about two weeks ago.

I don't think it is technique that Caroline is praising in *Aleck Maury* but a kind of nearness-to-life in nature. Stephen is abstract, but always has to "come to the surface" when he's spoken to. The old man has his affinities with the concrete. I haven't read that story ["Old Red"] in ten years of course. It merely introduced to me what I could be expected to do with a symbol and I sat down and wrote the first story I published . . .

I'll send back the story Monday along with any further comments I can think of.


## To Maryat Lee

31 January 57

Your brother came out Sunday night a week ago with the book and paid us a visit. I thought now this is a mighty nice man to come all the way out here to bring me a book, but by the time he left, I found myself engaged to talk in the GSCW chapel on the 7th of February. As I say, your brother will go far. I told him we were looking for you back and he allowed you doubtless will be back. Yesterday my mother met your mother and they engaged in polite conversation to a similar effect.

Well, I was fascinated by the little play—a real morality play if I ever saw one and altogether powerful in spite of it. I was able to fancy myself hanging from one of those fire-escapes and watching it with complete absorption. I am never willing to let well-enough alone and I now visualize that there ought to be a permanent vacant-lot repertory theatre to put on such plays all the time. Why don't these people like Baroness de Huek (sp?) sponsor such?

I hope the longer play picks up. I have the same feeling about my novel. I have parked it for a few weeks and am writing a lecture that I am going to have to give at Emory in the "Adult" education program—adult education calls for the most elementary things you can think of in not more than two-syllable words. The course is called "How the Writer Writes," and each week, if you please, they have a different writer come and lecture. If the poor souls are not confused in the beginning, they will be in the end. It got off to a big bang two weeks ago with a worthy, C.D., who produces a best-seller every year. I am going to end my lecture on the note that it is as noble not to write as to.

That is a shame about old Greene and his *Potting Shed*. The best thing I ever read on Greene was written by an English girl named Elizabeth Sewell and was published in *Thought*. She allowed that his sensibility was different from his convictions, the former being Manichean and the latter Catholic, and of course, you write with the sensibility. Her word for him was Neo-Romantic Decadent. What he does, I think, is try to make religion respectable to the modern unbeliever by making it seedy. He succeeds so well in making it seedy that then he has to save it by the miracle.

I am speculating that maybe by the time of your next visit, some of the local backwoodsmen will be irritated enough by things in general to stage a little cross burning on the Mansion lawn. But I'm afraid even that is infected with the general degeneration. The last time the Klan had a big gathering here, they set up a portable fiery cross in front of the Court House. That is to say, they plugged it in. It was lit by many red electric bulbs. When I saw that, I said to myself: this is mighty disheartening, it is later than I think. That was a notable Klan meeting too because the Grand Dragon attended and the Klansmen rode all over the county in a motorcade, distributing baskets to the needy . . .

*This letter was written in answer to Granville Hicks's request that Flannery contribute to* The Living Novel, *a symposium he was editing.*

## To Granville Hicks

21 February 57

I am sending you this talk just to show my appreciation for your having asked to see it; however, I think you will see at once that it is not what you are looking for. It was designed for a student audience—to combat their prejudices and if possible to keep them awake. Also it is not specifically about the novel.

If the talk had been for a serious audience, I would not have been making it. I'm not an intellectual and have a horror of making an idiot of myself with abstract statements and theories . . .

## To "A."

21 February 57

The window-washing incident I think is hilarious, just fine, and much better than the other. But that ending I cannot digest. That is too far to take Sutfoots. You might have him nosing around the exterior of some monastery, with his face pressed to a hole in the wall—but a lay brother *no*. No. Please, no. I don't deny God could do it but He is not the author of this story. This is a human invention. Reconsider it for heaven's sake. This is not a thoroughly naturalistic story and you don't want to destroy the tone at the end, which you do if you make Sutfoots a lay brother. This ending is too obvious. You can suggest something obvious is going to happen but you cannot have it happen in a story. You can't clobber any reader while he is looking. You divert his attention, then you clobber him, and he never knows what hit him.

I never told B. that [a correspondent Flannery never met] sent me those plays out of the blue. She had been writing me about two or three years before she sent them and had read all my stuff. She liked most of it but did not like "A Temple of the Holy Ghost." She wrote me that the It in there was a lie. She is full up to her ears of the Existentialists, Gide and Madame de Beauvoir and Sartre and Life and Loneliness and Alienation. I sympathize but sometimes it gets very maudlin and I wonder if she wasn't drunk when she was writing particular letters to me. The last letter she wrote me she said she had "lost her homosexuality," and was trying to be an artist. She is much absorbed with writing plays. As to the homosexuality I don't know if that is really a trouble of hers or if she is just like the rest of those arty people in the Village, who feel that all kinds of experimentation is necessary to discovering life and whatnot. She of course thinks my religion is my personal hallucination and in this last letter she said she knew I had lost my faith. I guess that was to irritate me.

A friend of [B.'s] apparently met her in a bar. [He] had announced his visit here to his NY connection. And she told the friend that I had helped her get her play published (I didn't, of course, though I wrote Arabel Porter a letter about it; however Arabel Porter would not have taken it if it hadn't been good). I am learning that I had better be careful what I say . . . as the simplest things are going to be repeated . . .

The *Commonweal* review of the O. Henry was pretty disgusting I thought, not only as it related to my story but to the rest too. I have the feeling sometimes that their reviewers are trying desperately to be clever because they have no other opportunity. Who cares that that gent found Jean Stafford's character insufferable (why?) or what he thinks about Mary McCarthy. They all—all the bright boys—love to take potshots at her because she is so much smarter than they are . . .

I hadn't read that Blum piece on "The Dead" [by James Joyce] but I liked it and also read "The Dead" over. If you don't have that collection *Dubliners* you should get it in Modern Libery and study those stories, as you can learn an awful lot from them.

In the *Constitution* on the 13th Celestine Sibley [Atlanta columnist] went over my performance at Emory, quoting me quoting the man who said when he finished his novel he felt as if he had given birth to a "sideways" piano. Which will teach me to open my bloody mouth so I can be understood. She also left the impression, which I did not intend to convey, that I had a great contempt for the audience. Anyway, it is over and I am glad. The little dinner beforehand was a table full of College Liberals and I sat at the head or the foot of the table and couldn't think of anything to say to them, expressionless as a clock. They were full of *Baby Doll*. Seems the Atlanta censors censored it.

The G.'s [farm help] have found greener pastures some eight miles away and are moving in two weeks. I am very glad as he was a poor dairyman and was wearing my mother down. The question is what will we have next? Good country people, poor white trash, nothing?

## To Maryat Lee

24 February 57

Your brother was not only there, he introduced me—as one who had been on and off the best-seller lists. I decided this was an innocent calumniation and ignored it.

I tried to decide if any of your agents could be mine—Mavis McIntosh and Elizabeth McKee. Miss McIntosh is an old lady who sits at her desk with her hat on and Miss McKee is a youngish lady who speaks out of the side of her mouth like a refined dead-end kid. Should you run onto them give them my regards.

Thanks for the Atkinson review. How weird to think that he would consider the cliché about the room from which faith had gone being like the marriage from which love had gone as sensitive! My my. What I would like to know is what did Walter Kerr say about *The Potting Shed?*

If you have Voices you'd better listen to them and let the form take care of itself. What does this appear to be heading up to—fiction you mean? I was startled at first when you asked me here something about how or where I got my material. At Emory they had a list of questions for me to answer and the first one was: Do you write from imagination or experience? My inclination at such a point is always to get deathly stupid and say, "Ah jus writes." This has anyway never occurred to me except as a theoretical consideration, of no concern to anybody seriously engaged in the act of writing. I draw the line at any kind of research and even object to looking up words in the dictionary. I think you probably collect most of your experience as a child—when you really had nothing else to do—and then transfer it to other situations when you write. The first story I wrote and sold was about an old man who went to live in a New York slum—no experience of mine as far as old men and slums went, but I did know what it meant to be homesick. I couldn't though have written a story about *my* being homesick. I wish I had Voices anyway, or anyway distinct voices. I have something that might be a continuing muttering snarl like cats courting under the house, but no clear Voice in years.

If you ever get in front of the television and you wish to see one of my stories rouged for an elegant interment, be in front of some set on Friday, March 1.

At Emory they had a little dinner party before I talked . . . One gent said, "I'm working with a group on interpersonal relations." Somebody asked what interpersonal relations were and one of the novelists said, "He means niggers and white folks."

*This letter initiated one of Flannery's treasured friendships, which started, like so many others, with a letter from a sympathetic and intelligent reader. Louise Abbot, of nearby Louisville, Georgia, had felt shy about asking to visit Flannery and considered pretending to be a "lady journalist." Fortunately, she abandoned the ruse, or this might have ensured Flannery's absence from home. They met quite often after the first visit.*

## To Louise Abbot

I'd be most pleased to have you come over and see me. I work in the mornings but I am at home every afternoon after 3:30. We live four miles outside of Milledgeville on the road to Eatonton (Hy 441 N.) in a two-story white house. The place is called Andalusia. You could drop me a card the week before you want to come so I could let you know if I'll be here. I usually am but occasionally I make trips. Or, we have a telephone . . .

In any case, I look forward to seeing you and I am very glad that you have decided not to be a lady-journalist because I am deathly afraid of the tribe.


## To Mrs. Rumsey Haynes

3 March 57

Thanks so much for the TV paper about brother [Gene] Kelly. Having now witnessed his performance, I must say that I am not overcome by his acting powers. We don't have a television but Sister, in town, does, so we went in to see the play. Now I am doubly glad we don't have one. The best I can say for it is that conceivably it could have been worse. Just conceivably.

Our [farm] family has got a better job and they are moving next week and so my mother is busy getting in another family. This is always a trying time because you never know what you are getting until you get them. This will provide her with an additional headache and me with an additional story probably. The new people seem to be several cuts below the Greenleafs. My imagination always precedes the events that take place here.

We are looking for the bulbs you sent us to come up daily. Things are already in bloom. Usually everything blooms in February and then gets killed in March. Also everything is laying and the other day I decided to eat a goose egg for breakfast. I fried it, ate it, and was galvanized for the rest of the day . . .


## To Granville Hicks

3 March 57

Since sending you that talk, I have been provided with the serious audience. Against my better judgment I have said I will talk at Notre Dame in April and I am at this point trying to write a talk that will do for the occasion. As the subject will be regionalism and religion in fiction, or anyway my experience of it, I think it might serve your purposes as well as the talk you have seen and that it should be a better paper. Anyway, if your deadline is not at once, I would like to send it to you when I finish it in about a week or ten days. If you don't like it, you can use the one you have, beginning it where you please. Having this other paper to do, I wouldn't have time to write another introduction.

I begin to feel like a displaced person myself, writing papers and not fiction.


## To Denver Lindley

6 March 57

I watched the TV play, disliking it heartily from first to last. However, that was not nearly so bad as having to sustain all manner of enthusiastic congratulations from the local citizens. They feel that I have arrived at last. They are willing to forget that the original story was not as good as the television play. Children now point to me on the street. It's mighty disheartening . . .

I have not read any good reviews of Madison Jones' book [*The Innocent*]. I wrote him a note about it and had one in return. He appears to be bearing up.

I have a friend named John Lynch who has written ten or twelve stories that he would like to have published in a collection. I suggested that he send them to you. I have seen three or four of them and think they are superior . . . I hope anyway that he will get around to sending them to you.


## To "A."

9 March 57

This new ending is right. Just right. And as I stack the whole thing up in my head it seems to me that the whole thing must be just right now. I suggested sending two out at a time but reconsidering it I don't much see why you don't go on and send this one out by itself. I am not so sure that any place will take it because I think the Mass scene might scare them off; however, the purpose of sending it around would be to show various people that you CAN write stories. After reading this, they will remember you and be interested to see the next one. Somebody might even take it. If I were doing it, I would first send it to Mrs. Arabel J. Porter, [editor of] *New World Writing* . . . If you will, I'll write her that it is coming so she will look at it herself. When she sends it back to you, I would send it to *Epoch* or *Accent* or the University of Kansas City *Review*, addresses of which I will furnish you, if you want them. This process of sending things out and getting them back depresses some people but it is necessary for a certain length of time. Don't send any letter with the manuscript, just a stamped, self-addressed return envelope, and always when you get it back, send it back out again the same day or the next. Practical advice from Practical Annie, the Writer's Friend.

Well, how did you like THAT picture in the *Bulletin*? They will all think that if my face is habitually that dirty I should not be writing for a Cathlick paper . . .

Yours truly is speaking at Notre Dame University on April 15 and those Jesuits are paying me a hundred bucks and my plane fare; also I will get to see Robert [Fitzgerald] who will meet me in Chicago. And that so help me will be the last talking I am going to do this season.

Yes I saw the television play. The college librarian who is a great friend had a supper party—me and six local old ladies and my mamma—and then we repaired to Sister's to see the play . . . All over town old ladies were gathered to witness it. And other groups too. Immediately it was over, the telephone rang and a friend of the family said, "Three generations . . . have just watched your television play and we were all spellbound!" My mother has been collecting congratulations all week like eggs in a basket. Several children have stopped me on the street and complimented me. Dogs who live in houses with television have paused to sniff me. The local city fathers think I am a credit now to the community. One old lady said, "That was a play that really made me think!" I didn't ask her what. As for me I stood the play a good deal better than I am standing the congratulations.

Sent you the book on Fénelon and the Edith Stein. Never any hurry about these and don't feel you have to read them just because they are sent. Also have a copy of *PR* with Lowell's first chapter of his autobiography in it to send.

Mr. G. [farm help] is gone and one Mr. F. is installed. Mr. F.'s family consists of himself, wife, two babies, mother and daddy, whose name is Buster. According to Mr. F., "There ain't a thang wrong with daddy but two thangs, heart trouble and asmer." And Mr. F. says he has heart trouble hisself, that sometimes he gets down and don't have the heart to get up. Mr. F. is twenty-four years of age but looks older. His wife is probably about eighteen. She dips and he chews. His mother is separated from Buster but also separated from her second husband so she has returned to

Mr. F.'s hearth. According to Mr. F. her second husband hit her in the stomach so hard that she had to be carried to the hospital. Mr. F. went to see him about this and told him that if he did it again that he would get two or three others and they would come and lynch him. My mother said she reckoned Mr. F. didn't really mean that but Mr. F. said yesm he did. He said he figured it that no matter how strong a woman was, she wasn't no match for a man and any man that come picking on any woman, Mr. F. wouldn't care if he lynched him or not. Therefore we are expecting to be adequately protected if nothing else. English is flowing freely now for the first time in three years. Mr. F. talks every minute that he is not spitting or that my mother is not talking. He also gets along very well with Jack and Shot. My mother told him that she wasn't going to hire anybody who would hit her Negroes in the head and Mr. F. said he didn't believe in doing nothing to nobody else that he wouldn't want done to him. The other morning Mr. F.'s wife would not get up and cook his breakfast and Mr. F. told her she could get up and cook it or she could get up and get the hell out of there. My mother told him she didn't want any fussing and feuding going on on our place and Mr. F. said wouldn't be none go on. Mr. F. has been on "public works" and so he hasn't been eating too regularly and is very glad to have the job. And we are very glad to have Mr. F.

My agent's seccetary has just written me that she saw the TV play and thought it "was as close to the original story as it could possibly have been"—which must mean she hasn't read the original. Anyway, she allowed that they were going to query Rodgers and Hammerstein and see if they would like to do a musical adaptation. I can't decide if this was supposed to be a joke or not. I rather think not. I would rather see it a musical than what it was on that TV program.

> The life you save may be your own
> Hand me that there tellyphone
> Hideho and hip hooray
> I am in this thang for pay.

I will submit same to Rodgers and Hammerstein.


## To Maryat Lee

10 March 57

The enclosed is for you to read on the Japanese freighter. I have heard about these freighters—you eat eleven times a day and all is elegance. Your companions according to my speculations will be wealthy widows and widowers and retired schoolteachers and there will be parlor games. Let me know if I am right.

The following is good Georgia advice: don't marry no foreigner. Even if his face is white, his heart is black.

Thanks for offering to let me use your apartment but I don't think on crutches I am up to the city alone and I intend this summer to try to force this novel somewhat. I am going to Notre Dame to talk on April 15, and so I have stopped to write that talk, but when that is over, I aim to get at it, and stay at it (two hours a day that is).

Well I'm glad you liked the rest of the stories. "The Artificial Nigger" is my favorite and probably the best thing I'll ever write. All I seem to be doing these days is writing these stinking talks.

Let me hear about this Japanese freighter, and be sure you book your return passage as there is nothing but cannibals, savages, Chinese and opium parlors in those parts, and we expect you to visit again in Milledgeville, a Bird Sanctuary, where all is culture, graciousness, refinement and bidnis-like common sense.

15 March 57

The enclosed is for you to yawn into while reclining on cushions on Japanese freighter, first-class division. I am haunted by those four devils who don't get to eat with the Captain—how the other half lives, etc. You can also use this for yawning into while reading honorable novel, *Wise Blood*.

Also, if you are stopping in Tokyo and should get into any difficulty there ???? I have just acquired a pen pal, [an] Assistant Professor of English at the Japanese Defense Academy. An airmail yesterday from [him] announces, "An unspeakably deep impression that the glamourous style used in the 'Greenleaf' allures me further to read your other writings, because I am sort of interested to the Contemporary American Literature." Nobody but this gentleman has ever called my style "glamourous" and I am much taken. I am sure [he] would get you out of any jam.

No, the confusion is in the language, it ain't in me; I can't come. Right now I am so distracted trying to get myself to Notre Dame and back that I doubt I will ever be tempted to take another trip. I am the kind that would like to *be* somewhere but don't like to *get* there.

So. It is you who have not only led astray your brother but five hundred and twenty innocent girls who are struggling to be truthfully educated. These innocent souls now labor under the impression that it is a worthy state to be on the best-seller list. I hope on the Japanese freighter you will have time to acquire a sense of guilt about this.

## To John Lynch

16 March 57

I'm much obliged to you for reinforcing my invitation to Notre Dame. I was hesitant to accept a speaking engagement until I got it from Robert [Fitzgerald] that I wouldn't be expected to be I. A. Richards. I can't talk literary. However, I am coming and talk the way I talk.

I wrote Denver Lindley that you had a book of stories that you might be sending him and he has written to get your address which, with your leave, I will send him. In fact I will send it to him without your leave as I have to write him. He has his mind on his business and will not keep your stories nine months I am sure . . .

I hope the chicken pox is over and that I'll get to see you and your wife when I am in Notre Dame.

## To "A."

23 March 57

I reckon the new title is better than the first, but I don't think it does much for it yet. There is no reference to the Donne use of "island" in the story and I don't know how the reader is going to draw the connection you want him to. The story however does very well on its own without the reader's having to accept your view of these characters. For my part, for instance, I find Zeke as guilty as Randall (at the opposite pole of pride) and had I been the jedge would have give him twenty years at hard labor instead of three. This is neither here nor there. I wouldn't use the Donne poem in the story as it is too well known and has been used to death since *For Whom the Bell Tolls*. Everybody knows it now and therefore it's unusable.

If you don't want Mrs. Porter written I won't write her; however, it is not a matter of "if I am any good, I'll get published," etc. What is liable to happen is that your story lands on the desk of some young man with his hair in his eyes and feet on his typewriter and Mrs. Porter never sees it. All my writing to her would do would be to make sure that she saw it herself. And she is a woman of taste. Having done this for [one] who is a bore and for [another] who gives me a pain and several others I have never seen or would care to, I naturally would like to make sure she sees yours. With yr. permission, I will; without it I willn't. Inform.

The *Commonweal* had a lousy review of *The Innocent* by Madison Jones. It's a very fine novel.

Mr. F. is doing fine. He is the kind who isn't happy unless he is working, and as my mother is the kind who isn't happy unless he is working, they get along just fine. His mother is a down-at-the-mouth type but we are not seeing much of her. Every Wednesday for the last four weeks somebody has had to take Shot in to try to get him a driver's license. He can drive but he can't pass the test. The first time he got 38. My mother did the writing and read him the questions.

"What is the speed limit in Georgia, Shot?" she says.

"Mr. Louis say I ain't to drive no more than 55."

"Well, I think it's a little more than that in the daytime, Shot."

"Yes'm, it's 40 in the daytime."

"Put down exactly what he says," says the Patrolman, standing over them. And so that went. This last time he took it, he got 40 and my mother was encouraged. If he keeps going up 2 points she says, he'll get it eventually.

The note from Harold C. says he hopes I won't mind the little editing he had to do on the piece in *America* and that he expects the piece to draw considerable comment. Probably every irate priest in the country will communicate with them about it. I don't want to be drawn into any arguments, but I'd be much obliged if you'd watch their letters column.

I am reading at Elizabeth Stevenson's book on Henry James. She's real intelligent and a very good writer . . .

3/26/57

Thanks for the issue of *America*. It was my mistake though, not Harold C.'s. He said if I saw the issue of the 23rd I'd see they were using my piece & I naturally thot he meant it was in there. It was announced. Anyway, the piece is in the issue of the 30th & I have seen it . . . One look is enough. You will see what his editing amounted to & where it was. I do not mind at all being corrected but I think I should have been asked to make the correction myself. Nevertheless, it don't amount to much & my pious reaction is: to hell with it, I have other things to do.

This afternoon has been a full horror as my mother elected to remove the rug from under me & my furniture and put another one down. Everything was wiped up with turpentine water & I am waiting for the seven other devils . . .

I trust you find my handwriting as bad as yr own. I ain't strong enough to hit a key tonight. Excelsior.

## To William Sessions

[Spring 1957]

[Regina] says don't you bring her a thing but yourself. The truth is she enjoys having you immensely as she likes your conversation and she also likes the fact you eat what is put on the table.

I didn't know Isaac Rosenfeld had died. I had thought he was relatively young . . . I don't really know anything about him. I suppose anyone who did not believe in the divinity of Christ would correctly say that Oedipus' words at Colonus and Christ's on the cross meant the same thing; but to the believer, Oedipus' words represent the known while Christ's represent the unknown and can only be a mystery.

We'll look for you on the 27th.

## To Maryat Lee

4 April 57

It is not known by everybody but: the peafowl is called peafowl because his favorite dish is peas—green peas, black-eyed peas, sweets or any peas that come to mind. Furthermore, the peacock sheds his tail every August and the alert owner goes behind with bucket and picks up each feather. You are the recipient of a last August's feather and it cost the bird in question no sqwark. (sp?) In fact I am sure he would be delighted to know it will be among first-class passengers as he has no use for the lower orders.

The other day I saw your brother who said, "Well are you going to New York?" "What for?" says I in my stupid way. "Oh," he says, "atmosphere and all that. I heard she asked you and I think that was awfully nice of her." I said I thought it was too but I reckoned I'd have to put up with the atmosphere around here.

My only other Japanese acquaintance is Mr. Sanobu Fujikawa, who several years ago lived in Kamakura City. He spent an afternoon on our porch one time, brought by some friends of mine from Nashville while he was there on a Fulbright. He too was interested to the Contemporary American Literature.

I would like you to bring me back one saber-toothed tiger (with cub) and a button off Mao's jacket and any chickens that you see that I don't have already, I mean kind of chickens. A few years ago the Atlanta Chamber of Commerce sent the equivalent in Tokyo a bag of grits, as a good-will gesture. Presently a thank-you letter arrived saying the Tokyo Chamber thanked the Atlanta Chamber for the grits seeds, that they had been planted but had not yet come up. That story is just to illustrate that you are going amongst a heathen people and that you may not always be understood. Frankly I will feel much relieved when you get back here.

I guess all the bumbling boys at Notre Dame will be forced in off the golf courses and football fields to squint at a live novelist. I may not say anything, I may just make faces. Anyway, the word *beauty* never crosses my lips.

Well, cheers and kindly keep me posted on your progress in the Ori-ent and do not neglect to see about your return passage. Sustained anxiety.

## To "A."

6 April 57

What his Reverence corrected was the paragraph about the responsibility of the artist (I had Mauriac's name to purify the source all right). He changed it to read that the artist would realize that he as well as the Church had a responsibility for souls. I had said that the responsibility for souls was the business of the Church and the responsibility of the artist was to his art. Now it seems to me that he is correct but that some explanation should be given of how the artist's responsibility for souls operates. Is it, for instance, the same in kind as the responsibility of the Church, is it to children, to idiots, to old ladies, to fifteen-year-old girls, to unbalanced people? If I had been consulted about this I would have changed the paragraph to suit him, but I would have tried to clarify the other as much as possible. The paragraph seems to slide over the problem to me, and to contradict itself. Just in the paragraph before I had said that this kind of responsibility would turn the artist to stone. He left that as it was. I don't by any means think he is a small or mean man, I think he just sees this as an abstract theoretical problem and from a great distance. Whereas the writer himself is traveling the rocky road, and feels every individual bump.

You needn't worry, I ain't going to perform for the [service clubs] but when something comes up where I am actually asked to do something for the Church, then it is right for me to do it even when it is a drop in the bucket. As for the *Bulletin,* I've gotten more out of that than I've given and probably will out of this *America* thing too. Doing these things is doing the only corporal work of mercy open to me. My mother takes care of all the visiting the sick and burying the dead that goes on around here. I can't fast on acct. of what I've got. I can't even kneel down to say my prayers. Every opportunity for performing any kind of charity is something to be snatched at. I have no notion that the artist should be above the common people; the question is who are the common people right now? I confess I don't know. I don't think the [service club people] are—they look down on the artist. I even dislike the concept *artist* when it sets you above, all it is is working in a certain kind of medium to make something right. The material is no more exalted than any other kind of material and the idea of making it right is what should be applied to all making. St. Thomas said the artist is concerned with the good of that which is made, that art is a good-in-itself. Are you familiar with *Art and Scholasticism?* I'll send you my copy if you want it. About the only good thing Dr. Johnson had to say about Milton was that he didn't scorn teaching Latin to schoolboys . . .

[The college at which she had just read] was rather dreary. They had it in a long basement room and set me in the middle of it with the inconsiderable audience strung out the length so that you couldn't possibly make them all hear at once. Then half of them came when I was half through the talk, bang bang and scrape scrape. I don't think the man who introduced me had ever read a word I'd written, but he averred they were very fortunate to have me there. I now await my check for $50.

Now I am sure that I didn't call your story a "study of pride." A story is never a study if it is any good and I took that one to be good. But any story can be looked at in the light of any quality and pride being the most fundamental to human nature, I generally look at characters in the light of it. Further to judge the character is not to judge the story. You think too much of interpreting and analyzing and all that. Learn to write a story and then learn some more from the story you have written . . .

With forty others, the Confirmation should be got over without undue strain. I am glad I got all my ceremonies over at a numb(er) age.

Mr. F.'s 16-month-old son had a recent intestinal spell and my mother asked Mr. F. what the little boy might have eaten. Mr. F. allowed that he hadn't eaten nothing out of the way, the night before he had had sausage. Sausage! says my mother. It wasn't the sausage, Mr. F. said, he's been eating sausage since he was 6-month-old. Mr. F. said that with some of his paycheck he was going to buy a second-hand git-tar although he owes money to almost everybody in town. My mother gave him a lecture entitled "A good name is better than a large bank account," so he agreed that he would pay his grocery bill first . . .

## To Maryat Lee

17 April 57

I daresay that being alone in Yokohama for you is equivalent to negotiating passage through the Chicago airport for me. There they also speak a foreign tongue. You have, I trust, arrived in Yokohama? I mean in one piece? Of steady mind and nerve I mean? I hope you have some kind of firearm. A sawed-off shotgun or a Kentucky rifle or something. All I know about the Ori-ent is *Terry and the Pirates* which I don't read anymore, being too old and advanced in wisdom and knowledge.

I found on arriving at Notre Dame that I wasn't to talk just to the students but was to give a Public Lecture at Night. This added an element of formality but I ignored it. The audience of about 250 or 300 consisted of 25% Bumbling Boys, 25% skirted and beretta-ed simmernarians, 25% higher clergy, 25% faculty and wives, 25% graduate students, 25% . . . I am over-extending the audience. Anyway, the operation was successful and I have a hundred bucks to compensate for any damage that may have been done to my nervous system.

My parent took advantage of my absence to clean up my room and install revolting ruffled curtains. I can't put the dust back but I have ultimated that the curtains have got to go, lest they ruin my prose. She looks forward to any departure of mine as an opportunity to ravage my room and it always looks shaken when I return to it.

The next Occasion for me will be at the local college on something they call Honors Day and at which me and another worthy are to be "honored." I can do without all honors that do not carry stipends with them but if you convey this crude sentiment to your brother, I shall consider you a Skunk of the Third Water and will declare in public that you are a lier.

Don't forgit my saber-toothed tiger.

*To "A."*

Enclose you the Notre Dame speech, though there ain't much new in it. Also Madame Fitzgerald on Gardiner. You would like Madame FitzG I am sure. The trip was entirely successful. I escaped the snow by exactly one day and made all the necessary connections, which was what had me worried. I had thought the speech was to be in the afternoon and for students, but when I arrived Robt. announced it was to be 8 p.m. Monday and a Public Lecture. The room was full and they had to go out for more chairs. It appeared I was an object of considerable curiosity, being a writer about "Southern degeneracy" and a Catholic at oncet and the same time. The audience was not ominously clerical though there was a sprinkling of baby faces under heavy black berettas. During the talk I trained my gaze on one of them and he trained his back on me as if he didn't believe a damm word of it; nevertheless they appeared impressed, though they didn't laugh in all the right places. After it a girl came up to me and said, "I'm not a Catholic, I'm a Lutheran but you've given me some hope for the first time that Catholic writers may do something." I said, "Well please pray that we will." And she said, "I will, I will in Christ." And she meant it and she will and it is that kind of thing that makes these trips worth the effort. I also saw a godchild of mine for the first time who lives in South Bend and a few other people that I am glad to have met.

Naw you didn't say the artist is above the common people, that was just my digression on the subject, but you do seem to exalt him above his place in the scheme of things though it is hard to put my finger on just how. The word "dreams" which you did use, always terrifies me. The artist dreams no dreams. That is precisely what he does not do, as you very well know. Every dream is an obstruction to his work. I have sent you *Art and Scholasticism*. It's the book I cut my aesthetic teeth on, though I think even some of the things he [Maritain] says get soft at times. He is a philosopher and not an artist but he does have great understanding of the nature of art, which he gets from St. Thomas.

B. sent his story, which I liked. The truth is that B. just has a natural gift for imitation and he has considerable technical competence and with the Church, he also has some purpose and point to use these things for. It may however be almost *too* easy a gift, too facile, I don't know but time will tell. I objected to his use of the word "magic" in the paragraph toward the end about confession. I also thought that their sexy talk would have been more effective if there had been less of it but I didn't tell him that as I think I might have thrown him off the track. It don't do to carp about trifles.

A friend of mine in Virginia is going to send me an extra copy he has of *The Red Priest.* He says Peter Russell (a British bookseller) wrote him that Lewis was dictating a novel before he died, that he would dictate a while, then lapse into a coma, then pick up when he came out of it at exactly where he had left it, but Russell said it was too confused to publish.

Yrs. truly has declined to talk to the Ga. Liberry Association in November.

You are right about the exhaustion but now that I don't have to think about any trip I hope to pick up. I am getting some award from GSCW that I have to say two pages of thanksgiving for but that should be no terrible burden, except that I also have to go to a coffee and a tea for it and shake innumerable paws. These things are fine for the people that like them and the people that don't, as my mother tells me, are just peculiar.


## To Elizabeth Fenwick Way

2 May 57

Well we were real disappointed to get that telegram. My mother had had the beds made up just in case and was ready to make arrangements for the dog at the dog hotel when the yellow paper arrived. But I hope you will come next year. You will know your way on the roads better. Let me know if the lupus rash goes away shortly. I still don't stay out long without my hat though I have not had the rash in several years, which is maybe why.

Notre Dame was fine and I had a good audience and beat it out there, making all the connections, between tornados . . . Robert Fitzgerald has the chair of poetry out there for these four months and he met me in Chicago and I got back by myself without assistance. I am back at work with a vengeance. Trips at least do that for me. I am so glad to get back that I go to work at once with real gusto . . .

I have just had a turkey to hatch a goose-egg laid there surreptitiously. She was too embarrassed to even come off the nest with it so the gobbler killed it and now they are relieved of that perplexity. I find like Alfred Lord T. (or whoever it was) that nature is red in tooth & claw.

## To "A."

I read three of Joyce Cary's novels about five years ago and liked them at the time, but don't remember much about them now except they were lively. Those last pictures of him were rather saintly looking—as if he enjoyed life in that state as much as in any other. I have been reading a book about the Eastern Fathers. One of them said, "All life is a holy festival." I am supposed to be reviewing it for *Ye Bullyton*. [They have] thousands of my reviews on stock and I keep waiting for her to print the one on the Walter Kerr book, but she just don't print any of them . . .

B. ran onto Dorothy Day at the monastery and drove her to Atlanta to catch her train and they discussed *The Malefactors*. D.D. had been to Koinonia* and had been shot at. All my thoughts on this subject are ugly and uncharitable—such as: that's a mighty long way to come to get shot at, etc. I admire her very much. I still think of the story about the Tennessee hillbilly who picked up his gun and said, "I'm going to Texas to fight fuhmuh rights." I hope that to be of two minds about some things is not to be neutral.

You are way off on the subject of Mrs. FitzG. She is anything but soothing. She has a legal mind which she applies to a conscience run day and night on the highest octane principles . . .

My Uncle Louis said he saw you. How was she, says I. "Fine, fine, fine," he says and adds, "I know about as much about her as I do about you." Good will without communication—a very satisfactory state. I am feeling much better but will feel better yet I trust as soon as this program is over at GSCW.

Yrs. truly is being given a grant of $1,000 by the National Institute of Arts & Letters. So is Robert Fitzgerald and Mary McCarthy and I don't know who all else. Anyway any honor sent through the mail and cashable is about the only kind I got any great respect for . . .

Peacock tail is at its best except that we are having a three-day rain and he can't get it dried out. With nineteen hollering in the tree every night it sounds as if the whole chorus is being murdered slowly, repeatedly, formally, etc.

How do you like Maritain? Strangle that word *dreams*. You don't dream up a form and put the truth in it. The truth creates its own form. Form is necessity in the work of art. You know what you mean but you ain't got the right words for it.

---

* *Koinonia is a utopian community near Americus, Georgia. It is still active.*

You must never apologize for sending me a story that don't work because that is the kind you learn on. I think you are right not to try to salvage that one—at this time—because I don't think it is your material. Whether you were or weren't trying to make— call it a "redemptive figure"—out of Malison, that is the impression the thing gives, and it's a bad impression. But you can learn a great deal from what you've done on this story. It's a step in the right direction. I write for months and months stuff that I simply have to tear up—but I don't know what I can do until I have found out the hard way what I can't do. There are several technical lessons that you should have learned from this one, and that is the way it has to go. My existence is full of stories that I had to put aside because I wasn't writing them the way they needed to be written. I can help you much more on the ones that don't work than on the ones that do . . .

Oh. Don't let this story's not working keep you from going into the one that revolves around Joe McCarthy—but remember that you don't write a story because you have an *idea* but because you have a believable character or just simply because you have a story. This has some bearing on the subject of the word "dream," which we have been using at cross purposes. The last thing I would like to convince you of is that form is an absolute lying somewhere in an esoteric mist to which only the artist has access. Heavens no. That is to me what the word "dreams" used untechnically summons up and that is one reason I don't like it. Another is that it is constantly on the tongues of the kinds of ladies who attend [literary conferences] and who love to talk also about the "loneliness" of the artist.

Fr. Tavard got your address from me so he could send you a reprint of one of his articles. He left one with me and I liked it very much. Your description fits him down to the ground. He didn't get a chance to say much. He has written an article on Simone Weil he said arguing with Fr. Oesterreicher's point about there being nothing Christian about her. Fr. Tavard thinks there was. However the article was botched in the *Third Hour*, he said, and didn't make sense when they got through tampering with it . . .

One of my peachickens turned up last week without a foot— cut plumb in two, I suspect by somebody's sling blade. It fell off in two days—or rather as it was just hanging by a thread I cut it off and now the victim is doing fine but I don't know what I am going to do with a one-legged peacock.

I wish somebody would write something sensible about

Koinonia—as you say it is something regressive which is getting all the benefit of martyrdom. I think they should be allowed to live in peace but that they deserve all this exaltation I highly doubt. D.D. [Dorothy Day] wrote up her trip there in the *CW* [*Catholic Worker*], which I duly enclose. It would have been all right if she hadn't had to stick in her plug for Their Way of Life for Everybody.

## To Maryat Lee

19 May 57

Greetings from historic Milledgeville where the ladies and gents wash in separate tubs. Are you sure you haven't caught anything; what I mean is, the blood disease and all, what I mean is there are certain advantages to being stiff-necked? Unadaptability is often a virtue. If I were in Japan, I would be pretty high by the time I left out of there as I wouldn't have washed during the trip. My standard is: when in Rome, do as you done in Milledgeville.

Last Friday week I stood in a receiving line with your brother and sister-in-law for a good hour, pressing the soggy paws of citizens from all over the state who have daughters in college. Your sister-in-law is a whiz bang at it. The guests had their names pinned on them and she never failed to see the name and say it. As for me, my eye was as glazed as the one on the fish served to Mr. K. by the Shinnahon Lines . . .

Well, you have a decision in front of you if you have to decide whether you will live your whole life with a man. I am sure it requires a metamorphosis for anybody and cannot be done without grace. My prayers are unfeeling but habitual, not to say dogged, and I do include you in them.

I hope you understand that it is not the tooth of the saber-toothed tiger I want, it is the *tiger*. I don't care if it's a old toothless tiger or not, just so it's alive. I intend to start a zoo.

*At this time, Flannery received a letter that interested her from a young woman who was then teaching at Stephens College, in Columbia, Missouri. Cecil Dawkins, an Alabaman, two years younger than Flannery, wrote to her on the subject of teaching literature in general, and Flannery's stories in particular. A writer herself, she was published in a number of literary quarterlies, and Flannery admired her work. Her collected stories,* The Quiet Enemy, *were published in 1964 and a novel,* The Live Goat, *appeared in 1971. With Flannery's encourage-*

*ment, she made a play weaving together a number of the O'Connor stories, and it was presented at the American Place Theatre in New York in 1965, under the title* The Displaced Person.

*She and Flannery shared a Southern Catholic background, as well as their literary interests, and she became one of her regular correspondents for most of the years until Flannery's death.*

## To Cecil Dawkins

19 May 57

Thank you for writing me—and for mailing the letter. It is fine to know that freshmen are being introduced to contemporary literature somewhere. I had never heard of K. A. Porter or Faulkner or Eudora Welty until I got to graduate school, which may have been time enough for me in as much as I got to graduate school, but so many do not; they leave college thinking that literature is anything written before 1900 and that contemporary literature is anything found on the best-seller list . . .

Of course I hear the complaint over and over that there is no sense in writing about people who disgust you. I think there is; but the fact is that the people I write about certainly don't disgust me entirely though I see them from a standard of judgment from which they fall short. Your freshman who said there was something religious here was correct. I take the Dogmas of the Church literally and this, I think, is what creates what you call the "missing link." The only concern, so far as I see it, is what Tillich calls the "ultimate concern." It is what makes the stories spare and what gives them any permanent quality they may have.

There is really only one answer to the people who complain about one's writing about "unpleasant" people—and that is that one writes what one can. Vocation implies limitation but few people realize it who don't actually practice an art. Your freshman might be improved by a look at Maritain's *Art and Scholasticism*. He dwells on St. Thomas' definition of art as a virtue of the practical intellect, etc.

. . . Milledgeville is a Bird Sanctuary, population 12,000 (people, not birds). I live four miles outside of it on a dairy farm. If you are ever in this direction, stop and see me, and thank you again for writing.

## To Ben Griffith

21 May 57

Come over and fish any time and visit me when you get through. I went down to that pond once and decided it wasn't worth it. Right now I am acting as bloodbank for every redbug on the Eatonton Road and I don't want to add ants to it. I'll look forward to a visit from you.

I haven't seen *The Town* yet. I used to like *The Hamlet*—but for obvious reasons it is better for me to give the Snopes a wide berth . . .

I hadn't realized they had published the juvenilia—done without my permission I assure you.


## To Denver Lindley

21 May 57

Thanks so much for sending me Fr. Bruckberger's pièce de théâtre which I am enjoying, slowly, on account of the condition of my French. I am also greatly enjoying the sketchbook and it has spurred me to buy some tempera and Kem-Tone which I intend to apply to Masonite with, I reckon, the usual doubtful results.

We enjoyed your visit and look forward to the next one. You came a day too soon as far as the excitement was concerned as on Wednesday, Mr. F. discovered a rattlesnake near the chicken yard; but all he did was throw a crate on top of it and run, so it is still at large and maybe we can produce it the next time you come.


## To "A."

1 June 57

. . . Well, Mr. F., his wife, children, mother and stepdaddy, along with his lares and penates, moved out of here forever on a pick-up truck last Tuesday. The full story of Mr. F. will have to be written and by me sometime in the future. Suffice it to say that he proved himself to be of the tribe of Mr. Tom T. The colored people have moved over and things are going very well with just them. The big problem is to get Shot that driver's license and my mother has decided he has to have PROFESSIONAL assistance, so the teacher of driving at the local high school is coaching him, and we are all holding our breath. He drives very well but I still don't think it's clear to him what a vehicle is, etc.

Fr. McCown and the Gossetts from Macon went down to

Koinonia last weekend and invited me to go along but I declined, it being inconvenient in more ways than one. But they are coming over here next Tuesday and tell me about the trip on which they said they had "fun." The Gossetts buy things for Koinonia that they can't get down there. The enclosed is Fr. McCown's latest newspaper controversy. He sent it and said he expected The Christian Brothers to send him a free case of brandy for this invaluable publicity.

I haven't arranged a wooden leg for the peachicken yet and I'm afraid it can't be done. He hops but he has to be confined in a separate apartment as the others will kill anything crippled. I let him out for a little while the other day and had to rescue him at once and put him back. He will have to be what my mother calls "a boarder." (Cows that don't produce are boarders.) I have one peahen setting and one chicken setting on four peafowl eggs that I just picked up. The two-year-old hens lay anywhere until they get used to the idea.

I have just bought a very cheap, yellow, four-room house on the way to the waterworks—this being the fruit of my savings from literary earnings over the last ten years. I feel I have took on stature being a property owner. Others may go to forein parts and broaden theirselves but I am going to get 15% on my money by staying at home.

I have a painting to send you for your Confirmation but it will not arrive until I succeed in finding a box to mail it in. I thought I had one but it's too little although the painting is small. I wanted to find a suitable pious article for the occasion but all the pious articles I see turn my stomach. This painting is the one of the chukar quail and they have a rather purgatorial look so maybe it will be somewhat suitable anyway. It is no great shakes as a painting and I have messed with the frame overmuch but you are going to be the recipient of it nevertheless. Sooner or later, that is . . .

Any Saturday that suits you will be fine for us. Cheers.

[P.S.] My uncle Louis allowed he saw *you* the other day but you didn't see him.


## To Louise Abbot

6/2/57

The Carolina quarterly arrived and I have read your story and the first-prize one and the Paul Green thing. Your story is much better than that first-prize thing but I suppose since they gave it to you once, they couldn't do it again. The story is highly imaginative and I like the conception and the quality of the writing very much. It doesn't quite "come off" as a complete story and I have been at some pains to try and figure out why. As near as I can get to it, there are two reasons. One is that this woman's revolt or realization or however you want to characterize her experience is not firmly rooted in her individual character—or so it seems to me. I mean that we don't know enough about her to make her experience believable. I feel that what happens to her, what she realizes, she realizes because the author wants her to, not because it is her character to realize it. If it is believable it is believable because you tell it well and we have to take your word, but it ought to be believable because from the woman's character it appears inevitable.

The other thing is the cactus—which I find too "literary," having too much the air of being there to be a symbol.

I think you do what many writers do who haven't written a great many stories—try to be subtle. Anyway, I like the writing and I think you ought to write a lot and that the more you write the more complete your stories will become.

## To "A."

Saturday (6/57)

. . . Wish to announce that Willie Shot Manson was granted license to drive a vehicle by the State of Georgia in Sparta, Georgia on June 3 at 4:31 p.m. EST, 1957 A.D. I tell Ma she should send out engraved announcements . . .

## To Maryat Lee

9 June 57

So it may be the South! You get no condolences from me. This is a Return I have faced and when I faced it I was roped and tied and resigned the way it is necessary to be resigned to death, and largely because I thought it would be the end of any creation, any writing, any WORK from me. And as I told you by the fence, it was only the beginning. And perhaps you will find it the same, if you don't look for beginnings to be too quick. Everything has to be diluted with time and with matter, even that love of yours which has to come down on many of us to be able to come down on one. It is grace and it is the blood of Christ and I thought, after I had seen you once, that you were full of it and didn't know what to do with it or perhaps even what it was. Even if you loved Foulkes [David Foulkes-Taylor] and [Donald] Ritchie and me and E. and E.'s brother and his girl friend equally and individually, it all has to be put somewhere finally. In the play [Wm. Alfred's *Agamemnon*] that some New England man wrote there is a line: "Pity the man who loves what death can touch." I don't know the play, only the line. But it is what we are to be pitied and praised for that we do, must, love what death can touch. Well, be busy about it and do not be afraid to be busy about it in the South.

But this Foulkes is nuts if he has the idea that it would be preferable to settle in a "progressive" Southern state. You might as well go to Moline or Rock Island and be done with it. I recommend Missippi.

Yes it was E. Wynn [who had visited]. I had the faces right anyhow and liked her best. She wrote me a letter and said, "If Maryat marries the man, I'd like to know." I mean to ask her to come back again but she probably won't. The people you would most like to have come back manage to be timid . . .

I bought the Wilbur Cash book once because it cost 95¢ and I have never read it for the same reason. I always get trapped in my own economies. But I lean, you know, in the other direction, towards the reactionaries, who got a better grip on the English language.

We are going around the countryside looking at Santa Gertrudis bulls because my mother is thinking of converting to beef. People are harder to handle than cows and white folks than niggers. If you have less complicated cows you have less complicated help. I hope the logic clear. I asked your brother what the man (this Foulkes) did and he said, "I think he has sheep ranches," and added, "but I don't think he has any personal contact with the sheep." I couldn't tell what his attitude toward this was. I don't much think they are expecting you to really get married, but of course I might be wrong about it.

When I come to Japan I will bring my own washtub and washrag and soap and handle it myself. Hell.


*To "A."*

15 June 57

My mother forgot and insured that package and I was sorry as I was afraid then you'd have to go after it. She knowing how it was wrapped up decided it was unlikely it would get there. Don't miss that picture of E.S.; also the old lady who runs the Third Hour is in there—her kinsman used to tell me that she was the ugliest woman in the world and that I reminded him of her which was why he liked me. She looks pretty beat up, but she was chased out of Russia by the Bolsheviks and then out of France by the Germans . . .

The thing about *The Spoils of Poynton* is that the vulgar couple is so much nicer than the furniture collectors. James must have known it. I love that about the boy's eyes looking like the lights in an open club (something like that) and those folks hanging the children's drawings on the wall etc. and that big blonde girl who got him—as she should have. He must have been making fun of the heroine throughout, else he was nuts. But the book is very ambiguous and you have to judge James on *The Portrait of a Lady*, not those nicknacks like the *S. of P.* and *The Sacred Fount* etc.

Report on Mr. F. will be forthcoming on the 25th. We will be waiting at the driveway on that bus—unless some cow gets stuck in the water trough at that precise time, in which case you start up it.

Monday week I had my semiannual X-ray and the doctor was much encouraged as the bone is no worse. To be no worse is in this case to be some better for they had expected it to get worse. It may be that these crutches are paying off.

Mary F. O'Connor sounds like somebody's washwoman. Did every one of you have an individual sponsor or proxy there? We read in the paper there were 204 or somesuch number and it looks like they would have had one proxy for everybody.

[P.S.] Wear some *old* shoes as this place is very muddy and manurey.

## To Cecil Dawkins

19 June 57

I had a friend who once applied for a teaching job at Sarah Lawrence and was interviewed and asked what novels she would teach and she named *The Portrait of a Lady* and suchlike but at everything she named, they said, "That's too hard for the kids." Around here Stevens [Stephens College] is thought of as a place where they teach how to behave on dates but I gather from what you say that this must not be entirely so.

I don't really think the standard of judgment, the missing link, you spoke of that you find in my stories emerges from any religion but Christianity, because it concerns specifically Christ and the Incarnation, the fact that there has been a unique intervention in history. It's not a matter in these stories of Do Unto Others. That can be found in any ethical culture series. It is the fact of the Word made flesh. As the Misfit said, "He thrown everything off balance and it's nothing for you to do but follow Him or find some meanness." That is the fulcrum that lifts my particular stories. I'm a Catholic but this is in orthodox Protestantism also, though out of context—which makes it grow into grotesque forms. The Catholic, using his own eyes and the eyes of the Church (when he is inclined to open them) is in a most favorable position to recognize the grotesque . . .

## To Maryat Lee

28 June 57

. . . Well however you work it out, you will continue to have my limp, obfuscating and airless prayers. You are of course entirely right that the reply was inadequate and cliché-ridden. It always will be. These are mysteries that I can in no way approach—except with the coin of the realm which has the face worn off it. I doubtless hate pious language worse than you because I believe the realities it hides. Nevertheless, you do misinterpret me if you think I mean that it all ends in tatattatum and a tragic little pie. I believe in the resurrection of the body. I also believe in it before it gets that way, dear girl, so don't put me down in yr Associate Reformed Presbyterian black books. It's my own & your own but also the Essential.

Anyway, what I said in the letter, I also said in "The Artificial Nigger," and that is the way I should keep on saying it, it being my vocation to say it that way.

·  What I want to know is, you mean you're going to produce this play in New York? Off-Broadway or something? I thought it took about a million dollars. Lord, I'm glad I'm a hermit novelist.

What did Ritchie write that impressed you on the boat? I am having to go to Athens at the end of the month to conduct a workshop. Senator Pappy O'Daniels used to conduct the Light Crust Dough Boys every Mother's Day over the radio and I feel this is the same bill of goods—haddeyer get an agent? etc. The last time, one old lady said, "Will you give me the technique for the frame-within-a-frame short story?"

Let me know if you make it legal, though I can't think it

would make the foggiest difference (as I only believe in making it sacramental) whether you did or not. But we won't hear about it around here I reckon until you do make it legal. About Aunt Attie. She won't kick off over the telegram. I had an 83-yr-old cousin that I was certain my first novel was going to kill, but it gave her a new lease. Her strength is as the strength of ten . . .

## To "A."

29 June 57

The Mailer [*The Deer Park*] arrived but I have been taken up with the St. Bonaventure, which I will finish first so as I can send it back to you. It is very fine and the sort of thing you will be able to read again next year and get just as much out of—having forgot it all in between. Same as *Cross Currents*, that is. That Fr. Tavard is a real genuine scholar.

A fast letter from Harold C. S.J. written on the same day he called me announces that NBC won't be able to come here to get the tape so for me to just write it out and they will read it in the studio for the July 14 broadcast [of the Catholic Hour]. After maybe knocking every other sentence upsidedown. Anyway, it suits me all right not to read it myself as I cannot stand the sound of my own voice over the radio, but it is really a lot of trouble to write and I have been at it for the last two days and haven't finished it yet, and it's only two pages . . .

If you are wasting any of your sympathy on that peafowl and his *loneliness*, desist. That is the Pathetic Fallacy I think you call it. All that peafowl knows in the way of emotions are two: where do I get the next thing to put in my craw, and where do I keep out of the way of something that wants to kill me until I can find something I want to kill. Right now he is outside, sitting in the cool, and not a social thought to his name . . .

Don't fail to come—and if it is before 11:30 that is all right. It's all right for you . . .

12 July 57

That is a considerable compliment to you that they are keeping that story to consider it longer and it means just what it says: that they are considering it. They could have saved postage sending them back together. They get hundreds of manuscripts and it's a rare one they keep to consider. I'm pleased if you ain't and whether they keep it or not, you know that it has given them pause.

I've finished *The Deer Park*, it being considerably easier to read than *Transiency and Permanence*. He's a very good writer. I think that section where Teppis talks to Whashisname and then Lulu and then has Bobby in is a very funny piece of writing. The least believable to me is all the sex stuff. He never goes into it, handles it aseptically as a monk might. He has the Church on the brain but never mentions Christ so that you wonder if he knows what the Church is about. You wonder where he will go next. I feel he's a satirist at bottom. All that spoiled-priest in Faye stuff was hard to believe. It sounds to me like neo-romantic decadent as Miss Sewell called the stuff, make-believe-spoiled-priest. Have you read *The Romantic Agony*, a study of decadent romanticism by Mario Praz? I got it if you ever want to. Lewis called it a "mass of satanic bric-a-brac" (the Praz book, that is) . . .

We have bought the Santa Gertrudis bull and he is supposed to come this weekend or early next week. He is supposed to be as tall as the man who has been owning him. He came originally off that King Ranch or was from their stock. He is eventually to get us into the beef and out of the dairy business, thereby putting an end to the possibility of other F.'s on this place.

I remember Powers' stories poorly as I haven't read *Prince of Darkness* since it came out. I do remember there was an awful story in there about an old couple and a baseball one I didn't like and I don't recollect that I liked the racial one. A very good friend of mine named Robie Macauley has written a collection of stories called *The End of Pity*, which I want you to see. It's not out yet but I have an advance copy which I'll send you in a few weeks. Not all the stories in this one are good but the good ones are as good as anybody's.

I'm still not sure about that title [*The Violent Bear It Away*] but it's something for me to lean on in my conception of the book. And more than ever now it seems that the kingdom of heaven has to be taken by violence, or not at all. You have to push as hard as the age that pushes against you.

The Santa Gertrudis bull reminds me that I still have your St. Gertrude half read. Every time I get around to her, something else comes up . . . The Tavard is being very fruitful for me, but I have to take it a little at a time.

## To Cecil Dawkins

You certainly are nice to want to give me that dog but I'll have to take the thought for the dog. I didn't tell you what I raise: I raise peacocks—and you can't keep dogs and peacocks on the same place. When people come to see us with a dog, we have to ask them to keep the dog in the car—else the peachickens will take to the trees and have nervous prostrations. I have 27 right now. This place sounds like the jungle at night as they yell and scream at the slightest atmospheric disturbance or mechanical noise. In addition to the peafowl I have ducks and geese and several different kinds of chickens but the peafowl are the main interest. I spend a good deal of my time sitting on the back steps with them. They have no proper sense of place; we have a very nice lawn that they could decorate to advantage but they prefer to sit on the tractors or the top of the chicken house or the garbage-can lid. So I adjust myself to their tastes, including being anti-dog. But I do appreciate your wanting to give it to me.

I am always vastly irritated by these people (I guess like [Wallace] Stegner) who know as much about the South as I do about lower Hobokin and on the strength of it advise Southern writers to leave it and forget the myth. Which myth? If you're a writer and the South is what you know, then it's what you'll write about and how you judge it will depend on how you judge yourself. It's perhaps good and necessary to get away from it physically for a while, but this is by no means to escape it. I stayed away from the time I was 20 until I was 25 with the notion that the life of my writing depended on my staying away. I would certainly have persisted in that delusion had I not got very ill and had to come home. The best of my writing has been done here.

This is not to say that what the South gives is enough, or that it is even significant in any but a practical way—as in providing the texture and the idiom and so forth. But these things have to be provided. So much depends on what you have an ear for. And I don't think you can have much of an ear for what you hear when you're over 20—that is, for a new kind of talk and life. The advantages and disadvantages of being a Southern writer can be endlessly debated but the fact remains that if you are, you are.

Catholicity has given me my perspective on the South and probably gives you yours. I know what you mean about being repulsed by the Church when you have only the Jansenist-Mechanical Catholic to judge it by. I think that the reason such

Catholics are so repulsive is that they don't really have faith but a kind of false certainty. They operate by the slide rule and the Church for them is not the body of Christ but the poor man's insurance system. It's never hard for them to believe because actually they never think about it. Faith has to take in all the other possibilities it can. Anyhow, I don't think it's a matter of wanting miracles. The miracles seem in fact to be the great embarrassment for the modern man, a kind of scandal. If the miracles could be argued away and Christ reduced to the status of a teacher, domesticated and fallible, then there'd be no problem. Anyway, to discover the Church you have to set out by yourself. The French Catholic novelists were a help to me in this—Bloy, Bernanos, Mauriac. In philosophy, Gilson, Maritain and Gabriel Marcel, an Existentialist. They all seemed to be French for a while and then I discovered the Germans—Max Picard, Romano Guardini and Karl Adam. The Americans seem just to be producing pamphlets for the back of the Church (to be avoided at all costs) and installing heating systems—though there are a few good sources like *Thought,* a quarterly published at Fordham. This spring I went to lecture at Notre Dame and met some very intelligent people. In any case, discovering the Church is apt to be a slow procedure but it can only take place if you have a free mind and no vested interest in disbelief . . .

Since you hadn't read Caroline Gordon, I'm sending you a copy of a quarterly that came out last year and was entirely devoted to her. You might find something in it that would be of use.


*To Thomas Stritch*

1 August 57

If I said the old souls wrote epics in Negro dialect, I was bad wrong. They don't know the South exists anymore. They are all writing television plays in television language and they are all nuts; and so was I after three hours of [a writer's conference]. However I was one of the lesser features. The big attractions were The New York Agent Who Sold *Gone with the Wind* to the Movies, and two giant-sized poetesses from South Georgia who conducted a panel on "The Religious Market." One old sister said she wrote true-confession stories with one hand and Sunday-school stories with the other—which sounds right to me as I always suspected the same mind produced them both. There was one bright spot in all this: an old man (the only man) from

Louvail, Ga., who attended every session and broke up every one that he attended. He quoted extensively from Dickens and the Bible and held the floor with a terrible tenacity. He hated the old ladies and they hated him. I can see that those sixty nuns would be wonderful.

## To Sally and Robert Fitzgerald

1 August 57

I conferred with Tom Stritch upon your address and he produced this one but said he wouldn't guarantee it. Anyway I wanted to inquire about yr states of health and send my mid-summer greetings. My mamma had to get rid of her white help as Mr. F. was selling the milk out of the cans between here and Eatonton and proving himself in general more trouble than the cows. So there is nobody here but us and the niggers and everything is very peaceful. Noblesse obleeege with a vengeance as my mama runs it but very peaceful. They are the only colored people around here with a white secretary and chauffer.

Several weeks ago, yr. friend & mine, Fr. Gardiner S.J. of *America* called me up over the long-distance telephone and said in a well-oiled voice, "Miss O'Connor, I hadn't heard from you since your excellent article in *America* and I wondered if you were mad at me." Ha ha. This boy is not calling me up to find out if I am mad with him, says I. What he wanted was for me to write a statement about Cathlic literature for a radio program; which I did for penance. He apologized for changing my article but allowed as how the pressures of getting out a weekly magazine sometimes made it necessary for them to make changes, he thought it was only a paragraph anyway.

At my last conference with the Scientist it appeared from the X-ray that my bone is mending and therefore has nothing to do with the lupus, and that I may look forward to getting rid of the sticks in two or three years. So that is fine. I want to stomp around when I get to be an old lady.

A letter from that Lynch boy at Notre Dame said he was on his way to New York to be interviewed for a job at McGraw-Hill. I'm afraid he is not going to die happy until he gets them all to New York. I thought Notre Dame was mighty nice myself and certainly wouldn't want to leave it for NYC . . .

[P.S.] I have 27 peachickens. My mother says some of them have got to go.

## To Elizabeth Fenwick Way

4 August 57

Well cheers for *Poor Hariet* [Elizabeth Fenwick's new novel]! I enjoyed her and also my mamma enjoyed her and I must say you are lucky on your jackets. Now about the ax. I am sure it was your old woman and that she ran either up or down into a basement and that she was wielding an ax. It had to be yours because I have never read anybody else's mystery stories and this made a big impression on me. I couldn't have dreamed it up, then you had better write it and send me a 10% cut when it gets the Crime of the Month Club Trophy or whatever.

Yes mam, I know all about renters. My papa was a real-estate man and my mamma has two apartment houses and we have gone nuts with renters for years. It's like when you've got 7 children, 1 more don't make any difference though. This is the first one I *own*. So far nothing has broken but the hot-water heater. I gave the renter a bucket of paint and she slapped it on the kitchen herself. I have a good renter right now but I expect the worst in years to come. Something to keep me in touch with reality and all and all.

I hope you got over yr spell in bed. The sun is no good for us, even though you may feel worse in the winter. I had me a little spell and took some pills as cost 60¢ a throw four times a day for four days and am now all right again. For the lupus, I am taking HYDELTRA, five 2.5 mg each per day, which they tell me is a very small maintenance dose. The heat here is pretty bad right now but I don't reckon as bad as in New York. I can work in the mornings but in the afternoons I can't do nothing but look at peachickens.

(My mother read *Poor Hariet* straight through and kept saying, "Well I just don't know how she figured all this out, I just couldn't do it.")

## To Cecil Dawkins

4 August 57

No hurry about the *Critique*. I've never seen another copy of that thing. I suppose it folded; if it didn't I hope it will before it gets around to me. It is awful disconcerting to read critical articles about what you've done—you find yourself writing like those people *think* you write. I listen to a few people I trust but not many.

Last week I went to give a talk on the short story at a

Jamboree [of aspiring regional writers]. They are mostly all over sixty, bloodthirsty to sell, they will take any amount of encouragement, and their works are heavily inspirational. At first I had thought: these will be the usual old ladies writing epics in negro dialect, old South stuff, etc. etc. Then they sent me 7 manuscripts and I was to select the best to read in this workshop. Well they were all television stories written in television language for the television world. The old souls don't know the South exists. I was right shocked. Terrible stories of course. I selected the least awful and someone read it and then they descended on it like buzzards. There was one old man there, a wool-hat boy (the only man present besides an official), and he made some long remarks about what Jesus had said to the woman taken in adultery. This was apropos of nothing but it somehow fitted into the general picture. There was also someone there who had come "to urge writers not to use degrading language." The big attraction was The Agent Who Had Sold *Gone with the Wind* to the Movies. She referred to me throughout as "You"—either couldn't pronounce my name or didn't think it was worth it. Altogether the Ringling Brothers couldn't have equalled it.

That farm sounds like a big undertaking. I watch what goes on on this one largely through the crack in the door. My contribution amounts to picking up a few eggs. I have had some bone trouble and for the last two years have been walking on crutches; I expect to be on them for two or three years more or longer—but when you can't be too active physically, there is nothing left to do but write so I may have a blessing in disguise. Anyway there is always something going on on a farm to watch . . .

I've never read Hermann Hesse. I'm sadly lacking on Germans.

## To "A."

9 August 57

I haven't seen *Modern Age* yet but I am trying to get hold of it and will send it along to you if I do. This is what was going to be the *Conservative Review*. I say Russell's articles will have to have permanent value as they will all be at least three years old before they appear. He had gotten a review from Ashley of *A Good Man Is Hard to Find* but that being no longer a new book, he asked him to expand it into a short piece for the second issue. A. said he was going to if he had time, but I don't think he has much faith in the appearance of a second issue. Russell had also got one of

John Lynch's poems. I don't know but what Lynch has asked for it back before now. When anybody wants to get hold of Russell he is always in Scotland.

I am sure they weren't referring to *The Malefactors* but to that book about Dylan Thomas, can't think who wrote it, but a friend of his (John Malcolm Brinnin??); I think it was called *Dylan Thomas in America,* or something like that, and now his wife Caitlin has written one. It's awful the way they pick on the dead, feast on the dead . . .

The jamboree was a real farce . . . There were forty or fifty [women] in the room and three men, the man who was running the thing . . . (he had to be there), a youth with the name of Mr. Phinizy Spalding, and an old man . . . who came from Louvail, Ga., sent I am sure by the Lord to be a plague to the penwomen. This was a poet and he had his poems in a paper bag from the ten-cent store; he attended every session he could and tried wherever possible to get the floor away from the ladies. After I had made my talk, we had read the best (the least awful) of the seven stories. This job fell to Mr. Phinizy Spalding as the author was not supposed to be known. Then when it was read, the girls discussed it. Their comments were of this kind: "I just thought that man was awful!" "I just loved him!" "I thought SHE was just right" etc. etc etc. This discussion went on for half an hour. [The old man] sitting quietly but his eyes getting glittery. Mrs. P. who had heard how he liked to get the floor continued to ignore him until the last minute. Then she let him talk. She should have let him talk sooner. He said he thought the problem should be looked at *historically,* and then he launched into a long account of what Jesus had said to the woman taken in adultery. There was nothing about adultery in the story but he seemed to be having a good time. After he had told that, he said he had discussed this passage from the Bible with a genteel and reefined Georgia lady, cutting his eyes around at the audience, and she said, "What do you think He meant by that?" "I think He meant some of them folks might be saved before you and me," said [he]. "You *know* he didn't!" she said. "I reckon I know He did," [he] said. Then I kind of saw the point: he hoped they might all be dammed, all penwomen. His eyes were glittering with a secret wisdom. The women were growling under their breaths for him to sit down, but he held on until the bell rang. He was worth my trip.

Mr. Phinizy Spalding [now a professor of history at the University of Georgia] must have been a graduate student. When he got home he wrote me a letter saying that as an undergraduate he had written a term paper entitled "Children in the Stories of

Flannery O'Connor," and that he liked my stories. I intend to invite him to drop in if he is ever in this direction. Anybody with a name like that could not but be welcome.

It's a little hard to imagine that Petry story in a straight version but I'll be anxious to look—at any number of versions. Thinking about your writing in general and what might be your "authentic" material, I suspect that the best story you have done is the one about the fellow who butts the plane and gets himself court-martialed, the one the NWW said the narrator kept from being dramatic. That story was the least strained as far as the characters were concerned and there was an authenticity about it that Uncle Petry lacks—because they were people and he is a two-dimensional illustration. I have been reading your friend Uncle Henry James' essay on de Maupassant and inspired by the same have written off for the Modern Library de Maupassant. To get back on course: you may ultimately be right that what you have to handle is your own neurosis (don't like that word though), but there are plenty of people who can handle their neurosises and can't write and plenty can write but can't handle etc. In any case, I would not be hasty to make two problems one and when I thought about the story I would forget about myself and when I thought about myself I would forget about the story.

E. sent s.o.s. saying her file was empty and could I send a review of anything—anything! So I promptly sent a review of Baron von Hügel's *Essays and Addresses*, omitting to mention that they were first published in 1921. The Petrine Claims incidentally are the claims of the Pope to be head of the Church, as opposed to you, me, Haze, and Hoover Shoats being supreme head. You want to see it, I'll send it.

We have got the bull, this one from Perry, the Mulachee Farms . . . My mother has named him Banjo. I couldn't say why. I always thought that if she had a dog she'd name him Spot—without irony. If I had a dog, I'd name him Spot, with irony. But for all practical purposes nobody would know the difference.

(LATER:) I liked most of Waugh's answers but he has too narrow a definition of what would be a Catholic novel. He says a novel that deals with the problems of the faith; I'd rather say a Catholic mind looking at anything, making the category generous enough to include myself.

I managed to be in good health throughout the visit of Mr. Ashley though I daresay he contributed to my subsequent decline by his ability to sit up until 1 o'clock and not know the difference. I go to bed at nine and am always glad to get there. Don't however refer to him as "your" A.; there are no claims there and none desired. He is very dry and very intelligent and it is always good to have somebody like that to talk to.

An old soul who heard the Catholic Hour last Sunday—seems it comes on at 6:30 a.m. of all ungodly hours. Anyways, my statement or such of it as was used was apparently read by Paul Horgan . . . At Iowa, I was only a student and Horgan never even knew I was in the room, I am sure—though once he noted forty things wrong with a story of mine and I thought him a fine teacher. Anyways, the old lady is going to write off for a transcript of the program, which it seems you can get for the asking, so I intend to read what I did not hear.

24 August 57

Sent you the *God's Heralds. The Two-Edged Sword* and *The Path through Genesis* are much more interesting books but I lent them to Tom Gossett last fall and he has not returned them and the Gossetts are now off on their vacation. He is a very nice man who teaches at Wesleyan and his wife at Mercer but it don't make any difference how nice a man is you should never lend him a book. I am learning. When they get back in the fall, I will write him and ask him if I didn't lend it to him. It's probably lost or forgotten or has never been read.

E. has lately sent me four books which I am reading at one time. One is the Mauriac novel, *Lines of Life*. It was first published in 1921, I think, under the name *Destinies*. I read it about ten years ago in the Skidmore College Library and remember nothing about it but the last sentence, which in that translation was: "And (she) was again one of those corpses floating down the stream of life." In this translation, it is "(She) had again become one of those dead who are carried down the stream of life." Now I have got to wondering if I am remembering the first translation right. The next time you are in the PL will you look and see if they have that old Mauriac? It would probably be under the title *Destinies*. And see what the last sentence is. They probably don't specialize in Mauriac at the PL but if they have it let me know what the translation was. Also have you read any Mauriac yourself? I have eight of his novels and would be glad to supply you.

I can't see Petry in a straight version either. I don't think you should force yourself but when you find something that comes with some ease then start working on it.

Mr. Phinizy Spalding told in his letter that he was writing his thesis on the poetry of William Alexander Percy, so when I answered him I asked who was Wm. Alex. Percy and a return postcard announced the arrival of Mr. Phinizy Spalding to take place the following Monday, he being horrified to learn that I didn't know who W.A.P. was, was bringing himself and a copy of Percy's masterpiece, *Lanterns on the Levee,* now in its 16th printing. So Monday in due time, he showed up with it and also a copy of one of Percy's books of poems. It turns out that our mutual admiration, Walker Percy, is one of two adopted sons of Wm. Alex. P., and that Mr. Phinizy Spalding is his nephew or cousin or something, I didn't get it quite clear. Anyway Walker Percy early in his way in the world came down with TB and had to be confined for a period during which he and St. Thomas became friends and he became a Catholic. He wrote a novel which Mr. Phinizy Spalding said he put aside as it was not good and is now writing some kind of philosophical treatese (sp?). He is a doctor but has to take it easy on account of the TB which gets active if he does. He is also (Walker Percy) a friend of Caroline's but I never got any of this from her.

If you pass down Peachtree [Street] you will probably see that my poor uncle is houseless. The Bell House is going to be bull-dozed, beginning Monday. He loves every rotten plank in it. He brought all the furniture out of it—largely monstrosities—and it is arriving here this afternoon in a van and he has been bringing out pieces of junk for the last six months and depositing them in the back hall. Everything sacred. It's just about as poignant to be torn away from a house as a person . . .

Did you like the story of Isobel English's in the *Commonweal?* I thought it was fine after I had got to the end, a really very effective thing.

Sent you Robie's novel. *Time* gave one of its nasty pats to Andrew's novel. I don't want to read it myself but I daresay it is better than they think.

26 Aug 57

Enclosed directed sent to you . . . The letter explains to me why [William Sessions] can be good writer—: he is a good writer.

Uncle has found himself a room somewhere in your neighbor-hood. So if you should see his smiling face, smile you back at him. He is homesick for those rotten boards.

## To Cecil Dawkins

27 August 57

What I can't decide is what you do with all that tomato juice. This is the only farm I've heard of that specializes in dogs, worms and tomato juice. If I ever get in that direction I'll certainly stop and investigate. Right now, what with my two aluminum legs, I don't have any urge to go out of the yard.

To tell you the truth I didn't even read all the articles in that *Critique.* I never remember a critical piece fifteen minutes after I've read it anyway. I'm blessed with Total Non-Retention, which means I have not been harmed by a sorry education—or that is my cheerful way of viewing it . . .

Point of view runs me crazy when I think about it but I believe that when you are writing well, you don't think about it. I seldom think about it when I am writing a short story, but on the novel it gets to be a considerable worry. There are so many parts of the novel that you have to get over with so you can get something else to happen, etc. etc. I seem to stay in a snarl with mine.

Wouldn't have been any good with the atheist either. I have a good many friends of this stripe and I have learned not to talk to them on the subject. They start with different premises and see the Church only from the outside and are generally afraid of anything that is serious and concrete enough to make a personal demand . . . This is not to say that faith isn't subject to reason or that you shouldn't inform yourself of ways to defend it; but such would be for your own sake; it would never much help you to win any arguments. I remembered something I had read about the co-existence of believers and unbelievers and looked it up and started to tear it out and send it to you; instead I will just send the whole quarterly as it is a magazine you might like to see. A good many of the articles in it are too professionally philosophic for me to be able to understand but there are always two or three in every issue that I can get.

I reckon "sensitive, moving, and strange" are adjectives that only an agent can use in combination. I don't have anything against agents except when they try to give literary advice. Fortunately mine does not; I tell her where I want the thing sent and she sends it. When I want it to go to a quarterly I send it myself and give her the commission because the editors of quarterlies will generally comment and sometimes this is helpful. Anyway, it's more fun.

The Hesse [*Magister Ludi*] I'll read with interest and if I could reciprocate with anything I've got, let me know.

## To William Sessions

1 September 57

I thought the enclosed characters might be some friends of yours, or that should you chance to be homesick for Carrollton they would dissipate the feeling. My mother keeps saying, "Poor Billy, poor Billy, he can't talk over there, he can't talk, the poor boy, write him a letter, just think, he can't talk. Poor Billy," etc. etc. etc. I tell her you doubtless ain't suffering but she is convinced you are [Sessions was then studying in Germany] . . .

My round uncle has brought all his beloved Things home [from the Bell House] . . . We have come into the front-porch rockers from there so our front porch now looks like the entrance to an old ladies' rest home. I hadn't rocked for years but I think I am going to excel at it with a little more practice . . .

Let us hear how and what you do and are studying. We cannot return information of a similar interest as all that happens here of importance occurs in the barnyard division; e.g. we have a new Santa Gertrudis bull . . . He is 17 months old. He is cherry red. He weighs 1,100 pounds. He has brown eyes. He has been tested for Bangs and TB. Cheers and Screams.


## To "A."

7 September 57

In regard to the one-footed peacock, he has been reabsorbed into the tribe. When the mating season is over, they calm down. He goes with the herd now and don't have more than a barely perceptible limp. He can also climb stairs and jump so as to snatch the tastiest scrap away from the nearest peahen. My mother says we have entirely too many of them and she is gunning to get rid of some of them. They wallow in her flower beds. Nobody wants to buy any so I think I'm safe for a while anyway.

I had never read Cozzens before. We have the same editor and the last time he was down, he was full of the Cozzens book and they sent me a copy. I have got about halfway through it so don't have any claim to an opinion. I don't like the way he writes—no detail is omitted—but there is power in it. All the nasty characters move in the direction of Rome, being nitwits, etc. or possibly just sexually motivated. What Cozzens said about *The Old Man and the Sea* reveals him—that it could be in *Little Folks Magazine*. He's a hack beside Hemmenway.

All what you say about *The Innocent* [by Madison Jones]

seems true to me though I didn't read it carefully enough to take all that in myself. I suffer from generalized admiration or generalized dislike . . .

21 September 57

No hurry for Robie's book or the *Thought* & don't feel you have to read either. Right now I feel swamped with too-much-to-read myself. From E. I have a biography of St. John of the Cross and one of Rabelais. I read a little of one and then a little of the other; edifying contrast.

*The Lines of Life* is full of ambiguities and as I felt incapable of going into them with competence (and that the *Bullytin* readers wouldn't have been interested anyway) I escaped the problem shortly by doing a notice of three books together—as you will see, saying as little about the Mauriac as possible. One thing I notice about Mauriac is that he often does it the opposite way—instead of the evil life intruding upon the good as a shock of grace, the good intrudes upon the evil. He did it that way in *The Lamb*—just the opposite of *Lines of Life*. Anyway, it seemed to me that the boy, Bob, was something to pry the woman's life open to spirit for a short space and that her life then closed up again and what you do in the book is stare into this wound while it is open. The force of habit and the weight of possessions close it up again. You accept grace the quickest when you have the least. Pierre and his scruples I feel is very close to Mauriac, probably the result of Mauriac examining his conscience, Mauriac seeing himself as he *could* be. He said somewhere that while scruples was a disease of the soul, it was at least an indication that the soul was alive.

Never heard of the Female Orphan Benevolent Society. Is this something the *Bulletin* advertises? Nothing could be bearable about it I am sure.

I am becoming convinced that anybody who gives anybody else any advice ought to spend forty days in the desert both before and after. Anyway, when I told you to write what was *easy* for you, what I should have said was what was *possible* for you. Now none of it is easy, none of it really *comes* easy except in a few rare cases on a few rare occasions. In my whole time of writing the only parts that have come easy for me were Enoch Emery and Hulga; the rest has been pushing a stone uphill with my nose. Now *Accent* to the contrary notwithstanding it is perfectly *possible* for you to write fiction; it may not be the thing for you to write. I don't know. Nobody can tell you that but yourself but you can't tell yourself too quick or on the basis of one or two rejection slips.

The traditional story is Hemingway got 200 before he sold a story (and the one he sold was lousy as I read it). Anyway, the question arises: if you are not going to write fiction what are you going to write?

Your reviews are very good indeed and you would write good commentary on life in general but these things require specific opportunity to do them; you have to have an excuse that you don't need when you write fiction. I can imagine your writing some literary articles for the *Commonweal* but that takes probably special invitation. The other things are poetry and autobiography and drama. Poetry I presume is its own reward. It don't take but six cents to send it around and get it back. Plays I don't know anything about but I imagine you might like to try your hand at one but I doubt if you'd like to write them. That . . . girl is apparently dead crazy to write plays. I guess it's a bug you have to have. Autobiography sounds very grand but I don't think grand folks are the ones to write it. I think no one should write one unless he's called on by the Lord to do so. Therefore, you perhaps would be the one to write one. At least you know to what end your experience has tended. The gist and the moral of all these unlucid remarks is that all writing is painful and that if it is not painful then it is not worth doing.

The *Register* weekly out of Denver should be used to wrap up the fish. Poor St. Therese. They [some dancing nuns] all look as if they're doing the Charleston.

## To Cecil Dawkins

22 September 57

I'm a full-time believer in writing habits, pedestrian as it all may sound. You may be able to do without them if you have genius but most of us only have talent and this is simply something that has to be assisted all the time by physical and mental habits or it dries up and blows away. I see it happen all the time. Of course you have to make your habits in this conform to what you *can* do. I write only about two hours every day because that's all the energy I have, but I don't let anything interfere with those two hours, at the same time and the same place. This doesn't mean I produce much out of the two hours. Sometimes I work for months and have to throw everything away, but I don't think any of that was time wasted. Something goes on that makes it easier when it does come well. And the fact is if you don't sit there every day, the day it would come well, you won't be sitting there.

Everybody has a different problem about finding a set time to do it, but you should do it while you have a fresh mind anyway. After you've taught all day, you must be too tired and what creative energy you have must have gone to the little ladies of Stevens. If I had to teach I think I'd rather teach the Peter Bells (what they call the unteachable ones at the local college) which end of the sentence you put the period on rather than teach the bright ones Literature. You can't be creative in all directions at once. Freshman English would suit me fine. I'd make them diagram sentences.

Guardini has a number of things on Dostoevsky and I like the one I enclose and here is also a thing Caroline wrote on her debt to the Greeks. This is one of Caroline's themes which in part I take with several grains of salt; anyway, I wrote her that I was still after mastering me English and would doubtless not be getting onto no Greek . . .

## To William Sessions

27 September 57

We were cheered to hear . . . My mother says we must save your letters and present them to you when you come back so you will have a record of all this. I say well I reckon old Billy is taking him some notes, etc. I sent your letter to me to Fr. McCown with instructions for him to return it, which he did, saying to send him some more as he certainly had enjoyed it and liked to travel even if vicariously. I think he is having a sad time at that retreat house. He said seagulls got to be tiresome and he felt as if his words bounced on the walls. Do write him if you have time . . .

We were wondering if there is anything you can't get there that we could send you. I send Madame Fitzgerald the home permanent wave and the gingerbread mix, both inappropriate for you, but there might be something else. Could you use some Instant Tea or Coffee? Supersuds, corn plaster, or Hadacol? Let us know.

The Ga. Literature Commission has just declared *God's Little Acre* to be obscene. They have been debating about whether a book called *The Dice of God* by an Alabama author is obscene or not. A group of gentlemen from Macon brought it to their attention, demanding that it be declared obscene. There was a hearing and it turned out the gentlemen had read only the obscene parts; asked when something was obscene they said it was obscene when it couldn't be read before a lady.

Are you going to see Heidegger on his mountain top? Are you

going to see Msgr. Guardini, Karl Adam, or Max Picard, or is Max Picard still living? What about Marcel and what about that lady critic that is so good—Claude Edmond Magny? I wrote the Fitz-geralds that you would likely show up and etc. I suggest that you write them a note to their present address and find out when they are going to move . . . They said they'd look forward to seeing you and you might be near this summer place.

The Bell House is now down and nothing left but two beech-trees on either side of the lot so it is going to be called The Beech-tree Parking Lot. Time Marches On. We have inherited their old birdbath, which is giving an antique look to the west side of the house. Excelsior.


## To "A."

5 October 57

But to turn to the Female Orphan's Benevolent Association. This is simply a case of I-didn't-know-I-done-it. Every year about Christmas time my mother says, without introduction or prelimi-nary, "Give me your three dollars for St. Mary's Home," at which I go and write out a painless check which she mails to a crony of hers in Savannah. This must be how I get to be a member but nobody has ever said the vile name to me. St. Mary's Home is the Catholic orphanage for girls in Savannah. When I was a child it was in a creaking house on a dreary street and I was occasionally taken there to visit the Sisters or some orphan distant-cousins; also probably as a salutary lesson. "See what you have to be thankful for. Suppose you were, etc."—a lesson my imagination played on exhaustively. I don't suppose that orphanage was so bad, there was doubtless plenty of love there but it was official, and you wouldn't have got yours from your own God-given source. Anyway, to me it was the ultimate horror. . . . I still remember. From time to time, they were allowed to spend the day with me—miserable occasions for me, as they were not other children, they were Orphans. I don't know if they enjoyed coming or not; probably not. Now St. Mary's Home has moved into a bigger and more elegant house on Victory Drive and I understand that most of the "orphans" are children of divorced parents where the mother has to work and that a good many of them are paid for. This is just as necessary a work I am sure. Anyway, I have been at least an Imaginary Orphan and that was probably my first view of hell. Children know by instinct that hell is an absence of love, and they can pick out theirs without missing.

( 244 )

This is very interesting about Mr. Q. whoever he is because Madame S. called me up over the telephone (over what else now?) and asked me if I would contribute a story to this new magazine. They would pay a hundred dollars. She said she was very enthusiastic about it, etc. They were going to reprint her [story] and were going to reprint other things of Jawger Authers. I allowed as how I didn't have anything being engaged upon the production of a novel and she asked if they could reprint one of my stories. Have to ast Harcourt, Brace, says I. And we exchanged a few other politenesses and she said she'd send me a copy of the magazine . . . I imagine she is a woman of considerable goodwill—helping the lepers and so forth—and very likely to be duped by a gent like Mr. Q. There is certainly a ripe field for an enterprising confidence man to work in among writers . . . Keep me posted.

I had never thought about Robie and his book in connection with any attitude of his about women. From what I've heard him say about her, his mamma was like all other mammas. He has a younger brother. When they were off at school he said his mother sent them clippings out of the local paper and they would always thank her, commenting on the wrong side of the clipping. It all sounded highly normal.

We have not seen the sun in nine consecutive days. Yesterday Jack drew a knife on Shot and my mother says it is all the weather. They never seem to hurt each other but they get mad and stay that way about six hours and then everything is dandy again and you can't separate them. There should be a break in this weather sometime and we would like you to come down if you could spare a Sareday during October or November—or if you and [an aunt] could drive down some Sunday and have dinner with us. We'd love to have her. Consider and let me know as any Sat. or Sun. is convenient.

[P.S.] . . . an item of fan mail. The old lady depresses me as much as I depress her; however, she don't deprive me of my sleep so I'm still one up on her. Cheers.

## To Maryat Lee

8 October 57

I was much cheered and relieved to hear from you though the vein was mysterious. I haven't received any crusty note. Maybe you didn't put enough postage on it and it's simmering on the high seas; anyway, if you sent it, I reckon I provoked it. I scrounged around in my trash system trying to find if I had a carbon of my last to you. I had, and reading it over, found it in part disagreeable, vain, and unclear. I take it at this point to have been one of my attempts to be funny. It was not, but was as I saw with horror open to many possible interpretations of a vulgar nature. None of these was intended so put it down to my native idiocy. I just don't have a highly developed sensibility and I don't know when I've hurt people until they tell me. To have caused you any pain is very painful to me and is the last thing I would have wanted to do, or to have seemed to doubt for an instant that you ever act in any way not according to your conscience.

The only thing that irked me about the last letter I did get from you was your use of the word eternity in the plural, with airless in front of it. I don't mind being a pathetic quaver but eternity means the beatific vision to me and my quaver, or anybody else's, has nothing to do with it. Anyway, it would be impossible for me not to want you as a friend. A ridiculous notion. I am not to be got rid of by crusty letters. I'm as insult-proof as my buff orpington hen and if the letter ever does show up, I doubtless won't know the difference.

Miss E. Wynn wrote me a card from NYC and said she had had an announcement of your marriage and I was glad to hear it as I had begun to think you might have drowned in a Japanese tub or been eaten by the saber-toothed tiger. I hope you made yourself a play in Hongkong. I read in the paper that Carson McCullers is going to have a play shortly to be called *The Square Root of Wonderful*—a title that makes me cringe.

The local institution is open again but I have not seen your brother or sister-in-law and I am wondering if he faces an inauguration this year. They inaugurated the last one within an inch of his life, only to have him depart within two years. This cured them of making haste and your brother's hair may be allowed to turn white in office before they make his position formally official; but when the occasion occurs hit will be great and you should plan to be here.

You must get your visit in anyhow before we secede from the Union. The Russian moon is just light diversion for us. The latest thing is the American Resettlement Association, whose object is to resettle Georgia colored families in refined Northern residential areas (only the best areas), lots in which will be bought up by the ARA with state funds. This is not quite as permanent as sending them all back to Africa but it has a lot of supporters.

I am keeping my mind on the important things, like peachickens. The season here has been terrifyingly productive. I used to say I wanted so many of them that every time I went out the door I stepped on one. Now every time I go out the door, one steps on me.

## To Denver Lindley

9 October 57

I am probably the only person in the country who prefers the works of Mr. Dillon Ripley to Mr. J. G. Cozzens. Anyway, I certainly have enjoyed his book and if you are speaking with him, tell him he has one ardent fan in the state of Georgia, but one so low in the duck world as to be practically not there.

As for Mr. Cozzens, I persevered through about 250 pages [of *By Love Possessed*]. I hesitate to find tedious what is giving such general satisfaction but I find it tedious. My mother says she is going to wait and read it in the *Reader's Digest*. An excellent decision, I told her.

## To "A."

19 October 57

Well, enclosed find my installment. How you reckon you answer a letter like that?* . . . I think this may just be a kind of piety that you find among people who read nothing but Catholic literature, have none but Catholic friends or indifferent Protestant ones. Maybe a kind of piety that feeds on itself. But then I can't call it wrong, or even vulgar. Needless to say, she's got the dramatic event to build on, all right. What keeps you away from the wrong kind of violence? I was reading that St. Thomas said Prudence was the highest of the virtues (those beyond Faith Hope & Charity, I presume) because it articulated all the others. Anyway, the older I get the more respect I have for old Prudence.

It's what Fr. H. ain't using right now. I think he should be sent for a reflective spell to the nearest Dominican Saltmine. Cogley had a point that they should have put him on their own platform and answered him, said put-up or shut-up, Dr. H. And a lot of what he said is doubtless true, such as that they have people explaining Catholic doctrine who don't know as much about it as a parochial-

_____

* *This paragraph refers to a tragic event in the life of a friend, who accepted it in a spirit—and described that acceptance in terms—that Flannery found baffling, fanciful, foreign to her own mode of thinking and speaking; and yet, as she says, neither wrong nor even vulgar.*

school pupil. But when he says such things as that Maritain has had no influence over Catholic students at Princeton, he is only saying in effect how stupid the Catholic students at Princeton must be. This is probably another situation that will get worse. I suppose Fr. H. is the kind of priest we need to pray for. I remind myself of this but I haven't done it.

I persuaded my mother this week that she didn't want to go to see *The Ten Commandments*. Told her she ought to read the book first anyway and presented her with Exodus. Then to salve my guilty conscience I went to see the *Three Faces of Eve* with her as she don't like to go by herself. First time I had been to the picter show in two or three years. It was not such a bad picture, but I ain't going again for another three years if I can possibly help it.

A very nice thing happened last night. Elizabeth Bishop called me up from Savannah. She was on a freighter going to Brazil where she lives and it docked unexpectedly in Savannah. I have never met her but last year she wrote me a letter and said she liked my stories. We have mutual friends in the Lowells and she had seen them this summer and their new baby. I asked her to come up but the freighter was leaving some time in the middle of the night so she couldn't have done that. She seemed like a most cordial pleasant soul and it was one of those things that you just don't expect. She said one of these times when she comes North she will get a stop-over and come to see me.

I have put up the novel for a short spell and am writing a story and it's like a vacation in the mountains.


## To Cecil Dawkins

27 October 57

Thanks so much for the picture. One of these days I'll send you one of me and two of my friends but my friends are not very cooperative about having their pictures struck—don't like to be seen with me or something.

I have heard that Katherine Anne Porter writes her stories in her head before she puts them down but I always tend to think such reports are exaggerated, perhaps just because they don't fit in with what I find I can do. I always have an idea of what I want to do when I write a story, but whether I'll be able to remains always to be seen. I am writing a story now and have proceeded at a regular rate of two pages a day, following my nose more or less. They have to work out some way or other, and I think you discover a good deal more in the process when you don't have too definite ideas about what you want to do. That is interesting about your reading some Shakespeare to limber up your language before you start; though I think that anything that makes you overly conscious of the language is bad for the story usually.

Your schedule sounds horrible and I suppose the worst of such a job is that something extra is always coming up. I find girls of that age awfully hard to talk to. I lectured at Wesleyan College in Macon last year and as a result some of their students who have a vague urge to "express themselves" began to come regularly to see me. When they appear, they do all the talking and they have fantastic but very positive ideas about how everything is and ought to be; and they are mighty sophisticated on the outside. The visits leave me exhausted and yearning to go sit with the chickens.

Anything having to do with this "learning for life" stuff turns my stomach permanently. I had to attend a "progressive" high-school here, one of those connected with a teachers' college. In the summer all the teachers went to T.C. and sat at the feet of an old boy named William Heard Kilpatrick and those who couldn't afford that went to Peabody and sat at the feet of somebody who had sat at the feet of William Heard Kilpatrick. In the winter they returned and asked us what, as mature children, we thought we ought to study. At that school we were always "planning." They would as soon have given us arsenic in the drinking fountains as let us study Greek. I know no history whatsoever. We studied that hindside foremost, beginning with the daily paper and tracing problems from it backward . . .


*To "A."*

2 November 57

I am much exercised to know what this book looks like that makes you think it has passed through my hands. Did chicken feathers fall out of it? Were there unintelligible comments in the margins? Did it smell rural? No mam. I never saw it. *War and Christianity Today* would be way beyond me anyhow. Usually she don't send me anything I don't ask for.

My agent has just sent me three copies of the British edition of the stories. I am under contract to apparently the worst British publisher as 17 houses turned down [*Wise Blood*] before they offered it to him and he took it. Anyway, without permission, he has changed the title of the collection to *The Artificial Nigger* and on the jacket has featured a big black African, apparently in agony, granite agony; which is supposed to be an artificial nigger. The agent thinks that changing the title is a breach of contract so she is going to try to get . . . me a good publisher.

The latest turn of events around here is that my cousin in Savannah insists that my mother and I go on that diocesan pilgrimage to Lourdes and Rome that Msgr. McNamara is conducting next spring. In addition to insisting upon it, she wishes to give us the trip—which is the basis of her insistence. (She is the child in the high chair in the picture in the parlor at home.) As this is about the only way either of us will ever get there, my mother is all for it. I am all for it too though I expect it to be a comic nightmare. It only lasts 17 days so I figure I should be able to stand it that long. What I see is a planeload of fortress-footed female Catholics pushed from shrine to shrine by the prelates McNamara and Bourke . . . I guess the way to stand it will be to indulge temporarily in Quietism, cut my motor off so to speak and be towed.

More about Thomas though this fellow falls flat on his face in the last paragraph ["The Comforts of Home"].

"A View of the Woods" was in the last *Partisan* and I have had the enclosed from Cal about it. He has wonderful insights and is probably right that this one was written by Mary Pitts herself, playing Jehovah. But Mary Pitts can't be anybody but Mary Pitts and can't write anything but what Mary Pitts would write. There are no children in the new one and I wouldn't know how it is coming, but I do know that the novel is coming better for my being away from it for a spell. Several things have fallen into place in my head. Meanwhile I am sailing on the Jellybolee with this story. I figure right now on calling it "The Enduring Chill."

I have ordered three Chinese geese, which may be here Saturday in time for me to display. If not, we have a fairly new colt and the Santa Gertrudis . . . And we will be at driveway at 12:10.


## To William Sessions

3 November 57

Yestiddy we got your hand-written communication from Italy and today the cards, which are very fine . . . Incidentally, my mother was much taken with the card with the hats on it and appreciated being thought of. That hand-wrote letter leaves much to be guessed at but I think I deciphered that today you will be visiting the Fitzgeralds. I hope so. If so, write me about them and if they have moved for the winter yet, let me know. I will write them at Levanto but I don't really know if they are in the same place there—or what that is or what or what.

Two Sundays back we were honored by a visit from your friend and mine . . . who sat regally on the sofa and told us that she was writing the History of West Georgia College, that she had heard from you twice, and other such bits of information. [She] always leaves me with a warm feeling—as if I had just been promoted to the fourth grade after having stayed in the third grade two years. She left intoning, "It's such a wonderful world we live in! So many things to do! So many interesting people!"

Last week my cousin in Savannah wrote my mother that she wanted . . . to give us this trip. She is very wealthy. It is a 17-day pilgrimage with stops in Ireland (some old castle), London (where the pilgrims will be welcomed by guess who—Gerald P. O'Hara Hisself, Papal Nuncio to England), Paris, Lourdes, Rome and Lisbon, and home again home again jiggity jig. As this is not going to cost me anything, I reckon I can endure it . . . I'll hope Sally Fitzgerald will get to Rome to see us. . . .

Regards to Heidegger.

## To Granville Hicks

7 November 57

I like the book very much and am glad to find myself in it [*The Living Novel, a Symposium*]. I haven't spent much time worrying about whether the novel is dead or not but only about whether the one I'm working on is dead.

You have any permissions that you may need from me about placing the volume elsewhere . . .

## To Elizabeth and Robert Lowell

10 November 57

Harriet looks capable of handling you both. I have a lot of advice for people with children (I mean about how to protect yourself and so forth) but nobody listens to me although I have the totally objective view. About three weeks ago Elizabeth Bishop called me up from Savannah . . . She told me about you all and Harriet and I was highly pleased to hear it all and to hear her. I would like to persuade her to stop over here on one of her trips up or down. Also, I think you all should bring Harriet to see this region and me, so as my kinfolks say, "she would be broad." It certainly is not good to raise a child in Boston . . . They think anybody who didn't go to Harvard or MIT is underprivileged.

Since her grandpa brained her, I guess Mary Pitts won't be playing Jehovah anymore—though I don't guarantee it. I guess she is like Powers' cat. I wrote Powers I hoped some Minneapolis motorist would run over that cat permanently, in the interests of literature, and he wrote me he wasn't going to use the cat anymore so I could quit praying for it to be dispatched.

The enclosed picture of me looks pretty much like Mary Pitts playing Jehovah though. I painted the self-portrait and friend (pheasant cock) a couple of years ago and I got tired of having people say it didn't look like me as I knew better it did. So I got a lady with a flashbulb thing to take me alongside of it and this is the proof . . .

Tell [your friend] to come to see me. A lot of people come. Some of them are nice but most of them are mighty peculiar and expect me to be too and go away greatly disappointed.

Thanks for the pictures and the word; and my love to you three.

## To "A."

16 November 57

Your visit was thoroughly enjoyed by us and is always good for me though I may look tired. The truth is I am tired every afternoon and there's nothing to be done about it. It's the nature of the disease. A lot of people decide I am bored or indifferent or uppity but at a certain hour of the day my motor cuts off automatically. I am really wondering if either my mother or I will be able to stand this trip. She is used to going all the time, but not that kind of going, and I don't think it would be worth any strain on her. However, it appears we are going . . .

She is reading the Lourdes book and every now and then announces a fact, such as, "It doesn't make any difference how much you beg and plead, they won't let you in." "Won't let you in where?" "In Lourdes with a short-sleeved dress on or low-cut." "I ain't got any low-cut dress." I am going to read it when she gets through . . .

It appears I may get to behold Madam Holzhauer after all. I had an invitation to give something they call a Matrix lecture to the something with Greek letters women's journalism fraternity at Marquette in Milwaukee in April. They don't know what the date is to be but I said that if it were early in April, I'd come. I can use practically the same thing I used at Notre Dame and they pay my way and gimme a hundred dollars and I get to see the horrors of Milwaukee; also I get to see Carol Johnson; also Madam H., as it seems it was she and no other who recommended me. Well, we shall see.

I am glad you [are getting] something decent to review instead of Sister Potluck and the Gravedigger's Grandmother. You have exactly the right idea of how such a heavy tome should be handled. You are not expected in 200 words to give any judgment. Just tellum it's Theology and who wrote it and why and then settle down to enjoy it yourself.

I see I should ride the bus more often. I used to when I went to school in Iowa, as I rode the train from Atl. and the bus from M'ville, but no more. Once I heard the driver say to the rear occupants, "All right, all you stove-pipe blonds, git on back ther." At which moment I became an integrationist.

I announce with wild pleasure that I have finished the story ["The Enduring Chill"] once through as of today and that when I go over it about three more times, I think I will have done it; another month, I guess. Right now I am highly satisfied with all its possibilities and all that's already in it. This can be a delusion. Monday it may appear hopeless to me, but I doubt it. Nobody appreciates my work the way I do.

Thursday morning we had a short sharp wind which Jack came and announced as a "twister." My mother didn't pay too much attention though he said it had hurt the barn roof and taken the washing machine off their porch and set it down in the woodpile. When she went down there, she found there practically wasn't any roof. The insurance people estimate about $800 or so damage. Henry lost his front porch. Later in the day, Pussonalities in the Noos called up and my mother announced the damage and so forth and at 12:35, we listened to her over the radio. She declared it was *not* her voice, that she didn't sound like that, but that she wasn't going to criticize anybody else's voice over the radio again. Having had the little experience myself, I sympathized. I am glad you got to hear the rural radio.

## To Cecil Dawkins

17 November 57

Except for one novel by Wright Morris I haven't read any of those people in that book [*The Living Novel*] either. . . . All I have read of Isak Dinesen are the twelve *Gothic Tales* and some of them I like right much—the one where the old woman and the money change places—but I can't take much of her at one time.

Do you mean to tell me you had to teach *Cress Delahanty* [Jessamyn West]? My Lord. I haven't read it but when I think of all the books they ought to be made familiar with—and then *Cress Delahanty*, I begin to wonder.

The other day I had the experience of talking to a young man of the same age as the girls I find I can't talk to. He was a little older perhaps, 23, just out of Harvard, and wanting to write. I had never heard of him but he called me up and asked if he could come down from Atlanta and spend the afternoon and after I had said, yes, he adds, "and I'll bring a manuscript." Well he came and spent the afternoon and it was not a question of my having to say anything; all I had to do was listen. He was writing a deeply philosophical novel (thought he) about a lad horribly like himself who was going to commit suicide in the last chapter. All the chapters leading up were devoted to his reasons for this action, full of stuff about the "sense of time." He explained that while there were long philosophical passages, he was cutting these up with scenes. I was treated to the reading of one scene which he announced was the "love" section. At that point I was too tired to laugh so I didn't disgrace myself. I discreetly tried to suggest that fiction was about people and not about the sense of time but I am sure made no impression.

I have noticed that the girls at the local college adore to have ceremonies in which they light candles or hold lighted candles. Any excuse will do—a ceremony for physical-fitness week or what have you. I have decided that this is because they have never been to a really liturgical religious service where these things have their proper place and are relegated to the background and have meaning.

I wouldn't be discouraged by the experience you had reading your story. Learning to write proceeds by such shocks and jolts and it's the people who *don't* have them who will never do anything. Elizabeth Hardwick told me once that all her first drafts sounded as if a chicken had written them. So do mine for the most part. It might be dangerous for you to have too much time to write. I mean if you took off a year and had nothing else to do but write and weren't used to doing it all the time then you might get discouraged too easily. Of course I don't know. But don't anyhow say to yourself that you will give yourself so long to find out what you can do—because these things don't work on time limits. Too much time is as bad as too little. I'd certainly try for all the fellowships and whatnot and I would keep sending my stories out. Agents are all right but when you send your stuff out yourself, you get comments that are sometimes very valuable. Do you try such places as *Accent?* My first story was published in *Accent,* so was J. F. Powers'. (I can't stand to read that story over now. It jolts me exactly as yours must have jolted you.)

Well regards to the dogs. I have bought myself three Chinese geese. I like the shape they have and the noise they make. They hold their heads almost straight up and step without looking.

## To Thomas Gossett

24 November 57

We certainly would like you all to come over and bring Miss [Maire] MacEntee. She sounds powerful formidable with all them degrees and whatnot but we'll look forward to the visit. I have been meaning to write anyway and ask you and Louise to come over some afternoon. I hear you are teaching something called Southern Literature. What is that?

Fr. McCown says there is nothing at Pass Christian but seagulls.

## To "A."

30 November 57

I enclose the Plunketts . . . Ruth looks a little like Mrs. Roosevelt as would be expected for anyone who has this intimacy with God. There are several things in their pursuits that interest me, that seem to be logical perversions of doctrines of the Church. I looked up Acts 19:11–12 and see that what they are talking about originated in things that had touched St. Paul. Your handkerchief, if you order one, will have touched Elridge, who is backed up with one quarter of a million hours of prayer since 1943. The awful thing about the Plunketts is that they may not be crooks. However, they both look pretty crooked to me . . .

If you intend to throw A.T. out as a poet, you are going to have to get you some better aesthetic grounds than that there is no color in his poems or none of the things that have color. This will not do. This is a confusion of one thing with another and a sentimental, or close to it, approach to poetry. If he goes on your grounds, so do almost all the Metaphysical poets. You take "Ode to the Confederate Dead"—as I remember it there is only one color used in that and it is really *used*—green—the insane grass and the green of the serpent in the last stanza. That is a poem in which any color but the greys and seres and drabs would be inappropriate. This is a

masterly poem; read it, forgetting who wrote it. Color is not necessary to all poetry. That depends entirely on the nature of the poem
and what the poet is trying to do and what he manages to do.
Your method tends to be to read the poem and judge the poet—
because I reckon you are more interested in people than in art,
which is as it should be, but when you read a poem you are only
entitled to comment on the poem as a poem. What you seem to do
is read the poem, judge the poet, and then the poem from your
judgment of the poet.

The scientist says I may take the shots, so that is the next
thing on the agenda. My mamma has finished the Lourdes book.
I am almost afraid to read it.

Caroline has sent me her latest called *How to Read a Novel*. I
had asked E. to get it for me to review. You want to see it? I think
you would find it valuable, it's really more for writers than readers,
and it is uneven I think, but you would still find it valuable. Will
send it if you want it. Also will send if you want it something called
*The Living Novel, a Symposium*, edited by Granville Hicks. He is
a friend of mine and I am in the book (a thing of mine that you've
already read anyhow), but there are nine others in it of varying
degrees of sense. As Ashley says, they have to have one colored
man and one Catholic.

I have a few things to do to the story ["The Enduring Chill"] yet
but you will see it shortly. I go from liking it to not liking it. When
I am in the liking-it stage I am tempted to send it to you, but when
I am in the not-liking-it stage I decide to keep it a while longer.


## To Sally and Robert Fitzgerald

1 December 57

We were highly pleased to know you could use a fruit cake
and sent you off one Friday. The gent at the P.O. said it would take
it 20 days to get there so you can be watchful on the 18th or
thereabouts. I would hate for some Eye-talian to getaholt to it
before you.

It appears that the pilgrumidge is from April 22 to May 7 . . .
My parent is currently worried about where you can drink water
and where you can't over there. All the ladies who have "been"
tell her something different. If you haven't been to Lourdes yet,
how come you don't meet us there? The geography is beyond me,
of course.

Do you know what the undertakers are doing with the ashes
of the folks they cremate? Well, they are sending them to the canni-

bals to make Instant People out of. My mother came home with that the other day. She circulates among all and sundry.

Our colored man, Jack, has had all his teeth pulled and is about ready now to get his new teeth. The dentist asked him what kind he wanted and he said he wanted "pearly white teeth." The dentist asked what kind of pearly white teeth and he said, "You know, like on the handle of a gun." He also wants some gold ones scattered through the plate. Regina has been trying to talk him out of this but he says he ain't going to spend his money for no ordinary-looking teeth.

## To Caroline Gordon Tate

10 December 57

I'm busy with the Holy Ghost. He is going to be a waterstain —very obvious but the only thing possible. I also have a fine visitor for Asbury to liven him up slightly. I'm highly obliged for your thoughts on this ["The Enduring Chill"] and I am making the most of them. When I get this finished I'd like you to see it again because it is already much improved—but I notice my stories get longer and longer and I'm afraid this one may be too long. If I've finished with it, I'd like to send it to the Cheneys for a Christmas card and will hope that you might have time to look at it there. If not, I'll send it to you after Christmas . . .

I have lately been getting dizzy because I am taking a new medicine and have got an overdose of it. So I figure I'll do my staggering around at home. It takes some time for the dose to get regulated. Every time something new is invented I get in on the ground floor with it. There have been five improvements in the medicine in the 7 years I've had the lupus, and they are all great improvements.

A friend of mine at Wesleyan, a Dr. Gossett, wrote me that he and his wife had just come from the Modern Language Asso. convention in Knoxville or somewhere and had heard Willard Thorpe read a paper on "The Grotesque in Southern Literature." He (Thorpe) allowed as how the roots of it were in antebellum Southern writings but that the grotesque you met with in Southern writing today was something else and has serious implications which the other didn't approach. He said he had no satisfactory explanation for the change. The Gossetts decided the reason he didn't was because he doesn't know enough theology. I seem to remember that he wrote one of the better reviews of *The Malefactors*, but I may be mixed up on the name.

You are more sanguine about this pilgrimage than I am. It's not that I'd rather be a tourist; I'd rather stay at home. You are good to ask us to stop by Princeton, but knowing the difficulties of getting anywhere, I doubt we could engineer it. I envy you that energy you have. I wish you would come to see us. We have a lovely place—as evidenced by my reluctance to leave it for 17 days of Holy Culture and Pious Exhaustion. Pray that the Lord will (gently) improve my attitude so I can at least endure it . . .

## To "A."

14 December 57

Wal, I can't argue with you or Caroline either about *The Golden Bowl* because haw haw I haven't read it. She probably exalts James overmuch out of admiration for his technical achievements, and you sell him short for never having had temptations. Now I think it is a great grace not to be tempted. I used to have a Swedenborgian friend who was very critical of the Lord's Prayer. "Imagine," said she, "asking not to be led into temptation! We should ask to be led into temptations so that we could grow strong and overcome them!" Which might be logical enough if we hadn't been instructed otherwise by Christ Himself. Apparently after a while in his life, St. Thomas was relieved of all temptations of the flesh and certainly this was necessary if he was to write a *Summa*. James apparently knew nothing of any real religion. Graham Greene has an essay on this subject in *The Lost Childhood* but I forget exactly what his view of it was . . .

About the Lourdes business. I am going as a pilgrim, not a patient. I will not be taking any bath. I am one of those people who could die for his religion easier than take a bath for it. The one thing in France I have a real desire to see is Matisse's chapel in Vence; but of course they won't be going near any suchlike as that . . . By my calculations we should see more airports than shrines, and I suspect that if you've seen one shrine you've seen them all. Aside from penance being a good thing for us, I'm sure religion can be served as well at home. I'll be glad when the 17 days are over. Also I am afraid I may miss the geese hatching. But back to the baths. If there were any danger of my having to take one, I would not go. I don't think I'd mind washing in somebody else's blood . . . but the lack of privacy would be what I couldn't stand. This is neither right nor holy of me but it is what is.

The time interfered with Chicago. It also interfered with an invitation to an Arts Festival in Colorado, where I'd like to go because I've never been there. I would have got 500 bucks for those two classes in Chicago, so even if I ain't taking a bath, I figure I am making a financial sacrifice. On second thought, what a lousy conclusion!

I have torn the story ["The Enduring Chill"] up and am doing it over or at least a good deal of it over. It bids fair to be very long. Parts of it are very funny and it contains a memorable Jesuit, but I haven't got it right yet. But I am anxious to send it to you & trust it will get there before Christmas. Also I am sending you a little book for Christmas . . .

## To Father J. H. McCown

20 December 57

Two or three things have come up on which I need some expert SOS spiritual advice. Not long ago the local Episcopal minister came out and wanted me to get up a group with him of people who were interested in talking about theology in modern literature. This suited me all right so about six or seven of them are coming out here every Monday night—a couple of Presbyterians, the rest Episcopalians of one stripe or another (scratch an Episcopalian and you're liable to find most anything) and me as the repersentative of the Holy Roman Catholic & Apostolic Church. The strain is telling on me. Anyway this minister is equipped with a list of what he would like us to read and upon the list is naturally Gide also listed on the Index. I despise Gide but if they read him I want to be able to put in my two cents worth . . . You said once you would see if you had the faculties to give me permission to read such as this. Do you and will you? All these Protestants will be shocked if I say I can't get permission to read Gide.

The other thing concerns a girl I am writing to . . . She says she found that instead of "make straight the way," it was "make tight the straight jacket," and that her family was very strict about trifles, etc. etc. . . . Anyway, apparently the straw that broke the camel's back with her was when a priest told her that it was a mortal sin to eat meat on Friday. She is real confused and I am trying to give her suggestions about reading some people like Maritain as she has obviously never read anything but the Do-Nots. Anyway, would eating meat on Friday be a mortal sin if she didn't understand it as an act of rebellion? I was afraid to make any pronouncement on this to her. You can't tell her to see a priest because she wouldn't but I could help her if I knew myself. Thanks & Happy New Year.

*To Cecil Dawkins*

Have you seen Caroline Gordon's latest book out (Viking) called *How to Read a Novel?* I think it's badly titled because it isn't really for readers but for writers. I think it would be good for your freshmen though. Whenever I finish a story I send it to Caroline before I consider myself really through with it. She's taught me more than anybody.

I never have met Miss K.A.P. All the men who know her seem to like her as I strongly gather she has a way with them, but I know a few women who seem to like her too. I have friends in Nashville who know her rather well and they say she's always pleasant. So many catty remarks circulate and people always suppose that there is rivalry between women writers. If so, I always figure they are not the best writers.

Elizabeth Hardwick is a Kentucky girl, married to Robert Lowell. Her last book was called *The Simple Truth*. I think she's a mighty good writer. She's a big friend of Mary McCarthy's and about the same vintage.

You have to be careful about whose manuscripts you read because if you get a similar idea yourself later and work it up in your own way, the person is liable to think you stole it from him. I got a letter from a young man I had never heard of before and he announced blandly that he was writing stories which he thought were very much like mine and he wondered if I would read them. He was also worried about sending them to editors because they were so very much like mine he was afraid the editors would think he had borrowed them. He was a Certified Public Accountant but wondered if he should drop that occupation and become a writer. Would I please advise him. I advised him to stick to Certified Public Accounting. I had a letter from [another] young man who gave his age, weight, the color of his eyes, and the information that he had recently broken his leg in Jacksonville, Florida. He being laid up in bed by this had a big idea for a novel which would be a fast-moving adventure story. Since he thought I was pretty good with words and he was pretty good with ideas, he wondered if we couldn't get together and collaborate. Through the mail, I guess on account of his leg broken in Jacksonville, Fla. I enclose a sample of my fan mail; send it back to me as I cherish it . . .

## To "A."

28 December 57

That book has saved me considerable social energy . . . I have the book on the dining-room table and insist that all comers sit down and look at it. It takes up a good half of the usual visit and I don't let them skip a picture. Some are quite willing, others reluctant, but none has escaped. I like the saint being sawed down the middle myself and with an obviously dull saw too. She doesn't look too terribly inconvenienced though. I also admire the animals and devils. Some of these remind me of Rousseau, some the Christs of Rouault.

Enclose a new front and back, but I have not changed the last sentence as no other way seems to improve it. I was supposed to go to Nashville to see the Cheneys on the weekend of the 20th but I didn't feel like getting myself in those Christmas crowds at the airport so I didn't go. Caroline and Allen [Tate] did and were there for all of them. Allen had read the story ["The Enduring Chill"] to them . . . When I talked to Allen he said do one thing to that story for me and I said what and he said get the Holy Ghost in the first page or two. That is very good advice and it is what I have proceeded to do. Lon said that he hadn't known whether Asbury was coming or going there at the end, that the Holy Ghost came too fast. I think there is something in that too. So I have let it be known that he undeniably realizes that he's going to live with the new knowledge that he knows nothing. That really is what he is frozen in—humility. Faith can come later. I have it in mind to take Asbury further maybe in other stories. I also think Mary George is a monster who ought to have a little comedown. I have carefully not killed anybody off, you observe, so that I can have more to do with them later. Besides I don't want to be known as a killer, though death is the end of us all as the old man said heartily from his coffin . . .

11 January 58

We are having a big funeral here tomorrow as Henry [old field hand] died last Saturday night—eight days between these events. He had been having trouble getting his breath and Regina went over there last Saturday and said she wanted to take him to the doctor but he said he would go Monday. She went back in the afternoon and tried to make him go but he said no, Paul said you must be swaded by your pinion and his pinion was that he would wait until Monday. He was sitting by the fire eating an apple. He

( 261 )

died that night still sitting in the chair. Shot said that when he died, he grabbed aholt of him Shot and he like to have never got away. He has a daughter in Macon and she has a policy on him. A niece arrived from Philadelphia yesterday and another daughter arrives from Detroit Sunday. The undertaker offered to send out chairs but Louise [the wife of Jack, who also worked at the farm until her death in 1977] said not to send no chairs out, she didn't have time to be sitting around talking to all those niggers. We'll miss him around here as he was kind of an institution. The pearly white teeth are appropriately in for the occasion. They seem to be satisfactory. Louise says Jack ain't got any business with those teeth, he can eat just as well without them.

Naw those two pieces of paper I sent you—the beginning and end—were no good and I have done them over in a different way. Caroline said that was not subtle enough and she is right. Allen says I am too flat-footed. This time I have really improved it. I'll send you a copy when I get it done. You are doubtless as sick of it as I am but this is what you get for agreeing to see something before it's published.

My opinion of the Irish has gone up. We had a visitor, one of the Irish delegates to the UN. The Gossetts brought her over and we had supper with them. This girl is about 35, a lawyer, and a poet (in Irish). I asked her what they had in Ireland to correspond with the angry young men in England. She said they had some angry young men but that they didn't have the class business to be angry over. Anti-clerical? I asked her. Yes and anti-religious too. Most of them go the way of Joyce, she said, but it is very painful to them because when they cut themselves off from the religion they cut themselves off from what they have grown up with—as the religion is so bound in with the rest of life. She has an uncle who is Master General of the Dominicans in Rome and she wants us to go see him. She said that when it was learned that the Irish delegation was going to vote with the Communist bloc on whether or not to debate the admission of Red China, they immediately had a call from Cardinal Spellman telling them not to do it. That, said she, confirmed them in their resolution. Of course they had their orders from home, and they voted with the Communist bloc as they had planned. She seems properly anti-clerical but not particularly anti-religious . . .

The chief result of the Monday night affairs is that we have to air the damm room all of the next day to get the stinking cigaret smell out of it. I like two or three of the people and of course nothing very strenuous goes on and they are all very polite, and theology is seldom mentioned because I don't think anybody knows anything about it. I have bought an airwick and I aim to set it in a conspicuous spot.

## To Father J. H. McCown

12 January 58

I enclose you my latest published work lest you fall behind in your pursuit of Modern Literature. I have just completed one as I said with a one-eyed Jesuit in it but that has not been published yet.

I am very much obliged for your taking the time to find out about the permissions etc. I will use the *epeikia** and also invoke that word, which is very fancy. I have for the time being led them away from Gide, with the good reason that he is to be had in no 35¢ edition and we are all in the 35¢ class. I am afraid though they are headed for Sartre—also on the Index. So if you can include him in with Gide, I'd be obliged. These meetings are marked by such excessive politeness that not much gets said; also nobody knows anything about theology . . .

For the other information I am also obliged. It sounds better on paper than it works out in fact, however, as you can never so well decide if a thing is deliberate or not, or if the delectation is morose or not. Then you begin to wonder if your confessions have been adequate and if you are compounding sin on sin. This probably all comes from faulty training and being taught by the Sisters to measure your sins with a slide rule. It drives some folks nuts and some folks to the Baptists. I feel sure it will drive me nuts and not to the Baptists.

That girl wrote me the other day that she had not gone home for Christmas . . . I sent her a book by Mauriac called *The Stumbling Block.* She is one of those you have to go at obliquely, because I think she is much relieved to think that she has, with a good conscience, got rid of her faith. She'd never read a book called *Rebuilding a Lost Faith* for fear that would happen and she be stuck with it again . . .

* Epeikia *is a dispensation based on reasonableness in the interpretation of a law, in accordance with the law's spirit rather than the letter.*

## To Cecil Dawkins

. . . I am back on my novel after a vacation from it writing a story. I have now sent the story off and have to get my mind back on the other which is always a chore. New Directions sent me a book of stories by a man named James Purdy, called *Color of Darkness*. You have probably read about them. He had them printed in England and sent copies to such people as Edith Sitwell and they all wrote him wildly enthusiastic blurbs. The book had been rejected by 17 American publishers but when all this broke in England, New Directions published it. The stories have a kind of physical impact of disgust that I have never seen before. After a while they get monotonous but there are some wonderful things in them.

I read the *Field of Vision* [by Wright Morris] too. To me the elaborate framework, and symbolism, was too much for such petty characters. I couldn't have cared less what happened to any of them, though I thought the little boy was funny . . .

My mother and I plan a short pilgrimage to Lourdes and Rome this spring. I expect conversation [of the other pilgrims] to be professionally rewarding to me. I'll probably be listening to them when I should be looking at the windows of Chartres.

Sent you a book of Mauriac's that you will probably find sympathetic to some of your difficulties with the Church. Maybe time will settle this for you in a better way. I hope so.

## To Elizabeth McKee

25 Jan 58

I was beforehanded as usual in sending you that story ["The Enduring Chill"]. I have made some significant changes in it, improved it greatly. If Miss Morris is still considering it, will you please send her these corrected sheets. She can merely substitute the new pages for the old and it will be in order. I am sorry to cause you this trouble but it results in a better story. If she doesn't want it, send it back quick as I know where I can get rid of it.

## To Maryat Lee

Ground Hog Day

The passages [in M.L.'s play] are plumb creamy and I'll hope one of these days to view the whole thing. I gather you have to be financial wizard, slave driver & artist rolled into one; but I presume you can stand the pace. Though Lord, I would hate to turn my good work over to a bunch of actors.

Yes yes we are apparently going to Rome. Mrs. Tate tells me that Rome will improve my prose. I would like to think so; however by the time we get to Rome, I expect to be of a blankness. When we get back from this excursion, I am supposed to go to the University of Missouri and read, at least I am trying to convince them that I should read instead of lecture, mainly because the element of ham in me seeks release. I have a secret desire to rival Charles Dickens upon the stage. This story has two colored characters, a pseudo-intellectual artist, a country schoolteacher, a matron and a one-eyed Jesuit in it, so I figure that if I fail to convey one, there will be several others that I may manage to do justice to.

My spare time is taken up these days observing the domestic arrangements of geese. I feel that I understand their world thoroughly.


## To Elizabeth Bishop

6 February 58

Thank you so much for sending me *The Diary of Helena Morley*. We've all enjoyed it. My mother got hold of it first and could not help reading it aloud every now and then so I feel I have read it twice already. It reminds me a little of a diary written by a young New York woman who came to live in Georgia before the War Between the States (designation preferred by the UDC). It took her considerable time to get used to living with "the black shadows" everywhere. I suppose the two races can live together more agreeably in a Catholic country.

It was awfully nice of you to call me up on your way to South America. Of course I misinformed you about the night May Sarton was to be in Savannah. It was the next night so I hope you didn't seek out the performance. Two of the college teachers here attended. One reported it was over her head—she teaches sociology; the other said it was a great waste of time to take poetry that seriously when there are so many important *present-day* problems to be discussed—she was a Doctor of Education and was only slumming that night . . .

We certainly hope that you will be able to stop over with us on your way north next time . . .

## To Maryat Lee

Here I am misinforming my dear friends a mile a minute. No I am not going to Rome nor nowhere else (except Missouri). The doctor as of yesterday says I can't go. You didn't know I had a DREAD DISEASE didja? Well I got one. My father died of the same stuff at the age of 44 but the scientists hope to keep me here until I am 96. I owe my existence and cheerful countenance to the pituitary glands of thousands of pigs butchered daily in Chicago Illinois at the Armour packing plant. If pigs wore garments I wouldn't be worthy to kiss the hems of them. They have been supporting my presence in this world for the last seven years. What you met here was a product of Artificial Energy. The name of my dread disease is Lupus Erythematosus, or as we litterary people prefer to call it, Red Wolf. Anyway, no Europe. I am bearing this with my usual magnificent fortitude.

I would be plumb charmed to get to read the play. We are having tornados and hurricanes here and if the roof blows off and the play blows all over Baldwin County, I seek not to be responsible. Don't send it unless you have another legible copy. One blow a few months ago took the roof off the barn, or did I inform you of that?

I understand your friend Mr. Tillich is going to be at Wesleyan this year, also Miss Katherine Anne Porter. Wesleyan is filthy rich and can pay the price for the best people.

My Chinese goose has now laid five eggs but they all froze so I shall eatum.

Only a half a page but afterall, this ain't New York City. I don't get to go to no Shakespear productions. I don't even have a television.

Well, love from the dear old dirty Southland.

## To Sally and Robert Fitzgerald

Well I will have to send your children their snuff and Procebrin through the mail because the Scientist says I can't go. We went yesterday for my X-ray and when he heard that this trip would be 7 places in 17 days, he said he thought it would be a grave mistake for me to take it. I didn't twist his arm or nothing. He said it would be all right had I just been going one place and stay there so when I make me some money, I shall come to see you and nothing else.

That trip would have been nothing but airports. Cousin Katie is going to be very disappointed when she gets the letter saying we can't go. My mother I think is relieved that we aren't going because she didn't want to have to leave the place with the kind of help we've got; and me, I am bearing it with my usual magnificent fortitude. Ha.

The X-ray was no better and he has decided now that this is a side effect of the lupus; but I say to hell with it. He wants me to go to the man that runs Warm Springs and have him look at it which we will probably get around to sooner or later.

The *Odessey* arrived to my great improvement. Caroline says the trouble with me is I ain't got a classical education and I say I got as much as I can get out of Fitts and Fitzgerald. I look forward to the carnage at the end. I'm reading Erich Auerbach, a good chapter on the style of the *Odessey* contrasted with the style of the Old Testament. Thanks for all typing. I got the three pieces of it together.

Naw I never had to put any *New York Times* between my blankets in Connecticut. Your consciences can relax. That was inspired by one time when I saw George Davis' cold-water flat. I have improved that story a good deal with Caroline's strictures. I now have another Jesuit in it, in Asbury's mind, this one a very different type and it brings the other one out better.

This week I got a letter from of all people [the directress of Yaddo] . . . She said that now was the time when many people were applying to come to Yaddo and that she remembered how well I had worked there and she wanted me to know that if I cared to apply she would be glad to take it up with the admissions committee. It was a very nice letter. Of course I've no notion of applying but I wrote her my thanks. I suspect Granville Hicks is at the back of this . . .

Caroline says Cal has had another spell lately. He sent one of his Georgia students to see me during the Christmas holidays. I gave her a peacock feather to take him back—five feet about. She said she gave it to him and he looked at it sleepily and said, "That's all I need—a peacock feather."


## To Cecil Dawkins

12 February 58

Thanks for offering to let me use your camera but the doctor has decided that this trip would be too strenuous for me so it is off. I am just as well satisfied as I was not looking forward to the exertion. If I ever get terribly rich, haw, I shall go at my leisure and stay in one place.

However, I am going somewhere. I have been invited to talk at the University of Missouri, May 21st. I am also supposed to read some student manuscripts while I am there. A Mr. [William] Peden invited me. Do you know him? Anyway I trust I will see you as I gather your place is near Columbia if not in it, and you have a car so you can come to see me. What will the weather be like there then? He said I could come any time this semester but I can't go anywhere that there is ice on the ground. He sent me a copy of their student magazine, which has some good stories in it. I suppose their students will know more than I do. I hate to talk but I force myself to do these things as it is a way to supplement your income and right now I don't have any income . . .

Didn't see Jean Stafford's story, but I bet she could take Stephens apart. She was at Iowa too.

I'm glad I wasn't present to listen to your students break down my stories. They will insist on over-analyzing everything. I don't know if I told you but I had a little story in the fall *Partisan*. It would horrify them, I feel sure . . .


### To Sally and Robert Fitzgerald

26 February 58

This seems to be one of those on-again off-again trips. Cousin Katie was so disappointed that she says we must go anyway and not stay with the tour. I don't know if this can be arranged or not but what we thought we would like to do, if it can be arranged, is to go with the tour to Ireland and skip all the England and Paris stuff and fly from Ireland to Milan and stay with you the week while they are doing those other things. I want you to say if this will be an inconvenience to you to have the two of us for a week. I mean sho nuf feel free to say so because if you don't have the room, we can get a room somewhere near you. You said Levanto was on the train line to Lourdes so I thought you might would go to Lourdes with us, and on to Rome with the tour. They stay in Rome three days and then go on to Lisbon. I don't know if this will work out but would it suit you if it would? Could you meet us in Milan? Let for two minutes alone in foreign parts, Regina and I would probably end up behind the Iron Curtain asking the way to Lourdes in sign language. I cannot bear to contemplate it. Cousin Katie has a will of iron. My will is apparently made out of a feather duster.

The Monsigneur (God help him) wants me to "write up" the

Lourdes part of the pilgrimage. I don't think he has thought this through.

Regina and I have just got out of the hospital where we spent a week in a double room with identical colds and sore throats, taking identical red mycins. She after being cured of the disease had to be cured of the medicine. No medicines affect me anymore. The colored orderly was named Ulysses and all day we heard over the loud speaker, "Ulysses to X-ray," "Ulysses to emergency," "Ulysses to surgery." Ulysses brought us our dinner once and came and took away the trays when we were finished. He . . . had a pea-green cotton hospital cap on his head and his only words were, "Yawl sho ain't et much."

Thanks for asking me to come in May and stay a while but I will be doing good if I get there for this week in April. I have to go to the University of Missouri in May. I'd like to see [Mario] Praz fine . . . Let me know what you think of all this and if you'll go with us to Lourdes.

## To Maryat Lee

Thurs. [undated]

I have the feeling that the synopsis is ill-advised. It suggests that you don't have enough faith in the play itself coming across, or else in the reader getting it. Furthermore, I think it will suggest to them even more strongly that this is the stuff of a novel.

If I were going to use the quote at bottom of page 3, I would use the longer one. You can get by with that "nigh" in the whole play, but you can't get by with it out of context like that.

Also your prose is awfully cluttered. If you are going to write a synopsis, you will have to think a little about syntax and such pedestrian matters.

I was wondering—and this is just idle wondering of the non-theatre mind—why, instead of a synopsis, you don't write this play without any of the monkey business, without any of the heightening of language or parallel talking or that kind of stuff. This doesn't mean that you should just write it without their emotions coming through, but it means that you would make their emotions come through their language and not yours—no "nighs" and such stuff. Then you could present both plays to be read and the reader could see which one he liked best, and anyway get a better idea of the heightened one from reading the other. Also you might find after you had done it that the other was the better play. I ain't saying you would, I'm saying you might.

We have no water, no electricity, all the trees are broken with ice and the peacocks' tails are frozen. My innocent face has not been washed in twenty-four hours.

Bob [Giroux] has just sent me a jazzy review from the San Francisco *Chronicle* which says my book is like "a superior hill-billy concert." The fellow obviously adores hillbilly concerts and advises everyone to read the book.

## To "A."

26 February 58

The elegant paper was provided by my aunt Mary so that I could write my few feeble lines. We just got out of the place Monday—one week in there. My mother after being cured of the disease had to be cured of the medicine . . . At six o'clock in the morning I heard the following conversation from two nurses in the hall. What have you done with them sheets? I ain't done nothing with them. Well I tole you what to do with them. You ain't never done no suchofva thing. I know what I done. I know what you done too. You may know what you done but you don't know what I done. This went on for some time. It was the first vacation my mother has had in years, this being in the hospital for a week . . .

Caroline is not so hollow-eyed as that picture makes her out to be but it still looks pretty much like her. It is just like them to get some dumb Sister to review her book. I also observe they reviewed *The Living Novel* and made no mention of one of them in it being concerned with Catholicism. Embarrassed probably. There is a type of Catholic critic who must ignore all things Catholic . . .

I am yet too weak to contemplate Robie or J. F. Powers or any other literary soul or subject. Tonight I cope with the Rev. Kirkland's little group. Fortunately they've forgotten all about theology and we talk about Ring Lardner and Stephen Potter and any old thing . . . .

All my goose eggs froze, popped, and were eaten by the Muscovy drake. We begin again.

I don't know what occasioned my mother's mysterious remark about Shot getting brighter every day. Jack says he [Shot] is going to be worse for the next two or three days because the moon has changed and he is a mooney nigger. This is one of Jack's favorite remarks.

## To Alice Morris

28 February 58

I'm glad poor Asbury [in "The Enduring Chill"] has found asylum with you. He wouldn't have cared to be in any lesser journal.

I want to be sure you got the *second* opening and closing and that that is the version you are buying—the one with Ignatious Vogle, S.J. in it. There are also one or two spots where I think the prose needs a little doctoring. Is it out of order for me to ask you to send it back to me for say a week or two and let me do a few things to it? I have been in correspondence with Caroline (Tate) about this one and she declares that there are spots where the prose could stand improvement. Nothing drastic, just spots.

I thought and thought about a sentence to introduce it with but to no avail. I can only write stories. However, I think I should prefer: "A wretched young man arrives at the point where his artistic delusions come face to face with reality." What I really mean is *arty* delusions, but you can maybe make it better. Why not just have an arrow or a hand on the left side of the page, pointing downward, indicating that the story is below. Those ladies under the dryer all consider themselves intelligent . . .

## To "A."

7 March 58

I enclose these letters from Caroline [Gordon] . . . I think that if you study these you may learn as much as I have learned writing this story. I have learned more on this one than on any in a long time, merely because she has had patience with me. I have a few instincts but she has a few more plus thirty more years of experience . . .

Much obliged to you for sending the picture of William to his mammy. Fancy how her mother's heart will swell with pride. He allows he wants to meet us at Lourdes so I hope he will. I'll introduce him to the Msgr. and he can write up Lourdes. He does have a great talent for that sort of thing. We have had our passport pictures made. My parent's was very good . . .

I haven't read Powers' first collection in ten or twelve years but I remember disliking the baseball story and the one about the old couple. The rest I must have liked. Robie's that I liked best are "The Legend of Two Swimmers" and the German ones and "The Chevigny Man." The last time the pseudo-literary&theological

gathering gathered, we read "The Chevigny Man" aloud and they seemed to like it. A very nice boy does the reading . . .

Did you read about how disgusting my works are in the *Commonweal* last week? The Paul Bowles with whom I form this Cult is a very good writer, not the Paul Boles from Atlanta. I think this boy Esty is the same one who took off on me in the O. Henry review. I ain't quite the darling of the Catholic press yet, huh?

## To Sally and Robert Fitzgerald

11 March 58

We were cheered to hear you can have us and meet us but that is horrifying news about Lourdes. It is Cousin Katie's end-all and be-all that I get to Lourdes and if I am dead upon arrival that's too bad but I still have to get there. A 22-hour train trip would be the end of me, so I have written the travel agent to route us to Lourdes some way by plane, even if we have to fly from Milan back to Paris and join the tour there on the 28th. We would love you to do this with us but if you can't I can understand. I had no notion all these distances were so great. I am in the hands of this travel-agent woman whom I imagine as the same sort of character that unloaded the garbadine stockings on Robt. Her letters to me get less and less cordial and I get the idea that by now she is convinced I am a moron. I am convinced of it too so she ain't by herself. As soon as she sends me the itinerary I will let you know what it is—if she don't throw up the whole idea of having us as customers. I suppose they get a rake-off in the deal somewhere and I should quit worrying about her. If you can't go to Paris with us and down to Lourdes, you can meet us in Rome we hope.

. . . I wanted to get Louis to get me some pocket knives to bring your boys and Regina said you'd kill me, that you wouldn't want boys that size to have knives. I don't want to cause bloodshed in your clan but are they too young to have knives? Is there anything else you need or want?

Last Sunday I was visited by a poet named James Dickey who is an admirer of Robert . . .

I am glad to hear it's not so cold. I told my mother that that long sweater you gave me plus a raincoat which is lined would be sufficient but I was making no headway with her until your letter. She is afraid my poor white trash look will disgrace you.

I will get out of my head seeing that Matisse chapel at Vence as I will be doing well if I get alive to Lourdes.

## To Alice Morris

I promise you this is absolutely the last time I'll send you a fresh last page, but this one is much better. My Princeton mentor, C. Tate, assures me it is and I see so myself.

Many thanks for your patience.


## To "A."

20 March 58
Did I lend you a copy of *Thought* with a piece in it on Kierkegaard and St. Thomas? You may have sent it back and I lent it to somebody else but for the moment I can't lay my hand on it. The Pseudo Theol. Society has started reading Kierkegaard and when I resurrect that copy I want to lend it to the minister. There is a psychiatrist from the state hospital who comes and he has slept through both times we have read K. Doesn't get it at all, he says. We also now have the student worker who is a bright girl. Have you read *Fear and Trembling*?

Ashley's thesis was on "Caroline Gordon and the Impressionistic Novel" and that is what she is talking about. Rutgers University Press is considering it and Allen wants him to send the chapter on *The Malefactors* to *Sewanee*. This he calls "The Novel as Christian Comedy," which he says is pretentious enough for anybody. He has some thesis about her using the pattern of the Purgatorio in *The Malefactors* but I haven't seen it. I don't know any more about the quality of Ashley's mind than you do but Caroline seems to think the thesis is pretty good. And she needs somebody to write sensibly about her stuff because nobody much has. She hasn't ever got the critical attention she deserves I am sure. I see Allen got some kind of medal . . .

Now about Joe Christmas. Joe Christmas is the hero of Faulkner's book *Light in August* which you better had get and read. It's a real sick-making book but I guess a classic. I read it a long time ago and only once so I'm in no position to say. I keep clear of Faulkner so my own little boat won't get swamped.


## To Sally and Robert Fitzgerald

21 March 58
We will arrive with no lethal weapons. Yesterday we went to Savannah to see Cousin Katie and I bearded the Travel Ogre over

the telephone. It appears that we cannot get a plane direct for Milan but will have to spend the night in London. This may be just as well as they tell me after you have been on one of the things for 14 hours you feel like you've been on it three weeks. We are supposed to get there [to Milan] Thurs. 24th, at 1:40 p.m. and this should avoid having to spend the night there. She has arranged for us to go by plane from Milan back to Paris on the 28th. That one leaves Milan at 8:45 in the evening but she says that's the only one that goes. She says we can take a train to catch that one but we have to change in Genova. I told her I would worry about that one when we got to it.

If you want to go to Lourdes I imagine they would put a cot or something in our room, which is at the Hotel de la Grotte. I have asked the lady to tell me the names of the air lines and the one from Rome to Lisbon but I haven't been able to get it out of her. The hotel in Rome is the Hotel de la Ville. One of Regina's friends went to Europe last year and kept a diary which she brought around for our edification. What has not been copied out of guide books consists in complaints about the cold—this was at the end of May. She also brought back some frightful descriptions of the plumbing, which she delivers orally.

The Cathlicks have given Allen Tate a medal, I forget the name of it but Maritain got it once and some other people . . .


## To "A."

I have been holding the fort alone since Sunday night. In the middle of the night my mother had a severe pain in her back, so bad that she went to the hospital in the middle of the night . . . She hit her back on the edge of the sink somehow Saturday when the telephone rang. She appears to be better and hopes to come home tomorrow. I don't know what this will lead to for her; pray that this will be the end of it . . . The doctor thinks she will be all right and able to go on the trip. She wants to go. Since I've never much wanted to go anyhow, I am more than willing to call it off, but we will just have to wait and see how she gets on when she gets home. This has convinced me of one thing: that I must learn to drive. Louise stays with me at night but as to getting in town I am dependent on Sister . . .

I haven't read [Caroline Gordon's] *None Shall Look Back* but I have heard Lon Cheney expound on it. He says that the antagonist in NSLB is Death—the foe we don't know but all care about. You will see I really haven't ever read Caroline, just a few things here and there. I agree that Tom and his dreams don't work—it's really abstract, too much like an equation.

About the novel of religious conversion. You can't have a stable character being converted, you are right, but I think you are wrong that heroes have to be stable. If they were stable there wouldn't be any story. It seems to me that all good stories are about conversion, about a character's changing. If it is the Church he's converted to, the Church remains stable and he has to change as you say—so why do you also say the character has to remain stable? The action of grace changes a character. Grace can't be experienced in itself. An example: when you go to Communion, you receive grace but you experience nothing; or if you do experience something, what you experience is not the grace but an emotion caused by it. Therefore in a story all you can do with grace is to show that it is changing the character. Mr. Head [in "The Artificial Nigger"] is changed by his experience even though he remains Mr. Head. He is stable but not the same man at the end of the story. Stable in the sense that he bears his same physical contours and peculiarities but they are all ordered to a new vision. Part of the difficulty of all this is that you write for an audience who doesn't know what grace is and don't recognize it when they see it. All my stories are about the action of grace on a character who is not very willing to support it, but most people think of these stories as hard, hopeless, brutal, etc.

Katherine Anne Porter read in Macon on the 27th and the next day the Gossetts brought her over to have lunch with us. She was very pleasant . . . When she asked me where we were going in Europe and I said Lourdes, a very strange expression came over her face, just a slight shock as if some sensitive spot had been touched. She said that she had always wanted to go to Lourdes, perhaps she would get there some day and make a novena that she would finish her novel [Ship of Fools]—she's been on it 27 years. After that the conversation somehow got on the subject of death— there were two professors from North Carolina and the Gossetts and us and her—in the way that death is discussed at dinner tables, as if it were a funny subject. She said she thought it was very nice to believe that we would all meet in heaven and she rather hoped we would but she didn't really know. She wished she knew who exactly was in charge of this universe, and where she was going. She would be glad to go where she was expected if she knew. All this accompanied by much banter from the gentlemen. It was a little coy and a little wistful but there was a terrible need evident underneath it . . .

*In the midst of making plans for her trip to Europe, Flannery suddenly learned that her editor had resigned from Harcourt, Brace.*

## To Sally and Robert Fitzgerald

10 April 1958

. . . A wild letter from Billy announced he was on the way to Greece but hoped to see the Fitzgeralds on the 20th. I hope he likewise informed you he did. He wanted me to ask the Monsignor where he could stay at Lourdes . . . We can surely put you in our room at the Hotel de la Grotte/Bethanie, but not Billy. If you want to go, I hope you'll consider it. I have been reading about that church they have there in a hole in the ground that they pump the air into. It sounds like entering a lung.

Denver Lindley has just left Harcourt, Brace so I am in search of a publisher. Two or three are in search of me and tomorrow the new forces at Harcourt are coming down here for "tea." I called my agent up to ask her what she thought and she said, "Put some poison in it."

If you don't hear from me again and the Lord continues willing we will alight at 12:10 p.m. in Milan on Thursday Apr. 24. My mother is reading such things as how you have to announce yourself to the police department if you are going to stay over 24 hours, etc.

## To Cecil Dawkins

14 April 58

Thanks so much for the picture book about Rome. I'll probably see more Rome in the picture book than I do in Rome. Anyhow, we are about ready to go, have our tickets and other paraphernalia, and are prepared to endure—more or less. I'll probably be a beady-eyed specter by the time I get to Missouri . . .

Miss Katherine Anne was very nice indeed. Very pleasant and agreeable, crazy about my peacocks; plowed all over the yard behind me in her spike-heeled shoes to see my various kinds of chickens. I didn't hear her read but most of the people I talked to who did thought she read well. They say she had on a black halter type dress sans back & long black gloves which interfered with her turning the pages. After each story, she made a kind of curtsy, which someone described as "wobbly." She's about sixty-five. She's been on her novel 27 years and says all her friends call it "you-know-what." I hope I won't be on mine 27 years from now . . .

I'm not going to judge any literary contest that I've heard of. I hate to do things like that. I'll have a hard enough time talking to their students. Students always know more than I do.

## To Ashley Brown

14 April 58

My temperature is still sub-normal though we have our tickets in hand. The doctor said I couldn't go on the whole pilgrimage so we have cut it down very agreeably. Instead of going to Ireland and England, we are going to Milan and be met by the Fitzgeralds, and spend four or five days with them in Levanto while the others disport themselves at the Baloney Castle or whatever it is. We'll have to spend the night in London but that's all. I would love to see the Van Eyck portraits but I don't reckon we can make it. About Van Eyck—did you read the footnote in the Gilson book (that you suggested I get to review and that I finally got) about Van Eyck's abstractionism, quoted from Bazaine? I think this has some analogy to the grotesque in fiction. Anyway, after the Fitzgeralds, we will fly to Paris and join the pilgrims—of which there will be only twelve. Then Lourdes, Barcelona, Rome, Lisbon and home May 8, and you'll probably never catch me out of the confines of the United States again.

I haven't read Peter Taylor's play, but I didn't like the story in *Kenyon* as well as his others. And what about Robie being the new editor of the *Kenyon Review*? I hope he livens it up a little instead of it dulling him down some.

Miss Katherine Anne read in Macon a few weeks ago and had lunch with us the next day . . . She was mighty pleasant and agreeable. She told somebody in Macon that my stories reminded her of Sacheverell Sitwell and George Garrett. Who please tell me is George Garrett? I hope nobody awful.

I hope that Ivor Winters has been got over with. I hear Kingsley Amis is going to be at Princeton next year teaching.

It appears that my connection with Harcourt, Brace is about to be severed. Denver Lindley has left them, and I have an escape clause in my contract that says I can leave if he is not my editor. I think I will take up where I left off when they began changing editors so fast—with Bob Giroux at Farrar, Straus.

When do you set off for Yugoslavia?

## To Maryat Lee

15 April 58

I thought I better read the Ford [Foundation] letter over again before I wrote out my nomination and when I did I came across this—"The playwright is not included at the present time because the problems of playwrights are shortly to be given the Foundation's attention in other ways." It distresses me that I didn't read that the first time, but I go over such communications with a hot eye. Anyway, I will keep the information and will nominate you when I find out what the "attention in other ways" is if nominations are called for, suitably pruning Poppy's [friend of Maryat Lee] prose to my more austere requirements.

You made your mark in Milledgeville. Several ladies remarked to me that you were "lightly dressed" and they wondered that you didn't get cold. One, who ain't even met you, asked me if you were going back to your husband, and another, likewise unacquainted with you, wanted to know if you were "any good" as a writer. "On and off the best-seller lists," says I and evened that score. I gave the one who asked about your husband an idiot look and told the others that I didn't know if you were cold, but that I found it quite hot. Of Poppy they observed accurately that she wore bangs—but as if there were some peculiar guilt attached. Well, I live four miles out with the birds and the bees and the prospect . . .

*Since the terms of Flannery's agreement with Harcourt, Brace provided for release from her contract if her editor left the firm, after Denver Lindley's resignation she asked her agent to arrange a new contract with Robert Giroux for her novel-in-progress,* The Violent Bear It Away. *Again she requested the release provision, and signed the contract on April 15, 1958. She remained with the firm, which later became Farrar, Straus and Giroux, for the rest of her life. When Harcourt's edition of* Wise Blood *went out of print, FSG reissued the book. On the eve of her departure for Europe, Flannery arranged to meet two members of the publishing firm.*

## To Robert Giroux

17 April 58

I'm delighted with these arrangements and feel as if I am properly back where I started from.

I am going to stop in New York on my way back, only just

long enough to get through the customs and get a plane to Atlanta, so if Miss [Sheila] Cudahy and Mr. [Roger] Straus are not busy Tuesday I'd like to try to meet them then . . .

The limousine to meet us at the airport would be a great help, as I am on crutches and haven't attempted the city before in this fashion.

I hope you and the Eliots [T.S. and his new wife, Valerie] enjoy Texas. A man I know in Austin sends me a paper called *The Lone Star Catholic* and I have a mental picture of what a lone star Catholic should look like.

## To "A."

19 April 58

. . . I judge Fr. C. belongs to the tribe that knows what's bad but don't know what's good. If he said anything about Rouault not being a good religious artist, he's pure nuts. I don't know what he said about emotion and I don't think I would know too well how to apply the word to paintings, but what I object to in so many prayers that you read in prayer-books is that the emotion is somebody else's fever-pitch emotion—particularly in the Stations of the Cross, the ones of St. Whatshisname Liguori—you are stuck with *his* emotion, and it's something you can't live up to. Our emotions in the 20th century are affected by different conditions than in the 13th. I have just read a large book called *Art and Reality* by [Etienne] Gilson and I don't believe the word emotion even came up in it.

We have our tickets in hand, our traveler's checks, our two satchels and what have you and by the time you are reading this we should be in New York . . .

I wrote E. not to send me any books during the time I'll be away and got a letter right back congratulating me on going to Lourdes, enclosing their Easter letter from the son who is a Trappist (as my mother says, "Can you beat that?") and asking me to send him a card from Lourdes. She hopes that what I will get out of the Lourdes trip is a vocation to belong to the Marist Third Order. All I can say is boy, that would be an appropriate penance but I hope I'll be spared.

I'm glad you are on the short novel. Let it be what it will. Miss Katherine Anne and her 27 years have been giving me nightmares. It's not so much perfectionism—it's that a novel is like a machine, it either runs or it don't. If it don't run, she's right to keep it with her until it does. If it never runs, she's right not to inflict it on the public; but how awful to spend 27 years on what won't run. This is what I hope I will be spared.

I have a new publisher. My editor at Harcourt, Brace resigned suddenly. Three editors I have had have resigned from there in 3 years. It seems the place is being taken over by the textbook end of the firm and these men don't know anything about literature . . . Tuesday in New York I'll sign a contract with Farrar, Straus & Cudahy. I'll be back with [Robert Giroux] the editor I had at Harcourt for both *Wise Blood* and *A Good Man*. He was the first one [to resign from Harcourt] and the best and a very nice person, so I am cheered by all this. They have given me a much better contract and when I get home, I'll bear down on getting this novel finished. Miss Katherine Anne's visit was very well timed.

Rome
Monday [5 May 58]

Yr. letter here when we arrived for which grateful. I have been accompanied throughout trip by an infection but have been taking the Msgr's aureomycin & so am enduring more or less. Have sent no postcards or other such & will be very glad to get my two feet on my own ground next Friday, God willing.

. . . Lourdes was not as bad as I expected. I took the bath. From a selection of bad motives, such as to prevent any bad conscience for not having done it, and because it seemed at the time that it must be what was wanted of me. I went early in the morning. Only about 40 ahead of me so the water looked pretty clean. They pass around the water for "les malades" to drink & everybody drinks out of the same cup. As somebody said, the miracle is that the place don't bring on epidemics. Well, I did it all and with very bad grace.

Yesterday in Rome we went to St. Peter's for the general audience. The archbishop (O'Hara) arranged things so that we were on the front row. When it was over the Pope came down, shook our hands & the archB asked him to give me a special blessing [on acct. the crutches] which he did. There is a wonderful radiance and liveliness about the old man. He fairly springs up and down the little steps to his chair. Whatever the special super-aliveness that holiness is, it is very apparent in him.

The fellow pilgrims consist in 4 old ladies who are always getting lost from the rest, 4 priests, 2 little boys 12 & 14, 2 secretaries, & me and ma. They are constantly buying junk of one kind or another for which they pay large sums. One of the old ladies has just lost her traveler's checks.

I can't write except on the typewriter.

## To Sally and Robert Fitzgerald

Milledgeville
11 May 58

I enjoyed most you all and the Pope, and we are certainly more than grateful to you for the days we spent with you and for your coming with us the rest of the way. It would have been an awful trip if you hadn't . . . The plane ride back home about finished me. Regina revived as soon as she hit the cow country.

The plane ride from Rome to Lisbon was on the Argentine Airways in which we set facing each other, me and Regina facing Slowburn and one of the little boys, with M. and Mrs. S. and the Monsignor and Fr. B. facing each other across. Slowburn took out his needle and thread and began to patch his pocket; then he put that up and put a monocle in his eye and took out a dime novel in Spanish called *Solo Tu, Veronica,* and began to read that, then finally he went to sleep with his mouth open and the little boy had a great time making as if to insert a coin in it . . .

We didn't go to Fatima as it was an all-day trip and R. had a bad cold. Shrines to the Virgin do not seem to increase my devotion to her and I was glad not to go. They left at eight in the morning and came back at eight at night, all beat except the B. sisters who declared they felt much better at the end of the pilgrimage than they had at the beginning. We left them in New York waiting to get on an Eastern Airlines plane for Charlotte where they were to change for Augusta. The next day I read that an Eastern plane with a broken landing gear had circled the field at Charlotte for three hours to use up fuel, then had crash-landed but nobody was hurt. I think it was the one they were on, which was fortunate as I am sure they could take it.

Fr. B. bid me goodby with the information that he had read my stories and that when I wrote one about the pilgrimage he hoped I would be kind to them—he preserved a kind of wary cordiality toward me.

Everybody thought you were a great addition to the pilgrimage and M. took your address so she could thank you for helping her get the bolt of cloth. We left her in Atlanta, lugging the can of Lourdes water. The little boys amused themselves all the way to

Lisbon telling her that if she would go out on the back of the plane she would find a little balcony where she could look out, that we were about to crash, that if she gave Mr. Slowburn a commission he would find her a husband, etc. etc. . . . . She kept telling Slowburn she wanted to take him home with her. G. bought three pairs of shoes in Rome. Mr. Y. spilled his liquor in his TWA bag and it went all over his clothes.

You can't know how much we appreciate all you did for us and all the trouble you took. Enclose some more Weigel [books by Gustave Weigle]. Excelsior to you and children.

## To "A."

17 May 58

Well I am not getting to Missouri: as a result of a high blood count and a hacking cough, but I am not in a state of decline. Now for the rest of my life I can forget about going to Europe, having went. Had I been ten years younger I might have enjoyed it. The pilgrims were all I could have wanted—old ladies made of pure steel . . .

No credit is owing to me for taking the bath at Lourdes. Sally went along with us and she was determined that I take it and gave me no peace. She made the arrangements. If she hadn't been there, the arrangements wouldn't have been made. She has a hyperthyroid moral imagination. If I hadn't taken it she said it would have been a failure to cooperate with grace and me, seeing myself plagued in the future by a bad conscience, took it.* Nobody I am sure prays in that water.

B. has sent you a plaque and a medal so why don't you pick yourself out a Saturday and come get them. So far as I know any Sat. will be fine.

From here on out my novel will have to be forced by will. There is not pleasure left in it for me. How I would like to be writing something I could enjoy.

I saw Caroline in New York before I left. She is studying to get into the Carmelite Third Order—the way she goes at everything, full steam . . .

---

* I did make her do it, not because of an overheated moral imagination, but because I was sure she would later feel she had disappointed her elderly cousin. She knew I would insist, and that was perhaps the reason she so much wanted me to come along. She dreaded the possibility of cure in those circumstances; I didn't think she had to worry. She was annoyed, briefly, but her irritation faded.

Can't recall what I said about being an artist in the school of experience. Don't have a thought on the matter. Doubtless George Eliot was going according to her own conscience and doubtless she never penetrated Christian morality in its true meaning.

Wal, what Saturday can we look for you in pusson?

## To Maryat Lee

20 May 58

. . . It distresses me about your being persona non grata . . . but let me give you the advice of an old and world-weary customer. Myself. This thing of demanding honesty of people is in the upper reaches of extreme Innocence. The only people of whom you can demand honesty are those you pay to get it from. When you ask [someone] to be honest with you, you are asking him to act like God, whom he is not, but whom he makes some attempt to be like in giving you what you want, and it doesn't make him show up too well, of course. Never, above all things, ask your *family* to be honest with you. This is putting a strain on the human frame it can't bear. [A person's] honesty is only honesty, not truth, and it can't be of much value to you intellectually or otherwise. To love people you have to ignore a good deal of what they say while they are being honest, because you are not living in the Garden of Eden any longer. The last thing I find I want of my kinfolks is their honesty. Oeeewarrrrhggghhh.

Enough from the Sage. I should think Elizabeth [McKee] is right that you will have to show somebody how [your play] will work and in doing it you will show yourself probably. It is good you have some energy and some Poppy. All the energy needed staggers me. Once a university playhouse asked me about writing something for them. Would you find any help in something like that—I mean convince them to put it on. I suppose the actors would be dreary but then there might be some good ones. It would be like using a university press????

All the books on the short-story form I distrust but when I was coming along I used Brooks & Warren's *Understanding Fiction*. It sounds elementary but it has its virtues in that it has a variety of stories in the book and you get some idea of the range of what can be done. Actually there is no such thing as the short-story form. A nutty phrase.

Our cousin who gave us the trip furnished us with leather-bound travel books which we were to fill up about our experiences abroad and let her read when we got back. Miraculous and marvelous ill health prevented me from filling mine but I have just finished typing up my mother's so that when we go to Savannah Saturday we can present it. The charity is a good deal stronger than the prose in it. Maybe some day I will write mine, when the reality has somewhat faded. Experience is the greatest deterrent to fiction.

Cheers, love, & if you will visit the Mansion again, I will doubtless visit New York City. 6 of one, half a dozen of the other.

## To Cecil Dawkins

22 May 58

I got your letter shortly after I sent you my last note and was sorry to hear that about your losing your father. I'm having a Mass said for him here.

I have about recovered from the trip to Europe but I haven't gotten over having to give up the Missouri business, particularly after I had spent a good five weeks writing myself a lecture for it. Mr. Peden was very nice and seemed to understand. From time to time I read reviews of his in the *New York Times*. They are usually on books of short stories, which seem to be his province. And he appears to have very good taste.

The little vacation from the Opus Nauseous [*The Violent Bear It Away*] seems to have done me some creative good anyway as I am at it with something like vigor, or anyway, have been for the last two days or so. The people at Harcourt sent me Kingsley Amis' three novels, which I had been wanting to read, having heard of them ad infinitum. The first one I liked, the second one I didn't, and I have not yet had at the third. Too many too fast for him, I should say. Reading other people's half-failures always gives me a new urge to start on my own.

Bear in mind that you are coming to see us this summer and when you know when let me know and I will tell you exactly how to get here. This place is very nice right now with the exception of snakes. A snake got all my Chinese goose eggs while I was gone and took off an entire duck clutch. The peafowl lay latest, only about four or five eggs, and then set. They will be coming off around the first of July.

## To Ashley Brown

26 May 58

. . . The first cold germ I met [in Europe] moved in and stayed for the 17 days so most everything I saw was through a fog. Seeing the Fitzgeralds was fine. They have got a place there for Peter [Taylor] and another for Randall Jarrell for the summer. We stayed there about four days and then went to Paris. My cold kept me in the hotel room but I was visited by a girl named Gabrielle Rolin who has written a couple of books that haven't been translated yet but probably will. Instead of seeing Paris I saw her. Lourdes is a beautiful little village pockmarked with religious junk shops. The heavy hand of the prelate smacks down on this free enterprise at the gates of the grotto however. This is always full of peasants milling around and of the sick being wheeled on stretchers. Mauriac wrote somewhere that the religious-goods stores were the devil's answer there to the Virgin Mary. Anyway, it's apparent that the devil has a good deal to answer to. We batted around Rome for a couple of days and stayed in Lisbon a day. When the reality has somewhat subsided I may be able to do something with it. At present, I am just relishing being at home . . .

Robie has invited me to do a piece for the *Kenyon* to be called "Conflict in Crane." This is conflict in Dr. Frank Crane. Unfortunately my paper doesn't carry him anymore . . .

At the Fitzgeralds I read the Nabokov thing, *Pnin*, which I thought was wonderful. I took their children a copy of *Uncle Remus* but the children it appears speak only Italian, so I read it myself. It's really very fine . . .

When you come back from Serbo-Croatia or wherever it is you are taking yourself, you will have to come to see us. Let me hear from you from there. I am sure you could live in Portugal for about 25¢ a day.

## To Elizabeth Bishop

1 June 58

We went to Europe and I lived through it but my capacity for staying at home has now been perfected, sealed & is going to last me the rest of my life. The crowds weren't so bad but it was much too fast. I found that the crutches were a great asset. Never a plane I wasn't let on first. My crutches are aluminum; apparently nobody over there has aluminum crutches. Everybody stared and took his time about it, particularly the Italians.

Lourdes was not as bad as I expected it to be . . . Somebody in Paris told me the miracle at Lourdes is that there are no epidemics and I found this to be the truth. Apparently nobody catches anything. The water in the baths is changed once a day, regardless of how many people . . . get into it. I went early in the morning and it was clean; sat in a long line of peasants to wait for my turn. They passed around a thermos bottle of Lourdes water and everybody had a drink out of the top. I had a nasty cold so I figured I left more germs than I took away. The sack you take the bath in is the same one the person before you took off, regardless of what ailed him. At least there are no society trappings along with the medieval hygiene. I saw nothing but peasants and was very conscious of the distinct odor of the crowd. The supernatural is a fact there but it displaces nothing natural; except maybe those germs.

I am sure the ceremonies at the convent would get me down. I am a long-standing avoider of May processions and such-like nun-inspired doings. I am always thankful the Church doesn't teach those things are necessary. I read somewhere about some South American old lady who was entering the Convent; perhaps it was the same one you know.

There is a rich school thirty miles from here that is always having visiting poets . . . [and] the fellow who invites the visiting poets wants to have you so I gave him your address, hoping you might pay us a visit if they made it worth your time to come there. They want to have Eliot next year. Tom Gossett, the one who does the inviting, told me he had to explain to the President very tactfully who Eliot is before he would consent to paying him $1,000, which is the fee [Giroux set] for Eliot.

Anyway, we hope that sooner or later we'll have sight of you here.

*Almost a year after their correspondence began, Cecil Dawkins sent one of her stories to Flannery, who was impressed.*

## To Cecil Dawkins

8 June 58

I really like the story ["Pop the Blue Balloon"] and don't think it is precious. If you wrote that well five years ago, you should certainly keep on with it. You have a very good ear and that means a lot.

I don't have a copy of *In Defence of Reason* [by Ivor Winters] and haven't read it either so I'll be very glad to get it. Thanks a lot.

My friend from Santa Barbara reported that Winters was a success there or that at least a good many people appeared to be afraid of him. This seems to amount to the same thing.

Thanks also for the copy of the Midlands book. I rather liked the piece with one or two reservations. But they always insist on calling me a convert. They get this information from an issue of *Commonweal* that contained a letter from a man named Dale Francis who informed the *Commonweal* readers that I was a convert. He thought somebody told him so, or some such thing, and ever since anybody that writes anything, announces I am a convert. This wouldn't make any difference except that I think there is usually a difference in the way converts write and the way the born-variety write. With the born variety the point of view is more naturally integrated into the personality, or such is my theory. Incidentally that magazine *Critique* that had the Caroline Gordon issue is going to have its Fall '58 issue devoted to me and J. F. Powers. Do you know Powers' stories? Powers' stories can be divided into two kinds—those that deal with the Catholic clergy and those that don't. Those that deal with the clergy are as good as any stories being written by anybody; those that don't are not so good . . .

My novel is going very well for a change so I must be off to be at it.

## To "A."

14 June 58

. . . My mother said to [the wife of a suicide] that she didn't see how anybody with any faith in God could do such a thing. [The widow] said oh she was sure he had faith in God, but he didn't have any faith in people—which is to accuse him of the great asininity . . . His tragedy was I suppose that he didn't know what to do with his suffering . . .

Sent you the Missouri thing. You are the only one who would possibly want to see it. I learn to my horror that there is going to be one in the summer *Georgia Review* by somebody named Jane Hart to be called, "Strange Earth: the Stories of F. O'C." That strange earth business kills me.

I have discovered a short-story writer who is better than any of them, including myself. Go to the library and see if they have a book called *The Magic Barrel* by Bernard Malamud. If they don't, let me know and I will send you mine.

What do you do with a gallstone? A lady around here had a

mustard jar full of them taken out of her and was no worse for the wear. However I hope you can get rid of yours in some less inconvenient way. Maybe I should send you B.'s offerings. I have a tile that I got you at the Cathedral at Barcelona and a small plastic Our Lady of Monserrat that Sally sent you (she having heard of you via both B. and me) but I am afraid to mail either of them; however B.'s thing is wood so I might mail that. Let me know if you want that and *The Magic Barrel.*

I am taking driving lessons from the professor of highway dynamics at the local high school. Shot had 11 lessons. I hope to do it on the same. I is just as hard to teach as he is.

Right now I don't want to read [Ronald] Firbank because without warning I am suddenly doing very well on my novel. I see the woods in spite of the trees; in fact I even see through the woods. I have now about 100 pages and 50 more should do it. Unfortunately not any 50 will do. However I am much heartened.

Peculiar but I never could stand *Alice in Wonderland* either. It was a terrifying book; so was *Pinocchio.* I was strictly a *Peter Rabbit* man myself. Children don't have near as good taste as the experts would like to think.

EXTRA: Banjo's first calf has arrived. It has ears like a rabbit, is very large, broad-shouldered & a heifer. Rejoicing hearts etc.

## To Father J. H. McCown

June 29, 1958

Your mother sounds just like my mother. You should bring her down some time as I feel sure there is nothing they wouldn't agree about . . .

If you ever get to read a book these days, read one called *The Magic Barrel* by a Bernard Malamud. The stories deal with Jews and they are the real thing. Really spiritual and very funny. Somebody was telling me yesterday that the reason Jews are ahead of Catholics in every intellectual pursuit is very simple: they have more brains. I believe it.

## To Maryat Lee

2 July 58

My latest accomplishment is that I flunked the driver's test last Wednesday. This was just to prove I ain't adjusted to the modern world. I drove the patrolman around the block. He sat crouched in the corner, picking his teeth nervously while I went up a hill in the wrong gear, came down on the other side with the car out of control and stopped abruptly on somebody's lawn. He said, "I think you need sommo practice." So I have to go back next Wednesday and try again. It's getting me down. I have a very unbuoyant attitude to motion and I am developing an ulcer. I did make a hundred on the written part, but this profiteth me nothing.

What you done with your story? If you send it to Arabel you should tell her that you published that play *Dope*. Thinking it over further, I think it sounds like a good beginning for a novel in which at your leisure you could do something with the father and brother . . .

Yesterday we killed a black diamond pilot rattler in the shrubbery by the front stairs. The serpent at Jolly Corners. I hope I am still alive if you ever deign to come down here again.

---

*A publisher in Germany asked permission to make a selection of stories "which [he deemed] suitable for the German reading public."*

## To Elizabeth McKee

5 July 58

I've signed these [contracts for German publication], which I guess is all right if it's the best we can do. I'm curious to find out now which stories are not suitable for the German public. Didn't know I was quite *that* vicious.

## To "A."

5 July 58

High thanks for the Malamud which I have started. The only reason I would ever like to live in the city would be so I could ramble around in the 35¢ bookracks.

I have been ruminating on "The Hypothesis for Catholic Fiction." I don't think you could get it published the way it stands but you might if you developed it and expressed it in plainer language and if you made the concepts broader. For instance, when you say that most all Cath. fiction that is literature falls into group 2—that which "in a *setting* which unquestionably assumes that the faith is the most prevailing and indisputable reality in all the world . . . etc." I couldn't agree less. Setting is not what you mean.

The setting in which most modern fiction takes place is exactly a setting in which nothing is so little felt to be true as the reality of a faith in Christ. I know what you mean here but you haven't said what you mean. Fiction may deal with faith implicitly but explicitly it deals only with faith-in-a-person, or persons. What must be unquestionable is what is implicitly implied as the author's attitude, and to do this the writer has to succeed in making the divinity of Christ seem consistent with the structure of all reality. This has to be got across implicitly in spite of a world that doesn't feel it, in spite of characters who don't live it.

Writers like myself who don't use Catholic settings or characters, good or bad, are trying to make it plain that personal loyalty to the person of Christ is imperative, is the structure of man's nature, his necessary direction, etc. The Church, as institution, doesn't come into it one way or another. Your thesis will have to have two parts, a part to take care of those who use what Fr. Simons called the Catholic "decor" and a part to take care of those who don't. At least you have to recognize a difference in the practical problem here even if at bottom it doesn't affect your thesis. You say, "It follows that the sound Catholic fiction writer must write about the faith as though anyone who questioned it would obviously be utterly foolish and irrelevant . . . perhaps even a little insane." What the Catholic fiction writer must realize is that those who question it are not insane at all, they are not utterly foolish and irrelevant, they are for the most part acting according to their lights. What he must get over is that they don't have the complete light. This it seems to me is what you mean, though I am not trying to tell you what you mean. It is a matter of getting across the reality of grace, or as you say later on "in examining the relationship of human beings to their God," plus making FIRST their God believable. To, as I have said before, an audience not adequately equipped to believe anything.

You probably wrote this four-page paper in a half an hour. But it is going to take a lot longer to get it right. I think the idea of a paper on the feeling of transcendence in a Jewish and a Catholic writer would be a better paper to do because more compact, concrete, and to hand. I think you could write a very good critical paper if you spent enough time on it.

Wait until my book comes out and see if you like it before you decide you want to review it. There is no guarantee that you are going to be satisfied with it. I have more hope for it than I used to but I am not counting any chickens before they hatch. As for biographies, there won't be any biographies of me because, for only one reason, lives spent between the house and the chicken yard do not make exciting copy. I would like someday to see you write something about *Wise Blood* or the stories or the Tarwater episode, but to leave me out of it. It can be done. I doubt, for instance, that it's as terrible about Purdy as you think. I've seen pictures of him. He looks like a happy rolling boy. Seventeen New York publishers turned his book down, so he had it privately printed himself and sent copies to such people as Edith Sitwell and they raved and hooped and hollered so much that old Purdy immediately got his book taken up by New Directions. More than one way to skin a cat. I think he has a fine talent . . .

19 July 58

I am greatly obliged for *The Victim* [by Saul Bellow]. I've started it and finished *The Assistant* [by Bernard Malamud]. I don't like his novel as well as his stories but it's still a good novel . . .

As for me I have risen greatly in my own estimation. I am now licensed to operate a motor vehicle in the state of Georgia, passing the driving test with the excellent grade of 77. I am now persuading my mother to buy a car with automatic transmission and power steering. I figure this will add some years to her life as well as making it easier on me. Right now we favor the Plymouth. She says she will not have one that looks like an Easter egg so we are looking for a black one.

Naw I don't think my work is controlled entirely by mind. I do think that emotion has to be controlled in a story by the critical intelligence, not that emotion controls the critical intelligence. I don't think what was wrong with your article was what you had to say, but I don't think you got what you had to say successfully outside. There is a good critical article on Powers in the last *Kenyon*. You got to be specific, one thing following from another, and every detail down there; also everything has to be defined.

Would you like to read a real surrealist novel? This boy John Hawkes who came to see me sent me two of his. He is a born writer which is signified by the fact that it is possible to read this book of his all the way through. I'll send it to you if you're interested. This is the grotesque with all stops out. I think you ought to see it.

## To John Hawkes

27 July 58

I haven't written and thanked you for the books because I have been reading them. I braved the Faulkner, without tragic results.

Probably the real reason I don't read him is because he makes me feel that with my one-cylinder syntax I should quit writing and raise chickens altogether.

I am very much taken with your books and their wonderful imaginative energy. The more fantastic the action the more precise the writing and this is the way it ought to be. I have a friend, James Dickey, a poet, who was down here recently to show his little boy the ponies. I told him I was reading your books and it turned out that he has read all of them, including ones called *The Owl* and *The Goose on the Grave*. He described a passage in one of them where a man flies—he was lost in admiration. It appears he reads your books as they come out. You may state without fear of contradiction that you now have two fans in Georgia.

Your student's story is amusing and shows a wonderful imagination at work. However, I think she makes a mistake to set it in Georgia. That seems to me to detract from the fantasy. A fantasy attached to Georgia ought to have something of Georgia about it, and of course this doesn't.

I am more than pleased that you stopped to see me and that I've been introduced to your writing. Remember me to your wife and please stop again when you are down this way.


*To "A."*

2 August 58

. . . I don't agree with you that Purdy is a craftsman. That I think is exactly what he is not. He does not have a good ear and with a few exceptions the stories seem to me merely thrown together. What he has is an immense natural talent that he is either too satisfied with or too lazy to make precise. In half the stories I felt he didn't know himself where he was coming out at. The best ones from a standpoint of unity seemed to me the one about the child who had to burn the pictures and the one about the paraplegic. Those two seem to me achievements as far as the writing goes. They have a single effect, they do exactly what he must have wanted them to do. On some of the others such as the one about the drinking women, the compassion is very fuzzy, almost sentimental, his getting mixed up with the characters' compassion for themselves. And believe me that "63 Dream Palace" is technically as sloppy as it could get to be. The one about the colored boy that turned white's mama interested me. There he is certainly not so satisfied with his vomit, as you delicately put it. But there is something poverty-stricken and monotonous about the book. But don't judge him by it. There may be more to come. I have tried to find the picture of him but I can't find it. It was in a *Harper's Bazaar* about three months ago, a full-page picture. I can't believe such a benign rollypolly countenance can conceal many more vices than self-satisfaction and the urge to shock.

Well, the [farm help] and family are coming back to us. In the interim they have acquired a washing machine, refrigerator, television set, and a dog . . . My mother is not happy over the dog and he is to be on probation. The first chicken he kills, he goes. They seem very desirous of getting back. The negroes will move down to the other house. The devil you know is better than the devil you don't, according to my mother.

Will send you the Hawkes book as soon as I can lay my hands on something to wrap it up in. Hawkes and his family stopped by here about two months ago on their way to Florida. He teaches at Harvard. I had never seen him before. I am wondering what you will think of Hawkes as compared to Purdy.

My mother's [workman's] cousin is going to the army and wanted to sell his car and [he] tried to sell it to us—he said, "It's so pretty that when you're in it, it's just like being in a funerl parlor." It was red & white. We didn't get it.

## To Maryat Lee

25 August 58

We seem to have elected to communicate at the same instant about. I return you herein the Ford stuff. If they should ever decide I could nominate you, lemme know. The program seems designed to weed out the weeds beforehand, really very dull.

When I read that last paragraph in print ["The Enduring Chill"] I knew instanter that it was too long. When I have another collection, I am going to do some operating on it before I put it in. The problem was to have the Holy Ghost descend by degrees throughout the story but unrecognized, but at the end recognized, coming down, implacable, with ice instead of fire. I see no reason to limit the Holy Ghost to fire. He's full of surprises.

Somebody sent me a copy of that book of *Paris Review* interviews. The funniest one is with Nelson Algren. The interviewer says, "I understand you showed Simone de Beauvoir around Chicago?" and Algren says, "Yeah. I showed her around. I showed her the electric chair and everything."

We are about to elect us a governor. We have a choice of three segregationists: 1) the present lieutenant governor whose only visible merit is good looks, 2) a hillybilly singer, Leroy the Boy Abernathy, and 3) a rabid preacher, who claims to be backed by the Bible. You live in the wrong place, girl, but I done told you before.

## To "A."

30 August 58

. . . When I got that brown envelope I said to myself, Cheers she is sending me a story. And then out comes that piece. I will be glad for them to put me on their sinners-and-reprobates list and pray for me, but as for joining up with any third order, it is not for me. It is hard enough to keep up with your present obligations without taking on more. I wish E. would use up all her Holy writing paper. One correspondence I got was on the back of a pink and purple Virgin with sequins or something like stuck about her and a baby doll smile. She ought to read that old boy, Conway, in the Davenport *Messenger*. He gets them told every now and then about such things. Treat em rough, he says. Burn em.

Our new car has arrived. It is black, hearse-like, dignified, a rolling memento mori. Brother Louis got it for us in Atlanta from a man named Young who called up to sell it to us and told us that he loved Brother Louis just like he was one of his brothers and made a slight reduction in price. The next time you arrive at our gate, I shall meet you in it and drive you up. Incidentally, any time you get ready to take a Satday off, let me know. In a few weeks the weather should be right decent . . .

Send me a story of yours. Not no more piece of E.'s.

*Dr. Ted R. Spivey, a professor of English at Georgia State University in Atlanta, is the author of two books on literature and myth. He had called on Flannery to pay his respects, and a long correspondence began with this letter.*

## To Dr. T. R. Spivey

9 September 58

I have just finished a book which I am sure you would find relevant to your train of thought. This is *Israel and Revelation* by Eric Voegelin . . . It has to do with history as being existence under God, the "leap in being," etc. He gets away from the Spengler-Toynbee business very effectively and instead of seeing history as civilizational cycles sees it as an exodus from civilization. This is the first volume in what will be a six-volume study. The next two are on the Greeks but I haven't got my hands on them yet. You may already know about Voegelin. He was at LSU for years after being put out of the University of Munich by the Nazis—bodily, sitting in his chair. He has now returned to the University of Munich.

I enjoyed your visit and hope you will stop in again if you find it convenient when you pass this way.

## To Cecil Dawkins

20 September 58

This story ["Hummers in the Larkspur"] is a good deal better than some of the ones in the current Martha Foley collection that I have been reading. I hesitate to say anything is wrong with the structure of it. I don't think it should end with Nathaly and the hummingbirds but with the sentence, "They told it over and over to themselves only never to strangers for it was private and of the town." This because the story is about The Town vs. Mrs. S. The town is more important than Nathaly and you should end on what is most important.

Then there are one or two places where I think a false note is struck. On p. 11 where you have N. say the niggers won't accept Luella because she has white blood. Now this is simply not true of Negroes and N. would know it. They are very proud of their white blood, the lighter their skin the higher they think of themselves, and I have never known a Negro who didn't accept one with white blood. There are some in M'ville that are about as white as I am but they are colored and go with colored people. There could be some other reason why L. isn't accepted.

On p. 14 somebody says "we in the South . . ." It would be better not to mention the South. It appears as if you were trying to make a point. Even though the person might well have said it, you shouldn't have it in there.

On p. 15, I think the episode of Little Barb is unnecessary. It is rather too much and do you actually want to give the idea that only freaks are attracted to these foreigners? You have enough without Little Barb anyway.

On p. 19 you as omniscient narrator say "then there was a fight beat any . . ." This is using colloquial language when you leave out *that* that belongs in there. This may seem a small matter but the omniscient narrator NEVER speaks colloquially. This is something it has taken me a long time to learn myself. Every time you do it you lower the tone. It took Caroline about five years to get this through my head. You get it through yours quicker. You haven't done it but once.

Somewhere you have one of the women call a child a "kid." "Kid" is pretty low-class and sounds urban. Usually small-town Southerners if they aren't too common, call children children. Eudora Welty lets them say churren, which is what they say. Children will do. Kid is midwestern though you hear it *occasionally* in the South. I notice the poor white trashy kind in the South call theirs "younguns." These people are above that and I am pretty sure they would call a child a child and not a kid.

These are just small things but they make a great deal of difference in the long run. This is a story that ought to be published. Send it to *Accent.* Send it yourself and you might add a note saying your other published story was in *Pacific Spectator.* I don't think there's anything bad wrong with it. I don't think it falls down in the last five pages, but I do think it ought to end with what the town thinks.

One more thing. When the town sees Ullus Wingo and the child come back, they leave silently. Maybe there should be some voice to sum up their perplexity, their exasperation, their still misunderstanding. Every now and then the story seems just to verge on being sentimental. I don't think the title does much for it, either.

I am a pretty insensitive soul for subtleties and so forth but then one never writes for a subtle reader. Or if you do, you shouldn't.

Let me know if any of this makes sense to you, and if it doesn't, ignore it. It's very dangerous to criticize stories that are this good.

Cheers. I think you are a fine writer.

## To Dr. T. R. Spivey

28 September 58

The Bernanos novel is *Diary of a Country Priest.* It's out in an Image book. The German theologians are Romano Guardini and Karl Adam. Guardini's best-known book is called *The Lord.* Recently there was one out called *The End of the Modern World,* but I haven't seen it. He also writes extensively on Dostoevsky. I have a reprint of an article of his on the Legend of the Grand Inquisitor which I'll lend you if you're interested in it.

This enclosed piece on [Gabriel] Marcel should put you onto one of the mystic-existentialist writers in the Church—although he doesn't call himself an existentialist. His Gifford lectures, *The Mystery of Being*, are readable but his notebooks are not, at least not by me. No Aristotle in him that I can detect.

I have that Torchbook Eckhart but for some reason I haven't brought myself to read it. At one time I got a double dose of the mystics, mostly Spanish and Italian, and I haven't had a taste for them since. I have always wanted to get hold of Baron von Hügel's book on St. Catherine of Genoa—*The Mystical Element in Religion*. This is supposed to be a classic on mysticism. Evelyn Underhill learnt what she did from him apparently. However the book is not obtainable.

I have just finished a book by an Anglican priest, M. Jarrett-Kerr, *Literature and Belief*. He disposes of Greene and Mauriac handily and contends that the last great Catholic novel was Manzoni's [*The Betrothed*]. This I doubt.

Voegelin, incidentally, is not a Catholic. He calls himself a "Pre-Reformation Christian." I don't know what that would be.


## To Cecil Dawkins

5 October 58

I'm writing you for Regina to thank you for the cheeze. We are crazy about cheeze and we certainly do appreciate it. I forthwith cut into each package and sampled some of each and I can tell you it's very good cheeze. About the only kind of cheeze you can get around here is rat cheeze so we are enjoying this immensely.

I'll be interested to see what Mr. Ransom thinks of as "hick talk." I have always listened with profit to what he has had to say about my stories—except when he wanted me to change the title of "The Artificial Nigger." I am wondering who will run the *Kenyon* next year, since Robie Macauley has a year's leave and Edgar Bogardus got asphixiated.

We are reading *Lie Down in Darkness* for our Wednesday night gathering and I find it very impressive so far . . .

9 October 58

My thoughts on this story ["Eminent Domain"] are tentative. I think it is wonderfully imaginative. It's a wonderful idea having the old woman think the devil is taking over. What chiefly worried me when I read it the first time was the occasional mannered use of the language, a sort of pseudo-poetic effect, such as "other portents too she had seen," "saw cold grey his face," using the word earth for ground, putting the verb last in the sentence, etc. Then Jethro uses words like presence, brow, fitting, dwelling, finery, neat little old pen of a house, neat and pretty, canny sly old thing, crocodile tears, etc.—words and phrases that sound like you, not like a Negro man. Then I thought the section where he tells about his early life with his real momma was sort of unnecessary, particularly when you load it up with where the niggers sit on the bus and how they look at the white man's beach. It sounds as if these things are dragged in to show where the author's sympathies lie; leave it to the NAACP.

That was all I could see wrong with it on the first go-round but I read it twice because I thought it deserved to be read twice. When I read it again I realized something else. Negroes just don't go live in the mountains. At least there are no Negroes in the Georgia or North Carolina mountains. Negroes never lived in the mountains in slavery times and now most mountain people are hostile to them. Anyway, they are gregarious and a Negro with Jethro's propensities is not going to buy a house way up in the mountains. In Georgia the sun doesn't set on a Negro in a mountain county. The people run them out.

At first I thought you might make these white people, but I don't know if an old white woman would go in for the voodoo. Maybe you could have him take her where it's not really mountainous. It's too good an idea to throw away. At the .first reading I wasn't sure whether she pulled him down from that ledge or what. That could be clearer. If she is supposed to kill him, then you might have it done some other way. I don't know.

Also as usual I don't like the title. It sounds too clever. But this is one of the most imaginative stories I've read and you ought to do something with it. I would fix it up and send it to *Mademoiselle*. I think they might like it. Last week I had a letter from somebody there named Cyrilly Abels asking me to send them something. I don't have anything to send them but when I write her, I am going to mention you and say I have suggested you send her something . . .

Well cheers. I am still eating cheeze.


*To "A."*

11 October 58

I like this Danielou very much. There are a lot of people I can think of that I'd like to see read it . . . Maw much appreciates *The Nun's Story*. The nun on the front almost made me throw up . . .

Yesterday I heard from that magazine *Critique* that is devoting the issue to Powers and me. Some of it has gone to press. I judge that the two on me will be Caroline's and a fellow named Louis Rubin who has written reviews of my stuff before that I thought were good . . . I enclose you Caroline's piece which the more I read the better I like . . .

[A friend] had supper with us and greatly diminished the banana bread, and we have about taken care of the rest of it. She is poorly and has been debating for several weeks whether she should take a dose of calomel. Her doctor advises against it but she is sort of making a canvas of opinions.

## To Dr. T. R. Spivey

19 October 58

You may be right about [Gabriel] Marcel but I would have to reread him to know. I've read three of his books and I remember a great deal being said in them about the "broken world," etc. I can't think of anybody really apocalyptic to offer you though. It's in the nature of the Church to survive all crises—in however battered a fashion. The Church can't be identified with Western culture and I suppose the wreck of it doesn't cause her much of a sense of crisis. We certainly have no crisis theologians but in the Eastern countries there are many martyrs, whose blood counts for more in the mystical order of things.

What you say about the story interests me. It's not so much a story of conversion as of self-knowledge, which I suppose has to be the first step in conversion. You can't tell about conversion until you live with it a while. I can take all you have to say about it except that about the "sudden switch to undulant fever" when he drinks the raw milk in the dairy and it's the knowledge that he has no high and tragic mortal illness but only a cow's disease that brings the shock of self-knowledge that clears the way for the Holy Ghost. I couldn't have written the story at all without the undulant fever. Everything has to operate first on the literal level. I've thought that maybe there is enough in these characters to make a novel out of them sometime but it would be a novel with this story as the first chapter and the rest of it would be concerned with the boy's effort to live with the Holy Ghost, which is a subject for a comic novel of no mean proportions.

I suppose what bothers us so much about writing about the return of modern people to a sense of the Holy Spirit is that the religious sense seems to be bred out of them in the kind of society we've lived in since the 18th century. And it's bred out of them double quick now by the religious substitutes for religion. There's nowhere to latch on to, in the characters or the audience. If there were in the public just a slight sense of ordinary theology (much less crisis theology), if they only believed at least that God has the power to do certain things. There is no sense of the power of God that could produce the Incarnation and the Resurrection. They are all so busy explaining away the virgin birth and such things, reducing everything to human proportions that in time they lose even the sense of the human itself, what they were aiming to reduce everything to. As for fiction, the meaning of a piece of fiction only begins where everything psychological and sociological has been explained.

All this is underlining the obvious but I am unaccustomed to finding anyone else interested in it.


## To "A."

25 October 58

I'll be very glad when Birmingham [Birmingham-Southern College] is over with and I can get my mind 100% on this novel. I have the progression I want in mind now and I think I can finish it. Or maybe this is just wishful thinking . . .

I have been reading of all things a history of Georgia written by the history professor at the local college. It is a very fine thing and very good for getting your sense of continuity established. I did not know that we live on the borders of what was once the Creek Nation. I am highly impressed with the Georgia past. I am trying to persuade my mother to read it and when she finishes it I will send it to you, if you care to see it. It is full of eye-gougers and duellists.


## To Cecil Dawkins

26 October 58

I don't think there's anything much wrong with this story [one written as an undergraduate and never published] but that mostly what's against it is just the kind of story it is. Stories with farm settings have got to be almost a parody on themselves. Full of things like drawing up the well bucket and Pa and Ma and words like a-going and aim, feather mattresses and cold floorboards, etc. You meet all the expected props and with the irritation of these things you can't keep your mind on the character. Even the name Joel seems a typical farm boy name. I think it's sort of a nice story but I can see why nobody has bought it.

When using dialect, use it lightly. A dialect word here and there is enough. All you want to do is suggest. Never let it call attention to itself. Where people make the mistake is letting the dialect overshadow the character. You get a real person down there and his talking will take care of itself, but if you get to thinking about dialect and would he say it this way or that way, then you are going off the track, it's going to sound self-conscious. Concentrate on the meaning.

Usually when something is set in a past time it has to be longer than just a short story. People will read historical novels but a historical short story you seldom see . . .

I suppose my novel too will be called another Southern Gothic. I have an idiot in it. I wish I could do it without the idiot but the idiot is necessary. In any case it's a very nice unobjectionable idiot . . .

Enclose the BS [Birmingham-Southern] remarks, most of which you have heard from me before. I hate to write this kind of thing.


## To "A."

8 November 58

. . . As for any comparison between *The Malefactors* and *Lucky Jim*, it isn't in order. Amis was writing with great success from the top of his head. Caroline with less success from much farther in. Amis is not burdened with a belief in God. Mrs. Tate is. Amis had no problem. *Lucky Jim* is his only good novel. I've read them all and they get progressively worse. This Iris Murdoch is very good. Have you tried her?

Six or seven years ago I read three of Cary's novels and I must have liked them or I wouldn't have read three but I don't remember too much about them now. *Herself Surprised, The Horse's Mouth*, and *To Be a Pilgrim*. The latter I keep racking my head to try to remember because it must have been the most interesting one. He has gusto. The pictures of him working at the end when he was all but paralyzed were very touching.

Harassed I am but if it weren't Tarwater it would be another one. This is the condition of man. And I am heading toward the end of Tarwater. The greatest gift of the writer is patience . . .

The article in the *Commonweal* on the Japanese was right in line with what you say—some kind of spiritual void there. I have never read any Japanese writers myself. Right now I am reading the Pasternak. It is really something. Also a travel book on Greece by Henry Miller. Never read Henry Miller before but this book is very fine. Also reading a book called *The Eclipse of God* by Martin Buber that Dr. Spivey sent me. I have introduced him to Bernanos whom he likes. Do you know any Catholic crisis theologians? Only crisis theologians seem to excite him. He has a very fine mind in spite of the apocalyptic tastes.

Yesterday I went to a lunch for Claire Huchet Bishop whom you have probably read in the *Commonweal*. She's here lecturing, giving three or four lectures all on different subjects. A very versatile woman. European education makes ours look sick.


## To Cecil Dawkins

8 November 58

This is the best story ["The Mourner"] you've sent me in every way. The texture particularly seems a great advance on the others. There's no softness here. I like it very much. The only word I feel is not right in the whole story is the word *cowering* to describe the priest's bow at the altar. The boy of course is prejudiced and would like to think that the priest cowers; however he is also an artist and for him to see the priest as cowering casts suspicion on the integrity of his eye. One cowers in fear and this is not the tone at all of any of the priest's motions on the altar. When you make the boy see the priest as cowering you make him succumb to his own prejudice, which makes him less of a sympathetic character than he ought to be. But I think it's a terrific story, visualized very beautifully. Don't see why you should have any trouble getting rid of this one . . .

I have worked some more on the Birmingham talk because it doesn't really suit me but I am too sick of it to do much with it. I mean universal religion as opposed to sect, the catholic as opposed to the parochial. The notion of the perfectibility of man came about at the time of the Enlightenment in the 18th century. This is what the South has traditionally opposed. "How far we have fallen" means the fall of Adam, the fall from innocence, from sanctifying grace. The South in other words still believes that man has fallen and that he is only perfectible by God's grace, not by his own unaided efforts. The Liberal approach is that man has never fallen, never incurred guilt, and is ultimately perfectible by his own efforts. Therefore, evil in this light is a problem of better housing, sanitation, health, etc. and all mysteries will eventually be cleared up. Judgment is out of place because man is not responsible. Of course there are degrees of adherence to this, all sorts of mixtures, but it is the direction the modern heads toward. Some syntax . . .

## To Father J. H. McCown

15 November 58

I certainly would like to come to see your mother but travelling is getting harder and harder for me. We don't have a driver anymore . . . When I get to be a rich old lady with a car and chauffeur, then I will go places. Thank your mother for me and tell her if I ever find an easy way to get there, I will take her up on the invitation.

I had you sent a magazine published at the University of Minnesota, the issue being devoted to J. F. Powers and me. Your brother might like to see it. The Sister's [Sr. Bernetta Quinn] is the best of the ones on me . . .

We have had to spend two days this week in Atlanta at the doctor's and when we came back there was a card in the door with Fr. Ware's name and the name of a Fr. Galvin. We called and found out Fr. Galvin was the priest at the colored church in Macon so I presume he is a friend of yours and we are terribly sorry we missed him.

I am reading a book called *The Eclipse of God* by the Jewish theologian, Martin Buber. These boys have a lot to offer us. At your bookstore I hope they sell a book called *Holy Pagans of the Old Testament* (Helicon Press) . . .

## To Dr. T. R. Spivey

16 November 58

I think this book you sent me is wonderful and I am so very much obliged to you. Buber is a good antidote to the prevailing tenor of Catholic philosophy which, as this Fr. Murchland points out in the enclosed review, is too often apologetic rather than dialogic. Buber is an artist. That is one thing. Thomism usually comes in a hideous wrapper, but Buber's thought is cast in a form that is always readable. Just from reading *The Eclipse of God*, I didn't realize that Buber doesn't believe that man can participate in the Divine life. There is for him the Encounter with the Other,

but no interpenetration, no "I live now not I but Christ in me."
Although I knew Jewish theology wouldn't countenance God made
man, I thought that the Holy Spirit might be considered to enter
in, or something. In this it is very far from Catholic theology (also
from Tillich) but closer at other points.

You are right about Guardini needing to take in the corrupt
organization. If he were writing about the Inquisition he would
agree with you as far as that goes. But in the Legend, Dostoevsky
is using the Inquisition as a figure for the whole Church. To him
the Church was one grand corrupt organization. For Guardini it is
the mystical body of Christ, in spite of its spots of corruption like
the Inquisition. I presume this is why he didn't consider the Inquisition. He doubtless should have.

I have started reading the *Diary of a Country Priest* to see what
I make of it after all these years. I must have read it ten or twelve
years ago, once and not since. So far it seems to be only a slight
framework of novel to hang Bernanos' religious reflections on. The
diary form gives him leave to do this, otherwise he would have a
hard time. I am wondering if this is not something you have had
to cope with in your own novel. It is futile to speculate from the
not-too-well-known-to-you person to the probable work, but nevertheless tempting, and I should just imagine from some of the
things you have said that your novel is more reflective than exter-
nalized. You said something about my stories dipping into life—as
if this were commendable but a trifle unusual; from which I get
the notion that you may dip largely into your head. This would be
in line with the Protestant temper—approaching the spiritual directly instead of through matter. This is something Buber is opposed
to and it is one of the points on which he is close to Catholic
theology.

Bernanos stands very high with Catholics, at least with the
ones who read. As for the Church itself, it takes no official notice
of writers unless the work is contrary to faith & morals, upon which
it is put on the Index.

I like Pascal but I don't think the Jansenist influence is healthy
in the Church. The Irish are notably infected with it because all
the Jansenist priests were chased out of France at the time of the
Revolution and ended up in Ireland. It was a bad day if you ask
me. I read a novel by Sean O'Faolain about the demise of the Irish
novel. Apparently someone had suggested that there wasn't enough
sin in Ireland to supply the need. O'Faolain said no, the Irish sinned
constantly but with no great emotion except fear. Jansenism
doesn't seem to breed so much a love of God as a love of asceticism.

I am reading the Pasternak book and it is something of what

you are looking for. I was suspicious of all the praise given it; I thought it was just because Pasternak was a "good" Russian. But not so. It is a great book. At one point he has Dr. Zhivago say: "Art has two constants, two unending concerns: it always meditates on death and thus creates life. All great, genuine art resembles and continues the Revelation of St. John." Perhaps it is right that this should have been wrung out of Russia. I can't fancy its being wrung out of America right now.

Very glad to get rid of the Miss-Dr. business. I felt as if I were writing to Dr. Johnson; and Miss O'Connor sounds like the Last Librarian. I shudder to think that might have gone on and on.


## To Caroline Gordon Tate

16 November 58

I guess they sent you a copy of *Critique*. It helped to have you say something good about the novel [*Wise Blood*] . . . On reading it over, I have discovered what is wrong in the name of the Church as you have it. I knew something was wrong but I have only just realized what it is. Hazes's church is always called simply The Church Without Christ, never the Church of Christ Without Christ. That one comes in with Hoover Shoates and is further lengthened to the Holy Church of Christ Without Christ by Onnie Jay Holy. This doesn't make any difference in the *Critique* but you will want to correct it in the [projected] introduction [to a new edition] or the book will contradict what you say. Also another detail I noted is that Haze reads the sign about Leora Watts' friendly bed in the train station, not on the train. M. Coindreau probably isn't through with the [French] translation. I mean to write him and ask him to visit us when he comes South . . .

Big news for me. The doctor says my hip bone is recalcifying. He is letting me walk around the room and for short spaces without the crutches. If it continues to improve, I may be off of them in a year or so. Maybe this is Lourdes. Anyway, it's something to be thankful to the same Source for.


## To "A."

22 November 58

. . . I am surprised you don't know anything about the crisis theologians; in any case don't make a virtue of this ignorance for it is not. They are the greatest of the Protestant theologians writing today and it is to our misfortune that they are much more alert and creative than their Catholic counterparts. We have very few thinkers to equal Barth and Tillich, perhaps none. This is not an age of great Catholic theology. We are living on our capital and it is past time for a new synthesis. What St. Thomas did for the new learning of the 13th century we are in bad need of someone to do for the 20th. Crisis means something different of course for the Catholic than for the Protestant. For them it is the dissolution of their churches; for us it is losing the world. We have produced artists that might be thought of as crisis artists, for instance Bernanos and Péguy. One American Catholic writer who has the sense of crisis is Fr. Murchland whom you have read in the *Commonweal*. Fortunately, some of the best commentaries on the Protestant theologians, and some of the most appreciative, have been written by Catholics, e.g. Fr. Weigel on Tillich . . .

The harshness with which you speak of C. is not justified. She may be basically irreligious but we are not judged by what we are basically. We are judged by how hard we use what we have been given. Success means nothing to the Lord, nor gracefulness. She tries and tries violently and has a great deal to struggle against and to overcome. The violent bear it away. She is much to be admired for not repeating [her earlier novel]. It is better to be young in your failures than old in your successes.

Our cousin who gave us the trip to Lourdes is dying in Savannah but before she lost consciousness she had the happiness of knowing that the trip to Lourdes has effected some improvement in my bones. Before we went they told me I would never be off the crutches. Since last week I am being allowed to walk around the house without them as the bone is beginning to recalcify.

## To Cecil Dawkins

9 December 58

. . . At interviews I always feel like a dry cow being milked. There is no telling what they will get out of you. She asked me who my favorite author was and I said I liked James and Conrad mighty well and in a minute she said, "And you said your favorite author was James Conrad, now . . ." If you do manage to say anything that makes sense, they put down the opposite.

Never read the fiction in the quarterlies expecting to see anything first-rate. Yours is better. Ignore the rejection slips and concentrate on what you are writing.

I am strapped up with a broken rib, of all things. I broke it coughing. I never knew such was possible but I warn you: if you get a cough, buy yourself some cough syrup, don't just sit around coughing.

Glibness is the great danger in answering people's questions about religion. I won't answer yours because you can answer them as well yourself but I will give you, for what it's worth, my own perspective on them. All your dissatisfaction with the Church seems to me to come from an incomplete understanding of sin. This will perhaps surprise you because you are very conscious of the sins of Catholics; however what you seem actually to demand is that the Church put the kingdom of heaven on earth right here now, that the Holy Ghost be translated at once into all flesh. The Holy Spirit very rarely shows Himself on the surface of anything. You are asking that man return at once to the state God created him in, you are leaving out the terrible radical human pride that causes death. Christ was crucified on earth and the Church is crucified in time, and the Church is crucified by all of us, by her members most particularly because she is a Church of sinners. Christ never said that the Church would be operated in a sinless or intelligent way, but that it would not teach error. This does not mean that each and every priest won't teach error but that the whole Church speaking through the Pope will not teach error in matters of faith. The Church is founded on Peter who denied Christ three times and couldn't walk on the water by himself. You are expecting his successors to walk on the water. All human nature vigorously re- sists grace because grace changes us and the change is painful. Priests resist it as well as others. To have the Church be what you want it to be would require the continuous miraculous meddling of God in human affairs, whereas it is our dignity that we are allowed more or less to get on with those graces that come through faith and the sacraments and which work through our human nature. God has chosen to operate in this manner. We can't under- stand this but we can't reject it without rejecting life.

Human nature is so faulty that it can resist any amount of grace and most of the time it does. The Church does well to hold her own; you are asking that she show a profit. When she shows a profit you have a saint, not necessarily a canonized one. I agree with you that you shouldn't have to go back centuries to find Catholic thought, and to be sure, you don't. But you are not going to find the highest principles of Catholicism exemplified on the surface of life nor the highest Protestant principles either. It is easy for any child to pick out the faults in the sermon on his way home from Church every Sunday. It is impossible for him to find out the hidden love that makes a man, in spite of his intellectual limitations, his neuroticism, his own lack of strength, give up his life to the service of God's people, however bumblingly he may go about it . . .

It is what is invisible that God sees and that the Christian must look for. Because he knows the consequences of sin, he knows how deep in you have to go to find love. We have our own responsibility for not being "little ones" too long, for not being scandalized. By being scandalized too long, you will scandalize others and the guilt for that will belong to you.

It's our business to try to change the external faults of the Church—the vulgarity, the lack of scholarship, the lack of intellectual honesty—wherever we find them and however we can. In the past ten years there has been a regular rash of Catholic self-criticism. It has generally come from high sources and been reviled by low. If the same knowledge could be shared uniformly in the Church we would live in a miraculous world or belong to a monolithic organization. Just in the last few years have Sisters teaching in parochial schools begun to get AB degrees. Doubtless the good soul who didn't know papal history would never believe it if she read it anyway, but there are plenty of Catholic sources, all with the Nihil Obstat, that she could pick it up in. The Church in America is largely an immigrant Church. Culturally it is not on its feet. But it will get there. In the meantime, the culture of the whole Church is ours and it is our business to see that it is disseminated throughout the Church in America. You don't serve God by saying: the Church is ineffective, I'll have none of it. Your pain at its lack of effectiveness is a sign of your nearness to God. We help overcome this lack of effectiveness simply by suffering on account of it.

To expect too much is to have a sentimental view of life and this is a softness that ends in bitterness. Charity is hard and endures; I don't want to discourage you from reading St. Thomas but don't read him with the notion that he is going to clear anything up for you. That is done by study but more by prayer. What you want, you have to be not above asking for. But homiletics isn't in my line, particularly with a broken rib . . .

## To "A."

20 December 58

. . . Brainard Cheney is Lon and it is high time they reviewed that book. I wrote B.L. about six weeks ago and asked her why it hadn't been reviewed and she asked her boss (Luchessi—yer fellow parishioner, I judge) and got the reply, "Sorry honey, but it was about niggers." I reported this to Lon who reported it to Ralph McGill, so finally we get the review. It is a very respectable book, nothing great, but respectable . . .

What you want to read *A Stillness at Appomattox* for? Buy it for me but don't send it to me. I never was one to go over the Civil War in a big way . . .

The Nashville deal will be more than a small fee I am happy to say—$350. That is why I had to accept it. I think I'll read "The Artificial Nigger." I will have to practice up on it.

Me blessings to you Christmas and thereafter.


## To Father J. H. McCown

23 December 58

I highly appreciate all the printed matter. I have been wanting to get my hands on one of those books that list paperbacks. I might could afford to get educated now that I know what's to be had. I am also very glad to have the Daniel-Rops in the paperback. I have read it but I have a heathen friend that I would like to give it to. In fact I seem to have nothing but friends who have left the Church. They have all left because they have been shocked by the intellectual dishonesty of some Catholic or other—or so they say, frequently of priests. It's only partly that but it does account for a good deal. I wish we would hear more preaching about the harm we do from the things we do not face and from all the questions that we give Instant Answers to. None of these poor children want Instant Answers and they are right.

There is a very good book called *Christian Thought and Action* by Dom Aelred Ghrame [Graham], the Abbot of Portsmouth Priory. I don't know if it is in paperback or not. I would send it to you but I sent it to one of my heathen friends who has left the Church. She said she was amazed that a Catholic writer could be so flexible. Apparently she has met nothing but idiot priests all her life, also idiot nuns. She graduated from a Catholic school (grammar).

I don't know what kind of conspiracy that was at Minnesota.* Powers and I are, I suppose, the only two young writers in this

---

* *For some unexplained reason J. F. Powers had not been invited to a reception given for Flannery when she read at Minnesota. Powers wrote me that he was somehow in the black books of the department at the time. In any case, the two writers did not meet then, and unfortunately there was no later occasion for a meeting.*

country who are well thought of *and* connected with the Church. We both have the same kind of horns.

The doctor tells me that my bone is beginning to recalcify. I can walk around the room a few times a day without the crutches but I'm not supposed to overdo it, lest I interfere with further progress. They told me last year that it wouldn't get any better. I am willing to lay this to Lourdes or somebody's prayers but I hope the improvement will continue.

I am at the most critical point in my novel and I need your prayers about it. I would rather finish this novel right than be able to walk at all. It requires a lot more than I have.

I'll send you *The Magic Barrel* right after Christmas. The more I read it, the better I like it . . .


## To "A."

25 Dec 58

This is a wonderful book [Nikos Kazantzakis's *The Odyssey: A Modern Sequel*] you have sent me. I have just finished Book I and have felt I was in the presence of something. I hope you read it before you sent it but if you did not I will send it to you when you get ready. It fits in rather well with what I am also reading, the 2nd volume of Voegelin, on the Greek *polis*. He has some masterful analyses of the *Iliad* & of Aeschylus but other large hunks are dull or over my head. Anyhow, I am very grateful for the Kazantzakis because I would never have got my hands on it otherwise.

Big doings here the other night in preparation for the Yuletide. Louise came over after supper and said she was afraid to go back home because Jack had the gun loaded and said he was going to kill her. He was eventually persuaded by my mother to bring the gun over and leave it in the back hall. After the liquor wore off them, they all calmed down and yesterday she gave him back his gun; but today, we had to stay home to make sure hostilities didn't redevelop. So far nothing. My mother gave them a snappy sermon on: "Thou shalt not kill during the Christmas season" when she gave them their presents last night and I guess it paid off . . .


*Flannery seemed fated to asceticism. The one time she decided that she should contribute to the frolics at Yaddo, she tripped and broke her bottle on her way to the party.*

## To Robert Lowell

25 December 58

It is mighty unseemly of you to enshrine me in your memory falling up the steps with a bottle of gin. I recollect the incident. It was not gin but rum (unopened) and the steps were slick . . . In our house the liquor is kept in the bathroom closet between the Draino and the plunger, and you don't get any unless you are about dead. The last time I had any was when I dropped the side of the chicken brooder on my foot and broke my toe.

This spring we spent four days with the Fitzgeralds in Levanto and then Sally went with us to Paris and Lourdes and then to Rome. Europe didn't affect me none, but since coming back my bone has begun to recalcify, an improvement that was not expected.

I would like to think I will finish my book this year but this may be just what I would like to think. I will hope to read yours.

My love to you and Elizabeth and Harriet. That Harriet is going to take over if you don't watch out. You ought to raise her in the South and then she wouldn't have to go to school. I am really looking forward to the next generation being uneducated.

# PART III

---

## "THE VIOLENT

## BEAR IT AWAY"

## 1959 – 1963

---

*Soon after New Year's Day, 1959, Flannery completed the first draft of her second novel,* The Violent Bear It Away, *on which she had been working for seven years. After asking several of her close friends to read it critically, she made important revisions and sent the ms. to her publishers in July. The book was issued six months later—in late January 1960.*

## To Sally and Robert Fitzgerald

1 January 59

The dress arrived yesterday in time for me to start the new year right. It is beautiful and fits fine; in fact I think Regina was disappointed that she couldn't tear it up and put it back together again. Never saw any material like this before but it is just right for the climate. I am most powerfully obliged to you. Nothing else in these parts like it.

We spent the holidays preventing bloodshed . . . Every day [Regina] says she is going out of the dairy business . . :

I only have to bear with the prophet Tarwater for about ten or twelve more pages. At least I will be through with a first draft then and will have to start bearing with him again from the beginning; but it is a very good feeling to see the end in sight even if I don't know whether it's any good or not . . .

## To "A."

I read *Man's Fate* but never have read anything else of Malraux's. I have just finished the second volume of Voegelin. I don't think you would like it because it's more full of technical stuff than the other one. Parts of it were very exciting but for the most part you need to be a Greek scholar to read it . . .

Three or four more pages and I'll have a first draft. This is a very good feeling I can tell you after so many years. Of course now I have to go back to the beginning. I'm by no means finished but at least I know that it's possible. I must say I attribute this to Lourdes more than the recalcifying bone. Anyway it means more to me.

## To Cecil Dawkins

14 January 59

I told you Eudora Welty was coming to the University of Chicago this year. She isn't. I am. Her brother got sick and they called me up and asked me to take her place and I foolishly accepted. I can live for a year on what they are paying me for the week. I . . . will have two workshop classes and give one public reading on Friday 13th. I have to live in the dormitory and confer with the young ladies as to how to attain their ideals—this being a clause in some old lady's will who is providing 2/7 of the money for this part of the engagement. Maybe you can get down. If it were not winter, I would come up to see you, but I am going to do good if I don't break my neck as it is. I foresee all sorts of awful weather, planes that don't fly, etc. Last year my aunt started out for Chicago and had to land in Milwaukee. Send me your telephone number and if any such thing happens to me, I will call you SOS and demand to be taken care of.

I have finished my novel. At least I think I have. Anyway I have come to the end of it and for celebration and necessity have bought myself a new typewriter. My mother is out coping with the water works which have all gone bust, and I must get about typing my novel so I can send it to Caroline.

## To "A."

31 January 59

The opus is still called *The Violent Bear It Away* and I am more and more satisfied with the title and less and less satisfied with the rest of it. I don't know when I'll send it to the publishers. After Caroline has had her say, I guess, and I have worked some more on it. This is not the time for me to get hasty, after seven years. When I send it to the publishers, I will also send it to you and the Fitzgeralds, and anything you all have to offer, I can clean up on the last proofs. It is only 43,000 words. When I get back from Chicago I'll have to face it again. Pray that I will get back from Chicago. I dread this kind of trip.

All I know about Chicago is going from the Dearborn Street Station to the LaSalle Street Station, a journey that never impressed me as beautiful. I ain't going to see any more of Chicago while I'm there than necessary. I am going to read "A Good Man Is Hard to Find," deleting the paragraph about the little nigger who doesn't have any britches on. I can write with ease what I forbear to read.

I am much cheered that you are writing a novel. I have thought all along that you needed that much room. Let James help your structure but not your style. I have reread "The Aspern Papers" and "The Beast in the Jungle." I particularly like "The Aspern Papers."

I have heard from M. Coindreau, the translator. He says don't worry about [the] introduction . . . but he says what is needed is some kind of article, which he hopes to write and publish in Paris before the translation comes out, about the role of the evangelist and the itinerant preacher in Southern life and American literature. He is going to write on this from *Elmer Gantry* to *Wise Blood.* Also he is coming down here around the 1st of April to see me and talk about it. I have no idea what I will do with an Elderly French gentleman for several days. He is going to Paris the last of April and take the manuscript with him. The French name will be *La Sagesse dans le Sang.* He says the French have absolutely no notion of this kind of preacher, that they won't know what Haze Motes is, unless there is some kind of preparation . . .

## To Father J. H. McCown

Ground Hog Day [February 2, 1959]
. . . Pray for me that I will get to and from Chicago whole and be unscathed by the city interleckchuls. They are paying me well and unfortunately I have to earn me bread. I wish I didn't have to earn it this way in February.

I wrote your brother and had a nice note from him. When my book comes out I will send the both of you advance copies but it is not even out of my hands yet and after I send it to the publishers, it takes six months. Anyway it is finished enough for me at least to know that it is going to BE, and this is something.

B. writes that all their contracts have been renewed for next year but the president tells them they're not worth the paper they're written on. The idiot legislature has just passed a bill that nobody over 21 can go to college or over 25 start graduate school. Those boys are really desperate. I hope they ain't so desperate yet in Mississippi.

## To Sally and Robert Fitzgerald

15 Feb 59
Cheers for the Ford Foundation. I hope yours was a lot. Mine was $8,000 for the two years which is just 8,000 more than I was expecting. I have just got back from the University of Chicago where I spent five days—conducted two workshops and gave a reading (which nobody attended) and got $700. I also had to live in the dormitory and be available to students as wished to talk— some old lady left a fund for it. I met Henry Rago [editor of *Poetry* magazine] at a party and he was the one told me about the grants, mine and yours, as my letter had come to Milledgeville and I didn't know about it. He asked most particularly for you and was very glad you got a grant. I think he said he suggested your name, but I guess a lot of people did.

I have finished the novel and when I do some doctoring on it, I am going to send it to you, and please kindly tell me what you think and mince no words . . . Caroline has seen it and is very enthusiastic but I have not caught her enthusiasm. I am not sure it works and I want a less enthusiastic view on it . . .

Cousin Katie left me the house in Savannah I was raised in. It is next to hers. She left hers to another cousin. All this financial swell has me bothered. I intend to live for ten years on the Ford money. My mother says she wants to visit Ireland but I think the whim will pass. Right now she is involved in selling timber for the estate, a thankless family job.

We hope yr children have run through the known diseases by now & Telemacus will be boosted by Ford.

## To Catharine Carver

18 February 59

It was real good to hear from you . . . The fact is I was just before writing you. You said once you would read my novel when I finished it, or at least I don't know whether I have finished it or not but I have come to the end of it. I wouldn't send it to you without asking if I may again as you may be very busy or going on your vacation or some such thing. But if you would read it, I would be very grateful because I need somebody to tell me if I really ought to publish it or not, or if I need to work on it some more. Caroline has seen it and she likes it but she shares my point of view on some things and I want somebody to read it who doesn't necessarily. It's not long, only about 45,000 words. Will you drop me a card if I may send it to you? I'll have the ms. ready in about three weeks. Incidentally, the name of it is *The Violent Bear It Away* . . .

If your peacock feathers are getting motheaten, I can send you some more this fall. I have thirty now and I am going to be drowned in feathers. Several old ladies about town have decorated their hats with feathers I have given them. Maybe they feel like peacocks but it don't make them look like them.

Cheers and many thanks if I may send you this ms. It will mean a lot to me to have your say-so on it.

## To Maryat Lee

18 February 59

The local telegram official just called me up and read your wire in a very flat voice, obviously disliking to say Wow. It cheered me no end. I got the card from Bermuda and was thinking you were sunning yourself. Do you get your mail? I've written you a couple of letters of negligible import but unanswered. Lemme hear from you . . .

Best wishes to Poppy, if they are in order. What are you doing for an assistant? I dare say you don't need one. Have you heard anything about this theatre program they have at the University of

Illinois? A man named Charles Shattuck runs it and every other year they do a play and pay the play-write to come out there and put it on or something and they are supposed to be very good. This is at Urbana, Illinois. A lot of people have told me about this lately.

It appears that I have finished my novel. I am not actually sure which is where the rub comes. Just in that state of not knowing whether it works or is the worst novel ever written. Somebody said you don't finish one you just say to hell with it. I am tempted. The name of it is going to be *The Violent Bear It Away*. They do and you know what . . .


## To Cecil Dawkins

Geo. Wash. Birthday [1959]

It sure added to my pleasure and eased my pain to see you and Betty [Littleton] in Chicago. The plane not only went but went on time and arrived on time and some of my faith was restored. I told Dick Stern about your writing on the way to the airport and he said if you would be interested to send him some stories to the *Chicago Review*. I haven't seen the *Chicago Review* but he said they published good stuff. Richard G. Stern is his name. I liked him very much. He seems to have sole charge of any writing program there, but there doesn't seem to be much of one. Their students tend to abstract speculation.

There is some kind of business at Iowa where Rockefeller money is given away. That Phillopino (sp?) gentleman I was talking to after the reading had come over from Iowa City and he told me he had Rockefeller money to write there. J. F. Powers also had some at one time. You might write Paul Engle and ask about it. If you apply and I can do anything to help, let me know. I can write him a letter. There is also a Eugene F. Saxton fellowship but I don't know much about it. You usually apply for these things in the fall and get them in the spring. It may be that if you have established the habit of writing in this year, you can write and teach both, but I don't know what the teaching takes out of you. I was flabbergasted to get home and learn how much the Ford grant is . . .

The verse is Matthew 11:12. Christ has been talking about John the Baptist and says, "What did you go out to see? A reed shaken by the wind?" Then there is something else, a couple of verses and He says, "Since the time of John the Baptist until now, the kingdom of heaven suffereth violence, and the violent bear it away." I am still picking at the novel, still don't really know what I think of it.

Vanderbilt is not until April 21–4 and I'll be glad when that is over too. I am thinking about reading "The Artificial Nigger" if I can keep going that long. I won't be hurting anybody's feelings. It is great to be at home in a region, even this one.


## To "A."

28 February 59

It would have done your heart good to see all the marks on the copy [of the typescript of *The Violent Bear It Away*], everything commented upon, doodles, exclamation points, cheers, growls. You can know that she [Caroline Gordon] enjoys reading it and reads every word and reacts to every one she reads. Also she sent a paper she had written and a couple of other things for me to remark on . . .

Mr. William Ready gives me the creeps. Have you read his book, *The Poor Hater*? All these moralists who condemn *Lolita* give me the creeps. Have you read *Lolita* yet? I go by the notion that a comic novel has its own criteria . . .

If I were you I would just write Elizabeth Stevenson a letter and tell her you liked her book and would like to talk about it. I just met her that once at the Writers' Thing, her and her mother, and they looked to me like real nice people and no foolishness. I don't know her address but they must be in the book. I imagine the people she would have any interest in talking to in Atlanta are few and far between and you would be one of them, but I judged her to be on the reserved side.

Haven't seen the new poems of Cal [*Life Studies*]. Ashley wrote they were weird, like sections of a free-form memoir. Farrar, Straus is going to bring out a book of his this year. I hear Miss K. A. Porter's is to be out in September. At the rate I am going, mine won't be out until January. I am again very dissatisfied with it, in spite of Caroline and her enthusiasm.

Rebarbative is not in my dictionary but it reminds me of something between regurgitate and vituperative. My novel must be rebarbative. If you find it, let me know.

My Chinese goose has laid two eggs. Things are beginning to pick up. Consider what Sareday you can come down and pick you up some country air.

## To Cecil Dawkins

I am right embarrassed to think every story is the best but I
believe this ["The Quiet Enemy"] is the best so far. I believe it's
better than the ranch one even. The only thing I don't like about
it are the last four words—"the adjustment of their difficulties."
This sounds too clever, too facetious. If the woman is thinking it,
it is too clever for her, and if the narrator is thinking it, it is too
condescending of you. It's a very touching story and it ought to be
straight at the end, or anyway that's my feeling. Those last four
words just don't sound right. It's really a terrific story. I believe
Mr. Ransom would take it. Or Monroe Spears. Have you ever sent
a story to Monroe Spears (*Sewanee*)? Why not try Alice Morris
at *Harper's Bazaar*? Or tell Elizabeth McKee to try her.

That's fine about the *Sat. Eve. Post* if they come through.
They pay a lot I've always heard and you ain't going to be fooled.
As to Elizabeth and whether she should get anything out of it, I
would write her, tell her the situation, and ask her what is customary under the circumstances. [C.D. wrote sometimes under a
pseudonym for popular magazines.] She ought to be impressed
and get to work for you. I pay her for my stories when I sell them
but then she has done a lot for me and she hasn't done anything
yet for you . . .

The sun is greatly restricting my activities right now and will
continue to do so, I'm afraid. The doctor says I can't go out of the
house without stockings, gloves, long sleeves and large hat.
(Sunlight influences lupus and causes joint symptoms etc.) The
spectacle of me in this get-up all summer is depressing to my
imagination. We are having green glass put in the car . . .

Well cheers. You should be very pleased with yourself over
this story. What are you going to name it?

## To Catharine Carver

I am sending you the novel today to Viking. This is a great
favor you are doing me. It is doubtful in my mind whether this
thing should be published by itself as a novel or whether it should
be published in a collection of stories. If it is too slight to stand
the attention it would get as a novel, then I should do it the other
way. Let me know which you think would be best, and anything

else you can tell me that I ought to know. I am 100% pure sick of the sight of it but having been with it this long, I can stay with it some more.

## To Sally and Robert Fitzgerald

24 March 59

This is it and I will be much obliged for your considered comments and consider that I want to know the worst before publication and not after . . . I cannot see it any longer and the only thing I can determine about it is that nobody else would have wanted to write it but me.

People are very respectful of me these days, thinking that $150,000 of Mr. Ford's money has been divided eleven ways. I even got an advertisement from an investment broker this morning . . .

I hope you are accustoming yourself to the pressure of the grant. I feel it myself.

## To "A."

27 March 59

The novel is your medium all right. I see now why your stories don't exactly come off—they want to be novels. This is extremely well-paced and dramatic throughout. You have room to relax. I also think that this opus has definite commercial possibilities, not on account of its better qualities, but that is no matter. You must have knocked this off in less than a few months.

Now the ending of course is in the O. Henry tradition which is not the best, but I would leave it alone. I think you can mitigate the effect of the last chapter by going to work on the first one. I think that the conversation between the man reading the book and Herbert should be longer, and more significant. I think it should foreshadow the whole novel and give us an indication of Herbert's need. I think it should also establish Herbert as an intelligent person, even though one without opportunities and in a rut. The 2nd, 3rd and 4th chapters give the impression that Herbert is not too bright, then later on he begins to talk like an intellectual of sorts and once in a while he sounds more [you] than himself. The intellectual conversation he has with Bobby—all that stuff about democracy—ought to be cut down or out. But the important part is that in his first conversation with the man reading, we should get a preview in miniature of Herbert's real problem and of his character.

Lona is handled beautifully and all the others are fine too and the background is fine.

The first chapter should be more leisurely. He rides by the seated figure reading. Something about the figure arrests him, he drives on wondering what, something presses him to turn back (all this time he is revealing himself), he turns back. Go slow. This is actually the crucial chapter.

When you get this finished, the thing to do is try to sell it. I would like my agent to read it and then you would get a professional opinion as to its commercial possibilities. If she likes it, she will try to sell it for you and if she don't, she will send it back. No obligation. If she does sell it, she gets 10%, which is little enough. This would be better for you than sending it out yourself. That takes forever with a novel. Anyway, think about it and if you want to send it to her, let me know and I will write her about it. She is honest and if she thinks it can't be published, she'll say so.

You will probably get this Saturday instead of Monday but I thought you would want to hear. Put out more flags!

## To Catharine Carver

27 March 59

I've rewritten the last pages so I'll enclose them as I think they're an improvement. When the grim reaper comes to get me, he'll have to give me a few extra hours to revise my last words. No end to this.

*Thomas Stritch, a professor at Notre Dame and a favorite friend, sent his congratulations on the Ford Foundation award, and a cautionary note. This is her reply.*

## To Thomas Stritch

28 March 59

No, I am not going away and eat up my money. I have bought me a comfortable chair and I am being tempted by an electric typewriter; for the rest I am seriously considering usury. They don't want me to work for two years but I don't *ever* want to work so it's up to me to multiply the talent. I had some Rocke-feller money a few years back and it is still contributing to my upkeep because I bought a five-room house on the way to the water-works. The house is subject to termites and poor white trash but I get $55 a month for it. I'm pretty sure Henry Ford would commend this course.

I have finished my novel for all practical purposes, but am still tinkering with it. Pretty soon I'll have to send it to the pub-lisher. The name of it is *The Violent Bear It Away*. Matthew 11:12 as the Protestants say.

## To Maryat Lee

29 March 59

Sound principle never to take any advice from an agent except about money. That is all they know anything about, and possibly how to talk over more than one telephone at a time. It's nice to have something to turn down. I imagine that it would be very uplifting to refuse an option . . .

. . . I have a friend who predicts that the school crisis in Georgia will take the following course: the issue will come to a head, the Governor will close all the schools, the people will realize that this means no more collegiate football and will force him to open them again. This is the most cheerful prognostication I have heard.

Next week we are going to have for guest the translator of *Wise Blood* into French, a M. Coindreau, an elderly French gentle-man who teaches at Princeton. What I am going to do with him for two or three days I haven't decided. After you have shown the local monuments, the reformatory, and the insane asylum, there is very little left to entertain a guest, unless you wish to go to Eatonton, the home of Uncle Remus . . .

## To Louise Abbot

30 March 59

Much as we would like to have you for a neighbor, I am glad you managed to avoid the local institution. We have a new local institution here called "Green Acres" for "Elders." They had a formal opening two Sundays ago and my mother must go; so we went. The place is divided into two sections—Magnolia Hall for rich elders, and Camelia Hall for poor elders. When I foresaw my future in Camelia Hall I decided at once that I would rather go to the State Hospital . . .

I don't have to go anywhere with the Ford grant. I am thinking about buying an electric typewriter. I hear tell it cuts the work in two, and I have just finished typing my novel through twice, and that puts me even more in the mind to do it.

Your friend Spivey breezed through here the other day and gave me a very cheerful view on the school situation . . . He awaits Armageddon in an excellent humor . . .

## To Cecil Dawkins

3 April 59

Cheers, cheers! $1,000. That is beyond my comprehension for a story. The most I have ever got is $425. Now that they have taken one, they'll probably take another and you won't never have to go to work. This is a nervous letter. I am congratulating you on the electric typewriter. It is very nice but I am not used to it yet. I keep thinking about all the electricity that is being wasted while I think what I am going to say next. I can see the value of it when you have a manuscript to type but for the ordinary daily grind, I'm not so sure. However it's pretty nice and while I have the money, maybe I ought to get it. You can write yourself another story for the *Post* and get you one . . .

Your sale to the *Post* ought to impress your mother greatly. It sure has impressed my mother who brought the post card home. The other day she asked me why I didn't try to write something that people liked instead of the kind of thing I do write. Do you think, she said, that you are really using the talent God gave you when you don't write something that a lot, a LOT, of people like? This always leaves me shaking and speechless, raises my blood pressure 140 degrees, etc. All I can ever say is, if you have to ask, you'll never know.

## To Elizabeth Bishop

9 April 59

I'll be cheered to have you review the book [*Wise Blood*]. It appears to be out of print but I have written Mrs. Porter at the Signet place to see if they can provide me with some. If so, I'll send you one myself. As for the music it's all one to me. I am a complete musical ignoramus, don't know Mozart from Spike Jones. I never hear any music and don't seek it out. I don't know whether I feel guilty or cynical about this cultural deficiency, but anyhow, I do nothing about it . . .

Last month I went to the University of Chicago to "assist" at two writing classes and give a public reading and live in the dormitory for five days. Some old lady left them money to have a woman-writer or some other female character live in the dormitory a week and be asked questions. The last one they had was a sculptor and she brought a piece of marble and hacked at it for them and this was apparently most entertaining, but I was less of a success. The girls were mostly freshmen and sophomores and their questions gave out long before my patience. I had to sit with them drinking tea every afternoon while they tried to think of something to ask me. The low point was reached when—after a good ten-minute silence—one little girl said, "Miss O'Connor, what are the Christmas customs in Georgia?" I was mighty glad to leave after five days. They didn't have much in the way of writing students and at the public reading there was no public. And the weather was revolting.

My friend at the Methodist college who was going to ask you there to read has been asked to leave (too good for them) but you must stop here anyway if you come in October. The only visitor we've had lately is Maurice Coindreau. He has been translating *Wise Blood* into French and brought the translation down for me to see before he takes it to Paris next month. We had no idea what we'd do with an elderly Frenchman for three days but he was quite a nice guest and amused himself taking pictures of the peafowl with a movie camera. We'd certainly love to have you come. Anyway, if you have a different address next fall, let me know because I'll want to send you a copy of my novel.

## To Catharine Carver

18 April 59

Everything you say makes wonderful sense to me; in fact, your first note made sense and I started at once rewriting Part II, doing about what you suggested in your second letter. Rayber has been the difficulty all along. I'll never manage to get him as alive as Tarwater and the old man but I can certainly improve on him. I sent the ms. to the Fitzgeralds in Italy and yesterday I heard from Robert. He said essentially the same thing you have, so that corroborates it. He put it this way: be sure you haven't made too much of a parody of Rayber, as if you do, you take away from the point and significance of what Tarwater sees.

I would probably never have got the end written if I hadn't telescoped the middle and got on with it, because I dallied with them in the city for about two years and got nowhere. But now that I have the end, I think I can get the middle, anyway get it better.

You have not seen the last of this. As soon as I get a new middle in it, I must send it to you again. I want Denver to read it but ask him to wait until I send you the new middle as there is no use his reading what isn't going to be like that. Keep the manuscript and you can add the middle to it when I send it to you and then show it to him. I am glad you haven't told anyone else you have it. It occurred to me that the people at FS&C might take it amiss that I have sent it to someone at Viking, even though it was to a friend and nobody's bidnis but mine.

You have done me an immense favor that nobody else could have or would have done. Caroline read it but her strictures always run to matters of style. She swallows a good many camels while she is swatting the flies—though what she has taught me has been invaluable and I can never thank her enough. Or you . . .

## To "A."

April 18/59

. . . My parent spent three days this week in the hospital . . . during which time I pioneered in driving the car, solo, in town and back. I transported my aunt Mary and her cook on two occasions and they didn't seem noticeably to hold their breaths. In fact the cook was very complimentary. Miss Mary is a bad driver herself so remarks from her would not have been in order. My mother is back no worse for the wear . . .

I have now to sit down and write a graduate student in Cleveland who wants to know why my stories are grotesque; are they grotesque because I am showing the frustration of grace? It's very hard to tell these innocents that they are grotesque because that is the nature of my talent. Anyway, if I have to contribute to many more student papers, I think I will deserve an honorary PH.D.

Miss Gum Spirits of Turpentine has just been elected for the year. This is an election I always wait for. They must hold it when the sap begins to run as I notice it every year about this time. The other one I look for is Miss North Georgia Chick.

## To Sally and Robert Fitzgerald

20 April 59

Much thanks for the notes and general thoughts. Rayber has been the trouble all along. I think one thing that is needed is to make his reactions to the boy more dramatic and have some of the stuff happen other than in flashbacks. Anyway I aim to do a good deal more work on the middle section. I've already improved the last chapter on those places where the prose was bad. I think I'll work on it the rest of the summer and then say to hell with it. Anyway, I'm hugely obliged to you all for yr pains taken etc. I saw one of those [characters in book] one time with yellow hair and black eyelashes—you can't look any more perverted than that . . .

I am sending my gawdchile and Hugh [Fitzgerald daughters] mustard seed necklaces for their birthdays, whenever those are. I don't know the significance of the mustard seed, but the saleslady assured me that Miss America wore one all during the recent competition in Atlantic City. I hesitated no longer.

Just tear the ms. up. Have other copies. I am going to renovate the whole thing. When you see the book, it will be improved. I can't think where I'll get the psychoanalytical information. Maybe leave it out.

## To Maryat Lee

25 April 59

No I can't see James Baldwin in Georgia. It would cause the greatest trouble and disturbance and disunion. In New York it would be nice to meet him; here it would not. I observe the traditions of the society I feed on—it's only fair. Might as well expect a mule to fly as me to see James Baldwin in Georgia. I have read one of his stories and it was a good one.

I am just back from Vanderbilt and have had enough of writers for a while, black or white. Whoever invented the cocktail party should have been drawn and quartered. It was a good symposium for the most part but one a year is enuf for me.

Thanks for asking your broker but it don't look like I am going to have any money any time soon to invest. My cousin left me a house in Savannah and I am now learning whatall it needs; among the items is a new roof. When you clip your cool coupons, think of me coping with my hot renter. I just had to buy a $129 hot-water heater for the other tenant who, bless his heart, isn't but two months behind in his rent . . .

Incidentally, I have a friend in Tennessee who would like to meet James Baldwin I am sure. His name is Brainard Cheney and he is writing a novel set in interracial circles in New York. So last month he took a trip to New York where he has a lot of liberal abolishionist friends to get them to introduce him to some interracial society. He stayed two weeks and pulled all his strings and wasn't able to meet one Negro socially. Well, at least down here we are benighted over the table not under it. If he comes to New York again, I'll get him to call you and maybe you could scout up a few. But don't worry, he's not coming. I think he's decided to rely on his imagination . . .


## To Dr. T. R. Spivey

26 April 59

The girl you write about seems both very young and poorly instructed. I don't doubt she needs a good spiritual director but this takes a kind of genius and much grace and they are as hard to find as any other rarity. As to a confessor—one is as good as another. The confessional is not a place to discuss problems.

Probably the worst thing she could have done was to go to a Catholic college. It takes a very tough Catholic to stand the good nuns—that is the average run of them. I have come across a few who are educated women of a high scholastic achievement, but for the most part they know nothing of the world and have a kind of hot-house innocence which is of very little help to anyone who has to be thrown into the problems of the modern world.

As for the bad Catholics, this is simply one of the facts of life. I am reviewing some sermons of St. Augustine on the psalms and ran across this: "Still I want to warn you about this, brothers; the Church in this world is a threshing floor, and as I have often said before and still say now, it is piled high with chaff and grain together. It is no use trying to be rid of all the chaff before the time comes for winnowing. Don't leave the threshing-floor before that, just because you are not going to put up with sinners. Otherwise you will be gobbled up by the birds before you can be brought into the barn." She probably sees more stupidity and vulgarity than she does sin and these are harder to put up with than sin, harder on the nerves.

I have an extra copy of Baron von Hügel's letters to his niece which if she hasn't read and would like to read I'll send you to look at yourself and then give to her. The Baron's spirit is an anti-dote to much of the vulgarity and rawness of American Catholics.

I enjoyed the Vanderbilt proceedings. There is a very nice atmosphere there in the English Department. Jesse Stuart's ego was like the light on the front of a train but as Warren remarked, we probably all have that much but just know how to keep it under cover better . . .

## To Maryat Lee

Friday 5/6/59

Congratulations. The next thing I expect to hear is that you have bought a cow and are in the dairy business yourself. It sounds a little too Walden-Pondish but it must be nice to get out of the city, the which I have been reminded of by the *Village Voice*. Thank you for that. It reminds me of my character, Asbury, and his life in the city and if I write more about Asbury, it should come in very handy. The last issue had an interview with Anaïs Nin in it which nearly made me throw up, but which gave me a lot of ideas about Asbury. Asbury and his mamma are good for something else but I haven't decided what. When you are about to finish one you always feel the next one dragging at you . . .

You are probably not your mother's chile for nothing. She sounds as if she takes after you. If any of my kin take to reading Freud or Dostoevsky in their old age, I am going to leave home . . .

What's the state of *Kairos* [Maryat Lee's play]? Is the other one going to be put on in the alleys again? I'm not yet satisfied with mine but working like mad. My editor [Robert Giroux] was down here lately and we didn't know what we would do with that much New York in the country but he immediately went to his room, put on a plaid shirt and moccasins, and came down with his movie camera and took pictures of the peafowl. Don't know how I could live without them birds.

If you must read novels, you ought to be able to do better than Marquand. I am reading a very lively one called *Memento Mori* by Muriel Spark. All the characters are over 75 . . .

## To Caroline Gordon Tate

10 May 59

You heard the subterranean note in [Robert Lowell's] voice correctly, I guess. Bob Giroux spent last Monday and Tuesday with us and said Cal hospitalized himself before the party. He thought it a good sign that he did it himself and didn't have to be forced to. Giroux had just been to Gethseminie (sp?). He stopped over in Atlanta and visited the Trappist monastery in Conyers, which he said was much better looking than the one in Kentucky, or at least will be when they complete it. All the people in the outlying areas go to look at the monks—like going to the zoo.

I'm glad you have set out on *The Air of the Country*. With all the other things you do I don't see how you find time for it but I suppose after teaching it is a real relief to do it. It will be a big treat for me to see it . . .

I am doing the whole middle section of the novel over. The beginning and the end suit me, but that middle is bad. It isn't dramatic enough. I telescoped that middle section so as to get on with the end, but now that I've got the end, I see there isn't enough middle . . .

While I was at the Cheneys' I read part of Ashley's thesis, the chapter on *The Malefactors*. Ashley ought to get to work on that book and publish it. I think it's the best thing I've read on *The Malefactors*. If you would give him a verbal shove, he might get on with it. He is leaving Santa Barbara after this term but I don't know where he will go.

We were real pleased to hear your word about M. Coindreau. I guess he has gone by now. I have some clippings for him about evangelistic goings-on. One ad says, "Thrill to the Music, Message and Magic of this team!"


*To "A."*

16 May 59

. . . James has no preoccupation about avoiding vulgarity. James is a master of vulgarity. A good part of all his books and the whole of many of his stories are studies in vulgarity. Certainly he recognized it in himself, but he *recognized* it, he was able to define it in the concrete, and being able to define it and to see where it was only adds to his greatness. And as for James' physical infirmity, that is negligible in the Christian order of things and it is not good to carry it over and make a criticism of his work. James said he had the "imagination of disaster." Read his books and look for it and you will carp about him less, or to more effect. Have you read *What Maisie Knew*? Several processes of parents and their successive divorces and lovers seen through the consciousness of a child. You sometimes think the child must have a bald head and a swallow-tail coat; nevertheless it is a very moving book . . .

I suppose I will work on Tarwater the rest of the summer. It is too good a book not to be a better one. It'll never be the way it ought to be but it will have to stand up straighter than it is now before I let it go . . .


## To Cecil Dawkins

21 May 59

I hate to disagree with you ladies but I think this is one of the best ["Benny Ricco's Search for the Truth"]. There are one or two spots that I'd question. The librarian doesn't have to be sibilant on every word, just now and then, because all you want that effect for is the name, Shart. And on page 11 when Thomas asks Benny what the soul is and Benny says, "It is a part of the spirit of God which accounts for man's likeness to him," this does not seem right. This is not the catechism definition of the soul, is it? I don't have a catechism handy but I don't remember anything like that and I don't think Benny would be likely to give anything but what he had got by rote; or he might confuse what he had got by rote in some such fashion. You could use the same answer and show it to be a confusion of his. If that is the catechism answer, it's an answer that doesn't go into any of the theological complexities of the problem, but it doesn't sound like the right answer to me. Toward the end I get the feeling that you are saying to hell with this let's get it over with as soon as possible. It seems right to me that he should end up praying to the governor of the state—just right, but if he is going to pieces to this extent in the end, I think you ought to indicate earlier that he is capable of going to pieces. Usually people who are this dumb can't be shattered. I think you have to give us some indication nearer the front that he's capable of going to pieces. Maybe it's all implicit in it already. I hate to say because I think it's a mighty good story and I wouldn't want you to tamper with it and ruin it. Caroline would say that on that last sentence you shouldn't say kept "right on" praying. *Right on* is colloquial and lowers the tone. You might say he continued to pray—or anything not colloquial.

The title don't do much for it.

I can't remember if I told you what Jesse Stuart said to a friend of mine after I had read "A Good Man Is Hard to Find"— at Vanderbilt. He said he didn't know why I ended it that way. Didn't I realize the audience identified with the grandmother? I should have kept it going until the cops got there and saved the grandmother!

## To Dr. T. R. Spivey

25 May 59

On the surface of it it doesn't seem appropriate sending you letters designed for [Baron von Hügel's] niece; however it may be appropriate after all as you are interested in the education of women and this is the way he thought a woman should be educated. But anyhow, don't judge him as to his real work by this. All the "darling Gwen-childs" have to be ignored.

Next month there is going to be a book out from the Helicon Press on Chardin—his thought. My editor from Farrar, Straus was down here to visit me last week and I was asking him about Chardin and it turned out he knew him for about a month in New York, before he died. He said he was very impressive.

I am reading a book I like called *The Disinherited Mind,* by Erich Heller—essays on Goethe, Nietzsche, Rilke, Spengler, Kafka, and a few others. I know practically nothing about German literature.

Week before last I went to Wesleyan and read "A Good Man Is Hard to Find." After it I went to one of the classes where I was asked questions. There were a couple of young teachers there and one of them, an earnest type, started asking the questions. "Miss O'Connor," he said, "why was the Misfit's hat *black*?" I said most countrymen in Georgia wore black hats. He looked pretty disappointed. Then he said, "Miss O'Connor, the Misfit represents Christ, does he not?" "He does not," I said. He looked crushed. "Well, Miss O'Connor," he said, "what is the significance of the Misfit's hat?" I said it was to cover his head; and after that he left me alone. Anyway, that's what's happening to the teaching of literature.

## To "A."

30 May 59

Yesterday we did finally get to the [Holy Ghost] monastery—taken there by Tom Gossett—and spent the afternoon with B.'s friend, Fr. Paul. B. is very fortunate to have such a person for a spiritual adviser. Strangely enough B. rather resembles him, in looks and otherwise. Fr. Paul appears to have all B.'s virtues and none of his failings—a kind of B. with the dross burnt out. My mother enjoyed him hugely as he is a gardener. She came back with various kinds of ivy. I hope to give them some peacocks for the place when they get ready for them . . .

Peace be to you on Henry James. If you like his work the man himself is nothing in it one way or the other

I am more than ever impressed with the greatness of Baron von Hügel although this may appear a contradiction as I only here again know the writings—but then this is not fiction, and he directly states his opinion on everything, in the most involved sentences. The book is concerned in great part with St. Catherine of Genoa and confirms my opinion on the positive charity business. Positive is a bad word, suggesting aggressive charity. They could have got a better one. According to St. Thomas an act can be derived from charity in one of two ways. The first way the act is elicited by charity and requires no other virtue—as in the case of loving the Good, rejoicing in it, etc. In the second way, an act proceeds from Charity in the sense of being commanded by it. After St. Catherine's conversion, she devoted four years to rather strenuous penitential practices, but for the next period of her life, which the Baron counts about 21 years, she abandoned these and practiced simply works of charity. And this was the major, fullest, and as he would say most "costing" period of her life. I share your lack of love for the race of man, but then this is only a sentiment and a sentiment falls before a command. Also incidentally, you have the succession of H. Motes' doings mixed up. He put lye in his eyes first, which left him in no state to practice charity (p.c.) (not I'm sure that he would have known to anyway), afterwards came the rocks and barbed wire . . .


13 June 59

. . . Miss Mary [Cline] is poorly and we are having to go in town and spend the nights with her. I drive out here at seven thirty in the morning just like a bloody adult and am mighty thankful that the Lord allowed me to learn to drive.

There was a big killing in our neighborhood this week and a posse of 75 were out all through the woods . . . However, it seems he blew his own head off shortly after he killed the white man. Regina asked Shot what people in Eatonton were saying about the boy who did the killing. Shot said, "They said he oughtn't to did it" . . .

Robert wrote that the picture of Cal on the back of *Life*

*Studies* made Sally want to cry. I have the book but haven't had time to look at it much. He put himself in the hospital just before the book came out.

## To John Lynch

14 June 59

I managed to be in Chicago for the most impossible week in the winter. If I had known you were teaching there I would have got somebody to call you up for me and invite you out . . .

The Ford things have been given. Robert Fitzgerald got one and I am happy to say, I got one myself. I didn't know anyone had nominated me. Robert and family will never come home now I reckon. They have their oldest child in a boarding school in Rome, the best, and they can send her there for $500 a year. Robert has about finished the *Odyssey* so now he faces writing some poetry of his own.

I have just about finished my novel so now I have to begin thinking of the next one—one damm book after another. Some Sisters at Winona—College of St. Theresa—have suggested I might come up there this fall and talk at some Catholic colleges in Minnesota on being a Cathlick writer an all.

This season we have had three peachickens to hatch and have killed one rattlesnake. Otherwise nothing goes on around here.

## To Dr. T. R. Spivey

21 June 59

I haven't read the article in *PR* or the beat writers themselves. That seems about the most appalling thing you could set yourself to do—read them. But reading about them and reading what they have to say about themselves makes me think that there is a lot of ill-directed good in them. Certainly some revolt against our exaggerated materialism is long overdue. They seem to know a good many of the right things to run away from, but to lack any necessary discipline. They call themselves holy but holiness costs and so far as I can see they pay nothing. It's true that grace is the free gift of God but in order to put yourself in the way of being receptive to it you have to practice self-denial. I observe that Baron von Hügel's most used words are derivatives of the word *cost*. As long as the beat people abandon themselves to all sensual satis-factions, on principle, you can't take them for anything but false mystics. A good look at St. John of the Cross makes them all look sick.

You can't trust them as poets either because they are too busy acting like poets. The true poet is anonymous, as to his habits, but these boys have to look, act, and apparently smell like poets.

I am reviewing a book . . . on Zen and Japanese Culture. I took it up as a burden but I find it very interesting and it's easy to see what attracts the beat people to Zen and where it leads them astray. If you took Christ, the Church, law and dogma out of Christianity, you would have something like Zen left. The beat people's need for it witnesses to their need for the contemplative life. Do you think it would be possible for Protestantism ever to come up with a form of monasticism? I asked a divine from Mercer that and he said No. In any case if there could be such a thing in Protestantism, a lot of these people could be salvaged from Zen.

I don't believe that if God intends for the world to be spared He'll have to lead a few select people into the wilderness to start things over again. I think that what He began when Moses and the children of Israel left Egypt continues today in the Church and is meant to continue that way. And I believe all this is accomplished in the patience of Christ in history and not with select people but with very ordinary ones—as ordinary as the vacillating children of Israel and the fishermen apostles. This comes from a different conception of the Church than yours. For us the Church is the body of Christ, Christ continuing in time, and as such a divine institution. The Protestant considers this idolatry. If the church is not a divine institution, it will turn into an Elks Club . . .

## To Catharine Carver

23 June 59

I do appreciate the wire and I am relieved you think this section [of the novel] is improved. I think so myself but since I sent it to you I have done some further things to it and it is more better, as our help around here says. I am going to send the improved version to you but don't feel you have to read it because I know this sort of thing to be a nuisance. But I feel much better about the whole thing now and am going to send it on to old Giroux by August.

I had a letter the other day from Dick Stern and he said you had advised him to do some more work on his novel. He seems to have a good many novels at various stages of development. He said he had Cary Grant picked out for his hero. I have Spencer Tracy picked out for old Tarwater but I am afraid I will not be able to interest Jerry Wald in this.

Many thanks although my debt to you can't be repaid.

## To "A."

. . . I sometimes wished that I lived near all that culture, all them art movies and little theatres and what all, but then I think about it twice and am screamingly glad I don't. I find that even when we have things here, and there is occasionally something, I don't go to them . . .

I read one of Iris Murdoch's early books—*Under the Net,* I think it was. It was well written but I don't remember it. Ashley thinks she is great stuff but I haven't heard him remark on *The Bell.*

The Church's stand on birth control is the most absolutely spiritual of all her stands and with all of us being materialists at heart, there is little wonder that it causes unease. I wish various fathers would quit trying to defend it by saying that the world can support 40 billion. I will rejoice in the day when they say: This is right, whether we all rot on top of each other or not, dear children, as we certainly may. Either practice restraint or be prepared for crowding . . .

I am on the road home. In another month I should be sending you me novel.

## To Sally and Robert Fitzgerald

1 July 59

This is the middle section of the book again and it seems so much better to me and so different that I want you to see it. I've also followed yr strictures on the first and third parts but there is no use sending all that. I think this new section does it myself but let me know what you find amiss in it.

Billy Sessions asked me if I thought you all would read his play & I allowed as I thot you would. I have read it and it seems to me to have many virtues, but I don't know anything about plays and particularly verse drama. It sounds like Eliot and Williams shook up together but he may overcome that in time.

## To Maryat Lee

It's too hot here right now for me to be on any posses but come fall maybe there'll be another opportunity. Right now we are busy being host to the junior underworld. The reformatory is about a mile away and the lads escape about this time of year. Last week we had six one day, one the next, and two the next. They track them down through the woods with other reformatory boys. We would much prefer they use dogs.

Sistuh is bettuh so we are back in our own beds at night. It's mamma's runabout. I don't have one . . .

I am about convinced now that my novel is finished. It has reached the stage where it is a pleasure for me to type it so I presume it is done. I sit all day typing and grinning like the Cheshire cat. There is nothing like being pleased with your own efforts—and this is the best stage—before it is published and begins to be misunderstood . . .

## To "A."

11 July 59

Now that you have the novel back from Macmillan, do not let it sit around the house. If it were mine I would do one of two things, either I would send it to my agent or I would send it to Miss Catharine Carver at the Viking Press. If you send it to Catharine Carver you will get the most intelligent reading you could get in New York. I don't think it's a Viking book but anything she said to you about it would be valuable . . . If you send it to my agent, you will get a combined reading. She wastes no time about knowing whether she wants to fool with a thing or not.

I don't know about an artful mystic but you might try Jacopone da Todi (a poet) and certainly St. John of the Cross. John Frederick Nims is either having or has already had out a translation of St. John's poems and it is supposed to be very fine, better than Roy Campbell's. I read some of Angus Wilson's earlier books and I have one called *Such Darling Dodos*, which somebody gave me and I never finished, if you want to borrow it. I have an advance copy of John Updike's short stories, which are a disappointment, and a copy of Nabokov's early novel, *The Real Life of Sebastian Knight*, which is being reissued by New Directions. I tell you if you don't know Nabokov, you ought to. Try the one called *Pnin*. I will send you *The Real Life of Sebastian Knight* if you are innerested. Peter Taylor has a story in the last *Kenyon* which I like better than the one that got the O. Henry.

Can't you come to see us one of these Saturdays of your choice or a weekday either if you have a vacation? My mother was saying we ain't seen you in some time . . .

## To Elizabeth McKee

17 July 59

BELIEVE IT OR NOT

I am mailing the manuscript of my novel to you today and will be much obliged if you will get it to Giroux with dispatch.

## To Cecil Dawkins

17 July 59

Well my novel is finished and on its way courtesy the US Postal Service to the publisher. Catharine Carver's final verdict was that it is the best thing I've done. The most I am willing to say is that it has taken more doing than anything else I've done. I dread all the reviews, all the misunderstanding of my intentions, etc. etc. Sometimes the most you can ask is to be ignored.

The current ordeal is that my mother is now in the process of reading it. She reads about two pages, gets up and goes to the back door for a conference with Shot, comes back, reads two more pages, gets up and goes to the barn. Yesterday she read a whole chapter. There are twelve chapters. All the time she is reading, I know she would like to be in the yard digging. I think the reason I am a short-story writer is so my mother can read my work in one sitting.

Well I don't envy your having to talk three hours a day. Did I tell you that one of the teachers around here asked her class to define "classicism"? One answer: work in class.

I have been sent a copy of John Updike's short stories from Knopf—to be published in August. I liked the novel right much and I like some of the stories but a great many of them seem too slight to be included. Anyway, I am sending you the book for the good ones.

If you all get to drive balls into the dean of women I see why you like to play golf. I can't imagine any other advantages to it.

## To Dr. T. R. Spivey

To continue in the same vein, I don't chide you for wanting to go into the wilderness. I am sure more people will have to want to go and get there before things will get better; it's the business of starting things all over again that I steer clear of. We mean entirely different things when we each say we believe the Church is Divine. You mean the invisible Church with somehow related to it many forms, whereas I mean one and one only visible Church. It is not logical to the Catholic to believe that Christ teaches through many visible forms all teaching contrary doctrine. You speak of the well-known facts of Christ's life—but these facts are hotly contested—the virgin birth, the resurrection, the very divinity of Christ. For us the one visible Church pronounces on these matters infallibly and we receive her doctrine whether subjectively it fits in with our surmises or not. We believe that Christ left the Church to speak for him, that it speaks with his voice, he the head and we the members.

If Christ actually teaches through many forms then for fifteen centuries, he taught that the Eucharist was his actual body and blood and thereafter he taught part of his people that it was only a symbol. The Catholic can't live with this kind of contradiction. I have seen it put that the Catholic is more interested in truth and the Protestant in goodness, but I don't think too much of the formula except that it suggests a partial truth.

The Catholic finds it easier to understand the atheist than the Protestant, but easier to love the Protestant than the atheist. The fact is though now that the fundamentalist Protestants, as far as doctrine goes, are closer to their traditional enemy, the Church of Rome, than they are to the advanced elements in Protestantism. You can know where I stand, what I believe because I am a practicing Catholic, but I can't know what you believe unless I ask you. You are right that *enjoy* is not exactly the right word for our talking about religion. As far as I know, it hurts like nothing else. We are at least together in the pain we share in this terrible division. It's the Catholic Church who calls you "separated brethren," she who feels the awful loss.

I am through with my novel and have sent it to the publishers and now I sit wondering what the reaction to it will be. It is built around a baptism, a subject not calculated to be of interest to many. A lot of arty people will read it and be revolted. I trust.

## To Catharine Carver

The sentence wasn't there but I'll see that it gets back in. I have already sent the ms. to Elizabeth McKee to send to Giroux, and I hope she makes haste and sends it. I thought perhaps that sentence gave Rayber away too much. Any extended analysis makes me nervous and I begin to get bored reading it and then start hacking it out. But there are times when you have to be explicit, I guess.

Robert [Fitzgerald] wrote today that he thought it immensely better and particularly liked the "missionary child." However, he didn't go into details as he has been having attacks of gall bladder trouble and is going to have to have it out. Lucette was part of a story I started a long time ago and saw it wasn't going to come off and put it up. I am glad I had it laid by.

You can keep the ms. and show it to Denver if you want to. However, I have made many improvements in the other two sections. I had already tried it in every conceivable position, but I did break it up with some indirect comments of Meeks on the pursuit of happiness. Also I changed that part where the old man remembers the sentence from Rayber's paper about him. Robert thought the sentence was too explicitly stage-Freud. I got the Freud out of it. Several other small things, but they give it a better look.

Now that I have stopped working on the novel, I feel like somebody fired from his job, unemployed, looking for work. Notwriting is a good deal worse than writing . . .

## To "A."

25 July 59

. . . Thank you for what you say about the novel. Your appreciation always adds something to my own. I will shore it up against the day when I am faced with the misunderstanding reviews. I expect this one to be pounced on and torn limb from limb. Nevertheless, I am pleased with it myself, everything in it seems to me to be inevitable in the economy of the situation.

Now about Tarwater's future. He must of course not live to realize his mission, but die to realize it. The children of God I daresay will dispatch him pretty quick. Nor am I saying that he has a great mission or that God's solution for the problems of our particular world are prophets like Tarwater. Tarwater's mission might only be to baptize a few more idiots. The prophets in the

Bible are only the great ones but there is doubtless unwritten sacred history like uncanonized saints. Someday if I get up enough courage I may write a story or a novella about Tarwater in the city. There would be no reformatory I assure you. That murder is forgotten by God and of no interest to society, and I would proceed quickly to show what the children of God do to him. I am much more interested in the nobility of unnaturalness than in the nobility of naturalness. As Robert [Fitzgerald] says, it is the business of the artist to uncover the strangeness of truth. The violent are not natural. St. Thomas's gloss on this verse is that the violent Christ is here talking about represent those ascetics who strain against mere nature. St. Augustine concurs.

I will take just as much naturalness as I need to accomplish my purposes, no more, but a Freudian could read this novel and explain it all on the basis of Freud. Many will think that the author shares Rayber's point of view and praise the book on account of it. This book is less grotesque than *Wise Blood* and as you say less funny. But if it had been funny, the tone would have been destroyed at once. In some places I may have gone too near the edge already. As you say, one distraction, one look aside or up or down, and the jig is up.

I will not be doing any more after the book is published than at any other time. I do not attend book parties . . .


## To John Hawkes

26 July 59

I had been wondering about you and was glad to hear and your address will come in handy when I get ready to send you a copy of my novel. It is at the publishers but I don't know when they mean to bring it out—probably in the spring. I thought I would never finish it. I never know where the next word is coming from and now I don't know where the next 60,000 are coming from or what they will be about. Not having something under way is worse than having something under way. The name of this novel is *The Violent Bear It Away*. I don't think many people will like it, but it will mean something to me if a few people do, such as yourself.

I've asked the college librarian to get me Andrew's [Lytle] book and she will show up with it in time. I have been reading *The Real Life of Sebastian Knight*. I have always liked Nabokov, beginning with one I read called *Bend Sinister*. That was a long time ago and I have forgotten everything about it except that I was impressed, even possibly influenced. But when I read your first book, *Bend Sinister* returned to my mind . . .

I'll look forward to the next time you all travel to Florida . . . Stop by here.

## To Elizabeth Bishop

2 August 59

I have at last got my novel out of the house and on the train and haven't yet self-employed myself back on anything serious . . . After you have worked on a thing seven years, it is too close for you to see it with precision. I see my stories much more clearly because they haven't exhausted me by the time I finish them . . . My book is about a boy who has been raised up in the backwoods by his great uncle to be a prophet. The book is about his struggle not to be a prophet—which he loses. I am resigned to the fact that I am going to be the book's greatest admirer . . .

Yesterday I sold a pair of [peacocks], the first time I have sold any. These people showed up in a long white car, the woman in short shorts. They obviously had plenty of money that they weren't used to. She flew a Piper Cub, kept two coons, and what she called a "Weimeraw" dog. He was going to start in on pheasants, peafowl and bullfrogs. They came in and admired the house and she said, "We was in Macon looking for some French Provincial furniture. I want me a love seat." The man was a structural engineer. He said he had a friend who was a writer in Mississippi and I said who was that. He said, "His name is Bill Faulkner. I don't know if he's any good or not but he's a mighty nice fellow." I told him he was right good . . .

Let us know if you are coming this way. We could likely come to Savannah and meet you and bring you up here . . .

## To Robert Giroux

9 August 59

I enclose a new page 104. I added a sentence that Catharine Carver had liked in the first version and that I cut out in the second and now add again.

On page 43 the line missing between lines 11 and 12 is:
Buford lifted his hand. "He needs to be rested," he said.
The other things I have checked on the sheet and enclose it.

Just spell the misspelled words right. I would never know the difference.

About the duplication of phrases in the scenes at the pool: this is intentional and I am not much inclined to change it. Did it worry you yourself or is this just something that Elizabeth brought up? It hasn't bothered anybody else that has seen it. Putting it in the pluperfect takes away from the immediacy of it. If it bothers you the way it is, I will change it . . .

Thank you for wiring me that you liked the book. It relieved my mind . . . February seems a good enough time [to publish the novel] and I will be glad when it is out and over with.

14 August 59

The change you want to make on page 146 will be all right with me . . . I am enclosing a new page 141 which you can use or not as you think best. On an earlier version I had NOT HIS SON for BELONGS TO HIS SELF. Sally Fitzgerald said she missed the former on the second version, that she thought "belongs to his self" was too self-conscious for Tarwater. She may be right but I can't make up my mind. If you think it is better use it, if not, leave it like it is . . .

Have you all reissued a book of Mauriac's called *Questions of Precedence*? If you have, I would very much appreciate it if you would send me a copy . . . Best and many thanks for your care of the book.

## To Dr. T. R. Spivey

19 August 59

I'll try to answer your questions but as they are not doctrinal questions, you must remember that this is just my opinion about these things.

The good Catholic acts upon the beliefs (assumptions if you want to call them that) that he receives from the Church and he does this in accordance with his degree of intelligence, his knowledge of what the Church teaches, and the grace, natural & supernatural, that he's been given. You seem to have met nothing but sorry or dissatisfied Catholics and abrupt priests with no understanding of what you want to find out. Any Catholic or Protestant either is defenseless before those who judge his religion by how well its members live up to it or are able to explain it. These things depend on too many entirely human elements. If you want to know what Catholic belief is you will have to study what the Church teaches in matters of faith and morals. And I feel that if you do, you will find that the doctrinal differences between Catholics and Protestants are a great deal more important than you think they are. I am not so naive as to think such an investigation would make a Catholic of you; it might even make you a better Protestant; but as you say, whatever way God leads you will be good. You speak of the Eucharist as if it were not important, as if it could wait until you are better able to practice the two great commandments. Christ gave us the sacraments in order that we might better keep the two great commandments. You will learn about Catholic belief by studying the sacramental life of the Church. The center of this is the Eucharist.

To get back to all the sorry Catholics. Sin is sin whether it is committed by Pope, bishops, priests, or lay people. The Pope goes to confession like the rest of us. I think of the Protestant churches as being composed of people who are good, and I don't mean this ironically. Most of the Protestants I know are good, if narrow sometimes. But the Catholic Church is composed of those who accept what she teaches, whether they are good or bad, and there is a constant struggle through the help of the sacraments to be good. For instance when we commit sin, we receive the sacrament of penance (there is an obligation to receive it once a year but the recommendation is every three weeks). This doesn't make it easier to commit sin as some Protestants think; it makes it harder. The things that we are obliged to do, such as hear Mass on Sunday, fast and abstain on the days appointed, etc. can become mechanical and merely habit. But it is better to be held to the Church by habit than not to be held at all. The Church is mighty realistic about human nature. Further it is not at all possible to tell what's going on inside the person who appears to be going about his obligations mechanically. We don't believe that grace is something you have to feel. The Catholic always distrusts his emotional reaction to the sacraments. Your friend is very far afield if she presumes to judge that most of the Catholics she knows go about their religion mechanically. This is something only God knows.

At the age of 15 one would come into the Church with possibly many expectations of perfections and little real knowledge of human nature, and from 15 to 18 is an age at which one is very sensitive to the sins of others, as I know from recollections of myself. At that age you don't look for what is hidden. It is a sign of maturity not to be scandalized and to try to find explanations in charity. I doubt that she has seen any "lying" nuns. What she is probably talking about is "intellectual honesty" and she is forgetting that in order to be intellectually honest, you have to have an intellect in the first place. Most nuns go into the convent right out of high school, they have no knowledge of the world, their ways of loving the Church are frequently unwise, they are unbelievably innocent, most usually ignorant, and victims of the edifying tendency; a lot of them who are teaching are competent at most to wash dishes; but I have been in the Church for 34 years and I know many nuns, have gone to school to them, correspond with a few, and I have never found one who deliberately lied. At the other end of the scale I know some who are both educated and intelligent and whom it would be a privilege to have for teachers.

As for the neurotic priests, neurosis is an illness and no one should be condemned for it. It takes a strong person to meet the responsibilities of the priesthood. They take vows for life of poverty, chastity, and obedience, and there are very few defections. Most of the priests I know are not neurotic but most are unimaginative and overworked. Also the education they get at the seminaries leaves much to be desired.

About the Church's political actions. God never promised her political infallibility or wisdom and sometimes she doesn't appear to have even elementary good sense. She seems always to be either on the wrong side politically or simply a couple of hundred years behind the world in her political thinking. She tries to get along with any form of government that does not set itself up as a religion. Communism is a religion of the state, committed to the extinction of the Church. Mussolini was only a gangster. The Church has been consorting with gangsters since the time of Constantine or before, sometimes wisely, sometimes not. She condemms Communism because it is a false religion, not because of the form of gvt. it is. The Spanish clergy seems to be shortsighted in much the same way that the French clergy was shortsighted in the 19th century, but you may be sure that the Pope is not going to issue a bull condemning the Spanish Church's support of Franco and destroy the Church's right to exist in Spain. The Spanish clergy has good and bad in it like any other. If Catholics in Hungary fight for freedom and Catholics in Spain don't, all I can tell you is that Catholics in Hungary have more sense or are more courageous or perhaps have their backs to the wall more than those in Spain. A Protestant habit is to condemm the Church for being authoritarian and then blame her for not being authoritarian enough. They object that politically all Catholics do not think alike but that religiously they all hold the same beliefs . . .

## To "A."

I don't know if I have mentioned George P. Elliott to you or not but I have read a lot of his stories in anthologies and so forth and they are always interesting stories and no two in any way alike. I didn't much go for the one in the O. Henry this year but it may have been my fault—too much thinking required to get it . . . E. I feel sure goes by the person and not by the story. He is a victim of all the vices of the age. In the *Life* before last he writes an article about him and his children being held in their house at knife-point by two escaped convicts. This happened about two weeks ago and he's really made the most of it. Get the *Life* and read it if you want to get a pretty good idea of him.

After you have told me that Baldwin is repulsively a whiner, yestiddy I get a letter from a friend of mine in NY who knows and admires him. She has just started to read *Go Tell It on the Mountain,* and from the first chapters she marvels at how much he and I have in common. So there is no accounting for opinions . . .

Madison Jones stopped by here a few Saturdays ago and sat a good while. He is having a novel out in January. It seems that his wife and four children are Catholics. He said he guessed he was intellectually convinced but just didn't have the faith. My cousin's husband who also teaches at Auburn came into the Church last week. He had been going to Mass with them but never showed any interest. We asked how he got interested and his answer was that the sermons were so horrible, he knew there must be something else there to make the people come . . .

## To Maryat Lee

Well thanks for the offer of yr. apartment but I ain't coming to New York unless somebody pays me to and nobody is liable to pay me to. I do not attend autograph parties etc. Once only was I roped into any such as that and now I would rather be drawn and quartered.

Been working on that book for seven years with time off occasionally to write a story. The relief of finishing it was extreme but I haven't spit up or anything. I am now writing a story ["The Partridge Festival"] that seems very lightweight indeed and don't seem anyhow much of a challenge. Next I intend to write me a lecture to deliver at yr brother's institution this fall and anywhere else I am asked, that is, paid, to deliver it.

I read about 80 pages of Dr. Pasternak but I am so slow that the book had to go back ere I had fairly begun. There were a lot of wonderful things in those 80 pages but I don't think I could have stood that much formlessness for however many hundred pages there were. A friend of mine reviewed it and said it was like a huge shipwreck with a lot of beautiful things floating in it. You are not supposed to feel at home or at ease in any of the forms you see around you. Create your own form out of what you've got, let it take care of itself.

I cut out the Feiffer cartoon about the Eisenhower speech and show it to everybody that comes. I also enjoyed the interview with [Lorraine] Hansberry; and there are such things as the information of Mr. [Allen] Ginsberg that the way to reach God is through marijuana. They are revoltingly sentimental about their own bohemianism sometimes . . .

The thing for you to do is write something with a delayed reaction like those capsules that take an hour to melt in your stomach. In this way, it could be performed on Monday and not make them vomit until Wednesday, by which time they would not be sure who was to blame. This is the principle I operate under and I find it works very well.

## To John Hawkes

13 September 59

Your letter made me want you to read my novel now, so much so that I was tempted to send it to you (carbon) but I think this would be an infringement on your time and friendship, so I am sparing you. If FS&C have bound half-galleys I'll get them to send you a set. Sometimes publishers send these to me and they are very easy to read. Anyway, I would like to tell you something about this novel (much of which you have rightly anticipated) and its kinship to *Wise Blood*.

I don't think you should write something as long as a novel around anything that is not of the gravest concern to you and everybody else and for me this is always the conflict between an attraction for the Holy and the disbelief in it that we breathe in with the air of the times. It's hard to believe always but more so in the world we live in now. There are some of us who have to pay for our faith every step of the way and who have to work out dramatically what it would be like without it and if being without it would be ultimately possible or not. I can't allow any of my characters, in a novel anyway, to stop in some halfway position. This doubtless comes of a Catholic education and a Catholic sense of history—everything works toward its true end or away from it, everything is ultimately saved or lost. Haze is saved by virtue of having wise blood; it's too wise for him ultimately to deny Christ. Wise blood has to be these people's means of grace—they have no sacraments. The religion of the South is a do-it-yourself religion, something which I as a Catholic find painful and touching and grimly comic. It's full of unconscious pride that lands them in all sorts of ridiculous religious predicaments. They have nothing to correct their practical heresies and so they work them out dramatically. If this were merely comic to me, it would be no good, but I accept the same fundamental doctrines of sin and redemption and judgment that they do.

Now in the new book, all this is still there but it is a more ambitious undertaking. The great-uncle is not a puritan here, as you saw. He is a prophet. And the boy doesn't just get himself saved by the skin of his teeth, he in the end prepares to be a prophet himself and to accept what prophets can expect from their earthly lives (the worst). That was a shortened version of the first chapter. In the real first chapter it is brought out that the old man considers himself a prophet and that he has stolen the boy away from the schoolteacher in order to raise him up to take his place as a prophet when he dies. As soon as the old man dies, the boy is left alone with the threat of the Lord's call. He heads for the schoolteacher and the burden of the book is taken up with the struggle for the boy's soul between the dead uncle and the schoolteacher.

The modern reader will identify himself with the schoolteacher, but it is the old man who speaks for me.

I hadn't thought about the cross-shaped face as meaning anything but that he was marked out for the Lord—or at least marked out as one who will have the struggle, who will know what the choice is. Haze knows what the choice is and the Misfit knows what the choice is—either throw away everything and follow Him or enjoy yourself by doing some meanness to somebody, and in the end there's no real pleasure in life, not even in meanness. I can fancy a character like the Misfit being redeemable, but a character like Mr. Shiftlet as being unredeemable. Mr. Head's redemption is all laid out inside the story.

This is too much about me and my works. I read *The Velvet Horn* [by Andrew Lytle] and I was entirely taken with it. I didn't follow all the intricacies of the symbolism but it had its effect without working it all out . . . I'll be waiting for *The Lime Twig* and will prepare the other two members of the Georgia Hawkes Appreciation Society. And I do appreciate your interest in this book of mine. It's not every book that gets itself understood before it has been read.

## To Cecil Dawkins

22 September 59

The cheeze arrived yesterday in good shape and we started in on it at once. My mother is much taken with that in the jar, and I am much taken with all of it. Thanks a lot.

I'll have to try to get aholt to *Henderson the Rain King.* I remember Dick Stern thought it was wonderful. Since you have already sold "The Quiet Enemy," I don't think I would worry about the similarity. Those things can't be helped. It fits your story.

I have started on another story and this time I am keeping out of bloody Milledgeville.

Galley proofs of the novel are supposed to be here October 1. I imagine this means the advance copies will be out sometime in December. I'll see that you get one . . .

We went to a Registered Guernsey Auction last week which is I guess the nearest thing to a dog show. The cows were slicked up and had manicured tails and picked up their feet like show horses. We came home with six . . .

## To "A."

3 October 59

. . . I have the galley proofs of my novel and have been correcting them and it is very depressing to see the thing in print. It is dull and half-done and I will not be able to blame anybody for not liking it. I can barely force myself along.

It will take about a month before [the Sunday supplement] thing appears. They took about a million pictures—me feeding geese, looking at calves, looking at a book (*Familiar Reptiles*), looking at nothing—and looking like all the time the witch of Endor. I thought that I would be prepared for the questions which are usually always the same, so I wrote down a list of answers before she came and handed them to her. This should make her work easier as well as assuring me a few intelligible sentences.

There were some questions however that I wasn't prepared for, such as How does being a Catholic affect your work? (She is now the religion editor and interested in such things.) I said it was a great help. Why? I sputtered out a lot of incoherencies, which I will really hate to see when they appear.

If [Cardinal John Henry] Newman is a saint, his saintliness didn't destroy his scrupulous intellect or his finickiness and you'll have to accept him as a finicky saint. Anyway, here he is dealing with [Charles] Kingsley, enough to bring out the finickiness in any-body. I didn't read the stuff in the back from Kingsley, couldn't stand it. You'd better learn to skip the extra stuff . . .

Jack Hawkes is going to lecture at Brandeis University soon on some aspect of grotesque writing and is going to include me along with West, Djuna Barnes and himself, so he asked to see my novel and I sent it to him. Now I am very sorry I did because any perception as fine as his will find it dull and he is so awfully polite, so much a gentleman, that he will not want to say what he really thinks. The more I hear from him, the more impressed I am.


*To John Hawkes*

6 October 59

You were awfully good to write me such a long and detailed letter about the book. The proofs came early and seeing the thing in print very nearly made me sick. It all seemed awful to me. There seemed too much to correct to make correcting anything feasible. I did what I could or could stand to and sent them back this morning and my mother brought your letter in after they were mailed. It may be that on the page proofs I can get rid of some more of the as-if and seems. I was terribly conscious of them, seeing it for the first time in print. This is what I have to *learn*, to keep the level of the prose up. Caroline Tate, who has taught me considerable, says I can't even write a complex sentence, but I do think that the first sentence and the last sentence in that book are mighty fine sentences and I cheer myself meditating on them.

Rayber, of course, was always the stumbling block. I had a version of this book about a year ago in which Rayber was really no more than a caricature. He may have been better that way but the book as a whole was not. It may just be a matter of giving the devil his due. As you say, your vision, though it doesn't come by way of theology, is the same as mine. You arrive at it by your own perception and sensitivity, but I have had it given me whole by faith because I couldn't possibly have arrived at it by my own powers. This perhaps creates a gap that I have to get over somehow or other. Anyway I am usually out of my depth, and I don't really know Rayber or have the ear for him.

It is strange that in both these novels, what makes them possible as novels, I mean what makes them work, is the same thing that detracts or lowers the interest. I couldn't have written *WB* without Enoch. It would have been impossible mechanically. I was five years on *Wise Blood* and seven on this one, and in that time you turn and twist and try it every possible way and only one thing works. What you are really twisting about in is your limitations, of course. I had no trouble writing the first chapter and the last thirty pages; I spent most of the seven years on Rayber . . .

People are always asking me if I am a Catholic writer and I am afraid that I sometimes say no and sometimes say yes, depending on who the visitor is. Actually, the question seems so remote from what I am doing when I am doing it, that it doesn't bother me at all. Very very many thanks.

### To Robert Giroux

10 October 59

I enclose the other galleys that I have made changes on. I had already marked these in green but I made the extra changes in red so that you can find them easily.

There is only one place that I think needs special explanation here. On the last galley, 82, I changed on the first set of proofs "His hunger was so great" to "He was so hungry." On the second set I changed it back. I want it to remain "His hunger was so great."

Thank you for sending Caroline [Gordon Tate] the set of galleys . . . There are several people that I would like to see the book when it gets all the corrections in it—Elizabeth Bishop, Granville Hicks, Alfred Kazin, Andrew Lytle, the Lowells and R. P. Warren.

I am really much obliged for the [James] Purdy book.

### To Louise Abbot

[undated] Sat. 1959

I think there is no suffering greater than what is caused by the doubts of those who want to believe. I know what torment this is, but I can only see it, in myself anyway, as the process by which faith is deepened. A faith that just accepts is a child's faith and all right for children, but eventually you have to grow religiously as every other way, though some never do.

What people don't realize is how much religion costs. They think faith is a big electric blanket, when of course it is the cross. It is much harder to believe than not to believe. If you feel you can't believe, you must at least do this: keep an open mind. Keep it open toward faith, keep wanting it, keep asking for it, and leave the rest to God.

Penance rightly considered is not acts performed in order to attract God's attention or get credit for oneself. It is something natural that follows sorrow. If I were you, I'd forget about penance until I felt called to perform it. Don't anticipate too much. I have the feeling that you irritate your soul with a lot of things that it isn't time to irritate it with.

My reading of the priest's article on hell was that hell is what God's love becomes to those who reject it. Now no one has to reject it. God made us to love Him. It takes two to love. It takes liberty. It takes the right to reject. If there were no hell, we would be like the animals. No hell, no dignity. And remember the mercy of God. It is easy to put this down as a formula and hard to believe it, but try believing the opposite, and you will find it too easy. Life has no meaning that way . . .

Whatever you do anyway, remember that these things are mysteries and that if they were such that we could understand them, they wouldn't be worth understanding. A God you understood would be less than yourself.

This letter is full of non-sequiturs (sp?). I don't set myself up to give spiritual advice but all I would like you to know is that I sympathize and I suffer this way myself. When we get our spiritual house in order, we'll be dead. This goes on. You arrive at enough certainty to be able to make your way, but it is making it in darkness. Don't expect faith to clear things up for you. It is trust, not certainty . . .

Come to see us whenever you can. We are building two extra rooms and a bath onto the house—a back parlor. We will let you set in it. Cheers.


## To Sally and Robert Fitzgerald

11 October 59

Well, thanks for St. Paul [a reproduction of the Masaccio painting]. I reckon the Lord knew that the only way to make a

Christian out of that one was to knock him off his horse. We hope you are settled in your new place of business. My mother hopes you have a refrigerator.

The [farm help] are back with us and my mother is dealing with their financial problems. The old man got himself so entangled with the loan sharks that he had to come back I guess to get a personal bookkeeper. They are, however, a two-car family now.

Caroline is coming to spend weekend after next with us. She is going to fly to Columbia, S.C. where Ashley Brown teaches and he is going to drive her over and they are going to spend the weekend . . .

I have corrected the proofs, restored NOT HIS SON according to your instructions, and await the critical reception with distaste and unanticipation.

## To "A."

17 October 59

The proofs are back in New York and I have recovered some of my insensitivity to it and hope I don't lose it again. I enclose Jack Hawkes' letter because it will interest you. It is a most tactful document. He has a strange and wonderful mind. I am not sure what he means by "demonic" as he uses it; frequently he leaves me behind, but I think what he says is just & good. Except that I am very partial to Enoch. In both cases what he thinks lowers the interest is the very thing that makes the book possible as a novel. This is inevitable I suppose when your creative energy just can't encompass but one bill of goods, metaphysically.

We don't have a Catholic literature in the sense that we have a group of writers gathered around a central motivating proposition, or a leader, but we do have something in that there are a very respectable number of good poets who are Catholics (as our friend Hawkes would have it) who are sitting in their own places writing good poetry. And this don't have to include dear Allen or Carol Johnson either. Raymond Roseliep, Ned O'Gorman, John Logan, John Frederick Nims, John Edward Hardy, a couple of interesting nuns, Leonie Adams, and Robert Fitzgerald and there may be others. This is not a movement or a school; but literature is produced by people writing. There are no literary geniuses in this bunch but those are given by the Lord now and again and can't be had by improving the culture or anything.

Can't recollect reading anything Anne Fremantle wrote on

[critic Martin] Turnell but I have a paperback copy of his *The Novel in France,* which is enjoyable if you want to see it. Also if you want to see Elizabeth Hardwick's article on book reviewers I have it as somebody sent me that issue of *Harper's* as I am thrown a bone in it by Alfred Kazin. The donor proper marked the passage, etc. The issue is very interesting.

I am one of the laymen who RESIST the congregation yapping out the Mass in English & my reason besides neurotic fear of change, anxiety, and laziness is that I do not like the raw sound of the human voice in unison unless it is under the discipline of music . . .

## To Cecil Dawkins

31 October 59

It is probably just as well you didn't get the Saxton as there might have been publishing strings attached. I once got something called the Rinehart-Iowa Fiction Fellowship and then I had to struggle getting away from Rinehart. I hope Elizabeth is coming in handy in all this. This is where agents can do you some good.

I hope you get paid for those reviews if they are going to cut them. Nothing but money makes that endurable.

A friend of mine . . . brought Caroline Gordon down for the weekend and she gave me several hours' lecture on my prose. I have just corrected the page proofs and I spent a lot of time getting *seems* and *as-if* constructions out of it. It was like getting ticks off a dog. I was blissfully unaware of all this while I was writing it . . .

I have read Styron's *Lie Down in Darkness.* To my way of thinking it was much too much the long tedious Freudian case history, though the boy can write and there were overtones of better things in it.

We had a big cutting here Sunday and three stitches had to be taken in Shot's head, but all is peaceful now.

## To "A."

31 October 59

The next time you are in the library look at the fall *Kenyon Review* and read the interview with Mauriac. I found it very moving but then Mauriac is one of my admirations. According to Dr. Spivey Mauriac wrote somewhere that he sat next to Cardinal

Spellman at some function and felt that he would have had more spiritual kinship with the Dalai Lama . . .

You are probably right about the dialogue Mass but I still think either chanting it or singing it would add the discipline necessary to make it endurable. There are always at least one or two loud voices, that make their business with the Lord loudly intimate, beseeching, aggressive, that destroy the feeling of the whole. This would be impossible if it were sung or chanted.

I meant it was me that couldn't encompass but one bill of goods metaphysically, not Hawkes; but it may simply be that I have a metaphysical bill of goods that is more complete, and he has only sensibility. I don't really know whether the lack of dramatization is a higher method aesthetically. With me it was not a matter of using a method but of doing it the only way that seemed possible to get it done. It was certainly a harder novel to write than the other and demanded more of me; whether it demands more of the reader, I doubt. The end of it of course isn't shockingly different at all but as he says the "general reader" may find it so. There is too much in there about Rayber's struggling against the seed that is in him to take him entirely for the devil. I would have liked for him to be saved, and it is ambiguous whether he may be or not . . .

Another letter from Hawkes says he talked and read at Brandeis for an hour and a half and felt like a man in the stocks while doing it. He read the section from Andrew's novel where Lucius visits his Aunt Amelie, the section from mine about Tarwater's violation in the woods, and a section from his where a man is murdered in a steambath. Then he said there was a question period and the first question was "Mr. Hawkes, are you the devil?" This pleased him as he said though we could not accept such words or roles, he was glad to have put up a little of the smoke of evil. Apparently he feels very much as I do—that he is speaking to an audience which does not believe in evil, or better, in the reality of a personal devil, in principalities and in powers.

He is very much taken with *The Velvet Horn*. With Andrew I have the sense always of a very brilliant artificiality, but *The Velvet Horn* was very readable for me. I usually can't read a book that long.

I read *The Straight and Narrow Path* [by Honor Tracy] and it was too long but better sustained than most funny books. *The Loved One* [by Evelyn Waugh] is the right length for that kind of book . . .

I have an idea about doing over the Partridge story as a peanut festival. What do you think? Calhoun could be very superior to a peanut festival for a while. It would eliminate the man from Chicago who as you say is not very good and the rest could more or less stand. I am thinking of it.

14 November 59

I am not afraid that the book will be controversial, I'm afraid it will not be controversial. I'm afraid it will just be dammed and dropped, genteelly sneered at, a few superior kicks from one or two and that will be that. But I don't feel Tarwater is such a monster. I feel that in his place I would have done everything he did. Tarwater is made up out of my saying: what would I do here? I don't think he's a caricature. I find him entirely believable, plausible, given his circumstances. Well, we will have to wait and see. I expect the worst. At least this is an individual book. I can't think of anybody else's that it might remind you of. Nobody would have been found dead writing it but me . . .

I liked Minna [a friend of William Sessions]. She was short, dumpy, old and cute, and I think probably has a lot of good sense. Once when B. was out of the room, Fr. Paul told us that he had written Minna to pray that B. would find a wife and that Minna had written him back not to pray that he would find a wife, to pray that he would fall in love . . .

## To Maryat Lee

14 November 59

I keep thinking about you in that cold place and hoping you will get out of there before you freeze in it. There is no percentage in freezing and it don't improve the quality of anybody's prose. Even out here with butane gas I get so cold sometimes in the winter, I can't work, and I near about ruined myself spending the winter in Connecticut once and getting cold when there was a storm for several days and no electricity. You get sick and you will be in the hands of the receiver.

I would send you that story ["The Partridge Festival"], but I am redoing it. I am going to make either a cotton or a peanut festival out of it. That way I don't think it will be recognizable and I can get away with it. Right now I am doing another one ["The Comforts of Home"] that I may send you sooner or later if it works out, as it appears to be doing.

A few Sundays ago the girl's interview with me appeared in the paper. They came down here and took about fifteen pictures and the ones they selected were designed to make us look like poor white trash. The Negro house in the background and no notation that I didn't live in it—me looking gimlet-eyed out across what must be a hogwaller—me feeding some geese. Anyway, my mail for the last two weeks has been from rural Georgia. Letter from a man in Macon who wants to buy two Chinese geese, letter from a girl in Jonesboro who has an idea for a musical comedy based on the Civil War but is "not versed in literary type writing" and would like me to write it for her, letter from a carpenter in Thomaston ("i seen the pece in paper about you") who would like to send me his picture, letter from lady in Toccoa enclosing three tracts of Oral Roberts and a magazine called *Healing* (crutches in picture). All these letters are from people I might have made up. I don't want to get any nearer to them than in the imagination either . . .

I hope you have overcome the scene that was putting you in the swivet. Your letter gave me the sense that you couldn't work for watching yourself work. I may be wrong but if that happens it is time to leave Walden Pond and seek out society. Whyn't you spend Christmas down here?

## To John Hawkes

20 November 59

I have been wanting to write and thank you for sending back the manuscript and for reading it and marking it and for all you did to help me. It was a great help . . .

I don't think I'll be able to keep out of the city and stick to what you call the pure whiskey and coffin and Bible land. The fact is that all the inhabitants of the coffin and Bible land have left it and are in the city. To write about Haze and Tarwater, that's where you have to go. I don't know that I am through writing about Tarwater. I've left him right at the beginning. I keep wondering about how the children of God will finish him off. The ones that will do it will be these country people in the city.

You set me to thinking if I had really intended three representations of the Devil. I had meant for Meeks and the pervert at the end to take on the form of Tarwater's Friend, and when I first set out I had in mind that Rayber would echo all his friend's sentiments in a form that the reader would identify himself with. With trial and error I found that making Rayber pure evil made him a caricature and took away from the role of the old prophet since it left him nothing worth trying to save. I have been reading about some cases of possession in the 19th century. It appears that we have a certain privacy from the Devil, who cannot read our thoughts directly but can only decide what we are thinking from our acts. Apparently the Devil possessing a man keeps his own name and personality and the possessed keeps his, and can keep his soul inviolate while being possessed. And the Devil is most tortured to have to call his own name. This has nothing to do with Rayber here, but I find it interesting. I want to be certain that the Devil gets identified as the Devil and not simply taken for this or that psychological tendency . . .

My best to you and Sophie.

## To Dr. T. R. Spivey

30 November 59

I was rather horrified to see that I had put the word *merely* before the word *spiritual*. This was inexcusably sloppy writing as, of course, I did not intend to delegate the spiritual to an inferior status. I mean the spiritual by itself alone or the spiritual not embodied in matter. God is pure Spirit but our salvation was accomplished when the Spirit was made flesh. I meant to imply no more than the traditional teaching of the Incarnation as Catholics see it in the Church. When the Spirit and the flesh are separated in theological thinking, the result is some form of Manicheism. The Catholic's end in worship is always God Who is Pure Spirit.

If your vision of the future is Manichean, or even if it is purely Protestant, I'm not ready for it on principle. I am also not ready to say that literature and knowledge have come to an end for all practical purposes. These things are good in themselves. They reflect the Creator. Mauriac says God does not care anything about what we write. He uses it. So much the more reason I think that we have to give Him the best we've got for His use and leave the uses to Him. I do not know from what you say whether you have departed from, or never considered worthy in the first place, a Christian humanism. The times do seem a bit apocalyptic for anything so sane. Anyway, regardless of the specifics of your vision of the future, I should think that in so far as it is the desire for the Kingdom to come, anyone who has been given the grace of hope could share in it. In this sense I am still with you.

About hiding in the Church. I suppose you mean by this that I am hiding in the Church from, not in, Christ. This is to accuse me of some pretty repulsive qualities and I hope you are wrong. It is certainly possible to hide from spiritual reality in the Church.

I know a few who succeed at it, but for me to do so would at least be against the currents of all I feel and hope for. Anyway, it is something to be alert against.

About trying to be a type of saint I can't be, you don't say what type this is. I believe there are as many types of saints as there are souls to be saved. I am quite interested in saving my soul but I see this as a long developmental evolutionary process, extending into Purgatory, and the only moment of it that concerns me in the least is the instant I am living in.

I haven't read Père Teilhard yet so I don't know whether I agree with you or not on *The Phenomenon of Man*. In any case, I doubt very much if his researches are a product of the "Jesuit mind." Some of the severest criticism I have read about it has come from other Jesuits.

I hope to be around in the middle of December and will look forward to seeing you. That is if I don't freeze in the meantime. It is so cold here I can barely work the typewriter.

## To Robert Giroux

5 December 59

I like the jacket. It somewhat reminds me of the jacket on the British edition of *Wise Blood*, but I think it is better.

I had a, to me, rather depressing letter from a George Hardinge at Longman's, Green. They wanted to know what the significance was of Tarwater's violation in the woods by the man in the motorcar. He said he was afraid he did not get the religious symbolism on account of his own ignorance. But if the modern reader is so far de-Christianized that he doesn't recognize the Devil when he sees him, I fear for the reception of the book. In any case, we shall soon see.

## To Cecil Dawkins

10 December 59

I don't have any three stories. I don't even have one, just two potentially. I did the one that couldn't be used, which I now don't like anyway and am trying to make into a peanut festival, but I got disgusted with that and decided it was too slight to fool with. And I finished the other one ["The Comforts of Home"] and sent a copy to Catharine Carver and one to Caroline. Caroline said it was fine and Catharine Carver said it didn't work at all and I always takes the negative view before a thing is published so I am doing it over. So that's two potentially. I'm in the same boat you are. This second one is worth writing and if I get it anywhere near what it ought to be I'll send it to you . . .

. . . I really think you ought to look into the Yaddo business. The food is very good. The quarters are elegant. The servants are very nice. The scenery is magnificent. Mrs. A. runs it efficiently. Skidmore College is down the road and has a good library, or anyway, good enough.

Well cheers. Start thinking about you a *little* novel.


## To "A."

Wed. [December 1959]

Yes'm she don't get the moral point. But the reason she don't is because I have failed to make it plain. I am into the story ["The Comforts of Home"] again and as I go through it I see how really undramatic it is. The very arrangement is undramatic; also the position of sentences in paragraphs; points are stated and then shown; it's full of waste. I don't pay any attention to anything but her physical, you might say, reaction to the story. She is Catharine Carver.

You understand Thomas because you know me; she doesn't understand Thomas because she just has the story to read and understand . . . I talk about Thomas in this story. What I've got to do is get Thomas to reveal himself more. A story has to have muscle as well as meaning, and the meaning has to be in the muscle.


## To Father J. H. McCown

18 December 59

. . . Where can I get hold of a discussion of what St. Ignatius meant when he said, "the end sanctifies the means" ? ? This Protestant teacher I write to has gone over the deep end on the subject of Jung and one of Jung's most cherished hates is St. Ignatius. Jung has something to offer religion but is at the same time very dangerous for it. Jung would say, for instance, that Christ did not rise from the dead literally but we must realize that we need this symbol, that the notion has significance for our lives symbolically, etc. The boy has given me a book of Jung's called *The Undiscovered Self* (Mentor paperback) which is full of this kind of thing. Also full of such things as equating the Communist idea of community with the Church's and Communist methods with Loyola's. You ought to get hold of it just to see what you have to combat in the modern mind. I need something that covers this end-sanctifies-means business . . .

## To "A."

19 December 59

Thanks for sending the Coffee article. I am going to talk at Spring Hill in April (Jesuit college in Mobile) so I have to be thinking of something to say to them and I may reuse some of the Coffee grounds—like Fr. McCown's mother who uses them over and over until they turn white and then serves them for grits. Happens all the time in the Cathlick press.

I have seen the jacket design for my book. On an evil red-lavender background, the face of Francis Marion Tarwater in black wool hat peers out through some clay-colored corn. Very suggestive of the School of Southern Degeneracy but it could be worse. The back jacket is devoted to a quote from Caroline's piece in *Critique*, which will be like waving the red flag in front of several bulls.

I have "The Comforts of Home" torn up more or less but when I get it back together, I'll send it to Robie and see what he says . . .

That review wasn't at all adequate for *The Devil's Advocate* and the last line was rather smug, but to tell you the truth, I hate to write reviews and can never think of anything intelligent to say about the book. I have it if you want me to send it to you. It's just lying around here.

I have a paperback copy of *Breakfast at Tiffany's* but I haven't got to read it yet. They say that Truman [Capote] is a very good reader. Sometimes he wears a velvet suit. He climbs up on a stool and Dick Stern said he has a voice like an eleven-year-old girl but that after he has read a little, you don't notice that anymore . . .

## To Cecil Dawkins

23 December 59

In my day at Yaddo the maids were all well over forty, large, grim and granite-jawed or shrivelled and shrunk. This man's re-mark sounds as if it were made by someone who feels dutybound to show that he has been about. Of course I was there in 1948 and this is 1960 almost. Things may now have changed but in my day the help was morally superior to the guests by all I could judge of.

Liquor was not served by the management but of course you could get your own and in any collection of so-called artists you will find a good percentage alcoholic in one degree or another. There were a good many parties at which everybody contributed something for the liquor. I went to one or two of these but always left before they began to break things. In such a place you have to expect them all to sleep around. This is not sin but Experience, and if you do not sleep with the opposite sex, it is assumed that you sleep with your own. This was in pre-beatnik days but I presume it is all about the same. At the breakfast table they talked about Seconal and barbiturates and now maybe it's marujana. You survive in this atmosphere by minding your own business and by having plenty of your own business to mind; and by not being afraid to be different from the rest of them.

I don't recall specifically that passage in Dom Aelred Graham's book; however, I read the whole thing and was not shocked by anything in it nor did I find anything in it I hadn't heard before. It has an imprimatur. I gather from what you say that you don't understand that doctrine *develops*. "Innovation" seems a bad word to me for it implies that this teaching was not implicit in the deposit of faith, but I would have to see the passage again to find out. In any case, you may not understand from this that Dom Aelred does not believe in the real presence or that a Catholic has a choice in this matter. The Mass is a memorial but it is a memorial in which Christ is "really, truly, and substantially" present under the forms of bread and wine.

From what you ask me I see that you do not have any real imaginative vision of what the Church is. I don't take this to be your fault—Catholic education being what it is—but it is time you were learning what it is . . . Besides not knowing what the Church is in the large sense, you don't know what she teaches. For example, where on earth did you get the notion that the Immaculate Conception means that the Virgin Mary was conceived sexlessly? You must be confusing this with the Virgin Birth which is not the birth of the Virgin but Christ's birth. The Immaculate Conception means that Mary was preserved free from Original Sin. Original Sin has nothing to do with sex. This is a spiritual doctrine. Her preservation from Original Sin was something God effected in her soul: it had nothing to do with the way she was conceived. The Assumption means that after her physical death, her body was not allowed to remain on earth and corrupt, but was assumed, or like Christ's body after the resurrection, was caused by God to come into its transfigured and glorified state. Now neither of these doctrines can be measured with a slide rule. You don't have to think of the Assumption as the artist has to paint it—with the Virgin rising on an invisible elevator into the clouds. We don't know how the Assumption or the Immaculate Conception were brought about nor is this a matter for science in any way. Dogma is the guardian of mystery. The doctrines are spiritually significant in ways that we cannot fathom. According to St. Thomas, prophetic vision is not a matter of seeing clearly, but of seeing what is distant, hidden. The Church's vision is prophetic vision; it is always widening the view. The ordinary person does not have prophetic vision but he can accept it on faith. St. Thomas also says that prophetic vision is a quality of the imagination, that it does not have anything to do with the moral life of the prophet. It is the imaginative vision itself that endorses the morality. The Church stands for and preserves always what is larger than human understanding. If you think of these doctrines in this sense, you will find them less arbitrary.

I think that what you want is not a Church that can be "liberalized" but one that can be "naturalized." If there were a scientific explanation or even suggestion for these supernatural doctrines, you could accept them. If you could fit them into what man can know by his own resources, you could accept them; if this were not religion but knowledge, or even hypothesis, you could accept it. All around you today you will find people accepting "religion" that has been rid of its religious elements. This is what you are asking: if you can be a Catholic and find a natural explanation for mysteries we can never comprehend, you are asking if you can be a Catholic and substitute something for faith. The answer is no.

What the Church has decided definitely on matters of faith and morals, all Catholics must accept. On what has not been decided definitely, you may follow what theologian seems most reasonable to you. On matters of policy you may disagree, or on matters of opinion. You do not have to accept everything your particular pastor says unless it is something that is accepted by the whole Church, i.e., defined or canon law. We are all bound by the Friday abstinence. This does not mean that the sin is in eating meat but that the sin is in refusing the penance; the sin is in disobedience to Christ who speaks to us through the Church; the same with missing Mass on Sunday. Catholicism is full of such inconveniences and you will not accept these until you have that larger imaginative view of what the Church is, or until you are more alive to spiritual reality and how it affects us in the flesh.

The Church has always been mindful of the relation between

spirit and flesh; this has shown up in her definitions of the double nature of Christ, as well as in her care for what may seem to us to have nothing to do with religion—such as contraception. The Church is all of a piece. Her prohibition against the frustration of the marriage act has its true center perhaps in the doctrine of the resurrection of the body. This again is a *spiritual* doctrine, and beyond our comprehension. The Church doesn't say what this body will look like, but the doctrine proclaims the value of what is least about us, our flesh. We are told that it will be transfigured in Christ, that what is human will flower when it is united with the Spirit.

The Catholic can't think of birth control in relation to expediency but in relation to the nature of man under God. He has to find another solution to the population problem. Not long ago a lady wrote a letter to *Time* and said the reason the Puerto Ricans were causing so much trouble in New York was on account of the Church's stand on birth control. This is a typical "liberal" view, but the Church is more liberal still.

Your thinking about the Church is from the standpoint of a kind of ethical sociology. You judge it by your own dimensions, want it to conform to what you can know and see and above all you want it to let you alone in your personal life. Also you judge it strictly by its human element, by unimaginative and half-dead Catholics who would be startled to know the nature of what they defend by formula. The miracle is that the Church's doctrine is kept pure both by and from such people. Nature is not prodigal of genius and the Church makes do with what nature gives her. At the age of 11, you encounter some old priest who calls you a heretic for inquiring about evolution; at about the same time Père Pierre Teilhard de Chardin, S.J. is in China discovering Peking man.

I am going to send you some books along that may clear up one thing or another. This is one part apostolic zeal and two parts horror at some of your misconceptions about what is taught. I probably have a lot of misconceptions myself and what I say to you is subject to correction by anybody more in command of the subject than I am; I mean by any competent Catholic theologian. I'm no theologian, but all this is vital to me, and I feel it's vital to you.

*To "A."*

. . . I have found a lucky find for me in St. Thomas's sections
of the *Summa* and the *De Veritate* on prophecy. I haven't seen them
in the original because that section of the *Summa* is not in the
Modern Library volume I have and I don't have the *De Veritate;*
this is only from a commentary of Victor White, O.P. Anyway, St.
T. says that prophetic vision is dependent on the *imagination* of
the prophet, not his moral life; and that there is a distinction that
must be made between having prophetic vision and the proclama-
tion of the same. More of this later. Meanwhile, know the terrific
pleasure these books are going to give me; and that your presence
in my existence gives me all the time.


*To John Hawkes*

26 December 59
I certainly do mean Tarwater's friend to be the Devil. If I
could have treated Rayber in the same way I treat Tarwater, then
it would have been possible to show to what extent Rayber, like
Tarw., accepts and resists the Devil; but I couldn't do this because
the Devil who prompts Rayber speaks a language I can't get down,
an idiom I just can't reproduce—maybe because it's so dull I can't
sustain any interest in it. The Devil that prompts Rayber would
never say, "How about all those drowned at sea that the fish have
et . . . ?" etc.

Several years ago a friend of mine in a writing class at Iowa
wrote me that his workshop had read and discussed the first chapter
of this novel (it was in *New World Writing*) and the discussion
revolved around who the voice was. Only one thought it was the
Devil. The rest of them thought it was a voice of light, there to
liberate Tarwater from that "horrible old man . . ."

Meeks is one of those comic characters but, like Mr. Shiftlet
[in "The Life You Save May Be Your Own"] of the Devil because
nothing in him resists the Devil. There's not much use to distinguish
between them. In general the Devil can always be a subject for my
kind of comedy one way or another. I suppose this is because he
is always accomplishing ends other than his own. More than in the
Devil I am interested in the indication of Grace, the moment when
you know that Grace has been offered and accepted—such as the
moment when the Grandmother realizes the Misfit is one of her
own children. These moments are prepared for (by me anyway)

by the intensity of the evil circumstances. It is the violation in the woods that brings home to Tarwater the real nature of his rejection. I couldn't have brought off the final vision without it.

This is too much talk about my own book. You should be getting an advance copy shortly as I think they are to be sent out some time after Jan. 1 and I hope you will see some improvement in the prose of the middle section, thanks to your advice. I'll be waiting on those chapters of yours with real anticipation and a feeling of kinship. And my best to you and Sophie for the new year.

## To "A."

2 January 60

Well you don't let any grass grow under my feet. Here is old Saint T. at my doorstep. I am going to write Regnery and see if I can get these volumes; meantime I heartily thank you for sending me this one. It is just what I need, want and must have . . . I keep the prophet in my mind but I am not ready to do anything with it yet. I might write a novella about life on the farm with plenty of niggers, poor white trash, and gentry of various kinds, but right now I have to get these hideous talks off my mind. I don't know how I get into these things, but I am going to take myself in hand and not get into any more this year . . .

Let me know when you get ready to read Teilhard's book and I will send it to you. It is hard to read if you don't know anything about chemistry and biology and I don't, but as you get on in it, it becomes very stimulating to the imagination. The review reprinted in the *Davenport Messenger* suggested that we better hurry on down and read it before it was put on the Index, which I gather will be no particular reflection on the book or Père Teilhard but merely to stifle the heresies that it may generate.

*The Muses Are Heard* [by Truman Capote] is probably good but I can barely force my way through *Breakfast at Tiffany's*. It is what I would not have expected him to be—dull.

I suppose half of writing is overcoming the revulsion you feel when you sit down to it. All through the middle section of this last novel I had to wade through tides of revulsion every day. It's the curse of any long piece of work. If you are ¾ through, the worst is behind you. Buy yourself a bunch of carrots and when you must eat, eat them raw, making as much noise as you can. The nearer you can sound like Bugs Bunny, the better. This will soon kill your desire for excess eating . . .

## To Robert Lowell

10 January 60

Thank you for the ancient animals. I feel like an ancient animal myself, having just finished one book and having now to think about another one. But I think so slow it doesn't bother me much.

I am sorry that all you have is Massachusetts peacock feathers. Very inferior and subject to moths in a way that Georgia peacock feathers are not. I give them to all my old-lady friends for their hats.

A happy new year to you and Elizabeth and Harriet. I give you my annual warning that you should bring that child South where she can get a good education.

## To Cecil Dawkins

11 January 60

Well the book [*The Violent Bear It Away*] came. The title page is a real mess. They try to be fancy and just create confusion. I haven't read it for misprints because I don't have the courage, but you will soon see. If you mark any misprints, let me know.

I am real glad you have quit writing in the Judas vein [reference to an early story regarding the "necessity of Judas to Christ"]. The thought behind this may be profound for all I know but I just couldn't get to the thought for being repulsed by the pretentiousness of the dialogue, etc. I have never found a writer who could make Christ talk. An early story like this should make you feel good to see how far you have come.

I sent you the Karl Adam book under the impression that you didn't know that the Virgin was conceived in the ordinary way. I thought it would have purely factual information in it, but you don't need it so don't read it. The dissecting language repels me too; this is what is known as The Pious Style. The worst I ever saw was a writer who said that if the Church was the body of Christ, the blessed Virgin could be thought of as His neck. This is purely of the writer, too comical to be taken seriously. In some pious writers there is a lot about the Church being the bride of Christ. This kind of metaphor may have helped that age to get a picture of a certain reality; it fails to help most of us. The metaphor can be dispensed with. I will try to send you something without the Pious Style. Also some discussion about reason and faith. There are many senses of faith; the baptized infant's faith is not that of the convert or of the Catholic who has been after it for some time. I think he only means that you must believe in order to understand, not understand in order to believe.

The only places you can really avoid the Pious Style are in the liturgy and in the Bible; and these are the places where the Church herself speaks . . .

They have just sent me the copies of the French translation of *Wise Blood*. French books are all paperbacks and very pretty. I think this would be a more literate country if our books were published that way.

## To Maryat Lee

Thursday   Jan. 13   1960

Dean showed up this afternoon with yr groggy note, the gent in the Viking suit, Act. II, & news of you. Last night, Deanie called, identifying herself as "Maryat's niece" and said you weren't dead yet [ML had undergone an operation]. I was gratified to hear it and gratified this afternoon to hear they hadn't got all of your insides, and am gratified all along to know they are getting none of your money. Now you won't be able to leave me that picture. There are bad angles to all things.

As I shall undoubtedly precede you now out of this world I leave you the following: my rooster painted on the cottonseed meal top, my set of St. T. *De Veritate* & what is then left of my easel. Present this at the proper time & collect your goods.

Meanwhile cheers and remember to comport yourself properly, or as I would do, and have done, myself in similar circumstances. If you will always remember to act as well as I act, you will never get in trouble of ANY kind.

[P.S.] The Act II will read tomorrow. It is already sundown and past my bedtime. Love.

## To "A."

16 January 60

. . . I have seen the first review of the book—in the Jan. *Library Journal* (they get proofs apparently)—completely unfavorable. Says there is too much argument and dialectic and not enough convincing action to bring this macabre tale to a successful conclusion. I write in fits and gasps and as one compelled more by a moral need than as an artist. Well. Hints of things to come.

The review is by a lady in the Concord P.L. She also says Tarwater is the latest edition to my "band of poor God-driven Southern whites." I am getting the connection between the God-driven and the underprivileged—God-drivenness being a form of Southern degeneracy . . .

I am sending you a couple of copies of the *Village Voice*. Usually there's nothing in it worth reading but occasionally there is a good interview and there is that man Feiffer, a cartoonist . . .

The enclosed is part of a paper Carol Johnson is going to read at North Carolina on philosophy in the novel. She sent it to me. I think it's very funny. I would like to hear her talk.

I have just finished doing over "The Comforts of Home" and will send it to you when I type it. I think you will see how it is better . . .

## To Katherine Anne Porter

22 January 1960

Thank you so much for your note and for wanting me to sign the card. Now that the book is in print, I see all the things that could have, should have, been done to it. Still it is a great relief to have it out of the way.

I wish you were about to see my Chinese geese. I don't think I had them when you were here. They have knobs at the top of their bills and a very handsome shape on them and terrible voices, and they are mortal enemies to the peacocks. The racket is sometimes unbelievable. Geese fight on the ground and peacocks about four feet above. So they have not managed to kill each other yet . . .

## To Cecil Dawkins

28 January 60

The worst misprint was actually on the next to the last page. It is supposed to be "he heard the command," and they have it, "he heard to command," which doesn't make sense. Anyway, thanks for reading it and for your honesty which I very much appreciate. I think your judgment is the conventional one and I expect to meet it on all sides. I wish the book were better but I am glad it is not another *Wise Blood*. You can't repeat yourself and I do prefer to go where few choose to follow.

Maybe you will like the enclosed better ["The Comforts of Home"]. It will be in the *Kenyon Review*, probably summer. The end still worries me somewhat. The end of "The Enduring Chill" also still worries me, particularly as someone who read it recently thought that Asbury died in the end. Because the bird began to move down, the person seemed to think Asbury started to move up.

We are into our new wing finally. We have sister's old drapes, Louis's old sofa, cousin Katie's old rug and chairs, and consequently it looks as if we have been living in it a hundred years. I have to hurry up and paint something to hang on the walls before my mother puts up somebody's old pictures.

Have you read Malraux's *The Voices of Silence*? I am working my way through it slowly. It is really fine.

## To "A."

30 January 60

. . . More about your review of my novel. It says something I can't expect anybody else to say, and I really appreciate it . . . I am prepared to read nothing but disappointed reviews—except in the Catholic press this time. I have heard from two enthusiastic Jesuits and Sister Bernetta Quinn, also Madison Jones. Madison too warned me that the reviews were likely to be unfavorable. His novel is coming out in February also and they are to send me a copy. Ashley has read the first chapter and says it is very fine. If you would like to read these letters I am getting, I will send them to you. It is instructive to me. None of them, except Cecil's possibly, can be taken at face value . . .

Probably just as well they didn't show Christ's face. They would have made it so inexcusably handsome, you would have thrown up. Did you ever hear of Stanley Kramer? One of these Jesuits who wrote me—a very jazzy Jesuit I gather—wants to show my book to Stanley Kramer's agent, who is a friend of his. The Jesuit thinks it would make a good movie. A real fantasy, if I ever heard one.

## To Robert Lowell

2 February 60

I'll keep your letter about the book nearby when the trouncing begins. After working on it so long, I lose sense and confidence and forget what my own struggle is about. I am not through with prophets, though. I think the next one will be about how the children of God finish off Tarwater in the city; and that one may finish me off. Prophecy is a matter of seeing, not saying, and is certainly the most terrible vocation. My prophet will be inarticulate and burnt by his own visions. He'll have to explode somewhere.

You at least ought to bring your daughter on a visit here, at which I would present her with a peacock and a Chinese goose— both very imperious birds themselves.

This is Ground Hog day.

## To Andrew Lytle

4 February 60

I feel better about the book, knowing you think it works. I expect it to get trounced but that won't make any difference if it really does work. There are not many people whose opinion on this I set store by.

I have got to the point now where I keep thinking more and more about the presentation of love and charity, or better call it grace, as love suggests tenderness, whereas grace can be violent or would have to be to compete with the kind of evil I can make concrete. At the same time, I keep seeing Elias in that cave, waiting to hear the voice of the Lord in the thunder and lightning and wind, and only hearing it finally in the gentle breeze, and I feel I'll have to be able to do that sooner or later, or anyway keep trying . . .

There is a moment of grace in most of the stories, or a moment where it is offered, and is usually rejected. Like when the Grand-mother recognizes the Misfit as one of her own children and reaches out to touch him. It's the moment of grace for her anyway —a silly old woman—but it leads him to shoot her. This moment of grace excites the devil to frenzy.

Besides the fact that nobody knows about the devil now, I have to reckon on the fact that baptism is just another idiocy to the general reader . . . Well anyway, I am most grateful to you and steadied by you. If you get up this way, please stop with us. Ashley enjoyed his visit with you all. That boy is on the road more than Kerouac, though in a more elegant manner.

*Reactions to* The Violent Bear It Away *began to reach Milledgeville, and she wrote to her editor.*

## To Robert Giroux

10 February 60

Thanks for the telegram about the good review. Maybe all the baptized will rally around this one. I have had letters from some of the people books were sent to. All the Jesuits and Sister Bernetta Quinn seem to approve; also Andrew Lytle.

I have a friend who lives up the road from Granville Hicks and she has been told by him that he has written a favorable piece on it for the *Saturday Review*. *Time* is sending a man down here tomorrow—which doesn't mean they like it.

Please have me sent another ten books charged to me. I hope my donations won't interfere with the general sales.

Catharine Carver is coming down on the 18th of March to visit us for a few days.


## To "A."

13 February 60

I would not give any thought to the fact that your novel does not express your convictions as a Catholic. The convert does not get to experience his convictions in the years that experience forms the imagination, so it is quite right that what you will reflect is your need; that is right and that is enough. In the other things you have written it may have been an attempt to express your now-convictions that marred the writing. This sounds like a highly interesting book and I await it with sympathy . . .

Thursday *Time* sent two men down here from Atlanta, one to take pictures and the other to ask questions sent from the NY office —so they are intending to do something with it and we shall wait patiently to see what. The man took about a million pictures, in all of which I am sure I looked like Bishop [the idiot child in her novel]. They will select the one that looks most like Bishop. Apparently there is a very favorable review in the February *Catholic World* by the Medieval Studies man at Boston University. I haven't seen it. And Granville Hicks is writing something favorable about it for the *Saturday Review*. So there will at least be a mixture . . .

After the interview with the *Time* man I am very much aware of how hard you have to try to escape labels. He wanted me to characterize myself so he would have something to write down. Are you a Southern writer? What kind of Catholic are you? etc. I asked him what kinds of Catholics there were. Liberal or conservative, says he. All I did for an hour was stammer and stutter and all night I was awake answering his questions with the necessary qualifications and reservations. Not only will I look like Bishop but will sound like him if he could talk.

## To Elizabeth Fenwick Way

14 February 60

. . . I wish the reviews were past and I was headed into the next one. I wish you could publish a book as quietly as a short story without having to hear from all the bright people in the Sunday papers.

That voice you object to is the Tempter, the Devil, the same as suggests possibilities to all of us, and he becomes actualized in the man who gives Tarwater the lift toward the end. But I like his language. His idiom appeals to me . . .

I didn't finish in a fever, just a small temperature, and afterwards I sat down and wrote me a short story which will be in the summer *Kenyon* or thereabouts. But after you finish a novel, a story don't seem worth the little trouble it takes.

## To Robert Giroux

16 February 60

Thank you for sending the Duhamel review and also the second order of books. The review is very interesting to come out of so unlikely a place as Boston . . .

The publication date [February 8] apparently means nothing. The books have been being sold here for about two weeks. One good soul bought four to send as Valentines—before reading it.

## To Cecil Dawkins

Geo Wash Birth [February 22, 1960]

. . . Maybe you ARE hearing too much Freudian talk. Oedipus never entered my head. I don't see Oedipus in it now even, without straining him a good deal. Oedipus killed his father and married his mother. But do we have to see Oedipus in every man who doesn't like his father? The old man's animosity is directed at the mother because she's his opposite as far as virtue goes. In any case if the Oedipus business is visible in it, it is so because it is in nature, not because I worked with that in mind. I don't think any good writer would do such a thing. Unless the Greenwich Village hack variety. I'll see if I can't catch the outside steps business and the other sentence on the proofs [of "The Comforts of Home"]. As for the structure I am satisfied with that, as I am also satisfied with it in the novel. I think your ideas about structure are too much applied from the outside, or at least too rigid.

I hope you are not tearing up stuff you write because it is not up to a par that really does not fit its particular nature. There is a danger here that you will forsake your instinct for general critical principles . . .

## To Maryat Lee

25 February 60

I hope you are in a profound and recuperative sleep, recovering from the bus and daily life in Georgia, recovering from our richness to which you are sensitive. Well, come back for you are already missed.

I am fixing to paint this afternoon and regardless of nature I will do a painting in the colors on this glass plate. The picture on the wall is constantly admired by us, though I am beginning to make out Dean's features in it.

Publication day came and went with nothing more unpleasant than the *Time* and *New York Times* reviews. I would have been a little uneasy had *Time* liked the book, but I do regret their making it and me so unhealthy-sounding.

I got to get to work.

## To Cecil Dawkins

28 February 60

Yep, you're right, it can be done but it's like the woman preaching and the dog standing on its hind legs. I wouldn't want nobody to have to strain hisself.

I am painting and hating it but we've got to have something to put on that wall. Every now and then my mother comes and looks and says, "Well now I like that. That's my kind of painting. I can tell exactly what that is." Which makes me feel like I'm as good as Eisenhower or Churchill. I make Grandma Moses look like an abstractionist.

Of reviews of the book I have seen to date, *Time, NYTimes* Sunday and *Herald Tribune* Sunday and Orville Prescott *NYTimes,* and the *Saturday Review.* With the exception of the *Saturday Review,* they are all as you predicted and as I knew they would be. It is to them all a trip in a glass-bottomed boat. One other exception is the Feb. *Catholic World* which has a long piece by the

Medieval Studies man at Boston College. Perhaps I have created a medieval study. Which reminds me, have you seen any films by this man Ingmar Bergman? People tell me they are mighty fine & that I would like them. They too are apparently medieval. I quit going to the movies long ago however as Roy Rogers don't appeal to me . . .

I don't know but it might be better for your future work if you let your mother read that story. Then she would have seen what would be to her the worst and you would know her shock was over. But I might be wrong. Everybody has to work that out his own way.

Hang on and somebody besides Harpers will be willing to publish your book of stories, or Harpers will if they see you getting away from them.

## To Maryat Lee

1 March 60

What I hate to think of is you with your talent wasting your energy fighting with idiots and crooks and such trifling people as you appear to have to grapple with to get anything done in the theatre. I presume that there is no help for it, that this is your particular vocation, but anyway I think you are right to say these won't be your problems at the moment. You still might just think of that prose, that novel that you wrote 900 pages a day of . . .

Letter just arrived from you which says you enclose your day's work but nothing is enclosed. Did you forget to enclose it or is this I-ro-ny, or something?

I don't really think it is discipline you lack, if you are thinking of discipline as the ability to sit down and work, to do it, to keep at it, etc. You seem to work awfully hard to me. Rather than something you lack, it may be something you have too much of. I will be thinking of what this is, or of how I could say it with any intelligence. If it is a lack of any kind, I think it is a lack of what you find in Francis Fergusson's book, a lack of learning that would put you in a larger framework than just your personal problems. By a lack of discipline, Madame Karlweis may mean that you simply don't know how to control your own sensibility—too much sensibility. I once said to Ashley that the writer required a certain grain of stupidity. "No," said he, "a certain fanaticism." A certain fanaticism is an automatic control to the sensibility. Now I am cooking with gas, on the front burner; I am getting hot.

Do you want me to send you these two *Violent Bears* you left?

Write me what you want writ in them and I will write it and send them on. I hear there is a good review in the *Atlantic Monthly* but I have not seen it.

Friday [March 1960]

I am in bed, confined, with the epizootic and taking two-toned pills so whilst confined I have occupied the occasion reading Euripides' *Alcestis*. Now is it this Alcestis you are doing or did you mean Orestes or somebody? Is it Alcestis, wife of Admetus? It's a pretty untragic play with only 1 dead body & that eventually brought back from the shades by Heracles. Having finished it, I am now reading *Medea*. More to my taste. Though something *could* be made of the other.

Today it is snowing here & were I not confined to my bed taking two-toned pills I would be painting a snow scene. This would be appropriate as I have this large tube of white and snow is white. On this truth, I will leave you.


## To Elizabeth Fenwick Way

3 March 60

. . . A friend of mine in New York who doesn't like the book anyway has sent me several of the unfavorable reviews—I think as a way to try to show me that I must mend my ways. I guess you saw *Time*. A full medical report. Lupus makes the news. That was a really sickening review and in very bad taste. Orville Prescott says I'm a white witch. There was a favorable one in the *Sat. Review* and I hear in the *Atlantic Monthly* though I have not seen that. The *New Yorker* always gives me a nasty half-paragraph so if you see it, please send it to me.

Get you a chauffeur and come right on down. Did I tell you I had learned to drive. I learned and got my license but I don't drive much, being afraid I will kill somebody . . .

I am reading a man named Wm. Golding—*Lord of the Flies* paperback. I think you would like it.

I'm glad you like the evangelical child. None of the reviewers mention her.

## To "A."

I enclose the latest in idiot reviews. I think this is the funniest to date. Return.

If you don't want it, I'd like to have "The Comforts of Home" back as I would like to send it to the Fitzgeralds who haven't seen it. I disagree entirely with your comments on both the sheriff's deputy and the piece of paper. I hope you are not developing these kinds of rigidities about stories, about mine anyway. The piece of paper floating down is there to dramatize one of the sheriff's silences. While he is saying nothing the sun changes from one side of the porch and the loiterers move into it and a piece of paper floats down. That this paper should be expected to have any meaning other than its simple function is not to be countenanced. As for the deputy, he is part of the sheriff's world and he slinks into the car because the sheriff has apparently been telling him what to do. The sheriff controls this amount of fat by a mere look. The deputy dramatizes the sheriff's power. You ought to read *Dubliners* again. These things have their functions but they are not functions leading to action, nor do they have to be . . .

During this last spell of weather, we had no water or lights and the peacocks came down from the tree in the morning with their tails frozen stiff and went limping about until the middle of the day looking very miserable.

I am wondering where you got the idea that my childhood was full of "endless illnesses." Besides the usual measles, chickenpox and mumps, I was never sick. You say there is love between man and God in the stories, but never between people—yet the grandmother is not in the least concerned with God but reaches out to touch the Misfit. As you say, there is very much the business of the characters not wishing to be swallowed up in another's will. Rayber's love for Bishop is the purest love I have ever dealt with. It is because of its terrifying purity that Rayber has to destroy it. Very interesting.

## To Maryat Lee

No, I am not pleased that B. should write *Time*, but don't pass this comment on because what she has done she has done. She asked them not to print it so if they don't no harm will be done. *Time* can't hurt me, but I don't want further attention called

*

to myself in this way. My lupus has no business in literary considerations. Yesterday, however, I received a letter from a lady in St. Augustine who has lupus and doesn't know much about it and would like me to write her something—cheering, I gather. The which I have done. I have also received in plain envelope without return address a bunch of pamphlets on how I may be saved from the Catholic Church. These from Ossining, New York. And also from a gent in Wisconsin an offer to swap a copy of my book for a copy of *Social Doctrines of the Catholic Church* which I gather is also an attempt to save my soul from the Scarlet Woman . . .

I went to the extreme of buying a couple of tubes of paint but I don't know that they improved the picture. I don't know if I am finished with it but every time I do anything else to it, it looks worse so I guess I am.

I read with much interest about the play put on at Manhattanville. The Mother Superior up there is, or the last time I heard was, a Mother O'Byone, originally from Savannah, whose father was a great friend of Cousin Katie's. Mother O'Byone is apparently a very remarkable woman from all I have heard.

We now have lights and water again & my face has been washed.

What does Madam Karlweis think of the play you finished down here? I am always inter-rested in local products. Maryat Lee, the Baldwin County playwright. I expect to write a critical piece with this title and publish it in the *Union Recorder* if that particular play is produced.


## To Robert Giroux

6 March 60

Thanks so much for the reviews. They are amusing. Even the ones who report favorably don't seem to have read the book. There was a very favorable one in the Savannah *Morning News* which called the hero Tarbutton throughout and said he was nine years old . . .

After Lent I would be obliged if you would send Fr. Paul at the monastery in Conyers a copy of my book, and if Fr. Louis [Thomas Merton] reads it, I'd like to know what he thinks.

## To "A."

Monday p.m. [postmarked March 8, 1960]

. . . I thinks it's a lot of baloney about having to love the characters in a book for them to be worth writing about. However, anybody that can't love Tarwater, there's something wrong with them. I find Tarwater distinctly lovable . . .

The jets will have to do better than they are doing for me to go to South America but maybe I can get her [Elizabeth Bishop] here sometime. If so, I will try to get you here at the same time.

[P.S.] Enclosed is review by your friend Harold, S.J. Wherever do you suppose he gets the idea that Tarwater drowned Bishop to put him out of his misery? A kindly interpretation but it would be news to Francis Marion [Tarwater].

## To Charlotte Gafford

16 March 60

I do so much appreciate your letter [about *The Violent Bear It Away*]. I have the feeling that while many people will read this book in some fashion or other, only a few will *really* read it, or see anything in it. The reviews prove this, even the favorable ones. The favorable ones are sometimes the worst. I have one from the *Boston Herald* which says this is a superbly written book about an old man's inhumanity to a poor boy, a real tragedy, for the boy never escapes the old man.

I am real glad to hear about the [new] baby who can go to Church with you. I'll pray that some of the others will eventually go with you too . . .

I hope you keep on writing and sending your stories to the quarterlies. That is where most of the good writing is when there is any.

My best to you and my very real thanks.

## To Dr. T. R. Spivey

16 March 60

Thank you for what you have to say about the novel. I am glad you can say this much good about it but I would not like to have you stop at that point. Get on with the rest of it. My feelings are not easily hurt and I am aware of some of the book's limitations, perhaps different ones than you are. Anyway, you have more to bring to it than most & I will listen to you even if I can't agree.

One thing I observe about the title is that the general reaction is to think that it has an Old Testament flavor. Even when they read the quotation, the fact that these are Christ's words makes no great impression. That this is the violence of love, of giving more than the law demands, of an asceticism like John the Baptist's, but in the face of which even John is less than the least in the kingdom—all this is overlooked. I am speaking of the verse, apart from my book; in the book I fail to make the title's significance clear, but the title is the best thing about the book. I had never paid much attention to that verse either until I read that it was one of the Eastern fathers' favorite passages—St. Basil, I think. Those desert fathers interest me very much.

I finished the Jung book. Jung is with the uncles and not the great uncles; which is not to condemn him. I admire him and as you can see by the date in the Goldbrunner, have been interested in the subject for some time. I have two other books that might interest you, one *God and the Unconscious* by Victor White, a Dominican, and another, *Religion and the Psychology of Jung*, by a Belgian Jesuit. Both are sympathetic to Jung and Jung contributes the introduction to the White book.

To my way of thinking, Goldbrunner has used Jung in the only way that I think he can be used, which is in helping the person face his own psychic realities, or those realities that the great mystics have always faced and that the Church teaches (in spite of Jung's constant contention that she does not) we must face. Goldbrunner can do this because he believes in the objective reality of God. St. Catherine of Genoa said "God is my best self," by which she realized probably what Jung means but a great deal more. The real religious person will accept the God of Abraham, Isaac and Jacob, but not one who is no more than psychic energy. The kind of "belief" that Jung offers the modern, sick, unbelieving world is simply belief in the psychic realities that are good for it. This is good medicine and a step in the right direction but it is not religion.

All of what Jung says about penance and accepting the world's sins as your own, and emphasizing evil and admitting the shadow, I can accept, because it is what I've always been taught by another source. When Jung says that the Church reduces evil to talk about original sin and Adam's relatively insignificant "slip-up" with Eve, he is showing that he knows nothing about what the Church teaches. In general when he wants to rant at the

Church he reduces it to some least common denominator of low practice, or misapplication of doctrine.

He is an old man now and this may be nearly his last book. It has a certain admirable desperation in it like a last cry to the world to save itself. I just don't think the world will save itself by outgrowing the Church. In 1911 Jung wrote that the Christian religion seems to have fulfilled its great *biological purpose* (his words) so far as he was able to judge. There are parallels between Jung and Teilhard that are striking. They have both the evolutionary view, except that Teilhard believes the Church fulfills a continuing evolutionary purpose that will be completed at the end of time in Christ. Your admiration for Jung and dislike of the other one is puzzling, unless it can be accounted for by your not really having read Teilhard thoroughly. Those two would have had much to say to each other, though one worked with psychic energy and the other dug up bones.

I hope this don't exhaust your patience. Love.

## To "A."

19 March 60

I agree with everything you say about Cecil's story ["The Quiet Enemy"] and I will tell her she has a fan. It would mean a lot to her if you would just drop her a note yourself, because she apparently can't write right now and it might give her a lift or something.

[A mutual acquaintance] finally got around to her duty, which I enclose for your edification. I will admit it is very hard to thank an author for his book when you didn't like it. Doubtless the Devil has a whole roomful of penmen in hell practicing such letters. Henry James was very good at it. You either do like Cecil, or you do it with art, or you fall in and start struggling like [the acquaintance].

I also enclose another . . . I would hesitate to show this to anyone but you, but I think it puts him in a better light than our conversation about him did. I requested the Devil's side, so that will be forthcoming too. I can imagine it. This is a fine man and one in need of your prayers.

Elizabeth is Elizabeth Fenwick . . . She writes novels, writes one to suit herself and then one mystery novel to make money, then one to suit herself, etc. She lives by a kind of rhythm, has nothing to say but is full of lovely feelings, giggles, is a big soft blond girl and real nice to be around except that she bats her eye-lashes. She has lupus like me. Or at least several doctors tell her she has it and several have told her she hasn't. I believe she has. I met her at Yaddo and lived next door to her in New York. Her reactions to my books are always peculiar. For instance, she didn't like Enoch at all. Didn't understand why he was even in the book. And in this one she doesn't understand the voice . . . She *is* a kind of complement to me, and we get on famously. I'll send you one of her mysteries and one of the ones she writes to suit herself if you would like to see them.

Did you read the article about Golding in the last *Common-weal?* If not, do. The last time Ashley was here he brought me the *Lord of the Flies.* Good old Ashley is a fan of people like Golding usually ten years before anyone else knows they exist, so for so long, he has been talking about Golding. I haven't finished *LOTF* but so far, it reminds me of you . . .

The only picture I have seen of E. Bishop is one Cal had one time. A very pretty mature brunette sitting on an open porch in a rocking chair. Last year he wrote me she had sent him one of herself standing next to a naked Indian woman and the caption said, "One of the rare photographs of the poet, Miss Bishop."


## To Cecil Dawkins

23 March 60

Got yr letter at dinnertime after my momma had gone to town with the note I scribbled yesterday from my own flu bed. I have been up and down with it, wishing I could really get it and get it over with. Today I'm up again.

I don't know what to advise you about this offer but all I can tell you is if it were mine, I'd turn it down. I wouldn't have them [Harper] telling me what stories I was going to include or rewrite. Catharine Carver says Hiram Haydn is the best. I think I would ask Mavis (Elizabeth is in Europe I think) to show it to him, if it were mine. I just don't think you are going to have any trouble getting a publisher. Also I wouldn't want a woman editor unless she was someone I knew and liked already. Catharine Carver is a great friend of mine and I would have her for my editor in a minute, but some strange woman—no.

I told a friend of mine . . . to go to the liberry and read your story. She went on her lunch hour and didn't get it finished, so she went back after supper. She was really impressed and she don't impress easy. She told me to tell you. I told her to write you herself, which she may or may not do. She writes but has never published anything but Elizabeth is sending two of her novels around. I think something will come of them eventually. If you & Betty [Littleton] come down this summer, I told her I would ask her down to meet you . . .

## To "A."

2 April 60

Well I thanks you for my birthday message. I am thirty-five years old and still have all my teeth. As for R.M.: he is a great admirer of Thomas Wolfe & in my opinion anybody that admires Thomas Wolfe can be expected to like good fiction only by accident . . . F.D. also used the speech in one of his columns and to mean the opposite of what I mean, or nearabouts. He's a nice man too. They're all nice. Nevertheless, I felt like the old man and the sea—there was nothing left of my fish when I got home.

You are right about Dr. S. The Devil's part arrived and I will send it to you when I answer it. As I thought, it was another analysis of my character: I am afraid of the Spirit. Who isn't, brother?

Naw I didn't see [a mutual acquaintance] and I haven't even got to answer her letters. I been sick. When these damm speeches are over, I may never make another one, or anyway not for three months.

Someone told me today that there was a nasty paragraph in the *New Yorker* about my book. If you see it let me know. Someone also said there was a review in the *New Republic* which was not favorable or unfavorable and I haven't seen that either . . .

I ain't strong enough yet to think about what is a great book. I think I'd rather not think about it. If I get shut of [the speeches and other distractions], maybe I can call my head my own again. I will have something to say about ritual too. Also I am thinking about the Lana Turner bidnis [a Hollywood murder of that year], your using it and all. I don't know. If I were you, I'd just let it lead me where it would.

## To Father J. H. McCown

6 April 60

Well yesterday I had dinner with your momma and I met your sister and brother and cousin and sister-in-law and cousin-in-law, and I think now I would know any McCown I met on the street. Your brother in New Orleans wasn't there but they said that he might get toward Georgia shortly so we will look to meet him too. I certainly enjoyed it and I hope I get to see them all again . . .

If Georgia is going to see you this summer, we will expect you to light here and my mother says she won't give you the bum's rush. If you manage to get here on time. I would like my mother to meet yours as they would have Everything to agree about.


## To "A."

9 April 60

Spring Hill was peachy. I enjoy these things once I get there. It will be back to civilization for B. and they seemed genuinely pleased with him. He made the impression of intellectual liveliness. . . . They begin their classes by saying the Our Father, end them by saying the Hail Mary. The students rise to speak. There were two grinning black faces in the class I talked to the day after my lecture. Fr. Murray is very funny, all are urbane in the good sense. They call the Bishop's house The Kremlin.

Fr. Watson met me at the plane and told me he had written a letter to *America* about Fr. Gardiner's review which he thought very bad, but they had not printed the letter so he had turned it into an article which he had sent to the *Commonweal*. I doubt if they print it either, but it would have rejoiced yr heart to see what he made of Fr. Gardiner's review.

Enclosed is the Devil's part. The problem in answering a letter like this is to admit your own sins without having them laid at the door of the Church. All this flow business he is filled to the gills with and the flow is considerably above reality. You can never put your finger on him. Those of us who deal with matter and form can be nailed to the wall, but these people who are always rising to flow with the spirit, just go on flowing. I wish you and he and B. could get together because I would like your opinion of him after you had viewed the flesh. There is considerable . . .

This ain't really my week to write you but I wanted to send you the enclosed, thank you for the above, & tell you to look in the autumn–winter *Paris Review* for Cecil's other story, "The Buffalo Ranch." More from me next Sareday.

## To Dr. T. R. Spivey

9 April 60

I don't think you are unfair to me in what you say about my stage of development etc. though I have a much less romantic view of how the Holy Spirit operates than you do. The sins of pride & selfishness and reluctance to wrestle with the Spirit are certainly mine but I have been working at them a long time and will be still doing it when I am on my deathbed. I believe that God's love for us is so great that He does not wait until we are purified to such a great extent before He allows us to receive Him. You miss a great deal of what is in my book, my feeling for the old man particularly, because the Eucharist does not mean the same to you as it does to me. There are two main symbols in the book— water and the bread that Christ is. The whole action of the novel is Tarwater's selfish will against all that the little lake (the baptismal font) and the bread stand for. This book is a very minor hymn to the Eucharist.

Water is a symbol of purification and fire is another. Water, it seems to me, is a symbol of the kind of purification that God gives irrespective of our efforts or worthiness, and fire is the kind of purification we bring on ourselves—as in Purgatory. It is our evil which is naturally burnt away when it comes anywhere near God.

If you mean that all I get out of the Jung book is the fact that he misrepresents the Church, you do me an injustice, but if in his book it is not out of order for him to misrepresent the Church again and again, it is not out of order for me to defend her.

Your friend's comment about my being more interested in the way the story is told than in the story itself seems very ignorant to me, as well as untrue. Stories get to be written in different ways, of course, but this particular story was discovered in the process of finding out what I was able to make live. Even if one were filled with the Holy Ghost, the Holy Ghost would work through the given talent. You see this in Biblical inspiration, so why think that it would be different in a lesser kind of inspiration? If the Holy Ghost dictated a novel, I doubt very much that all would be flow. I doubt that the writer would be relieved of his capacity for taking pains (which is all that technique is in the end); I doubt that he would lose the habit of art. I think it would only be perfected. The greater the love, the greater the pains he would take.

Now about Teilhard. *The Phenomenon of Man* is not a book about animals in the first place but about development. There is nothing in it about animals except the section on the development of the primates. The man is a scientist, writing as one. From your comments on him, I can't really believe you have read the book, or if you have, it was with a very hot eye and not enough sympathy to get his vision. The place to find out about his love of nature would be his autobiography. From sections of it I have read in Tremontant, I gather him to have been able to satisfy you on that score. This is a scientific age and Teilhard's direction is to face it toward Christ. His likeness to Jung is not in gnosticism. Talk about this man after you know something about him. I know you don't want it but I am going to send you a book on Teilhard's thought by a Frenchman, C. Tremontant.

When I was in Atlanta at that thing I met two very nice girls who were friends of yours, but I did not catch their names. Also on that trip I got to the Grant Park Zoo as I had a guest who must see the cyclorama. They have a nauseous Hollywoodish soundtrack that you have to view the cyclorama by. After the English teachers and the cyclorama I was too exhausted to see all of the zoo but I saw the ape division, which was very elegant. You wondered if the mandrill got that way by nature or from living in that tiled bathroom. I hope to go again sometime when I can devote my full energy to it.

Happy Easter to you and much joy.


## To Thomas Stritch

[April 1960]

I am real pleased you liked the book. Some folks I don't care whether they like it or not but it adds a certain glint to it for me that you do. I have the feeling that this book is going to make me known at last to the Baptized.


## To Elizabeth Fenwick Way

April 13, 1960

Thanks for the love letter from the *New Yorker* and the Japanese book. We are enjoying the Japanese book and will return it before too long, but if you want it before I get through with it, send an SOS. As for the *New Yorker*, it goes true to form, except for the word "majestic"—how did that get in there?

Yesterday and today I have been broken out in an interesting rash. I foresee a little spell. I also have one finger which has the feeling of being dead at the bottom, at the tip, I mean. I remember you had trouble with your fingers. Was it like that? Sort of as if the finger were packed in dry-ice or had Novocain in it?

In spite of your "bursitis" and them supersonic sound waves, I still give you credit for having Lupus with a capital L. The LE cells don't have to show up in the tests for you to have it. I hope some time you will go to Dr. Sofer there at Mt. Sinai. I get told from several sources that he is the lupus authority . . .


## To John Hawkes

14 April 60

Thanks for your letter of some time back. I have been busy keeping my blood pressure down while reading various reviews of my book. Some of the favorable ones are as bad as the unfavorable; most reviewers seem to have read the book in fifteen minutes and written the review in ten . . . I hope that when yours comes out you'll fare better.

It's interesting to me that your students naturally work their way to the idea that the Grandmother in "A Good Man" is not pure evil and may be a medium for Grace. If they were Southern students I would say this was because they all had grandmothers like her at home. These old ladies exactly reflect the banalities of the society and the effect is of the comical rather than the seriously evil. But Andrew [Lytle] insists that she is a witch, even down to the cat. These children, yr. students, know their grandmothers aren't witches.

Perhaps it is a difference in theology, or rather the difference that ingrained theology makes in the sensibility. Grace, to the Catholic way of thinking, can and does use as its medium the imperfect, purely human, and even hypocritical. Cutting yourself off from Grace is a very decided matter, requiring a real choice, act of will, and affecting the very ground of the soul. The Misfit is touched by the Grace that comes through the old lady when she recognizes him as her child, as she has been touched by the Grace that comes through him in his particular suffering. His shooting her is a recoil, a horror at her humanness, but after he has done it and cleaned his glasses, the Grace has worked in him and he pronounces his judgment: she would have been a good woman if *he* had been there every moment of her life. True enough. In the Protestant view, I think Grace and nature don't have much to do with each other. The old lady, because of her hypocrisy and humanness and banality couldn't be a medium for Grace. In the sense that I see things the other way, I'm a Catholic writer.

I hope you are writing and that *The Lime Twig* is on the way. Also that you all may be going to Florida this year and will stop for a longer visit with us.

## To "A."

16 April 60

I enclose some more letters. Don't feel you have to comment on all these. They are just for your entertainment, as considered preferable to television . . . The one from Paris from a Mlle. Gabrielle Rolin who has written three novels herself and who has been a correspondent of mine for a few years now. The carbon is one Caroline wrote to the *NYTimes* and didn't send . . . I think the idea that Tarwater is a hero who is not matriarchally conditioned is an innerresting idea. The one from Red [Robert Penn] Warren pleased me no end as I really didn't expect him to like the book . . .

Well I do not have to go to Savannah to talk to the NCCW as last week I broke out in the galloping hives and the Doctor said I could not go. After receiving this information, the hives subsided. Well the system makes its own adjustments to circumstances, and the moral of this story is do not make the National Council of Catholic Women your personal hairshirt or you will start itching, and have to take it off.

Cecil is I think 31. She wrote me she had had a fine letter from you and thanked me for the introduction. She wanted to know if you were a native of these parts as you said you knew the people talked the way she wrote it because you heard them on busses. It made me think how really stratified socially the South is. Cecil hasn't heard them on anything but busses and the like herself, nor have I theoretically, though living on a place like this I hear more . . .

Miss K.A.P. cuts away a lot of the grease around the Lady Chatterley business in the February *Encounter* . . . It's refreshing to see her take off on Lady Chatterley.

My mind is so free and unburdened that I am fixing to clean up my desk.

## To Elizabeth Bishop

23 April 60

The pictures are wonderful and I am glad to know you got back from looking at the Amazon and were not leaned upon by one of the tame buffalos and pushed over. I kept having that mental picture, sort of in snapshot form—"one of the rare photographs of the poet, Miss Bishop," and the tame buffalo, smiling, leaning you down. My notion of the jungle is all out of Frank Buck so tame buffalos seem very funny to me. Maybe it wasn't even jungle where you were. I would love to come to see you but I guess I will have to let the jets get it down to a fine point before I undertake a trip. Already they go from New York to Miami in 2 hrs & 40 min. We were going to take a trip to Europe again but instead we added a wing onto the house and my mother says we are sitting in our trip to Europe. I would just as soon sit in it, though I feel guilty about my attachment to comfort over culture.

My book has received considerable attention, most all of it simple-minded . . .

Caroline's comment on the back had really been written about *Wise Blood* and the stories. In the piece they took it from she went on to quote Blake's thing about oft in midnight streets I hear, about the harlot's curse blighting with plagues the marriage hearse etc.; so I suppose what she had in mind was Blake's vision of evil. Anyway, I would just as soon they had used a variety of quotes on the back, some from other points of view. Although I am a Catholic writer, I don't care to get labeled as such in the popular sense of it, as it is then assumed that you have some religious axe to grind. However, since the review in *Time*, my mail has been full of attempts to save me from the Church . . . and I have received an anonymous message in a shaky hand to the effect that my religion is phony. I suppose a book like mine attracts all the lunatics. I had one letter telling me that people such as I write about do not exist and in the same mail a friend sent me a clipping about a Rev. Mr. Pike of Lebanon, Tenn. who has got himself in the news for immolating a lamb, wired to a cross, at his "special" revival services; also one about a boy named Jimmy Sneed, a 13-year-old evangelist, who hung himself because his mother spanked him for sassing her. A neighbor was quoted as saying, "He was a good boy. He had been preaching around here some lately and was doing fine."

You asked about Catharine Carver. She saw the book when the middle section was composed of three instead of six chapters. She told me it wasn't long enough and that it broke apart in the middle and that Rayber didn't come through—all of which was true. So I added all the business about the child evangelist and the chase through the city at night and that helped it no end. After that, she thought it was fine. I value her opinion and she will tell me when something is bad. I have a horror of somebody publishing something of mine when it isn't fit to publish.

A few weeks ago she came down here from Philadelphia (she works for Lippincott there now) and spent the weekend with me. She said it was the first time she had gone anywhere in ten years . . . I think she liked it here and I hope to get her down here from time to time. The day she came I was to talk in Atlanta at something called The Georgia Council of Teachers of English—an unctuous order of high-school English teachers. Their project for the last two years has been getting up a "map of Georgia Authors." So after two years of hard labor, they had the thing ready to unveil at their annual luncheon meeting; I was the speaker. I got them to let me bring Catharine and this was her introduction to the South. They had the menu all worked in with Georgia literature—Tara Prime Ribs, Ransy Sniffle Potatoes, Tar Baby String Beans, Uncle Remus pecan pie, etc. There was a long eulogy of Georgia literature written by John Donald Wade and read for him by an old gentleman with a trembling voice; the program went on for about two hours until finally they unveiled the map, a hideous modernistic thing with twenty ugly little faces completely covering it; the rest of the Georgia writers were listed around the margin, a hundred or so. My talk was the last thing on the bill but it was a real anti-climax because they were all sleepy by then. But [Catharine] was amused by the whole thing and I was delighted to have such a silly occasion to entertain her with . . .

## To Maryat Lee

28 April 60

I have not seen your Parker pen but if I do I'll hock it at once and split the proceeds with you. The paintbrush and a book arrived back yesterday brought I think by Dean and not by Emmet. With two green-stamp books I got myself a fishing tackle box to keep my paints in. It has two trays in it and is very elegant and pretty soon I am going to start painting.

That certainly was a shame that colored woman on the bus had to get you. I sat down next to a colored woman in the waiting room at the Dearborn Street station in Chicago once. She was eating grapes and asked me to have some but I declined. She was very talkative and kept talking and eating grapes. Finally she asked me where I was from and I said, "Georgia," and she spit a mouthful of grape seeds out on the floor and said, "My God" and got up and left.

I can't tell from your rendition of it whether the sculptor's advice was good advice or not. A word stands for something else and is used for a purpose and if you play around with them irrespective of what they are supposed to *do*, your writing will become literary in the worst sense. On the other hand you do need to think much more than you do about how you use words. Wyndham Lewis said about Orwell's style (I believe it was Orwell) that he got it by putting down the first jolly old word that came into his jolly old head.

## To Cecil Dawkins

30 April 60

I have been in the hospital in Atlanta for the scientist to find out what is responsible for my feet swelling. He found out everything that was not responsible for their swelling so I figure we have accomplished something anyway.

You asked where "A." is from. She is from Georgia but you know you and I too hear the kind of people we sometimes write about only on the street or the bus or the back door. She is a very interesting girl, one of the brightest I know; though she didn't get to finish college, she is better read than most of my Ph.D. acquaintances. She [works] by day and by night she reads and writes. She has travelled about some and has had a very hard life . . . Her writing gets better and better and I hope to the Lord Elizabeth can start selling something of hers. I think the novel is her form. She went and read "The Buffalo Ranch" and is sold on your writing. When you come to see us, try to come at a time that will include Saturday so I can have her down to meet you. Saturday is the only day she can come on. If you came through Atlanta, you could just pick her up and bring her with you . . .

## To "A."

30 April 60

I almost called you up last week as I spent from Tuesday to Friday at the Emory Hospital, however I am not talented at working strange telephones so I called nobody up. I did not expect to be there but after an office visit the Scientist said I must go. They mostly drew blood from me & I am no worse for the wear.

Tomorrow we expect Fr. Paul and the Abbot for lunch. The Sisters at the Cancer Home in Atlanta had a child there with a cancer that grew out of one side of her face. She died year before last when she was twelve and they think she was a saintly child. They had her for about ten years. The Sister in charge wrote me about her, sent pictures of her, sent the Bishop's funeral sermon etc. and asked me if I would write a story about her—fiction, or otherwise. They want people to know about her. I said such a story shouldn't be fiction and wasn't in my line but suggested they write it themselves, by having a compilation of witnesses among the Sisters who had known the child, and maybe I could help them collect these pieces together to make a book, edit it, and if necessary contribute a foreword. It appears now that the Abbot is interested and is coming down here to talk to me about it, and dear Lord knows what I will be in for. What interests me in it is simply the mystery, the agony that is given in strange ways to children; they, I think, really feel she was a saint and want it known, and here I am about to write a book in collaboration with a convent.

Miss Katherine Anne's piece is not against Lawrence but against the publishing absurdity that has recently been made about Lady Chatterley. More pious slop has been written about that book by intelligent people than any other book I can think of and she says some very refreshing things . . .

My Jung friend is not a little bit in love with me but resents me rather thoroughly I think. Not that the two are mutually exclusive, I just don't think the first is so. I feel as if I may have given him a worse opinion of the Church than he had to start with and this worries me. The little I know is not enough to combat the little he knows and there are such differences in the meanings of things that when I say something like "The Church is a divine institution and stands for Christ in the world," he thinks this is sentimentality—whereas all that feminine principle stuff, eros, is a regression to me from what St. Paul means by charity.

I was pleased with the *Commonweal* review and amused by the one in the *Critic* . . .

## To Maryat Lee

Here is yr bruder with his academic teeth bared. I will try to keep you supplied with such photographs as I gather from the *Union Recorder.*

The recital must have been very good & Deanie was much perked up by your wires etc. My sit-upon was pleased it lasted exactly one hour & no more. An old lady dropped her cane in the middle of one of the pieces but nobody was so rude as to notice except me. There were a lot of folks there, dressed up as for church and afterwards considerable food. All that was lacking was you, padding around in your red sneakers and plaid pants.

My mother says you *cook* that ham.


## To "A."

14 May 60

Let me right now correct, stash & obliterate this revolting story about Lowell introducing me as a saint. I don't know who could have repeated such a thing, but I would be very much obliged if the next time you see him you would impress on him the impropriety of repeating this kind of slop. He may have got it from the Fitzgeralds and have taken it without the attendant details. At the time it was happening, poor Cal was about three steps from the asylum. He had the delusion that he had been called on some kind of mission of purification and he was canonizing everybody that had anything to do with his situation then. I was very close to him and so was Robert. I was too inexperienced to know he was mad, I just thought that was the way poets acted. Even Robert didn't know it, or at least didn't know how near collapse he was. In a couple of weeks he was safely locked up. It would be funny if it had not been so terrible. Anyway, it was during this time that he was behaving so. Robert and I both made fun of him when he said such things, but there was no deterring him. He mixed it all in with his wild humor. Things went faster and faster and faster for him until I guess the shock table took care of it. It was a grief for me as if he had died. When he came out of it, he was no longer a Catholic . . .

All [the Abbot] said about the little girl was that she was a strong character. We didn't get a chance to talk about her because when he was ready to, somebody else came in . . . I told him it was a perilous undertaking to deal with such a thing and Fr. Paul said yes it was full of pitfalls and shook his head and the Abbot said, "She was a strong character," and shook his head . . .

Dr. [Spivey] now tells me that I should have had more sympathy for Tarwater in my book because there is so much Tarwater in us all. Ah me . . .

## To Maryat Lee

Wednesday [May 20]

Dear Raybucket,

I have a mental picture of you at old Walden Pond again amongst the tomatuses. Why don't you take yourself a real vacation in that land of happy retreat, Milledgeville, a bird sanctuary? . . .

I'm glad you think what I said about your friend's novel was near the point. I don't like to criticize the work of people who are strangers to me. You never know when something you may say might make them go jump in the lake. I don't mean I go around saying things that make people jump in the lake, but you might just step on a deep wound or something. I hadn't heard from her until today when I got a note saying thank me for my kind letter and I would hear from her later. I don't think much of the kind of spontaneity you suggest unless it comes from someone who has developed the habit of art. Sooner or later anyhow, you have to mind how you say what you have to say. However, the thing she sent me was entirely too clever. I don't think she can spend her life doing 18th-century imitations. Has she ever done anything besides be justice of the peace at Wellesley and rebel from the Union Seminary?

[Robert Penn] Warren is a lovely man. That *Band of Angels* is probably not his best by far. I suggest you read *All the King's Men*. I have his long dramatic poem *Brother to Dragons* if you would like me to send it to you.

Cheers,
Waterbucket

## To Elizabeth Fenwick Way

22 May 60

Thanks for the clipping and if you run up on the horrifying one, don't fail to send it. I don't horrify easily. They say my bones aren't leaking calcium; there is some kind of blood test they gimme to determine that, but they believe that the lupus has affected those blood vessels that feed the top of the thigh bones, or anyway that is the likeliest possibility. But I will go along with you on that aspirin any day—the World's Finest Medicine. Last summer my jaw was popping out of the socket every time I opened my mouth and I couldn't chew good red meat for the pain. I took eight aspirin a day for a month and haven't had any more jaw trouble.

A lady I know said a lady she knew said a doctor who knew Dr. Sofer said Dr. Sofer said lupus sometimes just went away and stayed away for as long as ten years or so. One of these days I may yet take myself to be inspected by Dr. Sofer . . .

Await litry communication.


## To Cecil Dawkins

23 May 60

That is peachy about Atheneum . . . [Andre] Deutsch is supposed to be good in England. Have you ever sold the Benny Ricco story and the one about the man that killed the moron? Try the *Noble Savage* maybe—that is Bellow's magazine, costs $1.25 I think but I haven't read it. You might also try *New World Writing*, now under new management.

You can try earlier for the Yaddo business next year. You might write better at some less exciting place for the time being. I am strong on the belief that you can't write a story until you have a story to write, but then you sometimes find one by messing around with this and that.

[My friend] had a letter from this Minor girl at McIntosh and McKee saying that both she and Miss McIntosh had read her novel and felt they couldn't handle it but they would wait and let E. McKee satisfy herself that they couldn't when she got back next month. This is too bad. It's a real wild novel but it has a lot of virtues. I think there are two suicides and three murders in it, though I forget the exact count. Anyway, a lot worse stuff is published and there is a real mind behind this one.

Vitamins make me hungry and then I eat and have too much weight to carry around on my decaying hips. I take something called GEVRAL, geriatric food supplement. I am not yet exactly in the geriatric class but I'll know what to do when I get there. I take other pills for the foot-swelling.

Your mother's reaction to "The Buffalo Ranch" is right in line with what is to be expected. All my aunts think mine are sacrilegious. Pay it no mind and go about your bidnis . . .

## To Maryat Lee

24 May 60

Don't sit there and tell me that fellow returning yr wallet was anything but a bloody miracle. Ha ha.

I'll be pleased to meet your friend. Is she passing through here or what; or do you mean meet her through the mail?? My "helping" your writing was largely a matter of your pulling what you wanted out of my head while I sat there. Also a matter of there is a kinship between us, in spite of all the differences there are. But it is unlikely I would be any help to someone else—but anyway I would be glad to converse with her or whatever. I would rather not read the novel of anyone I don't know though because there is too much danger of hurting the person. I don't mean hurting his feelings, I mean hurting his writing. I never keep my mouth shut enough about things that temperamentally aren't to my taste.

I beat my brains out every morning on a story I am hacking at and in the afternoon I am exhausted is why I haven't got down to the typewriter. It takes great energy to typewrite something. When I typewrite something the critical instinct operates automatically and that slows me down. When I write it by hand, I don't pay much attention to it . . .

What do you mean—you were IN *Camino Real?* You acted in it? You watched it or what?

I don't know how you would tell anybody his writing was mannered, except you say, "Brother, this is mannered." I once had the sentence: "He ran through the field of dead cotton" and Allen Tate told me it was mannered; should have been "dead cotton field." I don't hold that against Allen. Give him something good to criticize and he would do better.

31 May 60

I hope you don't have friends who recommend Ayn Rand to you. The fiction of Ayn Rand is as low as you can get re fiction. I hope you picked it up off the floor of the subway and threw it in the nearest garbage pail. She makes Mickey Spillane look like Dostoevsky.

Your friend wrote and asked if I would read her novel and I suggested she send me four chapters of it first and let me see if I *could* read it. If it is temperamentally too much against my grain, it would be better for her if I didn't read it. This way I can tell.

That is interesting about the Kabuki. I knew them Japanese must do something besides all wash in the same tub. However, it's still theatre and over me head. What do you mean—that man Ritchie is over here talking the thing or he is over there and is recorded? . . .

I enclose a sample of yr br's prose. What did you ever do with that ham?

[P.S.] If you feel porely, get yourself a jar of GEVRAL. You take it in milk & put some coffee in it. It is for old people. I love it. Geriatrics!

## To Father J. H. McCown

2 June 60

Thanks for the reports of Miss O'Connor at Spring Hill and yr part in the Azalea Trail. I have written me a story set in an azalea festival and if I find it worthy to be published I will some-day send you a copy of it. All characters fictitious as usual.

You get some of those friends of yours to bring you over when you come to Macon and we will invite you and them to lunch. Macon has another big murder these days . . . A very exciting place to make a retreat in. I was recently over there to the Macon Writers Club breakfast and a half a dozen people asked for you. Some of them would bring you over. On the other hand, since the automobile has been invented never have I seen a grounded priest . . .

## To John Hawkes

2 June 60

Please do have New Directions send me the galleys to your book. It sounds like a real exciting book. It will be to me. I think you have nothing to lose by making it more realistic than your others. Cal Lowell wrote me something about my (last) novel that at the time I read it brought your work to my mind too. He said, "I have been thinking that we perhaps have something of the same problem—how to hold to one's true, though extreme vein without repetition; how to master conventional controls and content normal expectations without washing out all one has to say. This hurried way of saying it sounds cynical, but I think something like this happened to Shakespeare in moving from his clotted, odd, inspired *Troilus and Cressida* to the madder but more conventional *Lear*." I don't know whether this says anything to you about what you are doing but I thought of you when I read it. I feel myself that you have such a marvelous gift of sight that you can afford, almost like none of the rest of us, to content normal expectations.

As between me and Greene there is a difference of fictions certainly and probably a difference of theological emphasis as well. If Greene created an old lady, she would be sour through and through and if you dropped her, she would break, but if you dropped my old lady, she'd bounce back at you, screaming "Jesus loves me!" I think the basis of the way I see is comic regardless of what I do with it; Greene's is something else . . .

## To "A."

11 June 60

. . . Yesterday B.'s opus arrived in the mail . . . Instructions are to send it on to you when I finish with it. I am in medias res now with no opinion yet.

No the dog-book lady didn't come. I talked to her once about the award over the telephone but I never know who I'm talking to on the telephone and not until I hung up did I realize she was the dog-book lady. She sounded like a good old girl . . .

There was a nice paragraph about *The Violent Bear It Away* in the last *Partisan Review* in the Fiction Chronicle by a man I respect, R. W. Flint. He didn't say much but what he said was ok. The reviews get more favorable the farther away they are from publication date. This is as it should be.

The enclosed will amuse you. It is a section that Powers censored out of a book called *Conversations with Catholics* that Lippincott is going to publish soon—tape-recorded sessions with [Dwight] MacDonald . . . I can't understand why either of them should find the mummy hard to understand. I thought it dangerously obvious.

I've sent you *Christ and Apollo* [by Fr. Lynch S.J.] which has some good answers to the question of what-are-you-saying. But when people ask you this, there is no answer for them except to say you are saying what can't be said otherwise than with your whole book, that you can't substitute an abstraction and have the same thing . . .

## To Cecil Dawkins

22 June 60

Who should turn up yesterday but your friend W., his wife and four children. They are tenting on the lake and are on the way from Alabama back to Pennsylvania by way of various water spots. He is quite a talker and friendly pusson . . . He visited here three times yesterday, once preliminary or introductory at 10 in the morning, then went off and returned with a camera at 11, then returned with wife and children at 4. I think it would be great if the camera had not been invented, but apart from that and the morning visits, I enjoyed them. I can't tell from talking to him what he might write. He has a cousin who has published a lot of things in the *Atlantic* . . .

I am behind on everything from company. M. Coindreau, the gentleman who translated *Wise Blood* into French, has just spent four days with us, bringing with him the reviews of it from the French papers. One full-page one from *L'Observateur* illustrated in the middle with a picture of Billy Graham, one review of my book and Algren's (*A Walk on the Wild Side*, in French *La Rue Chaude*) with the favor going to mine. The reviews indicate it is a good translation and I was very pleased, so was M. Coindreau. He is now going to translate the last novel.

I finally finished my picture and it is hung, and I am still fiddling around with the farce and also have begun another thing that I don't know what it will be.

Viking sent me that *Walk Egypt* [by Vinnie Williams] because it is by a Georgia lady. Georgia ladies are supposed to read the books of other Georgia ladies, but I ain't read it yet. It sho does look long . . .

I am broke out with little peafowl—fourteen. Also many odd-looking biddies . . .

## To "A."

25 June 60

I enclose you Caroline's words on the "Partridge" story. At first reading I thought she was just being technical but on consideration I saw she was right, so I enclose you what I did about it and as you can plainly see it is much better. All critical minds seem to turn to the word nickel, mo-over, so I will hereinafter spell it in the traditional way . . .

The mummy was an idol to Enoch if you want to analyze it

but the fact is you can't analyze that kind of attraction. For the book as a whole, it was the figure for the new jesus—a shrivelled man.

There was a good review in *Jubilee* of my book written by somebody named Paul Levine. I didn't know who he was but when M. Coindreau came down last week, he had fifteen or twenty questions typed out to ask me from Paul Levine who it appears is preparing a book on 6 writers—McCullers, Capote, Buechner, Bellow, Salinger and me, the book to be published by Harcourt, Brace. The questions were very intelligent so I should hope something from the book . . .

I sent you the pamphlet from Carol. She wrote me she didn't get the Fulbright to Spain that she was expecting and I think this was probably a blow, but she is going anyway. What is Scamander? I am too ignorant to read this poetry . . .

## To Elizabeth McKee

26 June 60

I don't know how the rumor could have originated that I am dissatisfied with my publisher, because it certainly isn't true . . . If Giroux has got the notion I am dissatisfied, please tell him there is nothing to it. Mr. Dodds said he had been advised to write me by one Allen Jossey-Bass. A friend of mine brought a young man named Allen Something (never caught it) by here one afternoon but I can't recollect talking publishers with him . . . We have a constant stream of visitors and I suppose each takes something away in a version known to himself but not necessarily to me. Anyway, I thanked Mr. Dodds for his letter and told him I was tied up . . .

I have no notion of hastening my ways for the *Atlantic*. I have a story but I am still thinking about it . . .

Apparently *Time* magazine received a letter or so about that review they did of my book. They had their Atlanta office call up to check on a few things, mostly on whether they had got the nature of my disease wrong (which they had). They also wanted to know who all visited us and where all I had been to lecture. All this three months after the review. A secretary or something wrote me a desultory letter acknowledging the mistake.

I am glad you are back. I had begun to fear you might have given up the operation.

## To "A."

. . . I haven't read [Frederick] Buechner myself, but if I was writing it I would throw out Capote in favor of Malamud and Carson McCullers in favor of Powers . . .

There doesn't have to be any connection between Enoch and a criticism of humanism. As a fiction writer, I am interested first in Enoch as Enoch and Haze as Haze. Haze is repulsed by the shriveled man he sees merely because it is hideous. He has a picture of his new jesus—shriveled as it is. Therefore it certainly does have meaning for Haze. Why would he throw it away if it didn't? Its meaning is in its rejection. Haze, even though a primitive, is full of the poison of the modern world. This is in part responsible for some of the comic effect. Of course that isn't all there is in it and when I wrote it my mind was not primarily on these abstract things but only on what would Haze and Enoch do next, they being themselves . . .

Fr. Paul says he is afraid B.. thinks Jesuits are not made of the same frail stuff as the rest of us. If not, I daresay he will shortly find out.

## To Cecil Dawkins

11 July 60

. . . I'm not sorry you asked [your friends] to stop. Ask anybody you like to stop, as people stopping is about the only way I get to see anybody except for my little trips occasionally which I have less and less enthusiasm for—at least for the going. I like it all right after I get there. Anyway, it was just that everybody appeared to be stopping at once that was getting me down . . .

I find that one story a year is a good average, for me, anyway. You can't put one out right after another. Just write every day whether you know what you're doing or not. Right now I have a vague notion in my head about a novella or somesuch I want to write but it is all very vague indeed and I find myself approaching it from one direction and another and I'll just keep on until I have an entrance. This is just something you can't force. But don't do other things. Sit at yr machine.

## To "A."

. . . We had quite a gathering here Monday—six Sisters from the Cancer Home, the Trappist Abbot, and a Msgr. Dodwell. I was greatly impressed with the Sister Superior. She is one of the funniest women I have ever encountered and has all the rock-like qualities that you would have to have to do what they do. She brought two old Sisters, one of whom was Mary Ann's nurse, and three younger Sisters, one of whom draws . . . and the other two write . . . However, the Sister Superior is the one doing the writing on the book and she writes better than the others. She don't write like Shakespeare but she does well enough for this. What will come of the book, I wouldn't know but I am convinced that the child had an outsize cross and bore it with what most of us don't have and couldn't muster. The founder of their order was Hawthorne's daughter. I have just read a biography of her—very interesting if you'd like to see it . . .

That Haze rejects that mummy suggests everything. What he has been looking for with body and soul throughout the book is suddenly presented to him and he sees it has to be rejected, he sees it ain't really what he's looking for. I don't regard it in any abstracted sense at all . . .

Well poor old Jack [Kennedy]. I hope he gets [elected]. I think King Kong would be better than Nixon. We didn't see any of it, having no television, but one night I listened for a spell on the radio when we had company who must hear it. Fortunately the company soon left to seek out a television so we went to bed.

## To Cecil Dawkins

Herbert Hoover's Birthday [10 August 60]
The agents will send you the check from the publishers, having already do not fear taken out their one hundred bucks.

That's good that you may be coming this way in the fall. I hope it won't be the week of October 16 however as I have signed myself up to go to Minnesota that week to talk . . . The letters I've had from the Sisters there have been very intelligent and solicitous —in fact they offered to put me up in the infirmary but I declined. Always sound a little more decrepit than you are is my motto.

I finally finished that farce ["The Partridge Festival"] and made it less objectionable from the local standpoint; however, my mother still didn't want me to publish it where it would be read around here. So I told Elizabeth to send it to the *Critic*—a Catholic book-review magazine which is going to start publishing fiction in the fall. They took it, much to my surprise, and paid $400 for it, when their usual price is $300. If you have had no luck with "Benny Ricco" elsewhere, you might try them. They don't want the usual junk you find in Catholic magazines . . .

Elizabeth has written that *Holiday* would be interested in having me do an article for them on peafowl for $500. I hate articles but I like money so I am toying with it. I find there ain't much you can say about a peachicken; however, it makes me want to finish so I can write a story again . . .


## To "A."

3 September 60

I also thought: she ought to send that story to E. McKee at once and not send anything around herself because every time she gets anything back, she is going to get depressed. Write them, send them back to Elizabeth and forget them. If you need to "take" anything, it is a typing course. Ain't there some nine-day-wonder-Learn-You-To-Type course at some of those business schools? I know that in the 19th, 18th, 17th centuries they wrote with a goose quill and got along fine, but this is not the 19th, 18th, or 17th centuries and I think you need to see what you are doing while you are doing it.

. . . I had a letter from T. last week in which this occurred (same old stuff only worse): "The one thing I do believe is that we are headed for a true rebirth of the Spirit. My mind tells me very little about these matters, but in my soul I feel happier every day about these matters. I foresee soon the end of our present pessimistic climate and the birth of a new optimism as we move toward the moment of rebirth." . . . I am sure I'd prefer the philologist.

You probably read Richard Gilman's review of *The Leopard* [by Giuseppe de Lampedusa]. He came Thursday and left the next day, and I wish you had been here as you would have enjoyed him as much as I did . . . He wants to do a critical piece for either *Commonweal* or *Commentary*. I said *Commentary* would be better if they'd take it and he agreed. He also agreed we needed a word for what I do, but he didn't have one either.

I have read 100 pages of *The Bell* [by Iris Murdoch] and I am all for it. This is much better than *Under the Net* and I intend to go back to it today. I have worked all week on the Sisters' ms. and am beginning to talk baby talk. When I get shut of it, I'll go back over that speech and see what I can do about the dishwater realism—maybe just eliminate the word dishwater and leave it at realism.

Your visit was a treat for me. It was just good to know you were in the house.

## To Maryat Lee

6 September 60

Dear Rayverberator,

I ain't forgot you, you just have too damm many places of residence. Do I wish to send the products of me teeming intelligence to Chester and them set for three weeks getting cool whilst you are flim-flamming about in New York, or do I want to send same to New York and have them idle in your mailbox while you are picking cucumbers in Chester? For from me mail-getting you are not in a good position. Having just read your letter I am developing your style but will not retain it longer than one paragraph I do hope.

I saw your sister-in-the-law in the Piggly Wiggly yesterday and she and I was speaking of you and she said you might be here some time soon. She did not appear to have been shocked at *La Ronde*, only bored; I think she slept through most of it.

I am taking off either the 13th or the 17th of October for Minnesota for one week where I will tellum this and that as my prewrit paper directs me. Two convent schools—the Manhattan-villes of the Midwest, or so I trust. The letters from the Deans are very intelligent and the head of the English Dept. at one of them has written a book called *The Metamorphic Tradition in Modern Poetry*, it being a study of Auden, Jarrell, Williams (Wm. Carlos) and Stevens. I am very Country Bumpkinish in such society.

For my part I am sorry you ain't doing *Kairos* as planned to begin with. Did that lady get cold feet?

My chicken feed bill this month was $9.95. I must get back to imminent duties of which you are not one.

Your obt servant,
Tarfaulkner

## To William Sessions

I'm sorry the book [*The Violent Bear It Away*] didn't come off for you but I think it is no wonder it didn't since you see everything in terms of sex symbols, and in a way that would not enter my head—the lifted bough, the fork of the tree, the corkscrew. It doesn't seem to be conceivable to you that such things merely have a natural place in the story, a natural use. Your criticism sounds to me as if you have read too many critical books and are too smart in an artificial, destructive, and very limited way.

The lack of realism would be crucial if this were a realistic novel or if the novel demanded the kind of realism you demand. I don't believe it does. The old man is very obviously not a Southern Baptist, but an independent, a prophet in the true sense. The true prophet is inspired by the Holy Ghost, not necessarily by the dominant religion of his region. Further, the traditional Protestant bodies of the South are evaporating into secularism and respectability and are being replaced on the grass roots level by all sorts of strange sects that bear not much resemblance to traditional Protestantism—Jehovah's Witnesses, snake-handlers, Free Thinking Christians, Independent Prophets, the swindlers, the mad, and sometimes the genuinely inspired. A character has to be true to his own nature and I think the old man is that. He was a prophet, not a church-member. As a prophet, he has to be a natural Catholic. Hawthorne said he didn't write novels, he wrote romances; I am one of his descendants.

In any case, your critique is too far from the spirit of the book to make me want to go into it with you in detail. I do hope, however, that you will get over the kind of thinking that sees in every door handle a phallic symbol and that ascribes such intentions to those who have other fish to fry. The Freudian technique can be applied to anything at all with equally ridiculous results. The fork of the tree! My Lord, Billy, recover your simplicity. You ain't in Manhattan. Don't inflict that stuff on the poor students there; they deserve better.

We'll look for you for Thanksgiving day . . .

## To "A."

. . . I think what particularly appealed to me in *The Bell* was the picture of this rather dumb woman coming into the community and destroying it while at the same time absorbing a little of the good in it for herself. I want to read the rest of them but not until I get through with Minnesota, Mary Ann, and an Arts Festival at Wesleyan the last of October. Whew . . .

Just by chance I have come upon a book on the romance-novel which is very good—an Anchor book: *The American Novel and Its Tradition* by Richard Chase. I wish you would take a look at it if you haven't seen it.

I'm glad you have set to on another one, and if this is one that you just have to write out of yourself, I should say the less time spent on it the better. Has Elizabeth McKee commented on *Miss Nancy*? . . . She sent me six copies of the British *The Violent Bear It Away* and the cover looks a good deal worse than when I saw it in rough form, but it is a masterpiece compared to the British paperback cover of *Wise Blood.* Sabbath is thereon turned into Marilyn Monroe in underclothes. I am surprised that the British one is so much worse than the American, but the more lately I see of British doings, the more I respect our own, as being at least one degree less degraded.


## To Elizabeth McKee

28 September 60

I'm amused by the letter from *Holiday*. The fellow obviously thinks it's a great accomplishment to write something for them.

I'm no reporter and couldn't do anything on Jackson, Nashville or Birmingham. Milledgeville is the only Southern town I could write about and if I did that I'd not only have to please the editors of *Holiday* but the 10,000 citizens here. I'm afraid it would activate my lupus.

However, the next time I am feeling indigent and have nothing worthwhile to do, I may think of something that would interest them.

Let me know when this thing is coming out. I have never seen *Holiday* in my life and don't aim to put any money back in the firm except the price of one issue, that being the correct one. And thanks for thinking of this idea [of an article on peacocks]. My uncle is going to be horribly impressed; he can't stand peacocks.

## To Robert Giroux

Thank you for sending the ad. I have received my six copies of the Longman's edition of the book. The jacket appears to belong on a good Western; however, I passed on it myself in a rough stage so I have no one to blame. The rough stage was so rough that it didn't look so bad.

I am engaged in an odd project right now which I would like to solicit your professional advice about sooner or later. In Atlanta there is a home for incurable cancer patients run by the Dominican congregation of nuns that was founded by Hawthorne's daughter. In the early part of the summer, the Sister Superior there wrote me about a child with a face cancer whom they had kept for nine years. She came when she was three, died when she was twelve. Many people in Atlanta heard about her and became friends of the home through her. She apparently had considerable charm in addition to this outsize cross. The Sister Superior is determined that something must be written about her. She had written a man named Hugh Cave (because he had published a book about a little girl) and asked him to write about this child. He told her a Catholic ought to do it (I suppose to get her off his hands). Through the monastery she heard about me, so she wrote and asked me to write a story about a child like this one. Just my kind of thing.

I wrote her that this was not the sort of thing that made fiction and that if it had to be written, the Sisters should write it themselves and it should just be a factual account of the child's life and death in the Home. I told her if they did happen to write it, I'd be glad to go over the manuscript and would supply a little introduction if that would help. I thought that would be the last I'd hear of her. Never underestimate them. They forthwith sat down and wrote it and they are hellbent to see it through. The Abbot is interested in it and so is the Bishop who wants it to have the imprimatur. I hear he thinks the child was a saint.

The manuscript is not very good, of course. I set about to get the obnoxious pieties out of it and that proved almost impossible. I'm still working on it, and they are expecting me not only to turn it into a decent manuscript but to get them a publisher. Would you read it when I get it edited? I know I can't make it into the kind of thing you would publish but you might be able to tell me who might or if you think it's publishable at all.

Fr. Paul thinks it's quite comic that they have lit on me to do this. He asked them which of my murder stories gave them the idea I should help them with it . . .

*Flannery had been sought out by a student at GSCW, Roslyn Barnes, who interested her greatly. The course of their friendship, and Roslyn's eventual fate, are traced in future letters. At this time, Roslyn was studying in Iowa City.*

## To Roslyn Barnes

29 September 60

I know exactly where you are living as I lived for two years at 32 East Bloomington (now torn down I think) and for one year at 115 East Bloomington, a big grey house owned then by a Mrs. Guzeman. Some time ask your landlord what became of Mrs. Guzeman. She was most a hundred then so I suppose she is in the cemetery now.

Thanks for looking up Mr. Santos but it was not James but Bienvenido Santos. Paul [Engle] will doubtless know.

I wish I could visit you ladies but I will be doing well to get my old bones to Minnesota and back. I don't know why I do these things . . .

It's good you have both the radiation work and the writing out there. If you don't take to writing, you can switch over full time to the other.

Give my regards to Paul if you locate him again in the next six months. And keep me posted on your own doings.

## To William Sessions

29 September 60

. . . I'm glad to hear you don't generally make Freudian interpretations where something else applies better and that you are not dishing out that kind of stuff at Spring Hill.

I am alarmed, however, lest you have become an interpreter of Southern Protestantism along the lines of a Baptist orthodoxy. Surely you know that Methodists have an equal stake in this, in quality if not quantity, and that they believe in enfant baptism. There is one very dominant Protestant trait which old Tarwater exhibits. When the Protestant hears what he supposes to be the voice of the Lord, he follows it regardless of whether it runs counter to his church's teaching. The Catholic believes any voice he may hear comes from the Devil unless it is in accordance with the teachings of the Church. You are judging the old man as if he should act like a Catholic. The prophets were Jews and old Tarwater is a Protestant and his being a Protestant allows him to follow the voice he hears which speaks a truth held by Catholics. One of the good things about Protestantism is that it always contains the seeds of its own reversal. It is open at both ends—at one end to Catholicism, at the other to unbelief.

Both the old man and the child can be inspired to speak the truth in spite of their Protestantism or even because of it. If they can't then you are demanding that the novelist submit his characters and action to social determinisms. All right if that's what you want to do but it can't be demanded . . .


*To "A."*

1 October 60

I finished the Richard Chase book and liked it highly except his notions about the Christian novel. He seems to think the divisive American novel is strictly a product of the Enlightenment and that the Christian novel will be more in line with the British novel of manners—healing. Absolutely the opposite, in my estimation. This notion that grace is healing omits the fact that before it heals, it cuts with the sword Christ said he came to bring. I think Chase writes about the Christian novel with only the pagan's notion of Christianity. Somewhere else in there he calls the Christian view of history cyclical if I am not mistaken. It is not cyclical but evolutionary. Can it be possible that a man with this much learning knows so little about Christianity?

I have a novelist friend in Smiths, Ala. named Caroline Ivey who wrote me about Harper Lee. She knew her father who was a lawyer. Apparently the people in her town in Alabama (Mayborough) think she shouldn't have used the Boo Radley episode as there was apparently something like it in the town. Caroline Ivey was highly sympathetic to Miss Nelle Harper Lee and insisted on sending me the book . . . I think I see what it really is—a child's book. When I was fifteen I would have loved it. Take out the rape and you've got something like *Miss Minerva and William Green Hill* * I think for a child's book it does all right. It's interesting that all the folks that are buying it don't know they're reading a child's book. Somebody ought to say what it is . . .

*Holiday* took the peacock bait. $750—more than I have ever got for any piece of writing, by about half. Crime pays.

The current selection of the Catholic book club is something

* Miss Minerva and William Green Hill *was the first of a series of children's books about an aunt and nephew in a Southern small-town setting.*

called *The Secret of Dreams* by a Spanish Jesuit. I was curious (so bot it) having gone through several discussions of the dream bidnis with the worthy doctor [Spivey] . . . The book is not as bad as the title would suggest and has some useful information in it. If you would like to see it . . .

Are you looking at the Kennedy-Nixon debates and what do you think? We don't see them.


## To John Hawkes

9 October 60

This is about how much I like *The Lime Twig*. It came last Sunday and I read it that afternoon and evening in a sitting that was unwillingly interrupted once or twice. The action seems to take place at that point where dreams are lightest (and fastest?), just before you wake up. It seems to me that you have retained all the virtues of the other books in this one, but added something that will hold the reader to the reading. I can't make any intelligent comments about this book any more than I could about the others; but I can register my sensations.

You suffer this like a dream. It seems to be something that is happening to you, that you want to escape from but can't. It's quite remarkable. Your other books I could leave when I wanted to, but this one I might have been dreaming myself. The reader even has that slight feeling of suffocation that you have when you can't wake up and some evil is being worked on you. I don't know if you intended any of this, but it's the feeling I had when the book was happening to me.

I want to read it again in a month or so and see if the second time I can take it as observer and not victim. Meanwhile my admiration is 90% awe and wonder.

I am about to take off for Minnesota where I am going to talk at two Catholic colleges and read at the University—"A Good Man Is Hard to Find." I think when I read this story aloud I get over my interpretation of it—as against yours and Andrew's—fairly well, but I have an unfair advantage, since I sound pretty much like the old lady. After Minnesota, I am going to an Arts Festival thirty miles from here where Katherine Anne Porter, Caroline Gordon, Madison Jones and me are going to be paid (well) to swap clichés about Southern culture. An old lady left her sizable fortune for an Arts Festival every year at this college with the stipulation that the guests had to be Southerners and discuss Southern culture. The money goes on whether the culture does or not. I think it's programs like this that are going to hasten the end of it . . .

Again my admiration. Nobody else writes like you do.


14 October 60

You certainly can use that quotation if you like it better than the one I sent the fellow at New Directions. The one to you is more relaxed, more what I felt but wouldn't have said to a stranger. To him I said: "I hope that *The Lime Twig* will gain a wide audience for the work of John Hawkes. It retains all the visual power and intelligence of his other books but adds an element of suspense that should entrap readers who might otherwise have found his fiction 'difficult.' I think he is our most interesting writer. He is the only one I know of who isn't doing what is done every day of the week." Sounds very jacketish. If you prefer the other so do I. If you want to combine parts of both, do whatever you like.

I'm not skittish about Leslie Fiedler. He doubtless knows a good thing when he sees it, even if he does have to wrap it up in Freud.

The enclosed postcard I resurrected from under a glass, as it seems to be both your and my subject matter somehow. I would deal with the Free Thinking Christian Mission on Highway 80, but I think it would take you to handle the physical apparatus of the cart, carriers, etc. I particularly like the goat on the top of the heap.

Cheers and keep me posted on how the book does. I wish they could be written and deposited in a slot for the next century myself.


## To "A."


27 October 60

Some reviews enclosed. After reading these and then seeing myself put by Mr. Wm. Jay Smith in the "eccentric tradition that goes back to Peacock and Firbank and up to Iris Murdoch and Flannery O'Connor" I had a certain feeling of liberation. It is very nice to be classed as an eccentric and let alone. I understand there is an article called "The Fact in Fiction" by Mary McCarthy in the last *Partisan.* She says miracles aren't allowed in fiction and makes other statements of a like nature. I haven't read it so I don't know if she allows for the Eccentric Tradition. But I'm all for the Eccentric Tradition. I am glad you have decided to cut out the off-beat element in this projected novel of yours, however, and that you plan to have miracles. I am only really interested in a fiction of miracles. As for the off-beat business, it seems to me better for any number of reasons that you leave it out, and since you are going to leave it out, I applaud spending more time on what you are going to do.

I got back from Minnesota last Friday. I didn't see Mr. Wm. Van O'Connor, but I met some people of considerable interest . . . I was much impressed with [Sister Bernetta Quinn] and much impressed with all the Sisters I met out there. In the last *Critic* there is a poem by a William Goodreau—"Three Poems for Three Nuns"— the last in the series is Sister Bernetta. Mr. Goodreau I like very much. Also met a colored man named Al Miller who teaches Economics there but used to be book review editor of the *Critic*. According to Sister Bernetta he has the best mind of anybody on their faculty. I hope this wasn't race prejudice on her part. Anyway, I met no duds at either school . . .

This weekend we are steeling ourselves for Caroline and Ashley and a dinner party involving they two, K.A. Porter, Madison, Louis Rubin and Deen Hood, the lady from Florida with the lupus. She just sort of appeared. She thinks nothing of driving six hours up here if she takes the notion. This time she left the husband at home which is just as well as the table won't hold but ten . . .

## To Father J. H. McCown

28 October 60

Well, we were glad of a little evidence that we are still on yr list. The book I'll enjoy and return in good time. We were on the outlook the last of July for one of Mr. R.'s two-toned Cadillacs bearing yourself and were disappointed when none showed up . . .

If John Howard Griffin* gets to Georgia again, we would be delighted to see him; but not in blackface. I don't in the least blame any of the people who cringed when Griffin sat down beside them. He must have been a pretty horrible-looking object . . .

## To Elizabeth McKee

28 October 60

Someone has just called my attention to the fact that this Scott, Foresman Freshman English Program text which has "The

---

* *Griffin, author of* Black Like Me, *was the newspaperman who stained his skin and traveled the country as a black for several months.*

Life You Save" in it has it with the last paragraph omitted. I would be much obliged if you would call Harcourt and tell them. I think some kind of protest ought to be lodged. I suppose there is nothing that can be done about it now but I certainly don't like the idea of my story being in a textbook and the last paragraph omitted . . .

## To Robert Giroux

4 November 60

Thanks again for the reviews. It [*The Violent Bear It Away*] appears to be a book which no two people have the same thing to say about.

Thank you also for agreeing to read the Sisters' book [*A Memoir of Mary Ann*] when I get through with it. Caroline was here last weekend and I got her to read it. She said she thought that it was moving and ought to have a secular publisher. Right now the only thing that moves me is the desire to get it off my desk.

## To John Hawkes

6 November 60

I told you once you had three readers in Georgia. I know one of them very well and I sent her the proofs to *The Lime Twig* when I finished, figuring she was too poor anyway to buy the book. She wrote me the enclosed letter about it. Whether you agree with all her interpretations or not, I thought you would like to see that somebody you never heard tell of reads you with this much attention and pleasure . . .

The message on the other side of that card I sent you came from a couple who took up with me through the mails. Some very odd people turn up hereabouts, usually hoping to find me as unconventional as themselves. However, as I am highly conventional, most of them go away; but this couple have become fast friends of ours. They live in St. Augustine. The girl originally wrote me because she read in *Time* magazine that I had lupus (*Time* got the nature of the disease wrong but at least the name right). This girl had just been told that she had it and the week that she was told, she had also attended the funeral of somebody with it, so she was scared to death and wrote me to find out what she could about lupus. Then nothing would do but they must come to see me and since then, they have been here three times. I suppose it gives her confidence to see that the lupus does not deter me overmuch.

I have a story ["The Comforts of Home"] in the current *Kenyon*, which after reading in print, I am dissatisfied with, but it has a very interesting devil in it that might appeal to you. But I think the story itself don't come off.

## To Cecil Dawkins

8 November 60

I have been recuperating from Minnesota and then an Arts Festival at Wesleyan attended also by Caroline and Miss K. A. Porter. Caroline spent the weekend here after it . . . and one night of it, we had the lot of them to supper. Katherine Anne remembered to inquire about a chicken of mine that she had met here two years before. I call that really having a talent for winning friends and influencing people when you remember to inquire for a chicken that you met two years before. She was so sorry that it was night and she wouldn't get to see him again as she had particularly wanted to. I call that social grace . . .

R. writes that you have broken with the ranks of investment peddlers but gives no details. I was just about to write and congratulate you and ask for some financial advice. The trouble with writing is you make all your money at once and then don't get any for years. I have my two houses on the way to the waterworks but think I would like me some intangible investments; I keep wondering if Coca-Cola will be good for eternity, etc. . . .

I have seen the MVSEVM in St. Louis but it was too big to impress me. Last year when Catharine Carver visited me, we met her in Atlanta and took her to the cyclorama in the mvsevm where Enoch got the mummy. Catharine wanted to see the mummy herself, so she and Regina went upstairs to look for it and I waited downstairs. After a while they came back but hadn't found it. On the way out, Catharine asked the girl at the ticket place if there had used to be one and the girl said yes there had, but she didn't know what had happened to it. Catharine was satisfied then that Enoch had taken it . . .

## To "A."

12 November 60

. . . I am now writing the introduction to the Sisters' book and I am enjoying it extremely. I have thought about it enough I suppose to make the writing of it a real pleasure. Next week I will probably send it to you for your consideration; I need to be told where it begins to sound pompous. You don't have the trouble of being pompous when you write fiction, but when you, or I anyway, write something like this, inflation lurks around every paragraph. The introduction is quite opposite in tone to the book itself; which is I think as it ought to be . . .

If you are interested in reading James Purdy's *The Nephew* I have it. I really think it is quite a good book, on a small scale. I am in the midst of *The Leopard* and agree with you that that is very fine.


## To Robert Giroux

12 November 60

I'm obliged for the clipping from *TLS*. The only British review I have seen that you haven't sent me was one by Kingsley Amis in the *Observer*. It was extremely unfavorable but he ended up saying that I had convinced him that this is the way people were in Georgia. (Horrors!) Longman's has boldly quoted this in their ads, ignoring the fact that the review was unfavorable. I would send it but I can't lay hands on it at the moment. Did I tell you that Longman's wrote me they were disappointed in the way the book was selling—after a month it had sold only 1500 copies. That was about 1500 more than I would have expected.

Would you send a copy of *The Violent Bear It Away* to M. Maritain in Princeton? Last spring, M. Coindreau took his French translation of *Wise Blood* over to Maritain and according to him, Maritain was so much taken with it that he asked M. Coindreau to come over to talk about it. I would like him to be sent this last novel.

We are all highly pleased with the results of the election. All the Baptist ministers in Georgia are having to find a new subject.


## To Cecil Dawkins

12 November 60

. . . It is my considered opinion that one reason you are not writing is that you are allowing yourself to read in the time set aside to write. You ought to set aside three hours every morning in which you write or do nothing else; no reading, no talking, no cooking, no nothing, but you sit there. If you write all right and if you don't all right, but you do not read; whether you start something different every day and finish nothing makes no difference;

you sit there. It's the only way, I'm telling you. If inspiration comes you are there to receive it, you are not reading. And don't write letters during that time. If you don't write, don't do anything else. And get in a room by yourself. If there are two rooms in that house, get in the one where nobody else is . . .

I will not tell you anything interesting to read as you have no bidnis throwing away your time in that fashion.

## To Maryat Lee

Garfield's Birthday [November 19, 1960]

Your friend's story is fine. Its quality is largely visual and painterly. I couldn't say what she would do with characters. If I were you I would send this to *New World Writing* and such places . . .

I am glad you find me a good Protestant. That is indeed a compliment. All good Catholics have the best Protestant qualities about them; and a good deal more besides; my good deal more besides I try to keep from view lest it offend your delicate sensibilities. Elizabeth Wynn and her minister and his wife arrived in due course. I thought you had told me she was of an agnostic persuasion, so I was expecting a Unitarian or some pious liberal fraud; instead, bless us, a real man of God. I didn't have to tell him what I meant by the Christ-haunted South. He already knew.

The rich Milledgeville ladies had themselves a postmortem over the election next day. The chiefest comment was that now there would be a Kennedy in every office and that Mrs. Kennedy would never be able to grace the White House. You see, we keep in mind the really important things. My friend, George Haslam, wrote me that there was no truth in the rumor that the Kennedys were going to name their baby Martin Luther Kennedy. I presume this had its genesis in New York. It was not heard in the South. Now that we have elected him, we can begin to cuss him.

Lance Phillips is going to write the Secession Pageant. The returns are going to a Youth Center. And Susan Hayward of Hollywood California and Carrollton Georgia is going to come and hep us celebrate—January the 20th. You should make arrangements to be here. You would just love it . . .

*To "A."*

25 November 60

I was distressed you wouldn't come and have been worrying about what could be the matter. I started to call you up and try to persuade you to change your mind and then I decided I had better mind my own business and didn't do it. Now I am sorry I didn't because I think too many people and especially me mind their own business when their real business is somebody else's business. I feel very strongly that your business is my business, even if I don't always act quick enough on the feeling. I asked B. what he thought might be the matter and he said he thought you might be depressed because you had shown something you had written to some young man who had made a lot of criticisms of it that you thought were just. Then I doubly wished that I had called up and insisted that you come and I also wished I were up there so that in the spirit of Christian charity I could knock you in the head with the nearest stick of wood.

Of course B. may be wrong and I hope he was but assuming for the moment he wasn't, I have this to say. No matter how just the criticism, any criticism at all which depresses you to the extent that you feel you cannot ever write anything worth anything is from the Devil and to subject yourself to it is for you an occasion of sin. In you, the talent is there and you are expected to use it. Whether the work itself is completely successful, or whether you ever get any worldly success out of it, is a matter of no concern to you. It is like the Japanese swordsmen who are indifferent to getting slain in the duel. I feel that you are distracted, particularly when you say, for instance, that it is B.'s writing that interests you considerably more than he does. This is certainly not so, no matter how good a writer he gets to be, or how silly he gets to be himself. The human comes before art. You do not write the best you can for the sake of art but for the sake of returning your talent increased to the invisible God to use or not use as he sees fit. Resignation to the will of God does not mean that you stop resisting evil or obstacles, it means that you leave the outcome out of your personal considerations. It is the most concern coupled with the least concern. This sermon is now ended. It may be as wide of the mark as Pitty-pat's, in which case ignore it. But you owe me a visit . . .

I didn't know that copy of the introduction had that bad place in it. I guess that should teach me to look at the carbons. The Sisters were very pleased with it and even Regina liked it which means something . . . I enclose Caroline's comments. I have no intention of changing the opening, but I will do the smaller things she suggests. I feel that the opening is all right. I think she is right about putting myself in too much. This is supposed to be about Mary Ann, but correcting that is mostly a matter of taking out the I-thinks and I-feels . . .

[P.S.] I thought a bloody semicolon was for a long pause. What is it for?

## To Roslyn Barnes

28 November 60

Enclose you a clipping from the *Atlanta Journal* in case you might want to give it to your teacher . . . Do you think there are still any closed societies in the South? There are two official ones, Black and White, but they are about to be loosed upon one another. As for the others, I don't much think they exist in fact; they exist in the minds of some writers and perhaps that is enough . . .

Dr. Green [Helen Green, a professor at GSCW] has supper with us every now and then, but I have not seen her since school began. The last time she came out she appeared with one of her dresses in a brown paper bag and gave it to me as it was too small for her and I had admired it. She has two requirements for any dress she buys she says: it must be reduced and it must be navy blue . . .

## To Father J. H. McCown

4 December 60

Thanks for the interesting item. The one they took is probably not as good as your brother's, but I should appreciate the interest. Actually, I think they have very little literary judgment at that magazine. Whoever was responsible for that editorial on John Updike's novel, *Rabbit Run*, should be confined for a while. I suspect it was the Rev. Harold C. If you get a chance you might like to look at that book. It is true that the sex in it is laid on too heavy. It is so burdensome that you want to skip those parts from sheer boredom; but the fact is, that the book is the product of a real religious consciousness. It is the best book illustrating damnation that has come along in a great while . . .

Nothing doing around here. I am shortly going into Piedmont Hospital to have my bones inspected. They are melting or leaking or getting porous or something . . .

## To Maryat Lee

I daresay you have remounted your steed and are now galloping full ahead. Don't let People and their Opinions affect you so
much. I always count on a big percentage of Those Who Will Have
None of It and do not let myself be concerned about remarks within
that circle. When you do get something in production, you will be
subjected to a lot more adverse criticism than you are now so
you had better learn to ignore it.

Me I have other problems. My last X-rays were very bad and
it appears the jaw is going the same way the hip is. I had noticed
a marked change in the position of my mouth. Anyways, Tuesday I
enter your last year's hangout, Piedmont Hospital, for a general
inspection of my bones. If they don't turn up anything definite,
I'll have to go to Johns Hopkins . . .

## To Robert Giroux

8 December 60

Enclosed is the Sisters' manuscript. If you think there is any
possibility at all of its getting published anywhere, I might be able
to get them to improve it. After I had got the thing all typed for
them, they decided there were "a few other little things" they had
forgot to mention. So I told them to write them down and I would
insert them. Today they sent me the insertions, three of them.
Two I have inserted and the other I am sparing you. It had to do
with Mary Ann eating some applesauce.

Caroline proclaimed that this should be called *Death of a
Child*. I presented this to the Sisters but they did not take to it at
all. They then got together to think of titles and came up with
some that would curl your hair: *The Bridegroom Cometh, Song
without End, The Crooked Smile*. The Abbot, who is in on this
too, came up with the worst: *Scarred Angel*. I informed them that
none of these would do, and suggested the title I have put on it
[*A Memoir of Mary Ann*]. They accept this reluctantly but think it
is very "flat."

Now that they have produced a book, Sister Evangelist thinks
a movie should be made about Mary Ann. They are serious. I have
declined to take part in the production (for their postulants) of
the movie . . .

I hope you will have a Merry Christmas and thank you very
much for reading this. I think there is a great deal in this child

and wish her book were written better but I don't know anybody who would write it.

## To Roslyn Barnes

12 December 60

So Mr. Bienvenido Santos turned up right under your nose! Perhaps he is a permanent resident of Iowa City. You've found both him and Mrs. Guzeman so maybe if science and writing cease to interest you, you can be a private detective. I'll be glad to recommend you.

I am glad you are going to Mass because along with study there should be no better way of finding out if you are really interested in the Church. You don't join the Catholic Church. You *become* a Catholic. The study can prepare your mind but prayer and the Mass can prepare your whole personality. I wish that there were a book that you could give your parents that would prepare them for your interest because it seems to me you should at least try to cushion the blow if you are going to give them one. Perhaps they wouldn't read it, but if you think they would, you ought to look around for a book that would create interest in them without offending them. I think Msgr. Conway has a book—*Questions Catholics Are Asked,* or something. It might not do at all. Nothing might do, but at least you ought to look.

I don't know whether Msgr. Conway was there when I was or not. I never met him. I went to St. Mary's as it was right around the corner and I could get there practically every morning. I went there three years and never knew a soul in that congregation or any of the priests, but it was not necessary. As soon as I went in the door I was at home . . .

## To Maryat Lee

[from Piedmont Hospital, December 22, 1960]

I was cheered by the sound of that familer voice of yourn & today your letter came & tonight I may be chased through impassable white banks by a silent bus. Big Sister don't speak through the walls at night and I sleep very well. One of the Sisters at the Cancer Home has brought me a box of cresants, an aunt has brought me six egg custards, & my Florida friend sent me an artificial spider to put in the bed to frighten the nurses. It does not look like I will get home Friday. The old man says let's leave it on a day-to-day basis. My mother says when we leave, Piedmont will have my money, the doctors will have a lot more information and I will be about where I was when I came in. You can't get ahead of Mother.

All they do is draw my blood and X-ray my bones but they are learning. Another friend today brought me *A la recherche du temps perdu* in 2 volumes but I hope I won't be here long enough to read it. The food is lousy didn't you find?

When I came in & gave the information about myself at the admitting place, the woman, who had carrot-colored hair & eye-glasses to match, asked me by whom was I employed. "Self-employed," says I. "What's your bidnis?" she says. "I'm a writer," I says. She stopped typing & after a second said, "What?"

"Writer," I says.

She looked at me for a while, then she says, "How do you spell that?" . . .

I must leave you to eat an egg custard & a cresant as I have to stop eating & drinking at 12. Yours, O'Authwater


## To "A."

24 December 60

I read 50 pages of Proust in the hospital and was surprised how much I enjoyed it. We got home to find all my furniture piled in the middle of the room, newspapers and sheets all over every thing. Louise and [a workman] had had four days on the room and were about half finished. Also we had frozen pipes and all week we have been in a mess so I ain't got to any more of M. Proust, but I am going to enjoy it all next year and I trust by next Christmas to have it finished. I am still enjoying those Greek plays you gave me. From time to time I read one I haven't read yet.

What they found out at the hospital is that my bone disintegration is being caused by the steroid drugs which I have been taking for ten years to keep the lupus under control. So they are going to try to withdraw the steroids and see if I can get along without them. If I can't, as Dr. Merrill says, it is better to be alive with joint trouble than dead without it. Amen . . .

*Jubilee* accepted the introduction [to *Mary Ann*]. I was surprised. They will run it in February or March. The Sisters are tickled pink and maybe if the book don't get published, this will be something for them anyway.

Me, I am working on that story* I told you about and having the best time I have had in a spell of working. If I can work it out, I'll have something here . . .


## To Cecil Dawkins

29 December 60

I am plumb crazy about the peacock [in stained glass, made by Russell Green at Stephens]. My mother insists it is a partridge, but we had company and she said, "What would you call that?" and he said, "a peacock." We have it sitting in the center pane of one of the windows in the new part of the house, where it just fits . . . Tell Russell Green how pleased I am.

I have been in the hospital in Atlanta and they have discovered what is making my bones disintegrate . . . This brings on an interesting state of affairs. They are going to try to withdraw the steroids gradually and see if I can float without them, but at present my activities are limited. I can do nothing much but sit at home and write some stories, so I am at that.

"A." came to see me a couple of times in the hospital. She has started on a new novel which seems to be the right thing for her. If I could see that girl publish something I would be mighty happy . . .

I have recently undergone the repainting of my room. It was like the earthquake in Chile. It will never be done again while I live.

Tell Betty I appreciated her card and I don't know when they'll use the peacock story. I look every month and it ain't in there, but I have already spent the $750 . . .


## To John Hawkes

30 December 60

Did you happen to know that Thor's chariot is drawn by goats? And when he is visiting somewhere and there isn't enough to eat, he tells his host to kill and cook his goats but he makes them put the goatskins down in the middle of the floor and everybody has to throw the bones onto the skin and if anybody keeps a bone, one of the goats will limp after he has resuscitated them in the morning.

* A letter of 21 January 61 to "A." suggests that the story she was working on was "Parker's Back." It must have been abandoned and only taken up again several years later.

He will then knock in the head with his hammer whoever kept the bone. This information was casually passed to me by Caroline Gordon, who teaches a course in Mythology at the New School, so I sent her a postcard of the goat man and put on it, "These goats have been resuscitated several times." She also said that Frigga's chariot is drawn by cats and Venus's by doves. Anyway, this puts the Free Thinking Christian Mission in a more classical light . . .

I know it would mean a lot to [my friend] if you did write her. She has very little sense of her own worth and no outlets for the kind of mind and sensibility she has. My agent is sending around a novel she wrote, but there are no takers. Her imagination is more fertile than in good control yet, but with each book, she improves. It is my ambition to see her in print.

I have been in the hospital and my activities cut down upon. Midwestern trips are contraindicated for the present, so I intend to sit quietly and write me some stories. If it is necessary to conserve energy, I may buy an electric typewriter. Perhaps then my stories will electrify the general reader; or electricute him.

## To Elizabeth McKee

1/3/61

Thanks for your note before Christmas and for calling Harcourt, Brace. As for those Germans, they can omit "A Stroke of Good Fortune" and "A Temple of the Holy Ghost" but not "The Displaced Person" or as they call it, "Misplaced Person."

I am out of the hospital but not at full capacity yet.

## To Maryat Lee

[January 1961]

This is too bad about the fellow's play. The novelists continue to have it over you people. A lot of bad reviews & the play closes but a book stays around. You better had change your calling and learn to write proze as I have oft told you before.

I guess you are reading about how we are integrated now in our educated part. There is a marked change of atmosphere about all this in Georgia. They are fixing to junk the segregation laws and substitute a more local arrangement. Don't think now we will repeat New Orleans.

My stomach has somewhat recovered itself. It is no news around here.

## To Louise Abbot

1/13/61

I don't see how I could write what Miss R. wants because point of view never entered my head when I wrote that story ["A Good Man Is Hard to Find"]. I just wrote it. It's all seen from the eye of the omniscient narrator and that's that. I never gave it a thought. I'll look up that thing on the short story and have it when you come. Let us know when. Next Tuesday I am going to Atl. to the doctor & on the 20th & 21st, we have to go in town for the house opening in connection with celebrating the Civil War. I sure am sick of the Civil War.

*James Tate and his wife, Mary Barbara, were good friends of Flannery's in Milledgeville and members of the Wednesday evening group. Mr. Tate was in Iceland on military duty at this writing.*

## To James Tate

15 January 61

We were no end cheered to hear from you. I have a mental picture of you facing the winds in that baby-blue Parker [parka] (maybe it wasn't baby-blue but that's how I remember it) that Lance would have liked to have for himself. On account of my "incapacity" the Wednesday nights have not been meeting; but I don't think they would be much anyway without you, as nobody wants to come out in the cold to hear Brother Phillips discourse.

That worthy is striding about with a cat-like grin on his face these days, beingst he is the author of the pageant. He apparently goes to all the eating-meetings of the committee and is like to become our foremost authority on the War between the States, as the ladies like to call it. I have heard on the side some of them complain that the committee had no business "paying that Englishman to do what Katherine Scott [Milledgeville historian] could have done just as well"—for nothing, they mean.

Christmas morning my mother and I left the house in town and turned down in front of the Mansion. There we espied this walking creature, seven feet tall, in a flowing black karacul robe with a Russian hat a foot and a half high on its head. "What is that?" my mother said, stopping the car. We looked close and perceived it was Maryat. She had blown in in the middle of the night as is her wont. Some stage designer had made the clothes for her. She went to every party that the college people had the three days she was here and wore those clothes.

Somebody gave me the complete *Remembrance of Things Past* for Christmas and I am eating my way through it like a mole. I think it would make good Iceland reading for either you or the Captain. Maybe you could keep him quiet with it.

My mother was mighty pleased about what you said on the subject of Andalusia. We hope the months will go quickly for you and that you'll soon be fishing here again . . .

## To "A."

21 January 61

. . . I don't know if anybody can be converted without seeing themselves in a kind of blasting annihilating light, a blast that will last a lifetime. I would be afraid that a psychiatrist would make him lose the little he's gained, unless it was one who respected his beliefs. This girl . . . who shows up here from time to time, was a seminarian at Union in New York and quite snarled up in the emotions, etc. When the psychiatrist got through with her, her emotions flowed magnificently and she believes nothing and herself is her God, and everything for her depends on her success in the theatre—which I doubt if she'll ever have. She is charming and very generous but headed for some major crack-up if she doesn't somehow get back some of what she lost in the psychiatrist's office . . .

That letter he wrote me about my book was sex from beginning to end. Based the whole book on some half-baked Freudian symbols. I wrote him to try to recover his simplicity . . .

The nausea is better as my dose has been reduced, so when you get ready to come, come . . .

I am on page 513 in [the Proust novel]. I cain't get over it.

"Parker's Back" is not coming along too well. It is too funny to be as serious as it ought. I have a lot of trouble with getting the right tone . . .

I think that *Odyssey of a Demon* is a crackerjack title. You couldn't do better.

Special Special Special

[Farrar, Straus] are going to do the Mary Ann book. I am bowled over. The Sisters are dancing jigs up & down the hall . . . Whew!

## To Roslyn Barnes

23 Jan. 61

I finally got off *The Divine Milieu* to you.

We have been undergoing big doings here on account of Secession was passed in M'ville 100 years ago. A pageant for 3 days and a big parade in 20° weather with young ladies on floats freezing in their drafty dresses etc. etc. Long live the Wah Between the States.

I am sorry your parents are going to raise a ruckus but I guess those things can't be helped. Prayer will do more for them than argument.

I still feel only so-so.

## To Robert Giroux

23 January 61

The Sisters are dancing jigs all over the place. I bet them a pair of peafowl nobody would ever buy the book so I am out a pair of peafowl.

Sister Evangelist called up the Bishop at once and he was delighted. However, he wanted one thing in the manuscript out before he can give the imprimatur. The scene where Mary Ann goes to confession and the Sisters hear her say, "Fifty times, Monsignor." The Bishop says that can't be in there as you are not supposed to hear what goes on in the confessional. Bishops will be Bishops. Then there is one thing he wants added, which I think is a good idea and will improve the book. It seems that before she died, the Sisters allowed Mary Ann to become a Tertiary and she was buried in the Dominican habit. The Sisters had thought it better to suppress that as no one under fifteen is supposed to be a Tertiary and they were afraid they would get in trouble at headquarters. But the Bishop thinks it ought to be in and that this was a case of *in extremis* so it would have been permissible. I told the Sisters to write it up and indicate where it should come and send it to me. I will send it on in a few days.

Sister Evangelist wanted to know what "a free editorial hand" meant and I told her it meant you all would improve the book some, so she is all for a free editorial hand.

She is the one you should write to . . . She is being transferred in February sometime and will not be Superior after that, so if you could get the contract to her as soon as you can so that she can sign it herself, that will be best. She has written to the Head in Hawthorne to find out if it will be all right for her to sign it. She wants it fixed so the money will go to the Atlanta home, but has to get that okayed at Hawthorne . . .

Suggest to her whatever you think is right for my share in it. My share will have to go through Elizabeth, but not theirs. I'll write to Elizabeth about it.

Would you like a picture of Mary Ann to go in the front of the book? They have plenty of them at *Jubilee* that you can see. I enclose one for you. There are a million others because they were always taking pictures of her.

I like the idea of the brochure on my book because all the good reviews are stuck off where nobody will ever see them. If you do get it up, I wish you would include Richard Gilman's remarks on it in the Christmas book issue of *Commonweal*.

I'd also like to talk to you sometime about getting *Wise Blood* back in print. I get letters from college libraries asking where it can be found. You said once that you all might be willing to put it in print if Harcourt wouldn't.

[P.S.] I think the galleys on the Mary Ann book should be sent to me as the Sisters don't even know what they are. If you would like to have their original manuscript for the person who is going to edit this, I can send it to you.

28 January 61

I enclose what I received from Sister Evangelist today—some changes suggested by the Bishop, and the part about Mary Ann becoming a tertiary. I leave that like she sent it. Their writing kills me, but maybe you all can do something with it up there . . .

Mary Ann's sister, Sue, wrote a poem about her. The Sisters have sent it to me and wonder if it couldn't be put in a supplement. I enclose it.

In the front of the book they had wanted a quotation from *The Merchant of Venice*, Act 5, Scene 1—"How far that little candle throws its beams, / So shines a good deed in a naughty world." I had left it off because I thought enough was enough, but

I told them I would let you know they wanted it and you would do what you thought best about it.

The latest title they have cooked up is *Brief Candle*. I think it is awful, and hope you will insist upon *A Memoir of Mary Ann*.

There is also enclosed a Declaration that is supposed to be in the front of the book somewhere.

I told them to get a statement from the Longs [parents of Mary Ann] that they did not object to anything in the book. They told Sr. Evangelist they'd write her one.

Sister Evangelist thinks the Bishop is disappointed because his funeral sermon wasn't used in full. I thought it was mighty redundant and didn't deserve to be used in full; however I enclose the whole thing and if you all want to use it, it'll be all right with the Bishop.

They issue bulletins to me every other day, but I hope this will be the last.

## To "A."

4 February 61

I don't think the dead are held to any vow of obedience. As long as he [Teilhard de Chardin] lived he was faithful to his Jesuit superiors but I think he must have figured that in death he would be a citizen of some other sphere and that the fate of his books with the Church would rest with the Lord. After reading both books, I doubt that his work will be put on the Index, though I think some of the people who latch upon his thought and distort it may cause certain propositions in it to be condemned. I think myself he was a great mystic. The second volume complements the first and makes you see that even if there were errors in his thought, there were none in his heart.

In the matter of conversion, I think you are thinking about the initial conversion. I am thinking possibly about the deepening of conversion. I don't think of conversion as being once and for all and that's that. I think once the process is begun and continues that you are continually turning inward toward God and away from your own egocentricity and that you have to see this selfish side of yourself in order to turn away from it. I measure God by everything that I am not. I begin with that. Maybe this depends on the person and is different for different people.

I can't get over the Mary Ann business. I told the Sisters that if that child was a saint, her first miracle would be getting a publisher for their book. And now the more I think about the way that book was written, the more convinced I am that it is a genuine miracle. Giroux wrote, "I read the story with a few misgivings which somehow are not important." And I guess that about sums it up. They have asked for a free editorial hand, so I am hoping this will improve the book a little.

I have been reading Mauriac's *Mémoires Intérieurs,* which when I finish it I am going to send to you to read what he says about Emily Brontë. He sounds so much like you he might be you. He also has some good things to say about Hawthorne. I shall claim to be the only living person who doesn't have a theory about Emily Brontë. I don't know anything about her except she lived on the moor. I don't know what a moor is but I should guess a piece of land that was desolate and damp. I read *Wuthering Heights* once but I am going to have to read it again to see why it fascinates you so.

The only thing for apostate priests to do is to be violently anti-Catholic and write books against the Church or go on the sawdust trail with "I was a Catholic priest but I was saved by the Bible," etc. Perhaps this man's heart couldn't be in that.

The pageant was such a success, they are thinking of putting it on every year. There is no wound, my girl; this is merely a gorgeous way to make money.

## To Ashley Brown

13 February 61

This is the story that came out of that potato festival clipping ["The Partridge Festival"]. I am a receptive depository for clippings. The latest I have got to add to my collection is one of a man who has just had Christ tattooed on his back. This is obviously for artistic and not religious purposes as he also has a tiger and panther heads and an eagle perched on a cannon.

I have just got through reading *I Choose to Die,* by B. Cheney based on Sam Davis, boy hero of the Confederacy. It has several places in it for choreography by J.Z. I like it all but the song and dance.

We have been vigorously celebrating Secession here—parade, pageant, pilgrimages, etc. I sat over the hole in the upholstery in the living-room sofa and shook the hands of all and sundry. About 500 people showed up. Lance Phillips (the Englishman whose house we went to for tea) wrote the pageant and oddly enough it was a great success. Everybody is falling around now trying to get the copyright out of him, so they can make this thing like the

Paul Green business in North Carolina. He is holding out for a rising percentage of the net profits, which is certainly what he should get. They spent $1000 for fireworks and $600 for floats, and would not pay him but $200 for the pageant.

Louise recently stuck an icepick in Shot but otherwise we go on our peaceful way around here.

## To Roslyn Barnes

13 February 61

I am an insidious fudge-eater when I can get it but I can seldom get it. However you must have enough to do without starting a confectionary. I certainly hope the job comes through. The place out there seems to have had everything you wanted. I think now you were right to follow your instinct and go out there and ignore the Emory business and all its money. But at the time I had my doubts.

I forgot my own missal at Mass the other day and had to read a paper one placed in the pew. The Latin in it had been translated to make it appealing to idiots, everything in baby-English, enough to turn your stomach. So many of these attempts to get the Mass nearer the participants are misdirected.

We have at last got us a little decent weather and the peacocks, mistaking the season, have got their tails up.

## To Maryat Lee

2/14/61

I am glad you got shut of Mlle. N. She lived up to my expectations. You should take a leaf out of the book of us novelists and run your own rat race. Whyn't you take a vacation in Milledgeville, a bird sanctuary?

Lance's pageant was such a smashing success that the Chamber of Commerce hopes to put it on during the season and make this another Wm'burg. The Civil War is just beginning to pay off its investment.

I have bought 100 shares of Keystone B and 100 shares of Thriftimart & I feel like a bloody capitalist.

Enclose a farce of mine ["The Partridge Festival"].

## To Cecil Dawkins

15 February 61

I'd have to see those stories again to really be able to tell you what I think, but I do think this: that if there is any doubt in your mind, which there seems to be, you should wait. I have been sorry that I let "A Stroke of Good Fortune" be in my collection. I don't guess it made too much difference, but I do have the sense that it is not up to the rest of them. And I haven't decided if I'll include the enclosed one in my next collection. I don't think you should let anybody make you do anything faster than you are ready to do it. If you have copies of those stories and want to send them to me, I'll read them again as they all are sort of foggy in my mind at this point. What happened to "Benny Ricco"? I remember liking that one and never heard that you had sold it . . .

We are expecting the photographer from *Holiday* to come tomorrow to take the peafowls' pictures. I am sure that the scoundrels will sulk or spread only in front of the garbage can or all go off in the woods until he leaves, and as my mother points out, there is nowhere on this place that you can take a picture without having some ramshackle out-building get in it. In addition I fully expect it to rain.

The other day I received a call from Tennille, Georgia. A vigorous-sounding individual says, "This is L.A. I have written a novel!" Never heard of him but that is not unusual. He asked if he and his wife could come to see me the next afternoon and discuss the problems of publication. Well, it turned out that [he] is 87 years old with a wife about 40 who calls him "Sweetheart." He is writing a book about "a modern woman." My mother asked what was a modern woman. "One without scruples," he says. He says, "Frankly, Miss O'Connor, this is a very sexy book. I've come to the conclusion that if you want to reach a wide audience you must include a lot of sexy features." They stayed the better part of the afternoon and he gave us his receipt for stuffing duck.

Madison Jones teaches at Auburn. He writes good books that receive absolutely no notice. He has all sorts of schemes for getting out of teaching, but so far none of them have paid off. Last spring I gave him some geese, as he said he would like to build up a goose trade, but all the geese died. He wants to try again this spring. A very funny man.

## To John Hawkes

3 March 61

The enclosed is some Southern hot air to help melt the snow up there. This is the kind of silly business that ensues when Southern writers get together before an audience. Also enclosed is a story of mine, lighter than I usually write, but which will provide a view of some more metamorphoses.

Thanks so much for your article on Edwin Honig's poetry, which I enjoyed, without knowing the poetry, for the way it was written. R.J. is reading it now and will doubtless have something intelligent to say about it. It made me want to read the poetry it described. Elizabeth Way wrote me that David and Edwin Honig were going to start a poetry magazine. Maybe I can subscribe and read some of it . . .

From what I gather, Andrew has been quite influenced by Caroline. He wrote a fine essay on her work, which appeared in the issue of *Critique* (U. of Minn.) devoted to her . . . As I have learned a great deal from her, I preserved more or less a respectful silence.

The sheriff's vision is not meant to be taken literally, but to be the Devil's eye view. And nobody is "redeemed." I am afraid that one of the great disadvantages of being known as a Catholic writer is that no one thinks you can lift the pen without trying to show somebody redeemed. To me, the old lady is the character whose position is right and the one who is right is usually the victim. If there is any question of a symbolic redemption, it would be through the old lady who brings Thomas face to face with his own evil—which is that of putting his own comfort before charity (however foolish). His doing that destroys the one person his comfort depended on, his mother. The sheriff's view is as the world will see it, not as it is. Sarah Ham is like Enoch and Bishop—the innocent character, always unpredictable and for whom the intelligent characters are in some measure responsible (responsible in the sense of looking after them). I am much interested in this sort of innocent person who sets the havoc in motion . . .

## To Maryat Lee

Friday [c. 20 March 61]

I too have been prone on my couch this week, a victim of the common cold.

I'm cheered you liked ["The Partridge Festival"] but I must have it back as I have nary other copy.

If you really want to read somebody, read Proust for pity's sake. You have to read all 7 volumes before you get to see what he's about.

I am falling out of my chair.

## To Cecil Dawkins

22 March 61

I have been a victim of the common cold, which I then shared with my mother and so we have both been hacking and hooping for some time, me to such an extent that I think I broke my rib again, but now we appear to be on top of them.

I think writing plays is all right if you don't care much whether or not you fail at it. I have a friend who has put her whole life and sanity into the proposition that she must succeed in the theatre. She writes very experimental things and though she is quite brilliant, I don't think she has much chance. It is apparently the toughest thing to crack. But if you just do it for fun and don't get intense about it, I should think it would be fine. You are very versatile (sp?) and might be able to sail right through with a success. If you could, there would be a lot of money in it, or so my friend tells me . . .

The Sisters were so grateful to me for getting their book a publisher that they have presented me with a portable television. I was of course bowled over. One of them had a brother who gave it to her to give me. They don't have money of their own. So me and ma have entered the twentieth century at last. I can now tell you all about Geritol, Pepto-Bismol, Anacin, Bufferin, any kind of soap or floor wax, etc. etc. Fortunately we can get one station which is an educational network and has some interesting things.

My nest-watching activities have begun as I have four geese setting.

## To Maryat Lee

26 March 61

Yesterday was my birthday and in the midst of it arrived a Waring Blendor. I am bowled over and under. You only can be the donor of this instrument which makes me speechless. Ah, now my jaw can rot at its leisure. I am at once attracted in the book by something called bourbon balls and if I succeed in producing any, I will send you a sample. Are you coming here for Easter? If so, you can hold some demonstrations. My parent is equally took with it . . . Incidentally, did you know it was my birthday?

No story has showed up so I presume you are typing it. I have just written one and sold it to NWW that will be out in October. It is called "Everything That Rises Must Converge" and touches on a certain topical issue in these parts and takes place on a bus. When I get an extra copy, I will send it to you. I am highly pleased with it . . .

The Sisters that I got their book published came down week before last and picked up the two peafowl they won from me on the bet. They wanted to give me something to remember them by; they said, what did I want, and I said I didn't want anything; that I would have no difficulty remembering them. They don't have any money of their own. The Superior called up and said, We've found what we're going to send you. In fact we've already got it. My brother gave it to me to give you—a portable television. So now we have a portable television. One of the first things I saw on it was your brother. We get the University station and he was on it telling the folks about the needs of women's colleges, etc. The television didn't do much for him. His face looked like it had been slicked down the middle and not put together right.

I am about to get onto those liquor balls, having bought the stuff to do it with. Be on lookout for small reeking box.

*A professor of English had sent Flannery the following letter: "I am writing as spokesman for three members of our department and some ninety university students in three classes who for a week now have been discussing your story 'A Good Man Is Hard to Find.' We have debated at length several possible interpretations, none of which fully satisfies us. In general we believe that the appearance of the Misfit is not 'real' in the same sense that the incidents of the first half of the story are real. Bailey, we believe, imagines the appearance of the Misfit, whose activities have been called to his attention on the night before the trip and again during the stopover at the roadside restaurant. Bailey, we further believe, identifies himself with the Misfit and so plays two roles in the imaginary last half of the story. But we cannot, after great effort, determine the point at which reality fades into illusion or reverie. Does the accident literally occur, or is it a part of Bailey's dream? Please believe me when I say we are not seeking an easy way out of our difficulty. We admire your story and have examined it with great care, but we are convinced that we are missing something important which you intended for us to grasp. We will all be very grateful if you comment on the interpretation which I have outlined above and if you will give us further comments about your intention in writing 'A Good Man Is Hard to Find.'"*

*She replied:*

## To a Professor of English

28 March 61

The interpretation of your ninety students and three teachers is fantastic and about as far from my intentions as it could get to be. If it were a legitimate interpretation, the story would be little more than a trick and its interest would be simply for abnormal psychology. I am not interested in abnormal psychology.

There is a change of tension from the first part of the story to the second where the Misfit enters, but this is no lessening of reality. This story is, of course, not meant to be realistic in the sense that it portrays the everyday doings of people in Georgia. It is stylized and its conventions are comic even though its meaning is serious.

Bailey's only importance is as the Grandmother's boy and the driver of the car. It is the Grandmother who first recognizes the Misfit and who is most concerned with him throughout. The story is a duel of sorts between the Grandmother and her superficial beliefs and the Misfit's more profoundly felt involvement with Christ's action which set the world off balance for him.

The meaning of a story should go on expanding for the reader the more he thinks about it, but meaning cannot be captured in an interpretation. If teachers are in the habit of approaching a story as if it were a research problem for which any answer is believable so long as it is not obvious, then I think students will never learn to enjoy fiction. Too much interpretation is certainly worse than too little, and where feeling for a story is absent, theory will not supply it.

My tone is not meant to be obnoxious. I am in a state of shock.

## To Roslyn Barnes

29 March 61

I appear to be behind in everything these days but I hope I am in time anyway to wish you a happy Easter. It seems to be Iowa's time to get flooded. I hope the Iowa river will not creep up the hill to your doorstep. I have six geese setting so my cup runneth over. I have also written & sold to *New World Writing* a story called "Everything That Rises Must Converge," which is a physical proposition that I found in Père Teilhard and am applying to a certain situation in the Southern states & indeed in all the world.

## To Louise and Tom Gossett

10 April 61

Like all good farm folk, we get up in the morning as soon as the first chicken cackles. Let us know if you can't have breakfast with us on the 3rd. and what time to expect you. We will be counting on it.

Congratulations on having finally got educated. Now you can regress at your leisure. I like that theory of the reclamation of the novel. I have just read a review of my book, long and damming, which says it don't give us hope and courage and that all novels should give us hope and courage. I think if the novel is to give us virtue the selection of hope and courage is rather arbitrary—why not charity, peace, patience, joy, benignity, long-suffering and fear of the Lord? Or faith? The fact of the matter is that the modern mind opposes courage to faith. It also demands that the novel provide us with gifts that only religion can give. I don't think the novel can offend against truth, but I think its truths are more particular than general. But this is a large subject and I ain't no aesthetician. Is your thesis ever going to be available for reading by the hoipaloi (sp?)?

My mother is getting ready to sell out the dairy and go into beef cows. We are being done in by the local moonshine. The staff is non compos mentis every weekend and she HAS HAD ENOUGH . . .

## To John Hawkes

20 April 61

I was terribly pleased to know that Lillian Hellman likes my stories. I had never thought of her even remotely as a person who would read them. It is always a revelation to find out the people who like and dislike them. It is another way of reading the stories.

The enclosed is a horrible little piece of correspondence which please return to me as I feel it deserves a place in my files, possibly just as a lesson to me. I am conscience-stricken that I answered the man in such a harsh fashion. At the time, the thought of this interpretation multiplied by 93 was too much for me, but there was no excuse for this rudeness. I hope that before I die I either mend my manners or have less occasion to employ them.

The divine is probably the sum of what Singleton [the mad old man in "The Partridge Festival"] lacks and thereby suggests, but as he stands I look on him as another comic instance of the diabolical. I think that perhaps for you the diabolical is the divine, but I am a Thomist three times removed and live amongst many distinctions. (A Thomist three times removed is one who doesn't read Latin or St. Thomas but gets it by osmosis.) Fallen spirits are of course still spirits, and I suppose the Devil teaches most of the lessons that lead to self-knowledge . . .

*To "A."*

13 May 61

. . . I have only one complaint to make about you, I see only one blot on your character. This is the way you wrap up packages. By the time I got into these books, my fingers were bleeding and my disposition was shot for the day. I wished all your sticky paper in hell. Pulease get yourself a ball of string, a simple ball of string, and the next time you have occasion to post me a book, tie it up, just tie it up.

I have read *The Severed Head* and am a fourth through *The Flight from the Enchanter* [both by Iris Murdoch]. I read *The Severed Head* without wanting to put it down, but when I got through I did not see that it added up to anything. In fact, I found it completely hollow and with the exception of Honor Klein all the characters seemed to me composed of so much wind. The psychiatrist and the wife had no reality at all that I could see and were just farcical props to bring on Honor. I wouldn't attempt to figure out what she's getting at. But if she writes another book I will certainly read it . . .

A letter from Cecil. I think she would really like to write an introduction to *Wise Blood*, she said if she had a name, she would suggest it. Of course, I don't give a hoot about the name and I am going to tell her that if she wants to write one, write it, but that I can't guarantee that Giroux would like it or want to use it. I imagine she could get it published elsewhere if he didn't.

## To Elizabeth Fenwick Way

17 May 61

Thanks for the invite. If I weren't doing so well right now, I might come up and consult him [Dr. Sprung, a Providence, R.I., lupus specialist] but I have been doing better these last six months than any time since I have had the stuff. According to Dr. Merrill, it is in a recessive stage. If I have a relapse and get bad off again, I'll consult Dr. Sprung probably. If you keep having that rash, I would go to see him if I were you because you don't have to come clear up the en-tire Atlantic coast to do it, Dr. Merrill tells me that they can control the lupus skin rash (when it is just the skin-type of lupus and not systemic lupus) entirely with ARALEN. If you haven't taken ARALEN yet, ask your doctor about it. I am taking it. It takes away your appetite for about six weeks when you start taking it but then your system gets adjusted to it. It's a brand name for chloroquine and is not expensive like cortisone. I hope to have some further information from Mrs. B. about the drug, get the name of it if possible. I am hesitant about showing her letters to the doctors here. Doctors always think anybody doing something they aren't is a quack; also they think all patients are idiots.

About a month ago I had cortisone and Novocaine injections in both hips. It was a big help while it lasted but it didn't last but about two weeks; however, I don't believe they have gone back to hurting as much as they did before I had the injections. With some people these injections will last months.

If you go to Dr. Sprung maybe he will take color pictures of your rash. That sounds like a European doctor. If you know any-body in Providence, you might see what they think of him or if they've ever heard of him.

I hope Harpers takes the book as well as loves it . . .

## To "A."

27 May 61

. . . After we had B.'s letter, we had a note from Fr. Paul saying that B. had written him and asked him to break the news to us (presumably gently, said Fr. Paul). He had an idea that this was because B. knew Regina didn't approve of exotic romances; he was much amused—as were we. Anyway, B. couldn't wait and wrote us himself. I wrote him back that Regina approved heartily & we hoped he'd bring the girl back alive. I hope he comes back alive himself.

Ashley lent me *The Sand Castle* some time ago so I have already done read it. You ought to write an article on Iris Murdoch and send it to *Commonweal*. They would be very interested in the angle you have been approaching it by. I sure wish you would. Your only difficulty with that would be writing it clearly and not crowding your ideas.

I had a very nice note about the *Jubilee* piece [on *Mary Ann*] from Dr. Karl Stern [author of *Pillar of Fire*] in Montreal, also one from a young lady in Iowa who had seen it and wanted to know what my fee would be to read twelve of her short stories . . .

Your enthusiasm inspired me to read *A High Wind in Jamaica* again myself, and I am reentranced.

## To Maryat Lee

31 May 61

Mrs. B. had Dr. Sprung write the name of the drug down on one of his subscription blanks for me. It is SUBTILTRYPTASIN and is made by a Dutch pharmaceutical company called DYK—JULDEN (as far as I could make out that name) at Konstanz, Germany. She says there are over 400 letters concerning certified cures at the University of Munich. He has translated a couple of them to try to interest a pharmaceutical company here. I imagine that publishing in a medical journal is just like publishing anywhere else. She says he speaks very broken English. Also she says he is a man who is incapable of pushing anything or himself. What I think is he don't even need to try now that she is behind it. I suggested she write the Lupus Foundation. After some time, during which I am sure they were busy investigating Dr. Sprung, they have written him asking for all the information he can give them. It seems that the President of the Nat'l Lupus Foundation has a daughter thirty years old who has had it ten years and is in a very bad way. I wouldn't be surprised if the Foundation doesn't get busy on it now and do some of their own research. I find it all very interesting.

My miracle shots lasted just about two weeks. I am meditating those steel hips daily . . .

Tarlite

## To "A."

We had an awful accident here Thursday. Shot was sucked into the hay baylor up to his elbows. It was some time before he could be got out and he is pretty badly damaged but lucky to be alive. It didn't break any of his bones, but tore out some big gaps of flesh and gave him several third-degree belt burns. Regina and Lon Cheney, who was here at the time, stayed with him until the mechanic could come to get him out of the machine and the doctor could come. Then they took him to the hospital in her car and the doctor says he will be in there for some time. Of course he was fooling with the motor on—something she has told him a thousand times not to do. We are used to minor crises but this was major . . .

You ain't convinced me that there should be an introduction to *Wise Blood,* particularly one that announces the religious significance of the book. I would want no more said about that than that the book is seen from the standpoint of orthodox Christianity. Anything else would be pretentious and would only draw on me more attention by people such as [critic Robert O.] Bowen. The fewer claims made for a book, the better chance it has to stand on its own feet. "Explanations" are repugnant to me and to send out a book with directions for its enjoyment is terrible. In the future, anybody who writes anything about me is going to have to read everything I have written in order to make legitimate criticism, even and particularly the Mary Ann piece. It is not as if this book is any longer going to be judged alone. The man in the street ain't going to read it at all, and other people who read it will not be able to read it as naively as before. If I write a note to the second edition, it will be very light and oblique. No claims & very few assertions.

If you ever can get at the Atlanta Public Liberry Walker Percy's book, *The Moviegoer,* I wish you would check it out and send it to me. This is probably one we should both read . . .

Catharine Carver sent me this interview from the *Paris Review.* It's full of meat where most of them are not. Poor Cal [Lowell] is back in the hospital or was the last time I heard . . .

## To Ashley Brown

The Cheneys were here for a couple of days last week and announced that you were spending the summer in Columbia. I had thought you would have long since left for foreign parts. We had a crisis as usual while they were here . . .

A friend of mine in from Princeton tells Caroline is stuck with a boarder now who is a total alcoholic and a complete wreck and that she has to take care of him, coax him to eat, pick him up out of her pansy bed, see that he is met at the railroad station etc. . . . The last I heard from her she had taken him to a meeting of Alcoholics Anonymous which she had enjoyed very much but he had not . . .

I read Iris Murdoch's last novel and was fascinated as usual but as usual didn't know what it was all about. The next thing I want to read is Walker Percy's . . .

On the television I particularly enjoy the commercials. My favorite is the one for Tube Rose Snuff. There is one for The Loan Arranger which Regina cannot see without comment.

## To Roslyn Barnes

17 June 61

Can you tell me if the statement: "everything that rises must converge" is a true proposition in physics? I can easily see its moral, historical and evolutionary significance, but I want to know if it is also a correct physical statement. You are the only scientist I am acquainted with . . .

## To John Hawkes

22 June 61

. . . I don't think much of the traditional association of insanity with the Divine. That's for romantics. Quincy State Hospital is actually two miles out of Milledgeville, the same only bigger. A five-minute stroll through the grounds would dampen any enthusiasm you might have for the traditional association. I think you think I'm my own Mr. Parish, but actually I don't think we read Singleton so differently. I use Divine in the traditional Christian sense of the Holy and you don't. From that standpoint the old man is not divine. He's a lecherous old nut and stands for his own reality against the young people's absurd notions of him, and like you, I am all for Singleton in this, devil though I rightly consider him to be. He's one of those devils who go about piercing pretensions, not the devil who goes about like a roaring lion seeking whom he may devour. There is a hierarchy of devils surely . . .

Farrar, Straus have bought *Wise Blood* and are going to bring it out again and I am trying, unsuccessfully, to make myself write a foreword or note to the second edition or something like that, but I find I have nothing whatsoever to say about it . . .

## To Maryat Lee

6/24/61

You are probably right not to proceed until you see if Dr. Sprung really wants it. Deen Hood (the Florida girl) [who also had lupus] asked somebody she knew in Providence about Dr. Sprung. This person said he was regarded as a "wierdo." I fancy that anyone doing anything the least different & not having curtains in his office would be enough to attract that label. A term of honor like as not.

I thought I was going to have more shots this week but the doctor is on his vacation & I can't go until July 26. At that time I am going to make my assault about the [hip] operation, get it done this summer . . .

The [*New World Writing*] person in Phila. is probably my friend Catharine Carver. She's brighter than the lot of them put together. Listen to anything she has to say. Excelsior.

## To Marion Montgomery

9 July 61

I think your book [*The Wandering of Desire*] is wonderful, 100% solid and alive throughout. The Southern writer can outwrite anybody in the country because he has the Bible and a little history, but you've got more of both than most and a splendid gift besides. It all adds up to a really fine novel and I'll be proud to say the same or something similar to Miss Elizabeth Laurence who sent me the galleys. All I can say to you is you've done it.

## To Cecil Dawkins

17 July 61

. . . It is bad not to be able to write when you want to. I know the feeling and sometimes I feel I have written myself out and it's sheer drudgery. We have just had a weekend of Caroline. She read a story that I have been working on and pointed out to me how it was completely undramatic and a million other things that I could have seen myself if I had had the energy. It all goes to show that you can know something in your head and still not carry it out. I was writing the story in a hurry to see if I had a story to write. Now it'll probably take me three months to really dramatize the thing. So much of my trouble is laziness, not physical laziness so much as mental, not taking the trouble to think how a thing ought to be dramatized. I have written so many stories without thinking that when I have to think about one, it is painful. Caroline says I have been writing too many essays and it is affecting my style. Well I ain't going to write no more essays. I hope you get going soon. Don't socialize too much.

The Sisters' book [*A Memoir of Mary Ann*] is going to be a runaway. *Good Housekeeping* is going to feature it in their Christmas issue. They paid $4,500. I get $1,125 of that . . .

I have decided I'm not going to write an introduction to *Wise Blood*. The more I thought about it, the more repulsive the idea seemed to me.

Have you read *Where Angels Fear to Tread* of Forster's? *Passage to India* is still my favorite.

We have sold our dairy herd and are now in the beef bidnis. We went up the country a piece and bought up a purebred Shorthorn bull.


## To "A."

22 July 61

*Mary Ann* has now been bought by Burns & Oates of London. They asked permission to change the title to *The Death of a Child* and I persuaded the Sisters to give it. It is almost comical how speedily it is proceeding, this project of the Lord's. I feel it is that.

We went to the bone doctor Thursday and also the other one. The bone man would have been happy to give me a steel ball in both hips . . . The other one said no, I couldn't have it; so that is the end of that and I am stuck with what I got, which is all right. What you know you can't get rid of don't worry you as much as what you think you might get rid of. Old Warner (the bone man) could fix up that shoulder of yours right off with a little cortisone and Novocaine.

Ashley and Caroline were strenuous as usual. I had a story that I had written a first draft sort of on and Caroline thought as usual that it wasn't dramatic enough (and she was right) and told me all the things that I tell you when I read one of yours.

She did think the structure was good and the situation. All I got to do is write the story. This one is called "The Lame Shall Enter First."

Last week Houghton Mifflin sent me a book called *Clock Without Hands* by Carson McCullers. This long-awaited-by-the-faithful book will come out in September. I believe it is the worst book I have ever read. It is incredible. If you want to read it, I will send it to you. It must signal the complete disintegration of this woman's talent. I have forgotten how the other three were, but they were at least respectable from the writing standpoint . . .


## To Roslyn Barnes

26 July 61

I have been wanting to write and thank you for some time for writing me about the rising-converging business, but we have had one thing and another going on and I haven't done much that I wanted to. Anyway, what you said was helpful and follows my own line of thought on the subject, uneducated as that is.

I'll be delighted to recommend you for PAVLA [Papal Auxiliary Volunteers for Latin America] and I think you are wise to do something like this before you even think about becoming a Sister. And also wise to get the debts paid up. When people lend you money for your education, they are not very sympathetic to your becoming a missionary to any Indians before they get their money back. Not many people will understand your wanting to do this anyway—around here I mean—but I think it is fine . . .


## To "A."

5 August 61

That paperbook gallery has always been prompt enough with me. When they haven't had the book in stock, they've sent a slip to say it'll come later. I'd drop them a card if it was me.

We have had several ecstatic postcards from B. and I suppose you have had the same and everybody he knows in the 50 states. Ours detail the Church and the day (August 3) and his satisfaction with the lady and presumably her satisfaction with him. He says he is submitting gladly to the "capture"—as if the girl has indeed won a treasure. Well I hope she has and visa vussuh.

[Ford Madox] Ford's estimate of Caroline may have something to do with the fact that he taught her a great deal of what she knows and they were great friends. She is always quoting him on what he said about fiction. He raised up a disciple in her, suitable to his taste. I like *The Good Soldier,* but I couldn't read the Tietjens series. Also I don't like Ford's biography of Conrad, which Ashley sent me a secondhand copy of from England last year.

The latest word from Carol Johnson was that she was going through Greece on the back of some boy's motorbike. He wanted her to go to Israel with him but apparently she declined. I get cards from her all the time, about where she is and what she has seen and what she is reading and what she has written. I ain't got around to answering any of these but I suppose I will have to once she gets to Liverpool and stays put for a while . . .

Never read Spengler and never read *Mirror in the Roadway,* but I reckon I must read both sooner or later . . .

There is a lot of interest in Murdoch and I should think your article would go in *Commonweal* or possibly *Thought.*

## To Maryat Lee

Thursday [August 1961]
We are not coming to New York. The good Foundation cancelled the conference because so many people were in Europe, etc. That suits me fine as I was not looking forward to the trip.

This basophil business is interesting. The enclosed letter send back to me. Dr. Sprung's letter merely told him where he could get the stuff. I daresay by the time I may need Subtytriptsin old Merrill will know all about it.

You shouldn't take thyroid pills on your own advice. That is bad bidnis. Well, happy change if that is it.

I am writing a longish story in the morning & receiving on the front porch in the afternoon. Did you see the peacock article & picture in the Sept. *Holiday.* They changed the title to something stupid & cut out a necessary paragraph but otherwise it is unmauled. The picture is splendid.

## To "A."

19 August 61
Mama says did you notice that Billy's invitations said August 26 whereas he was married on the 3rd? We don't get it. He wrote us a card from Rhodes where they are enjoying the wedding trip and said the "two weddings were splendid, the Orthodox very beau-

tiful." I can just see Billy glorying in this dramatic ceremony twice . . .

Shot is still in the hospital. What he will be able to do when he gets out is a moot question. He has had his skin grafts so he should not be in there much longer. He don't have much use of his left arm, but it's possible that it will improve in time.

The Catholic Digest Book Club has taken the *Mary Ann* book. I don't know whether the Catholic Digest Book Club digests its books or leaves it to the reader to digest them. Anyway, we are going to reach the pious flotsam and jetsam if nobody else. The publication date is December 7th but the books will be sent to reviewers October 20. I am making up a list of reviewers for them to send books to and will include you on it . . .

## To Maryat Lee

25 August 61

You have even less sense than *I* gave you credit for. Nobody but a dope would prescribe for himself in the case of repeated sweats and general weakness. Have you had a blood count? Have you had a urinanalysis? Have you had your bloody head examined? When I was nearly dead with lupus I had these sweats. They are a sign of serious chemical imbalance. If you have bat brains you will go to a doctor—a good one—and quit messing around & experimenting with pills you know nothing about. Or come here and let Fancher do it. Anyway you are just playing with the health you've got & at this rate you won't have it long.

[P.S.] I have found a pair of swans cheap ($65) because the female is blind in one eye. Expect them to arrive next week.

## To Thomas Stritch

14 September 61

. . . You ought to see my swans. They are as moth-eaten a pair as you ever laid eyes on, but I am well pleased and expect them to improve under my supervision. They snort and hiss but are very slow on their feet and don't attempt to go anywhere but from the feed bucket to the water trough. This reminds me to tell you that if you do manage to cook up anything at Notre Dame, please also cook up a way to get me there from Chicago short of the airplane. I am sufficiently decrepit now to have retired myself from any but the simplest way of getting anywhere. But the way it looks to me, nobody will be travelling in May. We talk about the shelter and put it in a different place every day and haven't put it anywhere yet. And at night I dream of radiated bulls and peacocks and swans. But then, the Lord spared Nineveh where there were over a hundred and twenty thousand persons who didn't know their left hand from their right, and many beasts, so maybe there is a precedent for us to be spared too.

I don't know any new German theologians. All I know is Guardini and Adam and I reckon you know them—could hardly have escaped it. I'm much taken, though, with Père Teilhard. I don't understand the scientific end of it or the philosophical but even when you don't know those things, the man comes through. He was alive to everything there is to be alive to and in the right way. I've even taken a little from him—"Everything That Rises Must Converge" and am going to put it on my next collection of stories . . .


## To "A."

16 September 61

I am wondering if Beckett on Proust arrived. I'm sure I sent it, a couple of days, I think, after the *Critique*.

Next weekend will be peachy and we will meet you at the rural mailbox and reserve you a seat Sunday amongst the nail kegs.

Shot has been restored to us and our troubles have begun. He can't do anything yet and so he sits and decides what he is going to do with the wealth he has accumulated from his accident. This is a very demoralizing situation. A wealthy sitting Negro.

I am going to keep the swans in the back yard until they produce offspring. Then I am going to retire the parents to the pond and bring up the young ones myself. They seem very content to sit on the grass and show no disposition to walk anywhere. We may dig them a pool in the back yard, but I don't know. They snort and hiss but are really quite timid.

I would like to see that D. S. Savage book. Don't bother to mail it, just bring it when you come. The thing I am writing now is surely going to convince Jack that I am of the Devil's party. It is out of hand right now but I am hoping I can bring it into line. It is a composite of all the eccentricities of my writing and for this reason may not be any good, maybe almost a parody. But what you start, you ought to carry through and if it is no good, I don't have to publish it. I am thinking of changing the title to "The Lame

Will Carry Off the Prey." Anyway that analysis of yours about why Jack argues the way he does sounds pretty right to me. Entirely subjective. He says the artist leaves the herd and so becomes "evil." But whose eyes is he using here? The eyes of the herd. Abraham left the herd and did not become evil. Nuts.

Are we going to be seeing B. and Anna Magnani or what? We haven't heard from him, but I can't imagine him making anything but a triumphal tour of his journey to Mobile.

30 September 61

We sure will enjoy that candy and you sure shouldn't have sent it to us. We'll also enjoy the rum, and I hope you'll come again before it is gone. Louise came down from upstairs Monday and said, "Miss A. ain't slep in the bed." Regina asked her where she thought you had slept if you hadn't slept in the bed. She said she didn't know but you hadn't slep in the bed. She said maybe you slep on the flo. She said them sheets wasn't used. Regina has not convinced her yet that you slept in the bed. You will have to untangle this with her yourself the next time you come.

Since the Proust didn't come, I am worried that you may not get the library book. I know you don't want it insured so I will send it plain but with fear and trembling. And it was always me had this confidence in the Post Office Department. I'll send it Monday or Tuesday. I like it.

Mr. Coindreau said he put it in a kind of low argot, but perhaps it's just as well I don't know. As I think I recollect he didn't make the connection between the name Onnie Jay Holy and the Holy Church of Christ Without Christ. There are probably other things.

The Communist world sprouts from our sins of omission. The enclosed I haven't read myself but thought you would like to beinst this is within your present train of mind. You ought to write an article on this stuff you are delving into and send it somewhere . . .

The lady from *Good Housekeeping* told the Sisters that their book was very well written. They went down and took some pictures of them and are going to have a picture of Sister Evangelist as the "moving light" behind the book, which she certainly is, but she is going to be ready to kill them all for sending her picture . . .

14 October 61

Louise has been drunk for the past two Mondays. The first Monday, Regina was fooling around upstairs and found the dollar you left her, so she took it down and debated would she wait and give it to her when she was sober. However, she gave it to her at once. Louise didn't take it in for about an hour, then it penetrated the fog and she was all effusions. She is impossible when she is drunk, she insisted on polishing the sink with silver polish.

I sort of distrust anybody's defining what the novel is or even isn't. I am afraid somebody would define me out of it. People have to use it for what they have to use it for, Hemingway had to test his manhood with it and V. Woolf had to make it a laboratory, and A. Huxley a place to give lectures in. Given themselves I don't suppose any of them could have written any other way. You can criticize what they had to do with it, but you've got to leave the form vague enough to include them in it.

I received of all things two books from Dr. S. this week. One is Alan Watts' *Myth and Ritual in Christianity* which I gather is sort of his current Bible, and the other is a book I already have called *God and the Unconscious*, by a Dominican, Victor White, which he is apparently just discovering. He announces he will stop by on his way home at Christmas to see how I like the Watts, so I suppose that means I'll have to read it. I think it is full of psychological explanations of dogmas and rituals, which requires that he ignore the accepted meanings of them.

We had a letter from B., indicating that everything is hunky-dory and she is a pretty good cook and he is planning to start on his Ph.D., so maybe she is serving as a kind of anchor and will really be good for him. He'll have to quit flitting and get down to business.

A letter from Giroux says they are going to re-issue *Wise Blood* for the summer-fall season of next year and are there any corrections I would like to make. I can't even make myself read the thing again. I am just going to say NO there ain't any. You can't rewrite something you wrote ten years ago. Also there will be no introduction, as I can't even read the book, I sure can't write an introduction.

*About this time, Flannery's friend wrote that she had reached the conclusion that she could no longer remain in the Church. Their friendship was of course not endangered, but Flannery was greatly distressed.*

28 October 61

I don't know anything that could grieve us here like this news. I know that what you do you do because you think it is right, and I don't think any the less of you outside the Church than in it, but what is painful is the realization that this means a narrowing of life for you and a lessening of the desire for life. Faith is a gift, but the will has a great deal to do with it. The loss of it is basically a failure of appetite, assisted by sterile intellect. Some people when they lose their faith in Christ, substitute a swollen faith in themselves. I think you are too honest for that, that you never had much faith in yourself in the first place and that now that you don't believe in Christ, you will believe even less in yourself; which in itself is regrettable. But let me tell you this: faith comes and goes. It rises and falls like the tides of an invisible ocean. If it is presumptuous to think that faith will stay with you forever, it is just as presumptuous to think that unbelief will. Leaving the Church is not the solution, but since you think it is, all I can suggest to you, as your one-time sponsor, is that if you find in yourself the least return of a desire for faith, to go back to the Church with a light heart and without the conscience-raking to which you are probably subject. Subtlety is the curse of man. It is not found in the deity.

Now about the *Mary Ann* book—of course I want you to review it . . . if you can still say the same things about Mary Ann and the Sisters. But do not mention the introduction. The introduction is about the things that hold us fast in Christ when Christ is taken to be divine. It is worthless if it is not true.

We hear, via the grapevine, that Shot is going to sue us. Jack says, "I ain't so dumb, Miss, some nigger is putting him up to that." Shot hasn't said anything about it himself but he avoids us; sleeps all day and prowls all night. Regina consulted the insurance man and he said Shot couldn't sue because he had accepted the compensation insurance . . .

Cecil was going to try to meet me at Marillac but a letter from the Sister says the place is not open for the public because they are all nuns. So I reckon I won't see her. She can't make herself write, but the girl she lives with, who has no particular interest in it, sat down last summer and completed a novel in two months, and according to Cecil, it is a good one.


*To Maryat Lee*

3 Nov 61

. . . I can't read your letters very good but I gathered that you were suffering from exhaustion & weren't doing anything but rebuilding pianos & comparing the Synoptic Gospels & moving your mother over the mountains to give yrself a good rest. If you need any advice about resting, ask a professional rester like me.

Read my story ["Everything That Rises Must Converge"] in *NWW* 19.

Why don't you go back to NYC by way of Georgia?

Tartot

## To "A."

11 November 61

Your letter didn't come until Tuesday and when I didn't hear from you as usual on Monday, I thought, she's thrown out the Church and now she's going to throw me out with it. I was going to wait until Wednesday and issue a vigorous protest. I'm glad I didn't have to. I hadn't meant to imply that you felt any guilt over leaving. I presumed that if you had felt that, you wouldn't have left. I think your idea of why you left is ingenious. I am glad the Church has given you the ability to look at yourself and like yourself as you are. The natural comes before the supernatural and that is perhaps the first step toward finding the Church again. Then you will wonder why it was necessary to look at yourself or like or dislike yourself at all. You will have found Christ when you are concerned with other people's sufferings and not your own.

I have been having some correspondence with Andrew Lytle who has asked Jack [Hawkes], of all people, to write an article about my stories for the *Sewanee*. His idea about Jack surprised me. He said he had tremendous talent but wasn't concrete enough. He said he had just had to reject a story of Jack's because the evil in it was general; and evil, he says, is never general.

I enjoyed St. Louis. In fact it was quite an experience and I found more understanding of *The Violent Bear It Away* there than anywhere else. They all insisted that they had had the same experience as Tarwater and therefore they understood it. Their writing teacher is a Sr. Mariella Gable, whom I had heard of before. When I was in Minnesota last year one of the Sisters there told me that she had taught *The Catcher in the Rye* in her high school and parents had complained and the Bishop had told her to quit and she defended her position and was consequently sent to some outpost in the Dakotas. Anyway here she was here and in good odor. A fan of Iris Murdoch's.

I would like a full report on the representative of the ancient Greeks and of her Conway consort. I guess we will have to wait until Christmas for our own view . . .

I have just had a letter from a lady in Maryland who says her peafowl do not eat flowers and that if I want to see the article she wrote about peafowl, "Juno's Bird," published in the Garden Club annual, she will send it to me. I am writing her to send it at once.

## To Caroline Gordon Tate

16 November 61

Yesterday we went to the [Conyers] monastery for dinner and I met your friend Fr. Charles. We took two of our Protestant friends and as a surprise the Abbot invited my cousin, Msgr. O'Connor. I hadn't seen him in thirty years. He was an actor before he became a priest and afterward taught Sacred Oratory at the Catholic University for many years. It was quite a gathering. Afterwards we went to see the Church—which is unbelievable—and there was Fr. Charles. Apparently all the young monks are very excited about those records you are getting for them. He said you couldn't imagine how much it meant to them. He was eager to talk of course but didn't get too much of a chance. He said he heard a lot from Walker Percy, and that your letters meant a great deal to him. Fr. Paul was away getting a kiln. They are going to start doing pottery . . .

I have about finished that story ["The Lame Shall Enter First"] you saw a first draft of when you were here and I think you would approve of it now, but I am not going to afflict you with it because I know you have a million things to do.

We have decided that my swans are Polish swans because they have such even dispositions. I will be able to tell when they hatch. If they are Polish, they will be white; if mute, grey.

You said you wanted a picture of me and I enclose same. I had to have these taken. All teeth and spectacles.

## To "A."

25 November 61

Oh dear. However I expressed it, it had not occurred to me that you didn't feel for people. I wasn't thinking of feeling. I was thinking of something a good deal more radical. I don't really think it's too important what your feelings are. I doubt if even Miss Nancy and her strings deserves the feeling you lavish on her. People's suffering tears us up now in a way that in a healthier age it did not. And of course everybody weeps over loneliness. It is practically a disease. The kind of concern I mean is a doing, not a feeling, and it is the result of a grace which neither you nor I nor Elizabeth Bishop in the remotest sense possesses, but which Sister Evangelist, for example, does. It doesn't have to be associated with religious; I am just trying to isolate this kind of abandonment of self which is the result of sanctifying grace.

I see that I was wrong in my speculation that you would now have even less confidence in yourself. You have more, of course. Faith is blindness and now you can see. Faith is an over-reaching; now what you reach for is within your grasp. I think you are right to take off six months and I think that you will be able now to do anything you want—the novel or criticism or whatever you set your hand to, and believe me, nobody will rejoice in this like I will —not the heresy but in the success. Send me the Murdoch things. I don't know anything about her but I can at least tell you what I think about how it is written.

This has been one hellish week here. Thanksgiving began to be celebrated by the staff on Sat. 18th. On Monday Louise's niece, Shirley, turned up with a baby, which meant that Louise's mamma, Camilla, age 100, had to be sent out here to stay with Louise. The old woman and Shirley slept in the same bed and there wasn't but one so the baby had to have Camilla's half . . . When sober, [Louise] just wrings her hands and says, "What I going to do with that ole woman—mean and hateful as she can be." Regina asked her how Shirley liked the baby and she said, "She's just crazy about it—big ole black ugly thing."

I don't know what Andrew means by concrete in Jack's case but probably not what you are thinking because he admires *The Turn of the Screw*. He would probably be interested in your piece on Jack.

## To John Hawkes

28 November 61

I have been fixing to write you ever since last summer when we saw the goat man.* We went up to north Georgia to buy a bull and when we were somewhere above Conyers we saw up ahead a pile of rubble some eight feet high on the side of the road. When we got about fifty feet from it, we could begin to make out that

---

* *The founder of the Free Thinking Christian Mission, a wandering witness who traveled with a cart and a clutch of goats.*

some of the rubble was distributed around something like a cart and that some of it was alive. Then we began to make out the goats. We stopped in front of it and looked back. About half the goats were asleep, venerable and exhausted, in a kind of heap. I didn't see Chess. Then my mother located an arm around the neck of one of the goats. We also saw a knee. The old man was lying on the road, asleep amongst them, but we never located his face.

That is wonderful about the new baby. I can't equal that but I do have some new additions to my ménage. For the last few years I have been hunting a pair of swans that I could afford. Swans cost $250 a pair and that was beyond me. My friend in Florida, the one I wrote you about once, took upon herself to comb Florida for cheap swans. What she sets out to do, she does . . . So now I am the owner of a one-eyed swan and her consort. They are Polish, or immutable, swans and very tractable and I radiate satisfaction every time I look at them.

I had brief notes from Andrew [Lytle] a couple of times lately. In fact he has a story of mine but I haven't heard from him whether he's going to use it or not. He said he had asked you to write an article about my fiction and that if he used my story I might want to send it to you. If he does take it and you write an article and want to see the story ["The Lame Shall Enter First"], I'll send it. It's about one of Tarwater's terrible cousins, a lad named Rufus Johnson, and it will add fuel to your theory though not legitimately I think.

You haven't convinced me that I write with the Devil's will or belong in the romantic tradition and I'm prepared to argue some more with you on this if I can remember where we left off at. I think the reason we can't agree on this is because there is a difference in our two devils. My Devil has a name, a history and a definite plan. His name is Lucifer, he's a fallen angel, his sin is pride, and his aim is the destruction of the Divine plan. Now I judge that your Devil is co-equal to God, not his creature; that pride is his virtue, not his sin; and that his aim is not to destroy the Divine plan because there isn't any Divine plan to destroy. My Devil is objective and yours is subjective. You say one becomes "evil" when one leaves the herd. I say that depends entirely on what the herd is doing.

The herd has been known to be right, in which case the one who leaves it is doing evil. When the herd is wrong, the one who leaves it is not doing evil but the right thing. If I remember rightly, you put that word, evil, in quotation marks which means the standards you judge it by there are relative; in fact you would be looking at it there with the eyes of the herd.

I think I would admit to writing what Hawthorne called "romances," but I don't think that has anything to do with the romantic mentality. Hawthorne interests me considerably. I feel more of a kinship with him than with any other American, though some of what he wrote I can't make myself read through to the end.

I didn't write the note to *Wise Blood*. I just let it go as is. I thought here I am wasting my time saying what I've written when I've already written it and I could be writing something else. I couldn't hope to convince anybody anyway. A friend of mine wrote me that he had read a review in one of the university magazines of *The Violent Bear etc.* that said that since the seeds that had opened one at a time in Tarwater's blood were put there in the first place by the great uncle that the book was about homosexual incest. When you have a generation of students who are being taught to think like that, there's nothing to do but wait for another generation to come along and hope it won't be worse . . .

I've introduced *The Lime Twig* to several people and they're all enthusiastic. Somebody has gone off with my copy now. I hope you are at another one.


## To "A."

9 December 61

Just as well maybe that you ditch the paper at least until you really start being yourself. When I read it I said to myself: all she's doing now is trying to be Iris Murdoch. And your last letter only confirms this. Iris writes novels, she don't reduce things to ideas, therefore you won't either. But if anybody in God's creation was born with the brain to reduce the concrete to ideas, it is you. It is a gift and it's yours, but now you are going to put the lid on it. I daresay you can write novels too, but it is not as predominant a gift with you as the other. You are going to be intellectualizing all over the house and yard until your grave receives you. Right now you are confusing a personal psychological revolution with the eternal truth.

Many truths are represented by Iris Murdoch but that her truth and her morality are superior to the teachings of the Church I disbelieve—but then that is all you could expect of me. What I do wonder at is that you were in the Church five years and came out with such a poor understanding of what the Church teaches—that you confuse self-abandonment in the Christian sense with a refusal to be yourself, with self-torture, and suggest that it implies a scorn of God. Accepting oneself does not preclude an attempt to become better. It is, in fact, primary to that effort as the Church has always taught. Self-torture is abnormal; asceticism is not.

As for the success, my tongue was not in my cheek. Success means *being heard* and don't stand there and tell me you are indifferent to being heard. Everything about you screams to be heard. You may write for the joy of it, but the act of writing is not complete in itself. It has its end in its audience. Writing is a good example of self-abandonment. I never completely forget myself except when I am writing and I am never more completely myself than when I am writing. It is the same with Christian self-abandonment. The great difference between Christianity and the Eastern religions is the Christian insistence on the fulfillment of the individual person . . .

The M.'s [white farm help] finally moved Sunday. The old lady has been staying here while he worked in Eatonton and got the house up there ready. Louise was drunk when they took off and jumped in the cab of the truck with [the father and mother] and the two German police dogs (which when sober she is terrified of) and drove off with them. She returned two days later and could give no clear account of herself. Regina says it is a case of the Two Faces of Louise.

Some friends of mine in Texas wrote me that a friend of theirs went into a bookstore looking for a paperback copy of *A Good Man*. The clerk said, "We don't have that one but we have another by that author, called *The Bear That Ran Away With It*. I foresee the trouble I am going to have with "Everything That Rises Must Converge"—"Every Rabbit That Rises Is a Sage."

14 December 61

. . . We agree with you 100% about Jenny [Sessions]. They spent Monday and Monday night with us. Even Regina, who don't go in for the exotic, was completely convinced that this was a very fine girl and a very fine girl for Billy . . . Well we can all be very happy over that marriage.

The girl that lives with Cecil sent me her novel. It's what I call a prairie novel—you go through life with the woman on the prairie and nothing happens but there is a sense of time and space. It's well written but so low-keyed and even-toned that I am at a loss what to say about it. It's somehow readable though undramatic and rather dull. Totally opposite from Cecil, but at the same time sensitive. It's easy to see why she and Cecil get along.

Dr. Spivey arrived while Billy and Jenny were here and he was at his most hilarious, which entertained them and entertained him and kept me from having to entertain either of them. He was full of *La Dolce Vita,* which he went to see, taking someone with him to tell him what was going on, as he still suffers from psychosomatic blindness. The doctors have told him there is absolutely nothing wrong with his eyes, which delights him as it confirms all his theories. He thought it was a great movie. Have you seen it?

Cheers and more cheers for this book you sent us and Merry Christmas if you get this before & Happy New Year if you get it afterwards.

## To John Lynch

31 Dec. 61

I was cheered to hear from you and know you are still liking New England and I know the new baby will be a joy to you even so.

I make out as usual. This fall I acquired a pair of swans and I plan to become as great an authority on swans as I now am on peacocks.

If you all ever visit the South, I hope you come to see me and bring your seven children to visit my personal zoo.

A good new year to you and Gunny.

[P.S.] The Fitzgeralds have bought a farm in Perugia. Doubt if the U.S. will see them again.

## To Cecil Dawkins

10 January 62

I was cheered to hear from you at length. You seem to be sick a lot and I was somewhat concerned. I daresay you have the writer's stomach. I don't know no remedy.

I'll tell you what's with "A.," why all the exhilaration. She has left the Church. Those are the signs of release. She's high as a kite and all on pure air. This conversion was achieved by Miss Iris Murdoch, as you could doubtless see by that paper. [She] now sees through everything and loves everything and is a bundle of feelings of empathy for everything. She doesn't believe any longer that Christ is God and so she has found that he is "beautiful! beautiful!" Everything is in the eeeek eeek eureka stage. The effect of all this on me is pretty sick-making but I manage to keep my mouth shut. I even have restrained myself from telling her that if

Christ wasn't God he was merely pathetic, not beautiful. And such restraint for me is something! She is now against all intellectualism. She thinks she's at last discovered how to be herself and has at last accepted herself. She says she's always tried to be somebody else because she hated herself, but now she can be herself. It's as plain as the nose on her face that now she's being Iris Murdoch, but it is only plain to me, not her. What I am afraid of is that the reaction is going to set in in a couple of months, or maybe not that soon, but sometime, and when it does BANG. Everything runs to extremes with her as you can see . . . All I'm praying is that she'll come back to earth gradually so she won't realize the drop so much. You keep saying sane things to her. She'll take them from you where she won't from me right now, because she thinks all I see in it is the Church . . .

I have been writing on this same story ["The Lame Shall Enter First"] since the middle of last summer and I can't get it to suit me although Andrew Lytle has already said he'll take it for the summer issue of the *Sewanee* where he also plans to have a couple of essays on my fiction. I'll just keep on sweating, I guess. I have staring me in the face a lecture at North Carolina State College and one at Converse College in April and one in Chicago in May and I've got to write them and I've got to finish this story first and so I feel considerable pushed.

I'm real cheered to hear you are at it with vigor again. It is always a great temptation to write essays when you are writing fiction. I find it is a greater temptation the longer you write too. I have to watch it all the time. I also have to watch now a tendency to be too omniscient and not let things come enough through the characters.

The swans have learned to go and come from the pond now, and we have a goose who chases automobiles. I sure wish you all had come down here, but maybe next summer you can, and see all these wonders . . .


*To Ashley Brown*

12 January 62

I am really obliged to you for *The Moviegoer* and now I want to take my time and read it. I'm also obliged (and forgot to tell you so) for that passage from the *Purgatorio* [Canto XI]. It may well come in handy sooner or later, though I have more or less got the Sweet Briar thing out of the way, and now I'm trying to write an introduction to a reading of "A Good Man" that I am going to do at the University of Georgia. After this, I'm going to quit talking.

Lon spent a couple of days here this week. He thinks he'll write a piece about J. Hawkes' piece. We went through it, line for line, and there are some quite wild things in it, though he tries hard to cover his tracks ; . . .

Have you ever read a novel by Albert Guérard? Apparently he has written a good many. He sent me one suitably inscribed just before Christmas. He calls it a "comic" novel. I don't know precisely what to make of it, but I am faced with writing him a letter about it.

## To "A."

13 January 62

It seems we narrowly missed a visit from Cecil and Betty . . . Anyway, they will probably come in the summer. Cecil appears to be on the beam again as a result of the trip. In my opinion Cecil needs to live in the dear old dirty Southland and have more contact with the things she hates.

Louise's mama died last Sunday. The funeral will be this Sunday, conducted by People's Undertaking Parlor. I was wondering if they had to pay rent on the body since so much time elapses between the death and the funeral, but it seems not. They keep them in the back until the casket is selected, then they "brings them to the front." Lucy Mae, Louise's daughter, is going to call tonight from Miami to say whether she is coming. Whenever she comes, Louise always talks about going back with her, so I hope the threat will soon be over.

Did you read Styron's first book [Set This House on Fire]? . . . I don't think concern with guilt has too much to do with the traditional Christian artist's attempts at the novel. It may have a good deal to do with Styron's. Milner said there were very few Christian novelists in the South and I would agree with him.

The Last Chronicle of Barset is supposed to be Trollope's best but I have never been able to get my hands on it, but I like Trollope. Have you ever read his mother's account of her visit to America in the 1830s? Shouldn't be missed.

I've just had one of those poetically gentlemanly letters from Jack [Hawkes]. He is going to go to Utah this summer and handle the novel sessions at the Utah writers' conference and he's going to give a public lecture called "Wild Talents in the American Novel." I hope he includes himself. They have a new baby. Bernard Malamud and Albert Guérard got him the Utah job . . .

[P.S.] . . . James deploring the loss of a sense of mystery can be found I think in *The American Scene*, the section on Savannah. I do have this and if you want it sent, just drop me a card.

## To Maryat Lee

20 Jan 62

What's with you? I ain't got over yet how you didn't turn up here on Christmas day in your Russian hat. Did you get them nuts I sent you? . . .

I am on the trail of a new operation. This one they take a piece of bone out of your leg (bone with blood vessels in it) and graft it into your hip bone & that furnishes a blood supply to that hip. This is only performed by one man & he is at the University Hospital at Iowa City. They probably won't let me have this one either but I am looking into it . . .

## To Father J. H. McCown

24 January 62

. . . I've ordered Seán O'Faoláin's book of stories and will pass it on to you when I read it. He strikes me as a civilized man. You and the Gossetts ought to be getting copies of the last *New World Writing* that I have a story in as I asked the people in Philadelphia to send you one.

I had a letter from your mother this week about the Mary Ann book. She didn't know I had sent it to her as she lost the wrapping, but she allowed as how she liked the book. The Sisters are having a big bang at being authors . . .

Tom went to Mass with us one afternoon here. Afterwards he said he hadn't felt any warmth in it like he had when he heard you say Mass; no communion between priest and people. They look for that and we never think about it. I hope you get another opportunity.

I want to see the travelogue and I'll pray you get back here since that's where you want to go. I have a convert friend who has joined the Papal Volunteers and is going to Peru to teach the catechism to the Indians.

Cheers and many thanks again. You have relieved a lot of pain.

## To Maryat Lee

25 Jan 62

You don't sound in such excellent health to me. Let me hear if you have hypoglycemia. I would like to know somebody with that.

I'm an old fan of G. Marcel's. Have you read any of his plays? I had one in a magazine that I have looked for to send you but I can't come up with it. Naw, I couldn't ask all them Protestants to join me for an evening of Marcel. I'll get the Wm James lectures when they're published. Regnery is his publisher & I don't reckon they'll miss publishing these. I have his Gifford lecture, which meant a lot to me at one time and his *Metaphysical Journal* which I can't make head or tail of. Be glad to send you any of these if you haven't finished with him . . .

Me and Olivia [the Lees' cook] will expect you for Easter.

## To Cecil Dawkins

26 January 62

I've just sent off a note to Granville Hicks about your wanting to go to Yaddo. Now this may do some good but you'll still have to have sponsors for the application as mine is just sub rosa. I'd get both Haydn and Stegner. I shouldn't think you'd have any trouble with what all you've published.

Last week I met a gentleman your father delivered. He was a book salesman for Holt, Rinehart & Winston come to the college to see the English teachers. These salesmen often turn up here and when this one who was from Birmingham announced his origins, I asked him if he knew you, whereupon he said he knew *of* you and that one of his kinswomen had married in the Dawkins family and your father delivered him . . . He sure had an Alabama accent. He sounded like the man on television who advertizes Tube Rose Snuff . . .

She ["A"] had only been a Catholic for five years and the enthusiasm with which she entered had worn off and she hadn't penetrated far enough to be able to do without it. She must always be emotionally involved. Now she is emotionally involved in these new discoveries. I hope she is really writing. She has written me about some of the things she has read since she quit work—*Set This House on Fire, By Love Possessed, South Wind,* even a good deal of *Peyton Place.* She sees them all of course for what they are, but still if she's going to write she don't need to be reading stuff like that. I'm afraid she is doing more of such reading than any writing.

I don't know. Andrew might be glad for you to do an article for that issue of the *Sewanee*. He has asked Robert Fitzgerald and Robert said he would if he could get straight—they've just moved into a farmhouse in Perugia—but knowing Robert and his six children and his spouse, I doubt if he gets straight. Another one is to be written by Jack Hawkes and Andrew said he might write one himself if he could get straight. He too has moved in a new house. I don't think these will be from the Catholic angle, particularly not Hawkes who has a theory that my fictional voice is the voice of the Devil—a good insight as far as this last story is concerned. Do you know his fiction? I must have mentioned him to you. A very good friend of mine. The story came along fine after so long a time and I have sent it off. I hope he likes it. I agree that I must be seen as a writer and not just a Catholic writer, and I wish somebody would do it.


*To John Hawkes*

6 Feb 62

Here finally is the story that will be in *Sewanee* ["The Lame Shall Enter First"]. I've had the flu and ended up with less than my usual amount of energy, but I may make some minor changes here and there eventually. In this one, I'll admit that the Devil's voice is my own.

I'm cheered to be one of the "wild talents." Right now I feel something less.


*To "A."*

10 Feb 62

This is about all I'm capable of. I've had the flu and as far as energy goes, the bottom has dropped out. Regina can have flu shots so she didn't have the flu but she got a rousing cold in the head. She don't take gratefully to having to stay in the house. Anyway she is out now.

Thanks for the books. As I don't have the energy to do much but read them, I'll probably have them back in time.

You and your time worry me. Of course I've got no advice on these up and down times of elation & depression you seem to have, but I can tell you that time is very dangerous without a rigid routine. If you do the same thing every day at the same time for the same length of time, you'll save yourself from many a sink. Routine is a condition of survival.

Well on the 14th then I shall orbit with them & in the evening I shall tour the White House with Jackie. Regina says we will invite Mary Jo and Miss White out for this latter as they do not have a television. My, how them Sisters have changed my life.

## To Charlotte Gafford

10 February 62

This is good stuff [her thesis]. You ought to be able to give those Methodists [at Birmingham-Southern College] a run for their money. It's the moment of grace that makes a story work . . . The Misfit, of course, is a spoiled prophet. As you point out, he could go on to great things.

I see that telephone call those Vanderbilt students made has got around. What they wanted was for me to write their paper for them. They asked me such things as "Miss O'Connor, why did they stop at *the Tower?*"—trying to make something of the word *tower*. They try to make everything a symbol. It kills me. At one place where I talked, one of them said, "Miss O'Connor, why was the Misfit's hat *black*?" "Well," I said, "he stold it from a countryman and in Georgia they usually wear black hats." This sounded like a pretty stupid answer to him, but he wasn't through with it. In a few minutes he says, "Miss O'Connor, what is the significance of the Misfit's hat?" "To cover his head," I say. When the session was over they obviously thought I didn't have sense enough to have written the story I wrote.

One place in here I marked where I thought you could get on safer ground . . .

## To Marion Montgomery

16 February 62

Never introduced anybody in my life and I'm not quite sure how it ought to be done, but I will try to make it [introducing Mr. Montgomery's talk to the Macon Writers Club] painless. Couldn't you supply me with some fat piece of information about yourself that would bowl them over, I mean something besides being born in Upson County, Georgia? Have you ever been in trouble with the law? I feel I could really do something with a prison record. I don't want to waste my talents, of course.

What about that "peculiar sort of solemn neo-fundamentalism" that gives such comfort to our generation? Are you saved? I might do something along that line.

How is your health? Have you been feeling tired lately? Rundown? Out of sorts? Nothing like a good medical report.

I'll do my best with whatever information you give me.

This club will go for the history business. In fact, they frequently have the breakfast for some historian. There have been a couple from Athens but I forget their names. One of them was from Deepstep.


## To "A."

24 February 62

We have really had it this week. Last weekend Louise didn't come out of her house at all. Jack said she was "down in the back," which we took for the euphemism for "dead drunk." Monday he came over and said she couldn't get out the bed, so Regina went over there and sure enough, she was moaning and groaning and said she couldn't get up. Regina called the doctor and he said giver some aspirin. Regina made her take the aspirin and then went on in to town. When she came back at dinnertime, Jack said she wasn't no better and she'd have to go to the doctor so Regina called the doctor and made arrangements for her to come while he was still in his office, then went down to pick up Louise and Louise wouldn't come. Scared to death. Going to die. Fifty-six years old and never had been to no doctor. Regina couldn't do anything with her, so we went to town and got some Absorbine Jr. and Regina came back and rubbed her back. Didn't do any good, but Regina couldn't get her to the doctor. So finally we went up to Eatonton and got Shot's mama to come down and see what she could do. Her name is Ida. She talks in a high voice, constantly, and has a very high opinion of herself. On the way back she diagnosed the case as a "wranch back" and said she would make a poultice of mud and salt and that would take care of everything. She did this and administered a dose of Black Draught and then came over and said she had decided Louise would have to go to the doctor because she couldn't pass her water. So for about the fourth time that day Regina called the doctor and he said bring her in. All the way in she weeped and wailed and said she never had been to the doctor and to call Lucy Mae and she was fifty-six years old and had never been sick, never been to no doctor. "You on your way now," Ida says. They stayed in the doctor's office about an hour, and came out in high spirits. "How do you feel?" I said. "Feels better," she said, "I feels a heap better." "She didn't even know what a specimen was," Ida said and the rest of the way home Ida entertained us with how ignorant Louise was and how she had had to take charge and tell the doctor what was wrong with her etc. Ida said Louise's people were dropsical on her mother's side and on her father's side they went crazy. Anyway, what was wrong with her was the flu and the doctor had given her a shot of penicillin, and all week she has been recuperating. Regina says next year she is going to see she gets a flu shot.

Fr. Mayhew turned up the next day, thank the Lord not the one before . . .

*To Cecil Dawkins*

4 March 62

I think you'll like Yaddo . . . Granville Hicks is coming to Milledgeville in April with some friends of ours whose parents live here—my connection with him in late years.

I think Iris Murdoch is a fine stylist. What actually she is trying to do I wouldn't venture to say but she sure is readable, which is about all I ask, being of a non-critical temperament. "A." sounds very lethargic, no bounce, and a comment about being nearly thirty-nine and not able to learn new tricks. I think the job now is to keep her cheered up. She wrote me that you said Iris Murdoch was audacious and outrageous—and that pleased her very much.

My French translator is Maurice Coindreau. He did *Wise Blood* and is doing *The Violent Bear* but somebody else is doing the stories. They (the stories) have actually been done twice, but the first translation was so bad that M. Coindreau wouldn't let Gallimard use it . . . The German translation of the stories is apparently doing very well. Every week I get a batch of gibberish-reviews that I can't of course read. A German friend of mine here who teaches at the college read the translation and said it was a schizafrenic (sp?) experience for her to read about General Tennessee Flintrock Sash in German. She thought the translation was a good one. Someone else is doing the novel. It is a very odd feeling this of being someone else in a different language . . .

## To Father J. H. McCown

4 March 62

We loved your travelogue. Regina said to tell you it was her kind of literature—places and folks. She also likes to read about wild animals. I can't see something like this without visualizing it in print. Of course, if you abridged it some, you could probably send it to *Jubilee* as a Letter from Mexico. I don't know anything about Our Lady of Guadalupe. What's this about her painting her picture? Pious legend or what? My credulity is easily strained. Be sure to send us the next installment.

Thanks for the copies of *Catholic Mind*. That article in there on "Theology and Population" is the best I've read on that subject. I have a Protestant friend who is interested in the Church and naturally that subject as she is married and has three already. She got a Catholic in the town where she lives to get some pamphlets on the subject from the local priest. He produced some that horrified her—no theological basis given at all, just all this junk about how great it is to be a mother. She was pretty disgusted. I've sent her a copy of this, which should set things straight. The priest there came to see her and brought her a copy of another horror, a book called *I Had to Know*. She said it was terrible. I told her to tell him so so he wouldn't give it to somebody else like her.

I'm cheered you like "Everything That Rises Must Converge." I don't have another copy of it and I've lost your brother's address but if you will send me his address, I'll order him one from Philadelphia. I'd like to write a whole bunch of stories like that, but once you've said it, you've said it, and that about expresses what I have to say on That Issue. But pray that the Lord will send me some more. I've been writing for sixteen years and I have the sense of having exhausted my original potentiality and being now in need of the kind of grace that deepens perception, a new shot of life or something . . .

## To Charlotte Gafford

13 March 62

It may just be hopeless to try to convince the man who is directing your thesis as long as you use religious terms. *Magnificat* may be unintelligible to him. In my talks I have a way of approaching the subject of grace, as follows. The writer whose point of view is Catholic in the widest sense of the term reads nature the same way the medieval commentators read Scripture. They found three levels of meaning in the literal level of the sacred text—the allegorical, in which one thing stands for another; the moral, which has to do with what should be done; and the anagogical, which has to do with the Divine life and our participation in it, the level of grace.

Now if you use the word anagogical long enough, the idea of grace will become sufficiently disinfected for them to be able to take it. But maybe even that won't work.

Witness the enclosed review (which please send back to me). This appeared in the Catholic magazine *Renascence* and is written by a man who recently returned to the Church. I think there is considerable animosity behind it, but it is just an example of how even your own kind misinterpret. This is more pretentious than most and gratuitously ugly, however, many good people nodded their heads in agreement when they read it you may be sure . . .

## To Ashley Brown

18 March 62

I really liked this last one [last volume of the *Sword of Honor* trilogy] of Waugh's best and am very much obliged to you for lending it to me. I didn't get beyond the first book in *Parade's End*. I find Waugh more readable than Ford, except for *The Good Soldier*. You could write a good book on him. I tried to find you an interview with Waugh that I cut out of *Sign* magazine some years ago, but I can't lay hands on it. It was rather interesting. One of the questions was that Caroline Gordon had said that Mr. Waugh was "Christian in hope," before he became a Catholic and what did he think of this? I forget his words but the effect was he didn't think much of it. If you are interested in that interview, you could probably get it through the *Sign*, a sort of so-so Catholic magazine. Pretty so-so indeed, in fact, but occasionally they have something good like that interview.

Last week we had an overnight visit from Lon and Fanny, they both being in fine form, though Lon had had the flu and was spitting and blowing mightily and Fanny was taking penicillin for an abscessed tooth.

Fr. Charles at the monastery sent my parent the monastery copy of the Alice B. Toklas cookbook. She has been reading it, with appropriate comments, but our dishes have not got any more exotic . . .

## To Father J. H. McCown

27 March 62

The last episode was the best. I don't think you could possibly be too old to go to Mexico if you ain't too old to knock about the States. They just like your face and want to keep it in sight. I am getting pretty old myself—37 this week and to make it even more impressive, St. Mary's College at Notre Dame is going to give me an honorary Doctor of Letters. This makes me feel a mean hundred. Catholic colidge, note . . .

I am sorry to hear about your mamma. I wrote her a note. I guess they will put a pin in her hip.

## To Walker Percy

29 March 62

I'm glad we lost the War and you won the National Book Award. I didn't think the judges would have that much sense but they surprized me. Regards.

## To John Hawkes

5 April 62

I like the piece very very much and I hope Andrew takes it or if not him somebody else. This is not to say that you have convinced me at all that what you say is perverse is perverse. But you are very fine in pointing out where I disagree with you so I don't feel this does any damage to my views and the quality of the just plain textual insights is so wonderful that of course I hope this will be read. It doesn't seem stuffy to me.

I think what you do is to reduce the good and give what you take from it to the diabolical. Isn't it arbitrary to call these images such as the cat-faced baby and the old woman that looked like a cedar fence post and the grandfather who went around with Jesus hidden in his head like a stinger—perverse? They are right, accurate, so why perverse? I think you call them perverse because you like them. They may be perverse to the bourgeoise mind. Thomas Mann has said the grotesque is the true anti-bourgeoise style. But you don't have a bourgeoise mind and for you perverse means good. Nobody with a religious consciousness is going to call these images perverse and mean that they are really perverse. What

I mean to say is that when you call them perverse, you are departing from the word's traditional meaning.

This is a sloppy and hasty letter, but I want to send it right away because you seem to be in some doubt over the piece and I don't think you ought to be. Also I am fixing to take off on some bread-winning expeditions and don't have the time to sit down and write better, but I will later. I am going to Raleigh to talk at North Carolina State College next week, then the week after I am going to the Southern Literary Festival in Spartanburg. Andrew is going too so I'll ask him what he thought of your piece. Eudora Welty and Cleanth Brooks will be there as the other two guests. The week after that I am going to a Catholic college in Chicago and then down to Notre Dame and then home with my tongue hanging out and a firm resolve not to go anywhere else for as long as possible . . .

I hope Sophie is all right and you too. More later. I just wanted you to know that I appreciate what has gone into the piece and what has come out and I am touched and honored that you did it.


## To Cecil Dawkins

25 April 62

My editor has written me that he must have a note to the new edition of *Wise Blood* as this will enable him to [update the copyright] so I have had to do it. What do you think of the enclosed? It is as much as I can get out of myself.

The Hickses spent a week here recently and were asking about you and if you had got your acceptance yet. I hope you meet them when you go up there. I have a friend in Schenectady—[Rebekkah Poller], the one the Hickses came down with—an ex-liberrian . . . and I am going to ask her to ask you over or something when you are there.

I have just got back from Converse & the Southern Litry Festival where there was Eudora Welty, Cleanth Brooks, Andrew Lytle and me. I really liked Eudora Welty—no presence whatsoever, just a real nice woman. She read a paper on "Place in Fiction." It was very beautifully written but a little hard to listen to as anything like that . . . is written to be read. These affairs are powerful social. There was a coffee in the morning, a tea in the afternoon and a reception with a receiving line in the evening. She told a story about a beauty parlor operator in Jackson who writes novels about the Northwest Mounted Police. She sent one of her love scenes to Faulkner through the mail for criticism and when she didn't hear from him she called him up and said, "Mr. Faulkner, what did you think of that little love scene of mine?" He said, "Honey, it isn't the way I would do it, but you go right ahead, you go right ahead."

The week before Converse I went to North Carolina State. That is strictly a technical school, they don't give an AB or have any English majors, nevertheless have thirty people on the English faculty and the students are sharp.

Next week I go to Rosary College in Chicago and then to Notre Dame. Then the next week I have to go to Emory and talk to a Methodist Student congregation on "The South." Their choice of topic. Of course I don't know any more about the South than they do, but I hopes to pull it off. The first of June I go back to Notre Dame because I am being given a degree by St. Mary's College. Then after that, boy, I am going to stay at home and write me some fiction. A little of this honored guest bidnis goes a long way, but it sure does help my finances.

Everything is hatching around here in the goose line but no peafowl or swan eggs yet. I hope those swans don't disappoint me.


## To Thomas Stritch

7 May 62

I enjoyed it [visit to Notre Dame] an awful lot, particularly talking to you, but as I can't thank you enough I won't thank you at all. I'll just cherish what the dwarf said.*

I have instructions from my mamma to find out when I come back in June whether the nails in your plyboard walls are counter-sunk and filled with putty—which is what her carpenter tells her will have to be done here. (She is full of construction terms like "countersunk.")

She was on hand to meet me with, I regret to say, a wheel-chair, so I was rolled to the main concourse, feeling at least 102 years old. And you complain about being 49 . . .

---

* Tom Stritch had told her that the motto of the complete New York edition of Joseph Conrad, taken from Grimm, is, "No," said the dwarf. "Something human is dearer to me than all the gold in the world."

## To Sally and Robert Fitzgerald

7 May 62

We were cheered to hear from you and glad you are your own landlord though we wish you were landlords closer to home. I've just been to Notre Dame where I givem a talk and visited with Tom Stritch who will set out soon for Europe and be seeing you. I have to go back up there in three weeks to get myself a degree that St. Mary's College is going to give me. I reckon this is a non-negotiable degree, but perhaps it won't hurt.

Would you be so good as to look at the enclosed ["Preface to the Second Edition"] and tell me if you think it will do. Giroux has bought *Wise Blood* from Harcourt and is going to put it out this summer . . . I would just like to prevent some of the far-out interpretations.

Everything is in fine shape here since we are no longer in the dairy bidnis. Shot is still incapacitated so we get along with Jack and Louise, but Jack took off last week and stayed all week. He came back this morning, having been beat up at the Negro juke joint. Regina asked him where he had been and he said he had been plowing for a crippled man and he went because he knew the Lord would bless her for doing without him for the week. She said the Lord would have blessed me just the same if you had told me you were going. Around here it is not a matter of finding the truth but of deciding which lie you live with better.

## To Robert Giroux

9 May 62

I enclose a tentative note to the second edition. I want your opinion on this. I am not certain this is what I ought to write. If you think not, I can try again . . .

The Sisters didn't get any copy of the British [edition of] *Mary Ann*. Aren't they supposed to? I sent them one of mine but they would like another one or so.

I do appreciate the [I. B.] Singer book and I'm looking forward to the time when I can stay at home and read it.

*To "A."*

We'll be cheered to see you next Saturday and will be at the estate entrance at ten past high noon. Louis will be cheered to number you among his parcels Sunday.

I don't have the least objection to being put in the same sack with the other two ladies or to your writing about my work. My work, however, not my soul. I have almost no capacity to worship. What I have is the knowledge that it is my duty to worship and worship only what I believe to be true. This thing of it-doesn't-make-any-difference-what-but-only-how is a drain down which I hate to see you falling, if you are falling down it, which you may not be, because the Lord knows I am seldom subtle enough to make my way through your subjective considerations. In any case, the quality of human feeling has a great deal to do with grace, that much I'll grant you, and I certainly won't be praying for your failure.

The Sisters at Rosary had a copy of *The English Journal,* a rag I didn't know existed, and let me read it. I thought it was about as dumb as you could get. Not only did he say nothing happened to Haze and Tarwater, but that nothing happened to Mr. Head and Nelson! And that rot about the violence in the peacocks. Holy mother. The Sisters thought it was dumb too.

We were visited yesterday by Archbishop Hallinan [the new Archbishop of Atlanta]. He is a man after my own heart and he would be after yours . . . He has read everything I've written and in a speech last year he read something from *The Violent Bear.* All this is most gratifying, but he would be if he had never heard of me. Usually I think the Church's motto is The Wrong Man for the Job; but not this time . . .

I am reading Koestler's *The Lotus and the Robot.* I recommend it strongly.


*To Robert Giroux*

What do you think about eliminating that last sentence of the Author's Note—"It is hoped that this one does, agreeably." I don't think it really adds anything. [It was deleted.]

## To Granville Hicks

21 May 62

Everybody in Milledgeville was pleased with the interview and the idea that Milledgeville is really more interesting than Charleston so exhilarated the local editor that he reprinted the whole thing in the *Union Recorder*.

I have received one letter as a result of it—this from a lady poet in Oklahoma City who writes in purple ink and encloses several of her poems with a Biblical theme.

## To Maryat Lee

21 May 62

I have a plan for you. Come South at your own expense & let the White Citizens Council send you back. You could tell them that you was a little light but a guaranteed nigger. This would cut your expenses in half and give you a nice vacation in the land of sin and guilt. You could even go to Hyannisport. I wish this wasn't for real and then I could have made it up.

You never give me any information that will do me any good. What is the name of the colored man from Waycross? [Ossie Davis.] What is the name of his play? [*Purlie Victorious*.] What have the reviews said about it? . . .

Where's the short story? What's the clue? I've got to get down to it myself. I have been gallivanting fast and furious. You never read that story of mine "Everything That Rises Must Converge." The title should affect you with your affinities . . .

For Mother's Day I gave Regina a jackass named Ernest. It was what she wanted. We hope to raise little spotted mules.

## To Elizabeth McKee

28 May 62

. . . I have just corrected the proofs for the *Sewanee* story ["The Lame Shall Enter First"] that you haven't seen and I have decided that I don't like it and am going to try to persuade Andrew not to use it. However, I'm afraid it is too late.

I'm glad you're back.

*In the spring of 1962, Flannery gave a talk to an English class at Emory University in Atlanta. One of her hearers was a young poet much taken by what she had to say, and by her presence. Too shy to go up after the address, he wrote to her at home a little later, and received the following reply.*

## To Alfred Corn

30 May 62

I think that this experience you are having of losing your faith, or as you think, of having lost it, is an experience that in the long run belongs to faith; or at least it can belong to faith if faith is still valuable to you, and it must be or you would not have written me about this.

I don't know how the kind of faith required of a Christian living in the 20th century can be at all if it is not grounded on this experience that you are having right now of unbelief. This may be the case always and not just in the 20th century. Peter said, "Lord, I believe. Help my unbelief." It is the most natural and most human and most agonizing prayer in the gospels, and I think it is the foundation prayer of faith.

As a freshman in college you are bombarded with new ideas, or rather pieces of ideas, new frames of reference, an activation of the intellectual life which is only beginning, but which is already running ahead of your lived experience. After a year of this, you think you cannot believe. You are just beginning to realize how difficult it is to have faith and the measure of a commitment to it, but you are too young to decide you don't have faith just because you feel you can't believe. About the only way we know whether we believe or not is by what we do, and I think from your letter that you will not take the path of least resistance in this matter and simply decide that you have lost your faith and that there is nothing you can do about it.

One result of the stimulation of your intellectual life that takes place in college is usually a shrinking of the imaginative life. This sounds like a paradox, but I have often found it to be true. Students get so bound up with difficulties such as reconciling the clashing of so many different faiths such as Buddhism, Mohammedanism, etc., that they cease to look for God in other ways. Bridges once wrote Gerard Manley Hopkins and asked him to tell him how he, Bridges, could believe. He must have expected from Hopkins a long philosophical answer. Hopkins wrote back, "Give alms." He was trying to say to Bridges that God is to be experienced in Charity (in the sense of love for the divine image in human beings). Don't get so entangled with intellectual difficulties that you fail to look for God in this way.

The intellectual difficulties have to be met, however, and you will be meeting them for the rest of your life. When you get a reasonable hold on one, another will come to take its place. At one time, the clash of the different world religions was a difficulty for me. Where you have absolute solutions, however, you have no need of faith. Faith is what you have in the absence of knowledge. The reason this clash doesn't bother me any longer is because I have got, over the years, a sense of the immense sweep of creation, of the evolutionary process in everything, of how incomprehensible God must necessarily be to be the God of heaven and earth. You can't fit the Almighty into your intellectual categories. I might suggest that you look into some of the works of Pierre Teilhard de Chardin (*The Phenomenon of Man* et al.). He was a paleontologist —helped to discover Peking man—and also a man of God. I don't suggest you go to him for answers but for different questions, for that stretching of the imagination that you need to make you a sceptic in the face of much that you are learning, much of which is new and shocking but which when boiled down becomes less so and takes its place in the general scheme of things. What kept me a sceptic in college was precisely my Christian faith. It always said: wait, don't bite on this, get a wider picture, continue to read.

If you want your faith, you have to work for it. It is a gift, but for very few is it a gift given without any demand for equal time devoted to its cultivation. For every book you read that is anti-Christian, make it your business to read one that presents the other side of the picture; if one isn't satisfactory read others. Don't think that you have to abandon reason to be a Christian. A book that might help you is *The Unity of Philosophical Experience* by Etienne Gilson. Another is Newman's *The Grammar of Assent.* To find out about faith, you have to go to the people who have it and you have to go to the most intelligent ones if you are going to stand up intellectually to agnostics and the general run of pagans that you are going to find in the majority of people around you. Much of the criticism of belief that you find today comes from people who are judging it from the standpoint of another and narrower discipline. The Biblical criticism of the 19th century, for instance, was the product of historical disciplines. It has been entirely revamped in the 20th century by applying broader criteria to it, and those people who lost their faith in the 19th century because of it, could better have hung on in blind trust.

Even in the life of a Christian, faith rises and falls like the tides of an invisible sea. It's there, even when he can't see it or feel it, if he wants it to be there. You realize, I think, that it is more valuable, more mysterious, altogether more immense than anything you can learn or decide upon in college. Learn what you can, but cultivate Christian scepticism. It will keep you free—not free to do anything you please, but free to be formed by something larger than your own intellect or the intellects of those around you.

I don't know if this is the kind of answer that can help you, but any time you care to write me, I can try to do better.


## To "A."

9 June 62

That candy is being much enjoyed. Between Louis and M.J. it is fast disappearing. The bourbon, because of our abstemiousness, will last longer, but will be equally as much enjoyed, at least by me. But I wish you would come and bring nothing but yourself. You must come again soon and see these bookcases. They are so big that they have drained most of what is in my room and those now stand ready to be refilled, but at the rate publishers send me sorry first novels they soon will. Every now and then I collect these and present them to the local library with instructions that they had better read them and take out what is not fit to be read by the public. I believe in private censorship.

The degree-getting was dull but relatively painless. I got to be with Tom which was all the pleasure in it. They gimme the hood, which has now been wrapped up in newspaper against moths and put in the back reaches of the closet. So much for honorary degrees.

A lot of good news from Jack. He got a Guggenheim and also a grant from the National Institute of Arts and Letters and on the strength of these two, they are going to spend next year at Grenada, BWI. He did over the thing for Andrew, without changing his main thesis, and I gather Andrew is going to take it. I still dislike that story of mine . . .

Yesterday I had a visit from Dr. Spivey who is going to get married June 30 to a teacher in Sandy Springs. She too is interested in dreams and it seems that both their dreams prompted them to this action. He is as solemn as an owl about all this . . . He dreamed that I was out looking for some Negroes. It seems this means I am making spiritual progress. He congratulated me.

Regina has read *The Fox in the Attic*, not because she enjoyed it but because what she starts, she finishes. Now she is reading K.A.P., about two pages a night. I hope that the above principle will not operate in this. I am about half into the Hughes book, but haven't done anything with [*Ship of Fools*] yet . . .

## To Roslyn Barnes

10 June 62

. . . I've about finished the thesis and I'm impressed! As you say, the language is thesis language, using the technical jargon of writers on mysticism, whereas you need something more human for public presentation. However, this something you might be thinking about if in those jungles, or wherever it is, you have time on your hands.

Msgr. [Ivan] Illych is a friend of my friend Caroline Gordon. He is supposed to be a powerhouse. I will be wanting to hear about this.

The story I would have used [for the thesis] (but God forbid that I should have to) is "The Artificial Nigger."

## To Alfred Corn

16 June 62

I certainly don't think that the death required that "ye be born again," is the death of reason. If what the Church teaches is not true, then the security and emotional release and sense of purpose it gives you are of no value and you are right to reject it. One of the effects of modern liberal Protestantism has been gradually to turn religion into poetry and therapy, to make truth vaguer and vaguer and more and more relative, to banish intellectual distinctions, to depend on feeling instead of thought, and gradually to come to believe that God has no power, that he cannot communicate with us, cannot reveal himself to us, indeed has not done so, and that religion is our own sweet invention. This seems to be about where you find yourself now.

Of course, I am a Catholic and I believe the opposite of all this. I believe what the Church teaches—that God has given us reason to use and that it can lead us toward a knowledge of him, through analogy; that he has revealed himself in history and continues to do so through the Church, and that he is present (not just symbolically) in the Eucharist on our altars. To believe all this I don't take any leap into the absurd. I find it reasonable to believe, even though these beliefs are beyond reason.

If you are interested, the enclosed book [*Creative Evolution*, by Teilhard de Chardin] will give you one general line of reasoning about why I do. I'm not equipped to talk philosophically; this man is. I want it back sometime, but I am in no hurry for it. It shouldn't be read rapidly.

Satisfy your demand for reason always but remember that charity is beyond reason, and that God can be known through charity.

*The Dominicans in Atlanta kept in touch.*

## To Sister Julie

17 June 62

My head peacock sends you the tip of this feather which he regrets to say he lost in battle. I have too many cocks for the number of hens I have and they do nothing but fight all day. They scream all night but I don't hear them anymore.

I have been reading a book called *Word of God and the Word of Man*—about the trials of Biblical scholars since about 1880. Very enlightening to me. It's certainly easier to be a Bible reader in 1962 than in 1904.

I am writing every day but I don't know what, as the brew has not begun to thicken yet. Please pray it will. Sometimes it doesn't.

A man who runs a zoo in Florida has informed me through a friend that swans nest according to the weather, so I still have some hope that these two of mine will get with it before the summer is out.

## To "A."

23 June 62

I was sorry I didn't get in on the conversation last night. Report. This morning I sent you four Simone Weil books. There are two more, but I thought four made a big enough package for one trip, and I will send the other two (*The Notebooks*) next week along with *The Fox in the Attic*.

Cecil didn't seem to think much of *The Fox in the Attic*, said it was not as good as *A High Wind in Jamaica*. I can't agree with her. I think *A High Wind* is small enough to be perfect, but this other thing is part of something much larger and can't be judged by such standards. Regina is now reading *Ship of Fools* and she says they sure are fools all right. She says don't read it before you eat. She read the part about the bulldog being seasick just before we went to the Sanford House to eat. Then she read another such part before she ate another time. Her timing has been bad. I'll admit K.A. don't have the grace to see around the corner. What she does have aplenty is the ability to make things actual. [She] can create the sweating stinking life out of anything, the purely animal . . .

All I can tell you about that dream is that the nigger is The Instincts, according to Dr. Spivey. Whether he is anybody in particular's instincts I am not learned enough to say. Too bad I had to be entertaining an air plant though. Did I tell you the original air plant [Ashley Brown] is on his way to Africa?

What would you call *The Violent Bear It Away* if you couldn't call it that? Apparently that doesn't mean anything in German and they have written me for a new title. All they have come up with is *The Bursting Sun,* which they are not happy with, nor me neither. I am thinking of *Food for the Violent* or *The Prophet's Country.* I don't like either.

The Florida Hoods visited us this week. They got up early in the morning, made their coffee and took it to the pond with them in two mugs, which they set on the bank while they fished. Deen heard slurping. Ernest [the jackass] was drinking her coffee.


## To Charlotte Gafford

24 June 62

My coming to B'ham Southern in October was still just in the talking stage between me and [the former president of the college], so I should say the trip, if it was ever on, is now off . . .

Wild horses could not get me into the air in February—that is a dumb time to have a festival [the Birmingham Festival of Arts]. Local festivals are the worst of all. I would say without a quiver of compassion that it would cost them $300 plus travelling expenses for me in decent weather. I feel like R. P. Warren who was invited to some college in Pennsylvania and asked what his fee was. "$400 and I'm not worth it," he wrote back.

I have no use for panels or any collection of writers. One writer is enough for people to digest at one time . . .

## To Maryat Lee

26 June 62

We will be plumb charmed to put you up but as soon as we do your kinfolks will come out here & storm the fort to get you away as they are dying for you to come. Your invite here is always open.

As for the story, you worry about the wrong things.

The South is the place for you if you can keep yourself from running off to every sit-in or wade-in or kneel-in that is being held. Break a leg. I couldn't write any better prescription for your writing than to tell you to get out of New York and come South.

We will be looking for your face.


## To Roslyn Barnes

29 June 62

Well I'm glad you're really there. I've heard a lot about Msgr. Illych from two friends of mine who know him—Caroline Gordon and Eric Langkjaer [the nephew of Helene Iswolsky]. You must need somebody violent to run an outfit like that. I want to hear more. How many of you are there? Do you have a roommate? Will you study theology? . . .

We had the cub scouts yesterday and the nursery school this morning. Shot killed a 5-ft. water rattler while the nursery school was here but no one was any the wiser.

[P.S.] Is there anything you need that you can't get there that I could send you? Just let me know what I can do to support the troops.


## To Thomas Stritch

3 July 62

I hope you are having a good time and are not becoming converted to culture or anything. Dr. Crane, with whom I am in daily telepathic communication, says to tell you that the American traveler abroad is a salesman of the USA and that in Europe the Sincere Compliment is an important part of our foreign policy. Don't hesitate, he says, to use the same sincere compliment any number of times as sincerity is always fresh and useful.

My degree hasn't done a thing for me so far, hasn't increased my self-confidence or improved my personality or anything I expected it to do. The local wags have already got tired of calling me "Doctor." Regina wrapped the hood up in newspaper and put it away and unless I wear it Halloween, I guess it'll stay there . . .

## To Cecil Dawkins

19 July 62

It [Yaddo, where Cecil was now a guest] all sounds powerful familiar, even down to the studio squirril. I used to see chipmonks and a large important-looking woodchuck. I would have been happier writing in my room, but they seem to think it proper you go to a studio.

I heard that Mrs. Ames was not in favor of a swimming pool. I guess that was one battle she lost. She usually, I think, wins them.

Give my greetings to Jim and Nellie Shannon [of the staff at Yaddo in Flannery's time] if you meet them . . .

My female one-eyed swan turned over and died. I think it was old age and I don't think I had a mated pair. I think she was her supposed consort's mother. I am going to look for a young female for him just on the off chance he wasn't mated. My total of new peafowls for the year is eight, and the Abbot at the Trappist Monastery gave me three Muscovy ducks, so the general balance is kept . . .

I am having a great time writing I can't tell exactly what but maybe a short novel. It is good to be writing anything fictional at all after that spate of lecturing. This fall I am going to East Texas State College. I've never been to Texas . . .

I hope you are writing. Don't let all that time scare you.

## To "A."

21 July 62

. . . Did you happen to see the television program with Ray Moore and the five candidates for Governor? It was a kind of classical exhibition of Georgia politics. If I had written it myself it couldn't have been better. I saw the rerun because I missed it the first time, but if it is rerun again I'll see it again.

. . . What I mean about [Cecil] don't have anything to do with whether she is refreshingly relaxed or not. As I see it, we all have more innate capacity than we use, or more innate responsiveness than we use. Maryat was unable to respond to anything. Now she responds to everything, or anyway to much more. I daresay no one of us is free of these impediments to responsiveness. All education is a matter of getting rid of them. Some of them are conscious and some unconscious. The wrong kind of education can impose them. The reach may remain the same but we never reach the end of our individual reach, possibly not even idiots . . .

I am over two thirds the way across the Atlantic with Katherine Anne. It [*Ship of Fools*] may not be a great book but it is in many ways a fine one. It has a sculptured quality. I admire the bulldog in it the same way I would admire a bulldog carved to perfection. Essence of bulldog . . .

## To William Sessions

21 July 62

I took alarm at the word mononucleosis as I have always understood it was infectious, so I called Dr. Fulghum and asked him what he thought about us having a guest with it. He said he would not advise it, that it was infectious and remained infectious for some time after the person was apparently cured—he would set the time as three months he said. So this being the case, I think we will have to pass you up this time, though with much regret because we were looking forward to seeing you as I don't reckon we will for some time to come.

You had better check on this monoetc. and see what precautions you should take being around Jenny. I don't know what kind of a doctor you have but you had better get one that is more precautious . . .

## To Alfred Corn

25 July 62

What you ask about Rayber loving Bishop is interesting. He did love him, but throughout the book he was fighting his inherited tendency to mystical love. He had the idea that his love could be contained in Bishop but that if Bishop were gone, there would be nothing to contain it and he would then love everything and specifically Christ. The point where Tarwater is drowning Bishop is the point where he has to choose. He makes the Satanic choice, and the inability to feel the pain of his loss is the immediate result. His collapse then may indicate that he is not going to be able to sustain his choice—but that is another book maybe. Rayber and Tarwater are really fighting the same current in themselves. Rayber wins out against it and Tarwater loses; Rayber achieves his own will, and Tarwater submits to his vocation. Here if you like are two interpretations. There is still an authority to say which interpretation is right.

I hope you'll find the experience you need to make the leap toward Christianity seem the only one to you. Pascal had a good deal to say about this. Sometimes it may be as simple as asking for it, sometimes not; but don't neglect to ask for it.

Sometime when you are going to Emory, stop by here and pay me a visit. I would like to fit your face to your search. I don't remember which one of those students you were.

## To Maryat Lee

26 July 62

Cain't think of anything I would rather have immediately than this Japanese shirt with the starch in it. Can I wear it to the local teas? My mama will look at it and say, "Well that *looks* like Maryat" . . .

I can live without K.A.P.'s early stories myself. I like "Noon Wine" pretty good but the others tend to be coy.

When you come to visit Milledgeville bring your tent and you can bivouac on the mansion lawn. O Pioneers.

## To Cecil Dawkins

1 August 62

I'm real cheered you've been to Schenectady. I wish I had known the Pollers [see letter to "A." of 4 August 62] when I was there. The kind of people at Yaddo are so much all the same kind that it gets depressing.

When I was there I was upstairs in the big house during the summer and on the first floor of West House in the fall and winter. During the fall and winter I worked in another room in West House but in the summer I had one of those studios—a long single room with a fireplace and chaise longue in it and a couple of tables and straight chairs. Might well have been the one you have now. Where is the swimming pool going to be? There are nice walks around there as I guess you've found—around the lakes and back toward the race tracks. I used to walk into town.

Did you go to see Elizabeth McKee? I should have told you to tell her hello. I've written her twice asking her some questions about that movie contract I signed . . . and she hasn't answered so either she don't intend to or she's out of the office.

My reading isn't anything extra so send me anything you feel I could help about.

If "A." thinks you are conservative, what does she think about me? She is the kind for whom this doctrine of Murdoch's is particularly dangerous. I admire a saying of Braque's that he made about painting—"I like the rule that corrects the emotion" . . .


## To Robert Fitzgerald

3 August 62

I do like the piece in the *Sewanee Review* and I am awful obliged to you for writing it. I only wish mine in there was able to live up to it. Some time I would like to know what you think of Jack Hawkes' piece. I have argued with him for years about his Devil, which he don't know is an unfallen spirit of some purely literary kind.

Regina and govvermint are building another pond. She is even busier since she got rid of the dairy, but without so much tension . . .

The latest I have heard on Caroline is that she is going to California for nine months at $15,000 and teach a course on Emily Dickinson, Stephen Crane and HJ. My informant said she had discovered a streak of diabolism in Emily—I guess in preparation for the course . . .


## To Roslyn Barnes

4 Aug 62

I was very glad to hear this account of what Msgr. Illych is trying to do and I can see why he sends home half. He won't send you home I don't think. That is a school for sanctity and he must know that he can't create saints in 4 months though he has to try. This is surely what it means to bear away the kingdom of heaven with violence: the violence is directed inward.

The monitum on Teilhard was depressing at first but not after you considered it. Some say this method will replace the Index which would be a great thing. A warning on T. is necessary since his work is incomplete and unclear on the subject of grace—the idea may be inferred from it apparently that grace comes up from the bottom instead of down from the top. I don't think for a moment this was T.'s idea of course . . .

## To "A."

We were real sorry not to get to see Billy, but I am not about to expose myself to mononucleosis or Regina either. I called up the doctor to be sure I knew what I was doing and he said that even three months after you were apparently over the stuff, you could be carrying the virus—so I am worried that he might give it to Jenny . . .

Yes that was a good review of *Franny & Zooey*. I ask myself what you could expect a book called *Franny & Zooey* to be anyhow. I read two of the [stories] in the *New Yorker*. Dick Gilman had an even better review of it in *Jubilee* . . .

The Hickses got Cecil and took her down to dinner at the Pollers'—my friends in Schenectady—and she appeared to enjoy it—as I think she would because they are less arty people than what she is finding at Yaddo. The Pollers are insurance salesman and ex-librarian respectively and after a few weeks at Yaddo, you long to talk to an insurance salesman, dog-catcher, bricklayer—anybody who isn't talking about Form or sleeping pills. Hortense Calisher and her husband seem to be the biggest cheezes there. Cecil was going down last weekend and look at the city.

Last Saturday two of the Sisters came down and brought [Mary Ann's] family, all except [her sister], who has had a couple of tumors removed already and couldn't take any more riding. The father is dying of cancer and looked it. They brought Mary Ann very close. The mother has huge black eyes and the father has an over-large elongated head, the face covered with warts. I was much impressed with them. You hear of The Poor, but you seldom see them. I don't mean just poor folks, I mean people whose vocation it is to be poor and to have God touch them in just that way.

Odd about "The Temple of the Holy Ghost." Nobody notices it. It is never anthologized, never commented upon. A few nuns have mentioned it with pleasure, but nobody else besides you.

## To Father J. H. McCown

5 August 62

The enclosed is a letter from a young friend [Roslyn Barnes] of mine who is a Papal Volunteer at the school in Cuernavaca, and I am sending it to you because I know if you know about her you will pray for her. Send me the letter back but remember her. She's a convert of about two years, very bright, and with a real vocation. Her family are violently opposed to what she is doing but she goes her own way. She says Msgr. [Illych] is straight out of Dostoevsky . . .

I hope your mama is out of the wheelchair.

## To Alfred Corn

12 August 62

I think the strongest of Rayber's psychological pulls are in the direction that he does not ultimately choose, so I don't believe he exhibits in any sense a lack of free will. You might make out a case of sorts for Tarwater being determined since his great uncle has expressly trained him to be a prophet and to expect the Lord's call, but actually neither of them exhibits a lack of free will. An absence of free will in these characters would mean an absence of conflict in them, whereas they spend all their time fighting within themselves, drive against drive. Tarwater wrestles with the Lord and Rayber wins. Both examples of free will in action.

Free will has to be understood within its limits; possibly we all have some hinderances to free action but not enough to be able to call the world determined. In some people (psychotics) hinderances to free action may be so strong as to preclude free will in them, but the Church (Catholic) teaches that God does not judge those acts that are not free, and that he does not predestine any soul to hell—for his glory or any other reason. This doctrine of double predestination is strictly a Protestant phenomenon. Until Luther and Calvin, it was not countenanced. The Catholic Church has always condemned it. Romans IX is held by the Church to refer not to eternal reward or punishment but to our actual lives on earth, where one is given talent, wealth, education, made a "vessel of honor," and another is given the short end of the horn, so to speak—the "vessel of wrath."

This brings us naturally to the second question about priests and laity. It is the Bishops, not priests, who decide religious questions in the Catholic Church. Their job is to guard the deposit of faith. The coming Vatican Council is an example of how this works. The Bishop of Rome is the final authority. Catholics believe that Christ left the Church with a teaching authority and that this teaching authority is protected by the Holy Ghost; in other words that in matters of faith and morals the Church cannot err, that in these matters she is Christ speaking in time. So you can see that I don't find it an infringement of my independence to have the Church tell me what is true and what is not in regard to faith and what is right and what is wrong in regard to morals. Certainly I am no fit judge. If left to myself, I certainly wouldn't know how to interpret Romans IX. I don't believe Christ left us to chaos.

But to go back to determinism. I don't think literature would be possible in a determined world. We might go through the motions but the heart would be out of it. Nobody then could "smile darkly and ignore the howls." Even if there were no Church to teach me this, writing two novels would do it. I think the more you write, the less inclined you will be to rely on theories like determinism. Mystery isn't something that is gradually evaporating. It grows along with knowledge.

## To Maryat Lee

17 Aug 62

Book on way—a donation to the cause if there is a cause and if not, *spectacle est gratui* anyhow. I put to Helen Nash & after it was wrapped up I got to worrying if it shouldn't have been Dr. Helen Nash, but it was done wrapped up. I ain't supposed to know she's a doctor.

Did I tell you that the Ku Klux Klan met across the road Saturday night before last. They burned a cross—just for the sake of ceremony. We could have seen it out of our upstairs windows but we didn't know until it was over. You ought to be down to observe mid-August politics in Georgia. You would return with curled hair.

## To Roslyn Barnes

26 Aug 62

Well I am much cheered that you have got over the mid-term and are still there, not that I had any doubt about it. I have a Jesuit friend, Fr. McCown, whom I asked to pray for you. He is a great lover of Mexico and has done everything he could do to be sent there but he is 51 so they say he's too old (which seems ridiculous). Anyway he may write you a letter and tell you he's praying for you.*

This morning we had an illegible postcard from Helen Green [of GSCW]. I managed to make out your name on it. Now I am wondering if you saw her. She was going to bring back a Mexican girl named Rosario Somebody to live with her and work in the Sanford House. I had a card from Rosa Lee [Walston] from Dublin, a little more legible but not much.

Will you get to see us in October? Remember that anytime you are welcome . . .

## To Maryat Lee

6 Sept 62

According to my tellyvision the stock market is not cheering you up any. The dividends is all I'm interested in and mine haven't gone down. But that man can probably recoup your losses in time . . .

About old Proust. I read the whole bloody thing and liked the first books best and the last book. In the middle there were some drear spaces. As long as he kept it in society it was strong; great stuff, cheers. I have no desire to read any of it again . . .

## To Cecil Dawkins

6 September 62

I'm glad you're going to stay there for a while longer as it is beautiful in the fall and winter and most of the creepy characters take off at the end of the summer.

About the story ["The Lame Shall Enter First"] I certainly agree that it don't work and have never felt that it did, but in heaven's name where do you get the idea that Sheppard represents Freud? Freud never entered my mind and looking back over it, I can't make him fit now. The story is about a man who thought he was good and thought he was doing good when he wasn't. Freud was a great one, wasn't he, for bringing home to people the fact

---

* Fr. McCown did write to Roslyn Barnes, and it is to him that I am indebted for the letters Flannery wrote her. She gave them to Fr. McCown when she left for South America, where she disappeared in the course of her missionary work. All efforts to trace her or learn her fate have failed.

that they weren't what they thought they were, so if Freud were in this, which he is not, he would certainly be on the other side of the fence from Shepp. The story doesn't work because I don't know, don't sympathize, don't like Mr. Sheppard in the way that I know and like most of my other characters. This is a story, not a statement. I think you ought to look for simpler explanations of why things don't work and not mess around with philosophical ideas where they haven't been intended or don't apply. There's nothing *in* the story that could possibly suggest that Sheppard represents Freud. This is some theory of which you are possessed. I am wondering if this kind of theorizing could be what is interfering with your getting going on some writing. Don't mix up thought-knowledge with felt-knowledge. If Sheppard represents anything here, it is, as he realizes at the end of the story, the empty man who fills up his emptiness with good works. I just don't know such a man, don't have any felt-knowledge of him. I don't want to go on to higher mathematics, but to people I do know.

Elizabeth McKee wrote me that she had seen you and she seemed pleased with the visit. I'm cheered that the book is going to be published and if I can say anywhere that these shore are good stories, tell Mr. Haydn to let me know.

I have just read a review in the Chicago *Sun* about *Wise Blood* in which I am congratulated for producing a *Lolita* five or six years before Nabokov—so Freud is dogging my tracks all the way. I really have quite a respect for Freud when he isn't made into a philosopher. If I can lay hands on it, I will send you an article about him and St. Thomas in which they are rowing in the same boat. You probably hear a lot about Freud at Yaddo. To religion I think he is much less dangerous than Jung.

The army worms have eaten up my mamma's coastal bermuda . . .


## To "A."

8 September 62

I think that's great about going to New York if that's what I make out in the letter. I stayed there once very cheaply at the Y on 38th Street or 37th maybe off Lexington Avenue. Fourteen years ago that was and it was $2 a day and you could get your breakfast in the building. There was then a very good co-op cafeteria on 41st Street between Madison and Park. The only place in New York that I could afford to eat downtown where I didn't feel I was going home with pyoria . . .

We called B. on the phone when we got the news. He was at the hospital and sounded properly flustered. He told us Jenny was fine and then started right away telling us about his teeth, which it seems had been removed the week before and he had just got out of bed for the event. Not all his teeth removed, that is, just some embedded wisdom teeth. I hope you see him in New York . . .

On the basis of the fact that you use ten fingers to work a typewriter and only three to push a pen, I hold the typewriter to be the more personal instrument. Also on the basis of that you can read what comes off it.

## To Roslyn Barnes

17 Sept 62

Dr. Helen Green has not showed up yet. I have been meaning to call her but my mother is currently trying to get in hay with inadequate help so we will have to wait until that is over to ask her & Rosario to supper.

Thanks for the information about the teaching but I don't know enough to teach an English course. He might be able to find somebody through Caroline (Tate) whose current address is University of California at Davis. I know if [she] were free, she'd hop down there and teach it for him herself but she is presently engaged for the year at Davis.

I agree that you don't want to make leaders but denying them the pleasure of learning English is equivalent to denying us the pleasure of learning any other language. By denying them English, you are denying them an innocent pleasure. The more languages you know, the better you can appreciate your own. Better for them to learn English in Ecuador from you than spend a summer with Maestro Magnifico maybe. In other words I cain't for the life of me see how learning *anything,* unless it is evil, is going to make them less Ecuadorian. English or music or mathematics—all a discipline of the mind.

We have just completed a new pond so Junior and his crowd have a choice of two.

## To Sister Julie

19 Sept 62

I was cheered to hear from you. Katherine Anne looks mighty frail and wobbly in that picture you enclosed. The main emphasis of the conference must have been commercial. I think I prefer to go to colleges rather than conferences. That many writers gathered together can't be healthy.

I don't see the *Atlantic* so I haven't seen the poem of Br. Antoninus but I have seen others of his. Modern poetry largely escapes me anyway—not that I make much effort to read it . . .

The swan is still by himself and I must say doesn't seem to know the difference. We enjoy having him around . . .

My best to Sister Mary Brian and always to you.

## To Cecil Dawkins

20 September 62

Put me down for anything any time. You don't have to ask me about it. I recommend a couple of people every year for the Guggenheim, one year I recommended six, but nobody I ever recommend gets one. I have heard that you have to apply three times before they consider you eligible . . .

Some free advice from me is you don't want a job in New York City. You are on the right track about the South business. I have thought you needed to come back for a long time. It makes sense that you should. You'd be better off in any town population under 5,000 in south Alabama than you would be in New York City. That's where reality goes out the window. That is, when it ain't your reality.

I don't mean by this that you should come home and write "Southern," but only that you should be where you belong for a while, a part of a society that has some real extension outside of the mind.

The weather here has just started to turn, it's about 55 in the mornings and warms up to a nice 80 during the day and cools down again at night. We are fixing to go out and see a lady's white-face cows as Regina needs to buy some. She doesn't want white-face but she may come to it.

## To Roslyn Barnes

24 Sept 62

The enclosed is a graduation or survival present. Take yourself to dinner or something in honor of the occasion & consider me present in ghostly form.

H. I. Green finally appeared and gave us a very funny account

of her visit to Chula Vista. She took up the 1st 20 minutes expressing her relief that you were among nice people. All along she must
have been thinking that you had fallen in with cut-throats and
assassins. She seems to feel better about the religion too—that you
haven't been took. She thinks that man [Msgr. Illych] is the
"growing tip." According to her he is anti-American. She was most
impressed with the scantness of the meals. No foolishness. She said
you had a "little service" in the morning—I presumed this was
Mass—and a "little program" at night—everything was translated
into the language of WCG and I had to translate it back. I figured
the "little program" was benediction or compline. I wish she could
have stayed two months.

I am delighted with the minute bird—which she informed me
was a rooster. It's a dove and I will cherish it . . .


## To "A."

6 October 62

I am cheered you had a good time, and you seem to be on a
real art kick. Have you seen Malraux's *Voices of Silence*? And have
you seen Gilson's book on painting—I can't at the moment recollect
the name, but it is very fine and in a paperback. The Malraux is
wonderful. A month or so ago I ordered an art book that I thought
I would give you for Christmas and when it arrived I realized I
had ordered it because it was what I like and you wouldn't at all.
Also the jacket was half torn off it which always infuriates me as
it is just carelessness on their part wrapping it up. Anyway, this
was a book of Daumier's drawings. They kill me—but it isn't the
form, the motion or anything, just the expressions on their faces—
which is as far as I can get as per art. I am not going to afflict you
with it . . .

I am messed up again with Mrs. M., that indefatigable woman
. . . Last year she was sick and didn't have [the meeting] so this
year she is going it double and giving scrolls for books for both
years. This somehow puts *The Violent Bear* into it. I flatly declined
in a polite way to go to the Awards Dinner (at which they all come
dressed down) but agreed to pick up the scroll at a box lunch they
are having the day before at the Historical Society, but this requires
some words of thanksgiving on the spot which I am having to
write. I am telling them that awards are valuable in direct ratio
to how near they come from home. Don't give me no Nobel prize,
give me this here scroll, ahhhh. What I really mean is, and what

is true, is that the writer's check of himself is local where place still has meaning.

N. is better. We were up there Thursday to get me an injection in the hips and we went to see her. She was beginning to enjoy herself again. A big fat-faced Sister had just run in and said, "Why did the Governor of Mississippi shoot his wife? Because she wanted color TV." Poor N. will hate to come home to unheightened life.

We wish you would pick out a weekend to visit us inasmuch as you have already visited New York City and Washington, D.C.

## To Maryat Lee

9 Oct 62

You sure don't have any sense. That is no place for anybody that is sick and if you stay there messing around with New York doctors that you never know if they're crooks or not, you'll be borne back to your mama's on a stretcher. What you ought to do is come here and go to Dr. Burrell. In a small place they don't tolerate sorry doctors. When I lived in N.Y. I ran from one end of it to the other looking for an honest doctor. I know all about this. And I was borne home on a stretcher, all out helpless. Dr. Burrell is an internist, which is what you ought to see. You better listen to me.

I don't know Frank O'Connor and as he is connected with Harvard she'd probably have to go be enrolled to get his services. Why don't you try Hiram Haydn? He is editor at Atheneum. Get up a bunch of her stories and take them to him. You can tell him I suggested this if you like. He's publishing Cecil's stories this fall and he knows a good thing when he sees it. I gather Eileen [friend of M.L.] is not tied up with an agent. If so, the agent would have to do it, or get rid of the agent . . .

## To "A."

19 October 62

Thanks for the musicians. I started painting some a few years back and didn't complete them, but the Hoods took a fancy to them so here they are on their mantelpiece. It would be great to be able to paint what you wanted to paint. Can see, can't do.

Mrs. Hood has just sent me a Professional Beer Can Opener. It looks like something that in medieval times they might have opened heads with, but it works. I am like to drink up all my beer with this.

I had not expected to like the Powers book [*Morte D'Urban*] because I had read some chapters of it in the *New Yorker* and *Esquire* and elsewhere and they all sounded pretty much alike. Richard Gilman asked me to review it for *Commonweal* and I refused because I was afraid I wouldn't like it. I was sent two copies so if you should change your mind, I can supply you. As it turned out, I liked it very much. The whole adds up to a great deal more than the parts would suggest. It is probably much too cool for you to like, but it has many quiet virtues that should not be disdained. I think Powers precisely is a novelist.

Thanks for the offer of all them papers but I am trying to get rid of papers, not gather them in. I want to simplify my life. If the doctor were to say you have five years to live, it would take me all five to get my room in such shape that I could leave it. I'll also pass up Miss Sewell for the present. Somebody named Neville Braybrook, which name is familiar but I can't locate it, sent me his first novel, inscribed and mailed by himself from London, so I read it, and I imagine it is sort of like the Sewell thing—fog-bound. I mean you never see a face. You know what they're thinking but not what they look like or where they came from or where they're going to or how their thinking relates to anything. Most peculiar . . .

## To Maryat Lee

27 Oct 62

So this is THE Doctor Saltzer you are going to! I know you are in good hands. I ain't going to worry about you any more. Anybody with this taste in literature must know what he is doing in all other fields too. Tell him hello.

Since you can eat eggs and cheeze, you won't suffer. I think the diet is great. I'd like to be on it myself . . . I do highly hope you will get down before Nov. 15 or after Nov. 21 as between those dates I will be on the road, war permitting. I am going to East Texas State College, University of Southwest La., Loyola at New Orleans, & Southeast La. College, 4 talks in 6 days and too much too much. My bones are not up to it. Excelsior.

## To Charlotte Gafford

29 October 62

I was cheered to see you finally come out in the *Bulletin*— and in recommendation of *Wise Blood* too. I am afraid you have a hard audience to convince but I do thank you for going at it. I guess they have been sending you copies of the paper so you know we are slated to get Mr. Gerard Sherry as editor. I had never heard of him before this but other people seem to have. The *Bulletin* has been these years a wretched sheet and the Archbishop hopes to make something of it. I hope Gerard Sherry will let Leo keep on with the book page and give him a free hand. However, all that remains to be seen. All our heads may roll.

We really have a fine Archbishop. He has read my books and approves. He also has other qualifications for the office . . .

## To Father J. H. McCown

2 November 62

. . . Roslyn [Barnes] has just spent the week with us before being sent to Valparaiso to teach chemistry in a Jesuit university. She survived the Msgr. [Ivan Illych]. He left his imprint strongly on her. Regina was shocked at some of her tales. On bidding her goodby, the Msgr. said, "Don't try to be an Irish Catholic, but you'd better read some more theology." Roslyn was greatly puzzled by this and asked me what an Irish Catholic was. "You are in the presence of one," says I, bowing.

Her people are so opposed to what she is doing that she spent her week in Ga. with us and did not go home. Her mother is mentally upset in addition. The poor girl really has no home. She knows as much Spanish she says as a three-year-old and she is going to teach chemistry in it. Lord help us all . . .

## To "A."

3 November 62

As I recollect I sent you an article two or three years ago called "The Lady and the Issue" which said substantially the same things you are saying now about the sexes. The article offended you greatly though I couldn't see why it should. Anyway you appear to be approaching the mind of the Church on this in a roundabout way. The only difference being, as I see it, that you are erecting this truth into supreme position whereas it merely has its proper place in a hierarchy of truths. If you insist upon doing this, you will become that most unfeminine of creatures—the crank. It is strictly a male prerogative to be a crank. I do think you could get a good book out of this if you are careful not to accommodate the text to the theory. I don't know about Iris Murdoch's things, but anybody will point out to you in that story of mine ["The Lame Shall Enter First"] that the little boy wouldn't have been looking for his mother if she hadn't been a good one when she was alive. This of course could be debated, but it's nowhere suggested in the story that she wasn't a good one.

I don't have the *Voices of Silence*. I borrowed it from the Phillips. It may even be out of print.

We have had as guest this last week R., a mystical type. My mother does not suffer mystical types gladly. R. went outdoors to admire nature and Regina came upon her lying flat on the ground in the back yard. It was about 50 degrees. "Get up from there," Regina says. "You'll catch your death of cold. Can't you look at things standing up?" "Yes," R. says, "but it's so much more sacramental to lie on the ground." In two days she had a cold. You can't get ahead of mother . . .

M. Coindreau tells me that Styron's book, *Set This House on Fire*, was a great success in France—he translated it—and that the French think Styron is the greatest thing since Faulkner.

Can you fancy Steinbeck getting the Nobel prize. John O'Hara will be getting it next.


*To Robert Giroux*

5 November 62

I have seven stories but I don't think there is enough variety in them to make a good collection. I might as well wait and see what I come up with in the next year or two. I'm not in any hurry. I still want to call the book *Everything That Rises Must Converge*. Right now I am writing on something that may prove to be longer than I'd like. It's tentatively called "Why Do the Heathen Rage?" It's been inevitable I get around to that title sooner or later . . .

Mr. Coindreau tells me that he thinks Julian Green would be interested in seeing *A Memoir of Mary Ann*. He also thinks the Spanish would print it and is going to mention it to a Spanish publisher he knows. The Sisters had a letter from someone in Brazil who wants to put it into Portuguese.

Thank you for the Gogol book. I'm looking forward to reading it.

[P.S.] I saw the Swedish paperback [of *The Violent Bear It Away*].

## To Maryat Lee

I am cheered you're improved. Give old Saltzer a chance. You've probably got to make up for some lost time you wasted on those quacks and it will take a while. He wrote me a note to say that you were his patient and he recommended somebody for the lupus. Very nice of him. And asked about the swan. Expert hands you are in. If he doesn't do it, then get your mama to take you to Johns Hopkins or Mayo's or Boston. You are the heir to my *De Veritate* so it is imperative that *I* go first.

Right now I am in bed with the common cold. I am supposed to leave for Texas next Thursday so I hope I can throw it off. I have bit off more than I can chew this time.

I'm cheered you liked the converging one. I guess my mama liked it all right. My stories usually put her to sleep. She's accepting all the changes in her stride. The Church makes itself felt along those lines. I take several Catlic papers which are always yapping about racial justice. Actually *I* am the conservative in this family. Strictly a Kennedy conservative. I like the way that man is running the country.

What can I read on this disease you got? Or condition or whatever you call it.

My how you would love Texas. Just the place for you. Cure your interesting disease. The gentleman who met me at Dallas is from Greenville, Texas, where there is a big sign at the city limits, "Greenville, Texas, Home of the Blackest Dirt and the Whitest People." Their "white" means "fair & square," not Caucasian. In Greenville they say, "Our niggers are white too." I saw the home of General Walker in Dallas—a big two-story battleship-grey clapboard house with a giant picture window in front in which there is a lamp with a ceramic Uncle Sam for a base. There was a U.S. & a Texas flag flying on the lawn . . .

Right now I am in Louisiana where I haven't seen or heard anything that interesting yet but I shall keep my ears open. Travel is very broadening. I hope you are feeling better. Does it cost you $45 every time you get to hear Dr. Saltzer read? Is his poetry any good?

## To Father J. H. McCown

23 November 62

The enclosed check is for you to do something for the children with. Should I have made it out to the center? If so, send it back and I'll do that. I thought maybe if I made it out to you you could use it where you pleased—give them a party or something. I made some money on this trip and would like to get rid of a little of it . . .

Roslyn has got to Chile and she is in hog heaven too. Enclose the letter. These mystics.

I haven't heard about any book from the Gossetts. I suggested that if they were interested in the Council they read the Hans Küng book. I think the Council is great but I have to watch myself or I don't pray for the Council, I pray for those French and Germans, old Achille Cardinal Lienart and his team.

Thanks for the books. I'm glad to have them . . .

## To John Hawkes

24 November 62

I was much cheered to hear from you. Travel is very broadening. I have just got back from a trip to Texas and Louisiana . . . The first thing I was shown in Dallas was General Walker's house . . . Just like you would make it if you were writing a farce about General Walker. I talked to the Newman Forum at the University of Southwestern La. There a Prof. Wagner introduced me by quoting extensively from your essay in the *Sewanee*. It sounded good to me. I went on from there to Loyola in New Orleans, where the audience was superior to the others. I have a friend in New Orleans (originally from Milledgeville) whose distinguished title is Curator of the Jazz Museum at Tulane. He actually has a Ford grant to collect the stuff. In his charge I saw a lot of New Orleans that I wouldn't otherwise. We passed a Negro nightclub called "Baby Green's Evening in Paris," which I might some day like to investigate. If I had to live in a city I think I would prefer New Orleans to any other—both Southern and Catholic and with indications that the Devil's existence is freely recognized. I can somehow see you installed in that city very well.

The young lady you wrote about from Macon showed up and sat a while. She was a friend of a friend of mine so the friend brought her. I sent her away with some very vague answers to some very precise questions and with a bunch of peafowl feathers. She was quite nice. The more I see of students the vaguer my answers get. One of them in Texas fixed me with a seedy eye and said, "Miss O'Connor, what is your motivation in writing?" "Because I'm good at it," says I. He thought I hadn't understood him right . . .

The children of God are on the shelf right now. I'm writing something that requires my feeling around in it for a while before I will know what, or IF, it is supposed to be. I figure there is no hurry. I am isolated enough to have avoided the [critical piece by] Irving Malin. Do you think I ought to read it? The word *gothic* means nothing to me. I always use the word *grotesque*. Anyway, I don't want to raise my blood pressure if it's not necessary. I hope you'll give him what he deserves—whatever that might be . . .

## To Cecil Dawkins

24 November 62

The Guggenheim thing came and the enclosed is a carbon of my recommendation. I hope it does some good but I wouldn't count on it. They make some very odd choices and pass over some very good people. It didn't occur to me that you were still at Yaddo . . . "A." asked me for your address and I told her I didn't know, but I'll correct that shortly. She wants to correct something she said to you about I. Murdoch. Her letters seem pretty high to me these days. She is making all sorts of discoveries about the difference between men and women—a subject which interests her inordinately. Her latest discovery which will revolutionize human thought is that women are bigger than men. I listens, but I never get it.

No, Obolensky was never my publisher. They were Lon Cheney's publisher when [David] McDowell was there. He thought McDowell was the good man there. I don't know anything about them. Catharine Carver worked [at Lippincott] for the last several years. She is now with Viking in New York. If you are going to be in NY, I hope you will look her up. She lives in Princeton and commutes. I think she is very fine and you would like to know her.

I have just got back from Texas and Louisiana . . . Southern Louisiana fascinated me. I think if I could endure to live in any city it would be New Orleans. Fortunately I have a friend [there] . . . He opened a few doors for me. Not under his auspices I met Walker Percy whom I have corresponded with for a couple of years and whose book I like very much. Have you tried it—*The Moviegoer*?

I'm kind of playing around with something that may be a long story or may be a novel or may be nothing. I figure there's no hurry about anything.

## To Sister Julie

12 Dec 62

Thank you for the poem of Br. Antoninus. It's the only one I've read but I like it. If they were all like this, I'd be most enthusiastic. I haven't seen the *Atlantic* with the prize essay in it . . .

I wouldn't believe anything the *Atlantic* prints about the South. The radical right wing exists in pockets. There is much diversity of opinion in the South. I have just been to Texas and southern Louisiana and I witnessed some radical conservatism and some radical liberalism too.

The swan has taken up with three Muscovy ducks. They are the only birds around here he's not scared of. He goes to the pond with them & he acts like a large nursemaid trying to keep up with three lively children. When they feel like it, they fly away and leave him.

We are having a bad freeze here. All our pipes are frozen and we have no water. I'm just limber enough to wish you a Merry Christmas.


## To William Sessions

17 Dec. 62

We wish that youall, being this close, could get up and see us, but I reckon you are not motorized. We hope Master Andrew will observe his first Christmas with the proper aplomb but I wouldn't blame him if he ignored it altogether. We'll be thinking of you.

[P.S.] She [not identified] is full of Theory. The Theories are worse than the Furies.


## To "A."

21 December 62

I didn't open the package until I got your letter saying what was in it. It sure didn't occur to me that that was what it was and I was altogether clobbered. I thought it was out of print. I am more than pleased and the first thing I want to do with it is lend it back to you because you couldn't have had time to enjoy it properly before you sent it to me. What about it? Can I send it to you? Meanwhile I am enjoying it and indulging in what my Uncle Louis calls "pride of ownership."

About that candy jar, you are right about Regina having a hand in it. I think her artistic conscience probably hurts her about those vegetable dishes I sent you last year. This year she said, "You ought to give A. something *pretty*."

I am sold on the electric typewriter for busy work. This is not it I am using now. You can't compose on it as it don't wait for you, but I have a great deal of copying to do and the difference at the end of three hours when you haven't had to return a carriage every half second is absolutely perceivable.

With such things as office parties to your credit it's too bad you aren't writing fiction. Probably these "discoveries" of yours would bear out very well in fiction where the hardest thing for the writer to indicate is the presence of the anagogical which to my mind is the only thing that can cause the personality to change. Perhaps even here it changes within what it has been made. But I doubt if anyone ever touches the limits at either end of his personality. We are not our own light. You judge so much, so many, so fast, so constantly and with so little evidence that I don't doubt you are exhausted. Not that I'm not sure your human judgments are remarkable. I've always been convinced they were. That about Ashley is right. He knows nothing much beyond the rational about literature, but in other ways I have had glimpses of a good deal of tenderness and even some charity in him.

You would really have been exhausted by the visitor we just had—an artist from San Francisco that *Jubilee* sent down here to take a picture of me. A large creature with a big yellow mustache which I think maybe was designed to hide a young face. He didn't stay here but in a Volkswagen bus. I didn't ask him where he was staying but it turned out he stayed in our woods. Sort of an elegant artist-tramp. He was very intelligent and bubbled over with sensitivity for hours on end. He finally came to the conclusion that he couldn't take my picture because he senses too much resistance in me to letting my true self appear upon my mug. So he went off in his bus to pick fruit in Florida . . .

## To Sally and Robert Fitzgerald

1 January 63

I sure do like the head scarf and I will appear in it and my long sweater together. Regina has Cultivated Illiteracy and wants me to thank you for the handkerchief. She really uses them. I reckon it's the generation. Anyway, we both thank you.

Of late several visitors have come by here who knew you. The first was Claudio Gorlier [Italian writer and critic]. He spent the afternoon with us and stayed to supper. He is spending six months at Vanderbilt and six at Berkeley. He told us about being the gendarme for routing Michael [Fitzgerald] from his room. He also said you were disappointed in his position as regarded the Church. I gather his "position" was strictly political. We had grits and sausages for supper. He didn't appear to go for the grits but he ate many sausages and when there was only one left on the dish, I passed it to him and asked him to have it. A stricken look crossed his face and he said, "Oh no. I could not take the responsibility." We liked him . . .

I am about to get me a car that you drive without using your feet. Mine just don't work quick enough any more for me not to be afraid I'd kill somebody. I hate to drive but if R. got sick or something, we'd be stuck out here, so I guess it's the thing to do . . .

## To Elizabeth McKee

3 January 63

I enclose some peacock feathers for you and Ted along with my greetings for the New Year.

I have enough stories but I am not ready to think about a collection. I want to have more of a selection to choose from and I'm in no hurry. Too many people publishing too much anyhow.

## To Cecil Dawkins

13 January 63

I was cheered to hear you are not lost in the subways or something and I am all admiration over your ability to gin up a $1,000 piece of nostalgia. *Redbook* must have improved. Rita Smith is not supposed to be any drudge; maybe it's going littry like *Esquire*. Let me know the issue and I will away to the grocery sto and buy me a copy . . .

I am letting the Thing ["Why Do the Heathen Rage?"] I am writing set a while, while I write a piece for Sweet Briar. Then I have to write an introduction to the story "A Good Man Is Hard to Find" to read at the University of Georgia; also I have a tentative engagement to go to Troy State. They were supposed to write me in January about a date and I haven't heard from them and I fear I know why. In the fall I had a letter from one of their students saying she was too stupid to read my stories and she would be "graciously appreciative" if I would write her "just what enlightenment I expected her to get out of each of the stories." This is the kind of letter that leaves me beyond exasperation. I finally wrote her a note and said that my expectation of anyone's getting enlightenment out of them was mighty limited and I'd be glad if she could just enjoy them and not make problems in algebra out of them. Presently I get a letter back from her full of profuse thanks; she has shown the letter to the head of her department and he is profoundly shocked. Apparently they had a big argument about it before she produced the letter, then she produces it and he is properly clobbered. So I figure they don't want me now. I had this same trouble in Texas. Every story is a frog in a bottle to them. I suppose it has to be that way . . .

## To J. F. Powers

14 January 63

I wrote a review of your book [*Morte d'Urban*] for the diocesan paper but it has just got a new editor whose first act was to eliminate the book page, so the review never got printed and so I can't send it to you. I can't even find a copy of it. But it was so favorable someone might have thought I was in your employ. I chiefly said that it was a novel and all the people who said otherwise were nuts. I thought it really hung together as a whole piece and that it was worth holding on to for ten years or however long you held on to it. I sent a copy to the Fitzgeralds for Christmas. They are in Italy. They too were much taken with it and Robert said he didn't see how "anyone can ever again get windy about the Church in America without faltering at least once in tribute to Powers' work."

I don't have any proper address for you so I'll try this through the *Critic*. I just wanted to set down my vote of appreciation before the year starts piling up.

## To "A."

19 January 63
Gen. Robt. E. Lee's Birthday

I think I'll have to begin to inform you when it's anybody important's birthday as I have a calendar which informs me . . .

I haven't heard anything about the new *Bulletin*, but you've got to give the man more than one issue before you judge him in this fashion. The issue I read last night was much much better than the first one. Apparently Fr. Mayhew is going to do a regular column, which I call utilizing talent and discovering it quick. He has something in there this week on religious art that needs to be said. The fact that it has been said before has nothing to do with it. It will have to be said again as often as possible. And there is something good in there from Cardinal Bea. Not only has he got rid of B. and Miss E. but also of the Monsignor who tells you how to make converts and the Teen-Age Woman who answers questions. What distresses me is that he has also got rid of the book page. Whether this is temporary or permanent I don't know, and I can't get anything out of Leo [Zuber] about it . . . I am also afraid that this fellow Sherry is going to think that nothing is so important as stories about Racial Justice, datelined Chicago and Detroit and all of an abstract character. I am afraid in this matter he has come to preach to the heathen . . . I judge that it is going to take this man a while to understand that he is Somewhere not just Anywhere.

We have found out, we think, that we can get the instrument put on this car we've got so both of us can drive it, so I won't be buying one for a while anyhow. The lesson I have got to learn is that the evil of the day is sufficient thereof. It's my nature to prepare for future evils; sometimes they don't come and sometimes worse ones come than I prepared for . . .


## To Dr. T. R. Spivey

27 January 63

You have certainly got my intention down on this story ["The Lame Shall Enter First"]. I'm not sure myself that I carried out the intention dramatically so well. To tell you the truth, I haven't read the story over since it was published because I didn't want to be confronted too strongly with my failure with it: also I am still too close to it, but your analysis is cheering and makes me feel I'll be able to read it soon. The theme is a lot bigger than my powers to deal with it at this point, but I'll probably keep trying; people will say I don't have anything else to write about. Which is okay. You have to do what you have to do.

My only criticism is in certain things you imply about *The Violent Bear etc.* I don't think old Tarwater can quite be compared to Johnson's grandfather because old T. was really a fanatic by your definition of it. He wasn't all belief without deeds; he was a man who could act. I think you need to make a distinction between what the world calls a fanatic (anybody who believes and acts literally on his belief) and your own definition of a fanatic in this essay.

On page 1, you sort of leave the impression old T. is Calvinist and sees people as dammed by God. He sees them as dammed by themselves.

On page 2, you probably ought to make it clear that Tarwater escapes the Devil by accepting his vocation to be a prophet.

One minor thing on page 4—Sheppard didn't get that telescope until Johnson came. He wasn't interested in training his own child to reach the stars. Rufus was the incentive.

I guess the *South Atlantic* would be a good place to send it since you know somebody there, or maybe the *Ga. Review* or maybe the *Sewanee*, since this has considerable to do with the devil and they have already published one thing about me and the devil which was pretty off-center as far as I am concerned. Jack Hawkes' view of the devil is not a theological one. His devil is an impeccable literary spirit whom he makes responsible for all good literature. Anything good he thinks must come from the devil. He is a good friend of mine and I have had this out with him many times, to no avail.

I do thank you for writing this. It's a great help to me to know that somebody understands what I am after doing. Let me know when you all will be through again and I hope we can make better connections. Meanwhile cheers to you both.

*About this time Flannery received a letter from an admirer in New York, a teacher of the primary grades and an enthusiast who touched a responsive chord with her sincerity and perceptive response to Flannery's writings. The late Miss McKane eventually assumed a real importance for her, and was close to her throughout the last illness.*

## To Janet McKane

30 January 63

I am touched that you have had a Mass said for me and very pleased that you like my stories and think about them. That is all I could ask for as a writer.

I thought that you might like a copy of this book [an inscribed copy of *A Memoir of Mary Ann*] which, in a different way, says something about the mystery of suffering.

Thank you so much for your prayers. It will be a great help to me to know I have them.

*To "A."*

This is Ground Hog Day and I salute you. I think you ought
to go on full speed ahead on this idea that has got you. Out of the
head and onto the paper. That is the only way you can cope with
its intricacies or discover what you are doing. I have just read the
autobiography of a lady named Katharine Trevelyan of that British
Trevelyan family. It is subtitled, "the autobiography of a natural
mystic." It was interesting from the standpoint of your theory, but
I couldn't decide whether the woman was just batty at times or
whether she was advanced on the evolutionary ladder above the
average of us. Anyway, this thing was sent me in bound galleys
if you would like to look it over. It reminded me a little of Roslyn
too—these people who are always lying in the grass feeling God.

Mr. Sherry was to come down to see me yesterday but called
and said he didn't relish driving back after dark in the fog, so we
have reset the apintment for next Thursday. I have it roundabout
that he plans some kind of supplement once a month on the arts,
but I have not heard this from him.

This has been one of our weeks of complications with Louise.
The Negro's method of escape is foolproof. She can effect complete
mental absence when she wants to—she's there, grinning, agreeing, but gone gone. No white person can cope with this, not even
my parent. Least of all my parent . . .

The lady who don't believe in tithing because they didn't have
the income tax in Jesus' time met us . . . yesterday and screamed:
"Well, they're going to operate on Miss O. tomorrow and me and
D. are taking turns keeping her cook and if she don't pull through,
we'll get her. Of course I hope she pulls through but she's nearly
ninety and you know we might as well have her cook as anybody
else etc etc etc."

16 February 63
. . . Cecil is waiting to hear whether she is going to be accepted
for the job at the *New Yorker*. I hope for her sake she won't be.
I can't imagine anything that would be worse for her.

I found G. E. Sherry to be very nice and willing to listen to my
views on his conduct of the racial business in the paper. He says
he doesn't know anything about the region, wants to learn and
doesn't want to go off half-cocked. He has practically no help and
no money and he hopes for gradual improvements. The best thing
he's done so far is that movie column. For the book supplement

he hopes to get competent people to do the reviews and not any of us that have been doing them. I agree with this. Altogether I found him a modest man and able. The newspaperman has the same kind of a job as the housewife, eat it and forget it, read it and forget it . . .

## To William Sessions

23 Feb 63

We have not heard from you people in so long we want to be assured of your continued existence & well-being and So Forth.

We have so far survived the Georgia winter which is all that can be said about us.

How is my mama's God baby?

I hope you are working in a diligent manner so that you can become a Ph.D. and then go ignorant for the rest of your life . . .

## To Janet McKane

25 February 63

I am very happy to have both these books you sent me and your letter. I had not read either book, strange to say, but I had tried to get hold of the C. S. Lewis one without success. We have no bookstore here. I order books from Brentano's and they come, if at all, in six months. Anyway you couldn't have sent me two books that I would have appreciated more.

Père Teilhard talks about "passive diminishments" in *The Divine Milieu*. He means those afflictions that you can't get rid of and have to bear. Those that you can get rid of he believes you must bend every effort *to* get rid of. I think he was a very great man.

I've been to Lourdes once, as a patient not as a helper. I felt that being only on crutches I was probably the healthiest person there. I prayed there for the novel I was working on, not for my bones, which I care about less, but I guess my prayers were answered about the novel, inasmuch as I finished it.

I would like to send you *The Divine Milieu* but I lent my copy to somebody who didn't return it, so I'll send you instead a genuine work of the Lord, a feather from the tail of one of my peacocks. The peacock is a great comic bird with five different screaming squawks. The eyes in the tail stand for the eyes of the Church. I have a flock of about thirty so I am surrounded.

My best to you always and please continue to keep me and my work in your prayers.

## To "A."

. . . Quote from latest communication from Dr. A. Brown: "You can inform [your friend] that Iris Murdoch's annual novel will be out soon. This one is about a unicorn."

Mr. Sherry after his visit here went home and thought it over and then wrote and asked me if I would contribute an article every month to his supplement. I have told him no but that I will contribute an occasional one and have agreed to do something for the first issue. I have been right disgusted with all the sentimentality wasted on those teachers who were giving Steinbeck and Hersey to the 8th grade so I am writing on that. Ralph McGill had an idiot column on it in which he implied that Hersey was much better than Hawthorne.

Miss O. is still going strong, hanging on to her cook . . .

"Everything That Rises Must Converge" has got the O. Henry prize this year. I was much surprised as I had forgotten that that prize existed. Somebody from Harvard is now running it . . .

## To Sally and Robert Fitzgerald

I have just got back from the Symposium on Religion & Art at Sweet Briar and boy do I have a stomach full of liberal religion! The Devil had his day there. It began with Boas talking about "Art & Magic." I don't know what he meant to say but he left the impression that religion was good because it was art and magic. Nothing behind it but it's good for you. Then they had the Dean of Theological School at Drew. He was a Methodist-Universalist. I gather this means you don't drink but about theology you are as vague as possible and talk a lot about how the symbology has played out in Christianity and how it's up to artists to make up a new symbology. At these things you are considered great in direct proportion to how often you can repeat the word symbology. They wedged me and James Johnson Sweeney in there somewhere. He was above the fray as he confined himself to Art, but I waded in and gave them a nasty dose of orthodoxy, which I am sure they thought was pretty quaint. It ended with John Ciardi who told them why religion was no good—or so I hear, I didn't go to his lecture.

James Johnson Sweeney asked most especially for you when he found out I knew you. I didn't get a chance to say much to him as everywhere they sat me I was next to the Methodist-Universalist. He left in the middle of my talk. I don't think it was a protest gesture, I just think he thought he could live a useful life without it. I told them that when Emerson decided in 1832 that he could no longer celebrate the Lord's supper unless the bread and wine were removed that an important step in the vaporization of religion in America had taken place. It was somewhere after that I think that he left . . .

I haven't seen it in print but somebody told me he thought [Robert] got the Bollingen Prize. I congratulate you. You should have got it if you didn't. I guess you saw that Powers got the National Book Award. I was much cheered at that. I got the O. Henry this year. Walker Percy got the N'tl Book Award last year. Katherine Anne will probably get the Pulitzer Prize. I think you ought to judge the prize by the book but even so these hold up and all these people are Catlicks so this should be some kind of answer to the people who are saying we don't contribute to the arts.

[P.S.] Have you read about the lady in Texas who is having a chapel built in the shape of John Glenn's capsule?

*To "A."*

30 March 63

. . . I wouldn't go to battle for anything I could say, but there is much that I can't say that I would go to battle for. I've been writing for nearly twenty years and the one overwhelming sense I have had, constantly, is of my own inarticulateness.

Last Wednesday I went to the University of Georgia and read that night "A Good Man Is Hard to Find." It was a perfect audience because they caught everything, it all being familiar to them. When I reached the point where Red Sammy Butts comes in, there was an appreciable titter of another order that rolled through the audience. (That case interests me greatly.) Later somebody told me that the character of Red Sammy was not unlike the character of Wally [Butts, University of Georgia football coach].

Speaking of Red Sammy, in the French translation of the

stories which I have just recently got (*Les braves gens ne courent pas les rues*) Red Sam is called "le joyeux vetéran." I haven't got a chance yet to go through the rest of it but I am looking forward.

My Muscovy duck has come out from under the pampas grass with nine enfant Muscovys behind her, a grand sight. She is the only bird around here with impressive brains.

## To Janet McKane

31 March 63

Thank you so much for the Lourdes book and the book of Miss Tabor's poems. I have been sick in bed with my annual spring cold and I enjoyed them both then. I would like to show the poems to one of the chaplains at the state hospital here. I don't know if I mentioned it but we have in Milledgeville the largest mental institution in the world. They have just got into religion out there and now they have three Protestant chaplains. One of them, a Presbyterian, called on me not long ago. He had read some of my stories. He had been an engineering student before he went into the ministry and he didn't know much about literature but he was interested in poetry. I sent him off with a couple of Robert Lowell's books. Robert Lowell is a friend of mine who was in the Catholic Church for a while and who is plagued by recurring phases of mental illness. I told this minister that I thought every mental institution ought to have a resident writer. There are a lot of [patients] who are well enough to do more with themselves and their time than weave baskets. I think he would be much interested in this girl . . .

The "passive diminishment" is probably a bad translation of something more understandable. What he [Teilhard] means is that in the case he's talking about, the patient is passive in relation to the disease—he's done all he can to get rid of it and can't so he's passive and accepts it . . .

## To "A."

13 April 63

Catharine Carver sent me the copy of [Iris Murdoch's] *The Unicorn* so I pass it on. I presume the book ain't out yet. My sense of direction about what is out has been sadly askew since the NYTBR has been out of function. The first issue after the strike arrived yesterday and I will send it on in due time. I don't really read it, I just see what's being published. She also sent me a book they are publishing of Ivan Gold's called *Nickel Miseries*, which I think is a nice title. Ivan Gold arrived here one night for a literary conversation—unannounced . . . a Brooklyn boy. Now he has a beard I see by the dust jacket (which improves him considerably) and is an artist.

My post Easter company would doubtless wear you out with responses. The 15th, a Mr. F. from Maine, the 19th, a Dr. L. from Wheaton College, . . . a preacher-English teacher, and the 20th, a Franciscan Missionary Sister who proposes to write a paper. Then we are having a class from Shorter for an afternoon, the Newman Club for Supper, the Literary Guild for a picnic, and a selection of Methodists from Emory for a conversation (by them) on some Dostoevsky movies they have seen. All this will elicit very low-grade response from me, or let me say, I will try to keep my own counsel (sp?).

The other day I postponed my work an hour to look at W. C. Fields in *Never Give a Sucker an Even Break*. This indicates the measure of my respect for Mr. Fields. Anyway, I was disheartened that they put him in a picture that wasn't such a proper vehicle for him. I think I might have written a picture that would be good for him. But it would have been all him. There were some good scenes but not enough. At one point he is riding in an airplane, goes in the club car to have a snort and places his bottle on a table near the window. Bottle falls out the window and he dives out after it. As he falls, he catches the bottle, breathes a sigh of relief, uncorks it and has a drink. Another scene, two boys knock off his hat, he apprehends them and says, "You boys are about to fall heir to a stocking-kitten." "What's a stocking-kitten?!" they ask. "A sock in the puss," says Fields and dives for them.

My nine Muscovy ducks have been taken over by a bantam hen and their mother has gone on about her social life which consists in much tail-wagging with the two drakes. I figure I should have nine more in three months.

Your friends will endure your metaphysical speculations but doubtless with a minimum of attention. It's all wasted on me.

## To Father J. H. McCown

19 April 63

I'm cheered you're back with your proper fold. I only hope you dusted off the debutantes in good style with the aid of St. John Birch. I had just written the Gossetts that your address was Drujon

Lane, so I would be obliged if you would drop them a card and tell them your release has been effected. They were inquiring about you and your ulcer. I hope that is fine.

I am sure Roslyn would be pleased to hear from you . . . Just tell her that you are a friend of mine and have been praying for her since she was at Cuernavaca and that I showed you one of her letters and you would like to use it. I don't think she would mind. I had told her I had a friend who wanted to be sent to Mexico and couldn't be on account of being 50 years old and she was right indignant and said there were plenty of people there doing the job much older than that. Anyway, I think she is discouraged and don't like it where she is and it would probably be good for her to hear from you. In case you have forgot her last name it is Barnes. I haven't kept her letters to tell you the truth. About every two months I become oppressed by paper and I lay about me tearing up every scrap I can get my hands on. If I ever go beserk it will take this form, I'll be a maniac killer of public documents . . .

I don't say much about your book unless it's very bad. It wasn't. I await the next installment about which I hope I'll have even less to say . . .

## To Charlotte Gafford

21 April 63

Poor Madison [Jones]. I believe those things [an arts festival] are better endured in a state of coma, but it must have been mighty trying to be in and out of one. A lady called me up from Birmingham and asked me to something, maybe it was to the same thing. She seemed profoundly puzzled that I could find it in my heart not to come.

I was sorry that I was on my bed of affliction when your friend called as I would have liked to have asked him out. Anyway tell him if he passes through again to call me and I'll hope to be on my feet . . .

I wish you would take your children on an educational trip to the Okefenokee Swamp or somewhere and have to pass here. Our place looks very good right now. Everything is in bloom or hatching or strutting. One peacock stays in the middle of the road with his tail up as an obstruction to automobiles. It is necessary to get out of your car to dislodge him and when dislodged he makes a most ungodly noise, a kind of sustained curse in the treble octave. I think you would find the place congenial. If there's ever any possibility of your getting here, just let me know . . .

## To "A."

I meant you to keep the book but if you want it you can get it sometime. I read it and it held my attention about two-thirds of the way and then I began to feel I was reading a connundrum about some philosophical problem and not about folks and I got most weary. I thought the allegory was thin and rather oppressive in this one. This is a purely physical reaction of course.

I got shut of my last lecture this week and was feeling like somebody let out of the penitentiary when Regina gets a letter from her colored friend Annie that I am to write her a piece for Mother's Day at Flag Chapel (A.M.E.) entitled "Woman's Day." Last year I was summoned to write her one on "The Value of Sunday School," a subject much more to my liking. An invite to the White House I could decline, but not this, unsuited as the subject is to my taste. A friend of mine from Louisville who works on the paper there was telling me about one of the discussion topics that was sent in for a colored Baptist church anniversary church news—"Who Have the Soul of the World—Adam or Noah?" But I got to write her a paper on "Woman's Day."

No mam, she does not yet have the cook. Every time we see her she screams something like, "There's a heap worse things than death let me tell you. Poor Miss O., just laying up there. Now she thinks there's people in the room playing cards." A peculiarly horrible fantasy if you ask me. She has been somewhat deflected from that topic though because another lady here in town ran into her car.

Regina got her hand closed in somebody's car door week before last so she has been somewhat curbed. Only somewhat though.

I have a copy of *Man on a Donkey* [by H. F. M. Prescott] but I've never read it. I don't see how you read all you do. It seems to me I don't have much time to read. I intend to read Dostoevsky this summer . . .

## To Maryat Lee

You had better watch it as to the eating or you will end up again in Milledgeville a bird sanctuary. I hate to think of you back at that rat race instead of floating about the hinterland making the acquaintance of your colored kin.

I forgot to tell you that at Sweet Briar I met Mrs. Savage who had been in your apartment, friend of Cynthia's. I met about a million people and earned my $500 the hard way. Last week I went to Troy State in Alabama . . . Before that I went to the U. of Ga. where I had a great time. My kind of folks . . .

Last week I had a visit from a Baptist preacher from Wheaton (Billy Graham's alma mater I think). He & I got along great & sooner or later I'll go to Wheaton . . .

## To Sister Mariella Gable

4 May 63

Thank you so very much for your letter. I remember that at Marillac, you and I said we were easily defeated when it came to defending what we thought were necessary judgments about fiction in the face of people who didn't see them. I still am, and I'm much more liable to try to get out of the way as fast as possible than to struggle to make my views plain. I think though that it's the people and not the questions that defeat us.

When they ask you to make Christianity look desirable, they are asking you to describe its essence, not what you see. Ideal Christianity doesn't exist, because anything the human being touches, even Christian truth, he deforms slightly in his own image. Even the saints do this. I take it to be the effects of Original Sin, and I notice that Catholics often act as if that doctrine is always perverted and always an indication of Calvinism. They read a little corruption as total corruption. The writer has to make the corruption believable before he can make the grace meaningful.

The tendency of people who ask questions like this is always towards the abstract and therefore toward allegory, thinness, and ultimately what they are looking for is an apologetic fiction. The best of them think: make it look desirable because it is desirable. And the rest of them think: make it look desirable so I won't look like a fool for holding it. In a really Christian culture of real believers this wouldn't come up.

I know that the writer does call up the general and maybe the essential through the particular, but this general and essential is still deeply embedded in mystery. It is not answerable to any of our formulas. It doesn't rest finally in a statable kind of solution. It ought to throw you back on the living God. Our Catholic mentality is great on paraphrase, logic, formula, instant and correct answers. We judge before we experience and never trust our faith to be subjected to reality, because it is not strong enough. And maybe in this we are wise. I think this spirit is changing on account of the council but the changes will take a long time to soak through.

About the fanatics. People make a judgment of fanaticism by what they are themselves. To a lot of Protestants I know, monks and nuns are fanatics, none greater. And to a lot of the monks and nuns I know, my Protestant prophets are fanatics. For my part, I think the only difference between them is that if you are a Catholic and have this intensity of belief you join the convent and are heard from no more; whereas if you are a Protestant and have it, there is no convent for you to join and you go about in the world getting into all sorts of trouble and drawing the wrath of people who don't believe anything much at all down on your head.

This is one reason why I can write about Protestant believers better than Catholic believers—because they express their belief in diverse kinds of dramatic action which is obvious enough for me to catch. I can't write about anything subtle. Another thing, the prophet is a man apart. He is not typical of a group. Old Tarwater is not typical of the Southern Baptist or the Southern Methodist. Essentially, he's a crypto-Catholic. When you leave a man alone with his Bible and the Holy Ghost inspires him, he's going to be a Catholic one way or another, even though he knows nothing about the visible church. His kind of Christianity may not be socially desirable, but it will be real in the sight of God. If I set myself to write about a socially desirable Christianity, all the life would go out of what I do. And if I set myself to write about the essence of Christianity, I would have to quit writing fiction, or become another person.

I'll be glad when Catholic critics start looking at what they've got to criticize for what it is itself, for its sort of "inscape" as Hopkins would have had it. Instead they look for some ideal intention, and criticize you for not having it.

In the gospels it was the devils who first recognized Christ and the evangelists didn't censor this information. They apparently thought it was pretty good witness. It scandalizes us when we see the same thing in modern dress only because we have this defensive attitude toward the faith.

I probably have enough stories for a collection but I want to wait and see what this turns out to be that I am writing on now. Then perhaps if it ["Why Do the Heathen Rage?"] turns out to be a long story, I'll put them all together in a collection. I'm not in much of a hurry about publishing. I hate the racket that's made over a book and all the reviews. The praise as well as the blame— it's all bad for your writing.

I appreciate and need your prayers. I've been writing eighteen years and I've reached the point where I can't do again what I know I can do well, and the larger things that I need to do now, I doubt my capacity for doing.

I'm glad your paper is going to be on the ecumenic side of my writing. I am more and more impressed with the amount of Catholicism that fundamentalist Protestants have been able to retain. Theologically our differences with them are on the nature of the Church, not on the nature of God or our obligation to him.

## To "A."

11 May 63

I will attempt H. F. M. Prescott the next time I have the flu. It has always looked just too historical to open up. I have no idea where I got it. It's been here for a long time. I think you have an affinity for aging British ladies of unimpeachable integrity, or maybe there are just a lot of them. You don't find anything like them in France or Italy or Germany that I can think of. Madame de Beauvoir don't seem to fill the bill. On the other hand you don't find ladies like Simone Weil in England, or do you?

Have not read Bergson's or Meredith's essays on comedy and except for the fact that I don't remember what I read anyway, I think it would be a bad idea. The less self-conscious you are about what you are about, the better in a way, that is to say technically. You have to get it in the blood, not in the head.

My parent is back at large. In fact, she is putting up a creep-feeder. A creep-feeder is a feeder where the cows can't get at it but the calves can and as they eat the feed, more creeps out. Creep-feeder.

She and I are going to Boston for the weekend of the 31st of May to see my aunt and cousins and I am going to get another degree from one of the neighboring colleges [Smith]. This is really sort of oppressive and I am going to think of some way to render myself ineligible in the future . . . I hope to see Robert Fitzgerald though as he is in the country and going to be around there. He was at Notre Dame last week visiting Tom and they called me and I talked with them at some length. Robert is going to teach at Mt. Holyoke next year and put Benny [Benedict Fitzgerald] in Portsmouth Priory.

I had a letter from Elizabeth Bishop a month or so ago saying that she was sending me a present by a friend of hers, or rather getting him to bring it back to the States with him and mail it from his home in Ohio. She hoped I wouldn't be too appalled at it, a crucifix, she said, in a bottle. She is much interested in the things made by the natives. So a few days ago it came. It's not a crucifix at all, she just don't know what a crucifix is. It is an altar with Bible, chalice and two fat candles on it, a cross above this with a ladder and the instruments of the crucifixtion hung on it, and on top of the cross a rooster. It's all wood except the altar cloth and the rooster and these are paper, painstakingly cut out and a trifle dirty from the hands that did it. Anyway, it's very much to my taste, and you will have to see it when next you spend the weekend with us which I hope you will plan to do in June when I get shut of this Boston business.

## To Robert Fitzgerald

16 May 63

I wrote the secretary at Smith College to send you an invitation to the Harvard Club. This secretary hasn't answered any of my communications yet but I presume she does things eventually. They are supposed to meet me at the Hartford-Springfield airport on Saturday at 2:30. Regina and I are going to Boston the day before that and she will visit with her sister & niece. She and about a half a dozen cousins and aunts and uncles etc. will attend the thing on Sunday. R. says they will go *anywhere*. They'll take me back to Boston and the next day me & R. will fly home. She says that's a lot of money to spend for just a weekend but I tell her she'll be good and ready to come home by then . . .

T. Stritch and I agreed last year that these exercises are, quoth James, "rancid with veracity." Take something for boredom.

I just read a book by Dom Aelred Graham called *Zen-Catholicism*, with a picture of a Zen garden at Portsmouth Priory on the jacket. I hope they won't over-calm Benny there. We want you all to take one of yr vacations with us.

## To Janet McKane

17 May 63

I was amused at the price the gentleman was asking for his peacocks. I see them advertised frequently in the Georgia *Market Bulletin* for $17.50 apiece. I also enjoyed the issue of *Commonweal*. I take it, as a matter of fact, but I don't always read it well and I hadn't read the review of A[lice] B. Toklas' book or the review by

Alice Ellen Mayhew, so I was glad to have all that called to my notice. Alice Mayhew is the sister of a Fr. Mayhew stationed here in Georgia who is a friend of mine. He brought her over to have lunch with us last summer. They are native New Yorkers. It is always hard for a Southerner to realize that people are born and grow up in NYC. To us, it is a place that you go to, that you even may live in for a while, but which is totally unsuitable to grow up in. It doesn't seem at all odd to me that those children you teach don't know about New York State. I'm sure I wouldn't know about it either if I had grown up in New York City. I couldn't see over it. You and the Mayhews seem to have survived growing up in New York City so I suppose it can be done, but as a kind of miracle, not the normal thing surely. The sense of place is very highly developed in Southerners.

I was interested in what you said about your education being mostly all Catholic. Mine was in Catholic schools only through the first 6½ grades in Savannah. After that we moved to Milledgeville where there were none. I was always just as glad. In those days, the Catholic schools were not what they are today, I guess.

I read the Graham Greene book you mentioned but so long ago that I've forgotten it, but I feel that a novelist as good as Greene probably knows what he has to do better than any critic could tell him. However, I agree with W. Lynch's general theory. Truth, Goodness and Beauty are abstractions and abstractions lead to thinness and allegory whereas in good fiction and drama you need to go through the concrete situation to some experience of mystery. However again, I am no good at theory. Like Greene or any other writer, when I write I do what I have to with what I can. You are always bounded by what you can make live. I get weary with people like Hilda Graef who take Mauriac and Greene to task, for instance, for not writing about *Christian* marriage . . .

Georgia is full of Baptists named Kelly and the like. Maybe they lost it before they even got here, I don't know. But the ones who came with it intact have established it with some sacrifice. Mass was first said here in my great-grandfather's hotel room, later in his home on the piano. Now we have three Masses here every Sunday. But there's no school and so there's a lot of leakage as there is no school. We had one for three or four years but they took the Sisters away because they said they were needed more in the city . . .

Old Brentano's came through last week with the book I ordered before Christmas—*On the Theology of Death* by Karl Rahner. It is great but difficult to read. I read every sentence about three times and then have trouble connecting it with the next one. But every now and then I get the impact . . .

About the Ignatian method of meditation: it sounds fine but I can't do it. I am no good at meditating. This doesn't mean that I get right on with contemplating. I don't do either. If I attempt to keep my mind on the mysteries of the rosary, I am soon thinking about something else, entirely non-religious in nature. So I read my prayers out of the book, prime in the morning and compline at night. I like Teilhard's idea of the Mass upon the World.

I was interested to hear about the possible lupus. I am very content with mine. It's latent at the moment and well-behaved.


## To William Sessions

18 May 63

My mama did appreciate the card and directs me to tell you so. She is in the field, haying. She has recently been bit by two wasps and has caught her hand in a car door but is still in command.

Week before last we had Minna [Berg] & Fr. Paul for lunch. It was his birthday so we had a little cake etc. Minna looks fine and we all took your name in vain & wished you were present. We showed her pictures of Jenny & Andrew and she was highly impressed.


## To "A."

25 May 63

Well, I can report now that Miss O. has gone to her rest, accommodating her relatives to the extent that they can now attend the graduations of their children. For the last two weeks, [she] has been going around wailing, "It looks like the Lord *would* take Miss O. so M. could go to those graduations. It wouldn't be like this," she said, "if [the doctor] hadn't given her that transfusion. Didn't ask a one of us! Didn't say a thing to us, just gave it to her when she couldn't hardly breathe. She just rattled, just from the neck up and HE gave her a transfusion and etc. etc. etc." Both God and [the doctor] have been guilty of gross mismanagement in this case, but now that can be forgotten. The big thing is the Will and who will get the night nurse. [Her] big concern is that Miss C. hire the night nurse, but Miss C. who can't see her hand before her face is a stubborn type who don't realize that she needs a night nurse, and wouldn't want to pay one if she did realize she needed one. [She] thinks they ought to call [Miss C.'s son] and tell him he ought to pay the difference on the q.t. if Miss C. won't etc. etc. etc.

They finally got around to sending me the Philip Rahv anthology. There's never much money in those things but it's pretty good company to be in so I don't mind. Incidentally, I don't think any of Waugh's early things are in the same class with *Men at Arms*. Signet is going to put out my three books under one cover in October. They asked me to write an introduction to it but I said the note to *Wise Blood* ought to do for the lot of them and I am writing fiction now and don't want to interrupt myself to concoct some abstraction.

Never read Beauvoir. Never aim to. I think myself that Simone Weil is a trifle monstrous, but the kind of monstrosity that interests me. As for the blood and the head business, the blood and the head work together and what is not first in the blood can sometimes reach it by going first through the head and what is wrong in the blood can sometimes be tempered by the head.

I have taken up with reading C. Vann Woodward. Have you ever read this gentleman—*The Burden of Southern History* is what I have but I intend to order off after more. Southern history usually gives me a pain, but this man knows how to write English.

## To Janet McKane

5 June 63

Thanks for the Rumer Godden book and the papers and things that came yesterday. I'll read the book and return it but I am a slow reader and always have several things going at once, so should you want it before I get it back, just let me know. I guess we have about the same taste in magazines . . . The more I take, the less I read; even so, I read too much and in too slipshod a fashion, not stopping to let it soak in before I begin on something else.

I can understand your feeling about New York as I lived there for four months myself in 1949—in a room on the 12th floor of a building on the corner of Broadway and 108th. I liked riding the subways and the busses and all and there was a church on 107th and I got to Mass every day and was very much alone and liked it. Then I could get around, but I wouldn't like it now because I couldn't ride the subways or get around and I think a city is no good when you can't move around in it. I went to the Cloisters twice and I particularly remember one statue that I saw there. As I remember it was about four feet high and on a pedestal. It was the Virgin holding the Christ child and both were laughing; not smiling, laughing. I've never seen any models of it anywhere but I was greatly taken with it and should I ever get back to the Cloisters, which is unlikely, I mean to see if it is there. Do you know it?

I think you have a sense of place up there, but since it is not connected with a historical defeat, I don't think it touches as deep an emotion . . . It's not simply a matter of present-place, but a matter of the place's continuity and the shared experience of the people who live there . . .

Today I got in the mail Karl Barth's *Evangelical Theology: an Introduction,* to review for the diocesan paper. I can't review it intelligently but I'll just expound on the table of contents or something. I am anxious to read Barth and see how kin we are to him.

Yesterday one of my peahens hatched four chicks and a Muscovy duck came off with five ducklings. This is the best season around here, everything hatching or squawking or strutting. The other day I went out the door and counted fourteen peacocks with their tails up.

I know what you mean by light. There are a few people I can identify it in but I can never describe it.

*Referring to the Memorial Day race in Indianapolis, Tom Stritch told me that Flannery shared his interest in motor races, as well as in track events. This is one of the few times she mentions these diversions. The "portrait" of the Cardinal refers to something Tom was trying to write about his uncle, Cardinal Stritch of Chicago.*

## To Thomas Stritch

14 June 63

I'm glad you observed the holiday in a creditable way since you missed the race anyhow. I would love to see that crowd but I guess the nearest I'll get is on television. I watch the stock-car races sometimes but you don't see anything but cars. I know about Fireball Roberts though and I watched an interview with Tiny Lunn. He is a huge dead-serious innocent-faced boy who must have made it big, he had just won the one in Jacksonville when I saw him but he never smiled once. This is the kind I'd like to write a story about, like him. I have to write about the dumb ones as well as I'd have to teach that kind if I knew anything to teach, which I don't . . .

I watch the sportscast every day. A man named Savage interviews all the local athletes and others not so local when he can get them. He's kind of smirkey but they seldom smile. Last week there was a model railroaders' convention in Macon and he interviewed some of them, all rich retired businessmen. One old boy said, "People think this is a child's game (scowl). Well it isn't, it takes great skills and is very expensive."

I have some advice for you about the Cardinal's portrait. My advice is free, excellent, unsought after but given without stint. If you have only written it three times, it is still supposed to be no good. You have a defect of patience, not a defect of energy. But even if you have both you ought to keep on with it. He is not in the back of my missal but that don't mean that I don't take a proprietary interest in him. I have a defect of energy myself but not a lack of patience. I can wait on myself indefinitely.

We are real cheered you're coming to see us & suit yourself about the time. We'll take you when we can get you . . .


## To Marion Montgomery

16 June 63

You are absolutely right to consider nothing but major problems. My major problem is finding the next word. Do you intend to take this up? If so, I had better enroll at Converse for the summer.

I never wrote and thanked you for innerducing me at Georgia or for the copy of *The Sermon of Introduction*, but I liked them. They make up for my present lack of popularity with the *Atlanta Journal-Constitution* book page, that alert sheet of Sunday criticism. Did you see their mention of "Everything That Rises Must Converge"? Unsigned. I suspect somebody from Atlanta U. did it.

Remember me to the couple who used to be at Ga. but are now at Conv. and whose faces I can see like the back of my hand but whose names are nowhere in my head. Also to Andrew [Lytle] when he appears . . .


## To Janet McKane

19 June 63

. . . I hate like sin to have my picture taken and most of them don't look much like me, or maybe they look like I'll look after I've been dead a couple of days. Those in *Jubilee* were taken in winter by a very arty photographer whose favorite types of pictures were migrant fruit-pickers and the interiors of flophouses. We have a beautiful place here but he made it look like Oklahoma after the duststorm. I look like one of the Okies with the burden of world peace on my shoulders. The picture in the *Critic* is a little more like me but the interview is not very good. I hate to deliver opinions. On most things I don't deserve an opinion and on a lot of things I simply don't have an opinion.

In the self-portrait that is not a peacock. That's a pheasant cock. I used to raise pheasants but they got too much for me as they require attention and have to be caged. The peacocks take care of themselves. But I like very much the look of the pheasant cock. He has horns and a face like the Devil. The self-portrait was made ten years ago, after a very acute siege of lupus. I was taking cortisone which gives you what they call a moon-face and my hair had fallen out to a large extent from the high fever, so I looked pretty much like the portrait. When I painted it I didn't look either at myself in the mirror or at the bird. I knew what we both looked like.

I enjoyed the interview with Hans Küng in the *Cath. World*. Only the day before a Protestant friend sent me the May 29 issue of the *Christian Century* in which there is an attack on Küng accusing him of being anti-Semitic in *The Council, Reform & Reunion*. I guess you've read it. I thought it was wonderful and didn't observe any anti-Semitism in it, but this piece was by a Jew who had apparently been grievously offended by Küng's references to things Jewish. My friend who is an A.R.P. (Associate Reformed Presbyterian) with strong Catholic leanings was much upset by it. I sent her off the Freedom speech in *Commonweal* and I'll also show her this. I don't think Küng intended any anti-Semitism . . .

I've got all of Muriel Spark but strangely I've never read G. Fielding. I'll have to get around to it sooner or later. Right now I have Barth staring me in the face, plus a book of Pastor Lackmann's on the Augsburg Confession, one on Biblical studies and another on Biblical research and another by an Episcopalian on Teilhard. I like to read them but I loathe to write the reviews. I'll look forward to reading *An Episode of Sparrows* when I get some of this behind me.

I didn't see much of the city when I stayed in New York . . . I didn't go to a single play or even to the Frick museum. I went to the Natural History Museum but didn't do anything the least cultural. The public library was much too much for me. I did well to get out and get a meal or two a day. I finally ended up eating at the Columbia University student cafeteria. I looked enough like a student to get by with it, and it was one of the few places I suspected the food of being clean.

The peacocks are beginning slowly to shed so when I get a good bunch of fresh feathers, I'll send them to you and you can put them in a vase.

## To "A."

22 June 63

We appreciate the visit and the bottle and the candy. You are very good to come down here on a bus and go back with Louis [Cline]. It would be more than I could take. He does the best by the candy. He eats candy as I have probably said before by the handful not by the piece. He was on his third handful when Regina remarked "I don't see why you don't weigh a hundred more pounds than you do." "Man of discretion," he murmured.

The Hannah Arendt thing is all over the book section this time and I will send it to you shortly. Cal writes a good letter in her defense and a lot of other people . . .

I am much amused by the local reaction to my appearing in *Esquire* ["Why Do the Heathen Rage?"]. You would think that at last I was really going places. I didn't know so many people took the thing. Your friend Mailer is also displayed in this issue. I gather he is attacking a lot of selected writers but I haven't read it. These literary young men spend a great deal of time dissecting each other's failures . . .

Your views on morality are for never-never land. We don't live in it.

B. called up and talked a mile a minute but I can't remember anything he said but Regina found a card with the announcement of her godchild's birth so she is sleeping well again. We don't make at all good godparents. I always forget the Fitzgerald's birthday that I am godmother to and I can't for the life of me recall the first name of the other child I am godmother of.

The enclosed clipping I find very funny and a confirmation of my worst contentions about high-school English teaching . . .

## To Janet McKane

30 June 63

I'm always glad to see the Miss business ditched. I never feel much like Miss O'Connor.

I guess what you say about suffering being a shared experience with Christ is true, but then it should also be true of every experience that is not sinful. I mean that say, joy, may be a redemptive experience itself and not just the fruit of one. Perhaps however joy is the outgrowth of suffering in a special way. I am reading another book on Teilhard—by an Episcopalian. It's real good. I'd like to lend it to you when I get through if you're interested. It's a book I want to keep for the library I'm building up. When I die I'm going to leave this to the city library, a good Catholic collection for this good Protestant town. A very interesting thing in this book is about Teilhard's attitude toward devotion to the Sacred Heart of Jesus. It was apparently a focus for his ideas though the representation of it in popular devotion rather nauseated him. I have always thought it a shame that this devotion to the Sacred Heart couldn't be explained in some way that was not just sentimental piety.

Don't hesitate to tell me what you didn't agree with in the interviews. The answers are all half-answers, elliptical, incomplete and I am glad to hear the objections because I can see what probably should be brought up or added. I don't want any more copies. I look at them once to see there are no bad errors in the printing and then I don't look at them again. I don't know why the water tower except it's there and hard to avoid where he was taking the pictures. He probably thought it symbolized something.

I have a cousin who teaches the first grade in a school outside of Boston. She talks about how the children like to throw away things too.

It was *The Theology of Death* [by Karl Rahner] I was reading. I finished it but I could read it once a year and still not know exactly what he has said . . .


## To Thomas Stritch

4 July 63

I have this temptation to write you on the 4th of July though I usually don't celebrate it. However, don't be alarmed. You don't have to answer these things. I like it when you do but I know you have other bidnis to occupy yourself with. So do I and ought to be at it but I get weary writing, every day, what don't exist for who don't exist. We don't celebrate the 4th but the help does. Shot was at the back door early this morning to say he had a cousin who died last Friday and he must be off for the funeral today. He'll spend it riding up and down the road with a bad crowd that lives across the way and we also heard that they are going to barbecue a goat over there. R. let him go after giving a Jonathan Edwards-type sermon and letting him know she didn't accept the cousin story. He does love bad company.

The creep-feeder is a total bust. She got it up and they took it off down in the field and filled it up. The calves wouldn't have anything to do with it but the man at the feedstore said when they got hungry they'd go for it. So last week she went down to look at it and the peachickens were lined up at it like patrons at a diner. She claims they have eaten seventeen dollars and fifty cents worth of calf feed in the last month. It seems the geese have been at it too. I've got to pay for half the calf-feed now.

[P.S.] Katherine Anne sent me a review out of *L'Express* of *Les braves gens ne Whateveritis* [French edition of *A Good Man*]. It seems to be favorable but not sensible except it says I live on a *vast* estate among many beasts.

## To "A."

6 July 63

This will probably be an incoherent effort as [a workman] . . . is in my room putting up curtain rods for the drapes my mama has made. He is silent at the moment but he is never silent long.

I got the clipping about telephone-teaching from the teacher herself, an old Milledgeville gul who now holds forth at Columbus High. Last fall she brought the senior class of C. High on a tour of middle Georgia, historic sights and so forth. They went to Macon first and saw the Indian mounds, then they came here and saw the Mansion and me, then they went on to Eatonton and saw Turnwold, Joel Chandler Harris's home. Then they went back and wrote about what they liked best. One girl wrote that the O'Connor swan hissed at her. Anyway they learns by doing and looking and telephoning. She wanted to put my name on the telephone list but I declined to have it put there. Oh, she says, they ask very intelligent questions. One of them asked somebody what he thought of Absolutes. They had been reading Ayn Rand or somebody equally bad and had got interested in the question.

The fellow at Smith sent me Elizabeth Sewell's book of poems. The serious ones escape me but there are some lovely nonsense ones. I seem to think she has written a book on nonsense. There is a fine one to St. Thomas Aquinas about him sailing away with the owl and the pussycat. She has a very strong face on the back jacket. Will send you this if you are interested. I'd like to read the novel sometime if you've still got it.

Right now I am trying to get Madison Jones' new one read. It is a shame about his books. They are excellent and fall like lead clear out of sight the minute they are published.

[The workman] says he has a hemorrhage every three years. Maybe you have an ulcer, I says. No'm, he says. Hits out of my nose. The doctor says if hit didn't come out of my nose it would go into my brain and kill me.

## To Janet McKane

9 July 63

I enjoyed reading the children's comments on the poems. I really don't know much about children, that is to say, what goes on in their minds. I like to watch them from outside. I also appreciate the poems from the ark. They remind me a little of Péguy. The Virgin and Child on the card is not the one. It was stone or maybe it was wood but it wasn't colored. One reason I remember it particularly was because the Child had a face very much like the face of a friend of mine, Robert Fitzgerald. I lived with the Fitzgeralds in Connecticut for two years. They have six children and their three boys also looked like that—father's sharp nose. I think it is definitely the one in the Museum Bulletin. I think the ciborium in the form of a dove is wonderful. Back then their religious sense was not cut off from their artistic sense.

Walter [Walter Tilman, the son in "Why Do the Heathen Rage?"] is the character who appeared briefly in *Esquire*. My mornings are devoted to Walter. Poor Walter. We get on slowly if at all.

Rather than your sending down a copy of *The Violent Bear It Away*, I will send you up one. It didn't sell much in England and they sent me back a dozen or so copies, which are just sitting around here. I'm not much of an inscriber. My originality ends or is exhausted in writing the book, but I'll manage to make it plain that it's from me to you on the fly leaf. I can never think of quotations. The appropriate thing always comes to me too late.

I was very glad to get the picture. You look rather like an aunt of mine, dead now, but a force around here while she lived. My mother contends that you look like a friend of ours, also about 4'11" who has gone up to Hawthorne, N.Y. to see if she can stick it out in Rose Hawthorne's order of Dominican nuns. She's a Georgia girl, a convert, and is finding it awfully cold and severe.

You probably remember a lot of what you learned in college because you took it over a long period of time. I don't remember any of mine. I went during the war, summer and winter, and got through in three years. I like to say I have total non-retention. I enjoyed college and despised the progressive high school but only remember people and things from both.

That quote from Jeremiah: "The Lord is watching in the almond trees etc."—do you know the chapter and verse? I've begun at the beginning and haven't found it yet. I like it.

I'm also pleased to have the map of New York City. I never had one when I was there and all I knew was "uptown" and "downtown." I was there from April to September. The heat was much worse than Georgia. It's plenty bad here now. In the afternoons, I go out and scoot water on my swan.


## To "A."

20 July 63

Excuse me for forgetting the question about Robt.'s translation. Only the *Odyssey,* not the *Iliad.* It's in paperback now I believe. He has also translated the Theban cycle, two with Dudley Fitts and the *Oedipus at Collonus* (sp) by hisself. I much admire the latter. You also asked what I thought about Paul VI. I think Amen Amen Amen, but anyone would have done . . .

I started not to open that package, figuring it was just Simone Weil but I did and am glad. I haven't quite finished the novel but I think it's a very fine book [*Now Bless Thyself*, by Elizabeth Sewell], a poet's book sure enough. I very much like the notion she gets across that the poet deals exactly with the things that don't work out, that he's sort of a shock absorber, that he takes the first blows and mutes them through the imagination and makes things bearable. This must be a much younger picture on the novel jacket. The one on the book of poems is much more reserved and severe . . .

I've just recently had an ecstatic letter from Maryat about a book called *The Hands of Esau* by Hiram Haydn, he being the editor of the *American Scholar;* also Cecil's editor at Atheneum. According to Maryat if I want to see what her insides are like just read that book. I'm suspicious of books that look too much like anybody's insides, but I imagine there must be something to this one since it has set her off so . . .

## To Janet McKane

25 July 63

I was delighted to read the piece on Chagall. I never see the *Atlantic* so I would have missed it altogether and Chagall is one of my favorites. Last year I saw a television interview between Chagall and a young man from the museum in Boston I think it was—educational TV. The young man was very arty. He started out with a question about influences—very long and involved and exhibiting his own learning along the way, giving everybody including Chagall a lecture on the nature of influences on the artist. When he finally gave Chagall a chance to answer, Chagall said in the simplest way possible that his greatest influence was his mother. It took the poor young man an instant or two to get his bearings after that. Rouault doesn't come out very well in this does he? And when Chagall speaks of "the Spaniard" does he mean Picasso do you suppose? You see the Jewish sensitivity very well in this.

If there is a re-run of the program on the Irish in America I'll try to look at it. Between you and Mr. O'Gara it is already pretty vivid to me. I have never been greatly tied emotionally or sentimentally to my own Irish background. The Irish in America are sometimes more Irish than the Irish and I suppose some of my indifference is a reaction against that . . . On the other hand, all the Irish from Ireland that I have ever seen have been charming. About ten days ago someone brought a man named Thomas Kilroy and his wife to see us. He had been over here a year teaching at Notre Dame and was having a look at the South. His wife was from New York. They were going back to live in Dublin, he to write fiction. He was a friend of Mary Lavin whom he told me I should read. Anyway, here was the real thing, and I greatly prefer it. His wife from New York felt sort of like I did. I was brought up in Savannah where there was a colony of the Over-Irish. They have the biggest St. Patrick's Day parade anywhere around and generally go nutty on the subject. Thos. Kilroy said the South more than any other part of this country reminded him of Ireland—but he wasn't talking of places like Savannah. (Although I have heard it compared to Dublin!)

The last time I was really in New York was 1958 when we spent the night there on our way to Europe on the pilgrimage to Lourdes. Usually when I have to go somewhere I try to avoid it, because it is just too much getting in from the airport and out again and all that, but if I do ever get there we will have to have a meal together.

I had a cousin, now dead, who used to send me the Sacred Heart leaflets every month, but nobody sends them now. She called it her "band" or something like that. If you have a band, could you put me on it? I'd like to get them every month.

*The Violent Bear It Away* is from the Douay, also Confraternity versions. In a lot of instances the new ones are no improvement . . .

## To Richard Stern

27 July 63

What you ought to do is get you a Fulbright to Georgia and quit messing around with all those backward places you been at. Anyhow, don't pay a bit of attention to the Eyetalian papers. It's just like Cudden Rose says all us niggers and white folks over here are just getting along grand—at least in Georgia and Mississippi. I hear things are not so good in Chicago and Brooklyn but you wouldn't expect them to know what to do with theirself there. Down here is where all the writers come from and if you once come you would never want to leave it.

What are you fixing to do, publish another novel? Do you want to be known as One-a-year Stern? I am doing my best to create the impression that it takes 7 years to write a novel. The four-hour week. You are not helping the Brotherhood. Examine your conscience. Think. Meditate. Shilly-shally.

## To Maryat Lee

31 July 63

Where did you dig up a Hyperglycemia Foundation? I hope it has some sho-nuf doctors on it like Sofer, because any bunch of nuts can get up and call themselves a Foundation. Anyway what's being done for you? Why Red Bank, New Jersey? This doctor is doubtless a cousin to some Greenleafs I created. Ask her if she doesn't have Southern cousins. Is she black or white? Gimme the details when you feel like it. Corn at least is cheap. I feed it to everything out here. You may begin to cackle shortly though . . .

I see *The Hands of Esau* [by Hiram Haydn] in Marboro for a buck so I may invest but only to see your insides. Full of corn.

Do I have any books you would like to read or anything? Love & cheers.

## To "A."

I'm cheered to hear about the move and I hope you make it. I'd rather live in a less desirable neighborhood and have more space. I've usually had my own room but it's always been subject to intrusion. The only thing in mine that is not subject to intrusion is my desk. Nobody lays a hand on that, boy.

We have finally got us a new car which I can drive because it has power brakes and they are so positioned that you don't have to lift your foot to put them on. Now I don't feel so much like Billy Woodchuck in a house without a back door. I still hate to drive unfortunately.

Ashley inquired after you and said to tell you Iris Murdoch had written a play or was having one on in London or some such thing. He is full of such literary information which I promptly forget. He did say that Caroline was a friend of Elizabeth Sewell's. The latter wrote a book about Adonis or somebody that Caroline went nuts over and got in touch with her about. Possibly she looked like that picture on the novel and couldn't help herself. I find you are peculiarly helpless about pictures. You ought to see the ones that creature with the yellow and black mustache took of me. They are sinister. In them I look like one of the Okie women ready to shoot a revenuer . . .

I mean to send you sooner or later the copy of the *New York Review* that Ashley left here for me. In it Edmund Wilson airs his tastes about painting.

A friend of mine in Athens has written an essay entitled "Getting James Baldwin Off My Back."

Nothing doing here.

[P.S.] On *The Ring & the Book* I reckon I've read it. I had a course in college entitled "Tennyson, Browning" and it looks like they would have made us read it. I don't remember anything about it though. All I remember from the whole course is "Come into the garden, Maud, for the black bat, night, has flown." I thought that was hilarious.

## To Ashley Brown

Thanks a lot for the story of Eudora Welty's. Nobody else could have got away with it or made it work but her I think. I want to read it again. Do you want it back?

We got the car, complete with 327 engine and tires such as are found on police cars; power this and that. We wanted dark green but when it came it was light but it runs and I can drive it so as far as I am concerned it's okay.

Madison and Shalah (sp?) came over and spent the day and took back five Muscovy ducks. He has written that he is going to consult with the vet school at Auburn about my swan's "boils." I don't think they're exactly boils but anyway I'll be glad for any information I can get. Conn West consulted the Poultry Disease Center in Athens but they said they didn't make house calls.

I got sent Caroline's piece on [Ford Madox] Ford and MUST write her a letter, not about it, but just on general principles. I can't get up much enthusiasm over the White Goddess business . . .

I hope you enjoy San Francisco. I get a quarterly from Burlingame called *Genesis West* but I don't read it.


## To Maryat Lee

15 Aug 63

She begins to sound a little mo better. Hereafter I'll charge for my advice: $1 an hour medical, $5 literary. Herewith your well-preserved notes.

Are you any better?


## To "A."

17 August 63

. . . For "You are peculiarly helpless about pictures" read "one is peculiarly helpless about pictures." I wasn't meaning you. I was meaning me, and I ought to learn to use the "one is" formular but I just ain't a "one is" type. What I mean to say is any jerk can take a picture of you and do with it what he wills. I am sure there are now in existence hundreds of horrible pictures of me that I have no control over. Your face ought to be sacred to you but it sure is not. I am always glad when some judge stands out and won't let photographers into his courtroom. Photographers are the lowest breed of men.

We've had a bad week around here. Liquor has been coming in. Wednesday Louise threw scalding water on Shot and he had to be taken (by Regina) to the emergency room at the hospital and he's been more or less out all week from it. Louise was very pleased that she scalded him. Later in the day I asked Regina if she was still pleased with herself. Regina said no, she was sorry now she hadn't killed him . . .

*In this letter Flannery gives the first indication of a new health problem, anemia. This symptom was not then recognized as connected with the condition which would necessitate the operation that reactivated her lupus.*

## To Louise Abbot

18 Aug 63

Let us know when you get back and we'll get together. I hope the operation will not be bad if you have to have it. I guess those things are pretty safe now but tiresome to have to undergo, and nothing you'd exactly autosuggest yourself into. I have anemia from loss of blood and keep myself going with iron that has a special non-absorbent agent in it. Name of SIMRON. You might ask your doctor about this form of iron. It won't correct your trouble but it might make you feel better. It keeps my hemoglobin around 10— taking 6 a day . . .

## To Maryat Lee

23 Aug 63

You have to be very careful what you say to or show doctors. Remove any trace of imagination or anything not 20-20 facts. I waddn't born yesterday.

That sounds like a great boardinghouse. Do you have a sack of scratch feed in your square foot of space? You should make the acquaintance of the inmates. Better than reading probably.

We have a Chevrolet. I am supposed to drive it a little every day. I sure hate to drive but now I don't feel so much like Billy Woodchuck when he built him a house without a back-door (his mama told him never to do that again).

How come you ache in the joints? Isn't that new? Maybe all you have is lupus & don't know it. Cheers. How long you going to be there? Excelsior.

## To Janet McKane

27 August 63

Thanks so much for the museum bulletins with devilish dogs etc. The dog I like in painting is one in a painting of Rousseau. I don't know the name of it but the family is in a wagon, all looking ahead and there is one dog in the wagon and one underneath, kind of prim diabolical dogs. It's very funny. It used to hang in the Fitzgeralds' kitchen (the people I lived with in Connecticut) but I have never seen it anywhere else.

I don't much agree with you and your friend, the nun, about suffering teaching you much about the redemption. You learn about the redemption simply from listening to what the Church teaches about it and then following this to its logical conclusion. People are depressed by the ending of *The Violent Bear It Away* because they think: poor Tarwater, his mind has been warped by that old man and he's off to make a fool or a martyr of himself. They forget that the old man has taught him the truth and that now he's doing what is right, however crazy. I haven't suffered to speak of in my life and I don't know any more about the redemption than anybody else. All I do is follow it through literally in the lives of my characters. You understand this so the ending didn't depress you. People who are depressed by it believe that it would have been better if the schoolteacher had civilized Tarwater and sent him to college where he could have got an engineering degree or some such. A good many Catholics are put off because they think the old man, being a Protestant prophet, so to speak, has no hold on the truth. They look at everything in a confessional way . . .

I've been reading Shakespeare myself lately because I have found that the Marboro book stores are offering various volumes of the Arden Shakespeare for $1 a piece, which I think is a good bargain. I've got *King Lear, Richard II, Antony & Cleopatra* and *The Tempest* and I'm hoping they'll eventually put them all on the list. I get that Marboro sales sheet every month. A good deal of it junk (*Sex in the South Sea Islands*) but occasionally you find something worth having.

I like cartoons. I used to try to do them myself, sent a batch every week to the *New Yorker*, all rejected of course. I just couldn't draw very well. I like the ones that are drawn well better than the situations . . .

## To "A."

Them bookcases sound mighty adequate, mighty adequate, and I hope in your enthusiasm you waited to let the paint dry before you put the books on the shelves. Those birds are chukar (sp?) quail. I had about forgot that picture . . .

You are right about the Welty story. It's the kind of story that the more you think about it the less satisfactory it gets. What I hate most is its being in the *New Yorker* and all the stupid Yankee liberals smacking their lips over typical life in the dear old dirty Southland. The topical is poison. I got away with it in "Everything That Rises" but only because I' say a plague on everybody's house as far as the race business goes. I have just had my day smirched up slightly by reading something in the Atlanta magazine. B.F. sent me a list of questions, a lot about the race thing. She asked in one of them if I thought the *race* crisis was going to bring about a renascence (that wasn't the word she used but was what she meant) in Southern literature. I said I certainly did not, that I thought that was to romanticize the race business to a ridiculous degree. In the story that comes out they change the word *race* in the question to *social* so that none of it makes much sense. You can't get around newspaper people. I think they are the slobber-heartedest lily-mindedest piously conniving crowd in the modern world . . .

Tom has been here most of this week (Stritch) which is why I am communicating with you upon the Sabbath.

## To John Hawkes

I was much cheered to hear from you. I had been wondering for the last several months whether you were still being laved in the lap of that West Indian devil (care of Mrs. Miranda cum Gumbo) or whether you were back with Providence where the wind is fierce and the damp is acid. I'd glad you're back and glad to hear about the novel. I envy your get-down-to-itiveness. I have been working all summer just like a squirril on a treadmill, trying to make something of Walter and his affairs and the other heathens that rage but I think this is maybe not my material (don't like that word) but anyway I am committed to it for a spell at least . . .

I remember Hollis Summers and his wife very well and always liked them. They usually send me a poem at Christmas with no return address on it but I think they are somewhere like Kentucky or Ohio. An elderly nun I know wrote me last year and told me that a mutual friend of ours had gone to "Loaf of Bread." And I have never thought of it as anything but Loaf of Bread since . . . I am a veteran of Yaddo but I don't think I could take Loaf of Bread.

My swan is in good health in spite of having developed an unsightly tumor on his breastbone. I've had friends consult with the veterinary departments at the universities of Georgia and Alabama about him and it seems this is a common affliction of large ungainly birds. They sent word from Georgia that they didn't make house calls but if they were in the neighborhood would stop by to see him. We are expecting a baby burro any day and my Muscovy duck has set three times this year and presented me with her last hatch on Labor Day. She runs to holidays, the first hatch coming off on St. Patrick's Day and the second on Jefferson Davis's birthday. So you see everything is in a great harmony here . . .


## To Maryat Lee

10 September 63

Lord bless us, what next? Here I have been commiserating with my image of you that was so po and energyless it couldn't go to Washington to march for freedom with all its natural cousins and you all the time were fixing to hire yourself out as a super char to a super Catholic family. I can think of a lot of things I'd prefer your services at than housekeeping. No wonder she got another girl. You probably blended their garbage and baked it. The next book would have been *The Day We Were Poisoned by the House-keeper*. I never saw any of his [Jim Bishop's] columns and didn't know he wrote one. They don't penetrate down here I reckon. And I never read any of his books but them I have heard of. And they never heard of mine at all I would suppose, though they might have seen the Sisters' book about Mary Ann. If you would like a copy of that to give the 8 and 10-year-olds at your departure, I will send you one. Children read that in Catholic schools and apparently like it.

I'm glad he's making you write about the natural cousins. Seems to me that's all to the good. He might know exactly what to do with it after you had written it. It should be very good if you keep it objective and don't go rummaging around in people's heads, including your own.

We were in the car going around the corner the other day and a car was coming opposite in which was the Lee jaw. I thought for a minute it was you for sure but it was your brother.

I visited the bone doctor yesterday and he allowed after looking at my X-rays that my bones are sounder than of yore, last year to be exact. The heads are still flat and that won't change, but I can put a little more pressure on them. I'm glad I don't have no steel in me . . .


## To "A."

14 September 63

A letter from Jack Hawkes says they are back from their paradise and back in Providence where the wind is already fierce. He is having another novel out in January called *Second Skin,* a good Hawkesian title if I ever heard one.

. . . I have another one of these gentlemen of the movies on my trail, this one after "The Life You Save." He sent me his script. About the only change he had made was to have Mr. Shiftlet say he wouldn't marry Elizabeth Taylor unless he could take her to a restaurant and buy her something good to eat. Instead of the Duchesser Windsor, which is naturally much better, but I guess he is not of the Duchesser Windsor's generation. Only the use of an elegant tramp there would be funny though. Elizabeth Taylor, lacking it, is useless for style.

I am reading *Eichmann in Jerusalem,* which Tom [Stritch] sent me. Anything is credible after such a period of history. I've always been haunted by the boxcars, but they were actually the least of it. And old Hannah [Arendt] is as sharp as they come.


## To Cecil Dawkins

16 September 63

I bought me 500 sheets of this for 99¢ as I'm a great hand for a bargain. It reminded me of my school days but not what I put on it. I was cheered to hear from you and glad you're all right and glad to hear about Sister Foley getting you in *Best Stories.* Is this a story I know? I don't recollect any affirmative ones exactly, in the popular sense of the word; actually I calculate anything good to be affirmative. I'll be on the lookout for the book and will display it prominently in me antique bookcases which you have not seen so long it has been since you paid us a visit.

I've just been going on about my fictional bidnis this summer, staying doggedly on the wrong track I think, but I suppose you have to pursue the wrong road long enough to be able to identify it and then you can get and keep off it. Anyway, I'm in no hurry. Right now I've had to stop the fiction to work on a talk—always the same old talk but I refurbish it a little like an apartment for rent—which I'm going to give next month at Notre Dame of Maryland and Georgetown University. On the same trip I'm going to be at Hollins College for three days. They are filthy rich apparently and have a lot of writers there, one a month in fact, and pay exorbitantly. There I'll give a public reading and I guess answer questions like *Why is the Misfit's hat black?* I am in terrible shape with the govermint. I made more money than usual one year on the Sisters' book and the next year I had to talk at a lot of places to pay my income tax, which made me make more money again so I had to talk at a lot more places which made me make more etc. etc. I'm poor as they come and getting poorer and my income tax is getting higher every year and I think this must end somewhere short of the penitentiary or the poor house.

I liked Updike's first novel, *The Poorhouse Fair,* but that *Rabbit Run* thing you can have and the other one I didn't attempt. I just don't like people that are all that sensitive. I just never know if the thing they're being sensitive about is *there* or not. Everybody tells me to read *Catch-22* and I will when I find it in paperback. No bookstore here but I am going to Atlanta tomorrow and maybe I'll see it. Right now I'm reading *Eichmann in Jerusalem.* My what a book. I admire that old lady extremely . . .


*To Janet McKane*

20 September 63

I'm glad the feathers got there. If they bent it in half I hope they didn't break the stems. If you put some sand in the vase you put them in you can make them do the way you want; without it they mostly turn their faces to the wall. The birds are very ratty right now. The new tails are out about three inches and there are a few long feathers left from last year still in. Day before yesterday they made a big racket early in the morning. An owl had got into a pen where I have the Muscovy duck and her hatch and had taken a swipe at one of the ducks. Shot (the colored man who works for us) heard the commotion and came with his gun and shot the owl, a large hoot owl. It had a face very much like a cat's only the eyes were bigger. It had eyelashes. The colored folks ate it for supper. I asked Louise (the colored woman who works here) what it tasted like and she said "About like hawk." Which left me where I started at as I haven't eaten any hawk . . .

What do you think of that business of hauling children out of their neighborhood so that they can attend a "racially balanced" school? I should think it would be hard on all concerned, children and teachers, and do nothing to help the race situation . . .


## To "A."

28 September 63

I'm glad you've figured out free will or whatever. It's great to be able to figure it out but dangerous to put too much faith in your figuring.

Ernest [the burro] is a father. We've been waiting on this arrival since before I went to Smith and the other day I looked out from the chicken pen out into the oat field where Marquita had been waiting out this event and there she was, deep in conversation with a long-legged black creature, about an eighth of her size, who looked as if he were made up for a minstrel—all black with a white mouth. I took off on my own four legs and summoned everybody. Regina named him Equinox, to which I add O'Connor. You must plan to come to see him. Meanwhile I will shortly send you a photograph . . .

About dedicating books. You know I've been writing 18 years and have only published three. You sound like I had one a month at least on the presses. Maybe someday there will be one for Thos. [Stritch] but the next one is slated for Louis I. Cline, who is 70½, while Thos. is only 50½. I don't want them to die before I get around to them, though that may happen.

Yesterday we went to a luncheon at the college for the governor and got the official smile and the official handshake. My hand was being shaken while the last person got the smile and then I got the smile while somebody else's hand was shaken but this didn't worry me overly.


## To John Hawkes

29 September 63

You are mighty nice to engineer this invitation to Brown. I'd like to come if you all can wait to set the exact date in April until February which is when it will be set for B.C. Also if I could read

"A Good Man Is Hard to Find," with commentary, instead of giving a lecture. I have found this is much the best. It's better to try to make one story live for them than to tell them a lot of junk they'll forget in five minutes and that I have no confidence in anyhow . . .

I hope Providence is treating you better. Cheers to you and Sophie.

## To Janet McKane

11 October 63

I am really delighted with the big photograph of the smiling Virgin and Child. It came the other day. I can really see the detail now. I certainly do appreciate it.

I'm glad you liked Equinox. Actually the orchard is over to the left and you can't see it. He's actually in an oat patch, standing under a couple of apple trees that happen to be there. This is going to be a pecan grove some day if the trees (you see one boxed in) thrive. We don't raise peaches here, though we have a few trees. The so-called orchard is pear and plum. We have beef cows and raise only what they need to eat—bermuda grass, rye, fescue, etc. I mean to take some more pictures when I get back. Why I'm not in them is because I'm taking them. That's the back of the house you see in the picture.

I hope you don't start hearing about Milledgeville in the news. The local Negroes have just petitioned the city council to do the usual things—integrate the schools and eating places etc. However, they also wanted a Negro elementary school built, so I think this means, build us one and you won't be bothered. One item on their list was to integrate the library. It turns out that the library has been integrated for a year and they didn't know it. Nine Negroes had cards. That's the way things have to be done here—completely without publicity. Then there is no trouble. I hope the rest of it can be taken care of as well as the library did it, but I have my doubts about it. We shall see.

I am off Monday for my rounds and will be mighty glad when it's over. The brandy sounds like a good idea, but not for me on crutches. I just might over-relax myself . . .

## To "A."

. . . Love and understanding are one and the same only in God. Who do you think you understand? If anybody, you delude yourself. I love a lot of people, understand none of them. This is not perfect love but as much as a finite creature can be capable of. About people being stuck with those who don't love or understand them, I have read discussions of it but I can't think where at the moment. It all comes under the larger heading of what individuals have to suffer for the common good, a mystery, and part of the suffering of Christ.

I have been to Hollins, Notre Dame of Maryland and George-town; read at Hollins and talked at the other two places and came home with enough money to float me through the next six or eight months. I get a lot out of it besides money. I see how the other half thinks and I come home raring to write. This time I got a stomach full of reporters. The one in Roanoke attempted to imitate my accent—nawth for north, etc. The one in Baltimore informed me that he and I used the same style. No more than we use the same toothbrush I was tempted to say, but I was too tired at the time to be ugly. In Washington all they could ask you about was integration about which I managed to say nothing or I tried to say nothing and have not a very clear idea what I did say . . .

We are running back and forth to the hospital. Miss Mary [Cline] went to a concert the other night with the Garners [cousins] and Julia [an aunt] and after it keeled over on the pavement and cracked her head open. She has five stitches in it, claims she hasn't even had the headache, and is chomping at the bit to get out of there and get home. We are looking for somebody to stay with her. An unencumbered genteel female of 50, neither too fat nor too thin, who can drive an automobile, write business letters and sleep with an ear open, who does not cuss, spit in the street or smack chewing gum, and who can engage in polite conversation. Since I think this paragon is not to be found, Miss M. will probably have to spend her nights out here—a fate worse than death to her—after two days of which she may settle for something less than the afore-described.

## To Janet McKane

I had a good trip, not a cloud in the sky all the way. The little plane landed on the sides of mountains all over West Virginia and I enjoyed it all no end. Good audiences too, particularly at Georgetown. Thanks for your prayers. They were most certainly answered. And I always get back from these trips eager to get to work and I have almost finished a story since I got back. Though there is plenty to be done on it I suppose.

Thank you for the cards you sent me before I left and for the clippings that have come since I got back. I appreciate them all and will enjoy using the cards, probably on some of the many nuns I know. Every school I go to I end up with more friends among the Sisters—all highly individual too, they are. The one who runs the writing program at Notre Dame of Maryland is Sister Maura, a poet. As poets, when they are good they are very very good and when they are horrid—she is good . . .

It's been real hot here until the last two days, but I like the heat and hate the winter. We heat each room separately with butane gas, cut it off at night altogether and sleep under electric blankets. When it gets real cold, the pipes freeze and we have no water until the middle of the day . . .

## To Maryat Lee

31 October 63

Book has been sent. Mass has been said. How long you going to stay out there in them woods in Chester? It's already turned cold here. We're shivering beside our butane gas heaters.

Nothing doing so far on the integration front. I daresay a deal will be made under the table and maybe they'll get a new elementary school like they want. I hope so. Don't come down for any monkey bidnis or we'll put you in jail and hang you for inciting insurrections. I will personally volunteer to spring the trap or pull the rope or whatever you do.

## To Janet McKane

5 November 63

I did enjoy the children's letters and enclose one for them. I have been pretty tired since I got back and there is always a backlog of work to catch up with, letters that have to be attended to and so forth, but mostly it has been that I came home ready to write a story and I have put every bit of my energy into it. I finished it today, or at least I finished a first draft of it. Now I will rewrite it a lot and eventually decide if it's any good. Notice the review in this week's *NYT Book Section* of three story collections. The middle one is by a friend of mine from Alabama, Cecil Dawkins. She's a very good writer . . .

Saint Cecilia won't know what to do with me. I have the original tin ear. I cannot hear music; just don't know what to listen for. My playing the accordion had nothing to do with music. I liked it because it glittered and moved about. I had a twelve bass. I always wanted to be able to play (anything) but like Athena springing from the head of Zeus. Unfortunately it required practice and aptitude and other suchlike qualities that I did not have. I also tried the clarinet—I played middle C exclusively in the college orchestra—and the double bass, but I never got off middle C in anything but the accordion, and that was only because it glittered. And here you not only played it, but played it upside down! That never occurred to me to try.

Equinox is expecting the Humpty Dumpty Kindergarten Tuesday morning at nine-thirty. Every year we have the nursery school and the first grade and the various kindergartens and one year we had the "exceptional" children, which around here means the defective ones. Some of them asked very intelligent questions. The children go all over the yard and see the ponies and the peacocks and the swan and the geese and the ducks and then they come by my window and I stick my head out and the teacher says, "And this is Miss Flannery. Miss Flannery is an author." So they go home having seen a peacock and a donkey and a duck and a goose and an author . . .

*In explanation of the following letter, Cecil Dawkins writes: "I had written Flannery that I'd like to try an adaptation of several of her stories into a full-length play. This is her answer. The play, The Displaced Person, was produced at The American Place Theatre in NYC in 1966. I was almost through with the work in the summer of 1964. I recall we'd first planned that I'd go to Milledgeville in June and we'd read it together. But I saw I had a couple of more months of work on it yet, and she was in bad health. (I didn't know how bad.) When she died in August, I put the play away and didn't look at it again until Wynn Handman, producer at The American Place, phoned me to say he'd heard I had a play and would like to see it."*

## To Cecil Dawkins

5 November 63

I think it's a fine idea if you want to try it. My only qualm is your using that story "The Enduring Chill." I may incorporate that story in the long thing I'm doing now. I've been messing with it all summer and I just haven't made up my mind. It don't satisfy me as a story and I don't know whether I'll rewrite it as a story and use it in my next collection or make it a part of this thing I'm intermittently working on. Right now I've set all that aside and am working on a story ["Revelation"] that I like and am at the moment right enthusiastic about. It has one of those country women in it who just sort of springs to life; you can't hold them down or shut their mouths. Does it have to be the boy? What about the girl in "Good Country People"? I think I'd like to keep Father Finn from Purrrgatory off the stage until I'm sure he doesn't belong in this long thing I'm writing. You might use the girl in *GCP* and those two idiots in "Greenleaf" . . . Regina has all these stories put away where neither she nor I know where they are but I know you can get "Greenleaf" in *Southern Stories*, edited by Arlin Turner, a Rinehart paperback . . .

If you go to the Albee-McCullers [play] let me know what you think about it.

A copy of your book came [*The Quiet Enemy*] and I think it looks real good. Elizabeth sent me the Orville Prescott review which should help. "A." said she saw one in the London *Times Lit. Sup.* which was favorable. I'll keep my eye out for odd ones.

Did you ever consider *Wise Blood* as a possibility for dramatizing? If the times were different I would suggest that, but I think it would just be taken for the super-grotesque sub-Carson McCullers sort of thing that I couldn't stand the sight or sound of. But I can see where you could do something fine with the other. So as far as I'm concerned you can go ahead if you'd like to try it—just leave out Asbury and Fr. Finn.

8 November 63

The name Asbury don't interest me. What I had thought to do was use that story to help explain Walter's character (the thing in *Esquire*). I may not do it, I may go on and rewrite it as a story and use it in the collection. My trouble right now is that I am beset by too many possibilities and can't make up my mind. I'd really like to turn "Why Do the Heathen Rage?" into a long story, without the "Enduring Chill" section, and use it in the collection, but this all takes time. Anyway, I should think the successful intellectual would do you just as good. He can have out a slim volume of verse and he has a heart ailment too and is on a salt-free diet as I recollect. Who is H.C.? I have forgotten my own stories largely.

I would not be too squeamish about anything you did to this because I have no interest in the theatre for its own sake and all I would care about would be what money, if any, could be got out of it. It's nice to have something you can be completely crass about. The only thing I would positively object to would be somebody turning one of my colored idiots into a hero. Don't let any fool director work that on you. I wouldn't trust any of that bunch farther than I could hurl them. I guess I wouldn't want a Yankee doing this, money or no money.

About "The Enduring Chill," I am interested in keeping the situation of the boy coming home thinking he's going to die and in keeping the dialogue between him and Fr. Finn. If I find in the next month or so that I'm going to leave it as a story, I'll let you know . . .

Do you know that story of Andrew Lytle's where the old lady says, "I have a mule older than Birmingham"?

## To "A."

9 November 63

. . . [Cecil] seems to be seriously bit by the theatre bug and she says she wants to do an adaptation of "The Displaced Person," because this will give her some experience with the theatrical part of it and she won't have to think up the dialogue and so forth. I have told her she can do it if she wants to. If anybody is going to do it, I would rather have her. She intends to use several of the stories together, I mean other characters from them. I don't know what will come of it, but Cecil is plenty clever and E. McKee and Co. are handling plays now, so maybe something will . . .

We got a colored woman to come spend the nights with Miss M. but as soon as Miss M. got home and at the helm, she threw [her] overboard. [She] had worked previously for an old lady down the street to whom she read the Bible. Miss Mary . . . said she was not going to pay anybody 50¢ an hour to read the Bible. She also says she feels better than she's ever felt in her life, so there's no doing anything with her.

Since [your aunt] is retired, maybe you and [she] both could drive down some Saturday and eat dinner with us? Bear this in mind.

I was so polite to [someone who had written proposing an interpretation of "A Good Man Is Hard to Find"] I astonished even myself. Explained to him they were going to Florida and how come they couldn't possibly be going anywhere else. I have had a lot of bothersome letters from students lately asking tiresome questions like one who said writing was one of his "extracurricular pastimes" and he would like to know which was more involved in it, imagination or experience. A favorite question with them, but they deck it out in various degrees of pomposity.

I have writ a story ["Revelation"] since returning but have not decided yet if it is any good.


## To John Hawkes

10 November 63

I am back from my latest expedition, more convinced than ever that it is better to read than to lecture. And I forgot to say in my last note that I would be cheered to talk to the students in a class or whatever. That means answer questions—I can't just stand up and talk.

You are mighty nice to ask me to stay with you all but if Sophie has three devils and an angel and yourself to contend with, she doesn't need visitors. I make do very nicely with guest rooms. In fact, I collect them. The one at Hollins was a fully equipped apartment, even down to the electric dishwasher. The larder was stocked with Mt. Etna Ginger Ale and hushpuppy mix. Did they read my stuff and decide this was what I would eat? I haven't decided.

I got a folder from Boston College and see you have just read there lately. It said poetry. Was it poetry or fiction? What kind of an audience was it?

I came back from my trip with enough money to order me another pair of swans. They are on their way from Miami and Mr. Hood, the incumbent swan, little suspects that he is going to have to share his feed dish. He eats out of a vase, as a matter of fact, and has a private dining room. Since his wife died, he has been in love with the bird bath. Typical Southern sense of reality.


*The reception of* A Memoir of Mary Ann *had sowed the wild wind in the Dominican Home, and an impressive literary project was now proposed to Flannery's publishers, who later turned it down.*

## To Robert Giroux

Sister Evangelist rides again. She has become interested in the Bible and for the last two years with the ten minutes a day she has to give to it, she has worked up a book explaining each chapter with psalms interspersed for meditation. I encouraged her in this because I thought it was good for her and good in general for the Sisters to get interested in the Bible. Now it seems she is in dead earnest about getting the book published and has either convinced or beaten the Abbot at Conyers, Dom Augustine, into writing her an introduction for it. She has been writing the book in longhand, then sending it to a girl in Atlanta to type. The girl in Atlanta has then been sending it to me, chapter by chapter, to put in the punctuation. My further function is to get her a publisher. You will find her attitude to the whole business in the two letters enclosed, one to me and a copy of one she has written to Dom Augustine. I am supposed to ask you if you will look at the book with a view to publishing it. The Lord backs her projects and I only do what I am told.

Of course she has no idea of the time involved even supposing you did take the book, but I will tell her she couldn't have it out *this* Lent . . .


## To "A."

I been sick and am too weak at the moment to care about hitting this typewriter much. You have to be without energy to gauge whatall it takes. Anyway, I did finish a draft of this ["Revelation"] before I got sick but I am more or less anesthetized to it and have no idea if it works or not, particularly the last paragraph. I started to let it end where the hogs pant with a secret life, but I thought something else was needed. Maybe not what I've got. But anyway, anything you have to say will be helpful, provided it is within my ken.

We've heard all about the eclairs. Biggest eclairs he ever saw and he don't see how you ladies keep so thin eating as well as you do.

I am sad about the President [Kennedy]. But I like the new one.

## To Sally and Robert Fitzgerald

23 November 63

I hope you've got your various chirren stashed away in their various schools by now. Tell Benny if the Zen Garden gets too much for him and he elects to run away, to run South and visit us. It is much the better part of the country as we all know and we could take up on his education where the Rev. Aelred Graham left off at.

I am going to read at Brown (which is in Providence) in April before or after I go to Boston College so I'll hope maybe [get] to see you.

Regina is in command and sends you all her regards. Louise threw potash water on Shot last week (she keeps a supply for this purpose) and Regina told her that one of these days she was going to put his eyes out. "Yes'm," she says, "I hope I gets at least one of them."

I thought you all might enjoy this interview with [Conrad] Aiken who takes up residence part of the year in Savannah now and allows himself to be interviewed freely. Apparently he serves the interviewers martinis in frosted silver goblets and I guess this encourages the trade.

The President's death has cut the country up pretty bad. All commercial television is stopped until after the funeral and even the football games called off, which is about the extremest sign of grief possible. It's going to take all the wind out the sails of Southern politics, which has been operating exclusively on a "damm the Kennedys" basis . . .

## To Janet McKane

28 November 63

Well happy Thanksgiving, somewhat after the fact when you get this. I was interested in the reviews of the Carson McCullers adaptation. I dislike intensely the work of Carson McCullers but it is interesting to see what is made of it in the theatre, and by Edward Albee at that.

We spent most of the weekend looking at the sad events [President Kennedy's funeral] on television. It made me wonder if children draw any line between history and fiction. Murder in the living room. We saw Oswald killed three times, twice in slow motion. What do they make of it?

I'll be interested in the symposium on "The Jew in American

Culture." The declaration on the Jews and on religious liberty seems to have got sidetracked at the [Vatican] council. I hope they manage to get it going again.

I was much amused at your lyrics for the ladies and gents of PS 86 Br and marginal comments. It's real good to be able to do something like this; it fills a real social need. I used to do it when I was young but I guess now I have the cares that go with professionalism and the black heart as well.

Equinox [the burro] has been invited to be in the Hardwick Christian Church's Christmas crib. We think we will send his papa, Ernest, instead, as Ernest is more liable to enter into the spirit of it. Regina says he will eat all the hay out of the manger, but anyway he is easier to handle at this point. In fact demands all the attention he can get. I gave Ernest to my mother for a Mother's Day present two years ago. Somebody said that was for the mother who had everything . . .

## To Maryat Lee

29 Nov. 63

. . . A certain variety of Southern politics is at a standstill because now there's nobody to hate. Bobby no longer fills the bill and it's going to be hard for Southerners to hate Johnson. You should get you a television. I heartily recommend them.

I want to send you some pecans. Are you going to be there to receive them or are you potting off for the Piney Woods or Milledgeville or Chester or somers?

I have writ a story ["Revelation"] with which I am, for the time anyway, pleased pleased pleased.

## To Cecil Dawkins

1 December 63

. . . How are you coming? I finished my story and am pleased with it for the time being anyway. I'll let it set a spell now. I bought Bernard Malamud's collection (*Idiots First*) but I didn't like it as well as his first collection. It don't pay to buy books. I think I'll go back to my former policy of reading only what comes to me for nothing.

## To "A."

I'm much cheered that the story ["Revelation"] makes the right kind of noise in your head, though I am fearful other heads will be less reliable. If the story is taken to be one designed to make fun of Ruby, then it's worse than venal. The only other person I've sent it to is Catharine Carver and I haven't heard from her. She's a Yankee and a stoic, a woman whose only happiness seems to be in work and endurance, and that is not real happiness but just non-misery. What she makes of it will be a kind of acid test though I don't propose to pay too much attention if she makes nothing of it.

I wasn't thinking of Mary Grace as the Devil but then the whole story just sort of happened—though it took me about eight weeks to write it. It was one of those rare ones in which every gesture gave me great pleasure in the writing, from Claud pulling up his pants leg to show where the cow kicked him, right on through. The last time I went to the doctor here, Ruby and Claud were in there. It was just after Charlene and Walter announced their nuptials and that was the subject of conversation in the waiting room. I was just taken with the conversation—much better than anything I had in the story . . .

I didn't hear the two ambulance drivers interviewed but I heard everybody else and his brother. I think the funeral was a salutary tonic for this back-slapping gum-chewing hiya-kid nation. Mrs. Kennedy has a sense of history and of what is owing to death.

I'm better. My trouble is anemia . . .

I have just read the galleys to Jack Hawkes' latest—*Second Skin*—and will give you same when you come. It's a little easier to follow than the others but when it's over you don't know any more what you've got. At least I don't. You probably will. He got a Ford Grant for next year, for which I'm glad.

## To Cecil Dawkins

Sent you a box with a few nuts in it today. I forget if you eat them or not but you can always set obnoxious company to cracking them.

Elizabeth hasn't written me anything about an option but you couldn't afford an option anyhow. If Darryl F. Zanuck offers me 100 G for the rights I'll consult with you first and see can you match him; however, these stories have been in existence many years now and there've been no takers so I think you're safe.

The reviewers are the worst part of it, whether they're good or bad. I have a stack of German reviews and I'm always so pleased when one comes and I can't read it. Katherine Anne P. sent me one from France in which *A Good Man* was reviewed with *The Group* [by Mary McCarthy]. Fancy.

I hope you have a good Christmas. Maybe when you get the play finished, you will be coming this way and we can look it over together.

## To John Hawkes

12 December 63

I sent Mr. [James] Laughlin a little statement about *Second Skin* and I hope it'll meet with your approval. I think this one has an added power to keep the reader right there with it and I had the thought that you're about 90% magician. "A." is going to spend the weekend with us and I am going to give her the proofs to take home. She will come up then with a long and involved analysis and let me and you both know exactly what you've done. My appreciation is all on the level of what you make me see in a literal visual way. I don't know any other writer who can do it . . .

## To Janet McKane

13 December 63

. . . I tried to read *A Death in the Family* [by James Agee] but I couldn't go it but I like some other things of his and I imagine the letters to Fr. Flye are good. There was something called *The Morning Watch*, a short novel or maybe it was just a long story, that I liked.

You didn't enclose the picture of the two children but the little girl is the one in the picture with you I take it. Children have so many resources. They are crushed by things you don't notice and bounce up from what you think would crush them. I have a cousin who married a girl who apparently has some kind of mental trouble. He is a doctor but he doesn't have her hospitalized. She just sort of stays in bed and reads and lolls around, I gather, but the children are seemingly well-behaved and sturdy and thoughtful. The little girl writes poetry and sends me some occasionally.

Probably what he means about impounding "The Hound of Heaven" is that it ought not to be set up as THE type of religious poetry—lest the students think they had to have thous and thees and titanic glooms and whatnot in all religious poetry. I wouldn't impound "The Hound of Heaven," but I would impound "Trees" early on. Our pastor has a piece of bad verse to decorate most every sermon, all of which I feel sure was supplied him in some Catholic grammar school.

Your quoting a poem of R. P. T. Coffin took me back. He visited our college when I was about 18, read some poems of mine and came to our house for some kind of program. That was the only time in my life when I attempted to write poetry. All my poems sounded like "Miniver Cheevy." Mr. Coffin was a striking-looking old man. I believe he died a few years back . . .

*A new and somewhat ominous note is sounded in this letter, the first to suggest a possibly serious development in Flannery's fragile health. It seems not to have interested her as much as the reaction she had just received to "Revelation," with the ensuing and perennial problem of making her meaning quite clear. She scribbled this note in longhand to her friend.*

## To "A."

25 Dec. 63

I hope you're off your bed of affliction or if you're still sick I hope you're on it & not in that office. I'm on mine. Fainted the other night & gave my pore mother a turn, been in bed since. Not enough blood to run the engine or something. I'm going to take [new medication]. Wait a couple of weekends before you come—though I hope they'll lemme up next week.

Yes mam I heard from C. Carver. Can't send letter as it is somewhere on desk which might as well be in Wilkinson County as I am not supposed to walk to or around it. She thought it ["Revelation"] one of my most powerful stories and probably my *blackest*. Found Ruby evil. Found end vision to confirm same. Though suggested I leave it out.

I am not going to leave it out. I am going to deepen it so that there'll be no mistaking Ruby is not just an evil Glad Annie.

I've really been battling this problem all my writing days.

## To Janet McKane

The woodcarving came this morning and I do like and appreciate it . . . I can imagine that spending Christmas Day in the Y in Boston would be quite an experience. I spent mine in bed; didn't even get to Mass Christmas Day. I fainted the Monday before Christmas and have been in bed ever since. It seems my blood count is very low and I have to stay in bed until I get it built up. This week I am up a little and feel some better but there just isn't any energy. I do a little and I'm beat. I really can't write a decent letter because I can't think except on the typewriter and I don't have the energy for that, even though I have an electric one. That wouldn't do me much good today as we are having an ice storm and all the electricity is off.

Ernest—that is Equinox's pa—did the honors for the burros this Christmas and went both to the Christian manger and the Methodist pageant. He did very well in the Christian manger—in which there were also a cow a pig a Shetland pony & some sheep and he did all right at the Methodist dress rehearsal but when the big moment came and the church full of Methodists, he wouldn't put his foot inside the door. Doesn't care for "fellowship" I suppose. Balaam's ass.

Sent you a magazine in which a story of mine has been reprinted [*New World Writing,* containing "Everything That Rises Must Converge"]. Don't know if you had read this story or not. Anyway it's a right interesting magazine. What do you think of this business of abandoning Catholic elementary schools and concentrating on high schools?

A real happy new year and many thanks for everything, mostly for being.

# PART IV

---

# THE LAST YEAR

# 1964

*When the increased weakness and fainting spells suggesting a new threat to Flannery's health appeared, around Christmas of 1963, treatment for anemia was begun at once and she seemed to rally. She must have suspected that something was gravely wrong, but she was casual, even reassuring, in every mention of her state of being. She began working intensely, as her letters indicate, on the stories with which she hoped to round out the collection planned for the fall. Then, in early February, she learned that her anemia was caused by a benign but debilitating fibroid tumor. It had to go, although her internist, Dr. Merrill, was reluctant to allow any kind of surgery on a lupus patient. All her commitments were canceled, and on February 25, she entered Baldwin County Hospital for the operation, having refused to go to Atlanta, in order to spare her mother, who had to look after Miss Mary Cline in her declining health as well as Flannery.*

*Everything seemed to go well, but in fact what the internist had most feared happened. The lupus was reactivated, and Flannery's last battle to live began.*

*There was probably never much doubt of the outcome, and I find it hard to believe that Flannery didn't know it. Be that as it may, her chief concern was to finish the work on* Everything That Rises Must Converge. *And it was from the last year of her life that three unforgettable stories came: "Revelation," which was finished in late 1963, "Judgement Day," and "Parker's Back," both completed when she was more or less in extremis. "Judgement Day," the final treatment of a lonely, homesick old man—which had been the subject of her first published story, "The Geranium"—marks the distance she had traveled as an artist. With "Revelation" and "Parker's Back" she achieved her form as a writer, the realization of that potential body of work, uniquely her own, to which everything she had written before had contributed.*

*There is a sense of urgency throughout the last letters, but her mastery of herself was as established by now as the mastery of her craft shown in those last stories she had to tell. She never lost interest in her friends during the wearying year: her letters continued to pour out to them, and her light tone was deceptive. Most of us didn't realize how sick she was, though in retrospect her letters tell us more than they did at the time. Robert and I remember a letter she wrote us, now lost, very much in her vein, except that it ended with a request for prayers. Others received the same request. Mrs. O'Connor gallantly tried to keep the knowledge from Flannery herself, and perhaps Flannery was at the same time trying to keep it from her mother. In any case, she received Extreme Unction, now called the Sacrament of the Sick, at her own request, in July. It is painful, even now, to read in one of her letters—to someone she had never met—mention of Hopkins's poem,*

> *Margaret, are you grieving*
> *Over Goldengrove unleaving? . . .*

*She must have felt the natural sorrow of separation, and physical misery, too: "I've felt too bad to type . . ." but in her last note she is troubled for the safety of Maryat Lee, rather than for her own. For herself she was not so much stoical as quite serene; she had attained her personal form as well.*

## To Elizabeth McKee

3 January 64

I just want to let you know that I will shortly be sending a story ["Revelation"] to the *Sewanee Review* and if they take it will direct them to send the check to you. I'll also try to send you a copy of the story when I get one. I've spent the holidays in bed with a low blood count and am not up to much at the moment. This is a good story and *Esquire* would probably have taken it but it is one I prefer for various reasons to have appear in a Southern quarterly.

I suggested to a friend of mine, Robert Drake, that he send his stories to you. They've mostly been published in the *Christian Century* and I thought they might make a book that would have some kind of limited popular appeal.

All the best of the new year to you and Ted.

## To Janet McKane

5 Jan 64

Thanks so much for your letter & the card with the flowers from the Holy Land—when the Pope is there too! I feel some better but I'm not long on energy. My blood count has gone up to 9¼ however. I got to Mass today.

Whatever you sent from Boston hasn't come. The woodcarving came and I do like it, particularly the animal. Maybe the others will in due time. Whether they do or don't I appreciate all your thoughts of me.

The storm damage was bad in Milledgeville but we didn't suffer much out here.

Equinox's mama is named Marquita. She was named that when we got her. She's a Sicilian burro, has the cross on her back, supposed to be the kind that carried Christ into Jerusalem. Ernest is a Mexican burro. I guess Equinox is just a Milledgeville burro.

Cheers & thanks. I've exhausted my letter-writing energy for now.

## To Sally and Robert Fitzgerald

8 January 64

That was one more living ape [a bent-leather figure] you all sent me. I think it's a work of art and have it sitting in the parlor. We had a baby visiting us one afternoon last week and it got ahold of it and had the ape's entire head in its mouth before I wrested it away from it. But no damage was done. It's in as good shape as ever and I do like it and thank you.

I spent the holidays sick in bed with a low blood count but I am up again with instructions to just creep around . . .

The country is taking on some flamboyance now with Mr. [Lyndon] Johnson. All the furrin dignitaries go to Austin and thence to his ranch and get given Texas hats, or rather get them put on their heads by Mr. Johnson as the cameras click away. Sometimes they get the wrong head and somebody's face disappears and there are loud guffaws. I think state bidnis will never be the same after this administration.

Regina is fine and sends her best and we hope yours are getting educated right along and that Robert and Benny will come down in the spring and see us and some of the country . . .

## To Maryat Lee

18 Jan 64

I been sick. Fainted a few days before Christmas and was in bed about 10 days and not up to much thereafter. Blood count had gone down to 8 & you can't operate on that. It's up now & so am I but ain't operating yet on normal load. Ma has been in bed with intestinal flu this last week so if it hasn't been one thing it's been another. I'll try to get them nuts off before they get rancid.

Don't know which is worse, CORE or Young Republicans for Goldwater, but I reckon it is inevitable that they fall into the hands of one or the other. I guess this will get laid at your door though it is only nature taking its cose.

Glad you're picking up. Old doctor Greenleaf must not be a quack after all . . .

## To Thomas Stritch

22 Jan 64

. . . I never bought the record player. I saved up the money and then I thought this is a lot of money to spend for something you don't already appreciate and no guarantee that you ever will, so I ordered me a pair of swans instead. My old one died. Then after Christmas the Sisters in Atlanta called up and said somebody had given them a new record player for Christmas and they were sending their old one down for me by Louis, which they did. They said the automatic didn't work on the somethingorother but I don't see anything wrong with it. It makes a noise like popcorn is popping in it somewhere and Mary Jo says that is dust but I don't see any. Anyway, now that I've got it, I'm going to educate myself if possible . . .

## To "A."

25 Jan 64

General conditions hereabouts have improved. I am fully restored, Louise is prowling about as usual. I don't think Regina is all right yet but her policy is never to admit anything but perfect health. My aunt Julia who was near death in the hospital last week has rallied this and appears to be going to make it. I have hopes of everybody's survival.

Caroline was crazy about my story ["Revelation"]. She read

it to her class and they laughed until they cried or so she reported and Lord knows who she's reading it to now because she hasn't sent it back to me yet. This did not keep her from writing me six pages on the principles of grammar and on how to spell such words as horde which I spelled hoard but which means something else. She saw my second version which is really better and she understood it perfectly and thought it was probably the profoundest so far. So my mind is settled on that score. I also sent it to Ward Dorrance, an old friend of mine in Washington of whom I am very fond, and he allowed the same. So I hope in the next few weeks to get it typed up and send it on to the *Sewanee Review*. I could get $1500 for it from *Esquire* but I emulate my better characters and feel like Mr. Shiftlet that there should be some folks that some things mean more to them than money . . .

Very glad you are putting aside metaphysics if that's what you call what you're putting aside. Babies are no doubt healthier for women. Even chickens are healthier as a matter of fact.

I had a letter from Jack Hawkes who said he hoped I would give you the galleys of the novel because he really wasn't sure about that novel and he would like to have some of your impassioned analysis. So I really should have sent it to you and if I can jam it in a book I will so don't groan when you see it. It would be a good deed to read it and write him about it. I just pure didn't know what to say about it myself.

I have the original Tin Ear, that is to say, the First and Prime Tin Ear. So I like music that is guaranteed good because I have no way of finding out for myself. Old stuff like Haydn that there is positively no doubt about. On my own I wouldn't know it from Music to Clean Up By.


## To Robert Giroux

25 January 64

Thank you very much for the letter about Sr. Evangelist's project and the copy for her. I have sent it on and I hope it will give her a more realistic idea about what is involved in a book of this kind than I have been able to put over.

I am about ready to turn my own attention to a collection of stories. I have just completed another story ["Revelation"], which I think may possibly round it out. This makes eight finished and I am working on another which may or may not turn out. They are on the whole longer stories than in the last collection and I am wondering if there is any limit on the number of pages; whether it might be better to select six of these stories, or just what. I want to do some more rewriting on a few of them and I don't know when I can have it ready. Is there any particular time you would prefer to bring it out? [Giroux suggested the fall list.] . . .

## To Janet McKane

27 January 64

I liked the picture with the red scarf and the idea of your machinations with it in the interest of discipline. There's probably a little witch-doctoring left in the teaching profession, that has managed to stay out of the education textbooks. I had 3 education courses in college. Pure Wasted Time.

I don't think I thanked you for enrolling me in the year's novena of Masses. I do appreciate it. My blood count has gone up from 8.5 to 11.6 in a month and the doctor thinks that phenomenal. Around 13 is normal and I'll make it yet.

I'm rather glad the single folks, or left-overs as you call us, haven't been discovered by the Church. Think of the awful oratory that would flow over us . . .

11 Feb 64

My blood is back up now so I am working like mad and hope to keep it up so that *possibly* I can have a book of stories out in the fall. The ms. will have to be delivered in May if I do and there is much too much work needed to get it done but I am going to try anyway.

Maybe sooner or later I will get to write you a leisurely letter but I don't know when.

## To Thomas Stritch

11 February 64

Those records came Friday and we've been playing them ever since and haven't got to the bottom of the pack yet. It's a real gift to us even if not from your point of view. If I had known [Regina] would enjoy this thing so much I would have done something about getting one before now. I think she just likes some noise in the background, I don't know if she listens or not. Every now and then she says, that's pretty. This is the first time I've listened to music except once when I was at Yaddo, so I don't have any preference yet though I think I like the kind that is straight up and down better than what slides around, if you know what I mean . . .

The swans came too, week before last, but it has done nothing but rain and snow here so I haven't got to be out there with them any. I found out about the man where I could get these swans from Fr. Ginder of all people. He called me up from somewhere in Pennsylvania one Sunday last fall to know how he could get his peafowl down out of the trees. He had bought a pair from the Mother Superior and they had got out of the patio and been in the trees for three days. He was very genial and talked for twenty or twenty-five minutes on the long-distance telephone, which my parent said is just like them, no sense about money. I don't like his politics but I like him fine. I got the swans from the same place he got his peafowl. I couldn't tell him how to get them down out the trees so he says—to prove R.'s point—"Well, I think I'll just let them stay up there then and get her two new ones."


## To Elizabeth McKee

14 February 64

. . . I wrote Giroux that I was about ready to start thinking of another collection. He would like to bring it out in the fall but I don't know if I'll be able to have it ready by May; however, I am currently working with that in mind . . .

I still don't have a copy of that story ["Revelation"]. I've just now got it off to Andrew. We've been plagued with one thing and another this winter and nothing is on schedule.


*The first mention of the possible surgery her failing health would im-pose is contained in this letter.*

## To "A."

15 February 64

We appear to all have our nasal drips stopped for the moment by the right amounts of anti-histamine. Louise's and Shot's cases are complicated by liquor and a bucket of potash water which she keeps handy to throw on him. He gave her a bad blow over the eye, or at least she claims he did. He claims she was so drunk she fell down and hit her head on the fender. Anyway these trials are normal. Miss Mary is out of the hospital and R. appears okay. I may have to go into the hospital some time soon for [an operation] but that will have to await somebody else's decision. Meanwhile, I am trying to have out a book of short stories in the fall but doubt very much I will get it as the manuscript would have to be delivered in May and there is much work to be done on it..

What did you think of the Hawkes opus? I am supposed to go there in April and read on my way to Boston and if I get there, I will view them in their natural habitat but not stay with them.

My two new swans arrived and they look like a much younger pair than the last, have high voices and use them considerable. The weather has been too bad for me to get out and commune with them much.

Andrew Carl Sessions sent his godmother a picture of himself for Valentine's in which he appears in cowboy hat, six-shooters etc. and looks like the old man without the learning. She was much impressed.

We are broke out with records now as Thomas sent me a box full out of his basement. All I can say about it is that all classical music sounds alike to me and all the rest of it sounds like the Beatles.

I am reading for the first time *I'll Take My Stand* [Agrarian Movement Manifesto] which is out in a paperback. It's a very interesting document. It's futile of course like "woodman, spare that tree," but still, the only time real minds have got together to talk about the South . . .


*The decision to operate was confirmed in her next letter.*

## To Louise and Thomas Gossett

18 February 64

I sure do wish I could come but I have had to cancel all the lectures—Boston College, Brown and the University of Texas—and I have very shortly to go to the hospital and be cut upon by the doctors. I suggested they ask me again next year but I don't know. This is all fairly sudden. I wasn't looking for it . . .

Fr. McCown seems to be in Houston. He sho do move around aplenty. Tell him not to forget to send me your lunatic book. Just right for hospital or recuperative reading no doubt.

## To John Hawkes

20 February 64

All those plans make me feel worse than ever about not getting there. You all please invite me next year. My operation is scheduled for Tuesday. Meanwhile I am being loaded with cortisone to get ready for it . . .

It appears we are all taking to our beds. I hope you and Sophie manage to stay afoot.

## To Louise Abbot

21 Feb. 64

Well it looks as though I am going to arrive at the cutting table before you. [The medication] is still doing fine but I have a large tumor and if they don't make haste and get rid of it, they will have to remove me and leave it. So this operation is going to take place this Tuesday (the 25th). Pray for me.

I will miss another visit from the Spiveys (this is not why I am having the operation), who are scheduled to be through on the 14th. He sent me a paper on my stuff which he read recently at Georgia State. I liked it very much, much more than the last one. It seemed better put together, maybe because it had to be spoken.

When I get back on my four feet, we must definitely have that visit.

*Her first post-operative letter concerned a piece of news that greatly disturbed her.*

## To Robert Giroux

7 March 64

I have just got out of the hospital after having had serious surgery and am not yet up to the typewriter. I am shocked and disgusted by this turn of events.* Of course the Longs knew the book was being written and offered no objections. As soon as your letter came, Regina called Sister Josephine. She was looking through their files then for the letter written by the Longs saying

---

* *The parents of the child in* A Memoir of Mary Ann *had evidently been persuaded by a hungry lawyer to bring suit for harassment against the Sisters at the Cancer Home and Farrar, Straus, Giroux.*

they had no objection to the publication of the book. She said the letter had been written and she knew they had it . . .

We asked her if the Longs had been cool to them lately. She said, by no means: they had just recently sent the Longs $200(!). I think the Longs have just fallen into the hands of some shyster lawyer. They may not even be fully aware of what he is doing. Last summer the Sisters brought down Mr. & Mrs. Long and two of the girls and one of the girls' husband. They were feeling no harassment then that we heard of. They spent the afternoon with us and were very pleasant. Plain poor people and simple enough to get taken in. Sr. Josephine said Mr. Long had been trying to get Social Security but hadn't been able to.

Don't count on my book for the fall now. I'm not up to it. Cancelled lectures.

Please keep me posted on this Long mess because it certainly worries me.

## To Robert Fitzgerald

8 March 64

Cain't you and Benny pay us a visit Easter, especially if you are taking [your aunt] Agnes to St. Petersburg, you would naturally be moving in the right direction. We can send Joe* to Atlanta to meet you if you let us know in time to run him down. We hope you can.

Me, I just got out of the hospital where I had my middle entered by the surgeons. It was all a howling success from their point of view and one of them is going to write it up for a doctor magazine as you usually don't cut folks with lupus. But the trip in was necessary though nothing turned out malignant and I will soon be restored on turnip green potlicker. Right now I am just killing time and would be mighty proud to see you & Benedict. It's a good time of year to see these parts. Everything is in bloom . . .

R. says this is a joint invitation. I am the scribe around here, even in extremis—

---

* Joe Butts, who drove for the O'Connors, and who is still Mrs. O'Connor's right-hand man in Milledgeville.

## To Janet McKane

12 March 64

You are mighty nice to have the high Mass said for me in the Byzantine rite church and if I can't go on April 2, I'll read it in my missal. I do appreciate your doing it. I enjoyed looking at the Mass book with the music. Our congregation never sings, partly I think in protest at the awful hymns.

The IBM business would look better to you if you had ever seen a little atrocity called "A Check on the bank of Heaven." Some Sisters in Canada send me these: "Pay to the order of *Flannery O'Connor 300* Hail Marys." At one corner is a picture of the Christ Child & under this, the word *President*. On the other side is the Virgin—*Vice-President!* It takes a strong faith & a stronger stomach . . .

## To "A."

14 March 64

I think the most classic thing you could do with Jack's galleys would be to hang them out of your fourth-story windows and let the birds tear them into strips for their nests. If you have a better idea do anything you think appropriate. Just so I never lay eyes on them again. I hate galleys. The Monday before I was operated on on Tuesday here come galleys from the *Sewanee Review* for "Revelation" and I had to correct them there in the hospital. The story didn't seem so hot.

One of my nurses was a dead ringer for Mrs. Turpin. Her Claud was named Otis. She told me all the time about what a good nurse she was. Her favorite grammatical construction was "it were." She said she treated everybody alike whether it were a person with money or a black nigger. She told me all about the low life in Wilkinson County. I seldom know in any given circumstances whether the Lord is giving me a reward or a punishment. She didn't know she was funny and it was agony to laugh and I reckon she increased my pain about 100%. She was an LPN (licensed practical-nurse), the other two were R.N.s. There's great rivalry between the two. The R.N.s get more money. The night R.N. told me everything that had happened to Lassie for the last 3 Sundays. The day R.N. was the wife of the chief of police. So it was not an uneventful stay in the hospital. Nor unprofitable, I trust. But I ain't up to much yet & if you don't hear from me, you'll know the old energy just ain't there yet.

## To Dr. T. R. Spivey

17 March 64

Thank you for the invitation to talk at Georgia State. I appreciate it but . . . I'm not strong enough yet to undertake it. If I ever did talk or read there, it would have to be in the daytime. My idea about Atlanta is get in, get it over with and get out before dark.

I'd surely prefer to see you and Julia both here than just you, but lest I leave the wrong impression, let me tell you again that I have no interest whatsoever in all the dream business and don't want to hear about any dreams you all have had about me or my mother. Into that I can't go with you and there's an end to it . . .

## To Louise Abbot

20 March 64

We enjoyed very much our visit from Fr. Ellis yesterday. A most unassuming person he seemed and he appeared to genuinely like the people around there and what he was doing. Sometimes they can be pretty overbearing about Southerners but I got the idea he *tried* to understand.

I'm doing fine as far as the operation is concerned. It was a howling success but you always have aftereffects and mine are cystitis and [kidney infection]. Otherwise I'd be up & gone. I hope you manage to avoid this operation though. It's no fun . . .

## To Father J. H. McCown

21 March 64

I am back at home but more or less still in bed, entertaining all the little infections that follow an operation. I'm not really up to your request but you could tell them that anybody who wants to be introduced to Catholic fiction will have to start with the French —Mauriac and Bernanos. You can't dispose of a writer with a paragraph about his significance. I couldn't even compose such. You'd just better read them if you aim to say anything about them. The English are Waugh & Greene and Spark (Muriel) & the Americans: Powers, Percy (our friend Walker), Wilfrid Sheed . . . and some would include Edwin O'Connor. I don't know as I've never read him.

The most important non-fiction writer is Père Pierre Teilhard de Chardin, S.J. who died in 1955 and has so far escaped the Index, although a monition has been issued on him. If they are good, they are dangerous. I wish I could be of more help but I am not very good at this even when well, and right now I'm full of bugs. I do appreciate your prayers. I won't be out of the woods for a few months—until we are sure that all this stress is not going to re-activate the lupus . . .

## To "A."

I can scratch you out this kind of a note anyway but if you are like me when I see one of your handwritten communications, you will just wish it would go away. As far as the operation goes . . . I suspect it has kicked up the lupus again. Anyway, I am full of [infection] and am back on the steroids. Possibly I will end up at Piedmont. I hope not. Piedmont is a little more antiseptic socially than this country hospital here. You don't, as I recollect, hear what groans are being groaned in other rooms. Here there was an old lady across the hall from me who had been in the hospital since last November. She was about 92. Whenever they touched her, she roared LORD LORD LORD in the voice of a stevedore. At night when she coughed a nurse came in also in a voice you could hear any-where said "Pit that old stuff out, Sugar. Pit it out. Pit that old stuff out. Pit it out, Sugar," etc.

Yesterday we went to the doctor's office—same scene as in "Revelation" but nobody in there but us and two old countrymen—about 6 ft tall & skin and bones in overalls. They just had a talk. The first one said, "Six months from now this here room will be half full of niggers" . . . "Aw," says the other one, "it ain't the niggers so much. It's them high officials. Jest take the money away from them high officials & you won't have no trouble. All it is is money." Cassius Clay says he don't like all this talk about hate. Says, a tiger come in the room with you you gonna either run or shoot him. That don't mean you hate the tiger. It just means you know you and him can't make out. Did you see Cassius inter-viewed by Eric Sevareid on CBS? Worth seeing.

## To Janet McKane

2 April 64

I enjoyed seeing the pictures so much. Why don't I keep the one with you in it and return the others as you may not have copies? I'll await your instructions. I know Ridgewood, N.J., having visited once in Montclair and been driven around. We went to see somebody in Ridgewood but I don't remember who. I was 16 . . .

I read my Mass prayers this morning, not Byzantine by any means but with much appreciation of what you were doing for me.*

Five antibiotics have been tried out so far on my kidney infection and none have done anything to the infection though they have done several things to me—torn up my stomach and swollen shut my eyes. Then the cortisone comes along and undoes the swollen eyes but gives you a moon-like face. I went through all this in worse form in 1951 so I know about what to expect . . .

6 April 64

I think the rose quartz pendant is beautiful. I'll enjoy looking at it now and wearing it when I get out more. I went to Mass Sunday and have written some business letters on the typewriter but done no real work. When my dose of steroids gets regulated I'll be able to do more. I worked for ten years taking steroids and will just have to adjust to doing it again.

I was interested to hear about the Byzantine Mass and glad I was there by proxy. I do pray for you but in my fashion which is not a very good one. I am not a good prayer. I don't have a gift for it. My type of spirituality is almost completely shut-mouth. I really dislike books of piety most of all. They do nothing for me and they corrupt most people's ear if nothing else.

This book of C. S. Lewis on prayer is a good one but I don't like to pray any better for reading it. I also just read one of his called *Miracles*, which is very fine. Deceptively simple. You really need to read every sentence twice. Go among the Biblical scholars, says he, as a sheep among wolves.

My aunt in town aged 82 has been gravely ill this last week and all the family is here so things are rather disorganized. We don't expect her to live but she continues to hold her own.

My story ["Revelation"] has come out and I have ordered a copy for you and will send it to you when it comes. I haven't read it for errors in the type or for itself. I usually find plenty I'd like to change when it is too late . . .

[P.S.] I am a master of the messy letter.

* See letter of March 12, 1964. Robert Giroux told me that after Flannery's death he received an invitation to a Byzantine rite requiem Mass arranged by Janet McKane in a Second Avenue church in New York. He and she were the only ones who attended.

## To Louise and Tom Gossett

8 April 64

I am really enjoying reading your book. Fr. McCown breezed in here yesterday and appropriated the cover. I wouldn't let him have the book lest I never see it again. He was on his way to Macon to give a talk at the St. Joseph's Guild on "Literary Horizons of Catholic Thought," or some such grandiose title. He knows nothing whatsoever about the subject but was not letting that deter him. He will probably say your book is on the literary horizon of Catholic thought or something. I haven't finished it yet but it is a lot of fun to read . . .

My aunt Mary, the one in town, is critically ill and all the family is here because we don't know how long she can last—not long—so everything is at sixes and sevens here and my parent is running from here to the hospital to the house in town all day long.

I'm still reading *Out of Africa* [by Isak Dinesen] too. I'm still in bed on account of *Complications* so about all I can do is read and you all have provided my staple diet . . .

## To "A."

10 April 64

Mary Lou found Sister on the floor in her bedroom last Thursday week and we took her to the hospital with fever 103° which quickly went up to 106°. They gave her massive doses of cortisone and penicillin but really had no hope for her and Regina called the family. She's held her own for a week now but they still give us very little hope. She don't realize her condition, sleeps a good deal and when she is not sleeping is bright and gives orders right & left. As the doctor says, "She is still Miss Mary." They've got the fever down but can't keep her blood pressure up. I gather it's kind of a shock-state she is in. Anyway that's the way it is.

Don't call Louis and inquire for her because this is really a blow to him and his mind is better kept off it.

## To Richard Stern

[April 14]

I'm cheered my Chicago agent is keeping up with his duty to keep you informed on my state of being. It ain't much but I'm able to take nourishment and participate in a few Klan rallies. You're that much better off than me, scrapping Tuesday what you wrote Monday. All I've written this year have been a few letters. I have a little contribution to human understanding in the spring *Sewanee* but I wrote that last year. You might read something called "Gogol's Wife" if you haven't already—by one of those Eyetalians [Tommaso Landolfi], I forget which. As for me I don't read anything but the newspaper and the Bible. Everybody else did that it would be a better world.

Our spring's done come and gone. It is summer here. My Muscovy duck is setting under the back steps. I have two new swans who sit on the grass and converse with each other in low tones while the peacocks scream and holler. You just ought to leave that place you teach at and come teach in one of our excellent military colleges or female academies where you could get something good to eat. One of these days you will see the light and I'll be the first to shake your hand.

Keep me posted what you publish. Since you've slowed down, I might be able to keep up with you. I'm only one book behind now and if my head clears this year, I'm going to read it first thing.

Cheers and thanks for thinking of me. I think of you often in that cold place among them interleckchuls.

## To Maryat Lee

16 April 64

Miss Mary has astonished everybody by pulling out of it. Even at her sickest she never ceased giving instructions on how to treat her—but now she's sitting up in the bed doing it. This family is full of creakers. We creak along to about the age of 96. Look for me to be this kind too. I feel a lot better. Dr. Merrill was consulted over the phone & suggested Polycillin for the kidney bug & it seems to be working. For the last couple of days I've done a little work. My fingers swell and it's good for me to type. I can read anything I reckon. I'm more innerested in what I can write.

I guess you're right about that woman. You might up and throw something at her and get put in the penitentiary. Strategic retreat. I been doing it all my life and it works very well.

## To Elizabeth McKee

7 May 64

I have been thinking about this collection of my stories and what can be done to get it out with me sick. I am definitely out of commission for the summer and maybe longer with this lupus. I have to stay mostly in bed and am not supposed to get up and type except very short business letters. I was wondering if you have copies of the magazines the stories have been published in, if FS&G couldn't just print up the book from those? If I were well there is a lot of rewriting and polishing I could do, but in my present state of health I see no reason for me to spend my energies on old stories that are essentially all right as they are. Giroux seemed to want the book on their fall list and this is the only way I know to get it there. Will you call him up and discuss the matter with him and see what can be done? I think I'll be able to make any really necessary changes on the proofs.

If you don't have copies of all the magazines my mother may have the ones you don't. However she has her hands full right now as she has me in bed on one side of the house and my 81-year-old aunt, who has had a heart attack, on the other.

If we are going to make any money out of permissions, we'll have to get the book out.

The stories for inclusion are:

"Greenleaf" (*Kenyon*)
"A View of the Woods" (*PR?* or *Kenyon*)
"The Enduring Chill" (*Harper's Bazaar*)
"The Comforts of Home" (*Kenyon*)
"The Partridge Festival" (*The Critic*)
"The Lame Shall Enter First" (*Sewanee*)
"Everything That Rises Must Converge" (*NWW*)
"Revelation" (*Sewanee*)

This is not necessarily the order I want them in, but that can be worked out later with Giroux if he wants to go ahead and do it this way. Also which story I'll use for title.

## To Marion Montgomery

10 May 64

*Darrell* [his novel] took some of the curse offen the Baldwin County Hospital and eased my bed of affliction generally after I got home. I'm not stout enough yet for full-fledged comment à la Orville Prescott or that gent in the *Journal-Constitution* but I reckon I could do as well as either if my blood weren't low.

I was awful sorry to miss the Irish poet too but the day he came I had just got back from the hospital & I couldn't cope with ordinary white and colored folks, much less Irish poets. My orders now are to stay in bed and not have a lot of hooraw going on.

However I have an electric typewriter like I saw a picture of James Jones at and I hope to be creating my own hooraw in a month or two. Right now I'm just studying about it . . .

## To Charlotte Gafford

10 May 64

I'm intriegued (sp?) by the crystallized violets and delighted with the book of poems [*The Story Hour* by Sara Henderson Hay]. I enjoyed them thoroughly—the poems—and thought the illustrations were funny too. You reckon it would be in order for me to write her a note and tell her I enjoyed them?

I am at home again but am supposed to stay in bed and do nothing so I am writing me this story in my head and I hope by the time they let me up maybe I'll have it. But I'm not so sure. I have got so that I think on the typewriter (and almost nowhere else) . . .

## To Louise and Tom Gossett

12 May 64

Well our state has changed considerably since you last heard from me. I have been in the hospital again and now am in bed full-time. That operation started up the old trouble and I am back on the cortisone and doing none too well—though I feel no pain, only weakness. Yesterday I had a blood transfusion (you get up and go after hit) so today I got the energy to write some letters. In addition to me here, we have my aunt Mary. She grandly survived her heart attack and is out here with us. So my parent is running the Creaking Hill Nursing Home instead of the Andalusia Cow Plantation. Or rather she is running both.

If my trouble runs its predictable course, I reckon I will be in bed all summer. I haven't had it active since 1951 and it is something renewing acquaintance with it. I am not supposed to have company or go anywhere but to the doctor, which I do once a week. Maybe you all will be coming back this way in the fall. I sure hope for better things then. It's a good thing I cancelled that trip to Texas in May . . .

## To Janet McKane

15 May 64

I do appreciate the Mass that will be said for my intentions by the Paulist fathers. I don't know what my intentions are but I try to say that whatever suits the Lord suits me. So I reckon you might say my intentions are honorable anyway.

I hadn't seen these two memorial stamps and thanks for sending them. Do you collect them? I remember someone sending me one with a chicken on it once, commemorating Nat'l. Chicken Week. I should have saved it.

And thanks also for [Muriel Spark's] *The Girls of Slender Means*, which came at 12 o'clock noon and I finished before I went to bed. I really did like it, better than the others. Some of hers settle in the middle, but that one humps right along.

After trying out all the mugs I think the blue one with the stripes is the easiest to drink out of, but I like them all . . .

I feel better. Yesterday and today I worked one hour each. If I can keep that up, I'll be very pleased.

As for you I hope you keep your feet on the coffee table. Those viruses can linger on and pop up when you think you're through with them. Stop *before* you get tired, says my doctor.

Under separate cover I'm sending you the pages of a child's book that a publisher sent me to comment on. I thought you might like it for your class. I didn't comment on it. Don't know anything about children's literature. Throw it away if you can't use it.

## To Maryat Lee

15 May 64

Sure you are right. She [Ruby Turpin in "Revelation"] gets the vision. Wouldn't have been any point in that story if she hadn't. I like Mrs. Turpin as well as Mary Grace. You got to be a very big woman to shout at the Lord across a hogpen. She's a country female Jacob. And that vision is purgatorial. Purrrgatory and I don't reckon [your niece's] Presbyterian instincts operate on middling planes of glory. Anyhow the young are a trial to listen to. I'm very intolerant of them . . .

I had a blood transfusion Tuesday so I am feeling sommut better and for the last two days I have worked one hour each day and my my I do like to work. I et up that one hour like it was filet mignon.

Is your hemoglobin low? Mine was down to 8 is why the

transfusion. I just wish, if the rest at Chester don't do something for you, you would go to Dr. Sofer. Dr. Burrell says I have declared a moratorium on making blood—something that apparently happens in lupus.

In '51 I had about 10 transfusions. This time is not as bad as the last—because I know what's wrong with me. When I first came home May 1 from the hospital I was hearing the celestial chorus—"Clementine" is what it renders when I am weak enough to hear it. Over & over. "Wooden boxes without topses, They were shoes for Clementine." The transfusion cut that out. Must come from not enough blood getting to the head.

## To "A."

17 May 64

. . . I am feeling more pert than two weeks ago. What you say about my uncle is true enough and I wouldn't have been able to articulate it myself. He's never mentioned my father to me. If he did, he'd say something like, "He was a nice fellow," and wag his head. Do you know Conrad's story that featured Captain McWhirr? I forget which one it is, maybe *Typhoon*. He's a Captain McWhirr. You ought to read that story if you don't know it.

I'm surprised anybody in the city ever gets anywhere. I wouldn't have got to see [Hannah] Arendt unless somebody took me so I ain't surprised you didn't go. Would have been surprised if you had.

All the reaction I have got to "Revelation" has been favorable. It's in the spring *Sewanee*—except a letter I got from a girl . . . who, in schoolteacherly fashion, informed me it fell apart in the middle. Also she didn't understand the vision she said. They all interpit that to suit themselves. Maryat's niece asked her why I had made Mary Grace so ugly. "Because Flannery loves her," said Maryat. Very perceptive girl.

Miss Mary appears to be pretty satisfied here and I doubt myself if she is ever able to leave. It's easier on Regina to have all her worries under one roof anyway . . .

## To Cecil Dawkins

19 May 64

I was cheered to hear from you and I'll be proud to get *Catch-22*. I got nothing better to do than give it a running start. That operation in February started up my disseminated lupus and I have been in the hospital again recently with that. I'm at home now but as the TV personality says "I ain't doing nuttin, just settin around." In fact for almost all of the time except when I go to the doctor once a week. Last week I had a blood transfusion and that made me feel considerable stronger. No pain, just extreme weakness with this lupus as the other symptoms can be controlled with the steroid drugs.

"Revelation" was my reward for setting in the doctor's office. Mrs. Turpin I found in there last fall. Mary Grace I found in my head, doubtless as a result of reading too much theology.

My aunt Mary had a heart attack in March and she is out here with us now, also a cousin from Kansas City who is helping my mama do some of the work . . .

Are you still working on the play? I guess I'll be using that "Enduring Chill" story in the collection. I suggested to Elizabeth that maybe FS&G could print up the collection from the published stories. There's no use my wasting what little energy I can muster on busy-work. I do think some rewriting needs to be done on that particular story & I could do some on a couple of the others. However I haven't heard from her yet about it . . .

## To Maryat Lee

20 May 64

Going to Piedmont tomorrow to let Arthur J. Merrill take over. F. & B. give up, more or less, for the present anyways. Cheers,

Mrs. Turpin

## To Robert Giroux

21 May 64

Thanks for your letter. I'm glad we can go on with the collection in this fashion, though if I had more strength I would prefer to do it in the usual way.

I have found typewritten copies of "The Comforts of Home," "The Enduring Chill" and "The Lame Shall Enter First" and old galleys of "Everything That Rises" & if you need any of these I can send them. I have also found galleys of the one called "The Partridge Festival" and after reading it, I have decided that it is a very sorry story and I don't want it in. It's just not up to the others. However, there is a story ["Judgement Day"] that I have been working on off and on for several years that I may be able to finish in time to include. If not, I would rather have six or seven good stories than six or seven good and one bad . . .

My mother was talking to Sr. Josephine over the telephone the other day. She said they had not heard from the [parents of Mary Ann]. She thought they were embarrassed. I hope you haven't heard from them either. [The threatened lawsuit was dropped.]

## To Elizabeth McKee

21 May 64

Thanks for your letter. I've signed the contracts and my cousin will mail them tomorrow. I forgot to tell Giroux that the title *Everything That Rises Must Converge* is all right with me if he thinks that is what it ought to be . . .

I also told him that after reading "The Partridge Festival" I had decided I didn't want it in the collection.

## To Maryat Lee

21 May 64

That about [John Howard] Griffin was that Billy Sessions (you met him) was at the Monastery when Griffin in his black face hove in & Billy was on his way down & was going to bring Griffin but I forget what happened, they didn't get here. If I had been one of them white ladies Griffin sat down by on the bus, I would have got up PDQ preferring to sit by a genuine Negro. I read his other 2 books, one called *The Devil Rides Outside* (hysterical) (I don't mean hysterical ha ha but hystericaleeeek) and another called *Nuni* about some primitive tribe he fell in with. An interesting man but I wouldn't have liked him.

About the Negroes, the kind I don't like is the philosophizing prophesying pontificating kind, the James Baldwin kind. Very ignorant but never silent. Baldwin can tell us what it feels like to be a Negro in Harlem but he tries to tell us everything else too. [Martin Luther] King I don't think is the age's great saint but he's at least doing what he can do & has to do. Don't know anything about Ossie Davis except you like him but you probably like them all. My question is usually, would this person be endurable if white? If Baldwin were white nobody would stand him a minute. I prefer Cassius Clay . . . Cassius is too good for the Moslems.

You can have half interest in Mary Grace.

I think I'll have a book of stories out in the fall. I can't do the work on it, they'll have to print it up from the published stories, but I want to get it out of the way so I can use my limited energy for something new . . .

## To Robert Giroux

Piedmont Hospital
Atlanta
28 May 64

I've been in the hospital here since last Saturday but I hope to be out next week and I'll send you those manuscripts then.

I hope the other story will work out . . .

## To Louise Abbot

28 May 64

I'm in stir as the criminals say. That operation or its aftermath kicked up the lupus for me. I was in the hospital at home 10 days last month & it looks like I'll be in this one 10 days or so. I've been here since last Saturday. But when I get back home and on my feet, we'll set us a day for a visit.

I wouldn't spend much time worrying about dryness. It's hard to steer a path between indifference and presumption and [there's] a kind of constant spiritual temperature-taking that don't do any good or tell you anything either.

This evening I had a visit from the Abbot, bubbling over as usual. Regina (she's up here staying with my aunt) met him on his way in & told him he could stay 3 minutes (I got the high blood). He was here a full 30 I am sure.

[P.S.] Prayers requested. I am sick of being sick.

## To "A."

30 May 64

Don't pay too much attention to my good uncle in the matter of people's health. Rigor mortis has to have started setting in before he sees any serious difficulty. He was dying to call you up and tell you but I wouldn't let him as I have this real high blood [pressure] and am not supposed to have company, although the door has opened several times & somebody I haven't seen in twenty years has burst in. I'll tell him to bring you out [next week] if agreeable to you. They seem to think I'll be here another week. Cheers.

## To Janet McKane

6/5/64

I was distressed to hear you are sick but I guess the hospital is the best place for you.

I wish I could send you something or do something for you but it looks like that will have to wait. I said the rosary for you last night & actually managed to stay awake through all 5 decades. Very unusual. The Rosary is at least tangible.

I hope you will soon be out. My doctor seems in no hurry to let me go.

Cheers. I will see how many decades I last tonight on your behalf.

## To a Professor of English

6 June 64

Thank you for your note. I'm sorry I can't answer it more fully but I am in the hospital and not up to literary questions . . .

As for Mrs. May, I must have named her that because I knew some English teacher would write and ask me why. I think you folks sometimes strain the soup too thin . . .

## To Maryat Lee

8 June 64

I got three letters from you in one day all about Wellesley & colored folks & Marian Anderson and I bet she does say hellew. What are you doing working for Rockefeller or raising money for Mr. Check or what? I'm like Harry Truman, I don't care what happens to Republicans, including Rockefellers. Did you really give all them parties & stuff?

I am still here—into the 3rd week. I had a transfusion Sareday & another Sunday. I don't get any information out of them that I particularly understand but then I'd have to study medicine if I wanted to keep up with myself with this stuff. I don't know if I'm making progress or if there's any to be made. Let's hope they are learning something anyhow.

You will probably be wherever I don't send this.


## To Robert Giroux

9 June 64

I had thought I would be in the hospital here a week at most but it is going into the third week and so I haven't been able to send the manuscripts. I hope to be out next week but have no assurance of it. Since I am being so long delayed here, maybe it would be better to plan on a spring date for the book rather than before Christmas, and that will give me more time to try to finish another story ["Parker's Back"] when I get home. I am not apparently much better but with the blood transfusions I am getting I should be able to do some work when I get home.

I'm enjoying Xavier Rynne. Thanks for both. I haven't got the other one.


## To "A."

10 June 64

I'm afraid the telephone would finish me off for good. Letters I can do, company I can now have for 10 minutes but telephone clobbers me the thought of. Only thing I would be tempted to use it for is to call up & ask how I am & be told I am resting comfortably and have peaceful days & nights! That's the sweetest thing I ever heard, now ain't it. Peaceful days & nights. My.

Why don't you just come to see me this weekend, preferably in the afternoon & only if it is *not any trouble* whatsoever because you ain't going to be allowed to stay long enough to make it worth the trip . . .

It sure don't look like I'll ever get out of this joint. By now I know all the student nurses who "want to write,"—if they are sloppy & inefficient & can't make up the bed, that's them—they want to write. "Inspirational stuff I'm good at," said one of them. "I just get so taken up with it I forget what I'm writing."

( 583 )

## To Ashley Brown

6/15/64

I'm cheered you're going to Brazil. By all means take Elizabeth Bishop my best . . .

I'm up here in the hospital else I would send you some peafowl feathers to take her from me. She sent me an altar in a bottle.

I've been here 3 weeks. Caroline breezed in one weekend. She visited Fr. Charles at the monastery and they came out to see me. She has dyed her hair the color of funnytoor polish. Startling effect.

Report from Brazil and tell E. Bishop I'm hoping one of these days she'll pay me a visit.


## To Maryat Lee

16 June 64

I asked [the doctor] today when I could go home. Well he says we can begin to *think* about it now. Well you begin, says I, I been thinking about it all the time. So we are beginning to think about it. He has put me on a less rigid salt-free diet. For a while it was 2 grams a day, now it's about 5. I have to go slow on proteins because that is what the kidneys do not work on properly. They don't refine the poisons out of the proteins. So I can't eat as much meat & eggs & cheeze & such as I like.

I have a anecdote you can tell the next time you give a Southern party for Wellesley girls. A drove of cattle was coming down Constitution Ave. in Washington one day and Edward Everett said in the presence of Davy Crockett, "Those are Mr. Crockett's constituents. Where are they going, Mr. Crockett?" "They're going to Massachusetts, Mr. Everett," Davy Crockett said, "to teach school."

I got your number down but I won't call you. I can't afford it but even if I could, I don't think I could master the technical end of it yet. That *debilitates* me to think of.

That child in that picture is you all right. I'd have knowed you right off. Very happy-looking child. It's fortunate we didn't get together at that age. We would have blown something up. I would have found the matches and let you light the fuse.

## To Catharine Carver

I'm still stuck up here in the hospital. I thought I was coming for a week or ten days and I'll have been here a month Saturday. I wrote Giroux and asked him to hold off the publication date of the stories until spring. In that way I thought I could probably manage another story. I've got one ["Judgement Day"] that I'm not satisfied with that I finished about the same time as "Revelation" and when I get home I'm going to send it to you as is, and ask you to let me know what you think of it.

I have another in the making ["Parker's Back"] that I scratch on in longhand here at the hospital at night but that's not my idea of writing. How do those French ladies such as Madame Mallet-Joris write in cafés, for pity's sake? Anybody can write in a café is made different. No word from Giroux on making it spring.

I think when they finally let me out of here I'll be able to work if they ever let me out.

## To Maryat Lee

19 June 64

Going home tomorrow or so the old buzzard says today. Gave me a transfusion last night & I'll get another today & tomorrow will take my leave of Piedmont. At home I'll have to stay in bed & company will be restricted, but I'm looking forward to the cuisine.

## To Janet McKane

19 June 64

I go home tomorrow, praise the Lord. I'll have to stay in bed, even eat in bed for a while, but home is home . . .

The mail lady just arrived (they call them Pink Ladies here—they wear pink smocks & work 2 days a week voluntarily in hospitals—mostly society women with not enough to do at home—good souls really) with 3 letters from you which I was cheered to get. I do enjoy your letters. They are much more interesting than anything I have the energy to cook up in return. I realize I don't even answer half your questions. It is not lack of interest but lack of energy—mental & physical right now. I have always been a terrible conversationalist. I like to be around people who talk all the time because when somebody else is doing it, I don't have to.

I like Hopkins (to answer one) particularly a sonnet beginning

> Margaret, are you grieving
> Over Goldengrove unleaving? . . .

## To Maryat Lee

23 June 64

I must have left something out or else you just ain't sectionally small-minded enough to get it [anecdote in letter 16 June 64]. I think it is hilarious . . . That kills me, girl. You must be trying to give hit a fancy interpitation.

Dr. Fulghum is back in the driver's seat & Dr. M. has checked out. I'll see F. about Monday. Meantime, he says send him that story ["Revelation"] so he can see if he's going to sue me. Word of it has got around. It's your office, I said, but it's been thoroughly pickled before using . . .

## To Cecil Dawkins

Milledgeville
24 June 64

The books did come back but while I was in the hospital in Atlanta. I just got back Saturday after spending one month in Piedmont Hospital . . . I reckon it was no worse than any other hospital but that was an awful long time to have to stay, particularly as I was my own guest—no insurance for lupus. I'm all for Medicare myself.

Anyway my cousin eventually sent the books on and I enjoyed reading *Catch*-22 in the hospital though I haven't yet finished it. I think it gets funnier after page 36. I'm still on it. The [Grace] Paley I'm very glad to have too, though I think I will get this collection out of the way before I start reading it. Might make me dissatisfied with my offerings. I don't know if I'll include "You Can't Be Poorer Than Dead" or not. It'll be up to Giroux in any case. I'd like to, but it's a little as if it were just padding and I prefer to have enough without it. It would probably raise the price of the book & books are so high now you can't buy them except in paperback. However I mean to ask him what he thinks about including it . . .

I've had four blood transfusions in the last month. The trouble is mostly kidneys—they don't refine poisons out of the proteins & therefore you don't make blood like you should or you lose it like you shouldn't or something. As far as I am concerned, as long as I can get at that typewriter, I have enough. They expect me to improve, or so they say. I expect anything that happens . . .

## To Janet McKane

27 June 64

Thanks so much for the Russell stamps—particularly nice I thought—and for the leaflet. St. James will do nicely. I won't get to church again for a long time but I will have an eye to him when the day comes along. It is fine to be at home. I looked out the window this morning & T. Traveller & Equinox were chasing the swans off their pasture. No trespassing.

I hope you are better. My good wishes for you surpass my energy to do anything about it however. I am doing a lot of necessary rewriting on old stories and today in bed I did a day's work. This must be the result of my friends' prayers.

## To "A."

27 June 64

Lemme commend you and [your aunt] for yr fortitude & charity . . . All you say about B. is doubtless true but your great natural grace is finding the good in people. It's a real gift. I never been bothered with it myself.

My room has been judged not fit to house that piece of pottery you brought me so it is in the parlor. Tell [your aunt] and yourself I think it is the cat's ankle and feel a proper pride of ownership. Ma says it is a paperweight and if I ever come into my clean desk period, I'll use it there . . .

You asked what was done when we came back. Nothing. We left in a hurry without washing the tops of the breakfast pans or the coffeepot and everything was exactly like we left it. Rip Van Winkle didn't have it any different. Not even a glass of ice water to hand. Dust everywhere. The refrigerator full of rotten food. And Louise bowing & scraping and carrying on about how much she had missed us. Regina had told her hurriedly to take care of everything but nothing specific. Anyway even if she had it wouldn't have done any good. They had a month's vacation with pay . . .

[P.S.] I never read that controversy between Leavis & Snow, but Leavis is supposed to have got very impossible in his old age. It all reminds me of the Tates getting upset because Cardinal Spellman writes bad novels. I think it's charming that Cardinal Spellman writes bad novels. If he wrote good novels, I'd be worried about the Church.

## To Catharine Carver

27 June 64

Will you look at this one ["Judgement Day"] and say if you think it fitten for the collection or if you think it can be made so? It's a rewrite of a story that I have had around since 1946 and never been satisfied with, but I hope I have it now except for details maybe.

I have been home a week and feel I'm getting somewhere. I have to stay in these two rooms but R. has got me the table with the electric typewriter on it put so I get out of bed into the type-writer, so to speak, and every day I am able to do a little more.

Cecil Dawkins keeps telling me I ought to include "You Can't Be Any Poorer Than Dead" in this collection as a story—that's the first chapter of *The Violent Bear*. What do you think of that? I mean to write Giroux and ask him. I wouldn't want to use it just for padding but if I don't land in the hospital again before September, I believe I can write two more stories. I don't want any skimpy collection.

You are mighty good to read these for me . . .

## To Thomas Stritch

28 June 64

Here I am yours truly on the electric typewriter and I feel more or less like folks . . . I do what amounts to two hours of work a day and that is about as good as I ever did anyway. I asked the doctor if I could sit up at the electric typewriter and work. You can work, says he, but you can't exert yourself. I haven't quite figured this out yet; anyway I am confined to these two rooms and the porch so far and ain't allowed to wash the dishes. I guess that is exerting yourself where writing is officially not. When I was worst off I signed a contract for a book of stories and told FS&G they could get it out themselves; I didn't want Regina to have to fool with it. As soon as I got better I repented of that rash act, and I've now told them that I'll have to rewrite some of the stories so the collection won't be until spring, & I have the work to do.

The records are a real boon and when I'm not working, I'm listening to them which is in between times. There's no use fooling myself I know what's being worked out anywhere or what's dramatic. Of the ones you sent I think I like the 4-hand piano Chopin thing; there is a point in it where the peafowls join in . . .

*However depleted her energies, Flannery's mind was occupied with the planned new book of stories later published as* Everything That Rises Must Converge. *She wrote to Robert Giroux, who advised against the inclusion of "You Can't Be Any Poorer Than Dead" because it was an earlier version of the first chapter of her most recent book. He thought it belonged in a later book, and it appeared in* The Collected Stories.

## To Robert Giroux

28 June 64

I have been home a week from the hospital and can work a few hours a day. I've completed one story ["Judgement Day"] which I think will do in place of "The Partridge Festival" but I want to keep it a few weeks longer and think about it before I send it.

There is considerable rewriting I want to do on the one called "The Enduring Chill," so you might wait to put that in galleys until I get the new version.

"Greenleaf" is in the 1957 O. Henry collection, also in a paperback anthology edited by Arlin Turner and published by Rinehart, the title something about Southern Literature.

I am wondering what you think about including "You Can't Be Any Poorer Than Dead," which is a version of the first chapter of *The Violent Bear It Away* and was published in *New World Writing*. It holds up well as a story.

I also hope to write another story that I have in mind ["Parker's Back"], so I think there will be at least nine or ten stories and they are fairly long most of them . . .

## To Janet McKane

7/1/64

Thanks for the Mauriac book. I know it's fine and I hope I'll get to it sooner or later but right now I am rather cut in half by the drop in the dose of prednisone and want to use my little bit of energy on my work. It seems to be doing remarkably well & I know your prayers must be pushing it along. Do you know anything about St. Raphael besides his being an archangel? He leads you to the people you are supposed to meet and in the prayer to him composed I think by Ernest Hello, the words Light & Joy are found. It's a prayer I've said every day for many years. Will send you a copy if you don't know it.

## To Maryat Lee

7/1/64

I sort of reckon by now you must be in Chester but maybe you are not. Your friend [ballplayer] Jackie Robinson, I read, is in Albany—pronounced *All benny* if you ever take a notion to spend the weekend in one of their jails. I haven't heard about affairs of that order at W.C. because I can't have company & haven't seen anybody from over there. Sooner or later, if I live to see the day, I'll get an earful.

I'm pleased I can't have company because it means what energy I've got I can use for my own bidnis, getting this book out. I've got to get it out before I get worse & should I get better I'll have other & new stuff to work on. More to consider here than my habitual fiscal responsibility. My dose of prednisone has been cut in half on Dr. Merrill's orders because the nitrogen content of the blood has increased by a third. So far as I can see the medicine and the disease run neck & neck to kill you, but anyway I don't hear any choruses now, no more "Clementine" or "Coming for to Carry Me Home." I am likely some better. I hope you still are. And how is Rev. Check? I hope not disappointed still. Did you happen to read the story in that *Sewanee* I sent called "The Dalai Lama of Harlem"? It was too long but pretty good albeit. Read it.

Your sister-in-law is giving a luncheon to which I hear my parent & aunt are invited Saturday in honor of my cousin who is getting married. But we have our own problems here as Shot landed in jail Sunday for drunk driving in a borrowed car, leaving the scene of the accident & not having his license about him at the time. He is out on bond but I am afraid is headed for the chain gang, which he heartily deserves. Anyway, my parent is busy about his legal affairs so I doubt she gets to any luncheon.

## To Sister Mariella Gable

5 July 64

Thank you so much for sending the essay. I think Richard [Stern] has read your meaning incorrectly. I don't find anything in it that I could object to. Richard apparently dislikes the people of the Pentecostal religions with a certain vigor and for, I gather, purely personal reasons. I don't know what I said to him to give him the impression he seems to have taken away about my attitude toward them. I have the feeling that all my visitors go away with their own views confirmed. Half the time, I don't know what they're talking about and my answers are vague.

I do very much appreciate what you've put into the essay and I shall learn from it myself. And save my breath by referring other people to it.

The wolf, I'm afraid, is inside tearing up the place. I've been in the hospital 50 days already this year. At present I'm just home from the hospital and have to stay in bed. I have an electric typewriter and I write a little every day but I'm not allowed to do much.

I'll count on your prayers and when I have the strength I'll try to write you and Richard a joint letter about the Catholic Protestant inspiration problem in the stories. When critics get ahold of them the tail usually starts wagging the dog.

## To Janet McKane

8 July 64

I have been right weak since my dose was cut in half but now we are going back to smaller doses 4 times a day so I hope for some increase in energy. Yesterday the priest brought me Communion as it looks like a long time before I'm afoot. I also had him give me the now-called Sacrament of the Sick. Once known as Extreme Unction.

We passed a peaceful 4th of July, with most local restaurants either integrated or not tested. I'm cheered that bombshell is past.

## To Maryat Lee

10 July 64

Somebody gave me this paper—as being, I suppose, a reflection of my personality. Little stickers come with it as says such like as "Hi There!" and "Just a Note . . ." and you spit on them and stick them anywhere you please. I have decided to use it all up on you.

That grasshopper you left in the cage for me reminded me so much of the poor colored people in the jails that I let him out and fed him to a duck. I'm sure you'll understand. I'm enjoying old Günter Grass [*The Tin Drum*] and the Japanese pillow. That Grass is really something. I'll be all year reading it . . .

Miss Regina got Shot off with the lightest fine ($100) [for drunken driving] and paroled for a year to the court. She went with him. Otherwise he'd be at the prison farm tonight.


## To "A."

11 July 64

This here ["Parker's Back"] instead of a letter. Would you mind casting your eye over it and returning it on to me. I never know if what I do works until at least a year after it's written, at least I'm never *sure*. Cheers.


## To Janet McKane

14 July 64

Here's the prayer to St. [Raphael]. I think it was written by Ernest Hello. Don't recollect seeing that print of Rouault. Have seen the one of Christ standing at the boats with the sun in it. Maybe that's the one you have in mind. Thanks for sending the child's letter. I'll enclose it in case it's something you want back . . .

Thanks for the prayers. I do need them.

### PRAYER TO SAINT RAPHAEL

O Raphael, lead us toward those we are waiting for, those who are waiting for us: Raphael, Angel of happy meeting, lead us by the hand toward those we are looking for. May all our movements be guided by your Light and transfigured with your joy.

Angel, guide of Tobias, lay the request we now address to you at the feet of Him on whose unveiled Face you are privileged to gaze. Lonely and tired, crushed by the separations and sorrows of life, we feel the need of calling you and of pleading for the protection of your wings, so that we may not be as strangers in the province of joy, all ignorant of the concerns of our country. Remember the weak, you who are strong, you whose home lies

beyond the region of thunder, in a land that is always peaceful, always serene and bright with the resplendent glory of God.


## To Catharine Carver

15 July (64)

I do thank you and I'll get to work on this one ["Judgement Day"] you sent back. I can see the point about the daughter's coming being too close to his encounter with the doctor. As for the "on his back" business—that's a cherished Southern white assertion—that the Negro *is* on his back and in a way it's quite true. But you have to be born below the M.D. line to appreciate it fully.

I have drug another out of myself and I enclose it ["Parker's Back"]. I think it's much better than the last, but I want to know what you think. I think with these two new stories, I'll just leave it at 9 and forget about "You Can't Be Poorer Than Dead." I never thought much of including it anyway.

Have you read over the one called "The Enduring Chill"? I don't much like it but I am afraid once I get to messing with it, I'll make it worse than it is.

About the stroke right after the actor hits him: I have to immobilize him at once or he'd start walking home that minute. The old man in "A View of the Woods" was Mr. Fortune so I'm alright on Tanner.

This is certainly a great favor you're doing me reading these things. I'm still in bed but I climb out of it into the typewriter about 2 hours every morning.


## To "A."

17 July 64

I agree with all you got to say about this ["Parker's Back"] and enclose a better barroom scene. You sound like Caroline to the teeth. I sent it to her same time as I sent it to you and got a telegram back saying some mechanical details would follow but she thought it unique, that I had succeeded in dramatizing a heresy. Well not in those terms did I set out but only thinking that the spirit moveth where it listeth. I found out about tattooing from a book I found in the Marboro list called *Memoirs of a Tattooist*. The old man that wrote it took tattooing as a high art and a great profession. No nonsense. Picture of his wife in it—very demure

( 593 )

Victorian lady in off-shoulder gown. Everything you can see except her face & hands is tattooed. Looks like fabric. HE DID IT.

It's the other story that was published but this one ["Judgement Day"] is so different I aim to sell it again. I'll send that when I get up the steam to copy it. I can sit up at the typewriter about an hour at a time and I reckon I put in two and a half hours a day but you can't do much that way.

I'm cheered you got that raise. The Republican convention wasn't much. I look forward to the Democratic as they are better at the corn.

There's a right interesting review of Richard Hughes' *Fox in the Attic* by Walker Percy in the summer 64 *Sewanee*. Hate to subject you to this writing (hand) (mine). It's almost as bad as yours.


## To Maryat Lee

21 July 64

I seemed to be doing all right and then I got another spell [of kidney infection] and tomorrow I'm going to the Baldwin County to spend the day and have a blood transfusion as the hemoglobin has dropped to below eight again. I'll take *The Tin Drum* along.

The racial front appears to have switched momentarily to Harlem. Are you anticipating? Do you ride the subways at night by yourself? NY sounds to me like a lousy place to live now.

I'm still puttering on my story ["Parker's Back"] that I thought I'd finished but not long at a time. I go across the room & I'm exhausted.


## To "A."

25 July 64

No Caroline didn't mean the tattoos [in "Parker's Back"] were the heresy. Sarah Ruth was the heretic—the notion that you can worship in pure spirit. Caroline gave me a lot of advice about the story but most of it I'm ignoring. She thinks every story must be built according to the pattern of the Roman arch and she would enlarge the beginning and the end, but I'm letting it lay. I did well to write it at all. I had another transfusion Wednesday but it don't seem to have done much good.

We can worry about the interpitations of "Revelation" but not its fortunes. I had a letter from the O. Henry prize people & it got first.

## To Janet McKane

Thanks for the cards. I'll use up these before I start on the others. I like them all. I had better correct your barnyardology. There is no goose in that picture. That is a Muscovy duck named Sister. No religious significance. Sister sets about four times a year & hatches more than any of the others. The creature with the wattles is a guinea. The ones strolling on the steps are peahens (female of the peafowl). If I were you I'd throw away *The Art of Plain Talk* and keep at your Milton & Shakespeare. Sometime at your library you might see if you could find *The Ethics of Rhetoric* by R. M. Weaver. I once had a copy but I gave it to somebody for a graduation present and now I'm sorry I did.

## To Maryat Lee

26 July 64

As far as me and Senator Russell are concerned those riots couldn't be located in a better place than Harlem, not to mention Rochester and Brooklyn. And you seem to be daring the heat too. It ain't even hot here, very delightful. It don't do much but rain but it's very delightful.

I got a pint of blood or so last Wednesday and now I'm taking a double dose of antibiotic for the kidney . . . & they are withdrawing the cortisone. It's six of one and a half dozen of the other. I feel lousy but I don't have much idea how I really am.

That letterhead knocked me out—boy, that is some letterhead —so many folks there's almost no room for the letter. I hope those farm agents don't give you any trouble.

## To Janet McKane

27 July 64

The books & the burro came today and I do appreciate them. I'm not up to the books yet but I will be let us hope later on. I'm up to the burro. Equinox inside and out.

Today I went to the doctor and that always wears me out. He has had three coronaries and so his patients have to go to him.

*In an almost illegible scrawl, Flannery wrote her last letter, six days before her death on August 3, 1964, to Maryat Lee. It refers to an anonymous phone call. Found on the bedside table after her death, it was mailed by her mother.*


## To Maryat Lee

28 July 64

Dear Raybat,

Cowards can be just as vicious as those who declare themselves—more so. Dont take any romantic attitude toward that call. Be properly scared and go on doing what you have to do, but take the necessary precautions. And call the police. That might be a lead for them.

Dont know when I'll send those stories. I've felt too bad to type them.

Cheers,
Tarfunk

# INDEX

Georgia, University of, 461, 504, 511, 516

Georgia Writers' Association, 179, 183–4

"Geranium, The" (O'Connor), 3, 7, 74, 559

Gide, André, 116, 147, 149, 156, 202, 259, 263

Gill, Eric, 130

Gilman, Richard, 405, 429, 487, 496

Gilson, Etienne, 107, 231, 277, 279, 477, 494

Ginder, Father, 565

Ginsberg, Allen, 349

*Girls of Slender Means, The* (Spark), 577

Giroux, Robert, 8, 15, 20–1, 23–5, 27–37, 59, 62, 67, 71–7, 80, 85, 87, 113, 120, 122, 138, 270, 277–80, 286, 331–2, 334, 337, 340, 342, 344–5, 353, 361, 373–5, 380, 402, 409, 415, 417, 421–2, 428–31, 439, 451, 471, 473–4, 498, 549, 563–5, 567–8, 572, 575, 579–81, 583, 585–6, 588–9

Glenn, John, 511

"Gloom and Gold in Erza Pound" (Fitzgerald), 132

*Go Tell It on the Mountain* (Baldwin), 348

*God and Mammon* (Mauriac), 143–4

*God and the Unconscious* (White), 103, 382, 451

Godden, Rumer, 522

*God's Heralds*, 237

*God's Little Acre* (Caldwell), 243

Goethe, Johann von, 334

Gogol, Nicolai V., 44, 99, 498

"Gogol's Wife" (Landolfi), 574

Gold, Ivan, 513

Goldbrunner, Josef, 382

*Golden Bowl, The* (James), 86, 258

Golding, William, 378, 384

Gollancz, Victor, 88

"Good Country People" (O'Connor), 75–6, 78, 86, 111, 158, 160, 170–1, 546

*Good Housekeeping*, 445, 450

"Good Man Is Hard to Find, A" (O'Connor), 59–60, 85, 111, 317, 333–4, 389, 412, 426, 436–7, 460, 504, 511, 542, 548

*Good Man Is Hard to Find, A* (O'Connor), 65, 68, 71–6, 78–81, 85–91, 95–6, 101, 104, 108, 111, 114, 116, 133, 150, 178, 185, 197–8, 234, 249, 280, 291, 391, 458, 467, 512, 528, 533

*Good Soldier, The* (Ford), 447, 469

Goodreau, William, 414

*Goose on the Grave, The* (Hawkes), 292

Gordon, Caroline, *see* Tate, Caroline Gordon

Gorgeous George, 81

Gorlier, Claudio, 504

Gossett, Thomas and Louise, xi, 156, 222–3, 237, 255, 257, 262, 275, 286, 334, 438, 462, 500, 513, 566, 573, 576

*Gothic Tales* (Dinesen), 253

Graef, Hilda, 98, 520

Graham, Billy, 106, 401

Graham, Dom Aelred, 309, 364, 519, 550

*Grammar of Assent, The* (Newman), 477

Grant, Cary, 338

Grass, Gunter, 592

Grau, Shirley Ann, 121, 124, 159

Graves, Robert, 153

Green, Helen, 19, 420, 490, 492–4

Green, Julian, 498

Green, Paul, 223, 432

Green, Russell, 424

Greenberg, Martin, 42

Greene, Graham, 98, 108, 119, 121, 130, 137, 193, 201, 258, 297, 400, 520, 570

"Greenleaf" (O'Connor), 129, 146, 181–2, 191–2, 209, 546, 575, 589

Griffin, John Howard, 414, 580

Griffith, Ben, xviii, 68–70, 78–9, 83–4, 89, 118, 156, 186, 222

Grimm Brothers, 472

"Grotesque in Southern Literature, The" (Thorpe), 257

*Group, The* (McCarthy), 553

*Groves of Academe, The* (McCarthy), 37

Guardini, Romano, 74, 99, 104, 106–7, 126, 128, 131, 133, 150, 169, 173, 191, 231, 243–4, 296, 304, 449

Guérard, Albert, 461